펼쳐 보면 느껴집니다

단 한 줄도 배움의 공백이 생기지 않도록
문장 한 줄마다 20년이 넘는
해커스의 영어교육 노하우를 담았음을

덮고 나면 확신합니다

수많은 선생님의 목소리와
정확한 출제 데이터 분석으로 꽉 찬
교재 한 권이면 충분함을

해커스북 중·고등
HackersBook.com

기출로 적중

해커스 중학영문법 과 함께하면

점수가 확 오르는 이유!

기출 분석으로 완벽히 **적중**시키니까!

1 전국 중학교 내신
기출문제 빅데이터
철저히 분석 및 반영

2 최신 개정 교과서의
모든 문법 포인트
빠짐없이 반영

중학영문법
1학년

중학영문법
2학년

중학영문법
3학년

촘촘한 훈련으로 확실히 내 것이 되니까!

3 중간·기말·서술형
실전문제로
내신 완벽 대비

4 암기리스트·단어 암기장
+워크북으로
반복 훈련 가능

최신 개정 교과서 완벽 반영

기출로적중 해커스 중학영문법

1학년

이 책을 검토해주신 선생님들

강상훈 경기 평촌비상에듀학원 / 김가영 서울 송정중학교 / 김원덕 경기 올림피아드학원 / 박유정 서울 반포중학교 / 박윤정 경기 이지베스트학원

박은혜 서울 송파중학교 / 박정은 서울 대청중학교 / 양세희 서울 양세희수능영어학원 / 이계윤 서울 씨앤씨학원 / 이유빈 서울 잉글리쉬&매쓰매니저학원

이혜원 서울 대청중학교 / 정혜은 서울 용곡중학교 / 최다빈 서울 최강영어 / 최승복 경기 오른어학원 / 최지영 경기 다른영어학원

목차

CHAPTER 5 문장의 형식

CHAPTER 6 다양한 문장의 종류

CHAPTER 7 to부정사

CHAPTER 8 동명사

목차

구성 미리 보기

○ 시험에 나온, 또 나올 기출 적중 문법 POINT 학습

기출 적중 POINT

최신 개정 교과서와 전국 내신 기출 빅데이터에서 뽑아낸 문법 포인트를 빠짐없이 학습할 수 있습니다.

핵심 문법 사항

내신 시험 대비에 꼭 필요한 문법 사항을 명쾌한 설명과 예문을 통해 정확하게 이해할 수 있습니다.

심화 문법 TIP

어렵지만 실제 내신 시험에서 출제된 적이 있는 문법 사항을 학습하여 고난도 문제에 대비할 수 있습니다.

기출로적중 POINT 1 셀 수 있는 명사와 셀 수 없는 명사

정답 p.26

1. 셀 수 있는 명사가 단수일 때는 명사 앞에 a(n)을 붙이고, 복수일 때는 복수형으로 쓴다. 셀 수 있는 명사에는 보통명사와 집합명사가 있다.

보통명사	일반적인 사람·동물·사물을 나타내는 명사 boy, kid, student, cat, dog, bird, city, car, sandwich 등
집합명사	사람·동물·사물이 모인 집합을 나타내는 명사 class, family, team, group, band, club 등

He ate an apple and three pears. 그는 한 개의 사과와 세 개의 배를 먹었다.
Our team won the game. 우리의 팀은 그 경기를 이겼다.

2. 셀 수 없는 명사는 명사 앞에 a(n)을 붙일 수 없고, 복수형으로도 쓸 수 없다. 셀 수 없는 명사에는 고유명사, 추상명사, 물질명사가 있다.

고유명사	사람이나 장소 등의 고유한 이름을 나타내는 명사 Jack, Mr. Lee, Korea, Paris, Pacific Ocean, Hangang 등 (Tip) 고유명사의 첫 글자는 항상 대문자로 쓴다.
추상명사	눈에 보이지 않는 추상적인 개념을 나타내는 명사 peace, love, kindness, honesty, help, advice, information 등
물질명사	일정한 형태가 없는 물질을 나타내는 명사 water, tea, bread, rice, paper, rain, sand 등

Seoul is the capital city of Korea. 서울은 한국의 수도이다.
They need your help. 그들은 너의 도움이 필요하다.
Would you like tea? 너는 차를 원하니?

(Tip) furniture(가구), money(돈), clothing(의류), luggage(짐)와 같이 종류 전체를 대표하는 명사는 셀 수 없지만, 각 종류에 속하는 명사는 셀 수 있다.

종류 전체를 대표하는 명사: furniture – 종류에 속하는 명사: a chair, a desk, a table 등

연습문제 A 다음 명사가 셀 수 있는 명사이면 O, 셀 수 없는 명사이면 X를 쓰시오.

1 bag → _____   **2** love → _____

3 advice → _____   **4** school → _____

5 tree → _____   **6** oil → _____

7 clothing → _____   **8** teacher → _____

9 Spain → _____   **10** club → _____

11	tiger	→ _____	12	peace	→ _____
13	class	→ _____	14	salt	→ _____
15	skirt	→ _____	16	chair	→ _____
17	money	→ _____	18	team	→ _____
19	notebook	→ _____	20	Karen	→ _____
21	London	→ _____	22	sand	→ _____
23	luggage	→ _____	24	toy	→ _____
25	kindness	→ _____	26	paper	→ _____
27	family	→ _____	28	information	→ _____
29	Ms. Smith	→ _____	30	hat	→ _____

연습문제 B   괄호 안에서 알맞은 것을 고르시오.

1 Mr. Miller doesn't drink (coffee / coffees).

2 (Banana / Bananas) have important vitamins.

3 How did you meet (minho / Minho)?

4 Michael is putting (sugar / a sugar) in his tea.

5 Anna has four close (friend / friends).

6 Many (flower / flowers) are in the garden.

7 My aunt gave me (book / a book) about dinosaurs.

8 (Honesty / An honesty) is Tina's strength.

9 The store has different kinds of (furniture / furnitures).

10 I picked up (dollar / a dollar) on my way home.

11 My family is going to visit (Vietnam / a Vietnam).

12 Money cannot buy you (happiness / a happiness).

기출 적중문제

다음 중 밑줄 친 부분이 어법상 어색한 것은?

① A girl is looking for you.
② Brian is drinking milk.
③ Kate has a brother.
④ Let me give you an advice.
⑤ Water is necessary for our body.

셀 수 없는 명사는 a(n)과 함께 쓸 수 없어요.

연습문제

다양한 유형과 많은 양의 연습 문제를 통해 문법 사항을 암기 하지 않고도 자연스럽게 이해 할 수 있습니다.

기출 적중문제

빈출 포인트가 적용된 실전 문 제를 풀어보며 실제 내신 시험 의 출제 방식을 미리 경험해볼 수 있습니다.

기출 해결 TIP

빈출 포인트가 적용된 실전 문 제의 해결 TIP을 통해 실제 내 신 시험에서의 정답 적중률을 높일 수 있습니다.

구성 미리 보기

○ 체계적으로 시작하는 **기초 문법**

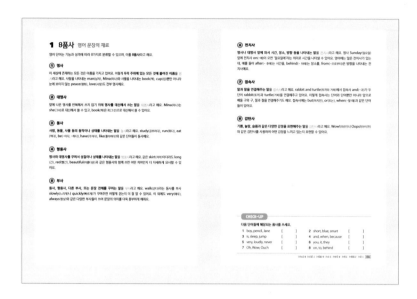

<< 중학영문법을 이해하기 위해 꼭 알아야 하는 기초 문법이 정리되어 있어 문법 실력이 부족한 학생들도 영문법을 체계적으로 학습할 수 있습니다.

○ 서술형 평가에 강해지는 **서술형 대비 문제**

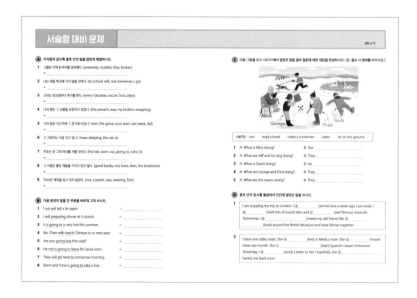

<< 다양한 유형의 서술형 대비 문제를 풀어보며 서술형을 강조하는 최근 내신 평가 트렌드에 대비할 수 있습니다.

○ 정답 적중률을 높이는 중간·기말고사 실전 문제

<< 전국 내신 기출문제의 빈출 유형과 문법 포인트가 반영된 객관식·주관식 문제를 풀어보며 실제 내신 시험에서의 정답 적중률을 높일 수 있습니다.

○ 학습 효과를 더욱 높이는 워크북과 부록

| 워크북 | 문법 암기리스트 | 단어 암기장 |

풍부한 양의 추가 문제를 풀면서 부족한 부분을 파악하고 보완할 수 있습니다.

교재에 수록된 문법 사항 중 꼭 암기해야 할 사항을 언제·어디서나 학습할 수 있습니다.

교재에서 사용된 중학 필수 단어 및 표현을 암기하며 어휘력을 향상할 수 있습니다.

기초 문법

영어 문법, 그 기초부터 알고 들어가자!

본격적인 학습 전에, 영어 문법의 기초가 되는 8품사, 문장 성분, 구와 절에 대해 배워보도록 해요!

1 8품사 영어 문장의 재료

영어 단어는 기능과 성격에 따라 8가지로 분류할 수 있으며, 이를 **8품사**라고 해요.

① 명사

이 세상에 존재하는 모든 것은 이름을 가지고 있어요. 이렇게 **우리 주위에 있는 모든 것에 붙여진 이름**을 명사라고 해요. 사람을 나타내는 man(남자), Mina(미나)와 사물을 나타내는 book(책), cup(컵)뿐만 아니라 눈에 보이지 않는 peace(평화), love(사랑)도 전부 명사예요.

② 대명사

앞에 나온 명사를 반복해서 쓰지 않기 위해 **명사를 대신해서 쓰는 말**을 대명사라고 해요. Mina(미나)는 she(그녀)로 대신해서 쓸 수 있고, book(책)은 it(그것)으로 대신해서 쓸 수 있어요.

③ 동사

사람, 동물, 사물 등의 동작이나 상태를 나타내는 말을 동사라고 해요. study(공부하다), run(뛰다), eat(먹다), be(~이다, ~하다), have(가지다), like(좋아하다)와 같은 단어들이 동사예요.

④ 형용사

명사와 대명사를 꾸며서 성질이나 상태를 나타내는 말을 형용사라고 해요. 같은 skirt(치마)이더라도 long(긴), red(빨간), beautiful(아름다운)과 같은 형용사와 함께 쓰면 어떤 치마인지 더 자세하게 묘사할 수 있어요.

⑤ 부사

동사, 형용사, 다른 부사, 또는 문장 전체를 꾸미는 말을 부사라고 해요. walk(걷다)라는 동사를 부사 slowly(느리게)나 quickly(빠르게)가 꾸며주면 어떻게 걷는지 더 잘 알 수 있어요. 이 외에도 very(매우), always(항상)와 같은 다양한 부사들이 쓰여 문장의 의미를 더욱 풍부하게 해줘요.

⑥ 전치사

명사나 대명사 앞에 와서 시간, 장소, 방향 등을 나타내는 말을 전치사라고 해요. 명사 Sunday(일요일) 앞에 전치사 on(~에)이 오면 '일요일에'라는 의미로 시간을 나타낼 수 있어요. 영어에는 많은 전치사가 있는데, 예를 들어 after(~ 후에)는 시간을, behind(~ 뒤에)는 장소를, from(~으로부터)은 방향을 나타내는 전치사예요.

⑦ 접속사

말과 말을 연결해주는 말을 접속사라고 해요. rabbit and turtle(토끼와 거북)에서 접속사 and(~과)가 두 단어 rabbit(토끼)과 turtle(거북)을 연결해주고 있어요. 이렇게 접속사는 단어와 단어뿐만 아니라 앞으로 배울 구와 구, 절과 절을 연결해주기도 해요. 접속사에는 but(하지만), or(또는), when(~할 때)과 같은 단어들이 있어요.

⑧ 감탄사

기쁨, 놀람, 슬픔과 같은 다양한 감정을 표현해주는 말을 감탄사라고 해요. Wow!(와우!)나 Oops!(아이쿠!)와 같은 감탄사를 사용하여 어떤 감정을 느끼고 있는지 표현할 수 있어요.

CHECK-UP

다음 단어들에 해당되는 품사를 쓰세요.

1 boy, pencil, Jane [ ]	2 short, blue, smart [ ]
3 is, sleep, jump [ ]	4 and, when, because [ ]
5 very, loudly, never [ ]	6 you, it, they [ ]
7 Oh, Wow, Ouch [ ]	8 on, to, behind [ ]

정답 1 명사 2 형용사 3 동사 4 접속사 5 부사 6 대명사 7 감탄사 8 전치사

2 문장 성분 영어 문장을 만드는 요소

영어에서 문장을 구성하는 여러 요소들을 **문장 성분**이라고 해요. 앞에서 배운 품사는 각 단어의 기능과 성격으로 구분되지만, 문장 성분은 문장 안에서의 역할에 따라 구분돼요.

① 주어와 동사

He(주어) + **smiles**(동사). 그는 웃는다.

하나의 문장을 만들기 위해서는 주어와 동사가 반드시 필요해요. 위 문장의 He처럼 **동작이나 상태의 주체가 되는 말**을 주어라고 하고, 이는 우리말의 '누가, 무엇이'에 해당해요. smiles처럼 **주어의 동작이나 상태를 나타내는 말**을 동사라고 하고, 이는 우리말의 '~이다, ~하다'에 해당해요.

② 목적어

I(주어) + watched(동사) + **a movie**(목적어). 나는 영화를 봤다.

위 문장에서 동사 watched 다음에 내가 본 대상인 a movie가 왔어요. 이렇게 **동사가 나타내는 동작의 대상이 되는 말**을 목적어라고 해요. 목적어는 주로 동사 뒤에 오며, 우리말의 '누구를, 무엇을'에 해당해요.

③ 보어

Jim(주어) + is(동사) + **a student**(보어). Jim은 학생이다.

위 문장에서 동사 is 뒤에 a student라는 대상이 왔는데 '학생을'이라고 해석하면 어색하죠? 위 문장의 a student는 주어 Jim을 보충 설명해주고 있어요. 이렇게 **주어나 목적어를 보충 설명해주는 말**을 보어라고 해요.

④ 수식어

My mom(주어) + jogs(동사) + **in the park**(수식어). 나의 엄마는 공원에서 조깅하신다.

위 문장의 in the park는 나의 엄마가 어디에서 조깅하시는지를 더 자세하게 설명해주고 있어요. 이렇게 문장에서 반드시 필요하지 않은 부가적인 요소이지만 **다른 문장 성분이나 문장 전체를 꾸며 의미를 더 풍부하게 해주는 말**을 수식어라고 해요.

CHECK-UP

다음 문장의 밑줄 친 부분의 성분을 쓰세요.

1 She likes roses.   [   ]   2 He bought a shirt.   [   ]
3 Amy plays the flute.   [   ]   4 I was sick yesterday.   [   ]
5 Mr. Kim is a teacher.   [   ]   6 The ducks swim well.   [   ]

정답 1 주어 2 목적어 3 목적어 4 수식어 5 보어 6 동사

3 구와 절 말 덩어리

두 개 이상의 단어가 모여 하나의 의미를 나타내는 말 덩어리를 **구**나 **절**이라고 해요.

① 구

I exercise in the gym. 나는 체육관에서 운동한다.

위 문장의 in the gym은 여러 단어가 모여 '체육관에서'라는 하나의 의미를 나타내고 있어요. 그런데 in the gym에는 앞에서 배운 주어와 동사가 없죠? 이렇게 **주어와 동사가 없으면서 두 개 이상의 단어가 모인 말 덩어리**를 구라고 해요.

② 절

Lisa was angry because I was late. 내가 늦었기 때문에 Lisa는 화가 났다.

위 문장의 because I was late도 여러 단어가 모여 '내가 늦었기 때문에'라는 의미를 나타내고 있어요. 그런데 위에서 배운 구와는 다르게 because I was late에는 주어 I와 동사 was가 포함되어 있죠? 이렇게 **주어와 동사가 있으면서 두 개 이상의 단어가 모인 말 덩어리**를 절이라고 해요.

CHECK-UP

다음 문장의 밑줄 친 부분이 구인지 절인지 쓰세요.

1 I need to buy a new bag.   [   ]
2 We like playing soccer.   [   ]
3 I know that Minji is kind.   [   ]
4 I'll call you when I arrive.   [   ]
5 She goes to work by subway.   [   ]
6 Brush your teeth after you eat.   [   ]
7 I read a book before I go to bed.   [   ]
8 The cookie on the plate smells nice.   [   ]

CHAPTER 1
be동사

Sara **is** a singer. Sara는 가수이다.

'Sara는 가수이다'라는 문장에서 '~이다'라는 의미를 나타내기 위해 **be동사**인 is를 썼어요. be동사는 주어의 상태를 나타내는 동사로 '~이다, ~(하)다, (~에) 있다'라는 의미이며, 나타내는 시점과 주어에 따라 형태가 달라져요.

기출로 적중 POINT

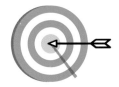

내신 100점 적중!
기출 출제율

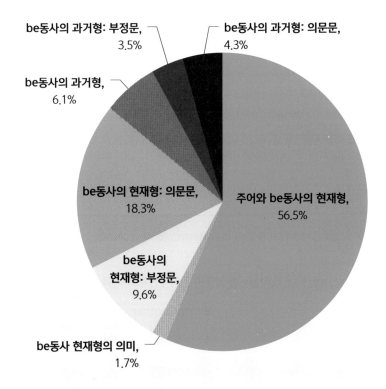

be동사의 과거형: 부정문,
3.5%

be동사의 과거형: 의문문,
4.3%

be동사의 과거형,
6.1%

be동사의 현재형: 의문문,
18.3%

주어와 be동사의 현재형,
56.5%

be동사의
현재형: 부정문,
9.6%

be동사 현재형의 의미,
1.7%

TOP 1 **주어와 be동사의 현재형 (56.5%)**
주어에 따라 형태가 변하는 be동사의 현재형을 묻는 문제가 자주 출제된다.

TOP 2 **be동사의 현재형: 의문문 (18.3%)**
be동사 현재형의 의문문과 대답의 형태를 묻는 문제가 자주 출제된다.

TOP 3 **be동사의 현재형: 부정문 (9.6%)**
be동사 현재형의 부정문의 형태를 묻는 문제가 자주 출제된다.

주어와 be동사의 현재형

정답 p.2

be동사의 현재형은 주어의 인칭과 수에 따라 am/is/are를 쓰며, 주어가 인칭대명사인 경우 줄여 쓸 수 있다.

인칭	수	주어(인칭대명사)	be동사의 현재형	줄임말
1인칭	단수	I	am	I'm
	복수	we	are	we're
2인칭	단수·복수	you	are	you're
3인칭	단수	he / she / it	is	he's / she's / it's
	복수	they	are	they're

I am a student. **I'm** 14 years old. 나는 학생이다. 나는 14살이다.
She is a teacher. **She's** kind. 그녀는 선생님이다. 그녀는 친절하다.
They are my cats. **They're** under the bed. 그것들은 나의 고양이들이다. 그것들은 침대 아래에 있다.

(Tip) 사람·동물·사물 대신 인칭대명사를 쓸 수 있다.

Mr. Smith, a boy → **he**	you and I, my friends and I → **we**
my aunt, a girl → **she**	you and she, you and Junho → **you**
a pencil, a library → **it**	Jenny and Paul, doctors, apples → **they**

연습문제 A 다음 말을 we, you, he, she, it, they 중 알맞은 인칭대명사로 바꿔 쓰시오.

1 Hana and I → _____

2 my mother → _____

3 the cups → _____

4 a piano → _____

5 you and Justin → _____

6 the tigers → _____

7 you and I → _____

8 Mr. Wilson → _____

9 his phone → _____

10 my friends → _____

11 her father → _____

12 books and pens → _____

13 Ms. Lee → _____

14 you and your brother → _____

15 your uncle → _____

16 coffee → _____

17 Mr. Kim and I → _____

18 Lisa, Daniel, and Karen → _____

연습문제 B 다음 빈칸에 알맞은 be동사의 현재형을 쓰시오.

1 She _____ my cousin.

2 You _____ smart.

3 We _____ at the church.

4 I _____ from Korea.

5 Andy _____ popular.

6 They _____ singers.

7 It _____ my favorite song.

8 Whales _____ so big.

9 This bridge _____ very long.

10 The boxes _____ on the floor.

11 Ms. White _____ a good swimmer.

12 Soyeon and I _____ in the movie theater.

연습문제 C 다음 문장의 밑줄 친 부분을 줄여 완전한 문장을 쓰시오.

1 You are brave. → _____

2 She is in her room. → _____

3 I am very thirsty. → _____

4 It is my book. → _____

5 They are busy now. → _____

6 We are late for school. → _____

7 He is a new student. → _____

기출 적중문제

다음 빈칸에 들어갈 알맞은 것은?

| _____ is at the bookstore. |

① They   ② Tom and I   ③ The students

④ We   ⑤ Michael

be동사가 is이므로 3인칭 단수 주어가 와야 해요.

be동사 현재형의 의미

정답 p.2

be동사의 현재형은 쓰임에 따라 여러 가지 의미를 나타낸다.

쓰임	의미	예문
be동사 + 명사	~이다	I **am a tennis player.** 나는 테니스 선수이다. These flowers **are tulips.** 이 꽃들은 튤립이다.
be동사 + 형용사	~(하)다	He **is tall.** 그는 키가 크다. Her eyes **are brown.** 그녀의 눈은 갈색이다.
be동사 + 전치사구	(~에) 있다	The keys **are on the table.** 그 열쇠들은 탁자 위에 있다. Lily **is at school** now. Lily는 지금 학교에 있다.

연습문제 밑줄 친 be동사의 의미와 같은 것을 <보기>에서 골라 그 기호를 쓰시오.

<보기> ⓐ He is a dancer.
        ⓑ Minji is smart.
        ⓒ They are in the museum.

1 My aunt is a pilot. [   ]

2 The story is scary. [   ]

3 Kelly and I are in Mexico. [   ]

4 I am hungry now. [   ]

5 He is a nice man. [   ]

6 It is her new jacket. [   ]

7 They are beautiful. [   ]

8 The dishes are on the shelf. [   ]

9 Mr. Davis is very angry. [   ]

10 She is my grandmother. [   ]

11 I am at the playground. [   ]

12 Your wallet is under the desk. [   ]

13 These cats are healthy. [   ]

14 His name is Steven. [   ]

15 The students are in the gym. [   ]

기출로적중 POINT 1-3 be동사의 현재형: 부정문

정답 p.2

be동사 현재형의 부정문은 am/is/are 뒤에 not을 붙이며, 줄여 쓸 수 있다.

주어(인칭대명사)	be동사의 현재형		not		줄임말
I	am				I'm not
he					he's not / he isn't
she	is				she's not / she isn't
it	+	+	not	→	it's not / it isn't
we					we're not / we aren't
you	are				you're not / you aren't
they					they're not / they aren't

He is not a high school student. 그는 고등학생이 아니다.
They're not in the classroom. 그들은 교실에 있지 않다.
The weather isn't hot today. 오늘은 날씨가 덥지 않다.

(Tip) am not은 줄여 쓸 수 없다.
   I (**am not**, ~~amn't~~) a soccer fan. 나는 축구 팬이 아니다.

연습문제 **A** 다음 문장의 밑줄 친 부분을 줄여 쓰시오.

1 He <u>is not</u> a dentist. → _____

2 We <u>are not</u> safe here. → _____

3 I <u>am not</u> twelve years old. → _____

4 <u>They are not</u> at home. → _____

5 <u>It is not</u> in my bag. → _____

6 <u>She is not</u> lazy. → _____

7 <u>You are not</u> alone. → _____

연습문제 **B** <보기>와 같이 다음 문장을 부정문으로 바꿔 쓰시오.

> **<보기>** Joseph is in Seoul now. → *Joseph is not[isn't]* in Seoul now.

1 I am sad today. → _____ sad today.

2 My mother is in the garden. → _____ in the garden.

3 Benny and I are neighbors. → _____ neighbors.

4 He is my classmate. → _____ my classmate.

5 A bee is on the flower. → _____ on the flower.

6 You are honest. → _____ honest.

7 We are good students. → _____ good students.

8 These gloves are cheap. → _____ cheap.

9 Jane is from Germany. → _____ from Germany.

10 History is my favorite subject. → _____ my favorite subject.

11 My sister and I are sleepy. → _____ sleepy.

12 This movie is popular in Korea. → _____ popular in Korea.

연습문제 C 다음 그림을 보고 괄호 안의 말과 be동사를 활용하여 빈칸에 알맞은 말을 쓰시오. (단, 줄임말로 쓰시오.)

1    **2**    **3**    **4**

1 _____ _____ on the boat. (Jessie)

2 _____ _____ _____ green. (the leaves)

3 _____ _____ a firefighter. (Adam)

4 _____ _____ _____ in the backpack. (the books)

기출 적중문제 ◎

다음 중 밑줄 친 부분을 줄여 쓸 수 <u>없는</u> 것은?

① He <u>is not</u> a liar.

② I <u>am not</u> a robot.

③ We <u>are not</u> tired.

④ That melon <u>is not</u> sweet.

⑤ They <u>are not</u> in the band.

be동사의 현재형: 의문문

1. **be동사 현재형의 의문문은 주어와 am/is/are의 순서를 바꾸고 문장 맨 뒤에 물음표를 붙인다.**

   They are baseball players. 그들은 야구 선수들이다.

   Are **they** baseball players? 그들은 야구 선수들이니?

2. **be동사 현재형의 의문문과 대답**

		의문문 (be동사 + 주어 ~?)	긍정의 대답 (Yes, 주어 + be동사.)	부정의 대답 (No, 주어 + be동사 + not.)
1인칭	단수	Am I ~?	Yes, you are.	No, you aren't.
	복수	Are we ~?	Yes, we are. / Yes, you are.	No, we aren't. / No, you aren't.
2인칭	단수	Are you ~?	Yes, I am.	No, I'm not.
	복수	Are you ~?	Yes, we are.	No, we aren't.
3인칭	단수	Is he/she/it ~?	Yes, he/she/it is.	No, he/she/it isn't.
	복수	Are they ~?	Yes, they are.	No, they aren't.

   Are **you** from Canada? 너는 캐나다에서 왔니?
   – Yes, **I** am. (= Yes, I am from Canada.) 응, 나는 캐나다에서 왔어.
   – No, **I'm** not. (= No, I'm not from Canada.) 아니, 나는 캐나다에서 오지 않았어.

   Is **James** your friend? James는 너의 친구니?
   – Yes, **he** is. (= Yes, he is my friend.) 응, 그는 나의 친구야.
   – No, **he** isn't. (= No, he isn't my friend.) 아니, 그는 나의 친구가 아니야.

   (Tip) 의문문에 대답할 때는 주어의 변화에 주의한다.
   Am I late? – No, **you** aren't. 내가 늦었니? – 아니, 너는 늦지 않았어.
   Are **you** students? – Yes, **we** are. 너희는 학생이니? – 응, 우리는 학생이야.

연습문제 A <보기>와 같이 다음 문장을 의문문으로 바꿔 쓰시오.

<보기> The river is deep. → *Is the river* deep?

1 You are free now. → _____ free now?

2 He is in the cafeteria. → _____ in the cafeteria?

3 Sally is your older sister. → _____ your older sister?

4 That tomato is fresh. → _____ fresh?

5 I am too noisy. → _____ too noisy?

6 It is a police car. → _____ a police car?

7 You are excited. → _____ excited?

8 The coins are in your pocket. → _____ in your pocket?

9 This yellow book is her diary. → _____ her diary?

10 The spoons are in the cabinet. → _____ in the cabinet?

11 They are on the plane now. → _____ on the plane now?

12 Jacob and I are the same age. → _____ the same age?

연습문제 B   다음 질문에 대한 대답을 완성하시오.

1 *A*: Is it spicy? *B*: No, _____ .

2 *A*: Am I in trouble? *B*: No, _____ .

3 *A*: Are you a student here? *B*: Yes, _____ .

4 *A*: Is your mother a writer? *B*: No, _____ .

5 *A*: Are the cookies ready? *B*: No, _____ .

6 *A*: Is the Eiffel Tower in Paris? *B*: Yes, _____ .

7 *A*: Is Mr. Carter at the basketball court? *B*: No, _____ .

8 *A*: Is your father with you? *B*: Yes, _____ .

9 *A*: Are you and your sister busy? *B*: No, _____ .

기출 적중문제

다음 그림을 보고 빈칸에 알맞은 말을 넣어 질문에 대한 대답을 완성하시오.

be동사의 의문문에 대답할 때는 대답의 내용이 긍정인지 부정인지 확인하세요.

A: Is your scarf blue?
B: _____, _____ _____ . It's red.

POINT 2-1 be동사의 과거형

기출로적중

정답 p.2

be동사의 과거형은 주어에 따라 was/were를 쓰며, '~이었다, ~(했)다, ~(에) 있었다'의 의미이다.

주어(인칭대명사)	be동사의 현재형		주어(인칭대명사)	be동사의 과거형
I	am		I	
he / she / it	+ is	→	he / she / it	+ was
we / you / they	are		we / you / they	were

I was an elementary school student last year. 나는 작년에 초등학생이었다.
He was really tired. 그는 정말 피곤했다.
The maps were on the wall. 그 지도들은 벽에 있었다.

연습문제 우리말과 같도록 be동사를 활용하여 빈칸에 쓰시오.

1 지우는 어젯밤에 아팠다. = Jiwoo _____ sick last night.

2 그녀의 귀걸이들은 그녀의 가방 안에 있었다. = Her earrings _____ in her bag.

3 어제는 나의 생일이었다. = Yesterday _____ my birthday.

4 그와 나는 일요일에 도서관에 있었다. = He and I _____ at the library on Sunday.

5 Emma와 Betty는 친한 친구였다. = Emma and Betty _____ close friends.

6 어제 그 신부는 아름다웠다. = The bride _____ beautiful yesterday.

7 이 카메라는 한 달 전에 할인 중이었다. = This camera _____ on sale a month ago.

8 우리는 지난 주말에 해변에 있었다. = We _____ at the beach last weekend.

9 나는 5분 전에 버스 정류장에 있었다. = I _____ at the bus stop five minutes ago.

기출 적중문제

다음 중 밑줄 친 부분이 어법상 어색한 것은?

① I was late for the movie.
② You and Sam were very kind to me.
③ Sophie and Joe was at home yesterday.
④ The birds were in the tree.
⑤ Ms. Miller was 30 years old last year.

be동사의 과거형은
주어가 하나일 때는 was를 쓰고,
여럿일 때는 were를 써요.

be동사의 과거형: 부정문

정답 p.3

be동사 과거형의 부정문은 was/were 뒤에 not을 붙이며, 줄여 쓸 수 있다.

주어(인칭대명사)		be동사의 과거형	not	줄임말
I / he / she / it	+	**was**	+ **not** →	I/he/she/it wasn't
we / you / they		**were**		we/you/they weren't

It was not my fault. 그것은 나의 잘못이 아니었다.
Max and Cindy weren't at the theater. Max와 Cindy는 극장에 있지 않았다.

연습문제 <보기>와 같이 다음 문장을 부정문으로 바꿔 쓰시오.

<보기> I was wrong yesterday. → *I was not[wasn't]* wrong yesterday.

1 He and I were English teachers. → _____ English teachers.

2 They were in China last week. → _____ in China last week.

3 The musical was amazing. → _____ amazing.

4 It was my choice. → _____ my choice.

5 You were at school last Friday. → _____ at school last Friday.

6 Emily was busy this morning. → _____ busy this morning.

7 The stars were bright. → _____ bright.

8 My room was dirty yesterday. → _____ dirty yesterday.

9 We were upset about the news. → _____ upset about the news.

10 The TV program was funny. → _____ funny.

11 Leo was a nurse ten years ago. → _____ a nurse ten years ago.

12 The sandwiches were delicious. → _____ delicious.

13 Those shoes were comfortable. → _____ comfortable.

14 The cats were very friendly. → _____ very friendly.

15 The magazine was helpful. → _____ helpful.

16 My neighbors were loud last night. → _____ loud last night.

정답 p.3

기출로적중 POINT 2-3 be동사의 과거형: 의문문

be동사 과거형의 의문문과 대답

의문문	긍정의 대답	부정의 대답
Was/Were + 주어 ~?	Yes, 주어 + was/were.	No, 주어 + wasn't/weren't.

Were you angry at me? 너는 나에게 화가 났었니?
- **Yes**, I **was**. (= Yes, I was angry at you.) 응, 나는 너에게 화가 났었어.
- **No**, I **wasn't**. (= No, I wasn't angry at you.) 아니, 나는 너에게 화가 나지 않았어.

Were Diana and her sister at the concert? Diana와 그녀의 언니는 그 콘서트에 있었니?
- **Yes**, **they were**. (= Yes, they were at the concert.) 응, 그들은 그 콘서트에 있었어.
- **No**, **they weren't**. (= No, they weren't at the concert.) 아니, 그들은 그 콘서트에 있지 않았어.

연습문제 A <보기>와 같이 다음 문장을 의문문으로 바꿔 쓰시오.

<보기> You were in the bathroom. → _Were you_ in the bathroom?

1 Debra was a musician. → _____ a musician?

2 The glasses were clean. → _____ clean?

3 The pictures were on the wall. → _____ on the wall?

4 The cupcake was delicious. → _____ delicious?

5 Her son was five years old last year. → _____ five years old last year?

6 Bananas were cheap many years ago. → _____ cheap many years ago?

연습문제 B 다음 질문에 대한 대답을 완성하시오.

1 A: Were you a dancer before? B: No, _____.

2 A: Were your grades good? B: Yes, _____.

3 A: Was the movie interesting? B: No, _____.

4 A: Were your parents doctors? B: No, _____.

5 A: Was Ms. Park in Boston last Monday? B: Yes, _____.

6 A: Was the math exam very difficult? B: Yes, _____.

7 A: Were my friends and I too noisy? B: No, _____.

A 다음 그림을 보고 be동사의 현재형을 활용하여 빈칸에 알맞은 말을 쓰시오. (단, 부정문에서는 줄임말을 쓰시오.)

1

It _____ a rabbit.
Its ears _____ white.

2

They _____ students.
Their teacher _____ in the classroom.

3

He _____ a baker.
His cookies _____ round.

4

The weather _____ sunny.
Her shoes _____ wet.

B 우리말과 같도록 괄호 안의 말과 be동사를 활용하여 문장을 완성하시오.

1 그 달력은 책상 위에 있다. (the calendar)   = _____ on the desk.

2 우리는 지금 춥지 않다. (we)   = _____ cold now.

3 소희와 나는 반 친구이다. (Sohee and I)   = _____ classmates.

4 그 접시들은 싱크대 안에 있었다. (the dishes)   = _____ in the sink.

5 그 공원은 사람들로 가득 차 있었다. (the park)   = _____ full of people.

6 그녀의 교실은 위층에 있니? (her classroom)   = _____ upstairs?

7 그들은 어젯밤에 집에 있었니? (they)   = _____ at home last night?

8 나의 삼촌은 의사가 아니다. (my uncle)   = _____ a doctor.

9 Helen은 지난 토요일에 아팠니? (Helen)   = _____ sick last Saturday?

10 그것들은 신선한 채소들이 아니었다. (they)   = _____ fresh vegetables.

11 그 가게는 어제 문을 열지 않았다. (the store)   = _____ open yesterday.

C <보기>와 같이 다음 문장을 괄호 안의 지시대로 바꿔 쓰시오.

> <보기>   He is in the hospital. (부정문으로)
> → *He is not[isn't] in the hospital.*

1 Her socks are purple. (부정문으로)

→ _____

2 They were on the train to Busan. (의문문으로)

→ _____

3 Alex and I were very surprised. (부정문으로)

→ _____

4 Your dog was in my yard yesterday. (의문문으로)

→ _____

5 This white building is his school. (의문문으로)

→ _____

6 It is a new smartphone model. (부정문으로)

→ _____

7 Jimmy was tired last weekend. (의문문으로)

→ _____

8 The weather was wonderful a month ago. (부정문으로)

→ _____

9 Mr. Brown is a movie director. (의문문으로)

→ _____

10 I am in the science room now. (부정문으로)

→ _____

11 These flowers are blue roses. (의문문으로)

→ _____

12 Beth is good at Korean. (부정문으로)

→ _____

13 The cats were on the roof this morning. (부정문으로)

→ _____

1 다음 중 주어와 be동사의 현재형이 잘못 짝지어진 것은?

① I – am
② Sumi and Jun – are
③ it – is
④ your bags – is
⑤ Ms. Lim – is

[2-3] 다음 빈칸에 들어갈 말로 어색한 것을 고르시오.

2

_____ are from England.

① You
② Jill and I
③ Her parents
④ He
⑤ Tony and his sister

3

_____ was absent yesterday.

① Mike and Kerry
② I
③ Yuna
④ My friend
⑤ He

4 다음 빈칸에 들어갈 말이 순서대로 짝지어진 것은?

| · Nate and I _____ cousins.
· His name _____ Brian. |
| --- |

① am – is
② am – are
③ are – is
④ are – are
⑤ is – is

5 다음 문장의 I를 Marie로 바꿔 완전한 문장을 쓰시오.

| I am a web designer.
→ _____ |
| --- |

6 다음 중 밑줄 친 be동사의 의미가 나머지 넷과 다른 것은?

① His eyes are green.
② The dogs are on the bed.
③ I am very sleepy right now.
④ This question is so difficult.
⑤ Sojin is brave and honest.

7 다음 빈칸에 들어갈 말이 나머지 넷과 다른 것은?

① She _____ nervous.
② Jackson _____ my neighbor.
③ My parents _____ busy.
④ The giraffe _____ very tall.
⑤ Matt _____ in Jejudo.

8 다음 중 밑줄 친 부분이 어법상 바른 것은?

① He are my older brother.
② Her sunglasses aren't cheap.
③ I amn't a great cook.
④ This chocolate cake not is delicious.
⑤ These flowers is colorful.

[9-10] 다음 글을 읽고 주어진 질문에 답하시오.

My classmates and I _____ all good friends, but we _____ also very different. (A) 나는 키가 작지만, Peter는 키가 크다. Jessica is a fast runner. However, Angela and Jimin _____ not fast runners.

9 위 글의 빈칸에 공통으로 들어갈 알맞은 말을 쓰시오.

→ _____

10 위 글의 밑줄 친 우리말 (A)와 같도록 문장을 완성하시오.

= _____ _____ short, but _____ _____ tall.

11 우리말과 같도록 괄호 안의 말을 활용하여 문장을 완성하시오.

나의 고양이는 지금 배고프지 않다. (be)

= _____ now.

12 다음 중 밑줄 친 부분을 줄여 쓸 수 없는 것은?

① Your phone <u>was not</u> here.
② They <u>are not</u> his new shoes.
③ I <u>am not</u> at home now.
④ Her friends <u>were not</u> bored.
⑤ Junho <u>is not</u> my boyfriend.

13 다음 표를 보고 빈칸에 알맞은 말을 <보기>에서 골라 쓰시오.

	Evan	Olivia
tall	O	O
dentist	O	X
in Seoul	X	X

| <보기> | is | isn't | are | aren't |

(1) Evan and Olivia _____ tall.

(2) Evan _____ a dentist, but Olivia _____ a dentist.

(3) Evan and Olivia _____ in Seoul.

14 다음 그림을 보고 질문에 대한 대답으로 가장 알맞은 것을 고르시오.

A: Is the living room clean?
B: _____

① Yes, it is.　　② Yes, it isn't.
③ No, it is.　　④ No, it isn't.
⑤ No, it aren't.

15 다음 중 자연스럽지 <u>않은</u> 대화를 <u>모두</u> 고르시오.

① A: Am I correct?

　B: Yes, you are.

② A: Were your puppies sick?

　B: No, they weren't.

③ A: Is Molly a violinist?

　B: Yes, she isn't.

④ A: Are you at the bank now?

　B: No, you aren't.

⑤ A: Was it hot in the summer last year?

　B: Yes, it was.

16 다음 문장을 주어진 지시대로 바꿔 쓰시오.

Danny is at the gym.

(1) 부정문으로

　→ _____

(2) 의문문으로

　→ _____

17 다음 중 밑줄 친 부분이 어법상 어색한 것은?

A: <u>Are</u> they baseball players? 　　 ① B: <u>No</u>, <u>we</u> <u>aren't</u>. They are <u>rugby</u> players. 　　② 　③ 　④ 　　　　 ⑤

18 다음 중 어법상 어색한 것은?

① I were in Paris a long time ago.

② My neighbors are very noisy.

③ She was a ballet dancer before.

④ Those houses are really huge.

⑤ It was windy and cloudy yesterday.

[19-20] 다음 글을 읽고 주어진 질문에 답하시오.

Gilbert was late for school yesterday. Kate was late, too. (A) <u>Their teacher was</u> <u>angry.</u>

19 다음 빈칸에 알맞은 말을 넣어 질문에 대한 대답을 완성하시오.

A: Were Gilbert and Kate late for school 　 yesterday? B: _____, _____ _____.

20 위 글의 밑줄 친 (A)를 의문문으로 바꿔 쓰시오.

→ _____

21 다음 중 어법상 바른 것끼리 묶인 것은?

ⓐ Juho and Tim aren't in the classroom. ⓑ Is interesting your job? ⓒ Was the soup too hot? ⓓ The baby not was sleepy. ⓔ Were you be busy last night?

① ⓐ, ⓒ　　　② ⓐ, ⓓ　　　③ ⓑ, ⓒ

④ ⓒ, ⓔ　　　⑤ ⓓ, ⓔ

22 다음 중 not이 들어갈 위치는?

① Ms. Jones ② is ③ a ④ gardener ⑤.

23 다음 중 밑줄 친 부분이 어법상 어색한 것은?

① We were awake all night.

② They are at the movie theater now.

③ That sweater is so expensive.

④ You and John are my best friends.

⑤ Bora and her brother was thirsty.

24 다음 우리말을 알맞게 영작한 것은?

> 너의 개들은 크니?

① Your dogs is big?

② You're dogs are big?

③ Is your dogs big?

④ Am you're dogs big?

⑤ Are your dogs big?

25 다음 질문에 대한 대답으로 알맞은 것은?

> A: Are you and Inho students?
> B: _____

① Yes, we aren't.　② No, we aren't.

③ Yes, you are.　④ No, we are.

⑤ Yes, you aren't.

[26-27] 다음 문장에서 틀린 부분을 바르게 고쳐 완전한 문장을 쓰시오.

26

> Is Jim and Liam on the soccer team?
> → _____

27

> Her birthday were last Saturday.
> → _____

28 다음 밑줄 친 부분을 인칭대명사로 바르게 바꾼 것은?

① Ron and Jake were at the shop. (→ You)

② Mr. Shaw was an Italian chef. (→ It)

③ You and Linda are very kind. (→ They)

④ Karl and I are a couple. (→ We)

⑤ The books are in my bag. (→ It)

29 다음은 Nick이 자신을 소개하는 글이다. 빈칸에 알맞은 말을 넣어 대화를 완성하시오.

> Hi, I'm Nick. I'm from Australia, but my parents are German. I'm twelve years old, and I'm a good hockey player.

> Anna: Is Nick from Germany?
> Ken : (A) _____, _____ _____.
> 　　　 (B) _____ _____ from Australia.
> Anna: Is he a good hockey player?
> Ken : (C) _____, _____ _____.

CHAPTER 2
일반동사

---

walk 걷다　　**like** 좋아하다　　**sing** 노래하다　　**know** 알다

walk, like, sing, know와 같이 주어의 동작이나 상태를 나타내는 동사를 **일반동사**라고 해요. 일반동사는 be동사
와 조동사를 제외한 모든 동사로, 나타내는 시점과 주어에 따라 형태가 달라져요.

기출로 적중 POINT

내신 100점 적중!
기출 출제율

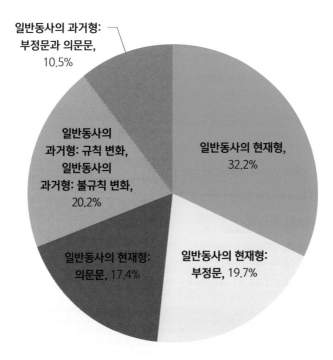

일반동사의 과거형:
부정문과 의문문,
10.5%

일반동사의
과거형: 규칙 변화,
일반동사의
과거형: 불규칙 변화,
20.2%

일반동사의 현재형,
32.2%

일반동사의 현재형:
의문문, 17.4%

일반동사의 현재형:
부정문, 19.7%

TOP 1 **일반동사의 현재형 (32.2%)**
주어에 따라 형태가 변하는 일반동사의 현재형과 일반동사의 3인칭 단수형을
묻는 문제가 자주 출제된다.

TOP 2 **일반동사의 과거형: 규칙 변화, 불규칙 변화 (20.2%)**
일반동사의 과거형을 묻는 문제가 자주 출제된다.

TOP 3 **일반동사의 현재형: 부정문 (19.7%)**
일반동사 현재형의 부정문의 형태를 묻는 문제가 자주 출제된다.

일반동사의 현재형

정답 p.5

1. 일반동사의 현재형은 주어가 3인칭 단수인 경우 동사원형에 -(e)s를 붙여 만들고, 그 외에는 동사원형을 쓴다.

❶ 주어가 1·2인칭 또는 3인칭 복수인 경우

I / we / you / they	+	동사원형	**I want** new socks. 나는 새 양말을 원한다.

❷ 주어가 3인칭 단수인 경우

he / she / it	+	동사원형 + -(e)s	**He likes** puppies. 그는 강아지를 좋아한다.

2. 일반동사의 3인칭 현재 단수형 만드는 법

대부분의 동사	동사원형 + -s	work – work**s** arrive – arrive**s**	love – love**s** speak – speak**s**
-o, -s, -x, -ch, -sh로 끝나는 동사	동사원형 + -es	go – go**es** mix – mix**es**	pass – pass**es** watch – watch**es**
「자음 + y」로 끝나는 동사	y를 i로 바꾸고 + -es	fly – fl**ies** carry – carr**ies** (Tip) 「모음 + y」로 끝나는 동사: buy – buy**s**	cry – cr**ies** study – stud**ies**
불규칙하게 변하는 동사	have – **has**		

Yuri speaks French well. 유리는 프랑스어를 잘 말한다.
My sister goes to bed at 11 o'clock. 나의 누나는 11시에 잔다.

연습문제 A 다음 동사의 3인칭 단수형을 쓰시오.

1 know – _____

2 do – _____

3 pass – _____

4 learn – _____

5 meet – _____

6 mix – _____

7 listen – _____

8 finish – _____

9 read – _____

10 walk – _____

11 hurry – _____

12 see – _____

13 look – _____

14 push – _____

15 smell – _____

16 carry – _____

17 try   – _____

18 brush   – _____

19 buy   – _____

20 fly   – _____

21 put   – _____

22 stay   – _____

23 touch   – _____

24 like   – _____

25 say   – _____

26 fix   – _____

27 watch   – _____

28 enjoy   – _____

29 run   – _____

30 give   – _____

31 pay   – _____

32 miss   – _____

33 taste   – _____

34 become   – _____

35 catch   – _____

36 think   – _____

37 make   – _____

38 feel   – _____

39 ask   – _____

40 worry   – _____

연습문제 B   괄호 안의 동사를 현재형으로 바꿔 빈칸에 쓰시오.

1 Josie _____ in London. (live)

2 He _____ English very hard. (study)

3 The bus _____ at 8:30 A.M. (arrive)

4 Gina _____ brown hair. (have)

5 I _____ my hands before meals. (wash)

6 Ms. Kwon _____ history at school. (teach)

7 The baby _____ every night. (cry)

8 Tom and I _____ basketball on Sundays. (play)

기출 적중문제

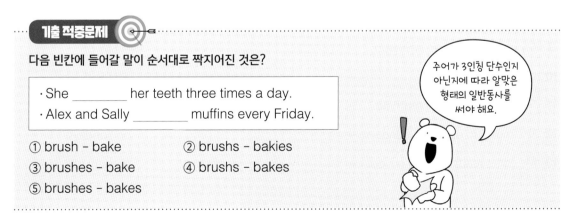

다음 빈칸에 들어갈 말이 순서대로 짝지어진 것은?

> · She _____ her teeth three times a day.
> · Alex and Sally _____ muffins every Friday.

① brush - bake   ② brushs - bakies

③ brushes - bake   ④ brushs - bakes

⑤ brushes - bakes

주어가 3인칭 단수인지 아닌지에 따라 알맞은 형태의 일반동사를 써야 해요.

일반동사 현재형의 부정문은 동사원형 앞에 do not[don't]/does not[doesn't]를 붙인다.

❶ 주어가 1·2인칭 또는 3인칭 복수인 경우

| I / we / you / they | + | **do not[don't]** | + | 동사원형 |

I do not eat breakfast. 나는 아침을 먹지 않는다.
My brothers don't play online games. 나의 형들은 온라인 게임을 하지 않는다.

❷ 주어가 3인칭 단수인 경우

| he / she / it | + | **does not[doesn't]** | + | 동사원형 |

She does not have class today. 그녀는 오늘 수업이 없다.
The movie doesn't start right now. 그 영화는 지금 당장 시작하지 않는다.

연습문제 A   <보기>와 같이 다음 문장을 부정문으로 바꿔 쓰시오.

| <보기> Jeremy speaks Russian. → *Jeremy does not[doesn't] speak* Russian. |

1 He sings very well. → _____ very well.

2 She goes to church. → _____ to church.

3 They exercise regularly. → _____ regularly.

4 Somin has a cat. → _____ a cat.

5 I know your phone number. → _____ your phone number.

6 Dan and his sister like sports. → _____ sports.

7 We need a new computer. → _____ a new computer.

8 Andy and Tina drink coffee. → _____ coffee.

9 My grandfather lives in Suwon. → _____ in Suwon.

10 It rains a lot in the fall. → _____ a lot in the fall.

11 Steve and I jog every morning. → _____ every morning.

12 The museum opens on Sundays. → _____ on Sundays.

13 Ms. Jones reads mystery novels. → _____ mystery novels.

다음 그림을 보고 괄호 안의 동사를 활용하여 빈칸에 알맞은 말을 쓰시오. (단, 현재형으로 쓰시오.)

1

(ride)

Jenny _____ a bicycle to school.

However, Leo _____ _____ a bicycle to school.

2

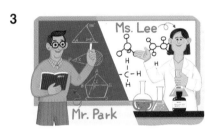

(practice)

Helen _____ the piano on weekends.

However, Josh and Ken _____ _____ the piano on weekends.

3

(teach)

Mr. Park _____ math at a middle school.

However, Ms. Lee _____ _____ math at a middle school.

4

(feel)

Kate _____ well today.

However, Peter _____ _____ well today.

기출 적중문제

다음 우리말을 알맞게 영작한 것은?

그녀는 우산을 가지고 있지 않다.

① She don't have an umbrella.
② She not has an umbrella.
③ She doesn't has an umbrella.
④ She don't has an umbrella.
⑤ She doesn't have an umbrella.

일반동사의 현재형: 의문문

정답 p.5

1. **일반동사 현재형의 의문문은 주어 앞에 Do/Does를 붙이고 주어 뒤에 동사원형을 쓴다.**

   ❶ 주어가 1·2인칭 또는 3인칭 복수인 경우

Do	+	I / we / you / they	+	동사원형	~?

   Do you know his name? 너는 그의 이름을 아니?
   Do tigers swim well? 호랑이들은 수영을 잘하니?

   ❷ 주어가 3인칭 단수인 경우

Does	+	he / she / it	+	동사원형	~?

   Does she live here? 그녀는 여기에 사니?
   Does Eunho watch TV a lot? 은호는 TV를 많이 보니?

2. **일반동사 현재형의 의문문에 대한 대답**

긍정의 대답 (Yes, 주어 + do/does.)	부정의 대답 (No, 주어 + don't/doesn't.)
Yes, I/we/you/they do.	No, I/we/you/they don't.
Yes, he/she/it does.	No, he/she/it doesn't.

   Do they like Korean food? 그들은 한국 음식을 좋아하니?
   – **Yes, they do.** 응, 그들은 좋아해. / **No, they don't.** 아니, 그들은 좋아하지 않아.

   Does Mr. Miller drive a car? Miller씨는 차를 운전하니?
   – **Yes, he does.** 응, 그는 운전해. / **No, he doesn't.** 아니, 그는 운전하지 않아.

연습문제 A <보기>와 같이 다음 문장을 의문문으로 바꿔 쓰시오.

> <보기> He likes pizza. → _Does he like_ pizza?

1 Liam has a fever. → _____ a fever?

2 Anne studies hard. → _____ hard?

3 She practices taekwondo. → _____ taekwondo?

4 They play basketball after school. → _____ basketball after school?

5 He locks the door at night. → _____ the door at night?

6 His grandparents raise animals. → _____ animals?

7 Batman wears a black suit. → _____ a black suit?

8 The laptop works now. → _____ now?

9 Minji and Junho know the address. → _____ the address?

10 You go to the gym on Sundays. → _____ to the gym on Sundays?

연습문제 B 괄호 안에서 알맞은 것을 고르시오.

1 (Do / Does) you want dessert now?

2 (Do / Does) he sleep late on weekends?

3 Does Woobin (run / runs) every morning?

4 (Do / Does) kangaroos jump high?

5 (Do / Does) Yerin have a winter coat?

6 Does your aunt (like / likes) her job?

7 Do the seats (have / has) enough space?

8 Does Lisa (break / breaks) her promises often?

9 (Do / Does) this sandwich taste good?

연습문제 C 다음 질문에 대한 대답을 완성하시오.

1 *A*: Does she like spicy food?　　　　　　　*B*: Yes, _____.

2 *A*: Does your brother love science?　　　　*B*: Yes, _____.

3 *A*: Do they know about the new student?　*B*: No, _____.

4 *A*: Does Minsu use hair spray?　　　　　　*B*: No, _____.

5 *A*: Do you and he have an umbrella?　　　*B*: Yes, _____.

6 *A*: Does Mary need our help?　　　　　　　*B*: Yes, _____.

7 *A*: Do your parents work at a hospital?　　*B*: No, _____.

8 *A*: Does the train to London leave from this platform?　*B*: No, _____.

기출 적중문제

다음 빈칸에 알맞은 말을 넣어 대화를 완성하시오.

A: _____ _____ _____ in Busan?
B: No, I don't. I live in Daegu.

일반동사의 과거형: 규칙 변화

정답 p.5

일반동사의 과거형은 대부분 동사원형에 -(e)d를 붙여 만든다.

대부분의 동사	동사원형 + -ed	call – call**ed** watch – watch**ed**	open – open**ed** cook – cook**ed**
-e로 끝나는 동사	동사원형 + -d	move – mov**ed** invite – invit**ed**	lie – li**ed** agree – agre**ed**
「자음 + y」로 끝나는 동사	y를 i로 바꾸고 + -ed	try – tr**ied** study – stud**ied**	copy – cop**ied** worry – worr**ied**
		Tip 「모음 + y」로 끝나는 동사: stay – stay**ed**	
「단모음 + 단자음」으로 끝나는 동사	마지막 자음을 한 번 더 쓰고 + -ed	stop – stop**ped** plan – plan**ned**	drop – drop**ped** grab – grab**bed**
		Tip 강세가 앞에 오는 2음절 동사: visit – visit**ed**	enter – enter**ed**

We **moved** to a new apartment. 우리는 새 아파트로 이사했다.

The snow finally **stopped**. 눈이 마침내 그쳤다.

Tip 과거형이 규칙적으로 변하는 일반동사의 과거형과 과거분사형(p.p.)은 형태가 같다.

원형　　과거형　　과거분사형
paint – **painted** – **painted**

연습문제 A　다음 동사의 과거형을 쓰시오.

1 talk　　–　_____

2 clean　　–　_____

3 love　　–　_____

4 cry　　–　_____

5 work　　–　_____

6 live　　–　_____

7 close　　–　_____

8 plan　　–　_____

9 open　　–　_____

10 hug　　–　_____

11 drop　　–　_____

12 like　　–　_____

13 wash　　–　_____

14 play　　–　_____

15 study　　–　_____

16 stop　　–　_____

17 raise　　–　_____

18 visit　　–　_____

19 arrive　　–　_____

20 marry　　–　_____

21 happen – _____ 22 want – _____

23 shop – _____ 24 dance – _____

25 decide – _____ 26 look – _____

27 worry – _____ 28 believe – _____

29 listen – _____ 30 enjoy – _____

31 taste – _____ 32 try – _____

33 save – _____ 34 stay – _____

35 invite – _____ 36 carry – _____

37 die – _____ 38 shout – _____

39 jog – _____ 40 smile – _____

41 copy – _____ 42 grab – _____

43 chat – _____ 44 hurry – _____

45 hate – _____ 46 jump – _____

47 hope – _____ 48 step – _____

49 enter – _____ 50 explain – _____

연습문제 B 괄호 안에서 알맞은 것을 고르시오.

1 The baby (smileed / smiled) at me.

2 I (planed / planned) my trip a week ago.

3 Jennifer (studyed / studied) at the library.

4 It (rained / rainned) heavily last night.

5 Lizzy (worryed / worried) about her final exam.

6 Cameron (played / plaied) the cello on the stage.

7 My family (stayed / staied) in Beijing last month.

8 Jack and Rose (chatted / chated) on the phone for hours.

기출 적중문제

다음 중 동사의 과거형이 잘못된 것은?

① like - liked ② start - started
③ cry - cried ④ hug - huged
⑤ play - played

일반동사의 과거형: 불규칙 변화

정답 p.6

일부 일반동사의 과거형과 과거분사형(p.p.)은 불규칙하게 변한다.

❶ A-A-A형: 원형−과거형−과거분사형이 모두 같다.

원형	과거형	과거분사형	원형	과거형	과거분사형
cost 비용이 들다	cost	cost	cut 베다, 자르다	cut	cut
hit 치다	hit	hit	hurt 다치게 하다	hurt	hurt
put 놓다	put	put	read [riːd] 읽다	read [red]	read [red]
set 놓다	set	set	spread 펼치다	spread	spread

Tracey **read** comic books last night. Tracey는 어젯밤에 만화책들을 읽었다.

❷ A-B-A형: 원형−과거분사형이 같다.

원형	과거형	과거분사형	원형	과거형	과거분사형
become ~이 되다	became	become	come 오다	came	come
overcome 극복하다	overcame	overcome	run 달리다	ran	run

Richard **came** from Germany. Richard는 독일에서 왔다.

❸ A-B-B형: 과거형−과거분사형이 같다.

원형	과거형	과거분사형	원형	과거형	과거분사형
bring 가져오다	brought	brought	build 짓다	built	built
buy 사다	bought	bought	catch 잡다	caught	caught
feed 먹이를 주다	fed	fed	fight 싸우다	fought	fought
find 찾다	found	found	get 얻다	got	got(ten)
have 가지다	had	had	hear 듣다	heard	heard
keep 유지하다	kept	kept	lay 놓다, 낳다	laid	laid
leave 떠나다	left	left	lose 잃다, 지다	lost	lost
make 만들다	made	made	meet 만나다	met	met
say 말하다	said	said	sell 팔다	sold	sold
send 보내다	sent	sent	sit 앉다	sat	sat
sleep 자다	slept	slept	spend 쓰다	spent	spent
stand 서다	stood	stood	teach 가르치다	taught	taught

원형	과거형	과거분사형	원형	과거형	과거분사형
tell 말하다	told	told	think 생각하다	thought	thought
understand 이해하다	understood	understood	win 이기다	won	won

Yujin lost her wallet yesterday. 유진이는 어제 그녀의 지갑을 잃어버렸다.

❹ A-B-C형: 원형-과거형-과거분사형이 모두 다르다.

원형	과거형	과거분사형	원형	과거형	과거분사형
begin 시작하다	began	begun	break 깨다	broke	broken
choose 선택하다	chose	chosen	do 하다	did	done
draw 그리다	drew	drawn	drink 마시다	drank	drunk
drive 운전하다	drove	driven	eat 먹다	ate	eaten
fall 떨어지다, 넘어지다	fell	fallen	fly 날다	flew	flown
forget 잊다	forgot	forgotten	give 주다	gave	given
go 가다	went	gone	grow 자라다	grew	grown
know 알다	knew	known	mistake 실수하다	mistook	mistaken
ride 타다	rode	ridden	rise 오르다	rose	risen
see 보다	saw	seen	sing 노래하다	sang	sung
speak 말하다	spoke	spoken	swim 수영하다	swam	swum
take 가지고 가다	took	taken	wake 깨우다	woke	woken
wear 입고 있다	wore	worn	write 쓰다	wrote	written

A large tree fell during the storm. 큰 나무가 폭풍우 중에 넘어졌다.

연습문제 A 다음 동사의 과거형과 과거분사형을 쓰시오.

1 lay – _____ – _____

2 sell – _____ – _____

3 draw – _____ – _____

4 buy – _____ – _____

5 tell – _____ – _____

6 cut – _____ – _____

7 speak – _____ – _____

8 become – _____ – _____

9 set – _____ – _____

10 eat – _____ – _____

11 run – _____ – _____

12 spend – _____ – _____

13 have	– _____ – _____	14 make	– _____ – _____
15 wake	– _____ – _____	16 hit	– _____ – _____
17 get	– _____ – _____	18 sleep	– _____ – _____
19 win	– _____ – _____	20 lose	– _____ – _____
21 meet	– _____ – _____	22 feed	– _____ – _____
23 find	– _____ – _____	24 put	– _____ – _____
25 read	– _____ – _____	26 write	– _____ – _____
27 build	– _____ – _____	28 hear	– _____ – _____
29 spread	– _____ – _____	30 fight	– _____ – _____
31 say	– _____ – _____	32 sing	– _____ – _____
33 catch	– _____ – _____	34 break	– _____ – _____
35 wear	– _____ – _____	36 take	– _____ – _____
37 do	– _____ – _____	38 hurt	– _____ – _____
39 go	– _____ – _____	40 think	– _____ – _____
41 swim	– _____ – _____	42 come	– _____ – _____
43 cost	– _____ – _____	44 see	– _____ – _____
45 teach	– _____ – _____	46 rise	– _____ – _____
47 understand	– _____ – _____	48 know	– _____ – _____
49 overcome	– _____ – _____	50 bring	– _____ – _____
51 choose	– _____ – _____	52 leave	– _____ – _____
53 fall	– _____ – _____	54 forget	– _____ – _____
55 fly	– _____ – _____	56 grow	– _____ – _____
57 ride	– _____ – _____	58 drink	– _____ – _____
59 sit	– _____ – _____	60 drive	– _____ – _____
61 begin	– _____ – _____	62 give	– _____ – _____
63 stand	– _____ – _____	64 keep	– _____ – _____
65 mistake	– _____ – _____	66 send	– _____ – _____

연습문제 B 괄호 안의 동사를 과거형으로 바꿔 빈칸에 쓰시오.

1 Randy _____ with us last week. (swim)

2 The player _____ the ball really hard. (hit)

3 Jintae _____ from his bike yesterday. (fall)

4 We _____ a present to Melissa. (give)

5 I _____ a big fish in the lake. (catch)

6 The man _____ a superhero in the movie. (become)

7 The chicken _____ an egg last night. (lay)

8 They _____ their apartment key. (lose)

9 My parents _____ a new fridge two years ago. (buy)

10 Mr. Murphy's dogs _____ on his bed. (sleep)

11 We _____ a lot of apple pies. (make)

12 He _____ the restaurant at 9 P.M. (leave)

13 The watermelon _____ sweet. (taste)

14 You _____ a great job in the dance contest. (do)

15 The lion _____ after the deer. (run)

16 She _____ the pizza on a plate. (put)

17 Adam _____ the news last evening. (watch)

18 A letter _____ for Harry this morning. (arrive)

19 Our football team _____ the final game. (win)

20 My sister _____ my phone on the floor. (drop)

기출 적중문제

다음 중 밑줄 친 동사의 과거형이 바른 것은?

① He reaaded the poem.

② I fed my cat an hour ago.

③ You saveed my life last night.

④ The car stoped at the red light.

⑤ Doyun faught with his mom yesterday.

1. 일반동사 과거형의 부정문은 동사원형 앞에 did not[didn't]를 붙인다.

주어 + **did not[didn't]** + 동사원형

We **did not have** time. 우리는 시간이 없었다.
It **didn't snow** much last year. 작년에는 눈이 많이 오지 않았다.

2. 일반동사 과거형의 의문문

❶ 일반동사 과거형의 의문문은 주어 앞에 Did를 붙이고 주어 뒤에 동사원형을 쓴다.

Did + 주어 + 동사원형 ~?

Did you find your phone? 너는 너의 전화기를 찾았니?
Did Fred study hard yesterday? Fred는 어제 열심히 공부했니?

❷ 일반동사 과거형의 의문문에 대한 대답

긍정의 대답	부정의 대답
Yes, 주어 + did.	No, 주어 + didn't.

Did they go to bed early? 그들은 일찍 잤니?
– **Yes, they did**. 응, 그들은 일찍 잤어. / **No, they didn't**. 아니, 그들은 일찍 자지 않았어.

Did Sandra play the piano last night? Sandra는 어젯밤에 피아노를 쳤니?
– **Yes, she did**. 응, 그녀는 피아노를 쳤어. / **No, she didn't**. 아니, 그녀는 피아노를 치지 않았어.

연습문제 A 우리말과 같도록 괄호 안의 동사를 활용하여 빈칸에 쓰시오.

1 그 쿠키는 그것 안에 설탕을 포함하고 있지 않았다. (have)
= The cookie ＿＿＿＿＿＿ ＿＿＿＿＿＿ sugar in it.

2 Monica는 새 동네로 이사했니? (move)
= ＿＿＿＿＿＿ Monica ＿＿＿＿＿＿ to a new town?

3 너는 지난 토요일에 그 콘서트를 즐겼니? (enjoy)
= ＿＿＿＿＿＿ you ＿＿＿＿＿＿ the concert last Saturday?

4 Max는 어제 그의 숙제를 끝냈니? (finish)
= ＿＿＿＿＿＿ Max ＿＿＿＿＿＿ his homework yesterday?

5 그녀의 어머니는 오늘 방과 후에 그녀를 태우러 가지 않으셨다. (pick)
= Her mother ＿＿＿＿＿＿ ＿＿＿＿＿＿ her up after school today.

연습문제 B 다음 문장을 괄호 안의 지시대로 바꿔 쓰시오.

1 Aaron went to tennis practice. (부정문으로)

→ _____ to tennis practice.

2 You forgot my birthday. (의문문으로)

→ _____ my birthday?

3 I met my friends at the movie theater. (부정문으로)

→ _____ my friends at the movie theater.

4 Carl took a shower this morning. (의문문으로)

→ _____ a shower this morning?

5 Yunho wanted cereal for breakfast. (부정문으로)

→ _____ cereal for breakfast.

6 Kevin's flight arrived around midnight yesterday. (의문문으로)

→ _____ around midnight yesterday?

연습문제 C 괄호 안에서 알맞은 것을 고르시오.

1 We didn't (had / have) lunch after the exam.

2 Mr. Wilson didn't (stay / stayed) at this hotel.

3 Did he (left / leave) a message? – Yes, he (did / didn't).

4 Linda didn't (tell / told) her secret to us.

5 Did you and Rachel (fight / fought) yesterday? – No, we (did / didn't).

6 Daniel didn't (believed / believe) my story.

7 Did you (hear / heard) anything about the fire? – No, I (did / didn't).

8 They didn't (close / closed) the garage door.

9 Did the kids (build / built) sandcastles at the beach? – Yes, they (did / didn't).

10 Did Amanda (sing / sang) in the contest? – No, she (did / didn't).

기출 적중문제

다음 문장을 주어진 지시대로 바꿔 쓰시오.

He sent a card to his parents.

(1) 부정문으로

→ _____

(2) 의문문으로

→ _____

> 일반동사의 부정문과 의문문에서 일반동사는 반드시 동사원형으로 써요.

서술형 대비 문제

A 괄호 안의 말을 활용하여 빈칸에 알맞은 말을 쓰시오. (단, 현재형으로 쓰시오.)

1 This cupcake _____ delicious. (look)

2 Patrick _____ his family and friends. (miss)

3 The store _____ _____ scissors. (not, sell)

4 _____ you _____ enough sleep? (get)

5 _____ Ms. Brown _____ safely? (drive)

6 _____ that egg _____ bad? (smell)

7 _____ Tommy and Pam _____ Korean? (speak)

8 I _____ _____ in Santa Claus. (not, believe)

9 Ms. Kim usually _____ for work at 7:30 A.M. (leave)

10 My brother _____ _____ his room regularly. (not, clean)

B 다음은 Amy, Ian, Nina가 하는 것과 하지 않는 것을 나타낸 표이다. 빈칸에 알맞은 말을 넣어 질문에 대한 대답을 완성하시오.

	Amy	Ian	Nina
play the guitar	O	X	O
like vegetables	O	X	X
have a pet	X	O	X
take a bus to school	O	O	X

1 *A*: Do Amy and Nina play the guitar?　　*B*: _____, _____.

2 *A*: Does Ian play the guitar?　　*B*: _____, _____.

3 *A*: Does Amy like vegetables?　　*B*: _____, _____.

4 *A*: Do Amy and Nina have a pet?　　*B*: _____, _____.

5 *A*: Does Ian have a pet?　　*B*: _____, _____.

6 *A*: Does Nina take a bus to school?　　*B*: _____, _____.

C 밑줄 친 부분이 어법상 맞으면 O를 쓰고, 틀리면 바르게 고쳐 쓰시오.

1 My team <u>losed</u> the game last month.　　→ _____

2 The monkey <u>fell</u> from the tree.　　→ _____

3 Did you <u>waked</u> up early this morning?　　→ _____

4 I didn't <u>fed</u> my horse today.　　→ _____

5 I <u>went</u> to Brazil three years ago.　　→ _____

6 Jason didn't <u>called</u> me yesterday.　　→ _____

7 Did he <u>gave</u> advice to you?　　→ _____

8 He <u>grew</u> up in a small village.　　→ _____

9 Emily didn't <u>make</u> any mistakes.　　→ _____

10 The police officer <u>stoped</u> her car last night.　　→ _____

D 다음 문장을 괄호 안의 지시대로 바꿔 쓰시오.

1 They bought a new sofa. (부정문으로)

　→ _____

2 This garden smells like roses. (의문문으로)

　→ _____

3 The baker bakes bread every morning. (부정문으로)

　→ _____

4 We watch horror movies. (부정문으로)

　→ _____

5 The class began at eight. (의문문으로)

　→ _____

6 Robert and Molly work out on weekends. (의문문으로)

　→ _____

7 She cut her finger last night. (의문문으로)

　→ _____

8 I broke the window yesterday. (부정문으로)

　→ _____

중간·기말고사 실전 문제

[1-2] 다음 중 동사의 3인칭 단수형이 <u>잘못된</u> 것을 고르시오.

1

① hurry – hurries   ② wash – washes

③ open – opens   ④ buy – buies

⑤ have – has

2

① pass – passes   ② meet – meets

③ mix – mixs   ④ fly – flies

⑤ become – becomes

3 다음 중 밑줄 친 부분이 어법상 <u>어색한</u> 것은?

> *A*: <u>Does</u> your <u>dog</u> <u>barks</u> a lot?
>   ①   ②   ③
> *B*: No, <u>it</u> <u>doesn't</u>.
>   ④   ⑤

4 다음 빈칸에 들어갈 말로 <u>어색한</u> 것은?

> _____ takes a yoga class every Friday.

① My friend   ② Suzie   ③ They

④ She   ⑤ Mr. Parker

5 다음 빈칸에 들어갈 말이 순서대로 짝지어진 것은?

> · They _____ the news at 8 o'clock.
> · She _____ in her room.

① watch – studies   ② watch – studyes

③ watch – study   ④ watches – studies

⑤ watches – study

6 다음은 Debra의 일정표이다. 표에 나온 표현을 활용하여 빈칸에 알맞은 말을 쓰시오.

7:30 A.M.	wake up
8:30 A.M.	arrive at school
12:30 P.M.	have lunch with friends
5:00 P.M.	play tennis with Beth
9:00 P.M.	do homework

> Debra wakes up at 7:30 A.M. She _____ at school at 8:30 A.M. She _____ lunch with friends at 12:30 P.M. She _____ tennis with Beth at 5:00 P.M. Finally, she _____ homework at 9:00 P.M.

[7-8] 다음 중 동사의 과거형이 <u>잘못된</u> 것을 고르시오.

7

① jump – jumpped   ② study – studied
③ begin – began   ④ hate – hated
⑤ stay – stayed

8

① ride – rode   ② plan – planned
③ hurt – hurted   ④ bring – brought
⑤ fly – flew

[9-10] 다음 중 동사의 과거형과 과거분사형이 <u>잘못된</u> 것을 고르시오.

9

① copy – copied – copied
② run – ran – run
③ spend – spent – spent
④ drive – drived – driven
⑤ see – saw – seen

10

① hurt – hurt – hurt
② grab – grabbed – grabbed
③ hear – heard – heard
④ hope – hoped – hoped
⑤ grow – grew – grewed

[11-12] 다음 글을 읽고 주어진 질문에 답하시오.

> Every Sunday morning, I ⓐgo to the park. In the park, I ⓑrun around the lake. Then, I ⓒsit on a bench and ⓓdrink some water. After a while, I walk back home and ⓔhave breakfast.

11 위 글의 주어 I를 Haley로 바꿀 때 빈칸에 알맞은 말을 쓰시오.

> Every Sunday morning, Haley ⓐ_____ to the park. In the park, she ⓑ_____ around the lake. Then, she ⓒ_____ on a bench and ⓓ_____ some water. After a while, she walks back home and ⓔ_____ breakfast.

12 위 글을 어제 있었던 일로 바꿀 때 빈칸에 알맞은 말을 쓰시오.

> Yesterday, I ⓐ_____ to the park. In the park, I ⓑ_____ around the lake. Then, I ⓒ_____ on a bench and ⓓ_____ some water. After a while, I walked back home and ⓔ_____ breakfast.

13 다음 중 어법상 바른 것은?

① My cat doesn't likes water.
② Jimin don't understand the question.
③ Tony don't watches TV much these days.
④ They don't be believe in fairy tales.
⑤ I don't fight with my friends.

14 다음 문장을 부정문으로 바르게 바꾼 것은?

We learn Spanish at school.

① We doesn't learn Spanish at school.
② We aren't learn Spanish at school.
③ We not learn Spanish at school.
④ We don't learn Spanish at school.
⑤ We isn't learn Spanish at school.

[15-16] 우리말과 같도록 괄호 안의 동사를 활용하여 문장을 완성하시오.

15

나의 여동생은 동물을 좋아한다. (like)

= My sister _____ animals.

16

Joseph과 Stella는 나를 믿지 않는다. (trust)

= Joseph and Stella _____ me.

17 다음 문장에서 어법상 어색한 부분을 찾아 쓰고 바르게 고쳐 쓰시오.

This elevator doesn't stops at the fourth floor.

_____ → _____

18 다음은 나와 유나가 좋아하는 과목을 나타낸 표이다. 동사 like를 활용하여 문장을 완성하시오.

	Science	English
I	O	X
Yuna	X	O

I _____ science, but I _____ _____ English. Yuna _____ _____ science, but she _____ English.

[19-20] 다음 문장을 주어진 조건에 맞게 바꿔 쓰시오.

I study history every day.

19 부정문으로 바꿔 쓰시오.

→ _____

20 주어 I를 Hyeri로 바꿔 완전한 문장을 쓰시오.

→ _____

21 다음 빈칸에 Do가 들어갈 수 없는 것은?

① _____ you miss your old teachers?
② _____ this train go to Seoul?
③ _____ they enjoy Mexican food?
④ _____ the flowers smell nice?
⑤ _____ Mark and Cindy walk to school?

22 다음 대화의 빈칸에 공통으로 들어갈 알맞은 것은?

> A: Does your brother _____ video games every day?
>
> B: No, he doesn't. But I _____ video games every day.

① play   ② plays   ③ played

④ plaies   ⑤ plaied

25 다음 그림을 보고 빈칸에 알맞은 말을 넣어 질문에 대한 대답을 완성하시오.

> Minha: Does Jake have red hair?
>
> Henry: _____ , _____
>
> _____ .

[23-24] 다음 대답에 대한 질문으로 알맞은 것을 고르시오.

23

> A: _____
>
> B: Yes, she does. She needs your help.

① Is she needs help with her report?

② Does she needs help with her report?

③ Does she need help with her report?

④ Do she need help with her report?

⑤ Do she needs help with her report?

26 다음 문장을 의문문으로 바꿔 쓰시오.

> Ms. Smith works at a huge company.
>
> → _____

24

> A: _____
>
> B: No, she didn't. It's still empty.

① Was she filled the basket with fruits?

② Was she fill the basket with fruits?

③ Did she fill the basket with fruits?

④ Did she filled the basket with fruits?

⑤ Does she filled the basket with fruits?

27 다음 글의 밑줄 친 부분을 어법에 맞게 고쳐 쓰시오.

> I ⓐhas one sister. Her name is Hannah. She ⓑget up late every morning. She doesn't ⓒstudies hard at all. She ⓓwatch dramas until midnight.

ⓐ _____   ⓑ _____

ⓒ _____   ⓓ _____

28 다음 문장을 괄호 안의 지시대로 바르게 바꾸지 못한 것은?

① Jackson has a pet lizard. (의문문으로)
→ Do Jackson have a pet lizard?
② Mindy takes piano lessons. (의문문으로)
→ Does Mindy take piano lessons?
③ I visited a temple in Vietnam. (부정문으로)
→ I didn't visit a temple in Vietnam.
④ Ron and I eat lunch together. (부정문으로)
→ Ron and I don't eat lunch together.
⑤ She went to Paris last year. (의문문으로)
→ Did she go to Paris last year?

29 다음 중 밑줄 친 부분이 어법상 어색한 것은?

Last year, I ①joined a cinema club
and had a wonderful time. Our club
members ②watched famous movies
together, and then we ③discussed the
movies. Lastly, we ④wrote movie diaries
and ⑤shareed them with one another.

30 다음 빈칸에 들어갈 말이 순서대로 짝지어진 것은?

· Oliver and I _____ the local art
museum yesterday.
· She _____ a fantasy novel last
night.

① visitted – read   ② visited – readed
③ visitted – readed   ④ visited – read
⑤ visitied – read

31 다음 중 밑줄 친 부분이 어법상 어색한 것은?

① I loved that song a long time ago.
② She breaked the chair by accident.
③ Did you wear a funny mask for the
festival?
④ We didn't visit our grandparents on
Chuseok.
⑤ Nari left her purse on the bus this
morning.

32 다음 (A)~(C)에 들어갈 말이 바르게 짝지어진 것은?

· Serena ___(A)___ a vacation yesterday.
· I ___(B)___ to school this morning.
· They ___(C)___ to my birthday party.

	(A)	(B)	(C)
①	took	walked	comed
②	took	walken	came
③	took	walked	came
④	taked	walken	came
⑤	taked	walked	comed

[33-34] 다음 질문에 대한 대답으로 알맞은 것을 고르시오.

33

A: Does this building have a parking lot?

B: _____

① Yes, it does.　② No, it does.

③ Yes, it is.　④ No, it isn't.

⑤ Yes, it didn't.

34

A: Did you and Alice win the game last week?

B: _____

① No, we aren't.　② Yes, we didn't.

③ No, we did.　④ Yes, we are.

⑤ No, we didn't.

35 다음 중 자연스럽지 <u>않은</u> 대화는?

① A: Does Joe read newspapers?

B: Yes, he does.

② A: Did Mr. Hall look tired?

B: Yes, he did.

③ A: Do they eat dinner at home?

B: No, they aren't.

④ A: Do you and Luke know her name?

B: No, we don't.

⑤ A: Did you go to the movies last night?

B: Yes, I did.

36 다음 문장을 의문문으로 바르게 바꾼 것은?

Your brother cooks well.

① Do your brother cook well?

② Do your brother cooks well?

③ Does your brother cook well?

④ Does your brother cooks well?

⑤ Did your brother cook well?

[37-38] 다음 문장을 주어진 조건에 맞게 바꿔 쓰시오.

Sam bought new sneakers yesterday.

37 부정문으로 바꿔 쓰시오.

→ _____

38 의문문으로 바꿔 쓰고, 그에 대한 부정의 대답을 쓰시오.

A: _____

B: _____

39 다음 중 어법상 바른 것끼리 묶인 것은?

ⓐ You didn't bring the right textbook.

ⓑ Did you enjoyed your lunch break?

ⓒ I not did meet Jisu last night.

ⓓ Did you and your friends have fun?

ⓔ Did study she at home yesterday?

① ⓐ, ⓑ　　② ⓐ, ⓓ　　③ ⓑ, ⓒ

④ ⓒ, ⓓ　　⑤ ⓓ, ⓔ

CHAPTER 3
시제

I **studied** English. 나는 영어를 공부했다.
I **will study** English. 나는 영어를 공부할 것이다.

동사 study(공부하다)의 형태를 **studied**(공부했다), **will study**(공부할 것이다)로 바꿔 내가 공부하는 시점을 나타냈어요. 이렇게 동사의 형태를 바꿔 행동이나 사건이 발생한 시간을 표현하는 것을 **시제**라고 해요.

기출로 적중 POINT

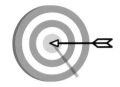

내신 100점 적중!
기출 출제율

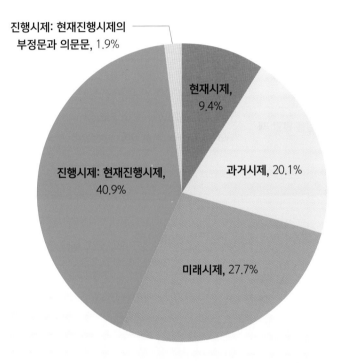

진행시제: 현재진행시제의
부정문과 의문문, 1.9%

현재시제,
9.4%

과거시제, 20.1%

진행시제: 현재진행시제,
40.9%

미래시제, 27.7%

TOP 1 **진행시제: 현재진행시제 (40.9%)**
현재진행시제의 형태와 동사의 V-ing형을 묻는 문제가 자주 출제된다.

TOP 2 **미래시제 (27.7%)**
미래시제의 쓰임과 형태를 묻는 문제가 자주 출제된다.

TOP 3 **과거시제 (20.1%)**
문장 안에서 과거시제가 쓰이는 경우를 묻는 문제가 자주 출제된다.

1. **현재시제는 '~이다, ~하다'의 의미이며, 동사의 현재형으로 나타낸다.**

They **are** my classmates. 그들은 나의 반 친구들이다.
She **runs** very fast. 그녀는 매우 빠르게 달린다.

Tip be동사의 현재형: am, is, are
일반동사의 현재형: 동사원형 또는 「동사원형 + (e)s」

2. **현재시제는 다음과 같을 때 쓴다.**

현재의 상태를 나타낼 때	Janet **lives** in Seattle now. Janet은 지금 시애틀에 산다.
현재의 습관이나 반복되는 일을 나타낼 때	Leo **wears** a suit every day. Leo는 매일 정장을 입는다. He always **wakes** up early. 그는 항상 일찍 일어난다. Tip 습관이나 반복을 나타내는 부사(구): every day, on Mondays, always, usually, once a week 등
일반적·과학적 사실을 말할 때	The Eiffel Tower **is** in Paris. 에펠탑은 파리에 있다. Water **freezes** at 0°C. 물은 섭씨 0도에서 언다.

연습문제 괄호 안의 동사를 활용하여 현재시제 문장을 완성하시오.

1 I _____ cheeseburgers. (like)

2 He usually _____ home at 9 P.M. (come)

3 Leaves _____ brown in autumn. (turn)

4 She _____ a middle school student. (be)

5 They _____ their grandparents once a month. (visit)

6 Mijin always _____ Saturdays with her family. (spend)

7 He _____ white teeth and a beautiful smile. (have)

기출 적중문제 ◎

우리말과 같도록 괄호 안의 말을 활용하여 문장을 완성하시오.

나는 매일 밤 책을 읽는다. (a book)

= _____ every night.

기출로적중 POINT 2 과거시제

정답 p.8

1. 과거시제는 '~이었다, ~했다'의 의미이며, 동사의 과거형으로 나타낸다.

He **was** a popular singer. 그는 인기 있는 가수였다.

They **went** to the library an hour ago. 그들은 한 시간 전에 도서관에 갔다.

(Tip) be동사의 과거형: was, were

일반동사의 과거형: 규칙 변화형(「동사원형 + (e)d」) 또는 불규칙 변화형

2. 과거시제는 다음과 같을 때 쓴다.

과거의 동작이나 상태를 나타낼 때	The weather **was** nice yesterday. 어제는 날씨가 좋았다. **Did** you **sleep** well last night? 너는 어젯밤에 잘 잤니?
역사적 사실을 말할 때	The Second World War **ended** in 1945. 제2차 세계 대전은 1945년에 끝났다. Lincoln **became** president in 1861. 링컨은 1861년에 대통령이 됐다.

(Tip) 과거시제와 주로 함께 쓰이는 부사(구): yesterday, last night, three hours ago, in 1993 등

연습문제 A │ 우리말과 같도록 괄호 안의 동사를 활용하여 빈칸에 쓰시오.

1 그들은 어제 영화를 봤다. (watch)

= They _____ a movie yesterday.

2 Lisa는 어젯밤에 많이 울었다. (cry)

= Lisa _____ a lot last night.

3 지난여름에는 비가 많이 오지 않았다. (rain)

= It _____ _____ much last summer.

4 그 연극은 매우 지루했다. (be)

= The play _____ very boring.

5 그들은 작년에 새 차를 샀니? (buy)

= _____ they _____ a new car last year?

6 그녀는 오늘 아침에 커피를 마시지 않았다. (drink)

= She _____ _____ coffee this morning.

7 나는 이틀 전에 민수에게 문자 메시지를 보냈다. (send)

= I _____ a text message to Minsu two days ago.

8 우리는 한 시간 전에 놀이 공원에 있었다. (be)

= We _____ in the amusement park an hour ago.

9 세종대왕은 1443년에 한글을 만들었다. (create)

= King Sejong _____ Hangeul in 1443.

10 Mark와 Diane은 어제 그 체육관에 있지 않았다. (be)

= Mark and Diane _____ at the gym yesterday.

11 Emily는 지난봄에 그 카페에서 일하지 않았다. (work)

= Emily _____ _____ at the café last spring.

연습문제 B 괄호 안에서 알맞은 것을 고르시오.

1 The sky (is / was) clear yesterday.

2 (Is / Was) your sister nine years old now?

3 Jina (studies / studied) for the test last night.

4 I (travel / traveled) to Europe four years ago.

5 They (are / were) in the restroom right now.

6 (Does / Did) your family move to America in 2005?

7 Joe (doesn't / didn't) go to school three days ago.

8 The sun (doesn't / didn't) rise in the west.

9 Seoul (is / was) the capital city of South Korea.

10 He (cries / cried) when he heard the news.

11 She lost her wallet, so she (walks / walked) home yesterday.

12 Hemingway (writes / wrote) *The Old Man and the Sea* in 1952.

13 It (is / was) cloudy an hour ago, but it (is / was) sunny now.

14 We (go / went) to the movie theater and watched an action movie.

15 Our volleyball team (doesn't / didn't) win the game last week.

16 I lived in Portugal three months ago, but I (live / lived) in Spain now.

기출 적중문제

다음 중 어법상 어색한 것은?

① He stayed home last night.

② My mother was sick yesterday.

③ I watched the TV show now.

④ Paul came to Korea two years ago.

⑤ We played football last Sunday.

특정 시제와 주로
함께 쓰이는 부사(구)에
주의하세요.

POINT 3 미래시제

정답 p.8

1. **미래시제는 '~일 것이다, ~할 것이다'의 의미이며, 「will + 동사원형」의 형태이다.**

   It **will be** cold tomorrow. 내일은 추울 것이다.
   I**'ll buy** a new phone next week. 나는 다음 주에 새 전화기를 살 것이다.

   (Tip) 미래시제와 주로 함께 쓰이는 부사(구): tomorrow, next month, next year, soon 등

2. **미래시제는 「be going to + 동사원형」의 형태로도 나타낼 수 있다.**

   He **is going to clean** his room. 그는 그의 방을 청소할 것이다.
   We**'re going to leave** soon. 우리는 곧 떠날 것이다.

3. **미래시제의 부정문과 의문문**

	부정문	의문문
will	will + not + 동사원형 → won't	Will + 주어 + 동사원형 ~? – Yes, 주어 + will. / No, 주어 + won't.
be going to	be동사 + not + going to + 동사원형	be동사 + 주어 + going to + 동사원형 ~? – Yes, 주어 + be동사. / No, 주어 + be동사 + not.

   The train **will not[won't] arrive** on time. 그 기차는 제시간에 도착하지 않을 것이다.
   I**'m not going to study** tonight. 나는 오늘 밤에 공부하지 않을 것이다.

   Will Somin go to middle school next year? 소민이는 내년에 중학교에 갈 거니?
     – **Yes**, **she will**. 응, 그녀는 갈 거야. / **No**, **she won't**. 아니, 그녀는 가지 않을 거야.

   Are you going to watch the movie? 너는 그 영화를 볼 거니?
     – **Yes**, **I am**. 응, 나는 볼 거야. / **No**, **I'm not**. 아니, 나는 보지 않을 거야.

연습문제 A <보기>와 같이 다음 문장을 will을 활용하여 미래시제로 바꿔 쓰시오.

<보기> It is cold today. → _It will be_ cold tomorrow.

1 I am 14 years old now.
   → _____ 14 years old next year.

2 Luke doesn't watch scary movies.
   → _____ scary movies.

3 Are you free now?
   → _____ free soon?

4 Eric and Jane go to the beach every summer.

→ _____ to the beach next summer.

연습문제 **B** | <보기>와 같이 다음 문장을 be going to를 활용하여 바꿔 쓰시오.

> **<보기>** Suji will join the book club. → *Suji is going to join the book club.*

1 Tommy will leave his home town tomorrow.

→ _____

2 I won't make a mistake again.

→ _____

3 Will you walk to school tomorrow?

→ _____

4 Matt and Kelly won't wait for me.

→ _____

연습문제 **C** | 괄호 안에서 알맞은 것을 고르시오.

1 She (not will / will not) like these shoes.

2 It is going to (rains / rain) a lot this Tuesday.

3 They (won't / aren't) going to sell their cat.

4 Will you (come / comes) to my birthday party? – Yes, I (will / won't).

5 Clark and I (will / are) going to travel around the world.

6 (Will / Are) our dinner be ready soon? – No, it (will / won't).

7 My parents (won't / aren't) eat out tonight.

8 He (is not / not is) going to buy a new bicycle.

기출 적중문제 ◎

다음은 Kate의 다음 주 주말 일정표이다. will을 활용하여 질문에
대한 대답을 완성하시오.

Saturday	do English homework
Sunday	go to the mall

A: What will Kate do next Sunday?
B: She _____ .

기출로 적중 POINT 4-1 진행시제: 현재진행시제

1. **현재진행시제는 '~하고 있다, ~하는 중이다'의 의미이며, 「am/is/are + V-ing」의 형태이다.**

   The birds **are flying** high. 새들이 높이 날고 있다.

   He **is writing** a letter now. 그는 지금 편지를 쓰고 있다.

   (Tip) 동사 have가 '가지다'라는 의미일 때는 진행형으로 쓸 수 없고, '먹다, 시간을 보내다'라는 의미일 때는 진행형으로 쓸 수 있다.

   She **has** brown eyes. 그녀는 갈색 눈을 가지고 있다.

   She **is having** breakfast now. 그녀는 지금 아침을 먹고 있다.

   (Tip) 현재진행시제는 미래를 나타내는 부사(구)와 주로 함께 쓰여 예정된 가까운 미래의 일을 나타낼 수 있다.

   I **am going** to the mall **tomorrow**. 나는 내일 쇼핑몰에 갈 예정이다.

2. **동사의 V-ing형은 대부분 동사원형에 -ing를 붙여 만든다.**

대부분의 동사	동사원형 + -ing	call – call**ing** sing – sing**ing**
「자음 + e」로 끝나는 동사	e를 빼고 + -ing	come – com**ing** make – mak**ing** (Tip) · 예외: be – be**ing** · 「모음 + e」로 끝나는 동사: see – see**ing**
-ie로 끝나는 동사	ie를 y로 바꾸고 + -ing	lie – l**ying** tie – t**ying**
「단모음 + 단자음」으로 끝나는 동사	마지막 자음을 한 번 더 쓰고 + -ing	run – run**ning** get – get**ting** (Tip) 강세가 앞에 오는 2음절 동사: visit – visit**ing** enter – enter**ing**

연습문제 A 다음 동사의 V-ing형을 쓰시오.

1 go – _____

2 jump – _____

3 sing – _____

4 sit – _____

5 dance – _____

6 begin – _____

7 make – _____

8 speak – _____

9 see – _____

10 write – _____

11 lie – _____

12 put – _____

13 run – _____

14 visit – _____

15	have	– _____	16	clap	– _____
17	ride	– _____	18	get	– _____
19	sleep	– _____	20	move	– _____
21	come	– _____	22	win	– _____
23	ski	– _____	24	study	– _____
25	watch	– _____	26	arrive	– _____
27	buy	– _____	28	talk	– _____
29	die	– _____	30	enjoy	– _____
31	be	– _____	32	close	– _____
33	play	– _____	34	draw	– _____
35	tie	– _____	36	cut	– _____
37	plan	– _____	38	work	– _____
39	build	– _____	40	fly	– _____

연습문제 B 괄호 안의 동사를 활용하여 현재진행시제 문장을 완성하시오.

1 The woman _____ an Italian restaurant. (enter)

2 The dolphins _____ in the sea. (swim)

3 Mr. Evans _____ strawberry cupcakes. (bake)

4 The students _____ the textbook. (read)

5 The cat _____ on my pillow. (lie)

6 He _____ a good time with his friends. (have)

7 The butterflies _____ in the field. (fly)

8 Some boys _____ on the boat. (sit)

기출 적중문제

다음 우리말을 영작할 때 빈칸에 들어갈 알맞은 것은?

그녀는 그녀의 선물을 개봉하고 있다.
= She _____ her presents.

① open ② is open ③ opening
④ be opening ⑤ is opening

기출로적중 POINT 4-2 | 진행시제: 현재진행시제의 부정문과 의문문

정답 p.9

1. 현재진행시제의 부정문: 「am/is/are + not + V-ing」

She **is not sleeping** now. 그녀는 지금 자고 있지 않다.
My friends **aren't watching** a movie. 나의 친구들은 영화를 보고 있지 않다.

2. 현재진행시제의 의문문과 대답

의문문	긍정의 대답	부정의 대답
Am/Is/Are + 주어 + V-ing ~?	Yes, 주어 + am/is/are.	No, 주어 + am/is/are + not.

Is Jason **playing** soccer now? Jason은 지금 축구를 하고 있니?
 – **Yes**, **he is**. 응, 그는 하고 있어. / **No**, **he isn't**. 아니, 그는 하고 있지 않아.

Are you **doing** your homework? 너는 너의 숙제를 하고 있니?
 – **Yes**, **I am**. 응, 나는 하고 있어. / **No**, **I'm not**. 아니, 나는 하고 있지 않아.

연습문제 A | 다음 문장을 괄호 안의 지시대로 바꿔 쓰시오.

1 Tim is taking a walk now. (의문문으로)

→ _____

2 Sally is dancing on the stage now. (부정문으로)

→ _____

3 They are enjoying the holiday. (의문문으로)

→ _____

4 The gardener is watering the flowers. (부정문으로)

→ _____

5 The camels are lying on the sand. (의문문으로)

→ _____

6 The guests are standing outside. (부정문으로)

→ _____

7 Your dog is jumping on the bed. (의문문으로)

→ _____

8 Sophie and Yunho are talking now. (부정문으로)

→ _____

다음 그림을 보고 빈칸에 알맞은 말을 넣어 질문에 대한 대답을 완성하시오.

1  **2**  **3**  **4**

1 *A*: Is she sitting on the chair?

   B: _____, _____ _____ . She _____ _____ on the floor.

2 *A*: Are the boys watching TV?

   B: _____, _____ _____ .

3 *A*: Are they painting the wall now?

   B: _____, _____ _____ . They _____ _____ the fence.

4 *A*: Is he eating pasta?

   B: _____, _____ _____ . He _____ _____ pizza.

연습문제 **C** 괄호 안에서 알맞은 것을 고르시오.

1 Patrick (isn't / doesn't) knocking on the door.

2 (Is / Does) your sister fixing your computer? – Yes, she (is / isn't).

3 They aren't (run / running) hard now.

4 (Are / Do) Sam and Carl sleeping? – No, they (are / aren't).

5 I'm not (washes / washing) the dishes now.

6 Sumin (is not / not is) staying at a hotel.

7 (Are / Do) they packing their bags? – Yes, they (are / aren't).

8 (Is / Does) your father parking the car right now? – No, he (is / isn't).

기출 적중문제 🎯

다음 중 어법상 바른 것은?

① Andy not is having breakfast.

② The students aren't listen to the teacher.

③ Are you and Michelle sing a song now?

④ They be clapping their hands.

⑤ Is she wearing a pink coat now?

진행시제: 과거진행시제

정답 p.9

1. **과거진행시제는 '~하고 있었다, ~하는 중이었다'의 의미이며, 「was/were + V-ing」의 형태이다.**

   He **was reading** a magazine. 그는 잡지를 읽고 있었다.
   The students **were waiting** for the bus. 그 학생들은 버스를 기다리고 있었다.

2. **과거진행시제의 부정문: 「was/were + not + V-ing」**

   She **was not cleaning** the bathroom then. 그녀는 그때 욕실을 청소하고 있지 않았다.
   We **weren't having** lunch at 2 o'clock. 우리는 2시에 점심을 먹고 있지 않았다.

3. **과거진행시제의 의문문과 대답**

의문문	긍정의 대답	부정의 대답
Was/Were + 주어 + V-ing ~?	Yes, 주어 + was/were.	No, 주어 + was/were + not.

   Was Michael **studying** math? Michael은 수학을 공부하고 있었니?
     – **Yes**, **he was**. 응, 그는 공부하고 있었어. / **No**, **he wasn't**. 아니, 그는 공부하고 있지 않았어.

   Were they **sleeping** at that time? 그들은 그때 자고 있었니?
     – **Yes**, **they were**. 응, 그들은 자고 있었어. / **No**, **they weren't**. 아니, 그들은 자고 있지 않았어.

연습문제 A   <보기>와 같이 다음 문장을 과거진행시제로 바꿔 쓰시오.

> <보기>   I met Susan at 5 o'clock. → _I was meeting_ Susan at 5 o'clock.

1 My classmates cleaned the classroom yesterday afternoon.
→ _____ the classroom yesterday afternoon.

2 Mina didn't have dinner with Jack last Friday.
→ _____ dinner with Jack last Friday.

3 Did the students take the exam then?
→ _____ the exam then?

4 Jamie walked to the train station two hours ago.
→ _____ to the train station two hours ago.

5 Did Luke do his science project yesterday?
→ _____ his science project yesterday?

6 We didn't play basketball last weekend.

→ _____ basketball last weekend.

7 The students didn't listen to the teacher.

→ _____ to the teacher.

8 My sister and I watched a horror movie last night.

→ _____ a horror movie last night.

연습문제 B 우리말과 같도록 괄호 안의 동사를 활용하여 빈칸에 쓰시오.

1 Peter는 한 시간 전에 운동하고 있었다. (exercise)

= Peter _____ _____ an hour ago.

2 나의 개는 어젯밤에 짖고 있지 않았다. (bark)

= My dog _____ _____ last night.

3 그들은 그때 전화로 수다를 떨고 있었다. (chat)

= They _____ _____ on the phone then.

4 John은 주스를 마시고 있었니? – 아니, 그는 마시고 있지 않았어. (drink)

= _____ John _____ juice? – No, he _____.

5 그 관광객들은 많은 사진을 찍고 있었다. (take)

= The tourists _____ _____ a lot of pictures.

6 그는 그때 샤워하고 있었니? – 응, 그는 샤워하고 있었어. (take)

= _____ he _____ a shower at that time? – Yes, he _____.

7 너는 샌드위치를 만들고 있었니? – 아니, 나는 만들고 있지 않았어. (make)

= _____ you _____ a sandwich? - No, I _____.

8 나의 친구와 나는 도서관에서 크게 이야기하고 있지 않았다. (talk)

= My friend and I _____ _____ loudly in the library.

기출 적중문제

다음 질문에 대한 대답으로 알맞은 것은?

> *A*: Were your brothers doing homework at nine?
> *B*: No, they weren't. _____

① They play computer games then.
② They will play computer games then.
③ They are playing computer games then.
④ They were playing computer games then.
⑤ They are going to play computer games then.

기출로적중 POINT 5 현재완료시제

정답 p.9

현재완료시제는 과거에 발생한 일이 현재까지 영향을 미칠 때 쓰며, 「have/has + p.p.(과거분사)」의 형태이다.

I **have lived** in Busan since 2008. 나는 2008년 이후로 부산에서 살아왔다.
(= I started to live in Busan in 2008. I still live there.)
　나는 2008년에 부산에서 살기 시작했다. 나는 여전히 거기에 산다.
Stacey **has lost** her watch. Stacey는 그녀의 시계를 잃어버렸다.
(= Stacey lost her watch. She doesn't have it now.)
　Stacey는 그녀의 시계를 잃어버렸다. 그녀는 지금 그것을 가지고 있지 않다.

(Tip) 현재완료시제는 과거에 발생하여 현재까지 영향을 미치는 일을 나타낼 때 쓰고, 과거시제는 과거에 발생하고 완료된 일을 나타낼 때 쓴다.
현재완료시제　Yura **has stayed** in Paris for two weeks. 유라는 파리에 2주 동안 머물러왔다.
과거시제　　　Yura **stayed** in Paris two weeks ago. 유라는 파리에 2주 전에 머물렀다.

연습문제 | 괄호 안의 동사를 활용하여 현재완료시제 문장을 완성하시오.

1 It _____ for two days. (snow)

2 Mr. Smith _____ China twice. (visit)

3 Jerry and Mindy _____ to Mexico. (go)

4 Ethan _____ just _____ the book. (start)

5 My parents _____ in Toronto since 1998. (live)

6 Jessica _____ cello lessons before. (take)

7 They _____ to Russia three times. (travel)

8 She _____ in that company since 2003. (work)

9 Lily _____ this letter several times. (read)

10 Alex _____ already _____ his science project. (finish)

11 Jinho and Sohee _____ each other for seven years. (know)

12 A man _____ just _____ in next door. (move)

13 I _____ Greek food, but I don't really like it. (try)

14 K-pop music _____ very popular around the world recently. (become)

Ⓐ 우리말과 같도록 괄호 안의 말을 알맞게 배열하시오.

1 그들은 어제 한국어를 공부했다. (yesterday, studied, they, Korean)

= _____

2 나는 내일 학교에 가지 않을 것이다. (to school, will, not, tomorrow, I, go)

= _____

3 소라는 토요일마다 축구를 한다. (every Saturday, soccer, Sora, plays)

= _____

4 나의 형은 그 선물을 포장하고 있었다. (the present, was, my brother, wrapping)

= _____

5 너의 팀은 지난주에 그 경기에 이겼니? (win, the game, your team, last week, did)

= _____

6 그 고양이는 지금 자고 있니? (now, sleeping, the cat, is)

= _____

7 주호는 곧 그의 머리를 자를 것이다. (his hair, soon, cut, going, to, Juho, is)

= _____

8 그 서점은 좋은 책들을 가지고 있지 않다. (good books, not, have, does, the bookstore)

= _____

9 Tom은 재킷을 입고 있지 않았다. (not, a jacket, was, wearing, Tom)

= _____

Ⓑ 다음 문장의 밑줄 친 부분을 바르게 고쳐 쓰시오.

1 I not will tell a lie again. → _____

2 I will preparing dinner at 5 o'clock. → _____

3 It is going to is very hot this summer. → _____

4 Ms. Chen wills teach Chinese to us next year. → _____

5 Are you going buy this coat? → _____

6 He not is going to leave for Seoul soon. → _____

7 They will are here by tomorrow morning. → _____

8 Kevin and Yuna is going to take a bus. → _____

C 다음 그림을 보고 <보기>에서 알맞은 말을 골라 질문에 대한 대답을 완성하시오. (단, 필요 시 형태를 바꾸시오.)

| <보기> | run | read a book | make a snowman | swim | lie on the ground |

1 A: What is Alice doing?　　　　　　　B: She _____ .

2 A: What are Jeff and his dog doing?　　B: They _____ .

3 A: What is David doing?　　　　　　　B: He _____ .

4 A: What are George and Fred doing?　　B: They _____ .

5 A: What are the swans doing?　　　　　B: They _____ .

D 괄호 안의 동사를 활용하여 빈칸에 알맞은 말을 쓰시오.

1
I am enjoying my trip to London. I ⓐ_____ (arrive) here a week ago. Last week, I ⓑ_____ (visit) lots of tourist sites and ⓒ_____ (see) famous musicals. Tomorrow, I ⓓ_____ _____ (meet) my old friend. We ⓔ_____ _____ (look) around the British Museum and have dinner together.

2
I have one older sister. She ⓐ_____ (live) in Mexico now. She ⓑ_____ (move) there last month. She ⓒ_____ _____ (start) Spanish classes tomorrow. Yesterday, I ⓓ_____ (send) a letter to her. Hopefully, she ⓔ_____ _____ (write) me back soon.

중간 · 기말고사 실전 문제

[1-2] 다음 빈칸에 들어갈 알맞은 것을 고르시오.

1

| Monica _____ spaghetti tomorrow. |

① make ② are making
③ will make ④ made
⑤ was making

2

| Last month, I _____ a new laptop. |

① buy ② buys
③ am buying ④ bought
⑤ will buy

3 다음 빈칸에 공통으로 들어갈 알맞은 것은?

| · The Earth _____ around the Sun.
· She _____ to church every Sunday. |

① go ② goes ③ went
④ was going ⑤ is going to go

[4-5] 다음 빈칸에 들어갈 알맞은 것을 <u>모두</u> 고르시오.

4

| Minho read a newspaper _____. |

① yesterday ② next week
③ two hours ago ④ now
⑤ soon

5

| Will they take the final exam _____? |

① yesterday ② last year
③ tomorrow ④ next month
⑤ five minutes ago

6 다음 대화의 빈칸에 들어갈 말이 순서대로 짝지어진 것은?

| A: What does Cindy do _____?
B: She _____ her friends. |

① last Monday - meets
② yesterday - will meet
③ every Sunday - meets
④ tomorrow - met
⑤ on weekends - met

7 다음 질문에 대한 대답으로 알맞은 것은?

> *A*: What did Minju and her brother do last weekend?
>
> *B*: _____

① They climb the mountain.
② They climbed the mountain.
③ They will climb the mountain.
④ They are climbing the mountain.
⑤ They are going to climb the mountain.

[10-11] 다음 문장을 괄호 안의 지시대로 바꿔 쓰시오.

10

> He will stay at my house next month.
> (부정문으로)
>
> → _____
>
> _____

11

> It is going to snow tomorrow. (의문문으로)
>
> → _____

8 괄호 안의 동사를 활용하여 다음 글의 빈칸에 알맞은 말을 쓰시오.

> My friends _____(come) to my house last night. We _____(eat) potato pizza and played table tennis together. It _____(be) really fun.

12 다음 중 어법상 바른 것끼리 묶인 것은?

> ⓐ Katie will is in Korea soon.
> ⓑ They not are going to go for a walk.
> ⓒ We are going to leave tomorrow.
> ⓓ Jiho will join our book club.
> ⓔ Is it going be sunny next week?
> ⓕ They will seeing many paintings there.

① ⓐ, ⓑ   ② ⓒ, ⓓ   ③ ⓐ, ⓑ, ⓒ
④ ⓐ, ⓓ, ⓔ   ⑤ ⓒ, ⓓ, ⓕ

9 우리말과 같도록 괄호 안의 말을 알맞게 배열하시오.

> 너는 이번 주말에 병원에 갈 거니? (will, to the hospital, this weekend, go, you)

= _____

13 다음 문장을 be going to를 활용하여 바꿔 쓰시오.

> Sarah will practice the violin tomorrow.
>
> → _____
>
> _____

14 다음 우리말을 알맞게 영작한 것은?

> Tony는 우산을 빌리지 않을 것이다.

① Tony didn't borrow an umbrella.
② Tony is going to borrow an umbrella.
③ Tony is borrowing an umbrella.
④ Tony won't borrow an umbrella.
⑤ Tony wasn't borrowing an umbrella.

15 다음은 Joan의 다음 주 일정표이다. 표를 보고 빈칸에 알맞은 말을 넣어 질문에 대한 대답을 완성하시오.

Monday	buy some books
Tuesday	prepare for the speech contest
Wednesday	participate in the speech contest
Thursday	have dinner with William
Friday	go to the amusement park

(1)
> *A*: What will Joan do next Tuesday?
> *B*: She _____ _____
> _____ _____
> _____ _____.

(2)
> *A*: Will Joan go to the amusement park next Monday?
> *B*: _____, she _____. She
> _____ _____ _____
> _____ next Monday.

16 다음 중 어법상 어색한 것은?

① I will watch a movie tomorrow.
② She was cooking in the kitchen then.
③ Andy was a high school student last year.
④ William is at home all day yesterday.
⑤ We weren't close friends a month ago.

17 다음 (A)~(C)에 들어갈 말이 바르게 짝지어진 것은?

> · We _____(A)_____ go to school yesterday.
> · _____(B)_____ Minseok start his homework soon?
> · People first _____(C)_____ on the Moon in 1969.

	(A)	(B)	(C)
①	didn't	Did	walked
②	didn't	Will	will walk
③	didn't	Will	walked
④	won't	Will	will walk
⑤	won't	Did	walked

18 다음 밑줄 친 ⓐ~ⓔ를 바르게 고치지 못한 것은?

> · They ⓐwere 20 years old next year.
> · We ⓑgo to a Korean restaurant yesterday.
> · My brother ⓒis very sick last night.
> · Thomas and his wife ⓓvisited Germany tomorrow.
> · Diana ⓔpasses the history exam last week.

① ⓐ were → will be
② ⓑ go → went
③ ⓒ is → will be
④ ⓓ visited → are going to visit
⑤ ⓔ passes → passed

19 다음 두 문장을 한 문장으로 바꿀 때 빈칸에 들어갈 알맞은 것은?

Sara first met Ken in 2000. Sara still knows him.
→ Sara _____ Ken since 2000.

① is knowing ② has known
③ knows ④ known
⑤ have known

20 다음 그림을 보고 be동사를 활용하여 빈칸에 알맞은 말을 쓰시오.

An Hour Ago	Now

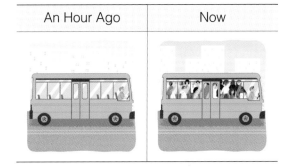

The bus _____ empty an hour ago, but it _____ full now.

21 <보기>와 같이 동사의 형태를 바꾼 것 중 잘못된 것은?

<보기> catch → catching

① jump → jumping ② swim → swimming
③ bring → bringing ④ tie → tying
⑤ have → haveing

22 다음 중 밑줄 친 부분이 어법상 어색한 것은?

① The baby is taking a nap.
② They are enjoying their vacation.
③ Everyone is claping at the concert.
④ Jake is using his cell phone.
⑤ Sue and Bob are putting on their shoes.

23 다음 중 밑줄 친 부분이 어법상 바른 것은?

It's Sunday morning. Birds are ①singging outside. My father and brother are ②makeing breakfast. My mother is ③watering flowers. I'm ④lieing under the tree. My dogs are ⑤runing in the garden.

24 다음 우리말을 영작할 때 빈칸에 들어갈 알맞은 것은?

그 학생들은 독후감을 쓰고 있다.
= The students _____ the book reports.

① writes ② are write ③ writing
④ are writing ⑤ wrote

25 다음 빈칸에 들어갈 말이 순서대로 짝지어진 것은?

· _____ Martin cleaning his room?
· Those kids weren't _____ shoes.

① Does – wear ② Is – wear
③ Does – wearing ④ Is – wearing
⑤ Are – wearing

26 다음 질문에 대한 대답으로 알맞은 것은?

> *A*: Is your father working in the office now?
>
> *B*: _____

① Yes, he does.　② No, he doesn't.
③ Yes, he is.　④ No, he wasn't.
⑤ Yes, he are.

[27-28] 다음 문장을 진행시제로 바꿔 쓰시오.

27

> Jackson ties a ribbon on the present.
>
> → _____
>
> _____

28

> My brother and I shopped at the mall 30 minutes ago.
>
> → _____
>
> _____

29 다음 대화의 빈칸에 들어갈 알맞은 것은?

> *A*: _____ with her dog?
>
> *B*: No, she isn't. She is just standing and talking on the phone.

① Is Ann run　② Does Ann run
③ Is Ann running　④ Will Ann run
⑤ Was Ann running

30 괄호 안의 동사를 활용하여 질문에 대한 대답을 완성하시오.

> *A*: What was your sister doing?
>
> *B*: She _____ _____ the flower pots. (move)

31 다음 그림을 보고 괄호 안의 동사를 활용하여 빈칸에 알맞은 말을 쓰시오.

> He (A)_____ _____ on the bench now and he (B)_____ curly hair. (sit, have)

32 다음 그림을 보고 <보기>의 말을 활용하여 주어진 질문에 답하시오.

> <보기>　eat　throw　take

(1) What is Jihee doing?
　→ She _____ a baseball.

(2) What are Molly and Glen doing?
　→ They _____ sandwiches.

(3) What is Owen doing?
　→ He _____ some photos.

33 다음 중 어법상 바른 것을 <u>모두</u> 고르시오.

① Was the monkey climbing up a tree now?
② Water boils at 100℃.
③ I didn't go to the dentist soon.
④ We were playing basketball an hour ago.
⑤ Are they enjoying the game yesterday?

34 다음 중 자연스럽지 <u>않은</u> 대화는?

① A: Was your sister studying?
   B: Yes, she was.
② A: Will it rain tomorrow?
   B: No, it won't.
③ A: Are you going to cook pasta?
   B: No, I'm not.
④ A: Are Betty and Jim dating?
   B: Yes, they are.
⑤ A: Did he break the window?
   B: Yes, he does.

35 다음 중 어법상 바른 것의 개수는?

ⓐ Are you watching TV right now?
ⓑ I don't have a smartphone last year.
ⓒ The show begins 20 minutes ago.
ⓓ Kyle visited Taiwan next year.
ⓔ I have a really warm winter coat.

① 1개   ② 2개   ③ 3개
④ 4개   ⑤ 5개

36 다음 중 어법상 <u>어색한</u> 것은?

① Beijing is the capital of China.
② Subin always eats desserts after dinner.
③ South Korea has four seasons.
④ The sun rises in the east.
⑤ Kim Yuna win the gold medal in 2010.

37 다음 중 밑줄 친 부분이 어법상 바른 것은?

① Jamie <u>has went</u> to America.
② She <u>have lost</u> her apartment key.
③ I <u>has played</u> baseball since March.
④ Ben <u>has watched</u> the show once.
⑤ We <u>have became</u> middle school students.

38 다음 문장을 괄호 안의 지시대로 바르게 바꾸지 <u>못</u>한 것은?

Sehee reads a poem.

① (과거시제로) Sehee read a poem.
② (미래시제로) Sehee will read a poem.
③ (현재진행시제로) Sehee is read a poem.
④ (과거진행시제로) Sehee was reading a poem.
⑤ (현재완료시제로) Sehee has read a poem.

39 다음 중 밑줄 친 부분의 쓰임이 나머지 넷과 <u>다른</u> 것은?

① He <u>is going to</u> practice the piano this afternoon.
② I <u>am going to</u> my grandpa's house now.
③ Dongha <u>is going to</u> study for the math test.
④ It <u>is going to</u> be sunny this weekend.
⑤ We <u>are going to</u> make dinner for our mom.

CHAPTER 4
조동사

Dan plays the violin. Dan은 바이올린을 연주한다.
Dan **can** play the violin. Dan은 바이올린을 연주할 수 있다.

'Dan은 바이올린을 연주한다.'라는 문장에 조동사 can(~할 수 있다)이 포함되어 'Dan은 바이올린을 연주할 수 있다.'라는 문장이 됐어요. 이렇게 다른 동사와 함께 쓰여 여러 가지 의미를 더하는 동사를 **조동사**라고 해요.

기출로 적중 POINT

내신 100점 적중!
기출 출제율

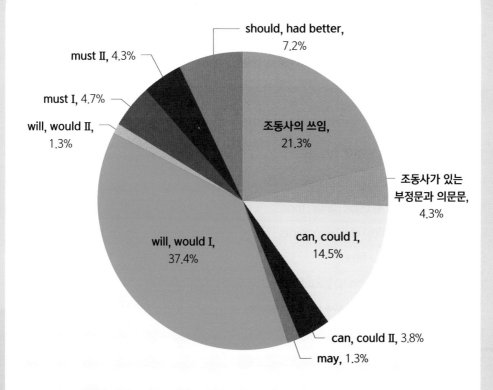

- should, had better, 7.2%
- must II, 4.3%
- must I, 4.7%
- will, would II, 1.3%
- 조동사의 쓰임, 21.3%
- 조동사가 있는 부정문과 의문문, 4.3%
- will, would I, 37.4%
- can, could I, 14.5%
- can, could II, 3.8%
- may, 1.3%

TOP 1 **will, would I (37.4%)**
조동사 will, would의 의미와 쓰임을 묻는 문제가 자주 출제된다.

TOP 2 **조동사의 쓰임 (21.3%)**
문장 안에서 조동사가 쓰이는 형태와 조동사의 특징을 묻는 문제가 자주 출제된다.

TOP 3 **can, could I (14.5%)**
조동사 can, could의 의미와 쓰임을 묻는 문제가 자주 출제된다.

조동사의 쓰임

1. **조동사는 「조동사 + 동사원형」의 형태로 쓴다.**

   I **can** speak English. 나는 영어를 말할 수 있다.

   Lisa **may** be at home. Lisa는 집에 있을지도 모른다.

   The musical **will** start soon. 그 뮤지컬은 곧 시작할 것이다.

   We **must** leave right now. 우리는 지금 당장 떠나야 한다.

2. **조동사는 주어의 인칭이나 수에 따라 형태가 변하지 않는다.**

   Mark (~~shoulds~~, **should**) eat more vegetables. Mark는 더 많은 채소를 먹어야 한다.

3. **조동사는 한 번에 하나만 쓴다.**

   He (~~will can~~, **will be able to**) pass the test. 그는 그 시험을 통과할 수 있을 것이다.

연습문제 괄호 안에서 알맞은 것을 고르시오.

1 He must (works / work) on Sunday.

2 My uncle (can / cans) cook Italian food.

3 Gary (should / shoulds) call his parents.

4 She can (ride / rode) a bike.

5 You should (be / are) kind to your friends.

6 We will (be able to / can) have some desserts.

7 Taylor (will / wills) be a great singer.

8 Sana and her family may (visit / visiting) Busan.

9 The baby will (can / be able to) walk soon.

10 Yuri must (wakes / wake) up early tomorrow.

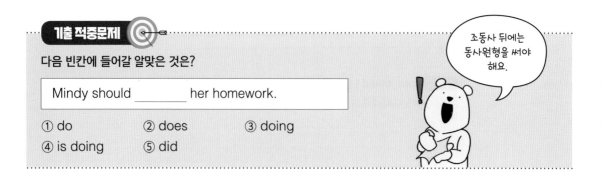

기출 적중문제

다음 빈칸에 들어갈 알맞은 것은?

> Mindy should _____ her homework.

① do   ② does   ③ doing

④ is doing   ⑤ did

조동사 뒤에는
동사원형을 써야
해요.

정답 p.12

기출로적중 POINT 1-2 조동사가 있는 부정문과 의문문

1. 조동사가 있는 부정문: 「조동사 + not + 동사원형」

I **cannot[can't] answer** the question. 나는 그 질문에 대답할 수 없다.

The story **may not be** true. 그 이야기는 사실이 아닐지도 모른다.

Mason **will not[won't] like** this shirt. Mason은 이 셔츠를 좋아하지 않을 것이다.

You **should not[shouldn't] be** selfish. 너는 이기적이면 안 된다.

2. 조동사가 있는 의문문과 대답

의문문	긍정의 대답	부정의 대답
조동사 + 주어 + 동사원형 ~?	Yes, 주어 + 조동사.	No, 주어 + 조동사 + not.

Can Steve **swim?** Steve는 수영할 수 있니?
　– **Yes**, he **can**. 응, 그는 수영할 수 있어. / **No**, he **can't**. 아니, 그는 수영할 수 없어.

Will you **meet** Emily tomorrow? 너는 내일 Emily를 만날 거니?
　– **Yes**, I **will**. 응, 나는 만날 거야. / **No**, I **won't**. 아니, 나는 만나지 않을 거야.

연습문제 A　다음 문장을 괄호 안의 지시대로 바꿔 쓰시오.

1　You should go to bed now. (부정문으로)
　→ _____ to bed now.

2　He can speak French well. (부정문으로)
　→ _____ French well.

3　Alice will play with us tomorrow. (의문문으로)
　→ _____ with us tomorrow?

4　We should order some food soon. (의문문으로)
　→ _____ some food soon?

5　Andrew may like spicy food. (부정문으로)
　→ _____ spicy food.

6　Lucas will watch the soccer game next week. (의문문으로)
　→ _____ the soccer game next week?

7　We must wait in line. (의문문으로)
　→ _____ in line?

8 They may be in the classroom. (부정문으로)

→ _____ in the classroom.

9 Linda can ride a bicycle. (의문문으로)

→ _____ a bicycle?

연습문제 **B** 다음 빈칸에 알맞은 말을 넣어 질문에 대한 대답을 완성하시오.

1 *A*: Can he ride a skateboard?   *B*: Yes, _____ _____ .

2 *A*: Should I wear a scarf?   *B*: Yes, _____ _____ .

3 *A*: Will you and Yura take a taxi?   *B*: No, _____ _____ .

4 *A*: Should I talk to him?   *B*: No, _____ _____ .

5 *A*: Must Ian and Cory buy tickets?   *B*: Yes, _____ _____ .

6 *A*: Will they arrive early today?   *B*: Yes, _____ _____ .

7 *A*: Can she read Chinese?   *B*: No, _____ _____ .

8 *A*: Must I stay in my room?   *B*: Yes, _____ _____ .

연습문제 **C** 밑줄 친 부분이 어법상 맞으면 O를 쓰고, 틀리면 바르게 고쳐 쓰시오.

1 <u>Wills she wash</u> the dishes?   → _____

2 You <u>can holding</u> my hand.   → _____

3 <u>Should we invite</u> them?   → _____

4 <u>Can you come</u> over now?   → _____

5 Sarah <u>not may be</u> good at sports.   → _____

6 We <u>shouldn't eat</u> too much sugar.   → _____

7 <u>Must clean I</u> the floor?   → _____

8 It <u>won't happens</u> again.   → _____

기출 적중문제 🎯

다음 중 어법상 바른 것은?

① Sophie not will stay here.

② Do you can see the stars?

③ They can dancing well.

④ Will it snow tomorrow?

⑤ Shoulds I go to the hospital?

정답 p.12

기출로적중 POINT 2-1 can, could I

1. can은 '~할 수 있다(능력·가능)'라는 의미이다.

He **can** ski well. 그는 스키를 잘 탈 수 있다.
Ostriches **cannot[can't]** fly. 타조는 날 수 없다.
Can you play the piano? 너는 피아노를 칠 수 있니?

2. could는 can의 과거형으로, '~할 수 있었다(능력·가능)'라는 의미이다.

Jane **could not[couldn't]** remember his name. Jane은 그의 이름을 기억할 수 없었다.

3. 능력·가능의 의미를 나타내는 can/could는 be able to로 바꿔 쓸 수 있다.

She **can** dance well. = She **is able to** dance well. 그녀는 춤을 잘 출 수 있다.
I **couldn't** sleep yesterday. = I **wasn't able to** sleep yesterday. 나는 어제 잘 수 없었다.
Can Peter climb trees? = **Is** Peter **able to** climb trees? Peter는 나무를 오를 수 있니?

연습문제 <보기>와 같이 다음 두 문장의 의미가 같도록 문장을 완성하시오.

<보기> He can speak Korean. = He _is able to speak_ Korean.

1 Jim can throw a ball very far.　　=　_____ a ball very far.

2 I can't understand him.　　=　_____ him.

3 Dogs can't see red.　　=　_____ red.

4 Can you hear the sound?　　=　_____ the sound?

5 We couldn't find the bus stop.　　=　_____ the bus stop.

6 They can sing in English.　　=　_____ in English.

7 Can Alex solve this problem?　　=　_____ this problem?

8 You and I can fix this machine.　　=　_____ this machine.

기출 적중문제 ◎

우리말과 같도록 괄호 안의 말을 알맞게 배열하시오.

우리는 그 경기를 이길 수 있다. (win, can, we, the game)

= _____

can은 허가나 요청의 의미도 나타낼 수 있다.

허가 (~해도 된다)	You **can** use my phone. 너는 나의 전화기를 써도 된다. **Can** I borrow your pen? 내가 너의 펜을 빌려도 되니? – Yes, you can. / Of course. / Sure. 응, 돼. / 물론이지. / 그럼. – No, you can't. / Sorry, you can't. 아니, 안 돼. / 미안, 안 돼. You **cannot[can't]** have dessert now. 너는 지금 후식을 먹으면 안 된다. └→ 허가를 나타내는 can의 부정형은 '~하면 안 된다(약한 금지)'라는 의미이다.
요청 (~해주겠니?)	**Can** you close the door? 문을 닫아주겠니? **Can** you please be quiet? 조용히 해주시겠어요?

Tip 허가나 요청의 의미로 질문할 때 could를 쓰면 더 정중한 표현이 된다.

허가 **Could** I sit here? 제가 여기에 앉아도 되나요?

요청 **Could** you please come inside? 안으로 들어와주시겠어요?

연습문제 **A** 밑줄 친 can의 의미를 <보기>에서 골라 그 기호를 쓰시오.

<보기> ⓐ ~할 수 있다   ⓑ ~해도 된다   ⓒ ~해주겠니?

1 Can I have some water?　　　　　　[　　　　　]

2 Some parrots can speak.　　　　　　[　　　　　]

3 Can you play the flute well?　　　　　[　　　　　]

4 Can I see a menu?　　　　　　　　[　　　　　]

5 Can you lend the book to me?　　　　[　　　　　]

6 Heejin can swim like a dolphin.　　　[　　　　　]

7 Can you wait for a moment?　　　　　[　　　　　]

8 Can I bring my friends to dinner?　　　[　　　　　]

9 You can take my umbrella.　　　　　[　　　　　]

10 He can speak five languages.　　　　[　　　　　]

11 Can you turn off the radio?　　　　　[　　　　　]

12 You can go home now.　　　　　　[　　　　　]

13 Can you please call me at 5 o'clock?　[　　　　　]

14 David can ride a motorcycle.　　　　[　　　　　]

우리말과 같도록 괄호 안의 말을 알맞게 배열하시오.

1 너는 나의 쿠키를 먹어도 된다. (can, you, my cookie, have)

= _____

2 우리를 도와주시겠어요? (help, you, us, could)

= _____

3 너는 극장 안에서 이야기하면 안 된다. (can't, in the theater, you, talk)

= _____

4 내가 여기에서 사진을 찍어도 되니? (can, here, a picture, I, take)

= _____

5 제가 당신의 이름을 물어봐도 되나요? (your name, I, could, ask)

= _____

6 지민이와 혜수는 소풍에 올 수 없었다. (Jimin and Hyesu, come, to the picnic, couldn't)

= _____

7 내가 이 창문을 열어도 되니? (open, can, this window, I)

= _____

8 호랑이는 수영을 잘 할 수 있니? (swim, can, well, tigers)

= _____

9 우리는 제시간에 도착할 수 있다. (can, we, on time, arrive)

= _____

10 엘리베이터를 잡아주겠니? (you, the elevator, hold, can)

= _____

11 그는 어제 그 일을 끝낼 수 없었다. (the work, couldn't, he, finish, yesterday)

= _____

12 너는 애완동물과 함께 이 건물에 들어가면 안 된다. (you, with a pet, cannot, this building, enter)

= _____

기출 적중문제 🎯

다음 중 밑줄 친 can의 의미가 나머지 넷과 다른 것은?

① Can I try on the shoes?
② I can cook spaghetti.
③ I can go to the concert with you.
④ Can you speak Chinese?
⑤ I can make a paper plane.

POINT 3 may

may는 약한 추측이나 허가의 의미를 나타낸다.

약한 추측 (~일지도 모른다)	Paul **may** be in his room. Paul은 그의 방에 있을지도 모른다. The answer **may not** be right. 그 답은 맞지 않을지도 모른다.
허가 (~해도 된다)	You **may** wear my jacket. 너는 나의 재킷을 입어도 된다. **May** I ask a question? 내가 질문을 해도 되니? – Yes, you may. / Of course. / Sure. 응, 돼. / 물론이지. / 그럼. – No, you may not. / Sorry, you may not. 아니, 안 돼. / 미안, 안 돼. You **may not** park here. 너는 여기에 주차하면 안 된다. └→ 허가를 나타내는 may의 부정형은 '~하면 안 된다(약한 금지)'라는 의미이다.

연습문제 밑줄 친 부분의 의미와 같은 것을 <보기>에서 골라 그 기호를 쓰시오.

<보기> ⓐ You <u>may</u> take a break.   ⓑ She <u>may</u> be angry.

1 <u>May</u> I take your order? [　]   **2** It <u>may</u> snow tomorrow. [　]

3 You <u>may</u> turn on the light. [　]   **4** He <u>may</u> be late for school. [　]

5 The man <u>may</u> be an actor. [　]   **6** <u>May</u> I speak to Hansu? [　]

7 <u>May</u> I try on the pants? [　]   **8** They <u>may</u> fail the exam. [　]

<보기> ⓐ You <u>may not</u> go outside now.   ⓑ He <u>may not</u> remember me.

9 Luke <u>may not</u> be free today. [　]   **10** You <u>may not</u> watch TV after 9 P.M. [　]

11 We <u>may not</u> touch the artwork. [　]   **12** It <u>may not</u> take much time. [　]

13 You <u>may not</u> smoke here. [　]   **14** He <u>may not</u> like the present. [　]

15 Silvia <u>may not</u> be thirsty. [　]   **16** We <u>may not</u> open that door. [　]

기출 적중문제 ◎

우리말과 같도록 괄호 안의 말을 활용하여 영작하시오.

내가 너의 컴퓨터를 써도 되니? (use, computer)

= _____

---

88 내신 점수와 영어 실력을 높여주는 추가 자료 제공 HackersBook.com

will, would I

정답 p.13

1. **will**은 '~할 것이다(미래)'라는 의미이며, 이때 be going to로 바꿔 쓸 수 있다.

   It **will** be sunny next weekend. 다음 주말에 화창할 것이다.
   = It**'s going to** be sunny next weekend.

   Will you go to the concert? 너는 그 콘서트에 갈 거니?
   = **Are** you **going to** go to the concert?

   (Tip) will은 주어의 의지를 나타낼 수도 있다.
   I **will** lose weight. 나는 살을 빼겠다.

2. 「**Will/Would** you ~?」는 '~해주겠니/~해주시겠어요?(요청)'라는 의미도 나타낼 수 있다.

   Will you be my friend? 나의 친구가 되어주겠니?
   Will you please turn off the light? 불을 꺼주시겠어요?
   Would you call a taxi for me? 저를 위해 택시를 불러주시겠어요?

연습문제 │ 우리말과 같도록 괄호 안의 말을 알맞게 배열하시오.

1 그녀는 우리의 밴드에 가입할 것이다. (our band, she, join, will)

= _____

2 나중에 나에게 전화해주겠니? (you, call, later, will, me)

= _____

3 지혜는 목걸이를 살 것이다. (a necklace, buy, Jihye, going, is, to)

= _____

4 문을 잡아주시겠어요? (would, hold, you, the door)

= _____

5 나의 남동생은 우리의 개에게 먹이를 줄 것이다. (will, our dog, feed, my brother)

= _____

기출 적중문제

다음 빈칸에 공통으로 들어갈 알맞은 것은?

> · Minha _____ go to Hanoi next summer.
> · I can't find my wallet. _____ you help me?

① is[Is]   ② does[Does]   ③ may[May]
④ will[Will]   ⑤ do[Do]

1. 「would like + 명사」는 '~을 원하다'라는 의미이며, 「want + 명사」로 바꿔 쓸 수 있다.

I **would like** some **coffee**. 나는 약간의 커피를 원한다.
= I **want** some **coffee**.

Would you **like** an **orange**? 너는 오렌지를 원하니?
= Do you **want** an **orange**?

2. 「would like to + 동사원형」은 '~하기를 원하다'라는 의미이며, 「want to + 동사원형」 으로 바꿔 쓸 수 있다.

I'd like to go for a walk. 나는 산책하러 가기를 원한다.
= I **want to go** for a walk.

Would you **like to know** the secret? 너는 그 비밀을 알기를 원하니?
= Do you **want to know** the secret?

연습문제 괄호 안의 주어와 would like (to)를 활용하여 문장을 완성하시오.

1 _____ wash my hands. (I)

2 _____ some grapes. (I)

3 _____ speak to you. (I)

4 _____ book a room? (you)

5 _____ a table for two. (I)

6 _____ some help? (you)

7 _____ drink something cold. (I)

8 _____ some dessert? (you)

9 _____ a laptop for my birthday present. (I)

10 _____ listen to this song? (you)

11 _____ more ice cream? (you)

12 _____ change my plans. (I)

13 _____ a glass of juice. (I)

14 _____ be a fashion model. (I)

기출로적중 POINT 5-1 must I

정답 p.13

1. must는 의무나 강한 추측의 의미를 나타낸다.

의무 (~해야 한다)	I **must** wear glasses. 나는 안경을 써야 한다. People **must** be honest. 사람들은 정직해야 한다.
강한 추측 (~임에 틀림없다)	He **must** be your brother. 그는 너의 남동생임에 틀림없다. You **must** have a problem. 너는 문제가 있음에 틀림없다. (Tip) 강한 추측을 나타내는 must의 부정은 can't(~일 리가 없다)를 쓴다. That movie **can't** be boring. 저 영화는 지루할 리가 없다.

2. must not은 '~하면 안 된다(강한 금지)'라는 의미이다.

You **must not** move. 너는 움직이면 안 된다.
Children **must not** swim alone. 아이들은 혼자 수영하면 안 된다.
We **must not** be late for class. 우리는 수업에 늦으면 안 된다.

연습문제 A 밑줄 친 부분의 의미를 <보기>에서 골라 그 기호를 쓰시오.

<보기> ⓐ ~해야 한다   ⓑ ~임에 틀림없다   ⓒ ~하면 안 된다

1 We <u>must</u> do our best. [   ]

2 The soccer players <u>must</u> be very thirsty. [   ]

3 You <u>must not</u> run in the hallway. [   ]

4 They <u>must</u> be nervous about the test. [   ]

5 Our mom <u>must</u> be in the kitchen now. [   ]

6 We <u>must not</u> eat on the subway. [   ]

7 She <u>must</u> be very popular. [   ]

8 The students <u>must</u> wear school uniforms. [   ]

9 You <u>must not</u> throw trash on the road. [   ]

10 The book <u>must</u> be a best seller. [   ]

11 You <u>must</u> wake up early tomorrow. [   ]

12 Kids <u>must</u> be careful with knives. [   ]

13 You <u>must not</u> be noisy in the library. [   ]

14 You <u>must</u> keep your promise. [   ]

우리말과 같도록 must 또는 can과 괄호 안의 동사를 활용하여 빈칸에 쓰시오.

1 청소년들은 충분한 잠을 자야 한다. (get)

= Teenagers _____ _____ enough sleep.

2 그들은 쌍둥이임에 틀림없다. (be)

= They _____ _____ twins.

3 그녀는 선생님일 리가 없다. (be)

= She _____ _____ a teacher.

4 방문객들은 박물관 안에 음료를 가져오면 안 된다. (bring)

= Visitors _____ _____ _____ drinks into the museum.

5 은호는 매우 행복함에 틀림없다. (be)

= Eunho _____ _____ very happy.

6 우리는 하루에 세 번 이를 닦아야 한다. (brush)

= We _____ _____ our teeth three times a day.

7 Jackson은 지금 교실에 있을 리가 없다. (be)

= Jackson _____ _____ in the classroom now.

연습문제 C 다음 빈칸에 must나 must not 중 알맞은 것을 쓰시오.

1 Tom is coughing a lot. He _____ see a doctor.

2 It's too cold outside. You _____ put on your coat.

3 The milk smells bad. You _____ drink it.

4 The light is red. We _____ cross the street.

5 The elevator is not working. We _____ use the stairs.

6 It's snowy and windy. You _____ open the window.

7 We missed a bus. We _____ wait for 15 minutes.

기출 적중문제

다음 표지판을 보고 괄호 안의 말을 활용하여 문장을 완성하시오.

You _____ here.
(must, ride a bike)

기출로적중 POINT 5-2 must II

정답 p.13

---

1. 의무를 나타내는 must는 have/has to로 바꿔 쓸 수 있다.

You **must** follow the rule. 너는 그 규칙을 따라야 한다.
= You **have to** follow the rule.

He **must** wear a tie. 그는 넥타이를 매야 한다.
= He **has to** wear a tie.

(Tip) have/has to가 있는 의문문: 「Do/Does + 주어 + have to ~?」
Do I **have to** go there? 내가 거기에 가야 하니?

(Tip) must의 과거형은 had to를 쓰고, 미래형은 will have to를 쓴다.
I **had to** return the shoes. 나는 그 신발을 반품해야 했다.
Jenny **will have to** tell the truth. Jenny는 진실을 말해야 할 것이다.

2. don't have to는 '~할 필요가 없다(불필요)'라는 의미이다.

We **don't have to** worry. 우리는 걱정할 필요가 없다.
Janet **doesn't have to** agree with him. Janet은 그에게 동의할 필요가 없다.

연습문제 A <보기>와 같이 다음 두 문장의 의미가 같도록 문장을 완성하시오.

<보기> We must arrive on time. = _We have to arrive_ on time.

1 I must wait for my friend. = _____ for my friend.

2 She must print her essay. = _____ her essay.

3 You must sign this form. = _____ this form.

4 We must think carefully. = _____ carefully.

5 You must be patient. = _____ patient.

6 They must finish the project soon. = _____ the project soon.

7 Adam must study math today. = _____ math today.

8 I must take this medicine. = _____ this medicine.

9 Ms. Han must buy some milk. = _____ some milk.

10 You and Jack must be quiet here. = _____ quiet here.

11 Uncle John must repair his truck. = _____ his truck.

12 My sister and I must clean our room. = _____ our room.

우리말과 같도록 must나 have to를 활용하여 문장을 완성하시오.

1 너는 오늘 밤에 저녁 식사를 준비할 필요가 없다.

= You _____ prepare dinner tonight.

2 사람들은 여기에 텐트를 치면 안 된다.

= People _____ put up tents here.

3 Jessie는 어제 교회에 가야 했다.

= Jessie _____ attend church yesterday.

4 그들은 다음 기차를 기다려야 할 것이다.

= They _____ wait for the next train.

5 Harry는 나를 도와줄 필요가 없다.

= Harry _____ help me.

6 소는 많은 물을 마셔야 한다.

= A cow _____ drink a lot of water.

7 너는 거기에 주차하면 안 된다.

= You _____ park there.

8 나는 아무것도 말할 필요가 없다.

= I _____ say anything.

9 나래는 일요일마다 일찍 일어날 필요가 없다.

= Narae _____ get up early on Sundays.

10 학생들은 수업 중에 그들의 모자를 벗어야 한다.

= Students _____ take off their hats in class.

11 그는 내일 종일 집에 머물러야 할 것이다.

= He _____ stay home all day tomorrow.

12 그의 가족은 밴쿠버로 이사해야 했다.

= His family _____ move to Vancouver.

기출 적중문제

다음 대화의 빈칸에 들어갈 가장 알맞은 것은?

> A: Do we have to take a taxi?
> B: No, we _____ take a taxi. We aren't late.

① can't   ② will   ③ must not
④ have to   ⑤ don't have to

기출로적중 POINT 6 — should, had better

정답 p.13

1. should는 '~해야 한다(충고·의무)'라는 의미이다.

You **should** exercise regularly. 너는 규칙적으로 운동해야 한다.
You **should not[shouldn't]** eat so fast. 너는 그렇게 빠르게 먹으면 안 된다.

2. had better는 '~하는 것이 낫다(강한 충고)'라는 의미이며, 주로 'd better의 형태로 줄여 쓴다. 부정형은 had better not이다.

We **had better** ask for help. 우리는 도움을 요청하는 것이 낫겠다.
You**'d better not** swim at night. 너는 밤에 수영하지 않는 것이 낫다.

연습문제 우리말과 같도록 should 또는 had better와 괄호 안의 동사를 활용하여 문장을 완성하시오.

1 너는 바다에서 구명조끼를 입어야 한다. (wear)

= You _____ a life jacket in the ocean.

2 우리는 그 컴퓨터를 수리해야 한다. (repair)

= We _____ the computer.

3 너는 오늘 그 도서관 책을 반납하는 것이 낫겠다. (return)

= You _____ the library book today.

4 그녀는 자정까지 깨어있지 않는 것이 낫다. (stay)

= She _____ awake until midnight.

5 너는 너의 시간과 돈을 낭비하면 안 된다. (waste)

= You _____ your time and money.

6 너는 너의 잠옷으로 갈아입는 것이 낫겠다. (change)

= You _____ into your pajamas.

7 학생들은 복도에서 시끄럽게 떠들면 안 된다. (make)

= Students _____ much noise in the hallway.

기출 적중문제

우리말과 같도록 괄호 안의 말을 알맞게 배열하시오.

> 너는 10시 전에 집에 와야 한다. (should, home, come, you)

= _____ before 10 o'clock.

A 다음 문장의 밑줄 친 부분을 바르게 고쳐 쓰시오.

1 Can I <u>plays</u> cards with you? → _____

2 Jake <u>musts</u> be very angry. → _____

3 He <u>not can</u> open the bottle. → _____

4 My sister <u>are</u> able to run fast. → _____

5 You <u>not have to</u> wait long. → _____

6 She would like <u>visit</u> Italy. → _____

7 May I <u>sat</u> next to you? → _____

8 You should <u>being</u> very careful. → _____

9 We <u>not must</u> pick the flowers. → _____

10 Can <u>turn you</u> on the lights? → _____

11 We <u>had not better</u> chew gum often. → _____

12 <u>Would do you</u> close the window, please? → _____

B 다음은 유나, 수호, 소민이가 할 수 있는 것과 할 수 없는 것을 나타낸 표이다. 표를 보고 빈칸에 알맞은 말을 넣어 대화를 완성하시오.

	ride a bicycle	speak Chinese	play baduk
Yuna	O	O	X
Suho	X	O	O
Somin	X	X	O

Suho: Yuna, can you ride a bicycle?

Yuna: ⓐ_____, I ⓑ_____. Can you ride a bicycle too?

Suho: ⓒ_____, I ⓓ_____. I never learned to ride a bike. However, I ⓔ_____ speak Chinese and play baduk well.

Yuna: Really? I ⓕ_____ speak Chinese too, but I ⓖ_____ play baduk.

Suho: Somin ⓗ_____ play baduk, so she and I sometimes play it together. You should learn baduk and join us.

C <보기>와 같이 빈칸에 알맞은 말을 넣어 질문에 대한 대답을 완성하시오.

> **<보기>** *A*: Can your brother use chopsticks?
> *B*: <u>No</u> , <u>he</u> <u>can't</u> . He is too young.

1 *A*: Will you eat lunch with us?
   B: _____ , _____ _____ . I'm not very hungry.

2 *A*: Can Minsu swim in the sea?
   B: _____ , _____ _____ . He is afraid of water.

3 *A*: Should we visit our grandmother?
   B: _____ , _____ _____ . She really misses us.

4 *A*: Can Jisun pass the science test?
   B: _____ , _____ _____ . She studied really hard.

5 *A*: May I go outside and play?
   B: _____ , _____ _____ _____ . It's too dark outside.

6 *A*: Will it rain this afternoon?
   B: _____ , _____ _____ . You should take an umbrella.

D 다음 그림을 보고 must와 괄호 안의 말을 활용하여 문장을 완성하시오.

1    **2**    **3**

1 *A*: You _____ here. (park your car)
   B: I'm sorry. I didn't see the sign.

2 *A*: What does this sign mean?
   B: We _____ . (fasten our seat belts)

3 *A*: The light just turned red.
   B: We _____ now. (cross the street)

중간·기말고사 실전 문제

[1-2] 다음 빈칸에 들어갈 알맞은 것을 고르시오.

1

> Hyeri _____ delicious chicken salad.

① can make ② cans make
③ can makes ④ cans makes
⑤ can made

2

> My puppies may _____ sick.

① is ② was
③ be ④ are
⑤ were

3 다음 중 어법상 바른 것은?

① He shoulds wake up early.
② Mary not can find her wallet.
③ Andy are able to ride a horse.
④ We must get there on time.
⑤ Do may I borrow your eraser?

4 다음 문장에서 어법상 어색한 부분을 찾아 쓰고 바르게 고쳐 쓰시오.

> Mr. Park will is our new English teacher.

_____ ➡ _____

[5-6] 우리말과 같도록 괄호 안의 말을 알맞게 배열하시오.

5

> Robert는 첼로를 연주할 수 있다. (play, can, Robert, the cello)

= _____

6

> 너는 너의 친구들과 싸우면 안 된다. (fight, not, with your friends, must, you)

= _____

7 다음 중 not이 들어갈 위치는?

> ① You ② had ③ better ④ trust ⑤ her.

8 다음 문장을 주어진 지시대로 바꿔 쓰시오.

> I should drink more water.

(1) 부정문으로

➡ _____

(2) 의문문으로

➡ _____

9 우리말과 같도록 괄호 안의 말을 배열할 때 세 번째에 오는 것을 쓰시오.

> 내가 너의 우비를 빌려도 되니? (raincoat, may, borrow, your, I)

→ _____

10 다음 질문에 대한 대답으로 알맞은 것은?

> A: Should I go to a dentist?
> B: _____

① Yes, I should.　　② No, I shouldn't.
③ Yes, you should.　④ No, you should.
⑤ Yes, you shouldn't.

[11-12] 다음 밑줄 친 부분과 바꿔 쓸 수 있는 것을 고르시오.

11

> Everyone <u>has to</u> finish their homework by tomorrow.

① shouldn't　　② don't have to
③ may　　　　④ must
⑤ can

12

> They <u>will</u> plant some trees in their garden.

① must not　　② are going to
③ are able to　④ should
⑤ may not

13 다음 중 짝지어진 두 문장의 의미가 <u>다른</u> 것은?

① Helen must look after her brother.
　= Helen has to look after her brother.
② I would like some coffee and biscuits.
　= I want some coffee and biscuits.
③ We must not turn off the heater.
　= We don't have to turn off the heater.
④ Can Theo play table tennis?
　= Is Theo able to play table tennis?
⑤ Will it snow tomorrow morning?
　= Is it going to snow tomorrow morning?

[14-16] 다음 두 문장의 의미가 같도록 빈칸에 알맞은 말을 쓰시오.

14

> Anton can speak lots of languages.
> = Anton _____ _____ _____ lots of languages.

15

> I want to have pasta for dinner.
> = I _____ _____ _____ have pasta for dinner.

16

> Cam couldn't fix his bicycle.
> = Cam _____ _____ _____ fix his bicycle.

17 다음 문장을 부정의 의미를 나타내는 문장으로 바꿔 쓰시오.

> They must be in Seoul right now.

→ _____

[18-19] 다음 우리말을 영작할 때 빈칸에 들어갈 알맞은 것을 고르시오.

18

> 나는 그의 이름을 기억할 수 없다.
> = I _____ remember his name.

① didn't   ② must not
③ may not   ④ shouldn't
⑤ can't

19

> 너는 건강에 좋은 음식을 먹는 것이 낫다.
> = You _____ eat healthy food.

① had better   ② would like to
③ don't have to   ④ must
⑤ may

20 다음 우리말을 알맞게 영작한 것은?

① 그들은 지금 배고플 리가 없다.
  = They don't have to be hungry now.
② 너는 매운 음식을 먹을 수 있니?
  = Will you eat spicy food?
③ Susie는 그의 여동생임에 틀림없다.
  = Susie must not be his sister.
④ 너는 오늘 밤에 나에게 전화할 필요가 없다.
  = You shouldn't call me tonight.
⑤ 우리는 눈 때문에 늦을지도 모른다.
  = We may be late because of the snow.

21 다음 대화의 빈칸에 들어갈 가장 알맞은 것은?

> A: I have a pain in my ear.
> B: You _____ listen to music loudly.

① can   ② don't have to
③ must   ④ had better
⑤ shouldn't

22 다음 표지판을 보고 must와 괄호 안의 말을 활용하여 문장을 완성하시오.

(1)    (2)

(1) You _____.
   (wear a helmet)

(2) You _____ in
   the library. (make a noise)

[23-24] 다음 빈칸에 들어갈 가장 알맞은 것을 고르시오.

23

> I _____ lift that box. It is too heavy.

① may   ② can't   ③ should
④ must   ⑤ will

24

> Don't go outside with wet hair. You
> _____ catch a cold.

① can't   ② should   ③ had better
④ won't   ⑤ may

25 다음 대화의 빈칸에 들어갈 말이 순서대로 짝지어진 것은?

> A: Where is Ms. Kim?
> B: She _____ be in the teacher's room.
> A: I went there, but I didn't see her.
> B: Oh, then you _____ wait for her.
>   She will be back soon.
> A: All right. Thanks.

① shouldn't – must not
② shouldn't – can't
③ must – should
④ must – can't
⑤ must not – should

26 다음 빈칸에 공통으로 들어갈 알맞은 것은?

> · I can't believe Juwon won the dance contest. He _____ be very happy.
> · You _____ get a haircut. Your hair is too long and messy.

① don't have to   ② can
③ may not   ④ would like to
⑤ must

27 다음 글의 빈칸에 가장 알맞은 말을 <보기>에서 한 번씩만 골라 쓰시오.

> <보기>   will   have to   can

> Now, I _____ take a bus to school because my house is far from my school. However, my family _____ move into a new apartment tomorrow. From tomorrow, I _____ walk to school.

28 다음은 소진이, 예리, 민호가 할 수 있는 것과 할 수 없는 것을 나타낸 표이다. 표를 보고 can을 활용하여 문장을 완성하시오.

	Sojin	Yeri	Minho
swim	O	O	O
play the drums	X	X	O

> Sojin, Yeri, and Minho _____ .
> Sojin and Yeri _____ .

29 다음 중 그림 속의 소년에게 할 말로 어색한 것은?

① You don't have to walk on the grass.
② You must not walk on the grass.
③ You may not walk on the grass.
④ You shouldn't walk on the grass.
⑤ You can't walk on the grass.

30 다음 대화의 빈칸에 공통으로 들어갈 알맞은 것은?

> A: Hello. _____ I help you with anything?
> B: Yes, I need a ticket to New York.
> A: OK. _____ you show me your passport?
> B: Of course. Here it is.

① Will   ② May   ③ Must
④ Can   ⑤ Should

31 다음 밑줄 친 can의 의미가 같은 것끼리 묶인 것은?

> ⓐ Can you turn on the TV?
> ⓑ She can cook Mexican food.
> ⓒ Some dogs can swim very well.
> ⓓ Can I play computer games now?
> ⓔ Can Samuel speak Korean?

① ⓐ, ⓑ   ② ⓐ, ⓔ
③ ⓑ, ⓒ, ⓔ   ④ ⓑ, ⓓ, ⓔ
⑤ ⓐ, ⓒ, ⓓ, ⓔ

32 다음 질문에 대한 대답으로 알맞지 <u>않은</u> 것을 모두 고르시오.

> A: May I borrow your pen for a minute?
> B: _____ You can use it.

① Sure.   ② Of course.
③ Yes, you may.   ④ No, you may not.
⑤ Sorry, you may not.

33 다음 중 자연스럽지 <u>않은</u> 대화는?

① A: Will you come to my party this Friday?
   B: Yes, I will. I'm free that day.
② A: Can I speak to Hana?
   B: Sorry, you can't. She's not home now.
③ A: Can you play the piano?
   B: No, I can't. I'm very good at it.
④ A: May I open the window?
   B: Sure. That's fine.
⑤ A: Will you pass the fork to me?
   B: Of course. Here it is.

34 다음은 영어 수업 시간에 지켜야 할 규칙이다. 밑줄 친 우리말 (A), (B)와 같도록 should와 괄호 안의 말을 활용하여 빈칸에 쓰시오.

> Welcome to English class! Before we start, I'd like to tell you about the class rules.
> 1. (A) 여러분들은 영어로 말해야 합니다. (speak)
> 2. You should bring your textbooks.
> 3. (B) 여러분들은 수업 중에 음식을 먹으면 안 됩니다. (eat, food)

(A) _____ _____ _____
    in English.
(B) _____ _____ _____
    _____ during class.

35 주어진 문장의 밑줄 친 may와 의미가 같은 것은?

> May I join you for lunch?

① You may leave now.
② The rumor may be true.
③ The trip may cost lots of money.
④ They may need more time.
⑤ It may snow on Christmas morning.

36 다음 문장을 과거시제로 바르게 바꾼 것은?

> Diana must apologize to me.

① Diana must apologized to me.
② Diana did must apologize to me.
③ Diana musted apologize to me.
④ Diana had to apologize to me.
⑤ Diana has to apologized to me.

37 다음 중 밑줄 친 must의 의미가 나머지 넷과 다른 것은?

① We must save money.
② Hazel must be very surprised.
③ I must go to bed early tonight.
④ All students must have student ID cards.
⑤ We must change trains at the next station.

40 다음 중 밑줄 친 부분이 어법상 바른 것은?

① You and Sam has to leave in five minutes.
② Billy has to do his homework yesterday.
③ He will must show his ticket at the gate.
④ Does she has to take the yoga class?
⑤ All students have to read this poem.

41 다음 중 밑줄 친 부분이 어법상 어색한 것의 개수는?

ⓐ Your phone may be in your bag.
ⓑ Tony would like to a sandwich.
ⓒ They should be not loud here.
ⓓ Will she can join our team?
ⓔ We must not act like babies.
ⓕ Will you giving this book to Luna?

① 2개 ② 3개 ③ 4개
④ 5개 ⑤ 6개

[38-39] 다음 대화를 읽고 주어진 질문에 답하시오.

Carl : (A) Can I use this computer?
Anne: Sure, you ⓐcan use it.
Carl : ⓑMay I use this printer too?
Anne: Sorry, it's broken.
Carl : But I really need a printer. I ⓒcan print my report.
Anne: Then you ⓓhad better try the printer over there. It ⓔmay work.

38 위 대화의 밑줄 친 (A)와 의미가 같은 것은?

① Will I use this computer?
② Must I use this computer?
③ Should I use this computer?
④ May I use this computer?
⑤ Do I have to use this computer?

39 위 대화의 밑줄 친 ⓐ~ⓔ 중 문맥상 어색한 것은?

① ⓐ ② ⓑ ③ ⓒ ④ ⓓ ⑤ ⓔ

[42-43] 밑줄 친 줄임말을 풀어 완전한 문장을 쓰시오.

42

I'd like to play outside with you.

→ _____

43

You'd better get some rest.

→ _____

CHAPTER 5
문장의 형식

Minho wants a new bag. 민호는 새 가방을 원한다.
　주어　　동사　　　목적어

위 문장은 주어 Minho, 동사 wants, 목적어 a new bag 으로 이루어진 완전한 문장이에요. 완전한 문장에는 필수적인 문장 요소가 포함되어야 하는데, 주어와 동사는 반드시 필요하며 동사의 성격에 따라 보어나 목적어가 필요하기도 해요. 이렇게 동사가 어떤 문장 요소를 필요로 하는지에 따라 다섯 가지로 **문장의 형식**이 나뉘어요.

기출로 적중 POINT

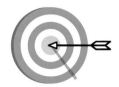

내신 100점 적중!
기출 출제율

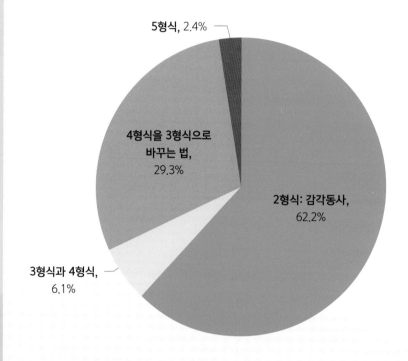

5형식, 2.4%

4형식을 3형식으로
바꾸는 법,
29.3%

2형식: 감각동사,
62.2%

3형식과 4형식,
6.1%

TOP 1 **2형식: 감각동사 (62.2%)**
감각동사의 종류와 감각동사의 주격 보어 자리에 올 수 있는 것을 묻는 문제가
자주 출제된다.

TOP 2 **4형식을 3형식으로 바꾸는 법 (29.3%)**
4형식 문장을 3형식으로 바꾸는 문제가 자주 출제된다.

TOP 3 **3형식과 4형식 (6.1%)**
3형식과 4형식 문장의 형태를 묻는 문제가 자주 출제된다.

1. **1형식 문장은 「주어 + 동사」의 형태로, 수식어(구)와 함께 쓰이기도 한다.**

   I smiled. 나는 웃었다.

   He talks loudly. 그는 큰 소리로 이야기한다.

   Snow fell from the sky. 눈이 하늘에서 떨어졌다.

2. **2형식 문장은 「주어 + 동사 + 주격 보어」의 형태이다. 주격 보어는 주어를 보충 설명하는 말로, 주격 보어 자리에는 명사나 형용사가 온다.**

   Juho became a soldier. 주호는 군인이 되었다.

   These cats are cute. 이 고양이들은 귀엽다.

연습문제 | 다음 문장이 1형식인지 2형식인지 고르시오.

1 The birds sang. (1형식 / 2형식)

2 My parents are angry. (1형식 / 2형식)

3 The mouse moved quickly. (1형식 / 2형식)

4 Hana's aunt is a designer. (1형식 / 2형식)

5 The bakery became popular. (1형식 / 2형식)

6 They studied really hard. (1형식 / 2형식)

7 The kids kept quiet. (1형식 / 2형식)

8 Mark and Joe sing well. (1형식 / 2형식)

9 Her teacher is very kind. (1형식 / 2형식)

10 The leaves turned red. (1형식 / 2형식)

11 Jamie exercised yesterday. (1형식 / 2형식)

12 I am a middle school student. (1형식 / 2형식)

13 Tradition is always important. (1형식 / 2형식)

14 The train arrived at the station. (1형식 / 2형식)

15 The dog jumped over the fence. (1형식 / 2형식)

16 Many stars shine in the sky. (1형식 / 2형식)

17 She became a news reporter. (1형식 / 2형식)

18 Kevin works at a library. (1형식 / 2형식)

기출로적중 POINT 1-2 2형식: 감각동사

정답 p.15

1. **감각동사는 감각을 나타내는 2형식 동사로, 감각동사의 주격 보어 자리에는 형용사만 온다.**

주어 + **look** ~하게 보이다 + 형용사
sound ~하게 들리다
smell ~한 냄새가 나다
taste ~한 맛이 나다
feel ~하게 느끼다

Sam **looks** happy. Sam은 행복하게 보인다.
His story **sounds** strange. 그의 이야기는 이상하게 들린다.
The flower **smells** nice. 그 꽃은 좋은 냄새가 난다.
Lemons **taste** sour. 레몬은 신맛이 난다.
I **feel** cold. 나는 춥게 느낀다.

(Tip) lovely(아름다운), friendly(친절한)와 같이 -ly로 끝나서 부사처럼 보이지만 형용사인 단어에 주의한다.
The necklace looks **lovely**. 그 목걸이는 아름답게 보인다.

2. **감각동사 뒤에 명사가 올 때는 전치사 like와 함께 「감각동사 + like + 명사」의 형태로 쓴다.**

The candy **tastes like** butter. 그 사탕은 버터 같은 맛이 난다.
It **sounds like** a good idea. 그것은 좋은 생각처럼 들린다.

연습문제 A | 괄호 안에서 알맞은 것을 고르시오.

1 Her voice sounds (softly / soft).

2 My grandparents feel (health / healthy).

3 The man looks (strong / strongly).

4 These cookies smell (delicious / deliciously).

5 Our teacher looks (happiness / happy).

6 This cupcake tastes (salty / salt).

7 Their songs sound (wonderful / wonderfully).

8 The watermelon tastes (sweet / sweetly).

9 This sofa feels (comfortable / comfortably).

10 Your dress looked (love / lovely).

11 Linda felt (hungry / hungrily).

다음 빈칸에 like가 필요하면 like를 쓰고, 필요하지 않으면 X를 쓰시오.

1 This soup tasted _____ spicy.

2 The bread smells _____ cheese.

3 His hands feel _____ rocks.

4 Amy's brother looks _____ friendly.

5 My puppy sounded _____ really sick.

6 Your milkshake tastes _____ strawberries.

7 A sheep looks _____ a small cloud.

우리말과 같도록 괄호 안의 말을 알맞게 배열하시오.

1 그 롤러코스터는 무섭게 보인다. (scary, looks, the roller coaster)
= _____

2 두리안은 지독한 냄새가 난다. (a durian, terrible, smells)
= _____

3 이 막대 사탕은 체리 같은 맛이 난다. (tastes, cherries, this lollipop, like)
= _____

4 나의 우비는 축축하게 느껴진다. (wet, my raincoat, feels)
= _____

5 그 책은 흥미롭게 들린다. (interesting, the book, sounds)
= _____

6 너의 머리는 장미 같은 냄새가 난다. (your hair, roses, like, smells)
= _____

7 그의 계획은 불가능하게 들렸다. (sounded, impossible, his plan)
= _____

기출 적중문제

다음 중 어법상 <u>어색한</u> 것은?

① It sounds very exciting.
② Those cats look hungry.
③ The mango tastes sweetly.
④ The milk smells strange.
⑤ This red scarf looks lovely.

감각동사의 주격 보어
자리에는 부사가 아닌
형용사가 와요.

정답 p.15

POINT 2-1 3형식과 4형식

1. **3형식 문장은 「주어 + 동사 + 목적어」의 형태이다. 목적어는 동사의 대상이 되는 말로, 목적어 자리에는 명사나 대명사 등이 온다.**

   I **rode** a bicycle. 나는 자전거를 탔다.
   James **plays** the piano well. James는 피아노를 잘 친다.
   Emily **met** him last week. Emily는 지난주에 그를 만났다.

2. **4형식 문장은 「주어 + 동사 + 간접 목적어(~에게) + 직접 목적어(-을)」의 형태이다. 4형식 문장의 동사는 두 개의 목적어를 필요로 하는 수여동사로, 수여동사는 '~에게 -을 (해)주다'라는 의미를 나타낸다.**

   give ~에게 -을 주다   send ~에게 -을 보내주다   bring ~에게 -을 가져다주다
   pass ~에게 -을 건네주다   show ~에게 -을 보여주다   teach ~에게 -을 가르쳐주다
   tell ~에게 -을 말해주다   write ~에게 -을 써주다   read ~에게 -을 읽어주다
   lend ~에게 -을 빌려주다   buy ~에게 -을 사주다   cook ~에게 -을 요리해주다
   find ~에게 -을 찾아주다   make ~에게 -을 만들어주다   get ~에게 -을 가져다주다
   build ~에게 -을 만들어주다 ask ~에게 -을 묻다

   She **will give** her brother a toy. 그녀는 그녀의 남동생에게 장난감을 줄 것이다.
   I **bought** Charlie new shoes. 나는 Charlie에게 새 신발을 사줬다.

연습문제 A <보기>와 같이 다음 문장의 목적어에 밑줄을 치시오. (단, 목적어가 두 개인 경우 각각 밑줄을 치시오.)

<보기> I sent her a text message.

1 I ate lunch.

2 We saw a butterfly.

3 Max brought his teacher a gift.

4 They built a big house.

5 Tommy passed her a pencil.

6 She gave me some advice.

7 My parents sold their old car.

8 Becky will teach them math.

9 Diana asked me a favor.

10 The patient took some medicine.

11 Ms. Rose cooked the kids pasta.

12 Dave showed us his new phone.

우리말과 같도록 괄호 안의 말을 알맞게 배열하시오.

1 그는 우리에게 영어를 가르쳐줬다. (us, taught, English)

= He _____ .

2 Marie는 스웨터를 샀다. (a sweater, bought)

= Marie _____ .

3 Fred는 그의 사촌에게 편지를 써줬다. (wrote, a letter, his cousin)

= Fred _____ .

4 그들의 할머니는 그들에게 호박 수프를 만들어주셨다. (them, made, pumpkin soup)

= Their grandmother _____ .

5 Alisha는 Lucas에게 많은 사진들을 보내줬다. (sent, many photos, Lucas)

= Alisha _____ .

6 그녀는 그녀의 딸에게 동화를 읽어줬다. (read, her daughter, a fairy tale)

= She _____ .

7 한 남자가 나에게 나의 이름을 물었다. (my name, asked, me)

= A man _____ .

8 그 아이는 종이비행기를 만들었다. (a paper airplane, made)

= The child _____ .

9 나의 가장 친한 친구는 나에게 비밀을 말해줬다. (me, a secret, told)

= My best friend _____ .

기출 적중문제

다음 그림을 보고 괄호 안의 말을 알맞게 배열하시오.

_____ (gave, flowers, the girl, the boy)

정답 p.16

POINT 2-2 4형식을 3형식으로 바꾸는 법

1. 4형식 문장은 동사에 따라 전치사 to/for/of 중 하나를 사용하여 3형식으로 바꿀 수 있다.

4형식	주어 + 동사 + 간접 목적어(~에게) + 직접 목적어(-을)

3형식	주어 + 동사 + 직접 목적어(-을) + 전치사 **to/for/of** + 간접 목적어(~에게)

Thomas gave his cousin a gift. Thomas는 그의 사촌에게 선물을 줬다.

→ Thomas gave a gift to his cousin.

2. 4형식 문장을 3형식으로 바꿀 때 쓰는 전치사는 동사에 따라 다르다.

to를 쓰는 동사	give, send, bring, pass, show, teach, tell, write, read, lend 등	Mr. Olson teaches students math. → Mr. Olson teaches math to students. Olson 선생님은 학생들에게 수학을 가르쳐준다.
for를 쓰는 동사	buy, cook, find, make, get, build 등	We made Bella a birthday cake. → We made a birthday cake for Bella. 우리는 Bella에게 생일 케이크를 만들어줬다.
of를 쓰는 동사	ask 등	Chad asked his teacher many questions. → Chad asked many questions of his teacher. Chad는 그의 선생님에게 많은 질문을 했다.

연습문제 A 다음 빈칸에 to, for, of 중 알맞은 것을 쓰시오.

1 William made sandwiches _____ me.

2 Lisa's boyfriend gave a rose _____ her.

3 He built a house _____ his family.

4 I showed my ID card _____ the police.

5 Derek passed the ball _____ his classmate.

6 I got a watch _____ my brother.

7 Mom showed a photo album _____ us.

8 The reporters asked some questions _____ the actor.

9 Ms. Shaw will buy some books _____ her son.

다음 4형식 문장을 3형식으로 바꿔 쓰시오.

1 He lent me some comic books.
→ He _____.

2 My father cooked us a delicious meal.
→ My father _____.

3 Angelina told Nancy the whole story.
→ Angelina _____.

4 May I ask you a favor?
→ May I _____?

5 Ms. White read the children a short novel.
→ Ms. White _____.

6 She bought her aunt a scarf.
→ She _____.

7 Frank wrote his parents a poem.
→ Frank _____.

8 I will find you a good job.
→ I will _____.

9 The tour guide brought us the maps.
→ The tour guide _____.

10 Subin made her classmates an apple pie.
→ Subin _____.

11 I sent my manager an e-mail.
→ I _____.

12 Can you give me some advice?
→ Can you _____?

기출 적중문제

다음 빈칸에 들어갈 전치사가 나머지 넷과 다른 것은?
① Cindy bought coffee _____ us.
② Harry lent his cap _____ Minjun.
③ Peter sent letters _____ his friends.
④ Could you pass the fork _____ me?
⑤ She gave her old necklace _____ her daughter.

4형식 문장을 3형식 문장
으로 바꿀 때는 동사에 따라
알맞은 전치사를 써야 해요.

5형식 문장은 「주어 + 동사 + 목적어 + 목적격 보어」의 형태이다. 목적격 보어는 목적어를 보충 설명하는 말로, 목적격 보어 자리에는 명사나 형용사가 온다.

My sister **calls** **the puppy Rufus**. 나의 언니는 그 강아지를 Rufus라고 부른다.

The film **made** **Jack a famous director**. 그 영화는 Jack을 유명한 감독으로 만들었다.

Exercise **makes** **us healthy**. 운동은 우리를 건강하게 만든다.

This coat **keeps** **me warm**. 이 코트는 나를 따뜻하게 유지한다.

(Tip) 목적격 보어 자리에는 동사에 따라 동사원형이나 「to + 동사원형」 등의 형태도 올 수 있다.

I **let** him **borrow** my laptop. 나는 그가 나의 노트북을 빌리도록 허락했다.

Mr. Kim **wants** us **to listen** carefully. 김 선생님은 우리가 주의 깊게 듣기를 원하신다.

연습문제 <보기>와 같이 다음 문장의 목적어에는 동그라미를 치고, 목적격 보어에는 밑줄을 치시오.

<보기> The rain made (my shoes) wet.

1 His friends call him Teddy.

2 Jessica keeps her room clean.

3 Sugar makes dishes sweet.

4 We call our fish Dory.

5 He always makes me angry.

6 I found the new chair comfortable.

7 The movie made the actor a star.

8 We must keep our minds open.

9 This cheesecake made the bakery popular.

10 Jake found the story interesting.

목적격 보어 자리에
부사는 올 수 없어요.

기출 적중문제

다음 문장에서 어법상 어색한 부분을 찾아 쓰고 바르게 고쳐 쓰시오.

The news made Emma sadly.

_____ → _____

A 다음 그림을 보고 <보기>에서 알맞은 말을 골라 질문에 대한 대답을 완성하시오.

1

2

3

4

5

6

<보기>　sour　sick　noisy　a cloud　a lion　peaches

1 A: How does Samuel look?　　　　B: He _____.

2 A: What does this shampoo smell like?　　B: It _____.

3 A: How does the lemon taste?　　　　B: It _____.

4 A: What does this sofa feel like?　　　B: It _____.

5 A: What does your pencil case look like?　B: It _____.

6 A: How does his song sound?　　　B: It _____.

B 다음 4형식 문장은 3형식으로, 3형식 문장은 4형식으로 바꿔 쓰시오.

1 I sent a card to Suzy.

→ _____

2 Mr. Smith teaches us history.

→ _____

3 He cooked a special dinner for his wife.

→ _____

4 My friend gave me her notes.

→ _____

5 The clown made balloon animals for the kids.

→ _____

6 Beth showed them her new shoes.

→ _____

7 Ms. Miller wrote a letter to the mayor.

→ _____

8 I will buy you the concert tickets.

→ _____

9 The waiter brought coffee to the customers.

→ _____

10 Can I ask you some difficult questions?

→ _____

C 우리말과 같도록 괄호 안의 말을 알맞게 배열하시오.

1 Kelly는 나를 거짓말쟁이라고 불렀다. (me, Kelly, called, a liar)

= _____

2 Henry는 그의 친구에게 돈을 빌려줬다. (money, lent, Henry, his friend)

= _____

3 우리의 삼촌은 우리에게 무서운 이야기를 말해줬다. (us, our uncle, a scary story, told)

= _____

4 경찰은 그 마을을 안전하게 유지한다. (the town, the police, keep, safe)

= _____

5 날씨가 그 조종사를 초조하게 만들었다. (made, the pilot, the weather, nervous)

= _____

6 그녀는 너에게 기회를 줄 것이다. (will give, a chance, you, she)

= _____

7 나는 수학 시험이 쉽다고 생각했다. (found, the math test, I, easy)

= _____

8 그는 그의 아들에게 장난감 자동차를 만들어줬다. (his son, made, he, a toy car)

= _____

[1-2] 다음 빈칸에 들어갈 알맞은 것을 <u>모두</u> 고르시오.

1

> Nate looks like _____.

① his grandfather ② nice
③ a model ④ beautifully
⑤ brave

2

> This soup tastes _____.

① greatly ② delicious
③ horribly ④ a potato
⑤ salty

3 다음 중 문장의 형식이 <u>잘못된</u> 것은?

① 1형식: I woke up late today.
② 2형식: The students listened carefully.
③ 3형식: My father fixed the laptop.
④ 4형식: The guide showed us the video.
⑤ 5형식: Christmas gifts make children happy.

4 다음 빈칸에 like가 들어갈 수 있는 것을 <u>모두</u> 고르시오.

① The wine smells _____ fantastic.
② This syrup tastes _____ chocolate.
③ Monica looks _____ friendly.
④ My hands feel _____ cold in winter.
⑤ That fruit looks _____ a star.

5 다음 중 2형식 문장끼리 묶인 것은?

> ⓐ Cassy dances well.
> ⓑ He laughed loudly.
> ⓒ That boy is very tall.
> ⓓ Jenny became a scientist.
> ⓔ We walked to the station.

① ⓐ, ⓑ ② ⓐ, ⓒ ③ ⓑ, ⓓ
④ ⓒ, ⓓ ⑤ ⓓ, ⓔ

6 다음 우리말을 영작한 것 중 <u>어색한</u> 것은?

① 그는 건강하게 보인다.
= He looks healthy.
② Jessie의 목소리는 화난 것처럼 들린다.
= Jessie's voice sounds angry.
③ 그 식물은 이상한 냄새가 난다.
= The plant smells strange.
④ 그 선수들은 지쳐 보인다.
= The players feel tired.
⑤ 그 레모네이드는 신맛이 난다.
= The lemonade tastes sour.

7 다음 중 어법상 <u>어색한</u> 것은?

① He looks like my classmate.
② Her new pillows feel soft.
③ Our coach sounded upset.
④ The singer felt like nervous.
⑤ The clouds look like ice cream.

8 다음 빈칸에 들어갈 알맞은 것은?

> Mr. Johnson made his kids a sandwich.
> = Mr. Johnson made _____.

① his kids for a sandwich
② his kids to a sandwich
③ a sandwich to his kids
④ a sandwich for his kids
⑤ a sandwich his kids

9 다음 문장에서 **틀린** 부분을 바르게 고쳐 완전한 문장을 쓰시오.

> That sounded thunder.
> → _____

10 다음 글의 빈칸에 들어갈 말이 순서대로 짝지어진 것은?

> I went to the shopping mall yesterday.
> I found a beautiful blue dress. I tried
> it on, and it looked _____ on me. I
> _____ a princess. I'm going to wear
> it for my birthday party next week.

① perfectly – felt like
② perfectly – felt
③ perfect – felt like
④ perfect – felt
⑤ perfection – felt like

11 다음 문장에서 어법상 <u>어색한</u> 부분을 찾아 쓰고 바르게 고쳐 쓰시오.

> Your new science project sounds very
> difficultly.

_____ → _____

[12-13] 우리말과 같도록 괄호 안의 말을 활용하여 문장을 완성하시오.

12

> 그녀의 집은 궁전처럼 보였다. (a palace)

= Her house _____.

13

> 저 가게의 케이크는 훌륭하게 보인다. (wonderful)

= That store's cake _____.

14 다음 중 밑줄 친 부분이 어법상 <u>어색한</u> 것은?

> I have a dog. She is very ①<u>young</u>. She
> is ②<u>cute</u> and ③<u>looks</u> a baby bear. She
> sounds ④<u>lovely</u> when she barks. Her
> white fur ⑤<u>feels</u> so soft.

15 다음 그림을 보고 괄호 안의 말을 알맞게 배열하시오.

_____
(Surin, passed, Jimin, the pepper)

19 다음 중 4형식 문장은 3형식으로, 3형식 문장은 4형식으로 바르게 바꾼 것은?

① I brought my dad a cup of coffee.
  → I brought a cup of coffee of my dad.
② I gave my homework to the teacher.
  → I gave my homework the teacher.
③ I showed the doctor my arm.
  → I showed my arm to the doctor.
④ Matt found a pencil for Carl.
  → Matt found for Carl a pencil.
⑤ He cooked his best friend dinner.
  → He cooked dinner to his best friend.

[16-17] 다음 빈칸에 공통으로 들어갈 알맞은 말을 쓰시오.

16

· This thing smells _____ garbage.
· The jelly tastes _____ grapes.

17

· Allie showed her pet _____ her classmates.
· Will you lend your pen _____ me?

18 다음 빈칸에 들어갈 말로 어색한 것은?

Nina _____ her sister an umbrella.

① gave   ② helped   ③ passed
④ lent   ⑤ brought

20 다음 (A)~(C)에 들어갈 말이 바르게 짝지어진 것은?

· Luke taught math ___(A)___ them.
· The tourist asked some questions ___(B)___ me.
· Janet gave some snacks ___(C)___ her friends.

	(A)	(B)	(C)
①	to	to	for
②	for	to	for
③	to	of	for
④	for	to	to
⑤	to	of	to

21 다음 빈칸에 들어갈 말이 나머지 넷과 다른 것은?

① Hilda sent a package _____ her nephew.
② She showed her new phone _____ them.
③ Mom told good news _____ me.
④ Wesley passed some paper _____ us.
⑤ Ms. Wilson got a watch _____ her husband.

내신 점수와 영어 실력을 높여주는 추가 자료 제공 HackersBook.com

22 우리말과 같도록 주어진 <조건>에 맞게 영작하시오.

나는 나의 형에게 생일 선물을 사줬다.

<조건>
1. buy, a birthday present를 활용하시오.
2. 전치사를 쓰지 마시오.
3. 시제에 주의하시오.

= _____

23 다음 중 어법상 바른 것의 개수는?

ⓐ Jisu sent text messages us.
ⓑ I passed my sister some towels.
ⓒ He built a snowman for his brother.
ⓓ Yuri bought new notebooks to me.
ⓔ The police officer asked some questions for the thief.

① 1개   ② 2개   ③ 3개
④ 4개   ⑤ 5개

[24-25] 다음 두 문장의 의미가 같도록 알맞은 전치사를 이용하여 문장을 완성하시오.

24

Our parents built us a tree house.
= Our parents _____ .

25

I showed the guests my artwork.
= I showed _____ .

26 괄호 안의 말을 알맞게 배열하시오.

A: Did you like the concert?
B: No, I didn't. _____
_____ (made, the concert, sleepy, me)

27 다음 중 주어진 문장과 문장의 형식이 <u>다른</u> 것은?

He rides a bike every morning.

① I put my coffee on the table.
② Natalie took a cookie from the jar.
③ Chris lent me his smartphone.
④ That store sells nice sneakers.
⑤ Roger met his friends at the theater.

28 우리말과 같도록 괄호 안의 말을 알맞게 배열하시오.

우리의 선생님은 Tony를 천재라고 불렀다. (Tony, called, a genius, our teacher)

= _____

29 다음 중 문장의 형식이 나머지 넷과 <u>다른</u> 것은?

① His story made him a hero.
② The wind makes me cold.
③ The snow made everything white.
④ Mr. Cooper made us some muffins.
⑤ The book made people uncomfortable.

CHAPTER 6
다양한 문장의 종류

He is from Italy. 그는 이탈리아에서 왔다.
Is he from Italy? 그는 이탈리아에서 왔니?

첫 번째 문장은 그가 이탈리아에서 왔다는 사실을 전달하는 평서문이에요. 하지만 주어와 동사의 위치를 바꾼 뒤 문장 맨 뒤에 물음표를 붙이면 그가 이탈리아에서 왔는지를 묻는 **의문문**이 돼요. 이렇게 특정한 의도를 나타내기 위해 의문문, 명령문, 감탄문 등 다양한 종류의 문장을 사용할 수 있어요.

기출로 적중 POINT

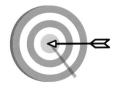

내신 100점 적중!
기출 출제율

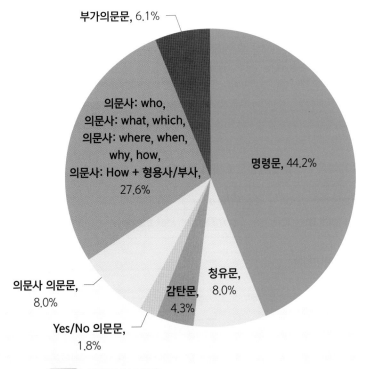

부가의문문, 6.1%

의문사: who,
의문사: what, which,
의문사: where, when,
why, how,
의문사: How + 형용사/부사,
27.6%

명령문, 44.2%

청유문,
8.0%

감탄문,
4.3%

의문사 의문문,
8.0%

Yes/No 의문문,
1.8%

TOP 1 **명령문 (44.2%)**
명령문의 의미와 형태를 묻는 문제가 자주 출제된다.

TOP 2 **의문사: who, what, which, where, when, why, how,**
How + 형용사/부사 (27.6%)
의문사 who, what, where, how 등의 의미와 쓰임을 묻는 문제가 자주 출제된다.

TOP 3 **청유문 (8%), 의문사 의문문 (8%)**
청유문의 의미와 형태를 묻는 문제가 자주 출제된다. 의문사 의문문의 형태를 묻는 문제가 자주 출제된다.

명령문은 상대방에게 지시하거나 요구하는 문장이며, 주어 You가 생략되어 있다.

긍정 명령문	'~해라'의 의미로, 동사원형을 문장 맨 앞에 쓰는 형태이다. **Wash** your hands. 너의 손을 씻어라. **Be** polite to everyone. 모든 사람에게 공손해라. **Take** off your shoes, <u>please</u>. 당신의 신발을 벗으세요. → 문장 맨 앞이나 맨 뒤에 please를 붙이면 더 정중한 표현이 된다.
부정 명령문	'~하지 마라'의 의미로, 「Don't[Do not] + 동사원형」의 형태이다. **Don't waste** food. 음식을 낭비하지 마라. **Do not be** late. 늦지 마라. Please **don't run** here. 여기에서 뛰지 마세요. (Tip) 「Never + 동사원형」은 '절대 ~하지 마라'라는 의미로, 강한 금지를 나타낸다. **Never be** rude. 절대 무례하지 마라.

연습문제 A <보기>와 같이 다음 문장을 명령문으로 바꿔 쓰시오.

> <보기> You should lock the door. → _Lock the door._
> You shouldn't lock the door. → _Don't[Do not] lock the door._

1 You should take this umbrella. → _____

2 You should try your best. → _____

3 You shouldn't tell a lie. → _____

4 You should keep a diary. → _____

5 You shouldn't miss class again. → _____

6 You should be a good person. → _____

7 You shouldn't walk on the grass. → _____

8 You should be friendly to others. → _____

9 You shouldn't be afraid of bugs. → _____

10 You should bring your swimsuit. → _____

11 You shouldn't be angry with him. → _____

12 You shouldn't use your phone in class. → _____

연습문제 B 다음 그림을 보고 <보기>에서 알맞은 동사를 골라 명령문을 완성하시오.

<보기> feed be go put take open

1

2

3

4

5

6

1 _____ careful of the car.

2 _____ straight for two blocks.

3 _____ the window.

4 _____ the birds.

5 _____ a picture here.

6 _____ the trash in the bin.

연습문제 C 밑줄 친 부분이 어법상 맞으면 O를 쓰고, 틀리면 바르게 고쳐 쓰시오.

1 Don't <u>is</u> selfish.   → _____

2 Never <u>yelling</u> at me.   → _____

3 <u>Be</u> quiet in the library.   → _____

4 <u>Cleans</u> your room.   → _____

5 <u>Not</u> worry about me.   → _____

6 Please <u>spoke</u> in English.   → _____

7 <u>Don't eat</u> too much sugar.   → _____

기출 적중문제

다음 빈칸에 들어갈 알맞은 것은?

Don't _____ on the air conditioner.

① turn   ② turns   ③ turned

④ turning   ⑤ to turn

청유문은 상대방에게 권유하거나 제안하는 문장이다.

긍정 청유문	'~하자'의 의미로, 「Let's + 동사원형」의 형태이다. **Let's order** pizza. 피자를 주문하자. **Let's move** to the science room. 과학실로 이동하자.
부정 청유문	'~하지 말자'의 의미로, 「Let's not + 동사원형」의 형태이다. **Let's not hurry.** 서두르지 말자. **Let's not be** nervous. 초조해하지 말자.

(Tip) 「Let me + 동사원형」은 '제가 ~할게요/~하게 해주세요'라는 의미이다.
Let me introduce my friend. 제가 저의 친구를 소개할게요.

연습문제 우리말과 같도록 괄호 안의 동사를 활용하여 문장을 완성하시오.

1 새 셔츠를 사자. = _____ a new shirt. (buy)

2 함께 저녁을 먹자. = _____ dinner together. (have)

3 지금은 택시를 타지 말자. = _____ a taxi now. (take)

4 제가 당신을 위해 그것을 해드릴게요. = _____ it for you. (do)

5 여기에 너무 오래 머무르지 말자. = _____ here too long. (stay)

6 7시에 만나자. = _____ at 7 o'clock. (meet)

7 그렇게 시끄럽게 하지 말자. = _____ so noisy. (be)

8 제가 저의 숙제를 끝내게 해주세요. = _____ my homework. (finish)

9 너의 문제에 관해 이야기하자. = _____ about your problem. (talk)

10 이 노래를 듣지 말자. = _____ to this song. (listen)

11 오늘 오후에 영화를 보자. = _____ a movie this afternoon. (see)

기출 적중문제 ◎—◁

다음 문장에서 어법상 어색한 부분을 찾아 쓰고 바르게 고쳐 쓰시오.

> Let's going to an Italian restaurant.

_____ → _____

POINT 3 감탄문

정답 p.18

감탄문은 '정말 ~이구나/하구나!'의 의미로, 기쁨이나 놀라움 등의 감정을 나타내는 문장이다.
문장 맨 뒤의 「주어 + 동사」는 생략할 수도 있다.

❶ What 감탄문은 명사를 강조한다.

| **What** | + | **(a/an)** | + | **형용사** | + | **명사** | + | **(주어 + 동사)** | **!** |

She is a very smart girl. 그녀는 매우 똑똑한 소녀이다.
→ **What** a smart girl (she is)! (그녀는) 정말 똑똑한 소녀구나!

(Tip) What 감탄문이 복수명사를 강조할 때는 a/an을 쓰지 않는다.
What boring books (these are)! (이것들은) 정말 지루한 책들이구나!

❷ How 감탄문은 형용사나 부사를 강조한다. How 감탄문이 부사를 강조할 때는 문장 맨 뒤의 「주어 + 동사」를 생략할 수 없다.

| **How** | + | **형용사** | + | **(주어 + 동사)** | **!** |

The test was really difficult. 그 시험은 아주 어려웠다.
→ **How** difficult (the test was)! (그 시험은) 정말 어려웠구나!

| **How** | + | **부사** | + | **주어 + 동사** | **!** |

He runs very fast. 그는 매우 빠르게 달린다.
→ **How** fast he runs! 그는 정말 빠르게 달리는구나!

연습문제 A 괄호 안에서 알맞은 것을 고르시오.

1 (What / How) a nice car!

2 (What / How) cold today is!

3 (What / How) a big tree this is!

4 (What / How) strange!

5 (What / How) a pretty flower!

6 (What / How) happy Amy looks!

7 (What / How) cute puppies!

8 (What / How) loudly Jamie talks!

9 (What / How) an exciting movie!

10 (What / How) lucky they were!

11 (What / How) slowly the turtle moves!

12 (What / How) a wonderful idea!

연습문제 B 다음 문장을 감탄문으로 바꿔 쓰시오.

1 The mountain is very high. → How _____!

2 It was a very hot day. → What _____!

3 They are very close friends. → What _____!

4 She was really brave. → How _____!

5 Cindy is a very good dancer. → What _____!

6 That is a really huge building. → What _____!

7 This umbrella is very colorful. → How _____!

8 It was a really hard question. → What _____!

9 You have really beautiful eyes. → What _____!

10 He swims very well. → How _____!

연습문제 C 우리말과 같도록 괄호 안의 말을 알맞게 배열하시오.

1 그것은 정말 무거운 배낭이구나! (backpack, is, heavy, a, what, it)

= _____

2 그 바람은 정말 강했구나! (strong, the wind, was, how)

= _____

3 이것은 정말 빠른 기차구나! (what, fast, is, this, a, train)

= _____

4 Andy는 정말 열심히 공부하는구나! (hard, how, Andy, studies)

= _____

5 그 원숭이들은 정말 영리하구나! (the monkeys, how, are, clever)

= _____

기출 적중문제

다음 빈칸에 공통으로 들어갈 알맞은 것은?

- _____ small shoes these are!
- _____ a terrible smell!

① Where　　② How　　③ Who

④ Those　　⑤ What

> What 감탄문은 명사를 강조하고, How 감탄문은 형용사나 부사를 강조해요.

기출로적중 POINT 4 Yes/No 의문문

정답 p.18

1. **be동사·일반동사·조동사가 있는 의문문은 대답의 내용이 긍정이면 Yes, 부정이면 No로 답한다.**

   Are you hungry? 너는 배고프니?
   – **Yes**, I am. 응, 나는 배고파. / **No**, I'm not. 아니, 나는 배고프지 않아.

   Did Henry miss the bus? Henry는 그 버스를 놓쳤니?
   – **Yes**, he did. 응, 그는 놓쳤어. / **No**, he didn't. 아니, 그는 놓치지 않았어.

   Can they come to the festival? 그들은 그 축제에 올 수 있니?
   – **Yes**, they can. 응, 그들은 올 수 있어. / **No**, they can't. 아니, 그들은 올 수 없어.

2. **부정의문문은 부정어 not을 포함한 의문문으로, '~하지 않니?'의 의미이다. 부정의문문에 대답할 때는 질문의 형태와 상관없이 대답의 내용이 긍정이면 Yes, 부정이면 No로 답한다.**

   Isn't she a pianist? 그녀는 피아니스트이지 않니?
   – **Yes**, she **is**. (= Yes, she is a pianist.) 아니, 그녀는 피아니스트야.
   – **No**, she **isn't**. (= No, she isn't a pianist.) 응, 그녀는 피아니스트가 아니야.

연습문제 <보기>와 같이 질문에 대한 대답이 괄호 안의 내용과 일치하도록 빈칸에 쓰시오.

<보기> A: Didn't you wake up early?   B: _Yes_ , _I_ _did_ . (I woke up early.)

1 A: Does Jim like cats?   B: _____, _____ _____. (He likes cats.)

2 A: Doesn't he know you?   B: _____, _____ _____. (He doesn't know me.)

3 A: Is the room dirty?   B: _____, _____ _____. (It isn't dirty.)

4 A: Didn't Lily use my pen?   B: _____, _____ _____. (She didn't use your pen.)

5 A: Weren't they at school?   B: _____, _____ _____. (They were at school.)

6 A: Can you show me the map?   B: _____, _____ _____. (I can show you the map.)

7 A: Do you agree with me?   B: _____, _____ _____. (I don't agree with you.)

8 A: Shouldn't we wait in line?   B: _____, _____ _____. (We should wait in line.)

9 A: Isn't your bag heavy?   B: _____, _____ _____. (It is heavy.)

10 A: Will it rain tomorrow?   B: _____, _____ _____. (It won't rain tomorrow.)

11 A: Aren't you from England?   B: _____, _____ _____. (I am from England.)

의문사 의문문

정답 p.18

1. **의문사 의문문은 구체적인 정보를 묻는 의문사로 시작하는 의문문이며, 의문사 의문문에는 Yes나 No가 아닌 각 의문사가 묻는 정보로 대답한다.**

who	what	which	where	when	why	how
누구	무엇	어느 것	어디에, 어디에서	언제	왜	어떻게

Who is that girl? – She is my sister. 저 소녀는 누구니? – 그녀는 나의 여동생이야.
When will the concert start? – At 8 o'clock. 그 콘서트는 언제 시작하니? – 8시에.

2. **의문사 의문문의 형태**

be동사가 있는 의문사 의문문	「의문사 + be동사 + 주어 ~?」	**Where** is the bakery? 그 빵집은 어디에 있니? **Why** were you late? 너는 왜 늦었니?
일반동사가 있는 의문사 의문문	「의문사 + do/does/did + 주어 + 동사원형 ~?」	**What** do you do on Sundays? 너는 일요일마다 무엇을 하니? **When** did Judy have dinner? Judy는 언제 저녁을 먹었니?
조동사가 있는 의문사 의문문	「의문사 + 조동사 + 주어 + 동사원형 ~?」	**Who** should we call? 우리는 누구를 불러야 하니? **How** can I get to the park? 내가 그 공원에 어떻게 갈 수 있니?

(Tip) 의문문의 주어가 의문사인 경우 「의문사 + 동사 ~?」의 형태이며, 의문사는 3인칭 단수 취급한다.
Who teaches this class? 누가 이 수업을 가르치니?

연습문제 A 우리말과 같도록 괄호 안의 말을 알맞게 배열하시오.

1 나의 머리가 어떻게 보이니? (does, my hair, how, look)

= _____

2 너는 왜 슬펐니? (sad, why, you, were)

= _____

3 버스는 언제 도착하니? (arrive, the bus, will, when)

= _____

4 네가 가장 좋아하는 배우는 누구니? (your favorite actor, who, is)

= _____

5 내가 화장실을 어디에서 찾을 수 있니? (can, I, a bathroom, where, find)

= _____

6 David는 무엇을 보고 있니? (is, David, what, watching)

= _____

7 너는 언제 자니? (you, do, sleep, when)

= _____

8 누가 이 창문을 열었니? (opened, this window, who)

= _____

9 그녀의 신발은 왜 더럽니? (why, dirty, her shoes, are)

= _____

10 내가 표를 어떻게 살 수 있니? (I, how, buy, can, a ticket)

= _____

11 무엇이 너를 행복하게 만드니? (makes, what, you, happy)

= _____

12 너는 어디에서 저 신발을 구했니? (did, you, where, those shoes, get)

= _____

연습문제 B | 밑줄 친 부분이 어법상 맞으면 O를 쓰고, 틀리면 바르게 고쳐 쓰시오.

1 What <u>she is</u> doing? → _____

2 Where <u>did you put</u> the keys? → _____

3 When <u>should I</u> leave? → _____

4 Who <u>speak</u> Spanish? → _____

5 Why <u>he looks</u> so surprised? → _____

6 <u>Can who</u> fix this door? → _____

기출 적중문제

다음 우리말을 알맞게 영작한 것은?

> John은 어디에 사니?

① John where lives?

② Do where John live?

③ Where is John live?

④ Where does John live?

⑤ Where do John lives?

의문사 who는 사람에 대해 물을 때 쓰며, 쓰임에 따라 whose나 whom으로 형태가 변한다.

who 누구	**Who** is your best friend? – My best friend is Jenna. 너의 가장 친한 친구는 누구니? – 나의 가장 친한 친구는 Jenna야. **Who** can answer this question? – Junho. 누가 이 질문에 대답할 수 있니? – 준호.
whose + 명사 누구의 ~	**Whose umbrella** is this? – It's my umbrella. 이것은 누구의 우산이니? – 그것은 나의 우산이야. (Tip) whose는 '누구의 것'이라는 의미로 명사 없이 단독으로 쓰이기도 한다. **Whose** is this umbrella? 이 우산은 누구의 것이니?
who(m) 누구를	**Who[Whom]** did you meet yesterday? – My uncle. 너는 어제 누구를 만났니? – 나의 삼촌.

연습문제 다음 빈칸에 Who, Whose, Who(m) 중 알맞은 것을 쓰시오.

1 _____ is that boy?

2 _____ is your favorite singer?

3 _____ idea was this?

4 _____ does Rosa like?

5 _____ did you see at the Christmas party?

6 _____ are those glasses?

7 _____ should I invite?

8 _____ called you this morning?

9 _____ can we trust?

10 _____ is the wallet on the table?

11 _____ is the best soccer player?

12 _____ shoes are these?

13 _____ is in the classroom?

14 _____ showed you the pictures?

15 _____ is Brad waiting for?

기출로적중 POINT 5-3 의문사: what, which

정답 p.19

what 무엇	what은 동물이나 사물, 또는 사람의 직업이나 성격에 대해 물을 때 쓴다. **What** is your favorite color? – Red. 네가 가장 좋아하는 색은 무엇이니? – 빨간색. **What** is he making? – Tomato soup. 그는 무엇을 만들고 있니? – 토마토 수프. **What** do you do? – I'm a teacher. 너는 무슨 일을 하니? – 나는 선생님이야. (Tip) what은 '무슨, 어떤'이라는 의미의 형용사로 쓰여 명사 앞에서 명사를 꾸밀 수 있다. **What flower** is that? – It's a lilac. 저것은 무슨 꽃이니? – 그것은 라일락이야.
which 어느 것	which는 정해진 범위 안에서의 선택을 물을 때 쓴다. **Which** do you want, water or juice? – I want water. 너는 물과 주스 중 어느 것을 원하니? – 나는 물을 원해. **Which** do you like better, tigers or lions? – Tigers. 너는 호랑이와 사자 중 어느 것을 더 좋아하니? – 호랑이. (Tip) which는 '어느, 어떤'이라는 의미의 형용사로 쓰여 명사 앞에서 명사를 꾸밀 수 있다. **Which subject** do you prefer, math or science? – I prefer math. 너는 수학과 과학 중 어느 과목을 선호하니? – 나는 수학을 선호해. **Which season** do you like? – Spring. 너는 어떤 계절을 좋아하니? – 봄.

(Tip) what은 정해지지 않은 범위에서 질문할 때 쓰고, which는 정해진 범위 안에서의 선택을 물을 때 쓴다.

What movie genre do you like? 너는 무슨 영화 장르를 좋아하니?
Which movie genre do you like better, comedies or romances?
너는 코미디와 로맨스 중 어느 영화 장르를 더 좋아하니?

연습문제 A 괄호 안에서 What이나 Which 중 알맞은 것을 골라 대화를 완성하시오.

1 A: (What / Which) does Ms. Evans do?
B: She is a dentist.

2 A: (What / Which) is faster, a ship or an airplane?
B: An airplane.

3 A: (What / Which) is your sister doing?
B: She is sleeping.

4 A: (What / Which) is his name?
B: Jimmy.

5 A: (What / Which) shirt is better, the green one or the blue one?
B: The green one is better.

6 A: (What / Which) are you going to do after school?

   B: I'm going to go to a yoga class.

7 A: (What / Which) beverage does Mr. Shaw want, coffee or tea?

   B: He wants tea.

8 A: (What / Which) did you buy at the market?

   B: I bought some strawberries and bananas.

9 A: (What / Which) country is larger, Russia or Korea?

   B: Russia.

10 A: (What / Which) do you prefer, e-books or paper books?

   B: I prefer paper books.

연습문제 **B** 자연스러운 대화가 되도록 질문과 대답을 연결하시오.

[1-5]

1 What is the date today? ·   · ⓐ Whales.

2 Who is the girl with a yellow ribbon? ·   · ⓑ Sujin.

3 Which are bigger, elephants or whales? ·   · ⓒ May 2.

4 Whose pens are these? ·   · ⓓ He's playing baseball.

5 What is Peter doing? ·   · ⓔ They're my pens.

[6-10]

6 Who is Jessica Taylor? ·   · ⓐ Tom Reed is my favorite player.

7 What was your Christmas gift? ·   · ⓑ She's a famous dancer.

8 What subject do you like best? ·   · ⓒ I live with my family.

9 Which player is your favorite in the team? ·   · ⓓ History.

10 Whom do you live with? ·   · ⓔ A sweater.

기출 적중문제

다음 빈칸에 들어갈 말이 나머지 넷과 <u>다른</u> 것은?

① _____ food does he like?

② _____ is the man next to Ann?

③ _____ was the news about?

④ _____ is your favorite sport?

⑤ _____ will you do tomorrow?

기출로 적중 POINT 5-4

의문사: where, when, why, how

정답 p.19

where 어디에, 어디에서	where는 장소를 물을 때 쓴다. **Where** is he now? – He's in his room. 그는 지금 어디에 있니? – 그는 그의 방에 있어. **Where** will you go this summer? – France. 너는 이번 여름에 어디에 갈 거니? – 프랑스.
when 언제	when은 시간이나 날짜를 물을 때 쓴다. **When** can you come home? – Around five. 너는 언제 집에 올 수 있니? – 5시 쯤. **When** is your birthday? – It's November 11. 너의 생일은 언제니? – 11월 11일이야. (Tip) 시간을 묻는 when은 what time으로 바꿔 쓸 수 있다. **What time** can you come home? 너는 몇 시에 집에 올 수 있니?
why 왜	why는 이유를 물을 때 쓴다. **Why** is it cold in here? – Because the window is open. 여기는 왜 춥니? – 창문이 열려 있기 때문이야. **Why** does she look so happy? – Because she passed the test. 그녀는 왜 그렇게 행복해 보이니? – 그녀가 그 시험을 통과했기 때문이야.
how 어떻게	how는 방법이나 상태를 물을 때 쓴다. **How** do you get to school? – I take the bus. 너는 어떻게 학교에 가니? – 나는 버스를 타. **How** was your vacation? – It was fun. 너의 휴가는 어땠니? – 그것은 재미있었어.

연습문제 A 다음 빈칸에 Where, When, Why, How 중 알맞은 것을 넣어 대화를 완성하시오.

1 A: _____ are you going to visit her?   B: Tomorrow.

2 A: _____ are you feeling now?   B: Very good.

3 A: _____ was Mr. Smith this morning?   B: He was at the hospital.

4 A: _____ do kangaroos have a pouch?   B: Because they carry their babies in it.

5 A: _____ does the baby look?   B: She looks very healthy.

6 A: _____ is Samuel from?   B: He's from Spain.

7 A: _____ didn't you call me last night?   B: Because I lost my phone.

8 A: _____ is the bank?   B: It's near the train station.

9 A: _____ will Daniel move into a new house?   B: June 8.

10 A: _____ are you going?   B: I'm going to the mall.

11 A: _____ was the weather in New York?   B: It was sunny.

12 *A:* _____ isn't Tom wearing a helmet?   *B:* Because his helmet is broken.

13 *A:* _____ is the fireworks festival?   *B:* Next Sunday.

14 *A:* _____ can I get to the airport?   *B:* You can take a shuttle bus.

15 *A:* _____ do you like summer?   *B:* Because I can swim in the ocean.

연습문제 **B** 자연스러운 대화가 되도록 질문과 대답을 연결하시오.

[1-5]

1 Where does Kenny live?   ·   ·ⓐ I can help you.

2 When is Hangeul Day?   ·   ·ⓑ October 9.

3 Why was Minjae absent?   ·   ·ⓒ By bus.

4 How did you get to Jeonju?   ·   ·ⓓ In Seattle.

5 Who can help me?   ·   ·ⓔ Because he was sick.

[6-10]

6 Where is my camera?   ·   ·ⓐ It's rainy and cold.

7 Why is your mom upset?   ·   ·ⓑ It's under your desk.

8 What do you do?   ·   ·ⓒ In three minutes.

9 How is the weather today?   ·   ·ⓓ Because I told her a lie.

10 When will the next train arrive? ·   ·ⓔ I'm a comedian.

기출 적중문제

다음 대화의 빈칸에 들어갈 말이 순서대로 짝지어진 것은?

> *A:* _____ were you late for class today?
> *B:* Because I missed the bus this morning.
> *A:* Oh no! How did you get to school?
> *B:* I walked all the way here.
> *A:* Really? _____ do you live?
> *B:* On Elm Street. It is ten blocks away.

주어진 대답에 따라 알맞은 의문사를 골라야 해요.

① Why – When   ② What – How
③ Why – Where   ④ What – Where
⑤ Who – Where

의문사: How + 형용사/부사

정답 p.19

「How + 형용사/부사 ~?」는 '얼마나 ~하니?'라는 의미로, 높이, 크기, 시간, 거리 등의 구체적인 정보를 물을 때 쓴다.

How tall ~?	높이, 키	How tall is the Eiffel Tower?	에펠탑은 얼마나 높니?
How big ~?	크기	How big are polar bears?	북극곰들은 얼마나 크니?
How long ~?	시간, 길이	How long did you stay there?	너는 거기에 얼마나 오래 머물렀니?
How far ~?	거리	How far is it from here to the bank?	여기에서 은행까지 얼마나 머니?
How old ~?	나이	How old is your brother?	너의 형은 몇 살이니?
How often ~?	빈도	How often does she exercise?	그녀는 얼마나 자주 운동하니?
How many ~?	개수	How many flowers did you buy?	너는 얼마나 많은 꽃을 샀니?
How much ~?	양, 가격	How much is this apple?	이 사과는 얼마니?

연습문제   다음 빈칸에 알맞은 말을 넣어 대화를 완성하시오.

1 A: How _____ is this pear? B: Two dollars.

2 A: How _____ is the bridge? B: It's almost 800 meters long.

3 A: How _____ does the bus come? B: Every 20 minutes.

4 A: How _____ is Jack? B: He is 165 cm tall.

5 A: How _____ is the tree? B: Almost a hundred years old.

6 A: How _____ books did you read last month? B: I read five books.

7 A: How _____ is it from here to the library? B: It's about five kilometers.

8 A: How _____ is Siwoo's house? B: It's really huge.

기출 적중문제

다음 빈칸에 공통으로 들어갈 알맞은 의문사를 쓰시오.

· _____ old are you?
· _____ can I get to the museum?
· _____ many clues did you find?

부가의문문

1. 부가의문문은 상대방에게 확인이나 동의를 구하기 위해 문장 뒤에 덧붙이는 의문문이다.

┌─── ①, ② ───┐
Sam is a singer, isn't he?
└──── ③ ────┘

Sam은 가수야, 그렇지 않니?

┌─── ①, ② ───┐
Sam isn't a singer, is he?
└──── ③ ────┘

Sam은 가수가 아니야, 그렇지?

① 긍정문 뒤에는 부정의 부가의문문을, 부정문 뒤에는 긍정의 부가의문문을 덧붙인다. (단, 부정형은 축약형으로 쓴다.)

② 앞 문장의 동사가 be동사면 be동사를, 일반동사면 do/does/did를, 조동사면 조동사를 사용한다.

③ 부가의문문의 주어는 앞 문장의 주어와 맞는 인칭대명사를 사용한다.

The students were in the library, **weren't they?** 그 학생들은 도서관에 있었어, 그렇지 않니?

She doesn't know Phil, **does she?** 그녀는 Phil을 알지 못해, 그렇지?

Minsu and Suji studied together, **didn't they?** 민수와 수지는 함께 공부했어, 그렇지 않니?

You can't drive, **can you?** 너는 운전할 수 없어, 그렇지?

(Tip) I'm으로 시작하는 문장의 부가의문문으로는 「aren't I?」를 쓴다.

I'm late, (~~amn't~~, **aren't**) I? 나는 늦었어, 그렇지 않니?

2. 명령문과 청유문의 부가의문문

명령문, will you?	Turn off the TV, **will you?** TV를 꺼라, 알겠니? Don't take pictures here, **will you?** 여기에서 사진을 찍지 마라, 알겠니?
청유문, shall we?	Let's take a walk, **shall we?** 산책하자, 어떠니?

연습문제 A 괄호 안에서 알맞은 것을 고르시오.

1 You're 14 years old, (are / aren't) you?

2 Gina doesn't live in London, (does / doesn't) she?

3 They don't drive a car, (do / don't) they?

4 The magic show was amazing, (was / wasn't) it?

5 Be quiet in the hallway, (will / aren't) you?

6 Steve bought you flowers yesterday, (did / didn't) he?

7 Linda can't speak Korean, (can / can't) she?

8 Let's go to the café, (shall / don't) we?

9 Ms. Jones is your art teacher, (is / isn't) she?

10 Don't touch the machine, (do / will) you?

11 You were playing a game, (were / weren't) you?

12 It will snow tomorrow, (will / won't) it?

13 I should come home before dinner, (should / shouldn't) I?

14 Joe and Luke aren't listening to the teacher, (are / aren't) they?

연습문제 B   다음 빈칸에 알맞은 부가의문문을 쓰시오.

1 It was windy yesterday, _____ _____ ?

2 The movie starts at six, _____ _____ ?

3 Mr. Kim got a haircut, _____ _____ ?

4 Give me a hint, _____ _____ ?

5 I don't have a fever, _____ _____ ?

6 They are swimming in the lake, _____ _____ ?

7 Arthur can play chess, _____ _____ ?

8 Let's talk about the details, _____ _____ ?

9 You and Jason are brothers, _____ _____ ?

10 I'm good at sports, _____ _____ ?

11 Yura is your best friend, _____ _____ ?

12 The spiders are very scary, _____ _____ ?

13 We weren't too loud in the theater, _____ _____ ?

14 Your sister doesn't like spicy food, _____ _____ ?

15 Ian, Jose, and Tina will eat lunch together, _____ _____ ?

기출 적중문제

다음 빈칸에 들어갈 알맞은 부가의문문은?

> Hailey can play the flute well, _____ ?

① does she   ② doesn't Hailey

③ can she   ④ can't Hailey

⑤ can't she

Ⓐ 다음 문장을 괄호 안의 지시대로 바꿔 쓰시오.

1 You turn down the volume. (긍정 명령문으로) → _____

2 This is a very popular book. (감탄문으로) → _____

3 Thomas runs really fast. (감탄문으로) → _____

4 You step on my foot. (부정 명령문으로) → _____

5 It is a very rainy day. (감탄문으로) → _____

6 You are late for the movie. (부정 명령문으로) → _____

7 You hang the pictures on the wall. (긍정 명령문으로) → _____

8 The classroom is very quiet. (감탄문으로) → _____

9 You get ready for school. (긍정 명령문으로) → _____

10 These are very big gloves. (감탄문으로) → _____

11 You take pictures in the gallery. (부정 명령문으로) → _____

12 The weather is very lovely. (감탄문으로) → _____

Ⓑ 다음 문장의 밑줄 친 부분을 바르게 고쳐 쓰시오.

1 <u>Let's going</u> on a field trip. → _____

2 She is a famous director, <u>is she</u>? → _____

3 <u>Let's be not</u> too hasty. → _____

4 Let's join the badminton club, <u>don't we</u>? → _____

5 <u>Talks</u> to your grandmother on the phone. → _____

6 He can't read without glasses, <u>can't he</u>? → _____

7 Mr. and Mrs. Long have three cats, <u>do they</u>? → _____

8 <u>Not do touch</u> the pot on the stove. → _____

9 Jihoon will travel to Mexico, <u>won't Jihoon</u>? → _____

10 Your parents weren't in the kitchen, <u>were you</u>? → _____

11 Hold the door for me, <u>do you</u>? → _____

C 다음 빈칸에 알맞은 의문사를 <보기>에서 골라 쓰시오.

<보기>   when   why   where   what

Alex : ⓐ_____ did you do on Sunday?

Sumi : I went to the shopping mall.

Alex : ⓑ_____ did you go there?

Sumi : Because I needed a new swimsuit for my vacation.

Alex : ⓒ_____ will you take your vacation?

Sumi : At the end of July.

Alex : ⓓ_____ are you going to go?

Sumi : I will go to Jejudo.

D <보기>와 같이 주어진 대답의 밑줄 친 부분에 대해 묻는 의문문을 완성하시오.

<보기>   A: _Who_ _is_ our new math teacher?
           B: Ms. Davis is our new math teacher.

1 A: _____ _____ we _____?

B: We should meet at your house.

2 A: _____ _____ her hobby?

B: Her hobby is basketball.

3 A: _____ _____ you _____ to the concert with?

B: I went to the concert with Jacob.

4 A: _____ _____ Emma _____ French?

B: She studies it because she will go to Paris next month.

5 A: _____ _____ you _____ Mike?

B: I saw him an hour ago.

6 A: _____ _____ the camera?

B: Liam and his brother broke it.

7 A: _____ _____ _____ the tower?

B: It is 65 meters tall.

중간·기말고사 실전 문제

1 다음 상황에 적절한 말을 <u>모두</u> 고르시오.

> 학생들이 빨간 불에 횡단보도를 건너고 있다.

① Ride a bicycle.
② Don't cross the street.
③ Turn on the red light.
④ Wait for the green light.
⑤ Don't be careful.

2 다음 중 어법상 바른 것은?

① Opens the window.
② Take off your hat, please.
③ Be not so mean to me.
④ Please be wait in line.
⑤ Don't late for class.

3 다음 빈칸에 들어갈 말로 <u>어색한</u> 것은?

> Don't _____.

① kick the trees
② pick the flowers
③ make the cat angry
④ rude to your teacher
⑤ forget my number

4 다음 우리말을 알맞게 영작한 것은?

> 그 새 학생에게 잘해주자.

① Be let's nice to the new student.
② Let nice to the new student.
③ Let be nice to the new student.
④ Let's be nice to the new student.
⑤ Let's are nice to the new student.

[5-6] 우리말과 같도록 괄호 안의 말을 알맞게 배열하시오.

5

> 그 시험에 대해 불안해하지 마라. (nervous, the test, be, don't, about)

= _____

6

> 그 지하철 역에서 만나자. (let's, the subway station, at, meet)

= _____

7 다음 빈칸에 들어갈 말이 나머지 넷과 <u>다른</u> 것은?

① _____ heavy your bag is!
② _____ bad the traffic is!
③ _____ a sunny day it is!
④ _____ hot the coffee is!
⑤ _____ fun this game is!

8 다음 대화의 빈칸에 들어갈 가장 알맞은 것은?

> A: _____ in mud again. There is dirt all over your pants.
> B: Sorry, Mom. I won't do it again.

① Play   ② Plays
③ Not plays   ④ Don't play
⑤ Doesn't play

9 다음 표지판을 보고 괄호 안의 말을 활용하여 명령문을 완성하시오.

_____ left. (turn)

10 다음 중 어법상 <u>어색한</u> 것은?

① How interesting is your story!
② What a noisy motorcycle!
③ What big eyes he has!
④ How tasty this cupcake is!
⑤ How hard my parents work!

11 다음 문장을 감탄문으로 바르게 바꾼 것은?

① This is a really huge house.
　→ How a huge house!
② I am very happy.
　→ How happy am I!
③ The sky is very clear.
　→ What clear!
④ The man is very wise.
　→ What wise the man is!
⑤ It is a very popular song.
　→ What a popular song!

12 다음 질문에 대한 대답으로 알맞은 것은?

> A: Didn't your brother win the race?
> B: _____ He got the first place.

① No, he wasn't.　② Yes, he did.
③ No, he didn't.　④ Yes, he didn't.
⑤ No, he did.

13 다음 문장을 감탄문으로 바꿔 쓰시오.

(1)
> You have a very great idea.
> → _____ _____
> _____ you have!

(2)
> The movie was really amazing.
> → _____ _____ the movie
> was!

14 다음 빈칸에 들어갈 알맞은 질문은?

> A: Mom bought me a sweater.
> B: _____
> A: It is red and white.

① What look like it does?
② Does what it look like?
③ What it does looks like?
④ Does it what look like?
⑤ What does it look like?

CHAPTER 6 다양한 문장의 종류　기출로 작중 해커스 중학영문법 1학년

15 다음 대화의 빈칸에 들어갈 말이 순서대로 짝지어진 것은?

> A: _____ apples do you have?
> B: I have three. You can eat one.
> A: Thanks. _____ did you buy them?
> B: At the market across the street.

① What – When
② How many – When
③ Who – Why
④ How many – Where
⑤ Who – Where

16 다음 중 밑줄 친 부분이 문맥상 어색한 것은?

① <u>Where</u> is the bus station?
② <u>What</u> are you having for lunch?
③ <u>Why</u> does she look so sad?
④ <u>How</u> are you feeling now?
⑤ <u>When</u> is that woman with the dog?

17 다음 중 자연스러운 대화는?

① A: Whom is Martha talking to?
   B: No, she isn't.
② A: Why are you standing outside?
   B: It's on July 4.
③ A: What did you eat this morning?
   B: It's next to the restaurant.
④ A: Whose hat is this?
   B: It's Sammy's hat.
⑤ A: What time is it now?
   B: Yes, it was. It was wonderful.

18 다음 빈칸에 들어갈 의문사가 나머지 넷과 다른 것은?

① _____ is our new teacher?
② _____ will you do tomorrow?
③ _____ day is it today?
④ _____ does Mr. Miller do?
⑤ _____ are you reading?

19 다음 빈칸에 들어갈 알맞은 의문사는?

> What time does the play start?
> = _____ does the play start?

① Where
② Who
③ When
④ Which
⑤ Why

20 다음 대화의 빈칸에 공통으로 들어갈 알맞은 것은?

> A: _____ are you watching on TV?
> B: I'm watching *Scary Mysteries*.
> A: _____ is it about?
> B: It's about aliens and ghosts.
> A: Wow. It sounds interesting!

① Why
② Where
③ How
④ What
⑤ When

21 다음 질문에 대한 대답으로 가장 알맞은 것은?

> A: Who is that girl over there?
> B: _____

① Eight years old.
② She is my cousin.
③ I was there too.
④ From America.
⑤ Because I know her.

22 다음 빈칸에 알맞은 의문사를 넣어 대화를 완성하시오.

> A: _____ color do you like better, blue or pink?
>
> B: I like pink better.

[23-24] 우리말과 같도록 괄호 안의 말을 알맞게 배열하시오.

23

> A: 너의 고양이는 몇 살이니? (your, is, old, how, cat)
>
> B: He is five years old.

= _____

24

> A: 너는 무슨 운동을 좋아하니? (like, do, sports, you, what)
>
> B: I like baseball.

= _____

25 다음 중 밑줄 친 부분이 어법상 바른 것은?

① He is a famous writer, <u>is he</u>?

② Anna likes melon, <u>doesn't Anna</u>?

③ She got your message, <u>did she</u>?

④ It was windy yesterday, <u>wasn't it</u>?

⑤ You didn't tell me the truth, <u>did I</u>?

26 다음 대화의 빈칸에 들어갈 말이 순서대로 짝지어진 것은?

> A: How _____ do you go to the library?
>
> B: Every weekend.
>
> A: How _____ is it from here?
>
> B: It's just two kilometers away.

① often – far   ② often – tall

③ long – far   ④ long – tall

⑤ old – far

27 다음 빈칸에 들어갈 알맞은 부가의문문은?

> Mr. Baker is your science teacher, _____?

① isn't he   ② is he

③ doesn't he   ④ do he

⑤ won't he

28 다음 중 밑줄 친 부분이 어법상 어색한 것은?

① He can't drink milk, <u>can he</u>?

② Clean your room, <u>will you</u>?

③ We won't fight again, <u>shall we</u>?

④ I am always right, <u>aren't I</u>?

⑤ Let's take a walk, <u>shall we</u>?

29 다음 빈칸에 들어갈 알맞은 것을 <u>모두</u> 고르시오.

> Alice _____, doesn't she?

① is very angry

② jogs every day

③ needs a new dress

④ had a stomachache

⑤ can speak Chinese

30 다음 중 어법상 바른 것을 모두 고르시오.

① Will goes Michael abroad?
② Write down your name here.
③ Let join the science club.
④ Don't drinks this old milk.
⑤ Is that novel boring?

34 다음 중 자연스럽지 않은 대화는?

① A: Why do you like this singer?
　B: Because she has a beautiful voice.
② A: When did you arrive in Seoul?
　B: A week ago.
③ A: Isn't Harry a musician?
　B: Yes, he is. He plays the drums.
④ A: Does Paula like dogs?
　B: No, she doesn't. She is afraid of them.
⑤ A: What is your favorite subject?
　B: No, it's not. I don't like math.

[31-32] 우리말과 같도록 빈칸에 알맞은 말을 쓰시오.

31

> Jane과 Sue는 친한 친구야, 그렇지 않니?

= Jane and Sue are close friends, _____
_____?

32

> 그 건물 안에서 담배를 피우지 마라, 알겠니?

= Don't smoke in the building, _____
_____?

35 다음은 민호가 좋아하는 과일과 좋아하지 않는 과일을 나타낸 표이다. 빈칸에 알맞은 말을 넣어 질문에 대한 대답을 완성하시오.

grapes	bananas	apples
X	O	X

(1) A: Doesn't Minho like apples?
　B: _____, _____ _____.

(2) A: Which fruit does Minho like?
　B: _____ _____ _____.

33 다음 중 어법상 바른 것의 개수는?

> ⓐ What size do he wears?
> ⓑ Didn't you lose your phone?
> ⓒ Where Monica is going now?
> ⓓ How do you make a paper plane?
> ⓔ Do you have any issues?
> ⓕ Why you were there alone?

① 없음　　　② 1개　　　③ 2개
④ 3개　　　⑤ 4개

36 다음 문장을 괄호 안의 지시대로 바르게 바꾼 것을 모두 고르시오.

① The tickets are really cheap. (감탄문으로)
　→ What cheap the tickets are!
② You stay up late. (부정 명령문으로)
　→ Not stay up late.
③ She is a really cute baby. (감탄문으로)
　→ What a cute baby she is!
④ It was a very exciting book. (감탄문으로)
　→ How an exciting book it was!
⑤ You clear the table. (긍정 명령문으로)
　→ Clear the table.

37 다음 중 밑줄 친 부분이 어법상 바른 것을 <u>모두</u> 고르시오.

A: I got a new pet yesterday.
B: ①<u>What kind of animal it is?</u>
A: Guess.
B: All right. ②<u>How big is it?</u>
A: It is very small.
B: ③<u>What it eats?</u>
A: Mostly seeds and vegetables.
B: It's a hamster, ④<u>is it?</u>
A: Yes, it is. Look at this photo.
B: Wow! ⑤<u>How cute it is!</u>

40 다음 중 어법상 <u>어색한</u> 것끼리 묶인 것은?

ⓐ What day does it is today?
ⓑ Please not do forget your homework.
ⓒ Where you hid the presents?
ⓓ Hold your father's hand.
ⓔ When did your sister turn 14?

① ⓐ, ⓑ, ⓒ   ② ⓐ, ⓑ, ⓔ   ③ ⓐ, ⓒ, ⓓ
④ ⓑ, ⓒ, ⓔ   ⑤ ⓒ, ⓓ, ⓔ

41 다음 (A)~(C)에 들어갈 말이 바르게 짝지어진 것은?

· ___(A)___ wallet is this?
· ___(B)___ are you looking for?
· ___(C)___ broke the window?

	(A)	(B)	(C)
①	Whose	Who	Whom
②	Whose	Whom	Who
③	Whose	Whom	Whom
④	Who	Whose	Who
⑤	Who	Whom	Whom

[38-39] 다음 문장에서 틀린 부분을 바르게 고쳐 완전한 문장을 쓰시오.

38

Turns off your cell phone.
→ _____

39

Did where you put the key?
→ _____

42 다음 글의 밑줄 친 ⓐ~ⓔ 중 어법상 <u>어색한</u> 것을 찾아 기호를 쓰고 바르게 고쳐 쓰시오.

You want to be healthy, ⓐ<u>do you</u>? So, ⓑ<u>will what</u> make you healthy? First, ⓒ<u>eat</u> lots of vegetables and fruit. Also, ⓓ<u>exercises</u> regularly. ⓔ<u>Do this</u> all the time.

(1) _____ → _____
(2) _____ → _____
(3) _____ → _____

CHAPTER 7
to부정사

I want **to sleep**. 나는 자기를 원한다.

'자다'라는 의미의 동사 sleep 앞에 to를 붙여 '자기'라는 의미를 나타냈어요. 이렇게 동사 앞에 to를 붙인 「to + 동사원형」의 형태를 **to부정사**라고 하며, to부정사는 문장 안에서 명사·형용사·부사 역할을 할 수 있어요.

기출로 적중 POINT

1 • **to부정사의 형태와 용법**

2-1 • **명사적 용법**

2-2 • **명사적 용법**: to부정사를 목적어로 쓰는 동사

2-3 • **명사적 용법**: 의문사 + to부정사

3 • **형용사적 용법**

4 • **부사적 용법**

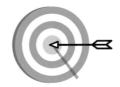

내신 100점 적중!
기출 출제율

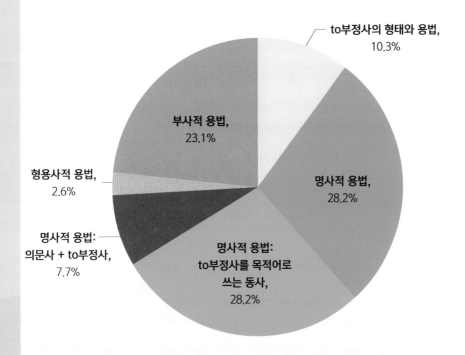

to부정사의 형태와 용법,
10.3%

부사적 용법,
23.1%

명사적 용법,
28.2%

형용사적 용법,
2.6%

명사적 용법:
의문사 + to부정사,
7.7%

명사적 용법:
to부정사를 목적어로
쓰는 동사,
28.2%

TOP 1 **명사적 용법 (28.2%)**
명사적 용법: to부정사를 목적어로 쓰는 동사 (28.2%)
to부정사의 명사적 용법을 묻는 문제가 자주 출제된다. 특정 동사 뒤에 to부정
사가 목적어로 쓰이는 경우를 묻는 문제가 자주 출제된다.

TOP 2 **부사적 용법 (23.1%)**
to부정사의 부사적 용법의 다양한 의미를 묻는 문제가 자주 출제된다.

TOP 3 **to부정사의 형태와 용법 (10.3%)**
to부정사의 형태와 용법을 묻는 문제가 자주 출제된다.

기출로적중 POINT 1 to부정사의 형태와 용법

to부정사는 「to + 동사원형」의 형태로, 문장 안에서 명사·형용사·부사 역할을 한다.

명사적 용법	My goal is **to be** healthy. 나의 목표는 건강해지는 것이다.
형용사적 용법	Let's buy some snacks **to eat**. 먹을 약간의 간식을 사자.
부사적 용법	She came here **to meet** her friend. 그녀는 그녀의 친구를 만나기 위해 여기에 왔다.

(Tip) to부정사의 부정형: 「not to + 동사원형」

I decided **not to buy** a new cell phone. 나는 새 휴대폰을 사지 않기로 결심했다.

(Tip) to 뒤에 동사가 오면 to부정사의 to이고, 명사가 오면 전치사 to이다.

to부정사   He likes **to take** pictures. 그는 사진 찍는 것을 좋아한다.

전치사 + 명사   He went **to the museum** yesterday. 그는 어제 박물관에 갔다.

연습문제 A   괄호 안의 동사를 to부정사로 바꿔 문장을 완성하시오.

1 They want _____ a bookshelf. (move)

2 Angela was happy _____ the news. (hear)

3 I have a book _____ on the plane. (read)

4 The city plans not _____ a new stadium. (build)

5 Minjun is saving money _____ Africa someday. (visit)

6 My hobby is _____ baseball with my friends. (play)

연습문제 B   밑줄 친 to의 쓰임과 같은 것을 <보기>에서 골라 그 기호를 쓰시오.

> <보기>   ⓐ We hope <u>to</u> see you again.
>   ⓑ Paul goes <u>to</u> school by subway.

1 Andy has something <u>to</u> tell us.   [   ]

2 Can you come <u>to</u> my birthday party?   [   ]

3 Their goal is <u>to</u> protect the environment.   [   ]

4 She showed an old picture <u>to</u> me.   [   ]

5 The movie was hard <u>to</u> understand.   [   ]

POINT 2-1 명사적 용법

정답 p.22

> **to부정사는 명사 역할을 할 때 주어·보어·목적어로 쓰일 수 있으며, 이때 '~하는 것, ~하기'의 의미이다.**

주어	**To speak** English is easy. 영어를 말하는 것은 쉽다. = **It** is easy **to speak** English. ↳ to부정사가 주어로 쓰일 때 주로 주어 자리에 가주어 it을 쓰고 원래 주어인 진주어 to부정사(구)를 뒤로 보낸다.
보어	**My hobby** is **to write** poems. 나의 취미는 시를 쓰는 것이다.
목적어	Cindy **wants to be** a vet. Cindy는 수의사가 되기를 원한다.

(Tip) 주어로 쓰인 to부정사(구)는 항상 단수 취급한다.
To have good friends is important. 좋은 친구들이 있는 것은 중요하다.

연습문제 **A**   우리말과 같도록 괄호 안의 말을 활용하여 빈칸에 쓰시오.

1 나는 과학을 공부하는 것을 싫어한다. (study)

= I hate ＿＿＿＿＿＿ ＿＿＿＿＿＿ science.

2 나의 소망은 축구 선수가 되는 것이다. (become)

= My wish is ＿＿＿＿＿＿ ＿＿＿＿＿＿ a soccer player.

3 소라는 그녀의 머리를 기르기로 결심했다. (grow)

= Sora decided ＿＿＿＿＿＿ ＿＿＿＿＿＿ her hair.

4 기타를 연주하는 것은 정말 재미있다. (play)

= ＿＿＿＿＿＿ ＿＿＿＿＿＿ the guitar is really fun.

5 Hall씨의 일은 건물을 설계하는 것이다. (design)

= Ms. Hall's job is ＿＿＿＿＿＿ ＿＿＿＿＿＿ buildings.

연습문제 **B**   <보기>와 같이 다음 문장을 가주어 it을 사용한 문장으로 바꿔 쓰시오.

<보기>   To watch a basketball game is exciting.

→ *It is exciting to watch a basketball game.*

1 To be an honest person is difficult.

→ ＿＿＿＿＿＿＿＿＿＿＿＿＿＿＿＿＿＿＿＿

2 To collect stamps is very interesting.

→ ＿＿＿＿＿＿＿＿＿＿＿＿＿＿＿＿＿＿＿＿

3 To learn many languages is my plan.

→ _____

4 To keep my room clean is impossible.

→ _____

5 To wake up early on Sundays is not easy.

→ _____

6 To read a lot of books is helpful.

→ _____

7 To watch too much TV is not good for your eyes .

→ _____

연습문제 **C** 밑줄 친 to부정사의 쓰임을 <보기>에서 골라 그 기호를 쓰시오.

<보기> ⓐ 주어 ⓑ 보어 ⓒ 목적어

1 It is safe <u>to swim</u> in this lake.   [   ]
2 Yuri's hobby is <u>to build</u> model ships.   [   ]
3 It is not easy <u>to be</u> creative.   [   ]
4 The cat hates <u>to get</u> wet.   [   ]
5 My plan is <u>to lose</u> three kilograms.   [   ]
6 My father likes <u>to read</u> newspapers.   [   ]
7 My advice is <u>to be</u> kind to others.   [   ]
8 The snow began <u>to fall</u> this morning.   [   ]
9 It is a bad habit <u>to smoke</u> cigarettes.   [   ]
10 <u>To exercise</u> regularly will make you healthy.   [   ]

기출 적중문제 ◎➤

주어진 문장의 밑줄 친 to부정사와 쓰임이 같은 것을 <u>모두</u> 고르시오.

I don't like <u>to eat</u> carrots.

① It is not safe <u>to travel</u> alone.
② My goal is <u>to read</u> 10 books this month.
③ Lola hopes <u>to meet</u> her favorite actor.
④ Bob's brother decided <u>to change</u> jobs.
⑤ It is really hard <u>to solve</u> this problem.

기출로적중 POINT 2-2

명사적 용법: to부정사를 목적어로 쓰는 동사

정답 p.22

다음 동사들은 to부정사를 목적어로 쓴다.

want	hope	decide	plan	need	would like
expect	like	love	hate	begin	start

She **wants to travel** to Berlin. 그녀는 베를린으로 여행하기를 원한다.

George **needed to finish** the book. George는 그 책을 다 읽을 필요가 있었다.

I **would like to invite** you to my home. 나는 너를 나의 집에 초대하기를 원한다.

연습문제 우리말과 같도록 괄호 안의 말을 활용하여 문장을 완성하시오.

1 그들은 그 경주에서 이기기를 기대한다. (win, expect)

= They _____ the race.

2 그 아기는 큰 소리로 울기 시작했다. (begin, cry)

= The baby _____ loudly.

3 Luna는 음악을 듣는 것을 좋아한다. (like, listen)

= Luna _____ to music.

4 그녀는 그녀의 반지를 팔기로 결심했다. (sell, decide)

= She _____ her ring.

5 Brad은 오늘 밤에 별을 보기를 원한다. (want, look)

= Brad _____ at the stars tonight.

6 그는 다음 주에 서울을 떠나기로 계획한다. (leave, plan)

= He _____ Seoul next week.

7 Victoria는 선생님이 되기를 바란다. (hope, be)

= Victoria _____ a teacher.

기출 적중문제

다음 중 어법상 어색한 것은?

① Amanda wants to ask you a question.

② He decided walking to school.

③ Nick expects to go to the movies with Lisa.

④ I would like to tell you a secret.

⑤ They are planning to clean the classroom.

기출로적중 POINT 2-3 명사적 용법: 의문사 + to부정사

「의문사 + to부정사」는 문장 안에서 명사처럼 쓰이며, 의문사에 따라 의미가 달라진다.

what + to부정사 무엇을 ~할지   when + to부정사 언제 ~할지
where + to부정사 어디에(서)/어디로 ~할지   how + to부정사 어떻게 ~할지

I don't know **what to do**. 나는 무엇을 해야 할지 모른다.
Did you decide **where to go** for vacation? 너는 휴가로 어디에 갈지 결정했니?
She taught me **how to play** the piano. 그녀는 나에게 어떻게 피아노를 치는지 가르쳐줬다.

연습문제 우리말과 같도록 괄호 안의 말을 활용하여 빈칸에 쓰시오.

1 나는 무엇을 먹을지 확실하지 않다. (eat)
= I'm not sure _____ _____ _____.

2 너는 바나나 빵을 어떻게 만드는지 아니? (make)
= Do you know _____ _____ _____ banana bread?

3 나의 발표를 언제 시작해야 할지 알려줘. (start)
= Tell me _____ _____ _____ my presentation.

4 Carla는 축제를 위해 무엇을 입을지 결정할 수 없다. (wear)
= Carla can't decide _____ _____ _____ for the festival.

5 나는 신선한 채소를 어디에서 살지 알기를 원한다. (buy)
= I want to know _____ _____ _____ fresh vegetables.

6 누군가가 나에게 어디에서 좋은 식당을 찾을지 말해줬다. (find)
= Someone told me _____ _____ _____ a nice restaurant.

7 토론 중에 언제 말해야 하는지 아는 것은 중요하다. (speak)
= It's important to know _____ _____ _____ during a debate.

기출 적중문제 ◎

다음 대화의 빈칸에 공통으로 들어갈 알맞은 의문사를 쓰시오.

A: I want to learn _____ to ski. Can you teach me?
B: Yes, I can. I'll teach you _____ to ski.

기출로적중 POINT 3 형용사적 용법

정답 p.22

to부정사는 형용사 역할을 할 때 명사나 대명사를 뒤에서 꾸밀 수 있으며, 이때 '~할, ~하는' 의 의미이다.

Nina needs **a jacket** to wear. Nina는 입을 재킷이 필요하다.

Let's choose **a movie** to watch. 볼 영화를 고르자.

Jinho is looking for **someone** to help him. 진호는 그를 도와줄 누군가를 찾고 있다.

연습문제 우리말과 같도록 괄호 안의 말을 알맞게 배열하시오.

1 찬호는 마실 약간의 차를 끓였다. (drink, to, some tea)

= Chanho made _____ .

2 저에게 먹을 무언가를 주세요. (to, something, eat)

= Please give me _____ .

3 나는 믿을 친구를 원한다. (trust, to, a friend)

= I want _____ .

4 우리는 우리의 미래에 대해 생각할 시간을 가져야 한다. (think, time, to)

= We have to take _____ about our future.

5 그들은 그들의 아기를 돌볼 누군가를 고용했다. (to, someone, look)

= They hired _____ after their baby.

6 이곳은 새로운 사람들을 만날 완벽한 장소이다. (a perfect place, meet, to)

= This is _____ new people.

7 Davis씨는 아이들에게 말해줄 많은 무서운 이야기들을 안다. (to, lots of scary stories, tell)

= Ms. Davis knows _____ the children.

기출 적중문제 🎯

우리말과 같도록 괄호 안의 말을 배열할 때 여섯 번째에 오는 것을 쓰시오.

> 그녀는 수영복을 살 약간의 돈을 가지고 있다. (buy, has, to, a, some, she, money, swimsuit)

→ _____

기출로적중 POINT 4 부사적 용법

to부정사는 부사 역할을 할 때 동사·형용사·부사·문장 전체를 수식할 수 있으며, 다양한 의미를 나타낸다.

목적	~하기 위해	목적을 나타낼 때 to 대신 in order to를 쓸 수 있다. I'll go to the library **to study**. 나는 공부하기 위해 도서관에 갈 것이다. = I'll go to the library **in order to study**.
형용사 수식	~하기에	The medicine is **safe to take**. 그 약은 먹기에 안전하다. The building wasn't **easy to find**. 그 건물은 찾기에 쉽지 않았다.
감정의 원인	~해서, ~하니	I'm **glad to see** my friends. 나는 나의 친구들을 봐서 기쁘다. She was **upset to hear** the news. 그녀는 그 소식을 들어서 속상했다.
결과	(…해서 결국) ~하다	Sam **grew up to be** a lawyer. Sam은 자라서 변호사가 되었다. My grandma **lived to be** 95 years old. 나의 할머니는 95세까지 사셨다.

연습문제 A 우리말과 같도록 괄호 안의 말을 활용하여 문장을 완성하시오.

1 Eric은 그의 부모님을 보기 위해 그의 고향을 방문할 것이다. (see, his parents)
= Eric will visit his hometown _____.

2 Brad는 생일 선물을 받아서 행복했다. (receive, happy)
= Brad was _____ a birthday gift.

3 Karen은 그 버스를 타기 위해 뛰었다. (the bus, catch)
= Karen ran _____.

4 그녀는 우유를 사기 위해 슈퍼마켓에 갔다. (milk, buy)
= She went to the supermarket _____.

5 이 수학 문제는 풀기에 어렵다. (solve, difficult)
= This math question is _____.

6 Harry는 그 사고에 대해 들어서 슬펐다. (sad, hear)
= Harry was _____ about the accident.

7 Elena는 자라서 유명한 스케이트 선수가 되었다. (grew up, be)
= Elena _____ a famous skater.

8 방콕은 방문하기에 정말 즐겁다. (fun, visit)
= Bangkok is really _____.

9 그 토끼는 사람들을 피하기 위해 나무 뒤에 숨었다. (people, avoid)

= The rabbit hid behind the tree _____.

10 그 농구 선수들은 경기에 져서 실망했다. (lose, disappointed)

= The basketball players were _____ the game.

연습문제 B 밑줄 친 to부정사의 역할을 <보기>에서 골라 그 기호를 쓰시오.

<보기> ⓐ 명사   ⓑ 형용사   ⓒ 부사

1 He is ready to take the test.   [   ]

2 My hobby is to collect coins.   [   ]

3 We wanted to get a new pet.   [   ]

4 I have some dishes to wash.   [   ]

5 It is easy to cook tomato pasta.   [   ]

6 Juho is choosing a laptop to buy.   [   ]

7 Abby came to my town to see me.   [   ]

8 She was happy to find out the truth.   [   ]

9 I took a subway to go to school.   [   ]

10 Do you have anything to say?   [   ]

11 I hope to save some money this year.   [   ]

12 The river is dangerous to swim in.   [   ]

13 My goal is to travel around the world.   [   ]

14 I don't have any friends to call.   [   ]

15 Alice exercises every day to stay healthy. [   ]

기출 적중문제 ⊙

주어진 문장의 밑줄 친 to부정사와 역할이 같은 것은?

Jane went to the mall to buy a shirt.

① My brother loves to play online games.

② You should wear gloves to protect your hands.

③ Mr. Harris wants to own a farm someday.

④ Henry hopes to be a good doctor.

⑤ I have some secrets to tell you.

서술형 대비 문제

A 밑줄 친 부분이 어법상 맞으면 O를 쓰고, 틀리면 바르게 고쳐 쓰시오.

1 My sister learned to <u>reads</u> last year. → _____

2 The principal wants to <u>see</u> you. → _____

3 I'm boiling the water to <u>making</u> tea. → _____

4 To shop online <u>are</u> convenient. → _____

5 There are many museums to <u>visit</u> in Paris. → _____

6 To play with my friends <u>is</u> really fun. → _____

7 The city planned <u>building</u> a new library. → _____

8 To eat vegetables <u>are</u> good for your health. → _____

9 Mr. and Mrs. Brown decided <u>buying</u> a house. → _____

B 우리말과 같도록 괄호 안의 말을 알맞게 배열하시오.

1 네 잎 클로버를 찾는 것은 행운이다. (a four-leaf clover, it, lucky, find, to, is)
= _____

2 Vicky는 쿠키를 만들기로 결심했다. (cookies, to, decided, make, Vicky)
= _____

3 나의 취미는 하프를 연주하는 것이다. (the harp, is, my hobby, play, to)
= _____

4 우리는 그 축제에 갈 계획이 있었다. (we, to the festival, had, a plan, go, to)
= _____

5 그 강의는 이해하기에 어렵다. (understand, the lecture, hard, to, is)
= _____

6 그는 변호사가 되기 위해 시험을 볼 것이다. (a lawyer, to, an exam, will take, become, he)
= _____

7 그녀는 벽에 쓸 노란 페인트를 샀다. (on the wall, to, bought, yellow paint, she, use)
= _____

8 나는 햇살을 즐기기 위해 밖으로 나갔다. (to, outside, went, I, the sunshine, enjoy)
= _____

C <보기>와 같이 괄호 안의 말을 활용하여 질문에 대한 대답을 완성하시오.

> <보기> A: What do you like to do on weekends?
>
> B: I *like to watch horror movies* . (watch horror movies)

1 A: What do you love to do in your free time?

B: I _____ . (play computer games)

2 A: Where do you want to go on your vacation?

B: I _____ . (travel to Germany)

3 A: What do you need to do right now?

B: I _____ . (walk my dog)

4 A: What do you hope to become?

B: I _____ . (be an astronaut)

5 A: What would you like to drink?

B: I _____ . (have a cup of coffee)

D <보기>와 같이 to부정사를 이용하여 다음 두 문장을 한 문장으로 연결하시오.

> <보기> My family climbed the mountain. We saw the sunrise.
>
> → My family climbed the mountain *to see the sunrise* .
>
> John was really excited. He met his cousin.
>
> → John was really excited *to meet his cousin* .

1 Ben sent me a text message. He asked me a question.

→ Ben sent me a text message _____ .

2 Ms. Clark was surprised. She saw her favorite movie star.

→ Ms. Clark was surprised _____ .

3 The old man was very sad. He left his hometown.

→ The old man was very sad _____ .

4 I went to Kevin's house. We did the homework together.

→ I went to Kevin's house _____ .

5 Jenny went to the post office. She sent a package to her grandparents.

→ Jenny went to the post office _____ .

1 다음 빈칸에 들어갈 알맞은 것은?

Tracy hoped _____ a diamond ring for her 30th birthday.

① buy   ② bought   ③ to buys

④ to buy   ⑤ to buying

2 다음 중 어법상 바른 것은?

① Drink too much coffee is bad.

② Judy's job is to taught children.

③ To read fantasy novels are fun.

④ My hobby is to play basketball.

⑤ It is important saves money.

3 다음 대화의 빈칸에 들어갈 말이 순서대로 짝지어진 것은?

A: I plan _____ abroad this spring. B: Did you decide where _____ yet? A: No, I didn't. I need to think about that more.

① to travel - visits

② traveling - visiting

③ to travel - to visit

④ traveling - to visit

⑤ to travel - to visiting

4 우리말과 같도록 괄호 안의 말을 알맞게 배열하시오.

밤에 자전거를 타는 것은 위험하다. (at night, to, a bike, ride, dangerous, is)

= It _____

5 다음 중 밑줄 친 to의 쓰임이 나머지 넷과 다른 것은?

① We go to the beach every summer.

② Would you like to have some pizza?

③ Kate plans to visit Sehun today.

④ It is very helpful to learn Chinese.

⑤ Tim likes to play tennis with his brother.

6 괄호 안의 말을 활용하여 다음 대화의 빈칸에 알맞은 말을 쓰시오.

A: What is your goal for the new year? B: I will start _____ Korean. (learn)

[7-8] 다음 두 문장의 의미가 같도록 빈칸에 알맞은 말을 쓰시오.

7

To finish my homework before dinner is my plan. = _____ is my plan _____ _____ _____ before dinner.

8

You should be a nice person to make friends. = You should be a nice person _____ _____ _____ friends.

9 다음 문장에서 어법상 어색한 부분을 찾아 쓰고 바르게 고쳐 쓰시오.

> Jack doesn't want drinking carrot juice.

_____ → _____

10 우리말과 같도록 빈칸에 알맞은 말을 쓰시오.

> 나는 그 진공청소기를 어떻게 사용하는지 모른다.

= I don't know _____ _____ _____ the vacuum cleaner.

11 다음 두 문장을 한 문장으로 바르게 연결한 것은?

> · Betty wants some cookies.
> · She will eat them.

① Betty wants some cookies to eat.
② Betty wants some cookies eat.
③ Betty wants some cookies eating.
④ Betty to wants some cookies eat.
⑤ Betty to want some cookies eat.

12 다음 중 밑줄 친 to부정사의 용법이 나머지 넷과 다른 것은?

① I know a funny story <u>to tell</u> you.
② The guests wanted something <u>to drink</u>.
③ I didn't have a chance <u>to meet</u> him.
④ Narae hopes <u>to become</u> an engineer.
⑤ Ken told me a good place <u>to buy</u> a dress.

13 다음 중 밑줄 친 부분이 어법상 어색한 것은?

> ①<u>Michelle's dream</u> ②<u>is</u> to ③<u>winning</u> the figure skating contest ④<u>in Russia</u> ⑤<u>next year</u>.

14 우리말과 같도록 괄호 안의 말을 활용하여 문장을 완성하시오.

> 나는 케이크를 만들기 위해 버터를 샀다. (buy, make a cake)

= I _____.

15 주어진 <조건>에 맞게 다음 두 문장을 한 문장으로 연결하시오.

> · I was surprised.
> · I saw Bill Gates.

<조건>
1. to부정사를 이용하시오.
2. 7단어로 쓰시오.

→ _____

16 우리말과 같도록 괄호 안의 말을 배열할 때 다섯 번째에 오는 것은?

> 그 영화는 보기에 무섭다. (watch, scary, the, is, movie, to)

① movie ② to ③ scary
④ the ⑤ watch

17 다음 중 어법상 바른 것끼리 묶인 것은?

> ⓐ Jisu went to the theater to watch a movie.
> ⓑ Leo needs to borrowing a pencil.
> ⓒ The snow began to falls last night.
> ⓓ To talk with my parents is always helpful.
> ⓔ I have some questions to ask.

① ⓐ, ⓑ   ② ⓐ, ⓒ   ③ ⓑ, ⓒ
④ ⓐ, ⓑ, ⓓ   ⑤ ⓐ, ⓓ, ⓔ

[18-19] 주어진 문장의 밑줄 친 to부정사와 용법이 같은 것을 고르시오.

18

> It is rude to talk loudly in an airplane.

① These pants are comfortable to wear.
② Robert made some cupcakes to sell.
③ I often light a candle to relax.
④ Amy ran quickly to arrive on time.
⑤ To remember her name wasn't easy.

19

> Matt left the classroom to wash his hands.

① The police searched the forest to find the lost child.
② My friends and I go to the park every Sunday.
③ Her wish is to make some new friends.
④ The children loved to build a snowman.
⑤ It is helpful to use a computer for research.

20 다음은 John의 일기이다. 다음 중 밑줄 친 부분의 역할이 나머지 넷과 다른 것은?

> December 25, 2006
> Dear Diary,
>
> Today is Christmas. I woke up early and went to the living room. My parents were waiting ①to give me presents. I was happy ②to see so many presents. The first one was a bicycle. I was excited ③to ride it. I also got a board game ④to play with my friends. Later, we went to the kitchen ⑤to eat breakfast. It was a great morning.

[21-22] 다음 문장을 우리말로 가장 알맞게 해석한 것은?

21

> Her daughter grew up to be a teacher.

① 그녀의 딸은 선생님이 될 것이다.
② 그녀의 딸은 선생님과 자랐다.
③ 그녀의 딸은 자라서 선생님이 되었다.
④ 그녀의 딸은 선생님이 되기를 원했다.
⑤ 그녀의 딸은 선생님이 되기 위해 자랐다.

22

> Bill listens to classical music to relax.

① Bill은 클래식 음악을 들어서 쉴 수 있었다.
② Bill은 클래식 음악을 듣기 위해 쉬었다.
③ Bill은 쉬기 때문에 클래식 음악을 들을 수 있다.
④ Bill은 쉬기 위해 클래식 음악을 듣는다.
⑤ Bill은 쉬면서 클래식 음악을 듣는다.

23 주어진 문장의 밑줄 친 to부정사와 쓰임이 같은 것은?

> To swim in the sea is exciting.

① The teacher decided to give a quiz.
② Abigail loves to play tennis on Sundays.
③ Santa's job is to give presents to kids.
④ It is fun to ride a big roller coaster.
⑤ My plan is to finish this book today.

[24-25] 다음 글을 읽고 주어진 질문에 답하시오.

> _____ (A) _____ **a peanut butter sandwich**
>
>
>
> 1. Toast two slices of bread to make them warm.
> 2. (B) 빵 한 조각 위에 땅콩버터를 바르기 위해 칼을 사용해라.
> 3. Spread some strawberry jam on the other slice of bread.
> 4. Put the two slices of bread together.

24 위 글의 빈칸 (A)에 들어갈 가장 알맞은 것은?

① What to make
② What to making
③ Where to make
④ How to make
⑤ How to making

25 위 글의 밑줄 친 우리말 (B)와 같도록 주어진 <조건>에 맞게 문장을 완성하시오.

> **<조건>**
> 1. 명령문으로 쓰시오.
> 2. use, a knife, spread를 활용하시오.

= _____ peanut butter on one slice of bread.

[26-27] 다음 글을 읽고 주어진 질문에 답하시오.

> I like to sing songs. My dream is ⓐto be a singer. So, I entered my school's talent show to sing in front of my friends. I came in first place. (A) 나는 그 대회에서 이겨서 기뻤다. (happy, win the competition)
>
> *talent show 장기자랑

26 위 글의 밑줄 친 ⓐ와 용법이 같은 것을 고르시오.

① That novel is fun to read.
② Linda stopped at a café to buy coffee.
③ I have a sandwich to eat.
④ His job is to sell jewelry.
⑤ Charlie was glad to find his phone.

27 위 글의 밑줄 친 우리말 (A)와 같도록 괄호 안의 말을 활용하여 영작하시오.

= _____

28 다음 밑줄 친 to부정사의 용법이 같은 것끼리 묶인 것은?

> ⓐ Minsu studied hard to pass the test.
> ⓑ Gloria's plan is to leave home at 5 o'clock.
> ⓒ Mary raised her hand to ask a question.
> ⓓ It is dangerous to play with fire.
> ⓔ We have a lot of boxes to carry.
> ⓕ My father woke up early to play golf with his friends.

① ⓐ, ⓑ, ⓔ
② ⓐ, ⓒ, ⓕ
③ ⓑ, ⓒ, ⓓ
④ ⓑ, ⓓ, ⓔ
⑤ ⓓ, ⓔ, ⓕ

CHAPTER 8
동명사

Cooking is fun. 요리하는 것은 재미있다.

'요리하다'라는 의미의 동사 cook을 V-ing형으로 바꿔 '요리하는 것'이라는 의미를 나타냈어요. 이렇게 동사가 V-ing형으로 쓰여 문장 안에서 명사 역할을 하는 것을 **동명사**라고 해요.

기출로 적중 POINT

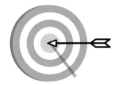

내신 100점 적중!
기출 출제율

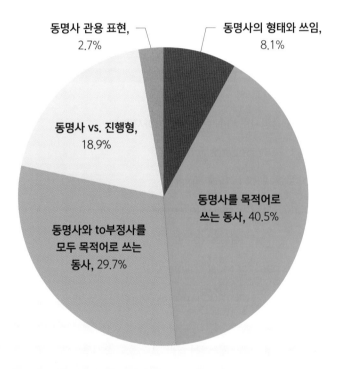

동명사 관용 표현, 2.7%

동명사의 형태와 쓰임, 8.1%

동명사 vs. 진행형, 18.9%

동명사를 목적어로 쓰는 동사, 40.5%

동명사와 to부정사를 모두 목적어로 쓰는 동사, 29.7%

TOP 1 **동명사를 목적어로 쓰는 동사 (40.5%)**
특정 동사 뒤에 동명사가 목적어로 쓰이는 경우를 묻는 문제가 자주 출제된다.

TOP 2 **동명사와 to부정사를 모두 목적어로 쓰는 동사 (29.7%)**
특정 동사 뒤에 동명사와 to부정사가 모두 목적어로 쓰이는 경우를 묻는 문제가 자주 출제된다.

TOP 3 **동명사 vs. 진행형 (18.9%)**
문장 안의 V-ing형이 동명사인지 진행형인지 구별하는 문제가 자주 출제된다.

POINT 1 동명사의 형태와 쓰임

동명사는 V-ing의 형태로 문장 안에서 명사처럼 주어·보어·목적어로 쓰이며, '~하는 것, ~하기'의 의미이다.

주어	**Swimming** in the sea is dangerous. 바다에서 수영하는 것은 위험하다.
보어	Her dream is **becoming** a singer. 그녀의 꿈은 가수가 되는 것이다.
동사의 목적어	Joe **enjoys** **listening** to music. Joe는 음악을 듣는 것을 즐긴다.
전치사의 목적어	I'm looking forward **to** **seeing** you. 나는 너를 보는 것을 기대하고 있다.

(Tip) 주어로 쓰인 동명사는 항상 단수 취급한다.

Watching comedy movies is fun. 코미디 영화를 보는 것은 재미있다.

연습문제 A 괄호 안의 동사를 동명사로 바꿔 문장을 완성하시오.

1 My hobby is _____ postcards. (collect)

2 _____ a trip takes a lot of time. (plan)

3 Do you like _____ at the gym? (exercise)

4 Jamie is good at _____ chess. (play)

5 _____ quietly is hard for most children. (sit)

6 His problem is _____ too much money. (spend)

연습문제 B 밑줄 친 동명사의 쓰임을 <보기>에서 골라 그 기호를 쓰시오.

<보기> ⓐ 주어 ⓑ 보어 ⓒ 동사의 목적어 ⓓ 전치사의 목적어

1 Thank you for helping us. [   ]

2 Brenda enjoys shopping online. [   ]

3 His plan is buying a new computer. [   ]

4 My favorite activity is climbing mountains. [   ]

5 The bird kept feeding its babies. [   ]

6 I'm thinking about studying Chinese. [   ]

7 Playing video games makes me happy. [   ]

8 Being polite to other people is important. [   ]

정답 p.24

기출로적중 POINT 2-1 동명사를 목적어로 쓰는 동사

다음 동사는 동명사를 목적어로 쓴다.

enjoy   finish   avoid   keep   mind   give up   stop   practice   recommend

Luke **finished** cleaning his room. Luke는 그의 방을 청소하는 것을 끝냈다.
I don't **mind** waiting for you. 나는 너를 기다리는 것을 꺼리지 않는다.
Could you **stop** talking so loudly? 그렇게 큰 소리로 말하는 것을 멈춰주시겠어요?

연습문제 우리말과 같도록 괄호 안의 말을 활용하여 문장을 완성하시오.

1 Miranda는 매일 춤추는 것을 연습한다. (dance, practice)
= Miranda ＿＿＿＿＿＿＿＿＿＿＿ every day.

2 그는 전 세계를 여행하는 것을 즐긴다. (enjoy, travel)
= He ＿＿＿＿＿＿＿＿＿＿ around the world.

3 그 개는 밤새도록 짖는 것을 계속했다. (bark, keep)
= The dog ＿＿＿＿＿＿＿＿＿＿ all night.

4 Dale은 편지를 쓰는 것을 끝냈니? (finish, write)
= Did Dale ＿＿＿＿＿＿＿＿＿＿ the letter?

5 나는 콘서트 동안 서 있는 것을 꺼리지 않는다. (mind, stand)
= I don't ＿＿＿＿＿＿＿＿＿＿ during the concert.

6 나는 이 식당에서 감자수프를 주문하는 것을 추천한다. (order, recommend)
= I ＿＿＿＿＿＿＿＿＿＿ the potato soup at this restaurant.

7 저녁 식사 전에 단것을 먹는 것을 피하세요. (avoid, eat)
= Please ＿＿＿＿＿＿＿＿＿＿ sweets before dinner.

기출 적중문제

다음 빈칸에 들어갈 말로 어색한 것은?

Lina ＿＿＿＿ playing the flute.

① enjoyed   ② practiced   ③ stopped
④ wanted   ⑤ gave up

다음 동사는 동명사와 to부정사를 모두 목적어로 쓰며, 둘 중 무엇을 써도 의미가 달라지지 않는다.

like   love   hate   begin   start   continue

I **love** drinking coffee. 나는 커피를 마시는 것을 좋아한다.
= I **love** to drink coffee.

Tom **started** painting a picture. Tom은 그림을 그리기 시작했다.
= Tom **started** to paint a picture.

연습문제 A 우리말과 같도록 괄호 안의 말을 활용하여 문장을 완성하시오.

1 Harris씨는 밤에 운전하는 것을 싫어한다. (drive, hate)
= Mr. Harris ＿＿＿＿＿＿＿＿＿＿＿＿＿＿ at night.

2 선호는 돈을 모으기 시작해야 한다. (begin, save)
= Sunho should ＿＿＿＿＿＿＿＿＿＿＿＿＿ money.

3 너는 음악을 듣는 것을 좋아하니? (like, listen)
= Do you ＿＿＿＿＿＿＿＿＿＿＿＿＿ to music?

4 나는 나의 영어 실력을 계속 키울 것이다. (continue, improve)
= I will ＿＿＿＿＿＿＿＿＿＿＿＿＿ my English.

연습문제 B 괄호 안에서 알맞은 것을 모두 고르시오.

1 My brother loves (cycling / to cycle).

2 The snow began (falling / to fall) yesterday.

3 Ms. Brown gave up (smoking / to smoke).

4 I want (asking / to ask) him something.

5 Don't avoid (going / to go) to the dentist.

6 Sharon likes (watching / to watch) musicals.

7 Sandra enjoys (hiking / to hike) on the weekends.

8 Does Pete hate (exercising / to exercise)?

9 The musician started (playing / to play) the guitar.

10 When do you plan (going / to go) abroad?

11 Mary and David kept (waiting / to wait) for you.

12 The students will continue (doing / to do) their homework.

연습문제 **C** 다음 그림을 보고 <보기>의 말을 활용하여 문장을 완성하시오.

<보기>	close the window	clean the kitchen	watch TV
	buy a new laptop	cry loudly	eat your salad

1

Do you mind _____ ?

2

The baby started _____ .

3

Cindy enjoys _____ .

4

Jimin wants _____ .

5

You should finish _____ .

6

Luna plans _____ .

 기출 적중문제

우리말과 같도록 괄호 안의 말을 활용하여 빈칸에 쓰시오.

Dora는 그녀의 친구들에게 편지를 써주는 것을 좋아한다.
(like)

= Dora _____ _____ letters to her friends.

= Dora _____ _____ _____ letters to her friends.

동명사 vs. 진행형

정답 p.25

V-ing형은 문장 안에서 동명사 외에 진행형(「be + V-ing」)을 나타내기 위해서도 쓰인다. 동명사로 쓰일 때는 '~하는 것, ~하기'의 의미이고, 진행형으로 쓰일 때는 '~하고 있다, ~하는 중이다'의 의미이다.

동명사	Studying English is interesting. 영어를 공부하는 것은 흥미롭다.
	My hobby is baking cakes. 나의 취미는 케이크를 굽는 것이다.
	She enjoys singing pop songs. 그녀는 팝송을 부르는 것을 즐긴다.
진행형	The students are studying English. 그 학생들은 영어를 공부하고 있다.
	I am baking a cake. 나는 케이크를 굽고 있다.
	She is singing a pop song. 그녀는 팝송을 부르고 있다.

연습문제 밑줄 친 부분의 쓰임과 같은 것을 <보기>에서 골라 그 기호를 쓰시오.

<보기> ⓐ We kept waiting for our friend.
ⓑ Frank is reading a magazine.

1 My dream is writing a novel. [   ]
2 The plane is landing at Incheon Airport now. [   ]
3 Drinking too much milk is not good. [   ]
4 My brother's wish is having a cute pet. [   ]
5 Dad is cooking breakfast in the kitchen. [   ]
6 Linda's goal is learning German. [   ]
7 I recommend eating fresh fruit every day. [   ]
8 Is Nate putting on his jacket? [   ]
9 The dog is chewing on a bone under the table. [   ]

기출 적중문제

다음 중 밑줄 친 부분의 쓰임이 나머지 넷과 다른 것은?

① Kate is sleeping on the sofa.
② She is washing her face now.
③ They are cleaning the room.
④ His goal is winning the game.
⑤ The nurse is calling the patient.

V-ing형이 동명사로 쓰일 때와 진행형으로 쓰일 때를 구별해야 해요.

POINT 4 동명사 관용 표현

정답 p.25

> be good at + V-ing ~하는 것을 잘하다
> look forward to + V-ing ~하는 것을 기대하다
> go + V-ing ~하러 가다
> How[What] about + V-ing? ~하는 게 어때?
>
> be afraid of + V-ing ~하는 것을 무서워하다
> be busy + V-ing ~하느라 바쁘다
> spend + 시간/돈 + V-ing ~하는 데 시간/돈을 쓰다
> thank … for + V-ing ~한 것에 대해 …에게 감사해하다
>
> Let's **go** shopping this afternoon. 오늘 오후에 쇼핑하러 가자.
> Leo **is busy** planting flowers. Leo는 꽃을 심느라 바쁘다.

연습문제 우리말과 같도록 괄호 안의 말을 활용하여 문장을 완성하시오.

1 나의 누나는 내일 스키를 타러 갈 것이다. (ski)
= My sister will _____ tomorrow.

2 펭귄은 수영하는 것을 잘한다. (swim)
= Penguins _____ .

3 우리는 너의 여자친구를 만나는 것을 기대한다. (meet)
= We _____ your girlfriend.

4 Andy는 혼자 자는 것을 무서워한다. (sleep)
= Andy _____ alone.

5 뜨거운 코코아를 주문하는 게 어때? (order)
= _____ hot cocoa?

6 Wood씨는 그 차를 수리하느라 바쁘다. (fix)
= Mr. Wood _____ the car.

7 나의 질문에 대답한 것에 대해 너에게 감사하다. (answer)
= _____ my question.

8 곰은 겨울 전에 먹는 데 많은 시간을 쓴다. (a lot of time, eat)
= Bears _____ before the winter.

기출 적중문제

다음 문장에서 어법상 어색한 부분을 찾아 쓰고 바르게 고쳐 쓰시오.

My grandpa is not good at use a smartphone.

_____ → _____

A 밑줄 친 부분이 어법상 맞으면 O를 쓰고, 틀리면 바르게 고쳐 쓰시오.

1 <u>To running</u> is a great way to exercise.　　→ _____

2 My plan is <u>finishing</u> the puzzles.　　→ _____

3 Talking to Jason <u>is</u> always helpful.　　→ _____

4 His job is <u>design</u> children's clothes.　　→ _____

5 Please finish <u>to paint</u> the kid's room today.　　→ _____

6 <u>Staying</u> up late is not a good habit.　　→ _____

7 Brushing your teeth <u>are</u> important.　　→ _____

8 She enjoyed <u>to open</u> her birthday gifts.　　→ _____

9 Ray's goal is <u>woke</u> up on time.　　→ _____

10 We couldn't avoid <u>to cancel</u> our trip.　　→ _____

B <보기>와 같이 대화에 나온 표현을 활용하여 문장을 완성하시오.

> <보기>
>
> Dan: Do you often eat cupcakes?　　Emma: Yes, I do.
>
> → Emma enjoys _eating cupcakes_ .

1 Stella: Do you skate every day?　　Yunho: Yes, I do.

→ Yunho practices _____ every day.

2 Jay: Do you often listen to jazz music?　　Gloria: Yes, I do.

→ Gloria loves _____ .

3 Karen: Will you have dinner with Ken?　　Tina: Yes, I will.

→ Tina plans _____ .

4

Susie: Are you still studying Chinese?

Colin: Yes, I am.

→ Colin will continue _____.

5

Jihye: Do you still play the violin?

Owen: No, I don't.

→ Owen gave up _____.

6

Robert: Can you close the door?

Suho: Yes, I can.

→ Suho doesn't mind _____.

7

Bobby: Will you join the band?

Amelia: Yes, I will.

→ Amelia has already decided _____.

C 괄호 안의 말을 활용하여 대화를 완성하시오.

1

A: What do you ⓐ_____ this weekend? (plan, do)

B: Nothing. Why?

A: ⓑ_____ to an amusement park? (how about, go)

B: That sounds great. I ⓒ_____ parades. (like, watch)

A: Me too! I'll buy the tickets.

2

A: I have to go shopping. I need a new purse.

B: I ⓐ_____ to Fiesta Mall. (recommend, go)

A: OK. Do you ⓑ_____ with me? (want, come)

B: Why not? I ⓒ_____ a new bicycle helmet. (need, buy)

A: Oh. Do you often ride your bike?

B: Yes, I do. I ⓓ_____ my bike every weekend. (enjoy, ride)

A: Really? I didn't know that!

중간 · 기말고사 실전 문제

[1-2] 다음 빈칸에 들어갈 말로 <u>어색한</u> 것을 고르시오.

1

> Jenny _____ painting pictures.

① likes ② plans ③ enjoys
④ begins ⑤ continues

2

> Mitch _____ singing the song.

① gave up ② practiced ③ started
④ wanted ⑤ finished

3 다음 중 밑줄 친 부분이 어법상 바른 것은?

① Michael is thinking of <u>to watch</u> a movie.
② Do you mind <u>to open</u> the window?
③ Brad decided <u>diving</u> into the pool.
④ Please stop <u>driving</u> so fast.
⑤ Let's finish <u>to make</u> the kites.

4 주어진 문장의 밑줄 친 부분과 쓰임이 <u>다른</u> 것은?

> <u>Riding</u> a horse is not easy.

① My goal is <u>losing</u> weight.
② <u>Fishing</u> in the lake is peaceful.
③ Many children enjoy <u>playing</u> games.
④ Clyde hates <u>fighting</u> with his friends.
⑤ Paul is <u>ordering</u> pizza on the phone.

5 다음 글에서 어법상 <u>어색한</u> 부분을 찾아 쓰고 바르게 고쳐 쓰시오.

> Raymond enjoys to hike. So, he loves spend time in the mountains.

(1) _____ → _____
(2) _____ → _____

6 다음 중 밑줄 친 부분의 쓰임이 나머지 넷과 <u>다른</u> 것은?

> A: Something is ①<u>moving</u>. What is it?
> B: It looks like an ant. What is it ②<u>doing</u>?
> A: It's ③<u>eating</u> the food.
> B: Wow. It's so tiny.
> A: Look! It's ④<u>going</u> somewhere.
> B: How about ⑤<u>following</u> it?
> A: That sounds fun!

7 다음 밑줄 친 부분을 바르게 고치지 <u>못한</u> 것은?

① What about visit Hanok Village?
   ↳ visiting
② Jack plans waking up early tomorrow.
   ↳ to wake
③ The baby kept to cry last night.
   ↳ cries
④ Thank you for to drive me to school.
   ↳ driving
⑤ You should practice play the guitar.
   ↳ playing

[8-9] 다음 빈칸에 들어갈 말이 순서대로 짝지어진 것을 고르시오.

8

> · Do you mind _____ the goldfish?
> · My plan is _____ a perfect score.

① feeding – get
② feeding – getting
③ feed – get
④ to feed – getting
⑤ feed – to getting

9

> · Molly continued _____ Charles.
> · I don't mind _____ here.

① to call – to sit
② to call – sit
③ calling – to sit
④ calling – sitting
⑤ to calling – sitting

10 괄호 안의 말을 활용하여 다음 글의 빈칸에 알맞은 말을 쓰시오.

> The Statue of Liberty was a gift from France to the United States. Workers finished ⓐ_____(build) it in 1886. Today, people enjoy ⓑ_____ (take) photos in front of it. They also love ⓒ_____(climb) up to the statue's head. In order to do this, they must walk up 377 steps.
>
> *The Statue of Liberty 자유의 여신상

11 다음 중 어법상 어색한 것은?

① The train to Busan started to move.
② Are you looking forward to visiting me?
③ She is afraid of being in the dark.
④ My dad is upset about losing his wallet.
⑤ It kept to rain all day yesterday.

12 다음 (A)~(C)에 들어갈 말이 바르게 짝지어진 것은?

> · Monica enjoys ___(A)___ in the ocean.
> · I gave up ___(B)___ this long book.
> · Jinho wants ___(C)___ to the cinema.

	(A)	(B)	(C)
①	swimming	reading	going
②	to swim	to read	going
③	swimming	reading	to go
④	to swim	reading	going
⑤	swimming	to read	to go

13 다음 대화의 밑줄 친 우리말과 같도록 주어진 <조건>에 맞게 영작하시오.

> A: Did you read this book yet?
> B: No, I didn't. 나는 그것을 읽는 것을 기대하고 있다.

> **<조건>**
> 1. 7단어로 쓰시오.
> 2. look, forward, read를 활용하시오.
> 3. 진행시제로 쓰시오.

= _____

14 다음 (A)~(C)에 들어갈 말이 바르게 짝지어진 것은?

> · I dream about ___(A)___ like a bird.
> · We will keep ___(B)___ on this science project.
> · Beth recommended ___(C)___ that play.

	(A)	(B)	(C)
①	flying	to work	watching
②	to fly	to work	to watch
③	flying	working	watching
④	flying	working	to watch
⑤	to fly	working	to watch

15 다음 중 밑줄 친 부분의 쓰임이 나머지 넷과 <u>다른</u> 것은?

① <u>Opening</u> the present was wonderful.
② Mark enjoyed <u>dancing</u> at the festival.
③ The lion is <u>running</u> in the field.
④ How about <u>taking</u> a trip together?
⑤ Does Anne like <u>trying</u> new foods?

16 다음 글의 밑줄 친 ⓐ~ⓔ 중 어법상 어색한 것을 찾아 기호를 쓰고 바르게 고쳐 쓰시오.

> Sarah hopes ⓐto travel to France. Visiting Paris ⓑare her dream. She enjoys ⓒto have French food. And she wants ⓓto visit the Eiffel Tower too. She will keep ⓔsave money for the trip.

(1) _____ → _____
(2) _____ → _____
(3) _____ → _____

[17-18] 우리말과 같도록 괄호 안의 말을 알맞게 배열하시오.

17

> 그녀는 요리하는 데 매일 두 시간을 쓴다. (spends, cooking, two hours, she)

= _____ every day.

18

> Josh는 재미있는 영상을 만드는 것을 잘한다. (at, making, good, funny videos, is)

= Josh _____.

19 다음 대화의 밑줄 친 ⓐ~ⓔ를 바르게 고친 것은?

> A: Did you finish ⓐwrite the report?
> B: No. The problem is ⓑfinds time.
> A: Did you start ⓒto working on it?
> B: No. I was busy ⓓplay video games.
> A: ⓔDo homework is more important.
> B: I know, but it's too boring.

① ⓐ write → to write
② ⓑ finds → find
③ ⓒ to working → work
④ ⓓ play → playing
⑤ ⓔ Do → To doing

20 다음 빈칸에 들어갈 알맞은 것을 <u>모두</u> 고르시오.

> My sister likes _____ sushi for dinner.

① eat　　② to eat　　③ ate
④ eats　　⑤ eating

21 다음 글의 밑줄 친 ⓐ~ⓔ 중 어법상 <u>어색한</u> 것의 개수는?

> Catching a cold ⓐis common, and here is some advice. Doctors recommend ⓑdrinking lots of water. You should avoid ⓒto move around so you can rest. ⓓTake medicine also helps. You will start ⓔfeeling better after a few days.

① 1개　　② 2개　　③ 3개
④ 4개　　⑤ 5개

22 다음 대화에서 어법상 <u>어색한</u> 부분을 찾아 쓰고 바르게 고쳐 쓰시오.

> A: How about to go to the park?
> B: Sure. Play soccer will be fun.

(1) _____ → _____
(2) _____ → _____

23 다음 중 밑줄 친 부분이 어법상 <u>어색한</u> 것은?

① How about <u>hanging</u> out with me?
② Julie will begin <u>to learning</u> Korean.
③ The student is busy <u>writing</u> his report.
④ I love <u>to wear</u> a hanbok on New Year's Day.
⑤ My brother was afraid of <u>singing</u> in front of people.

24 다음 빈칸에 들어갈 알맞은 것은?

> The police officers are busy _____ for the missing children.

① look　　② looks　　③ looked
④ to look　　⑤ looking

25 다음은 Janice가 Greg에게 보내는 편지이다. 밑줄 친 우리말 (A), (B)와 같도록 괄호 안의 말을 활용하여 문장을 완성하시오.

> Dear Greg,
>
> (A) <u>나를 너의 파티에 초대해준 것에 대해 너에게 고마워.</u> (invite, thank, for) I had a great time, and I met lots of interesting people. The food was also really good. (B) <u>특히, 나는 그 초콜릿케이크를 먹는 것을 즐겼어.</u> (eat, enjoy) I'm looking forward to seeing you again.
>
> Take care,
> Janice

(A) _____ me to your party.
(B) Especially, _____ the chocolate cake.

CHAPTER 9
명사와 관사

Monica and her **dog** are jogging along the **lake**.
Monica와 그녀의 개는 호수를 따라서 조깅하고 있다.

Monica, **dog**, **lake**와 같이 사람, 사물, 장소 등의 이름을 나타내는 말을 **명사**라고 해요. 명사는 **dog**나 **lake**와 같이 셀 수 있는 명사와 **Monica**와 같이 셀 수 없는 명사로 구분할 수 있어요.

기출로 적중 POINT

내신 100점 적중!
기출 출제율

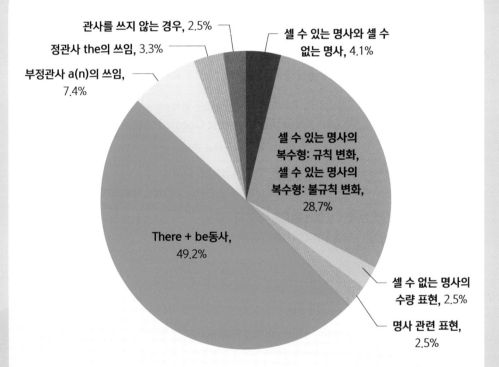

관사를 쓰지 않는 경우, 2.5%

정관사 the의 쓰임, 3.3%

부정관사 a(n)의 쓰임,
7.4%

셀 수 있는 명사와 셀 수
없는 명사, 4.1%

셀 수 있는 명사의
복수형: 규칙 변화,
셀 수 있는 명사의
복수형: 불규칙 변화,
28.7%

There + be동사,
49.2%

셀 수 없는 명사의
수량 표현, 2.5%

명사 관련 표현,
2.5%

TOP 1 **There + be동사 (49.2%)**
「There + be동사」의 형태와 be동사의 수를 묻는 문제가 자주 출제된다.

TOP 2 **셀 수 있는 명사의 복수형: 규칙 변화, 불규칙 변화 (28.7%)**
셀 수 있는 명사의 복수형을 묻는 문제가 자주 출제된다.

TOP 3 **부정관사 a(n)의 쓰임 (7.4%)**
부정관사 a(n)의 쓰임을 묻는 문제가 자주 출제된다.

POINT 1 셀 수 있는 명사와 셀 수 없는 명사

1. 셀 수 있는 명사가 단수일 때는 명사 앞에 a(n)을 붙이고, 복수일 때는 복수형으로 쓴다. 셀 수 있는 명사에는 보통명사와 집합명사가 있다.

보통명사	일반적인 사람·동물·사물을 나타내는 명사 boy, kid, student, cat, dog, bird, city, car, sandwich 등
집합명사	사람·동물·사물이 모인 집합을 나타내는 명사 class, family, team, group, band, club 등

He ate an **apple** and three **pears**. 그는 한 개의 사과와 세 개의 배를 먹었다.
Our **team** won the **game**. 우리의 팀은 그 경기를 이겼다.

2. 셀 수 없는 명사는 명사 앞에 a(n)을 붙일 수 없고, 복수형으로도 쓸 수 없다. 셀 수 없는 명사에는 고유명사, 추상명사, 물질명사가 있다.

고유명사	사람이나 장소 등의 고유한 이름을 나타내는 명사 Jack, Mr. Lee, Korea, Paris, Pacific Ocean, Hangang 등 (Tip) 고유명사의 첫 글자는 항상 대문자로 쓴다.
추상명사	눈에 보이지 않는 추상적인 개념을 나타내는 명사 peace, love, kindness, honesty, help, advice, information 등
물질명사	일정한 형태가 없는 물질을 나타내는 명사 water, tea, bread, rice, paper, rain, sand 등

Seoul is the capital city of **Korea**. 서울은 한국의 수도이다.
They need your **help**. 그들은 너의 도움이 필요하다.
Would you like **tea**? 너는 차를 원하니?

(Tip) furniture(가구), money(돈), clothing(의류), luggage(짐)와 같이 종류 전체를 대표하는 명사는 셀 수 없지만, 각 종류에 속하는 명사는 셀 수 있다.
종류 전체를 대표하는 명사: furniture – 종류에 속하는 명사: a chair, a desk, a table 등

연습문제 A 다음 명사가 셀 수 있는 명사이면 O, 셀 수 없는 명사이면 X를 쓰시오.

1 bag → _____

2 love → _____

3 advice → _____

4 school → _____

5 tree → _____

6 oil → _____

7 clothing → _____

8 teacher → _____

9 Spain → _____

10 club → _____

11 tiger	→ _____	12 peace	→ _____
13 class	→ _____	14 salt	→ _____
15 skirt	→ _____	16 chair	→ _____
17 money	→ _____	18 team	→ _____
19 notebook	→ _____	20 Karen	→ _____
21 London	→ _____	22 sand	→ _____
23 luggage	→ _____	24 toy	→ _____
25 kindness	→ _____	26 paper	→ _____
27 family	→ _____	28 information	→ _____
29 Ms. Smith	→ _____	30 hat	→ _____

연습문제 **B** 괄호 안에서 알맞은 것을 고르시오.

1 Mr. Miller doesn't drink (coffee / coffees).

2 (Banana / Bananas) have important vitamins.

3 How did you meet (minho / Minho)?

4 Michael is putting (sugar / a sugar) in his tea.

5 Anna has four close (friend / friends).

6 Many (flower / flowers) are in the garden.

7 My aunt gave me (book / a book) about dinosaurs.

8 (Honesty / An honesty) is Tina's strength.

9 The store has different kinds of (furniture / furnitures).

10 I picked up (dollar / a dollar) on my way home.

11 My family is going to visit (Vietnam / a Vietnam).

12 Money cannot buy you (happiness / a happiness).

기출 적중문제

다음 중 밑줄 친 부분이 어법상 어색한 것은?

① A girl is looking for you.

② Brian is drinking milk.

③ Kate has a brother.

④ Let me give you an advice.

⑤ Water is necessary for our body.

셀 수 없는 명사는
a(n)과 함께 쓸 수
없어요.

셀 수 있는 명사의 복수형: 규칙 변화

정답 p.26

셀 수 있는 명사의 복수형은 대부분 명사에 -(e)s를 붙여 만든다.

대부분의 명사	명사 + -s	book – books egg – eggs	cookie – cookies tree – trees
-s, -x, -ch, -sh로 끝나는 명사	명사 + -es	bus – buses church – churches	box – boxes dish – dishes
「자음 + o」로 끝나는 명사	명사 + -es	potato – potatoes (Tip) · 예외: piano – pianos · 「모음 + o」로 끝나는 명사	tomato – tomatoes photo – photos : radio – radios
「자음 + y」로 끝나는 명사	y를 i로 바꾸고 + -es	baby – babies diary – diaries (Tip) 「모음 + y」로 끝나는 명사	story – stories country – countries : key – keys
-f, -fe로 끝나는 명사	f, fe를 v로 바꾸고 + -es	leaf – leaves (Tip) 예외: roof – roofs	knife – knives cliff – cliffs

Please carry the boxes outside. 그 상자들을 밖으로 날라주세요.
Four tomatoes and two cookies are on the plate. 네 개의 토마토와 두 개의 쿠키가 접시 위에 있다.

연습문제 A 다음 명사의 복수형을 쓰시오.

1 dish – _____ **2** key – _____

3 city – _____ **4** cookie – _____

5 tomato – _____ **6** leaf – _____

7 butterfly – _____ **8** photo – _____

9 roof – _____ **10** cup – _____

11 baby – _____ **12** knife – _____

13 shirt – _____ **14** box – _____

15 bus – _____ **16** diary – _____

17 wife – _____ **18** wolf – _____

19 story – _____ **20** radio – _____

21 game – _____ **22** church – _____

23 star   – _____

25 address   – _____

27 leg   – _____

29 bench   – _____

31 piano   – _____

33 bottle   – _____

35 holiday   – _____

37 life   – _____

39 cliff   – _____

41 watch   – _____

43 boat   – _____

45 tree   – _____

47 brush   – _____

49 party   – _____

24 potato   – _____

26 doll   – _____

28 video   – _____

30 fox   – _____

32 book   – _____

34 peach   – _____

36 glass   – _____

38 lady   – _____

40 class   – _____

42 loaf   – _____

44 country   – _____

46 shelf   – _____

48 question   – _____

50 dictionary   – _____

연습문제 B   괄호 안의 명사를 알맞은 형태로 바꿔 빈칸에 쓰시오.

1 The girl gave me two _____. (potato)

2 I bought a _____ to read on a plane. (book)

3 Rebecca knows many scary _____. (story)

4 _____ fall from trees in winter. (leaf)

5 You should use _____ carefully. (knife)

6 The _____ of those houses are all green. (roof)

7 I visited three _____ in Europe. (country)

8 He can't find a nice _____ for his apartment. (sofa)

기출 적중문제

다음 중 명사의 복수형이 <u>잘못된</u> 것은?

① dog – dogs   ② knife – knives

③ tomato – tomatoes   ④ day – days

⑤ sandwich – sandwichs

일부 셀 수 있는 명사의 복수형은 불규칙하게 변한다.

❶ 단수형과 복수형이 다른 명사

man – men	woman – women	child – children	mouse – mice
ox – oxen	goose – geese	foot – feet	tooth – teeth

A **child** is looking for his toy. 한 아이가 그의 장난감을 찾고 있다.
I played soccer with many **children**. 나는 많은 아이들과 축구를 했다.

❷ 단수형과 복수형이 같은 명사

sheep – sheep   deer – deer   fish – fish   salmon – salmon

Look at that **sheep** on the grass. 잔디 위에 있는 저 양을 봐라.
Lots of **sheep** are resting in this field. 많은 양들이 이 들판에서 쉬고 있다.

연습문제 A 다음 명사의 복수형을 쓰시오.

1 man   – _____

2 mouse   – _____

3 sheep   – _____

4 ox   – _____

5 fish   – _____

6 foot   – _____

7 tooth   – _____

8 deer   – _____

9 woman   – _____

10 child   – _____

11 goose   – _____

12 salmon   – _____

연습문제 B 우리말과 같도록 빈칸에 알맞은 말을 쓰시오.

1 많은 여자들은 저 배우를 좋아한다.
= A lot of _____ like that actor.

2 고릴라는 서른두 개의 이빨을 가지고 있다.
= Gorillas have 32 _____ .

3 나는 한 마리의 물고기를 잡았지만 그것을 놓쳤다.
= I caught a _____ but lost it.

4 너는 이 농장에서 많은 사슴들을 볼 수 있다.

= You can see many _____ in this farm.

5 캥거루는 얼마나 많은 발들을 가지고 있니?

= How many _____ does a kangaroo have?

6 그 운동장은 아이들로 가득 차 있다.

= The playground is full of _____.

7 갑자기, 두 명의 키가 큰 남자들이 그 방 안으로 걸어 들어왔다.

= Suddenly, two tall _____ walked into the room.

8 세 마리의 양이 산에서 뛰어다니고 있다.

= Three _____ are running on the mountain.

연습문제 **C** 다음 그림을 보고 빈칸에 알맞은 말을 쓰시오.

[1-5]

1 A _____ is painting the fence.

2 A cat is chasing some _____.

3 Two _____ are playing with toys.

4 _____ are falling from the tree.

5 Three _____ are lying under the tree.

[6-10]

6 A _____ is jumping in the mud.

7 Three _____ are talking to one another.

8 Two _____ are sleeping.

9 The dog's _____ are dirty.

10 Some _____ are walking to the pond.

🎯 **기출 적중문제**

다음 문장에서 어법상 <u>어색한</u> 부분을 찾아 쓰고 바르게 고쳐 쓰시오.

Where are the oxes going?

_____ → _____

셀 수 없는 명사의 수량 표현

정답 p.27

셀 수 없는 명사는 그것을 담는 그릇이나 단위를 나타내는 명사를 활용하여 수량을 나타내고, 복수형은 그릇이나 단위를 나타내는 단위명사에 -(e)s를 붙여 만든다.

수량 표현	함께 쓰이는 명사	예시
a glass of 한 잔	water, milk, juice	**a glass of water** 물 한 잔
a cup of 한 컵	water, tea, coffee	**a cup of tea** 차 한 컵
a bottle of 한 병	water, milk, juice, ink	**three bottles of milk** 우유 세 병
a can of 한 캔	coke, soda, paint	**five cans of coke** 콜라 다섯 캔
a bowl of 한 그릇	soup, rice, salad, cereal	**two bowls of soup** 수프 두 그릇
a slice of 한 조각	pizza, ham, cheese, bread, cake	**eight slices of pizza** 피자 여덟 조각
a piece of 한 장/조각	pizza, cheese, bread, cake, paper, furniture	**a piece of paper** 종이 한 장
a loaf of 한 덩어리	bread	**six loaves of bread** 빵 여섯 덩어리

Can I drink a glass of juice? 내가 주스 한 잔을 마셔도 되니?
Bring us two bowls of salad, please. 저희에게 샐러드 두 그릇을 가져다주세요.
She ordered a piece of cake. 그녀는 케이크 한 조각을 주문했다.
I want three slices of cheese in my hamburger. 나는 나의 햄버거에 치즈 세 조각을 원한다.

연습문제 A 다음 말의 복수형을 쓰시오.

1 a bottle of water – five _____

2 a glass of juice – two _____

3 a cup of coffee – ten _____

4 a piece of furniture – three _____

5 a can of soda – four _____

6 a bowl of rice – nine _____

7 a slice of ham – three _____

8 a loaf of bread – six _____

연습문제 B 괄호 안에서 알맞은 것을 고르시오.

1 Charlie drank a (piece / glass) of milk this morning.

2 Two (slices / bowls) of pizza are on the plate.

3 Can you give me a (cup / loaf) of coffee?

4 I broke five (pieces / bottles) of ink yesterday.

5 He brought two (loaves / bowls) of soup for lunch.

6 I'd like to have two (pieces / glasses) of cake.

7 Sarah needs three (cans / slices) of paint.

8 The customer bought ten (loaves / bottles) of bread.

연습문제 C 우리말과 같도록 괄호 안의 말을 활용하여 문장을 완성하시오. (단, 숫자는 영어로 쓰시오.)

1 우리는 차 세 컵을 마실 것이다. (tea)

= We'll have _____ .

2 매일 물 여덟 잔을 마셔라. (water)

= Drink _____ every day.

3 저의 샌드위치에는 치즈 한 조각을 넣어주세요. (cheese)

= Please put _____ in my sandwich.

4 저에게 빵 다섯 덩어리를 싸주시겠어요? (bread)

= Would you pack _____ for me?

5 그는 이 책을 쓰기 위해 잉크 여섯 병을 썼다. (ink)

= He used _____ to write this book.

6 콜라 네 캔을 너의 친구들과 나눠라. (coke)

= Share _____ with your friends.

7 나의 누나는 아침으로 보통 시리얼 한 그릇을 먹는다. (cereal)

= My sister usually has _____ for breakfast.

8 너는 이 요리법을 위해 햄 세 장이 필요하다. (ham)

= You need _____ for this recipe.

기출 적중문제 ◎←⊏

우리말과 같도록 괄호 안의 말을 활용하여 문장을 완성하시오. (단, 숫자는 영어로 쓰시오.)

저희에게 주스 세 잔을 가져다주시겠어요? (glass)

= Would you bring us _____ ?

---

1. 한 쌍이 짝을 이루는 명사는 항상 복수형으로 쓰고, a pair of를 활용하여 수량을 나타낸다.

수량 표현	한 쌍이 짝을 이루는 명사	예시
a pair of	glasses, sunglasses, gloves, shoes, sneakers, socks, pants, scissors	**a pair of glasses** 안경 한 쌍 **two pairs of socks** 양말 두 켤레

I bought **a pair of sunglasses**. 나는 선글라스 한 쌍을 샀다.
Alex has **five pairs of pants**. Alex는 바지 다섯 벌을 가지고 있다.

(Tip) 한 쌍 중 하나만 나타낼 때는 단수형으로 쓴다.
I lost **a sock**. 나는 양말 한 짝을 잃어버렸다.

2. 숫자 + 단위명사는 하이픈(-)으로 연결되어 형용사처럼 명사 앞에서 명사를 꾸밀 수 있다. 이때 단위명사는 항상 단수형으로 쓴다.

My dad has a **two-door car**. 나의 아빠는 문이 두 개인 차를 가지고 계신다.
My dad has a two-doors car. (X)

Judy is a **sixteen-year-old girl**. Judy는 16살짜리 소녀이다.
Judy is a sixteen-years-old girl. (X)

3. 명사나 대명사 뒤에 콤마(,)를 써서 부연 설명을 덧붙일 수 있으며, 이를 동격이라고 한다.

Mr. Kim, **my homeroom teacher**, is very tall. 나의 담임 선생님인 김 선생님은 매우 키가 크시다.
 └──── = ────┘

This is **my pet parrot**, **Polly**. 이것은 나의 애완 앵무새인 Polly이다.
     └──── = ────┘

연습문제 **A** 괄호 안에서 알맞은 것을 고르시오.

1 She gave me a new pair of (glove / gloves).

2 I have a (six-year-old / six-years-old) cousin.

3 The children need five (pair / pairs) of scissors.

4 We must write a (ten-page / ten-pages) essay.

5 We will have a (two-month / two-months) vacation.

6 Sam packed two pairs of (sock / socks) in his backpack.

7 I'm going to buy a pair of (glass / glasses) for my grandmother.

8 Ms. Sanders designed this (twelve-story / twelve-stories) building.

연습문제 B 다음 그림을 보고 괄호 안의 말을 활용하여 문장을 완성하시오.

1

2

3

4

5

6

1 Pass me _____, please. (pair, scissor)

2 Tim is a _____ boy. (year, old)

3 Julie has _____. (pair, glove)

4 I found a _____ clover. (leaf)

5 This hospital is a _____ building. (story)

6 _____ are in the drawer. (pair, sock)

연습문제 C 다음 문장의 밑줄 친 부분과 동격인 부분에 밑줄을 치시오.

1 I was playing with my dog, Merry.

2 Her husband, Mr. Parker, is really kind.

3 I love William Shakespeare, a great writer.

4 Jinseo, a student in my class, is good at dancing.

5 Marcus and his brother, the football players, exercise every day.

기출 적중문제

다음 중 밑줄 친 부분이 어법상 바른 것은?

① Jane lost four pair of shoes.

② He has a two-years-old cat.

③ Give me three bottles of milks.

④ This is a ten-chapter book.

⑤ I bought a pair of pant.

There + be동사

1. 「There + be동사」는 '~이 있다/있었다'라는 의미로, 뒤따라오는 명사에 be동사를 수일치시킨다.

There	+	is / was	+	셀 수 있는 명사의 단수형 또는 셀 수 없는 명사
		are / were		셀 수 있는 명사의 복수형

There is **a spoon** on the table. 식탁 위에 한 개의 숟가락이 있다.
There was **orange juice** in a glass. 잔 안에 오렌지 주스가 있었다.
There are **some students** in the classroom. 교실에 몇몇의 학생들이 있다.

2. 「There + be동사」의 부정문과 의문문

	형태	예문
부정문	There + be동사 + not	There aren't **many cars** on the road. 도로 위에 차가 많지 않다.
의문문	be동사 + there ~? – Yes, there + be동사. – No, there + be동사 + not.	Is there **a cat** under the desk? 책상 아래에 고양이가 있니? – Yes, there is. 응, 있어. – No, there isn't. 아니, 없어.

연습문제 A 괄호 안에서 알맞은 것을 고르시오.

1 There (is / are) an ant on my ice cream.

2 There (is / are) four seasons in Korea.

3 (Is / Are) there any butter in the refrigerator? – No, there (isn't / aren't).

4 There (is / are) a lot of money in Jack's wallet.

5 (Is / Are) there a poster on the wall? – Yes, there (is / are).

6 There (is / are) a big baseball game tomorrow.

7 There (wasn't / weren't) any sugar in the coffee.

8 (Is / Are) there some pears in the basket? – Yes, there (is / are).

9 There (wasn't / weren't) any horses on the farm.

10 There (wasn't / weren't) much furniture in his house.

11 (Was / Were) there many flowers in the garden? – No, there (wasn't / weren't).

12 There (is / are) many visitors in the museum.

연습문제 B 다음 그림을 보고 빈칸에 알맞은 말을 넣어 질문에 대한 대답을 완성하시오.

1    **2**    **3**    **4**

1 *A*: Is there a lamp on the table?   *B*: _____, _____.

2 *A*: Are there any dogs under the sofa?   *B*: _____, _____.

3 *A*: Is there a notebook in the bag?   *B*: _____, _____.

4 *A*: Are there any birds on the roof?   *B*: _____, _____.

연습문제 C 우리말과 같도록 괄호 안의 말을 활용하여 빈칸에 쓰시오.

1 나의 침대 위에 세 개의 베개가 있다. (three, pillow)

= _____ _____ _____ on my bed.

2 놀이터에 아이들이 많지 않았다. (many, child)

= _____ _____ _____ in the playground.

3 병 안에 우유가 많이 있니? (much, milk)

= _____ _____ _____ in the bottle?

4 식탁 위에 두 개의 컵이 있었다. (two, cup)

= _____ _____ _____ on the kitchen table.

5 팬케이크를 만들기 위한 밀가루가 전혀 없다. (any, flour)

= _____ _____ _____ to make pancakes.

6 이 반에 학생들이 많이 있니? (many, student)

= _____ _____ _____ in this class?

 **기출 적중문제**

다음 빈칸에 들어갈 말이 나머지 넷과 다른 것은?

① There _____ some pens in the drawer.

② There _____ two sofas in the living room.

③ There _____ many people on the road.

④ There _____ a cookie on the plate.

⑤ There _____ ten dollars in the wallet.

「There + be동사」에서 be동사는 뒤따라오는 명사에 수일치시켜요.

부정관사 a(n)의 쓰임

정답 p.27

1. **부정관사 a(n)은 정해지지 않은 막연한 것을 가리킬 때 쓰며, 셀 수 있는 명사의 단수형 앞에만 쓴다.**

   Do you have **a** **map**? 너는 지도를 가지고 있니?

2. **부정관사 a(n)은 다음과 같은 경우에도 쓴다.**

'하나의(one)'를 나타낼 때	I ate **an** **apple** for breakfast. 나는 아침으로 한 개의 사과를 먹었다.
'~마다(per)'를 나타낼 때	Sumin usually goes to the gym once **a** **week**. 수민이는 보통 일주일에 한 번 체육관에 간다.
종족 전체를 대표할 때	**A** **shark** is a kind of fish. 상어는 물고기의 한 종류이다.

3. **a와 an은 뒤따라오는 단어의 첫소리에 따라 구별해서 쓴다.**

첫소리가 자음으로 발음되는 단어 앞에는 a	**a** book, **a** cat, **a** melon, **a** black shirt
첫소리가 모음으로 발음되는 단어 앞에는 an	**an** orange, **an** egg, **an** umbrella, **an** empty bottle

   (Tip) · 첫소리의 철자가 모음이지만 자음으로 발음되면 a를 쓴다.
   a university[jùːnəvə́ːrsəti]   **a** European [jùərəpíən]

   · 첫소리의 철자가 자음이지만 모음으로 발음되면 an을 쓴다.
   an hour[auər]   **an** honest[ánist] girl

연습문제 A   괄호 안에서 a나 an 중 알맞은 것을 고르시오.

1 (a / an) animal

2 (a / an) computer

3 (a / an) nurse

4 (a / an) orange

5 (a / an) uniform

6 (a / an) child

7 (a / an) fresh tomato

8 (a / an) honest student

9 (a / an) umbrella

10 (a / an) empty room

11 (a / an) good idea

12 (a / an) blue truck

13 (a / an) hour

14 (a / an) eraser

15 (a / an) useful tip

16 (a / an) old friend

17 (a / an) English teacher

18 (a / an) university

19 (a / an) interesting movie

20 (a / an) elementary school

연습문제 B 밑줄 친 a(n)의 의미와 같은 것을 <보기>에서 골라 그 기호를 쓰시오.

<보기> ⓐ Ms. Long has a brother.
ⓑ I go to the museum twice a year.
ⓒ An elephant is a very large animal.

1 She bought a dress and two skirts. [   ]

2 I try to work out four times a week. [   ]

3 A chicken is a bird, but it can't fly. [   ]

4 You should stretch once an hour. [   ]

5 There are twelve months in a year. [   ]

6 A wolf is a member of the dog family. [   ]

7 Susan gets a haircut three times a year. [   ]

연습문제 C 다음 빈칸에 a나 an 중 알맞은 것을 쓰고, 필요하지 않으면 X를 쓰시오.

1 Sojin ran for _____ hour.

2 There was _____ butterfly on the flower.

3 We can't live without _____ air.

4 She climbs the mountain once _____ week.

5 My family is raising _____ cats and dogs.

6 Let's try _____ bowl of pumpkin soup.

7 Mary has to buy _____ furniture.

8 We saw _____ owl on our way home.

9 This printer is out of _____ ink.

10 There is _____ fish in the fishbowl.

기출 적중문제

다음 빈칸에 들어갈 말이 순서대로 짝지어진 것은?

· Hansu is _____ honest boy.
· I saw _____ painting in the gallery.

① an - a ② an - an ③ the - an
④ a - the ⑤ a - a

정관사 the의 쓰임

정답 p.28

정관사 the는 정해진 특정한 것을 가리킬 때 쓰며, 셀 수 있는 명사와 셀 수 없는 명사 앞에 모두 쓸 수 있다.

앞에서 언급된 명사가 반복될 때	We watched a movie last night. **The movie** was scary. 우리는 어젯밤에 영화를 봤다. 그 영화는 무서웠다.
서로 알고 있는 것을 말할 때	Can you open **the windows**? 그 창문들을 열어주겠니?
유일한 것을 말할 때	**The sun** rises in the east. 태양은 동쪽에서 뜬다.
종족 전체를 대표할 때	**The raccoon** hunts at night. 너구리는 밤에 사냥한다.
악기 이름 앞에	He can play **the guitar** well. 그는 기타를 잘 연주할 수 있다.
서수, last, only 앞에	My classroom is on **the second** floor. 나의 교실은 2층에 있다.

연습문제 괄호 안에서 a(n)이나 the 중 알맞은 것을 고르시오.

1 It's too cold outside. Close (a / the) door.

2 The Moon moves around (a / the) Earth.

3 I ordered soup. (A / The) soup was delicious.

4 Could you pass me (a / the) ketchup?

5 Mr. Clark goes to the bakery twice (a / the) month.

6 Can I use (an / the) eraser on your desk?

7 My father enjoys playing (a / the) trumpet after work.

8 (A / The) last day of October is Halloween.

9 (A / The) day has 24 hours.

10 This is (an / the) only nice restaurant in my town.

기출 적중문제 🎯

다음 문장에서 어법상 어색한 부분을 찾아 쓰고 바르게 고쳐 쓰시오.

> Do you know how to play a harp?

_____ → _____

기출로적중 POINT 6-3 관사를 쓰지 않는 경우

정답 p.28

다음과 같은 경우에는 명사 앞에 관사를 쓰지 않는다.

운동, 식사, 과목 이름 앞에	We played **badminton** all day. 우리는 종일 배드민턴을 쳤다. I will meet Tom for **lunch**. 나는 점심 식사를 위해 Tom을 만날 것이다. **Science** is a difficult subject for me. 과학은 나에게 어려운 과목이다.
「by + 교통·통신수단」	Let's go there **by taxi**. 거기에 택시로 가자. You can reach me **by phone**. 너는 전화로 나에게 연락할 수 있다.
장소나 건물이 본래의 목적으로 쓰일 때	Students go to **school** on weekdays. 학생들은 평일에 학교에 간다. (Tip) 장소나 건물이 본래의 목적으로 쓰이지 않을 때는 관사를 써야 한다. Bob's mother went to **the school** to meet his teacher. Bob의 어머니는 그의 선생님을 만나기 위해 학교에 가셨다.

연습문제 다음 빈칸에 a(n)이나 the 중 알맞은 것을 쓰고, 필요하지 않으면 X를 쓰시오.

1 You can go to Jejudo by _____ ship.

2 My favorite subject is _____ history.

3 I usually go to the library once _____ week.

4 Hyeri can play _____ violin very well.

5 Please contact me by _____ e-mail.

6 We have to go to _____ bed early today.

7 I went to _____ church for my cousin's wedding.

8 Minjun doesn't play _____ soccer these days.

기출 적중문제

다음 중 어법상 어색한 것은?

① I'm going to school now.
② We'll get there by the train.
③ Jenny will learn how to play the cello.
④ Kenny bought a new basketball.
⑤ How about eating lunch together?

A 밑줄 친 부분이 어법상 맞으면 O를 쓰고, 틀리면 바르게 고쳐 쓰시오.

1 I put too much <u>salts</u> in my soup. → _____

2 Be careful when you use <u>knifes</u>. → _____

3 How white your <u>tooth</u> are! → _____

4 I couldn't see many <u>oxes</u> on this farm. → _____

5 Jill is a <u>sixteen-years-old</u> girl. → _____

6 Can I have six <u>glasses of water</u>? → _____

7 We have a lot of <u>happinesses</u> in our life. → _____

8 The <u>geese</u> are flying south for winter. → _____

9 Let's order two <u>bowl of salad</u>. → _____

10 It was a <u>three-weeks</u> journey by train. → _____

11 There are eight <u>slices of pizzas</u> in the box. → _____

12 They took many <u>photoes</u> of wildflowers. → _____

13 I bought <u>a pair of glove</u> for my sister. → _____

14 How much <u>money</u> do we need to buy tickets? → _____

15 Did you see two <u>pair of sneakers</u> in front of the door? → _____

B 다음은 Sally의 심부름 목록이다. 그림을 보고 빈칸에 알맞은 말을 쓰시오.

〈Sally의 심부름 목록〉

• five slices of cheese
• ⓐ _____ bread
• ⓑ _____ scissors
• ⓒ _____ juice
• two onions
• ⓓ _____ paint

ⓒ 다음 그림을 보고 <보기>와 같이 괄호 안의 명사를 활용하여 빈칸에 알맞은 말을 쓰시오.

| <보기> | *There* | *are* | *two* | *pictures* | on the wall. (picture) |

1 _____ _____ _____ _____ in the room. (child)

2 _____ _____ _____ _____ next to the window. (slide)

3 _____ _____ _____ on the table. (cookie)

4 _____ _____ _____ _____ in the fish tank. (orange fish)

5 _____ _____ _____ _____ in the room. (funny clown)

6 _____ _____ _____ on the floor. (book)

ⓓ 다음 빈칸에 a(n)이나 the 중 알맞은 것을 쓰고, 필요하지 않으면 X를 쓰시오.

1

Today, Justin did his science homework after ⓐ_____ school. He found some
information about ⓑ_____ Sun on the Internet. After he finished his homework, he had
ⓒ_____ dinner and ate ⓓ_____ last piece of cake in the fridge. He also practiced
playing ⓔ_____ clarinet before bed.

2

My apartment is on ⓐ_____ 20th floor. The elevator was broken, so I spent a lot of time
walking down the stairs. I usually go to ⓑ_____ school on foot, but I had to go by
ⓒ_____ bus today. Luckily, I wasn't late. After I ate ⓓ_____ banana for breakfast, I
played ⓔ_____ table tennis with my friend.

중간·기말고사 실전 문제

1 다음 중 명사의 종류가 서로 <u>다른</u> 것끼리 짝지어진 것은?

① boy, cat   ② love, beauty

③ team, class   ④ house, kindness

⑤ water, bread

2 다음 빈칸에 들어갈 알맞은 것은?

Jinsu wants to have a _____.

① rice   ② juice   ③ cookie

④ peace   ⑤ paper

[3-4] 다음 중 명사의 복수형이 <u>잘못된</u> 것을 고르시오.

3

① cup – cups   ② story – stories

③ fox – foxes   ④ bench – benches

⑤ leaf – leafes

4

① man – men   ② plane – planes

③ ox – oxes   ④ foot – feet

⑤ friend – friends

5 다음 <보기> 중 빈칸에 들어갈 수 있는 것의 개수는?

<보기>   girl   butter   apple   furniture   cars   book   building

There is a _____.

① 2개   ② 3개   ③ 4개

④ 5개   ⑤ 6개

[6-7] 다음 중 밑줄 친 부분이 어법상 바른 것을 고르시오.

6

① I gave beautiful <u>floweres</u> to my mom.

② We took many <u>photoes</u> in the forest.

③ Are you going to wash the <u>dishes</u>?

④ Karen doesn't eat <u>tomatos</u> at all.

⑤ Would you like some <u>sandwichs</u>?

7

① You need to get <u>a fresh air</u>.

② I'd like to drink <u>coffee</u>.

③ The park is full of <u>tree</u>.

④ <u>Five student</u> are absent today.

⑤ Ask your teacher for <u>an advice</u>.

8 be동사를 활용하여 다음 글의 빈칸에 알맞은 말을 쓰시오.

Yesterday was our school festival. There _____ clowns with balloons at the festival. There _____ a famous singer too.

[9-11] 다음 빈칸에 들어갈 말이 순서대로 짝지어진 것을 고르시오.

9

· _____ is important in a friendship.
· _____ is running in the park.

① An honesty – Boys
② Honesty – A boy
③ Honesties – A boy
④ Honesties – Boy
⑤ Honesty – Boys

10

· There is a can of _____ on the counter.
· Could you pass me a pair of _____ ?

① salad – pants
② bread – pencil
③ paint – scarf
④ soda – scissors
⑤ paper – gloves

11

· I bought two pairs of _____ .
· We're going on a _____ trip.

① sunglasses – three-days
② sunglass – three-days
③ sunglasses – three-dayes
④ sunglass – three-day
⑤ sunglasses – three-day

12 다음 그림을 보고 빈칸에 알맞은 말을 쓰시오.

Look at the big farm. There are four
ⓐ _____ on the hill. Two
ⓑ _____ are lying on the grass.
Three ⓒ _____ are feeding cows.

13 다음 중 명사의 복수형이 바른 것끼리 짝지어진 것을 <u>모두</u> 고르시오.

① dogs, knives, deers
② foots, dollars, babies
③ women, churches, brushes
④ cups, maps, boxes
⑤ classes, toothes, geese

14 다음 (A)~(C)에 들어갈 말이 바르게 짝지어진 것은?

· Four ___(A)___ of juice are in the fridge.
· I ate a ___(B)___ of cereal for breakfast.
· This room has three ___(C)___ of furniture.

	(A)	(B)	(C)
①	bottles	bowls	pieces
②	bottles	bowl	pieces
③	bottles	bowl	piece
④	bottle	bowl	piece
⑤	bottle	bowls	piece

15 우리말과 같도록 주어진 <조건>에 맞게 문장을 완성하시오.

바구니 안에 다섯 개의 토마토가 있다.

<조건>
1. there, tomato, be를 활용하시오.
2. 숫자는 영어로 쓰시오.

= _____ in the basket.

16 다음 중 밑줄 친 부분이 어법상 바른 것끼리 묶인 것은?

ⓐ Their wives are talking to each other.
ⓑ He has two pianoes in his home.
ⓒ Are the keyes in your pocket?
ⓓ They bought diarys for next year.
ⓔ I'm looking for some peaches.

① ⓐ, ⓑ   ② ⓐ, ⓔ   ③ ⓑ, ⓒ
④ ⓐ, ⓒ, ⓓ   ⑤ ⓒ, ⓓ, ⓔ

[17-18] 다음 문장에서 어법상 어색한 부분을 찾아 쓰고 바르게 고쳐 쓰시오.

17

There is a five-stories building next to the shopping mall.

_____ → _____

18

Kathleen is good at playing a guitar.

_____ → _____

19 다음 빈칸에 들어갈 말로 어색한 것은?

There are _____ .

① lots of new members in our club
② many people at the market
③ some cars in the garage
④ four deer in the field
⑤ ink in this bottle

20 다음은 Mark가 구매한 물품에 대한 영수증이다. 영수증에 나온 표현을 활용하여 빈칸에 알맞은 말을 쓰시오.

JJ SUPERMARKET

Items	Qty	$
Knife	2	$60.00
Potato	3	$12.00
Cookie	10	$20.00

TOTAL : $92.00

Mark bought two ⓐ_____, three ⓑ_____, and ten ⓒ_____.

21 다음 빈칸에 알맞은 말을 넣어 질문에 대한 대답을 완성하시오.

(1)
A: Is there any tea in the mug?
B: No, _____ _____.

(2)
A: Are there a lot of shirts in your closet?
B: Yes, _____ _____.

22 우리말과 같도록 빈칸에 알맞은 형태의 be동사를 쓰시오.

(1)
> 이 집 안에 두 개의 화장실이 있다.

= There _____ two bathrooms in this house.

(2)
> 병 안에 기름이 많이 없다.

= There _____ much oil in the bottle.

23 우리말과 같도록 괄호 안의 말을 활용하여 문장을 완성하시오.

> 지수는 매일 아침 물 세 잔을 마신다. (water)

= Jisu drinks _____
every morning.

24 다음 중 어법상 어색한 것은?

① There isn't any dust in the air today.
② There is an old tree in my backyard.
③ Were there lots of sheep on the farm?
④ There weren't many guests at the event.
⑤ Are there any butter on your toast?

25 다음 우리말을 알맞게 영작한 것은?

> 접시 위에 세 조각의 피자가 있다.

① There is three slice of pizza on the plate.
② There is three slices of pizza on the plate.
③ There are three slice of pizza on the plate.
④ There are three slices of pizzas on the plate.
⑤ There are three slices of pizza on the plate.

26 다음 그림을 보고 빈칸에 알맞은 말을 넣어 질문에 대한 대답을 완성하시오.

> A: Are there any squirrels in the tree?
> B: _____, _____ _____.

27 다음 중 어법상 바른 것은?

① Five piece of paper are in the printer.
② I ate two bowls of rices.
③ Bring us three glass of milks, please.
④ Would you like a can of coke?
⑤ Can you get me a loaves of bread?

28 다음 중 밑줄 친 부분의 의미가 나머지 넷과 다른 것은?

① There are some red dresses in my closet.
② Is there any hot chocolate in your cup?
③ Look at that man over there.
④ Are there many paintings in this museum?
⑤ There isn't lots of snow on the road.

[29-30] <보기>와 같이 다음 두 문장의 의미가 같도록 빈칸에 알맞은 말을 쓰시오.

<보기>
My house has a beautiful garden.
= <u>There</u> <u>is</u> <u>a</u> <u>beautiful</u> <u>garden</u> at my house.

29

My room has two computers.
= _____ _____ _____
_____ in my room.

30

This building doesn't have a parking lot.
= _____ _____ _____
_____ _____ at this
building.

31 다음 그림을 잘못 표현한 것은?

① There is a sofa in the room.
② There are two cats under the table.
③ There are three birds in the cage.
④ There is a flower vase on the table.
⑤ There is a television on the wall.

[32-33] 다음 빈칸에 들어갈 말이 나머지 넷과 <u>다른</u> 것을 고르시오.

32

① I have _____ blue chair in my room.
② Lucy bought _____ expensive watch.
③ What _____ huge pumpkin!
④ I want _____ new smartphone.
⑤ Could you give me _____ glass of water?

33

① There _____ a toy train in the box.
② There _____ an apple on the table.
③ There _____ a lot of ducks in the pond.
④ There _____ a phone on the desk.
⑤ There _____ a puppy under my bed.

34 다음 빈칸에 들어갈 수 있는 a와 an의 개수가 순서대로 짝지어진 것은?

· Our club will have _____ meeting soon.
· There is _____ egg in my salad.
· Do you go hiking once _____ month?
· _____ child is sitting on the bench.
· He is _____ English teacher.
· _____ man was waiting for Ms. Wilson.

① 2개 – 4개   ② 3개 – 3개   ③ 4개 – 2개
④ 5개 – 1개   ⑤ 6개 – 없음

35 다음 중 밑줄 친 the가 어법상 어색한 것은?

① <u>The</u> moon looks really big tonight.
② I have <u>the</u> breakfast at 8 A.M. every day.
③ Should I give <u>the</u> blanket to her?
④ Yerin is able to play <u>the</u> cello well.
⑤ Did he get on <u>the</u> last train?

36 다음 빈칸에 알맞은 관사를 쓰시오.

· January is _____ first month of the year.
· Maria takes ballet lessons twice _____ week.

37 다음 중 밑줄 친 부분이 어법상 어색한 것은?

① There is a butterfly on the fence.
② My friend's house is on the third floor.
③ My brother drinks juice every day.
④ John usually takes a nap after lunch.
⑤ My sister and I go to the church every Sunday.

38 다음 문장에서 어법상 어색한 부분을 찾아 쓰고 바르게 고쳐 쓰시오.

Two woman and three child are waiting in the line.

(1) _____ → _____
(2) _____ → _____

39 주어진 문장의 밑줄 친 부분과 의미가 다른 것은?

You should take a break once an hour.

① We visit our grandfather once a week.
② Do the kittens eat three times a day?
③ The city holds the festival twice a year.
④ Does he exercise four times a week?
⑤ Molly practiced the flute for an hour yesterday

40 다음 빈칸에 공통으로 들어갈 알맞은 말을 쓰시오.

· Could you open _____ door for me?
· Chicken salad is _____ only thing to eat at this restaurant.

[41-42] 다음 중 밑줄 친 부분이 어법상 어색한 것을 고르시오.

41

I need two onions, four mushrooms,
              ①   ②
cheeses, salt, and sugar.
  ③   ④   ⑤

42

There is three girls and a boy in the
    ①   ②   ③   ④   ⑤
chess club.

43 다음 밑줄 친 부분을 바르게 고치지 못한 것은?

① My grandparents play the tennis twice a week. (→ a tennis)
② I'm eating a piece of cakes. (→ cake)
③ I have a history tests tomorrow. (→ test)
④ The sky is blue and sun is shining brightly. (→ the sun)
⑤ Can I have two slice of cheese in my burger? (→ slices)

CHAPTER 10
대명사

a pink hat = it

Mom bought me a pink hat. I really like it.
엄마가 나에게 분홍색 모자를 사주셨다. 나는 그것이 정말 마음에 든다.

두 번째 문장에서 첫 번째 문장의 **a pink hat** 대신에 **it**을 썼어요. 이렇게 앞에서 언급된 특정한 명사를 반복하지 않기 위해 대신해서 쓰는 말을 **대명사**라고 해요.

기출로 적중 POINT

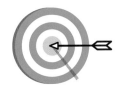

내신 100점 적중!
기출 출제율

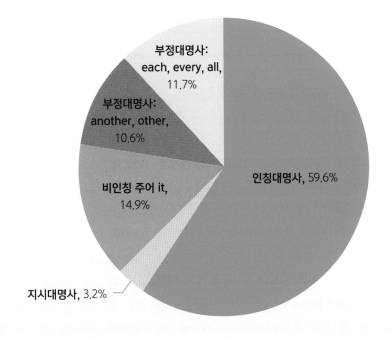

부정대명사:
each, every, all,
11.7%

부정대명사:
another, other,
10.6%

비인칭 주어 it,
14.9%

인칭대명사, 59.6%

지시대명사, 3.2%

TOP 1 **인칭대명사 (59.6%)**
문장 안에서 인칭·수·격에 따른 알맞은 인칭대명사를 쓰는 문제가 자주 출제
된다.

TOP 2 **비인칭 주어 it (14.9%)**
비인칭 주어 it의 쓰임을 묻는 문제가 자주 출제된다.

TOP 3 **부정대명사: each, every, all (11.7%)**
부정대명사 each, every, all의 의미와 쓰임을 묻는 문제가 자주 출제된다.

인칭대명사는 사람이나 사물의 이름을 대신하는 말로, 인칭·수·격에 따라 형태가 다르다.

인칭·수	격	주격	소유격	목적격	소유대명사
1인칭	단수	I	my	me	mine
	복수	we	our	us	ours
2인칭	단수·복수	you	your	you	yours
3인칭	단수	he	his	him	his
		she	her	her	hers
		it	its	it	–
	복수	they	their	them	theirs

❶ 주격은 '~은, ~이'의 의미로, 문장의 주어 역할을 한다.

I am a baseball fan. 나는 야구 팬이다.

He is in the kitchen. 그는 부엌에 있다.

❷ 소유격은 '~의'의 의미로, 명사 앞에서 명사와의 소유 관계를 나타낸다.

My chair is comfortable. 나의 의자는 편안하다.

Susie likes **her** English teacher. Susie는 그녀의 영어 선생님을 좋아한다.

(Tip) 명사의 소유격은 명사에 's를 붙여서 만들며, -s로 끝나는 복수명사에는 '만 붙인다.

Jack's bicycle Jack의 자전거   **my parents'** house 나의 부모님의 집

❸ 목적격은 '~을, ~에게'의 의미로, 동사나 전치사의 목적어 역할을 한다.

James doesn't **know me**. James는 나를 알지 못한다.

The test is very important **to them**. 그 시험은 그들에게 매우 중요하다.

❹ 소유대명사는 '~의 것'의 의미로, 「소유격 + 명사」를 대신한다.

These socks are **mine**. 이 양말은 나의 것이다.

= These socks are **my socks**. 이 양말은 나의 양말이다.

Your bag is heavy, but **his** is light. 너의 가방은 무겁지만, 그의 것은 가볍다.

= Your bag is heavy, but **his bag** is light. 너의 가방은 무겁지만, 그의 가방은 가볍다.

연습문제 A 다음 문장의 밑줄 친 부분을 인칭대명사로 바꿔 쓰시오.

1 The <u>Earth</u> is round. → _____

2 Linda loves <u>animals</u>. → _____

3 <u>My mother's</u> bag is expensive. → _____

4 <u>You and I</u> are middle school students. → _____

5 <u>The boy's</u> hair is red and curly. → _____

6 Alex gave <u>his girlfriend</u> a flower. → _____

7 <u>Sarah, Minho, and Kevin</u> are playing outside. → _____

8 <u>You and Somi</u> are on my team. → _____

9 <u>The children's</u> smiles are very beautiful. → _____

10 Mark told <u>me</u> the movie's ending. → _____

11 Mr. Clark helped <u>me and my classmates</u> a lot. → _____

연습문제 B 우리말과 같도록 괄호 안의 인칭대명사를 알맞은 형태로 바꿔 빈칸에 쓰시오.

1 (I) ① 나의 신발은 검은색이다. = _____ shoes are black.
　　　 ② 그 검은 신발은 나의 것이다. = The black shoes are _____.

2 (you) ① 이 노트북은 너의 것이다. = This laptop is _____.
　　　 ② 내가 너의 노트북을 빌려도 되니? = Can I borrow _____ laptop?

3 (he) ① 그의 집은 아주 크다. = _____ house is really big.
　　　 ② 저 큰 집은 그의 것이다. = That big house is _____.

4 (we) ① 식탁 위에 있는 피자는 우리의 것이다. = The pizza on the table is _____.
　　　 ② 우리의 피자는 맛있었다. = _____ pizza was delicious.

5 (they) ① 그들의 정원에는 많은 꽃들이 있다. = There are many flowers in _____ garden.
　　　 ② 이 아름다운 정원은 그들의 것이다. = This beautiful garden is _____.

기출 적중문제 ◎

다음 글의 빈칸에 들어갈 알맞은 것은?

Minsu is my best friend. _____ favorite subject is math, and he is really good at it.

① We　　② Us　　③ He
④ His　　⑤ Him

인칭·수·격에 따라 알맞은 인칭대명사를 써요.

1. **재귀대명사는 '~ 자신, ~ 자체'의 의미로, 인칭대명사의 소유격이나 목적격에 -self(단수)/ -selves(복수)를 붙인 형태이다.**

인칭 ＼ 수	단수	복수
1인칭	I - **my**self	we - **our**selves
2인칭	you - **your**self	you - **your**selves
3인칭	he - **him**self / she - **her**self / it - **it**self	they - **them**selves

2. **재귀대명사는 재귀 용법이나 강조 용법으로 쓰인다.**

재귀 용법	동사나 전치사의 목적어가 주어와 같은 대상일 때 목적어로 재귀대명사를 쓴다. 이때 재귀대명사는 생략할 수 없다. **I love myself.** 나는 나 자신을 사랑한다. **She looked at herself in the mirror.** 그녀는 거울에서 그녀 자신을 봤다.
강조 용법	문장의 주어·보어·목적어를 강조하기 위해 강조하는 말 바로 뒤나 문장 맨 뒤에 재귀대명사를 쓴다. 이때 재귀대명사는 생략할 수 있다. **I (myself) made dinner. = I made dinner (myself).** 나는 저녁 식사를 직접 만들었다. **We met the actor (himself).** 우리는 그 배우 본인을 만났다.

연습문제 A 우리말과 같도록 빈칸에 알맞은 재귀대명사를 쓰시오.

1 그녀는 그녀 자신을 잘 안다. = She knows ＿＿＿＿＿＿ well.

2 너는 너 자신을 믿어야 한다. = You should trust ＿＿＿＿＿＿.

3 나는 저 그림을 직접 그렸다. = I drew that picture ＿＿＿＿＿＿.

4 Max는 설거지를 직접 했다. = Max ＿＿＿＿＿＿ washed the dishes.

5 Cindy는 그녀 자신에게 화가 났다. = Cindy is upset at ＿＿＿＿＿＿.

6 그들은 그들 자신을 자랑스러워했다. = They were proud of ＿＿＿＿＿＿.

7 Davis씨 본인이 나에게 전화했다. = Ms. Davis ＿＿＿＿＿＿ called me.

8 우리는 우리 자신을 운이 좋다고 생각했다. = We thought ＿＿＿＿＿＿ lucky.

9 그 뮤지컬 자체는 환상적이었다. = The musical ＿＿＿＿＿＿ was fantastic.

10 나의 부모님은 이 집을 직접 지으셨다. = My parents built this house ＿＿＿＿＿＿.

연습문제 B 밑줄 친 부분을 생략할 수 있으면 O를 쓰고, 생략할 수 없으면 X를 쓰시오.

1 Anna cut <u>herself</u> by accident. → _____

2 They <u>themselves</u> solved the problem. → _____

3 She was talking to <u>herself</u>. → _____

4 The rumor <u>itself</u> is not a big problem. → _____

5 I interviewed the president <u>himself</u>. → _____

6 Help <u>yourself</u> to some cookies. → _____

7 I <u>myself</u> taught my brother English. → _____

8 Jason introduced <u>himself</u> to us. → _____

9 Marie and I cleaned our room <u>ourselves</u>. → _____

10 She calls <u>herself</u> a genius. → _____

11 Harry likes <u>himself</u> in a black suit. → _____

12 I felt proud of <u>myself</u> after I won the contest. → _____

연습문제 C 괄호 안에서 알맞은 것을 고르시오.

1 I like talking about (myself / himself).

2 She saw (herself / itself) in the water.

3 My father baked this cake (him / himself).

4 Rachel taught (us / ourselves) how to swim.

5 The queen (her / herself) visited my city.

6 You should take care of (ourselves / yourself).

7 He (myself / himself) wrote the letter.

8 We enjoyed (ourselves / themselves) at the rock concert.

9 Did you cook this pasta (you / yourself)?

10 Pedro wrote a song about (them / themselves).

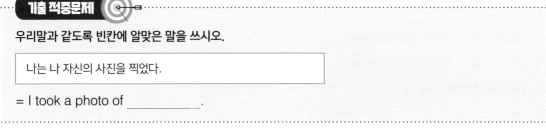

기출 적중문제

우리말과 같도록 빈칸에 알맞은 말을 쓰시오.

나는 나 자신의 사진을 찍었다.

= I took a photo of _____.

1. 지시대명사 this/these/that/those는 특정한 사람이나 사물을 가리킬 때 쓴다.

가까이 있는 사람·사물	단수	this 이 사람, 이것	This is my uncle. 이 사람은 나의 삼촌이다.
	복수	these 이 사람들, 이것들	These are delicious peaches. 이것들은 맛있는 복숭아들이다.
멀리 있는 사람·사물	단수	that 저 사람, 저것	That is not Sara's dog. 저것은 Sara의 개가 아니다.
	복수	those 저 사람들, 저것들	Those are your pants. 저것들은 너의 바지이다.

(Tip) 지시대명사가 있는 의문문에 Yes나 No로 짧게 대답할 때는 주어로 it/they를 쓴다.
Is **that** a new bakery? – Yes, **it** is. 저것은 새 빵집이니? – 응, 그래.
Are **these** your books? – No, **they** aren't. 이것들은 너의 책들이니? – 아니, 그렇지 않아.

2. this/these/that/those는 '이 ~, 저 ~'라는 의미의 지시형용사로 쓰여 명사 앞에서 명사를 꾸밀 수 있다.

This T-shirt looks small for you. 이 티셔츠는 너에게 작아 보인다.
Let's ask **those** students for directions. 저 학생들에게 길을 물어보자.

연습문제 A | 괄호 안에서 알맞은 것을 고르시오.

1 (That / Those) is a basketball.

2 Who is (that / those) kid under the tree?

3 I took (this / these) pictures yesterday.

4 How much are (this / these) gloves?

5 Is (this / these) Katie's house? – No, (it isn't / they aren't).

6 (This / These) is my cousin, Jimmy.

7 Are (that / those) earrings expensive? – Yes, (it is / they are).

8 Can I borrow (this / these) textbooks?

9 What is (that / those) on the wall?

10 (This / These) calendar is last year's.

11 Are (this / these) his sunglasses? – No, (it isn't / they aren't).

12 Take a look at (that / those) tall buildings.

연습문제 B 밑줄 친 부분의 쓰임과 같은 것을 <보기>에서 골라 그 기호를 쓰시오.

<보기> ⓐ This is a nice camera.
        ⓑ Let's feed this cat.

1 This is my family.   [   ]
2 Where did you buy that skirt?   [   ]
3 That is Mina's backpack.   [   ]
4 Those penguins look so active.   [   ]
5 Could you do this for me?   [   ]
6 Are these your sneakers?   [   ]
7 Did you paint those pictures yourself?   [   ]
8 Those are my tennis club members.   [   ]
9 Mr. Martin read his son this poem before bed. [   ]
10 These mufflers are for my grandparents.   [   ]

연습문제 C 우리말과 같도록 괄호 안의 말을 활용하여 빈칸에 쓰시오.

1 저 토끼는 Earl의 것이다. (rabbit)   = _____ _____ belongs to Earl.
2 너는 이 반지를 사기를 원하니? (ring)   = Do you want to buy _____ _____?
3 저 소방관들은 정말 용감했다. (firefighter) = _____ _____ were really brave.
4 너는 이 사진들을 보기를 원하니? (photo)   = Would you like to look at _____ _____?
5 Sandy는 저 사과들을 먹을 것이다. (apple) = Sandy is going to eat _____ _____.
6 나는 이 노래를 듣는 것을 좋아한다. (song)   = I like listening to _____ _____.

기출 적중문제

주어진 문장의 밑줄 친 that과 쓰임이 같은 것을 모두 고르시오.

That is my dog, Toby.

① That's a good idea.
② Let's watch that video.
③ That is my purse.
④ What kind of plant is that?
⑤ Who is that girl?

비인칭 주어 it

정답 p.30

비인칭 주어 it은 날씨·계절·시간·요일·날짜·명암·거리를 나타낼 때 쓰며, '그것'이라고 해석하지 않는다.

날씨	It is warm today.	오늘은 따뜻하다.
계절	It is spring now.	이제 봄이다.
시간	What time is it? – It is 7 o'clock.	몇 시니? – 7시야.
요일	What day is it? – It is Monday.	무슨 요일이니? – 월요일이야.
날짜	What date is it today? – It is January 13.	오늘은 며칠이니? – 1월 13일이야.
명암	It is bright in here.	여기는 밝다.
거리	It is four kilometers to the library.	그 도서관까지 4킬로미터이다.

(Tip) 대명사 it은 특정한 대상을 가리킬 때 쓰며, '그것'이라고 해석한다.
There is **a big house** on the hill. **It** is very beautiful. 언덕 위에 큰 집이 있다. 그것은 매우 아름답다.

연습문제 A 밑줄 친 it의 쓰임과 같은 것을 <보기>에서 골라 그 기호를 쓰시오.

<보기> ⓐ It was hot yesterday.
　　　　ⓑ It is my smartphone.

1 It is summer now. [　　　]

2 It is not his idea. [　　　]

3 It's eight thirty. [　　　]

4 It is snowing heavily. [　　　]

5 Where did you find it? [　　　]

6 It's my birthday today. [　　　]

7 You can buy it in the market. [　　　]

8 It is Saturday. [　　　]

9 It's bright outside. [　　　]

10 It takes only five minutes on foot. [　　　]

11 It's a hard decision to make. [　　　]

12 How far is it from here to your apartment? [　　　]

13 Let's order it right now. [　　　]

14 What a funny story it was! [　　　]

연습문제 B 다음 질문에 대한 대답을 <보기>에서 골라 그 기호를 쓰시오.

<보기>
ⓐ It's Friday.
ⓑ It's about ten miles.
ⓒ It takes 20 minutes.
ⓓ It is 5 o'clock.
ⓔ It is sunny.
ⓕ It's March 9.

1 A: What date is it?   B: _____

2 A: How long does it take to get to school?   B: _____

3 A: What time is it now?   B: _____

4 A: How is the weather today?   B: _____

5 A: What day is it?   B: _____

6 A: How many miles is it from here to the airport?   B: _____

연습문제 C 다음 그림을 보고 빈칸에 알맞은 말을 쓰시오.

1

A: What is the weather like?
B: _____ _____ today.

2

A: What day is it today?
B: _____ _____.

3

A: What season is it in Canada now?
B: _____ _____ there.

기출 적중문제 🎯

다음 중 밑줄 친 it의 쓰임이 나머지 넷과 <u>다른</u> 것은?

① It is my favorite color.
② It is too cold here.
③ It is February 26.
④ It is Saturday.
⑤ It is autumn.

it이 비인칭 주어로 쓰이면 '그것'이라고 해석하지 않고, 대명사로 쓰이면 '그것' 이라고 해석해요.

부정대명사: one

정답 p.30

> **one은 앞에서 언급된 명사와 같은 종류의 불특정한 사람이나 사물을 가리킬 때 쓰며, 복수형은 ones이다.**
>
> Does anyone have **an umbrella**? 누구 우산을 가지고 있니?
>   – Yes, I have **one**. – 응, 내가 가지고 있어.
>   (= an umbrella)
>
> I lost my **glasses**. I have to buy new **ones**. 나는 나의 안경을 잃어버렸다. 나는 새것을 사야 한다.
>   (= glasses)
>
> (Tip) 앞에서 언급된 특정한 대상을 가리킬 때는 it이나 they/them을 쓴다.
>   I bought **a new bag**. I like **it**. 나는 새 가방을 샀다. 나는 그것이 마음에 든다.
>   He made a lot of **cookies**. **They** were tasty. 그는 많은 쿠키들을 만들었다. 그것들은 맛있었다.

연습문제 괄호 안에서 알맞은 것을 고르시오.

1 I didn't bring my pen today. Could you lend me (one / it)?

2 He watched a movie last night. (One / It) was a horror movie.

3 I can't find my tennis racket. I need a new (one / it).

4 Dad gave me his old gloves. (Ones / They) feel very soft.

5 Where is your cell phone? – I put (one / it) on the sofa.

6 I'd like to buy a hat. May I see the brown (one / it) over there?

7 I baked some blueberry cupcakes. Would you like to try (ones / them)?

8 Someone left this coat in the classroom. – (One / It) is not mine.

9 Are you going to borrow that book? – No. I'm going to borrow this (one / it).

10 These shoes don't fit me. Do you have any bigger (ones / them)?

11 Hyemin likes cold drinks, but her sister likes hot (ones / them).

기출 적중문제 🎯

다음 대화의 빈칸에 알맞은 말을 <보기>에서 골라 쓰시오.

<보기>	one	ones	it	them

A: How about buying this white dress?
B: I don't like _____. Can I see the blue
_____?

기출로 적중 POINT 5-2 부정대명사: another, other

정답 p.30

1. another는 '하나 더, 또 다른 하나'라는 의미이다.

This shirt doesn't fit me. Please show me another.
이 셔츠는 나에게 맞지 않아요. 저에게 다른 것을 보여주세요.

(Tip) 「another + 단수명사」는 '또 다른 ~'이라는 의미이다.
   Would you like to see another skirt? 또 다른 치마를 보기를 원하시나요?

2. other는 '(불특정한) 다른 사람들/것들'이라는 의미이며, 주로 복수형인 others로 쓰인다. 「the + other(s)」는 '나머지'라는 의미이다.

You should be kind to others. 너는 다른 사람들에게 친절해야 한다.
There were two oranges. Dave ate one and gave me the other.
두 개의 오렌지가 있었다. Dave가 하나를 먹었고 나에게 나머지 하나를 줬다.

(Tip) 「other + 복수명사」는 '다른 ~'이라는 의미이다.
   I like Mr. Scott, but other students don't like him.
   나는 Scott 선생님을 좋아하지만, 다른 학생들은 그를 좋아하지 않는다.

3. one, another, other(s), some을 써서 여럿 중 일부를 나타낼 수 있다.

one ~, the other -	one ~, another -, the other ···
(둘 중) 하나는 ~, 나머지 하나는 -	(셋 중) 하나는 ~, 다른 하나는 -, 나머지 하나는 ···
There are two cats. One is black, and the other is white. 두 마리의 고양이가 있다. 하나는 검은색이고, 나머지 하나는 흰색이다.	There are three cats. One is black, another is white, and the other is brown. 세 마리의 고양이가 있다. 하나는 검은색이고, 다른 하나는 흰색이고, 나머지 하나는 갈색이다.
some ~, others -	**some ~, the others -**
(여럿 중) 몇몇은 ~, 다른 사람들/것들은 -	(여럿 중) 몇몇은 ~, 나머지 전부는 -
There are lots of cats. Some are black, and others are white. 많은 고양이가 있다. 몇몇은 검은색이고, 다른 것들은 흰색이다.	There are five cats. Some are black, and the others are white. 다섯 마리의 고양이가 있다. 몇몇은 검은색이고, 나머지 전부는 흰색이다.

괄호 안에서 알맞은 것을 고르시오.

1 My laptop is broken. I need to buy (another / other).

2 I finished my cream soup. May I have (another / other) bowl?

3 Richard always makes (another / others) happy.

4 Giant pandas only eat bamboo. They don't eat (another / other) plants.

연습문제 B 다음 그림을 보고 빈칸에 알맞은 말을 <보기>에서 골라 쓰시오.

<보기>	one	another	others	the other	the others	some

1

2

3

4

1 She bought two flowers. _____ is a rose and _____ is a tulip.

2 There are five students in the classroom. _____ are reading books, and _____ are talking.

3 There are many students in the gym. _____ are playing badminton, and _____ are sitting on the floor.

4 I have three friends from different countries. _____ is from China, _____ is from Canada, and _____ is from India.

기출 적중문제 🎯

다음 글의 밑줄 친 우리말과 같도록 문장을 완성하시오.

> There are two dolls in the room. 하나는 피아노 위에 있고, 나머지 하나는 침대 옆에 있다.

= _____ is on the piano, and _____ is next to the bed.

정답 p.31

기출로적중 POINT 5-3 · 부정대명사: each, every, all

부정대명사 each, every, all의 쓰임은 다음과 같다.

		쓰임	예문
each 각각의	단수 취급	each + 단수명사	**Each country has** its own culture. 각각의 나라는 그것의 고유한 문화를 가지고 있다.
every 모든	단수 취급	every + 단수명사	**Every song** on his new album **is** sad. 그의 새 앨범에 있는 모든 노래는 슬프다.
		everything / everybody / everyone	**Everyone looks** excited about the trip. 모든 사람은 그 여행에 대해 신이 나 보인다.
all 모든	복수 취급	all + 복수명사	**All mammals have** fur. 모든 포유류는 털이 있다.
	단수 취급	all + 셀 수 없는 명사	**All information** on this website **is** free. 이 웹사이트에 있는 모든 정보는 무료이다.

연습문제 괄호 안에서 알맞은 것을 고르시오.

1 Every (cloud / clouds) has a silver lining.

2 Each person (has / have) a different voice.

3 I know every (student / students) in my school.

4 All guests (has / have) to wear a suit.

5 Each (ticket / tickets) costs only 15 dollars.

6 Everybody (need / needs) someone to talk to.

7 I dropped the basket and broke all the (egg / eggs).

8 Everything (seem / seems) fine to me.

9 All the furniture in this store (is / are) so luxurious.

10 All the students (is / are) listening carefully to the teacher.

기출 적중문제 ◎

다음 밑줄 친 ⓐ~ⓔ 중 어법상 어색한 것을 찾아 기호를 쓰고 바르게 고쳐 쓰시오.

Every child need love and care.
ⓐ   ⓑ   ⓒ   ⓓ   ⓔ

_____ → _____

A 다음 문장의 밑줄 친 부분을 인칭대명사로 바꿔 쓰시오. (단, 인칭대명사의 격에 주의하시오.)

1 I have a <u>sister</u>. _____ name is Christina.

2 Allen made <u>the sandwiches</u>. _____ were really delicious.

3 <u>Ms. Lee</u> broke her leg. We should help _____.

4 I saw a <u>movie</u> last night. _____ title was *Finding Nemo*.

5 <u>All my new friends</u> are great. I like _____ a lot.

6 <u>Matt and I</u> are free now. _____ can go swimming.

7 <u>My brother</u> can't read this book. It's hard for _____.

8 <u>Mr. Kim's</u> car isn't the red one. _____ car is the black one.

9 <u>Stephen and Jose</u> are brothers. _____ father is a pianist.

B 다음 그림을 보고 빈칸에 알맞은 말을 <보기>에서 한 번씩만 골라 쓰시오.

| <보기> | this | these | that | those |

1 _____ children look so happy.

2 Who is _____ boy over there?

3 What a huge house _____ is!

4 I should buy _____ apples.

C 우리말과 같도록 괄호 안의 말을 활용하여 빈칸에 쓰시오.

1 밖이 쌀쌀하다. (be, chilly)

= _____ _____ _____ outside.

2 눈이 온 후에 모든 것이 아름다워 보인다. (everything, look)

= _____ _____ beautiful after it snows.

3 그녀의 정원에 있는 모든 꽃들은 좋은 냄새가 난다. (all, the flower, smell)

= _____ _____ _____ in her garden _____ good.

4 그곳에 가기 위해 버스로 10분이 걸린다. (take)

= _____ _____ ten minutes by bus to go there.

5 이 방 안은 어둡다. (be, dark)

= _____ _____ _____ in this room.

6 우리 학교에 계신 모든 선생님은 친절하다. (every, teacher, be)

= _____ _____ at our school _____ kind.

D 우리말과 같도록 괄호 안의 말을 알맞게 배열하시오.

1 그들은 두 명의 딸이 있다. 한 명은 선생님이고, 나머지 한 명은 작가이다.

(the other, a writer, is, a teacher, one, is)

= They have two daughters. _____ , and _____ .

2 나는 세 개의 선물을 받았다. 하나는 기타였고, 다른 하나는 가방이었고, 나머지 하나는 책이었다.

(was, the other, a bag, was, another, a book)

= I got three presents. One was a guitar, _____ , and _____ .

3 여섯 명의 아이들이 있다. 몇몇은 음악을 듣고 있고, 나머지 전부는 게임을 하고 있다.

(playing, are, listening, the others, some, are)

= There are six kids. _____ to music, and _____ games.

4 많은 사람들이 병원에 있다. 몇몇은 의사들이고, 다른 사람들은 환자들이다.

(are, others, doctors, some, are, patients)

= Many people are in the hospital. _____ , and _____ .

5 Alice는 두 개의 모자를 샀다. 하나는 노란색이었고, 나머지 하나는 검은색이었다.

(yellow, was, one, was, the other, black)

= Alice bought two caps. _____ , and _____ .

중간·기말고사 실전 문제

[1-2] 다음 글의 빈칸에 알맞은 인칭대명사를 쓰시오.

1

> Look at those big buildings. I designed
> _____ ten years ago.

2

> A girl called you this morning. _____
> name was Jinju.

3 다음 중 밑줄 친 부분이 어법상 바른 것은?

① <u>She's</u> eyes are brown.
② <u>It</u> neck is very long and thin.
③ They're <u>his</u> new sunglasses.
④ <u>We</u> teacher is very strict.
⑤ Tony will bring <u>their</u> here.

4 다음 중 밑줄 친 부분을 인칭대명사로 바르게 바꾸지 못한 것은?

① <u>Ms. Jones</u> is my neighbor. (→ She)
② I fought with <u>my brother</u>. (→ he)
③ Jimin is wearing <u>a scarf</u>. (→ it)
④ They gave <u>the girl</u> a prize. (→ her)
⑤ We can help <u>Mark and Brian</u>. (→ them)

5 다음 글의 빈칸에 알맞은 인칭대명사를 쓰시오.

> I want to introduce my friend. His name
> is Jackson. _____ hometown is
> New York. _____ enjoys reading
> comic books in his free time. I am very
> happy to know _____.

6 다음 대화의 밑줄 친 부분과 바꿔 쓸 수 있는 것은?

> *A*: Whose house is this?
> *B*: You know Mr. and Mrs. Sanders,
> don't you? It's <u>their house</u>.

① his   ② hers   ③ their
④ them   ⑤ theirs

7 다음 두 문장의 의미가 같도록 빈칸에 알맞은 말을 쓰시오.

> Is this your diary?
> = Is this diary _____?

8 다음 빈칸에 들어갈 알맞은 것은?

> Ms. Hill taught history to _____ last
> year.

① his   ② hers   ③ I
④ us   ⑤ their

[9-10] 다음 중 밑줄 친 부분의 쓰임이 나머지 넷과 다른 것을 고르시오.

9

① She is talking with her parents.
② All my classmates like her.
③ Her father is a police officer.
④ She came back from her trip.
⑤ Her dress is really beautiful.

10

① His shoes aren't expensive.
② I can't remember his name.
③ Is this textbook his or yours?
④ Minji and Jinsu are his cousins.
⑤ Is his uniform black or blue?

11 다음 빈칸에 공통으로 들어갈 알맞은 말을 쓰시오.

· _____ is my favorite color.
· _____ is getting bright.

12 다음 빈칸에 공통으로 들어갈 알맞은 것은?

· She saw _____ in a dream.
· My sister wrote the song _____ .

① she ② her ③ hers
④ herself ⑤ herselves

13 다음 대화의 빈칸에 들어갈 말이 순서대로 짝지어진 것은?

A: Whose bag is this? Is it yours, Suji?
B: Yes, it's _____ . Whose bag is that?
A: Do you know Hana? Maybe it's _____ bag.

① yours – she ② yours – hers
③ mine – her ④ mine – hers
⑤ hers – her

14 다음 중 주격 인칭대명사와 재귀대명사가 잘못 짝지어진 것은?

① I – myself ② he – himself
③ it – itselves ④ we – ourselves
⑤ they – themselves

15 다음 중 밑줄 친 부분이 어법상 어색한 것은?

① I made sandwiches for them.
② Did you fix this computer yourself?
③ I should calm myself down.
④ Would you like to come with ourselves?
⑤ Lisa helped us with our project.

16 다음 빈칸에 들어갈 알맞은 것은?

We took many pictures of _____ during the picnic.

① myself ② yourself
③ herself ④ themselves
⑤ ourselves

17 다음 중 밑줄 친 부분을 생략할 수 있는 것끼리 묶인 것은?

> ⓐ She hurt underline herself by mistake.
> ⓑ The service underline itself was great.
> ⓒ We underline ourselves made this pasta.
> ⓓ They introduced underline themselves to us.
> ⓔ Isaac created the game underline himself.

① ⓐ, ⓑ   ② ⓐ, ⓒ   ③ ⓑ, ⓓ
④ ⓑ, ⓒ, ⓔ   ⑤ ⓒ, ⓓ, ⓔ

18 다음 글의 밑줄 친 우리말과 같도록 괄호 안의 말을 활용하여 문장을 완성하시오.

> I have two favorite subjects. 하나는 수학이고, 나머지 하나는 역사이다. (math, history)

= _____, and _____ .

19 다음 중 밑줄 친 부분이 어법상 바른 것은?

① Are that your pants?
② Please keep these rule in mind.
③ Is these red pencil hers?
④ Did you buy those eggs yesterday?
⑤ Those is a really long bridge.

20 우리말과 같도록 괄호 안의 말을 활용하여 문장을 완성하시오.

> 내일은 추울 것이다. (will, cold)

= _____ tomorrow.

21 다음 질문에 대한 대답으로 가장 알맞은 것은?

> A: Are those cheetahs?
> B: _____ Those are leopards.

① Yes, it is.   ② Yes, they are.
③ No, it isn't.   ④ No, they aren't.
⑤ No, those aren't.

22 다음 대화의 밑줄 친 this와 쓰임이 같은 것을 모두 고르시오.

> A: Oh, look at this kitten.
> B: How small she is!

① What kind of flower is this?
② This is Joe's bicycle.
③ Is this umbrella yours?
④ This is my brother, John.
⑤ This watch is not mine.

23 주어진 문장의 밑줄 친 it과 쓰임이 다른 것은?

> It is winter in Korea.

① It tastes too spicy.
② It's going to be rainy.
③ What day is it today?
④ It's about five miles.
⑤ It is October 30.

24 다음 밑줄 친 it의 쓰임이 같은 것끼리 묶인 것은?

ⓐ Would you bring it to me?
ⓑ It takes an hour by bus.
ⓒ It's 5 o'clock right now.
ⓓ It is a little dark in this room.
ⓔ It's very rare and expensive.

① ⓐ, ⓑ   ② ⓐ, ⓓ   ③ ⓑ, ⓔ
④ ⓑ, ⓒ, ⓓ   ⑤ ⓒ, ⓓ, ⓔ

25 다음 글의 밑줄 친 우리말과 같도록 빈칸에 알맞은 말을 쓰시오.

I'll give you and your brother these two toys. 그 인형은 너의 것이고, 그 로봇은 그의 것이다.

= The doll is _____, and the robot is _____.

26 다음 문장의 밑줄 친 부분을 purses로 바꿀 때 빈칸에 알맞은 말을 쓰시오.

Is that your new purse?
→ _____ _____ your new purses?

27 괄호 안의 말을 활용하여 질문에 대한 대답을 완성하시오.

(1)
A: What season is it in Italy? (spring)
B: _____ _____
_____.

(2)
A: What day was it yesterday?
(Thursday)
B: _____ _____
_____.

28 다음 대화의 밑줄 친 ⓐ~ⓔ에 대한 설명이 잘못된 것을 모두 고르시오.

A: ⓐIt's too hot today!
B: I know. I'm sweating. ⓑIt is summer now.
A: Take this fan. ⓒIt will keep you cool.
B: But, don't you need ⓓit?
A: I have another one. You can use ⓔit.
B: Thanks!

① ⓐ는 날씨를 나타내는 비인칭 주어이다.
② ⓑ는 계절을 나타내는 비인칭 주어이다.
③ ⓒ와 ⓓ는 '그것'이라고 해석한다.
④ ⓐ와 ⓔ는 '그것'이라고 해석하지 않는다.
⑤ ⓒ와 ⓔ는 'summer'를 가리키는 대명사이다.

29 다음 빈칸에 들어갈 말이 나머지 넷과 다른 것은?

① This shirt doesn't fit. Let's find a different _____.
② I lost my pen. I will buy a new _____.
③ I don't have an eraser. Can you please lend me _____?
④ Don't throw away the paper. You can reuse _____.
⑤ My bed is too small for me. I would like a bigger _____.

30 다음 대화의 빈칸에 들어갈 알맞은 것은?

A: These muffins smell delicious.
B: I baked _____. Would you like to try some?

① it   ② them   ③ one
④ ones   ⑤ that

31 우리말과 같도록 주어진 <조건>에 맞게 문장을 완성하시오.

그는 그 자신을 예술가라고 부른다.

<조건>　call, an artist를 활용하시오.

= He _____.

32 다음 글의 빈칸에 들어갈 알맞은 것은?

Dora has three dogs. One is big and black. Another is white and fluffy. _____ is small and brown.

① One
② Another
③ Other
④ The other
⑤ Others

33 다음 글의 빈칸에 들어갈 말이 순서대로 짝지어진 것은?

Where do dolphins live? _____ dolphins live in the sea, and _____ live in rivers. River dolphins are rare, but they are real.

① One – other
② One – others
③ Some – another
④ Another – other
⑤ Some – others

34 다음 그림을 보고 빈칸에 알맞은 부정대명사를 넣어 문장을 완성하시오.

There are many people at the party.
_____ are singing, and
_____ are dancing.

35 다음 빈칸에 공통으로 들어갈 알맞은 것은?

· Can I ask you _____ question?
· This blouse does not fit me. Please show me _____.

① others
② another
③ other
④ these
⑤ them

36 다음 빈칸에 들어갈 알맞은 것은?

Everyone on the street _____ the Christmas tree.

① look at
② is looking at
③ be looking at
④ are looking at
⑤ were looking at

37 다음 (A)~(C)에 들어갈 말이 바르게 짝지어진 것은?

> · Every ____(A)____ is studying hard.
> · All ____(B)____ get a free gift at this store.
> · Each room ____(C)____ a great view of the ocean.

	(A)	(B)	(C)
①	student	customer	has
②	students	customers	has
③	student	customers	has
④	students	customers	have
⑤	student	customer	have

38 우리말과 같도록 괄호 안의 말을 활용하여 빈칸에 쓰시오.

> 그 밴드의 모든 가수는 좋은 목소리를 가지고 있다.
> (singer, have)

= Every _____ in the band _____ a good voice.

39 다음 밑줄 친 ⓐ~ⓔ 중 어법상 어색한 것을 찾아 기호를 쓰고 바르게 고쳐 쓰시오.

> Each person have a different look and
> ⓐ   ⓑ   ⓒ   ⓓ   ⓔ
> personality.

_____ → _____

40 다음 빈칸에 알맞은 말을 <보기>에서 한 번씩만 골라 그 기호를 쓰시오.

> <보기> ⓐ one   ⓑ ones
>   ⓒ another   ⓓ the other
>   ⓔ the others   ⓕ some

(1) Victoria bought eleven red roses and three white _____.

(2) I have three cousins. _____ is 5 years old, _____ is 13 years old, and _____ is 19 years old.

(3) There are ten members in the book club. _____ wear glasses, and _____ don't.

41 다음 중 어법상 바른 것의 개수는?

> ⓐ Each necklaces costs $100.
> ⓑ All experience are helpful.
> ⓒ Everyone needs friends.
> ⓓ All players have to follow the rules.
> ⓔ Every moment with you are fun.

① 1개   ② 2개   ③ 3개
④ 4개   ⑤ 5개

CHAPTER 11
형용사

a **delicious** pizza 맛있는 피자

Pizza is **delicious**. 피자는 맛있다.

그냥 '피자'라고 말하는 것보다 '맛있는 피자' 또는 '피자는 맛있다.'라고 말하면 어떤 피자인지 더 자세하게 알 수 있어요. 이렇게 사람이나 사물의 모양, 상태 등을 설명해주는 것을 **형용사**라고 해요. 형용사는 크기, 색깔, 모양, 감정, 상태, 날씨, 숫자 등을 나타낼 수 있어요.

기출로 적중 POINT

내신 100점 적중!
기출 출제율

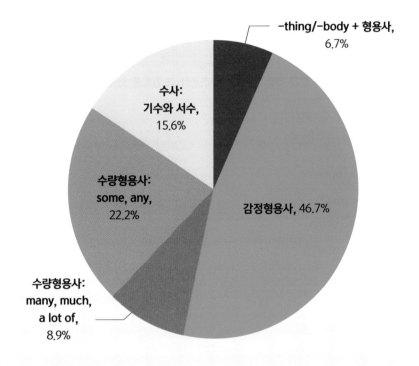

-thing/-body + 형용사,
6.7%

수사:
기수와 서수,
15.6%

수량형용사:
some, any,
22.2%

감정형용사, 46.7%

수량형용사:
many, much,
a lot of,
8.9%

TOP 1 **감정형용사 (46.7%)**
감정형용사의 의미에 따라 알맞은 형태를 쓰는 문제가 자주 출제된다.

TOP 2 **수량형용사: some, any (22.2%)**
수량형용사 some, any의 의미와 쓰임을 묻는 문제가 자주 출제된다.

TOP 3 **수사: 기수와 서수 (15.6%)**
기수와 서수를 영어로 나타내는 문제가 자주 출제된다.

형용사의 용법

정답 p.33

1. 한정적 용법: 형용사는 주로 명사 앞에서 명사를 꾸민다.

There is a **big box**. 큰 상자가 있다.

They are **famous actors**. 그들은 유명한 배우들이다.

2. 서술적 용법: 형용사는 보어로 쓰여 주어나 목적어를 보충 설명한다.

주격 보어   **The necklace is beautiful.** 그 목걸이는 아름답다.

목적격 보어   **Sally keeps her room warm.** Sally는 그녀의 방을 따뜻하게 유지한다.

연습문제   밑줄 친 형용사의 쓰임과 같은 것을 <보기>에서 골라 그 기호를 쓰시오.

> **<보기>**   ⓐ A dog has <u>good</u> eyesight.
>   ⓑ These carrots are <u>fresh</u>.

1   The classroom was <u>empty</u>.   [   ]

2   This is an <u>expensive</u> watch.   [   ]

3   Olivia is wearing a <u>red</u> dress.   [   ]

4   The sky was <u>clear</u> yesterday.   [   ]

5   We visited a <u>huge</u> palace.   [   ]

6   The book made her <u>sleepy</u>.   [   ]

7   We are very <u>hungry</u> now.   [   ]

8   I hope to buy some <u>fancy</u> shoes.   [   ]

9   That cat's tail is really <u>long</u>.   [   ]

10   My father told me some <u>good</u> news.   [   ]

11   Henry made his friends <u>angry</u>.   [   ]

12   Mom's tomato soup smells <u>delicious</u>.   [   ]

13   Are these <u>round</u> glasses yours?   [   ]

14   I want to buy the <u>wooden</u> table.   [   ]

15   I gave water to the <u>thirsty</u> dog.   [   ]

16   Mina's backpack was too <u>heavy</u>.   [   ]

기출로적중 POINT 2 형용사의 어순

정답 p.33

두 개 이상의 형용사를 함께 쓸 때는 주로 다음과 같은 순서로 쓴다.

판단		길이, 크기, 형태		나이, 오래된 정도		색깔, 재료
beautiful, great, useful 등	→	long, tall, small, round 등	→	young, old, new 등	→	blue, red, glass, wooden 등

Jinho is a **tall young** man. 진호는 키가 크고 젊은 남자이다.
The house has **round wooden** windows. 그 집은 둥글고 나무로 된 창문들을 가지고 있다.
Maria has **beautiful long brown** hair. Maria는 아름답고 긴 갈색 머리를 가지고 있다.
He drives a **small new blue** car. 그는 작고 새로운 파란 차를 운전한다.

연습문제 다음 그림을 보고 괄호 안의 말을 알맞게 배열하시오.

1

2

3

4

5

6

1 George is eating a _____. (apple, red, big)

2 This is a _____. (plastic, chair, square)

3 Kate has a _____. (cat, three-year-old, cute)

4 There is a _____. (brick, castle, old, huge)

5 My father made me a _____. (wooden, doll, small)

6 I looked at the _____. (round, moon, white, wonderful)

-thing/-body + 형용사

정답 p.33

> **-thing이나 -body로 끝나는 대명사를 꾸밀 때는 형용사가 대명사 뒤에 온다.**
>
> He wants **something** sweet. 그는 달콤한 무언가를 원한다.
> The toy store has **nothing** new. 그 장난감 가게는 새로운 것이 아무것도 없다.
> Let's ask **somebody** clever. 똑똑한 누군가에게 물어보자.
> Do you know **anybody** strong? 너는 힘센 누군가를 알고 있니?
>
> (Tip) 명사 thing(것, 물건)을 꾸밀 때는 형용사가 명사 앞에 온다.
> Jake can lift heavy **things**. Jake는 무거운 것들을 들 수 있다.

연습문제 괄호 안에서 알맞은 것을 고르시오.

1 Paul saw (nobody famous / famous nobody) there.

2 How about (something spicy / spicy something) for dinner?

3 (Somebody rude / Rude somebody) yelled at me on the bus.

4 Angela did (things great / great things) in her life.

5 The shopping mall had (nice nothing / nothing nice).

6 Do you have (anything cold / cold anything) to drink?

7 Magic is a (thing mysterious / mysterious thing).

8 Can you find me (pink something / something pink)?

9 It was a (thing difficult / difficult thing) to do.

10 I didn't notice (strange anything / anything strange) about the photo.

11 Did (something good / good something) happen to you today?

12 There isn't (anything useful / useful anything) in the box.

13 Jihye and I think it is (serious nothing / nothing serious).

14 We can't find (happy anybody / anybody happy) about the schedule change.

기출 적중문제 🎯

다음 문장에서 어법상 <u>어색한</u> 부분을 찾아 쓰고 바르게 고쳐 쓰시오.

> There was fun nothing on TV, so my friends and
> I went outside.

_____ → _____

> -thing으로 끝나는
> 대명사는 형용사가
> 뒤에서 꾸며줘요.

기출로 작중 POINT 4 감정형용사

정답 p.33

-ing나 -ed로 끝나는 형용사로 감정을 나타낼 수 있다.

V-ing(~한 감정을 일으키는)		V-ed(~한 감정을 느끼는)	
surprising	놀라게 하는	surprised	놀란
amazing	놀라게 하는	amazed	놀란
worrying	걱정하게 하는	worried	걱정하는
interesting	흥미롭게 하는	interested	흥미로워하는
boring	지루하게 하는	bored	지루해하는
exciting	신이 나게 하는	excited	신이 난
tiring	피곤하게 하는	tired	피곤해하는
moving	감동하게 하는	moved	감동한
shocking	충격을 주는	shocked	충격을 받은
annoying	짜증나게 하는	annoyed	짜증이 난
confusing	혼란스럽게 하는	confused	혼란스러워하는
disappointing	실망스럽게 하는	disappointed	실망스러워하는

He heard an **interesting** story. 그는 흥미로운 이야기를 들었다.
He was **interested** in the story. 그는 그 이야기에 흥미로워했다.

The TV show is **boring**. 그 TV 쇼는 지루하다.
I am **bored** with the TV show. 나는 그 TV 쇼에 지루해한다.

연습문제 A 다음 그림을 보고 괄호 안에서 알맞은 감정형용사를 골라 빈칸에 쓰시오.

1

(surprising / surprised)
① The magic show was _____.
② Jisu was _____.

2

(exciting / excited)
① The basketball game is _____.
② People are _____.

3

(amazing / amazed)

① The painting is _____.

② Minho is _____.

4

(shocking / shocked)

① Everyone was _____.

② The news was _____.

5

(boring / bored)

① The students are _____.

② The class is very _____.

6

(disappointing / disappointed)

① The pizza is _____.

② The kids are _____.

연습문제 B 괄호 안에서 알맞은 것을 고르시오.

1 What a (boring / bored) book this is!

2 I gave some water to the (tiring / tired) players.

3 Matthew was (confusing / confused) by the math class.

4 Teenagers aren't usually (interesting / interested) in politics.

5 People were (moving / moved) because of the movie's sad ending.

6 We watched an (interesting / interested) documentary about aliens.

7 He was (annoying / annoyed) with himself for losing the race.

8 They looked very (surprising / surprised) when the result came out.

기출 적중문제

괄호 안의 말을 활용하여 다음 글의 빈칸에 알맞은 말을 쓰시오.

There was a lot of water on the floor of the restaurant. The manager asked, "Oh, what happened to the floor?" He was _____. (surprise)

감정을 일으키면 V-ing, 감정을 느끼면 V-ed 형태의 감정형용사를 써요.

기출로 적중 POINT 5-1   수사: 기수와 서수

정답 p.33

1. 기수는 개수를 말할 때 쓰고, 서수는 순서를 말할 때 쓴다.

기수		서수		기수		서수	
1	one	1st	first	12	twelve	12th	twelfth
2	two	2nd	second	20	twenty	20th	twentieth
3	three	3rd	third	30	thirty	30th	thirtieth
4	four	4th	fourth	50	fifty	50th	fiftieth
5	five	5th	fifth	51	fifty-one	51st	fifty-first
6	six	6th	sixth	52	fifty-two	52nd	fifty-second
7	seven	7th	seventh	53	fifty-three	53rd	fifty-third
8	eight	8th	eighth	90	ninety	90th	ninetieth
9	nine	9th	ninth	100	a[one] hundred	100th	one hundredth
10	ten	10th	tenth	1,000	a[one] thousand	1,000th	one thousandth

Ms. Brown has three sons. Brown씨는 세 명의 아들이 있다.

Her third son is a barista. 그녀의 세 번째 아들은 바리스타이다.

(Tip) 100,000(10만)과 1,000,000(100만)은 기수로 다음과 같이 쓴다.

a[one] hundred thousand 100,000(10만)   a[one] million 1,000,000(100만)

2. 「hundreds/thousands/millions + of + 복수명사」는 막연하게 큰 숫자를 나타낸다.

Emma spent hundreds of dollars on her new laptop.
Emma는 그녀의 새 노트북에 수백 달러를 썼다.

I have thousands of ideas. 나는 수천 개의 아이디어가 있다.

There are millions of roses in the garden. 그 정원에는 수백만 송이의 장미가 있다.

(Tip) 정해진 큰 숫자를 나타낼 때는 hundred/thousand/million에 -s를 붙이지 않는다.

There are five hundred guests in this hotel. 이 호텔에는 500명의 투숙객들이 있다.

연습문제 A   다음 기수는 서수로, 서수는 기수로 바꿔 쓰시오. (단, 영어로 쓰시오.)

1 second   → _____

2 sixtieth   → _____

3 forty   → _____

4 twelve   → _____

5 nine   → _____

6 fifth   → _____

7 fifteen → _____ **8** one → _____

9 thirteenth → _____ **10** sixty-sixth → _____

11 forty-second → _____ **12** twenty-two → _____

13 thirty-three → _____ **14** one hundredth → _____

연습문제 **B** 우리말과 같도록 괄호 안의 말을 활용하여 문장을 완성하시오. (단, 숫자는 영어로 쓰시오.)

1 나는 세 개의 나라로 여행을 갈 것이다. 세 번째 나라는 스페인일 것이다. (country)

= I'm going on a trip to _____. The _____ will be Spain.

2 나는 일곱 개의 초가 필요하다. 오늘은 나의 여동생의 일곱 번째 생일이다. (candle, birthday)

= I need _____. Today is my sister's _____.

3 일 년에는 열두 개의 달이 있다. 열두 번째 달은 12월이다. (month)

= A year has _____. The _____ is December.

4 우리는 방문객들을 위해 스물 한 개의 선물을 준비했다. 스물 한 번째 방문객은 특별상도 받았다. (present, visitor)

= We prepared _____ for visitors. The _____ got the special prize too.

연습문제 **C** 우리말과 같도록 문장을 완성하시오. (단, 숫자는 영어로 쓰시오.)

1 그 식당은 100개의 유리잔을 주문했다.

= The restaurant ordered _____ glasses.

2 우리는 우리의 집을 고치는 데 수천 달러를 썼다.

= We spent _____ dollars fixing our house.

3 우리는 어제 하늘에서 수백 개의 별을 볼 수 있었다.

= We could see _____ stars in the sky yesterday.

4 뉴욕에서 로스앤젤레스까지는 거의 3,000마일이다.

= It is almost _____ miles from New York to Los Angeles.

기출 적중문제

우리말과 같도록 빈칸에 알맞은 말을 쓰시오.

나의 사무실은 아홉 번째 층에 있다.

= My office is on the _____ floor.

수사: 정수, 소수, 분수

정답 p.33

1. **정수는 세 자리씩 끊어서 기수로 읽는다.**

   651 → six hundred (and) fifty-one

   4,515 → four thousand, five hundred (and) fifteen

   8,912,345 → eight million, nine hundred (and) twelve thousand, three hundred (and) forty-five

2. **소수점은 point라고 읽고, 소수점 뒤는 한 자리씩 기수로 읽는다. 소수점 앞이 0인 경우 zero를 생략할 수 있다.**

   0.14 → (zero) point one four

   16.032 → sixteen point zero three two

3. **분수는 분자를 먼저 기수로 읽고, 다음으로 분모를 서수로 읽는다. 단, 분자가 2 이상일 때는 분모에 -s를 붙인다.**

   $\frac{1}{3}$ → one-third[a third] $\frac{3}{5}$ → three-fifths $\frac{5}{7}$ → five-sevenths

   $\frac{1}{2}$ → one-half[a half] $\frac{1}{4}$ → one-quarter[a quarter] 또는 one-fourth[a fourth]

   $4\frac{2}{3}$ → four and two-thirds $2\frac{11}{12}$ → two and eleven-twelfths

---

연습문제 | 다음 숫자를 영어로 쓰시오.

1 0.21 → _____

2 317 → _____

3 9,654 → _____

4 93.37 → _____

5 24,205 → _____

6 50,340,829 → _____

7 2.968 → _____

8 $\frac{8}{15}$ → _____

9 $3\frac{1}{2}$ → _____

10 $\frac{3}{4}$ → _____

11 $5\frac{4}{7}$ → _____

1. **시각은 시간과 분을 끊어서 순서대로 읽는다.**

   1:05 → one-o-five   2:23 → two twenty-three
   3:15 → three fifteen   5:30 → five thirty
   7:45 → seven forty-five   9:56 → nine fifty-six
   11:00 → eleven (o'clock) → o'clock은 정각인 경우에만 쓴다.

2. **시각을 읽을 때는 '~을 지나'라는 의미의 after/past나, '~ 전에'라는 의미의 to를 쓸 수 있다. 이때 15분과 30분은 각각 (a) quarter와 half를 주로 쓴다.**

   1:05 → five after[past] one   2:10 → ten after[past] two
   3:15 → (a) quarter after[past] three   5:30 → half after[past] five
   7:45 → (a) quarter to eight   10:50 → ten to eleven

연습문제 A 다음 시각을 영어로 쓰시오. (단, after, past, to는 쓰지 마시오.)

1 6시 23분 → _____ **2** 7시 35분 → _____

3 8시 15분 → _____ **4** 12시 03분 → _____

5 10시 52분 → _____ **6** 3시 00분 → _____

연습문제 B 다음 그림을 보고 괄호 안의 말을 활용하여 시각을 영어로 쓰시오.

1

2

3

_____ (after)   _____ (past)   _____ (to)

4

5

6

_____ (to)   _____ (after) _____ (past)

수사: 연도와 날짜

정답 p.34

1. 연도는 주로 두 자리씩 끊어 읽는다. 단, 2000년 이상은 끊어 읽지 않기도 한다.

1632년 → sixteen thirty-two

2005년 → two thousand (and) five

2012년 → two thousand (and) twelve 또는 twenty twelve

> (Tip) 연대는 연도에 -(e)s를 붙여 읽는다.
>
> 1900년대 → the nineteen hundreds 또는 1900s
>
> 1560년대 → the fifteen sixties 또는 1560s

2. 날짜는 서수로 읽는다.

5월 11일 → May (the) eleventh 또는 the eleventh of May

3. 연도와 날짜를 함께 읽을 때는 월과 일을 먼저 읽고, 다음으로 연도를 읽는다.

1989년 6월 29일 → June (the) twenty-ninth, nineteen eighty-nine

또는 the twenty-ninth of June, nineteen eighty-nine

연습문제 다음 연도와 날짜를 영어로 쓰시오.

1 1715년 → _____

2 8월 9일 → _____

3 1월 3일 → _____

4 2001년 → _____

5 1378년 → _____

6 2017년 → _____

7 10월 15일 → _____

8 12월 27일 → _____

9 2002년 6월 13일 → _____

10 1930년대 → _____

11 1842년 7월 31일 → _____

12 1700년대 → _____

13 2026년 3월 20일 → _____

수량형용사: many, much, a lot of

정답 p.34

many/much/a lot of는 모두 '많은'이라는 의미이다. many는 셀 수 있는 명사와 함께 쓰고, much는 셀 수 없는 명사와 함께 쓴다. a lot of는 셀 수 있는 명사, 셀 수 없는 명사 모두와 함께 쓸 수 있다.

many (수가) 많은	+ 셀 수 있는 명사의 복수형	**Many children** enjoy computer games. 많은 아이들은 컴퓨터 게임을 즐긴다.
much (양이) 많은	+ 셀 수 없는 명사	Do you have **much homework** to do? 너는 해야 할 많은 숙제가 있니?
a lot of = lots of (수·양이) 많은	+ 셀 수 있는 명사의 복수형/ 셀 수 없는 명사	He planted **a lot of flowers**. 그는 많은 꽃들을 심었다. There is **lots of sand** in her shoes. 그녀의 신발 안에 많은 모래가 있다.

연습문제 A 괄호 안에서 알맞은 것을 고르시오.

1 An octopus has (many / much) legs.

2 There isn't (many / much) milk in the bottle.

3 Don't drink too (many / much) water at night.

4 How (many / much) cans of paint do we need?

연습문제 B 다음 밑줄 친 부분을 many나 much로 바꿔 쓰시오.

1 There are <u>a lot of</u> plants in the garden. → _____

2 Amanda doesn't have <u>a lot of</u> interest in chess. → _____

3 You can see <u>lots of</u> historic buildings in this town. → _____

4 The chef doesn't need <u>a lot of</u> butter to make this pasta. → _____

기출 적중문제 🎯

다음 빈칸에 들어갈 말로 <u>어색한</u> 것을 <u>모두</u> 고르시오.

> _____ students like going on picnics.

① Many ② A lot of ③ Much
④ Lots of ⑤ Lot of

셀 수 있는 명사인지 셀 수 없는 명사인지에 따라 알맞은 수량형용사를 사용해요.

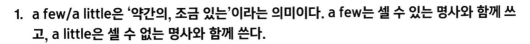

POINT 6-2 수량형용사: (a) few, (a) little

정답 p.34

1. **a few/a little은 '약간의, 조금 있는'이라는 의미이다. a few는 셀 수 있는 명사와 함께 쓰고, a little은 셀 수 없는 명사와 함께 쓴다.**

a few + 셀 수 있는 명사의 복수형	a little + 셀 수 없는 명사

There are a few **cookies** on the plate. 접시 위에 약간의 쿠키가 있다.	There is a little **milk** in the bottle. 병 안에 약간의 우유가 있다.

2. **few/little은 '거의 없는'이라는 의미이다. few는 셀 수 있는 명사와 함께 쓰고, little은 셀 수 없는 명사와 함께 쓴다.**

few + 셀 수 있는 명사의 복수형	little + 셀 수 없는 명사

There are few **cookies** on the plate. 접시 위에 쿠키가 거의 없다.	There is little **milk** in the bottle. 병 안에 우유가 거의 없다.

연습문제 A 괄호 안에서 알맞은 것을 고르시오.

1 There is still (a few / a little) tea in the pot.

2 (A few / A little) boys are waiting at the bus stop.

3 Mr. Kim took (few / little) pictures during summer vacation.

4 Sarah gave (a few / a little) bread to the monkey.

5 There is (few / little) apple juice in my glass.

6 It is (a few / a little) minutes before midnight.

7 Nick drank (a few / a little) water today.

8 Sue bought (a few / a little) fashion magazines.

9 We had (few / little) snow this year.

10 There were (few / little) children in the playground.

연습문제 B 우리말과 같도록 <보기>의 말과 괄호 안의 명사를 활용하여 문장을 완성하시오.

<보기> a few   a little   few   little

1 그 아이들은 하늘에서 약간의 별들을 봤다. (star)

= The kids saw _____ in the sky.

2 나는 시험을 위해 공부할 시간이 거의 없다. (time)

= I have _____ to study for the exam.

3 민하는 그녀의 커피에 약간의 설탕을 넣었다. (sugar)

= Minha put _____ in her coffee.

4 일요일 아침에는 버스에 학생들이 거의 없었다. (student)

= There were _____ on the bus on Sunday morning.

5 너는 이 요리를 만들기 위해 약간의 버터가 필요할 것이다. (butter)

= You'll need _____ to make this dish.

6 나의 팬케이크에는 시럽이 거의 없다. (syrup)

= There is _____ on my pancake.

7 나의 내성적인 남동생은 친구들이 거의 없다. (friend)

= My shy brother has _____.

8 서울에서 대구까지 가는 것은 약간의 시간이 걸린다. (hour)

= It takes _____ to go to Daegu from Seoul.

기출 적중문제

다음 글의 빈칸에 들어갈 말이 순서대로 짝지어진 것은?

Sunmi wanted to drink _____ soda, so she went to a supermarket. However, there were _____ coins in her purse. She had to come home without anything.

① a little – little   ② a few – few

③ a little – few   ④ a few – little

⑤ little – a little

POINT 6-3 수량형용사: some, any

정답 p.34

some/any는 '약간의, 조금의'라는 의미로, 셀 수 있는 명사, 셀 수 없는 명사 모두와 함께 쓸 수 있다.

❶ some은 주로 긍정문에 쓴다.

Peter will buy some notebooks. Peter는 약간의 공책을 살 것이다.
My uncle is drinking some coffee. 나의 삼촌은 약간의 커피를 마시고 계신다.

❷ any는 주로 부정문과 의문문에 쓴다.

I didn't have any water today. 나는 오늘 약간의 물도 마시지 않았다.
Do you need any boxes? 너는 약간의 상자들이 필요하니?

(Tip) 권유나 요청을 나타내는 의문문에는 some을 쓴다.

Would you like some snacks? 너는 약간의 간식을 원하니?
Can you lend me some money? 나에게 약간의 돈을 빌려줄 수 있니?

연습문제 괄호 안에서 알맞은 것을 고르시오.

1 I spilled (some / any) milk on the keyboard.

2 Do you have (some / any) brothers or sisters?

3 The farmer planted (some / any) rice and corn.

4 Sammy doesn't have (some / any) classes today.

5 Could you get me (some / any) chicken salad?

6 My grandmother showed me (some / any) old pictures.

7 Would you like to drink (some / any) tea?

8 There isn't (some / any) homework to do today.

기출 적중문제

다음 우리말을 알맞게 영작한 것은?

나는 오늘 약간의 시간도 없다.

① I have some time today.
② I don't have some time today.
③ I have any time today.
④ I don't have any time today.
⑤ I don't have no time today.

some은 주로 긍정문, any는 주로 부정문과 의문문에 써요.

서술형 대비 문제

A 밑줄 친 부분이 어법상 맞으면 O를 쓰고, 틀리면 바르게 고쳐 쓰시오.

1 I gave the <u>tired</u> horse some water. → _____

2 Sumin told me <u>nothing bad</u> about you. → _____

3 Is there <u>new anybody</u> in your class? → _____

4 There are almost two <u>hundreds</u> photos in my phone. → _____

5 John told me a <u>shocked</u> story about his friend. → _____

6 The winner got five <u>million</u> dollars. → _____

7 We couldn't find anything <u>excited</u> in the theme park. → _____

8 Lots of students are <u>interesting</u> in the book club. → _____

9 I want to talk about <u>important something</u>. → _____

10 There were seven <u>thousands</u> people at the concert. → _____

B 괄호 안의 명사와 many 또는 much를 활용하여 문장을 완성하시오.

1 Don't put too _____ in the soup. (salt)

2 I have _____ to ask. (question)

3 We didn't have _____ last summer. (rain)

4 _____ are interested in sports. (child)

5 How _____ do you want? (coffee)

6 There isn't _____ in this room. (furniture)

7 She has _____ in Busan. (good friend)

8 I didn't get _____ last night. (sleep)

9 Are there _____ about flowers in this store? (book)

10 You can see _____ on my farm. (sheep)

11 There are _____ along the beach. (nice restaurant)

ⓒ 우리말과 같도록 빈칸에 알맞은 말을 <보기>에서 골라 쓰시오.

> <보기>   many   much   a few   a little   few   little

1 내가 버스를 탈 약간의 돈을 빌려도 되니?

= Can I borrow _____ money to take the bus?

2 어제는 하늘에 구름들이 거의 없었다.

= There were _____ clouds in the sky yesterday.

3 관광객들은 이 지역에 대한 정보가 거의 없다.

= Tourists have _____ information about this area.

4 많은 팬들은 그의 새 앨범을 기다리고 있다.

= _____ fans are waiting for his new album.

5 그들은 대구로 가는 기차에서 약간의 좌석들을 발견했다.

= They found _____ seats on the train to Daegu.

6 Sophie는 요즘 많은 운동을 하지 않는다.

= Sophie doesn't do _____ exercise these days.

ⓓ 다음은 유라의 영국 여행 일정표이다. 빈칸에 알맞은 날짜를 영어로 쓰시오. (단, ⓐ에는 연도를 포함하시오.)

2016년				
7월 29일	7월 30일	7월 31일	8월 1일	8월 2일
런던으로 출발	런던 도착	Sam 만나기	뮤지컬 '라이온 킹' 보기	한국 도착
	해리포터 스튜디오 가기	Sam과 타워 브리지 가기	한국으로 출발	

Yura left for London on ⓐ _____
_____. She arrived the next day, on ⓑ _____. On her
first day in London, she went to the Harry Potter Studio. On ⓒ _____
_____, she met her friend, Sam. They went to the Tower Bridge together. On ⓓ _____
_____, she saw the musical *The Lion King*. Later that day, she took a flight and
arrived in Korea on ⓔ _____.

중간·기말고사 실전 문제

1 다음 빈칸에 들어갈 말로 <u>어색한</u> 것은?

Are there _____ schools in your town?

① much　　　② many　　　③ any
④ a few　　　⑤ a lot of

[2-3] 다음 그림을 보고 질문에 대한 대답을 완성하시오. (단, 숫자는 영어로 쓰시오.)

2

A: What time is it now?
B: It's _____.

3

A: What date is it today?
B: It's _____.

4 우리말과 같도록 괄호 안의 말을 알맞게 배열하시오.

오늘 밤에 재미있는 무언가를 하자. (do, tonight, something, let's, fun)

= _____

[5-6] 괄호 안의 말을 배열할 때 두 번째에 오는 것을 쓰시오.

5

Hazel is wearing a _____.
(long, jacket, nice, purple)

→ _____

6

Pour the milk in this _____.
(cup, round, glass, new)

→ _____

7 다음 문장과 의미가 같은 것은?

It's five forty-five.

① It's a quarter past five.
② It's a quarter to six.
③ It's a quarter past six.
④ It's a half to six.
⑤ It's a half past five.

8 다음 (A)~(C)에 들어갈 말이 바르게 짝지어진 것은?

> · I didn't see ___(A)___ birds in the sky today.
> · The marathon was ___(B)___ .
> · I learned ___(C)___ in science class.

	(A)	(B)	(C)
①	any	tiring	something new
②	any	tired	something new
③	some	tiring	new something
④	any	tiring	new something
⑤	some	tired	something new

9 다음 중 밑줄 친 부분이 어법상 어색한 것은?

> A: How was the K-pop concert?
> B: It was ①amazing. There were ②many fans in the concert hall.
> A: Did you have a good seat?
> B: Yes. I was ③a few rows away from the stage.
> A: Did you spend ④many money there?
> B: No. I just bought ⑤some posters.

10 우리말과 같도록 빈칸에 알맞은 말을 쓰시오.

> 그 팀은 방금 다섯 번째 골을 넣었다.

= The team just scored the _____ goal.

11 다음 글의 밑줄 친 ⓐ~ⓔ 중 어법상 어색한 것을 찾아 기호를 쓰고 바르게 고쳐 쓰시오.

> Every second week, Kevin goes to the dog shelter. ⓐMany dogs are staying there, but the ⓑpoor old dogs have ⓒfew toys. He wants to do ⓓnice something for them. So, he will buy them ⓔmuch toys this weekend.
>
> *shelter 보호소

(1) _____ → _____

(2) _____ → _____

12 다음 대화의 밑줄 친 우리말을 알맞게 영작한 것을 모두 고르시오.

> A: When is your birthday?
> B: 6월 23일이야.

① It's June twenty-threes.
② It's June twenty-third.
③ It's June twentieth-third.
④ It's the twenty-third of June.
⑤ It's the twenty-three of June.

13 다음 빈칸에 들어갈 말이 순서대로 짝지어진 것은?

> · I gave my sister _____ dolls.
> · Can I have _____ orange juice?

① many – a few
② much – a few
③ much – little
④ many – a little
⑤ much – a little

14 다음 빈칸에 들어갈 말이 순서대로 짝지어진 것은?

· This street has _____ coffee shops.
· There isn't _____ bread on the plate.

① some – any
② some – a few
③ any – some
④ any – any
⑤ some – some

15 다음 빈칸에 들어갈 말이 순서대로 짝지어진 것은?

· This map is too _____ .
· We are _____ about the field trip.

① confuse – excited
② confused – excite
③ confused – exciting
④ confusing – exciting
⑤ confusing – excited

16 우리말과 같도록 문장을 완성하시오.

공룡들은 수백만 년 전에 멸종됐다.

= Dinosaurs died out _____
ago.

[17-18] 다음 중 영어로 <u>잘못</u> 읽은 것을 고르시오.

17

① 10시 15분 = a quarter past ten
② 2008년 = two thousand eight
③ 3시 20분 = twenty to three
④ 2시 43분 = two forty-three
⑤ 1971년 11월 25일 = November twenty-fifth, nineteen seventy-one

18

① 0.454 = zero point four five four
② 20,036 = twenty thousand and thirty-six
③ 4,300,001 = four million, three hundred thousand and one
④ $\frac{2}{3}$ = two-third
⑤ $\frac{1}{6}$ = a sixth

19 다음 우리말을 영작할 때 빈칸에 들어갈 말이 순서대로 짝지어진 것은?

· 그 공원에는 수천 그루의 나무가 있다.
  = There are _____ of trees in the park.
· 우리 학교에는 500명이 넘는 학생이 있다.
  = Our school has over five _____ .

① thousand – hundreds students
② thousand – hundreds student
③ thousands – hundred students
④ thousands – hundred student
⑤ thousand – hundred students

20 다음 중 밑줄 친 형용사의 용법이 나머지 넷과 다른 것은?

① I am looking at the <u>modern</u> building.
② Jinsu wants to see his <u>favorite</u> singer.
③ My father bought me <u>brown</u> gloves.
④ Your shoes are not very <u>clean</u>.
⑤ There are <u>sweet</u> doughnuts on the table.

21 <보기>와 같이 다음 두 문장의 의미가 같도록 문장을 완성하시오.

> <보기> This apple is green.
>   = This is *a green apple* .

This magic show is fantastic.
= This is _____ .

22 다음 중 기수와 서수의 형태가 잘못 짝지어진 것은?

① two – second
② nine – nineth
③ twelve – twelfth
④ forty – fortieth
⑤ seventy-three – seventy-third

23 다음 중 밑줄 친 부분이 어법상 어색한 것은?

① Do you have <u>any</u> plans for this summer?
② The library has <u>some</u> good books.
③ There isn't <u>any</u> shampoo in the bottle.
④ Could you lend me <u>some</u> pens?
⑤ I didn't make <u>some</u> cake for my mom on her birthday.

24 다음 우리말을 알맞게 영작한 것은?

> 그의 새 소설은 매우 실망스러웠다.

① It was his very disappointing novel.
② It was his very disappointed novel.
③ His new novel was very disappoint.
④ His new novel was very disappointing.
⑤ His new novel was very disappointed.

25 다음 빈칸에 many가 들어갈 수 <u>없는</u> 것은?

① I got _____ presents from Santa Claus.
② How _____ planets are in our solar system?
③ Jane doesn't drink _____ coffee.
④ There are _____ dishes to do.
⑤ Tom saw _____ animals in the forest.

26 다음 빈칸에 들어갈 알맞은 것을 <u>모두</u> 고르시오.

> We planted _____ trees on April fifth.

① a little   ② a few   ③ any
④ lots of   ⑤ much

27 다음 빈칸에 들어갈 말로 어색한 것은?

> My brother had much _____ last night.

① chocolate   ② water
③ green tea   ④ hamburgers
⑤ cream soup

28 다음 밑줄 친 부분과 바꿔 쓸 수 있는 것은?

The dog doesn't have a lot of energy.

① some ② few ③ much
④ many ⑤ a little

29 다음 빈칸에 공통으로 들어갈 알맞은 것은?

· Do you listen to _____ music these days?
· We need _____ cups for the party.

① many ② much ③ a few
④ a little ⑤ lots of

30 다음 중 밑줄 친 부분이 어법상 어색한 것의 개수는?

ⓐ Timmy likes to drink cold coffee.
ⓑ Anything yellow looks great on you.
ⓒ I met great somebody at the dance club.
ⓓ There is special nothing about this letter.
ⓔ The forest is full of tall trees.

① 없음 ② 1개 ③ 2개
④ 3개 ⑤ 4개

[31-32] 다음 문장에서 어법상 어색한 부분을 찾아 쓰고 바르게 고쳐 쓰시오.

31

I took any medicine an hour ago, but I don't feel better.

_____ → _____

32

Minha could find cheap nothing at the souvenir shop.

_____ → _____

33 다음 중 밑줄 친 부분이 어법상 바른 것은?

① He sent me lots of letter last year.
② Little rains falls in the desert.
③ I bought many shirts yesterday.
④ There isn't any sugars in the tea.
⑤ Would you like some apple?

34 주어진 문장의 밑줄 친 형용사와 용법이 다른 것은?

Chicago is a large city.

① Rabbits have long ears.
② The chef makes delicious pasta.
③ The warm air made me sleepy.
④ Susan has short red hair.
⑤ Koalas are very popular animals.

35 다음 중 밑줄 친 부분이 어법상 어색한 것은?

① He grew up in a small wooden house.
② I am wearing a beautiful pink dress.
③ Please bring a plastic large bag.
④ She showed me some old black-and-white photos.
⑤ Let's buy that tiny round silver plate.

36 다음 대화의 빈칸에 공통으로 들어갈 가장 알맞은 것은?

> A: Are you all right? You seem _____ today.
> B: I am _____ because I didn't sleep well last night.

① tiring ② tired ③ exciting
④ excited ⑤ shocking

[37-38] 우리말과 같도록 괄호 안의 말을 활용하여 빈칸에 쓰시오.

37

> Alice는 나의 나이를 알고 놀랐다. (surprise)

= Alice was _____ to learn my age.

38

> 어젯밤의 연극은 감동적이었다. (move)

= Last night's play was _____.

[39-40] 다음 문장에서 틀린 부분을 바르게 고쳐 완전한 문장을 쓰시오.

39

> This puzzle makes me confusing.
> → _____

40

> The chef's pasta was amazed.
> → _____

41 다음 중 밑줄 친 부분이 어법상 어색한 것은?

① It was a really boring book.
② I was worried about my grade.
③ The news was shocking.
④ Charlie is interested in baseball.
⑤ Waking up early is tired.

42 다음 빈칸에 들어갈 말로 어색한 것을 모두 고르시오.

> The movie sounds _____.

① annoyed ② disappointed
③ helpful ④ amazing
⑤ interesting

CHAPTER 12
부사

Turtles move **slowly**. 거북은 느리게 움직인다.

그냥 '움직인다'라고 말하는 것보다 '느리게 움직인다'라고 말하면 어떻게 움직이는지 더 자세하게 알 수 있어요. 이렇게 다른 품사를 꾸며 의미를 강조하거나 풍부하게 하는 것을 **부사**라고 해요.

기출로 적중 POINT

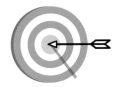

내신 100점 적중!
기출 출제율

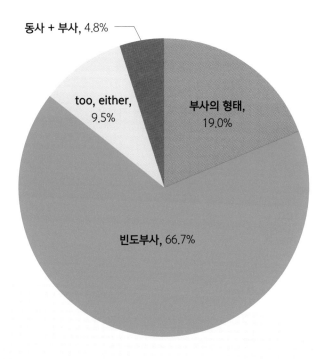

동사 + 부사, 4.8%

too, either, 9.5%

부사의 형태, 19.0%

빈도부사, 66.7%

TOP 1 빈도부사 (66.7%)
빈도부사의 종류와 문장 안에서의 위치를 묻는 문제가 자주 출제된다.

TOP 2 부사의 형태 (19%)
부사의 형태를 묻는 문제가 자주 출제된다.

TOP 3 too, either (9.5%)
부사 too, either의 쓰임을 묻는 문제가 자주 출제된다.

부사의 쓰임

정답 p.36

부사는 동사·형용사·다른 부사·문장 전체를 꾸민다.

동사 수식	Linda **speaks** quietly. Linda는 조용히 말한다.
형용사 수식	You are really **kind**. 너는 아주 친절하다.
다른 부사 수식	They sing very **well**. 그들은 노래를 매우 잘한다.
문장 전체 수식	Finally, **her dream came true.** 마침내, 그녀의 꿈은 이루어졌다.

연습문제 다음 문장의 밑줄 친 부사가 수식하는 부분에 밑줄을 치시오.

1 It rained heavily.

2 I was very tired yesterday.

3 Tommy studies hard.

4 Luckily, I passed the test.

5 Don't drink milk too much.

6 Please listen carefully.

7 The breakfast was really good.

8 You always make me so happy.

9 Sadly, it is time to say goodbye.

10 The movie was terribly boring.

11 Walk quietly in the hall.

12 Suddenly, someone knocked on the door.

13 The sun shines brightly in summer.

14 My brother speaks English quite well.

15 We ate the dessert too fast.

기출로적중 POINT 2-1 부사의 형태

정답 p.36

부사는 대부분 형용사에 -ly를 붙여 만든다.

대부분의 형용사	형용사 + -ly	slow – slow**ly** kind – kind**ly**	sad – sad**ly** poor – poor**ly**
「자음 + y」로 끝나는 형용사	y를 i로 바꾸고 + -ly	easy – eas**ily**	lucky – luck**ily**
-le로 끝나는 형용사	e를 없애고 + -y	simple – simpl**y**	terrible – terribl**y**
불규칙 변화	good – well		

Hazel ate her lunch **slowly**. Hazel은 그녀의 점심을 천천히 먹었다.
Luckily, they found their bags. 다행히도, 그들은 그들의 가방들을 찾았다.

(Tip) 다음 단어는 -ly로 끝나지만 부사가 아닌 형용사이다.

friendly 친절한　　**lovely** 사랑스러운　　**lonely** 외로운　　**weekly** 주간의　　**likely** 그럴듯한

연습문제 **A**　다음 형용사를 부사로 바꿔 쓰시오.

1 loud　　–　_____

2 real　　–　_____

3 happy　　–　_____

4 sad　　–　_____

5 bad　　–　_____

6 gentle　　–　_____

7 nervous　　–　_____

8 special　　–　_____

9 perfect　　–　_____

10 strange　　–　_____

11 similar　　–　_____

12 regular　　–　_____

13 strong　　–　_____

14 serious　　–　_____

15 wonderful　　–　_____

16 sudden　　–　_____

17 quiet　　–　_____

18 good　　–　_____

19 careful　　–　_____

20 different　　–　_____

21 clear　　–　_____

22 surprising　　–　_____

23 comfortable　–　_____

24 heavy　　–　_____

25 noisy　　–　_____

26 safe　　–　_____

27 nice　　–　_____

28 angry　　–　_____

29 wise   – _____   **30** deep   – _____

31 possible   – _____   **32** honest   – _____

연습문제 B   우리말과 같도록 괄호 안에서 알맞은 것을 고르시오.

1 주의해서 들어주세요.

= Please listen (careful / carefully).

2 모든 일을 완벽하게 끝내자.

= Let's finish all the work (perfect / perfectly).

3 오늘은 지독하게 춥다.

= It is (terrible / terribly) cold today.

4 소윤이는 아름다운 드레스를 샀다.

= Soyoon bought a (beautiful / beautifully) dress.

5 불행히도, 나의 아버지는 그의 신용카드를 잃어버리셨다.

= (Unfortunate / Unfortunately), my father lost his credit card.

6 그 영화는 나를 몹시 슬프게 만들었다.

= The movie made me (deep / deeply) sad.

7 모든 사람들은 그 가게의 친절한 주인을 좋아한다.

= Everyone likes the shop's (friend / friendly) owner.

8 Liam은 나에게 은행으로 가는 길을 친절하게 알려줬다.

= Liam (kind / kindly) showed me the way to the bank.

9 그녀는 오늘 정말 다르게 보이지 않니?

= Doesn't she look so (different / differently) today?

10 놀랍게도, 그는 지난달에 복권에 당첨됐다.

= (Amazing / Amazingly), he won the lottery last month.

11 Peter와 나는 방 밖으로 조용히 걸어 나왔다.

= Peter and I (quiet / quietly) walked out of the room.

기출 적중문제 ◎

우리말과 같도록 괄호 안의 말을 활용하여 문장을 완성하시오.

도서관에서 큰 소리로 말하지 마라. (speak, loud)

= _____ in the library.

POINT 2-2 형용사와 형태가 같은 부사

정답 p.36

다음 단어는 형용사와 부사의 형태가 같다.

late	형 늦은	부 늦게	high	형 높은	부 높이
early	형 이른	부 일찍	long	형 긴	부 길게, 오래
fast	형 빠른	부 빠르게			

You are late for school. 너는 학교에 늦었다.
I came home late last night. 나는 어젯밤에 집에 늦게 왔다.

Tina is wearing a long skirt. Tina는 긴 치마를 입고 있다.
We waited very long. 우리는 매우 오래 기다렸다.

Tip 형용사와 형태가 같지만 의미가 달라지는 부사에 주의한다.

hard 형 어려운, 단단한 부 열심히　　pretty 형 예쁜 부 꽤

It is a hard book to understand. 그것은 이해하기에 어려운 책이다.
The students are studying hard. 그 학생들은 열심히 공부하고 있다.

연습문제 다음 중 밑줄 친 부분의 품사가 나머지 둘과 다른 것을 고르시오.

1 ① I wake up early on weekdays.
② He called me in the early morning.
③ It is early in Canada now.

2 ① We arrived late for the game.
② Lilacs bloom in late spring.
③ I watched a scary movie late at night.

3 ① The price is too high.
② The airplane is flying high.
③ How high is the mountain?

4 ① You look so pretty in that dress.
② Look at the pretty house on the corner.
③ It was pretty cold this morning.

5 ① The boy with long arms is Timmy.
② I hope my dog lives long.
③ It took so long to get here.

6 ① The bread was hard like a rock.
② This is a really hard question.
③ Let's try hard to protect the environment.

7 ① Junsu ran too fast and fell over.
② My dad wants to buy a fast car.
③ She talked very fast, so I couldn't understand her.

-ly가 붙으면 의미가 달라지는 부사

정답 p.37

다음 부사에 -ly가 붙으면 의미가 다른 부사가 된다.

late 늦게 – lately 최근에

hard 열심히 – hardly 거의 ~않다

high 높이 – highly 매우, 대단히

close 가까이 – closely 면밀히

Kangaroos can jump **high**. 캥거루는 높이 뛸 수 있다.

I **highly** recommend this album. 나는 이 앨범을 매우 추천한다.

They live **close** to my house. 그들은 나의 집에 가까이 산다.

He looked at the painting very **closely**. 그는 그 그림을 매우 면밀히 살펴봤다.

연습문제 | 다음 빈칸에 알맞은 말을 괄호 안에서 골라 쓰시오.

1 (high / highly)

① Raise your hand _____.

② Yunho was _____ active in gym class.

③ She is a _____ successful writer.

④ An eagle flew _____ above the mountain.

2 (hard / hardly)

① Sarah pushed the button _____.

② We practiced _____ before the final game.

③ I can _____ speak because of a sore throat.

④ The accident was _____ surprising.

3 (late / lately)

① He has read many books _____.

② My brother worked _____ all last week.

③ _____, Susan has felt tired.

④ The plane arrived an hour _____.

4 (close / closely)

① Please read the directions _____.

② Daniel stood _____ to the main gate.

③ My cats like to sit _____ to the fireplace.

④ I checked my essay _____ for mistakes.

기출로 적중 POINT 3 빈도부사

1. 빈도부사는 어떤 일이 얼마나 자주 발생하는지를 나타내는 부사이다.

100%   0%

always	usually	often	sometimes	seldom	never
항상	보통, 대개	종종, 자주	때때로, 가끔	거의 ~않다	결코 ~않다

Noah is **usually** shy.   Noah는 보통 수줍어한다.
I **seldom** go swimming in the ocean.   나는 거의 바다로 수영하러 가지 않는다.

2. 빈도부사는 be동사나 조동사 뒤 또는 일반동사 앞에 온다.

be동사나 조동사 뒤	She **is** often late for school. 그녀는 종종 학교에 늦는다. We **can** always trust Minho. 우리는 항상 민호를 믿을 수 있다.
일반동사 앞	I sometimes **go** to the gym. 나는 때때로 체육관에 간다. The store never **opens** on Mondays. 그 가게는 월요일에 결코 문을 열지 않는다.

연습문제 A   우리말과 같도록 빈칸에 알맞은 빈도부사를 쓰시오.

1 Samantha는 항상 쾌활하다.
= Samantha is _____ cheerful.

2 Lily는 결코 나의 생일을 잊어버리지 않을 것이다.
= Lily will _____ forget my birthday.

3 산 속에서 공기는 보통 차다.
= The air is _____ cold in the mountains.

4 나의 가족은 저 식당에서 종종 저녁을 먹는다.
= My family _____ has dinner at that restaurant.

5 그 강은 겨울에 때때로 언다.
= The river _____ freezes in winter.

6 너는 보통 평일에 바쁘니?
= Are you _____ busy on weekdays?

7 나는 온라인으로 결코 옷을 사지 않는다.
= I _____ buy clothes online.

8 부산에는 12월에 거의 눈이 오지 않는다.
= It _____ snows in December in Busan.

9 Ken은 결코 커피를 마시지 않니?

= Does Ken _____ drink coffee?

연습문제 **B** 괄호 안의 빈도부사가 들어갈 위치에 V 표시를 하시오.

1 Birds build nests in trees. (often)

2 Do you eat breakfast at home? (usually)

3 Will you love me? (always)

4 My sister's room is clean. (seldom)

5 I will lie to my parents again. (never)

6 Does Sally go to the café? (often)

7 Bears can catch fish in rivers. (usually)

8 The restaurant serves unhealthy food. (never)

9 The subway is empty in the afternoon. (sometimes)

10 Would you work out with me? (often)

연습문제 **C** 다음 표를 보고 빈칸에 알맞은 빈도부사를 <보기>에서 골라 쓰시오.

<보기> never   often   always   sometimes

	Mina	Dan	Jiho	Dora
Mon	✓	✓		
Tue	✓	✓	✓	
Wed	✓	✓	✓	
Thu	✓			
Fri	✓	✓		
Sat	✓	✓		
Sun	✓		✓	

1 *A*: How often does Mina read a book?

   B: She _____ reads a book.

2 *A*: How often does Dan read a book?

   B: He _____ reads a book.

3 *A*: How often does Jiho read a book?

   B: He _____ reads a book.

4 *A*: How often does Dora read a book?

   B: She _____ reads a book.

기출 적중문제

우리말과 같도록 괄호 안의 말을 알맞게 배열하시오.

나는 주말에 보통 축구를 한다. (play, usually, I, soccer)

= _____ on weekends.

빈도부사는 be동사나
조동사의 뒤, 일반동사의
앞에 와요.

POINT 4 too, either

정답 p.37

> too/either는 '또한, 역시'라는 의미이다. too는 긍정문에 대한 동의를 나타내고, either는 부정문에 대한 동의를 나타낸다.

too	My brother **hates** carrots. I **hate** carrots, too. 나의 남동생은 당근을 싫어한다. 나 또한 당근을 싫어한다.
either	Mark **can't speak** Korean. Paula **can't speak** Korean, either. Mark는 한국어를 말할 수 없다. Paula 또한 한국어를 말할 수 없다.

연습문제 다음 빈칸에 too나 either를 넣어 대화를 완성하시오.

1 A: I like K-pop.   B: I like K-pop, _____.

2 A: I don't feel so well.   B: She doesn't feel so well, _____.

3 A: I can finish my homework.   B: I can finish my homework, _____.

4 A: He is ready to go now.   B: Diane is ready to go now, _____.

5 A: I won't go out this weekend.   B: I won't go out this weekend, _____.

6 A: We are middle school students.   B: They are middle school students, _____.

7 A: Nate doesn't have any pets.   B: I don't have any pets, _____.

8 A: This bag is very expensive.   B: These shoes are very expensive, _____.

9 A: We didn't go to school today.   B: They didn't go to school today, _____.

10 A: Jill couldn't solve the problem.   B: Owen couldn't solve the problem, _____.

기출 적중문제

다음 빈칸에 too가 들어갈 수 <u>없는</u> 것은?

① I loved the book, _____.

② She isn't very tall, _____.

③ Joe watched that movie, _____.

④ Patrick will join the club, _____.

⑤ My father can drive well, _____.

1. 다음은 목적어를 가질 수 있는 「동사 + 부사」이다.

turn on ~을 켜다	turn off ~을 끄다	put on ~을 입다/쓰다
take off ~을 벗다	try on ~을 입어보다/신어보다	pick up ~을 줍다/들어 올리다
wake up ~를 깨우다	give up ~을 포기하다/그만두다	write down ~을 적다
throw away ~을 버리다	put off ~을 미루다	hand in ~을 제출하다

I **turned off** the radio. 나는 라디오를 껐다.

Marie **picked up** a purse on the street. Marie는 길에서 지갑을 주웠다.

My father will **give up** smoking. 나의 아버지는 담배 피우는 것을 그만두실 것이다.

2. 「동사 + 부사」는 목적어가 명사인지 대명사인지에 따라 어순이 달라진다.

목적어	어순	예문
명사	「동사 + 부사 + 목적어」 / 「동사 + 목적어 + 부사」	He **turned on** his phone. 그는 그의 전화기를 켰다. = He **turned** his phone **on**. Can I **try on** these pants? 내가 이 바지를 입어봐도 되니? = Can I **try** these pants **on**?
대명사	「동사 + 목적어 + 부사」	Please **wake me up** at 7 A.M. 오전 7시에 저를 깨워주세요. You should **write it down** now. 너는 지금 그것을 적어야 한다.

연습문제 A 우리말과 같도록 빈칸에 알맞은 말을 쓰시오.

1 소민이는 그녀의 모자를 벗고 싶지 않았다.

= Somin didn't want to _____ _____ her hat.

2 여기에 쓰레기를 버리지 마라.

= Don't _____ _____ trash here.

3 종이에 당신의 주소를 적어주세요.

= Please _____ _____ your address on the paper.

4 나는 내일 아침에 유진이를 깨워야 한다.

= I must _____ _____ Yujin tomorrow morning.

5 지금 당장 에어컨을 켜자.

= Let's _____ _____ the air conditioner right now.

6 Ruby는 금요일까지 그녀의 숙제를 제출할 것이다.

= Ruby will _____ _____ her homework by Friday.

7 그들은 그 야구 경기를 미뤄야 했다.

= They had to _____ _____ the baseball game.

8 너는 그 흰 블라우스를 입어보기를 원하니?

= Would you like to _____ _____ the white blouse?

9 자기 전에 TV를 꺼라.

= _____ _____ the TV before you go to bed.

10 우리는 황사 때문에 마스크를 써야 한다.

= We should _____ _____ a mask because of the yellow dust.

11 너의 꿈을 좇는 것을 포기하지 마라.

= Don't _____ _____ following your dreams.

12 저를 위해 그 신문을 주워주시겠어요?

= Could you _____ _____ the newspaper for me?

연습문제 B 괄호 안에서 알맞은 것을 모두 고르시오.

1 David (turned on it / turned on the computer).

2 Sadly, Beth will have to (give it up / give up it).

3 You can (try them on / try on them) in the dressing room.

4 Did you (turn all the lights off / turn them off)?

5 His child wants to (take off it / take it off).

6 Please (pick your trash up / pick it up).

7 Minsun (put off her trip / put it off).

8 Could you (write down your name / write down it)?

9 (Hand it in / Hand in it) by the end of next week.

10 He (put a jacket on / put it on) before going outside.

11 You shouldn't (wake the baby up / wake him up) so early.

12 Could you (throw away them / throw them away)?

기출 적중문제

다음 문장에서 <u>틀린</u> 부분을 바르게 고쳐 완전한 문장을 쓰시오.

The loud noise woke up her last night.

→ _____

「동사 + 부사」의 목적어가 대명사인 경우「동사 + 대명사 + 부사」의 어순으로 써요.

서술형 대비 문제

Ⓐ 괄호 안의 형용사를 부사로 바꿔 빈칸에 쓰시오.

1 The men _____ yelled at each other. (angry)

2 The girl _____ apologized for her mistake. (polite)

3 You should spend your money _____. (wise)

4 The firefighter _____ went into the building. (brave)

5 The child stood _____ close to the cliff. (dangerous)

6 Jack sang really _____ at the concert. (good)

7 The vet _____ picked up the cat. (careful)

8 The student _____ answered all of the questions. (correct)

9 The twins like to dress _____. (similar)

10 _____, they found the treasure on the island. (lucky)

Ⓑ 다음 빈칸에 알맞은 말을 <보기>에서 골라 쓰시오.

<보기> late lately hard hardly

1 My grandfather can _____ drive anymore.

2 Young children shouldn't go to bed too _____.

3 The players tried really _____ to win the game.

4 My father has looked very tired _____.

<보기> high highly close closely

5 This diamond necklace is _____ expensive.

6 The kid stayed _____ to her father in the mall.

7 You must listen to the lecture _____.

8 Can dogs jump _____ like cats?

C 우리말과 같도록 괄호 안의 말을 알맞게 배열하시오.

1 Monica는 항상 친절하다. (friendly, is, Monica, always)

= _____

2 나의 아빠는 때때로 나의 엄마에게 꽃을 사주신다. (sometimes, my mom, my dad, flowers, buys)

= _____

3 Carl은 건강에 좋은 음식을 결코 먹지 않는다. (eats, healthy food, never, Carl)

= _____

4 너는 너의 부모님께 종종 전화해야 한다. (you, your parents, often, call, should)

= _____

5 너는 보통 아침에 운동하니? (exercise, do, in the morning, you, usually)

= _____

6 너는 항상 진실을 말할 거니? (tell, you, will, the truth, always)

= _____

7 그 빵집은 월요일에 거의 붐비지 않는다. (on Mondays, the bakery, crowded, is, seldom)

= _____

8 그는 주차 공간을 결코 찾을 수 없었다. (a parking space, he, never, could, find)

= _____

D 밑줄 친 부분이 어법상 맞으면 O를 쓰고, 틀리면 바르게 고쳐 쓰시오.

1 Can I try on them? → _____

2 Don't turn it on. → _____

3 When will you hand in the report? → _____

4 Mom wakes up me every morning. → _____

5 He put on it and went out. → _____

6 They had to put the festival off for a week. → _____

7 Throw away it in that trash can. → _____

8 Take your hat off during class. → _____

9 Don't forget to write down it. → _____

1 다음 중 형용사와 부사의 형태가 잘못 짝지어진 것은?

① smart – smartly ② gentle – gently
③ strong – strongly ④ easy – easyly
⑤ good – well

2 다음 대화의 빈칸에 들어갈 알맞은 것은?

A: I didn't watch that movie.
B: I didn't watch it, _____.

① too   ② either   ③ well
④ so   ⑤ do

3 다음 중 밑줄 친 부분이 어법상 어색한 것은?

Redwoods are very large trees. They
①mainly grow in Northern California.
Redwoods are ②usually over 30 meters
tall. They live for a ③pretty long time.
④Amazingly, some are over 1,000 years
old. We should protect them ⑤careful.

*redwood 미국삼나무

4 다음 중 짝지어진 관계가 <보기>와 다른 것은?

<보기> heavy – heavily

① noisy – noisily   ② strange – strangely
③ bad – badly   ④ love – lovely
⑤ similar – similarly

5 다음 문장에서 어법상 어색한 부분을 찾아 쓰고 바르게 고쳐 쓰시오.

Toby shouted angry at his brother.

_____ → _____

6 다음 우리말을 영작한 것 중 어색한 것은?

① Diana는 정기적으로 그 식물들에 물을 준다.
   → Diana waters the plants regularly.
② 소라는 천천히 유리 조각을 주웠다.
   → Sora slowly picked up a piece of glass.
③ 마침내, 나는 부엌을 청소하는 것을 끝냈다.
   → Finally, I finished cleaning the kitchen.
④ 그 운동화는 나에게 완벽하게 맞는다.
   → The sneakers perfect fit me.
⑤ 저 건물은 정말 오래됐다.
   → That building is really old.

[7-8] 다음 중 밑줄 친 부분의 쓰임이 나머지 넷과 다른 것을 고르시오.

7

① Minjun came late to the concert.
② The bus arrived at the station late.
③ Benny was late for school today.
④ The movie started ten minutes late.
⑤ My sister wakes up late every morning.

8

① Cheetahs can run very fast.
② My family eats dinner early.
③ Every child behaved well.
④ The cake tasted pretty good.
⑤ A turtle has a hard shell.

9 다음 중 밑줄 친 부분이 어법상 어색한 것은?

① Tornadoes are terribly dangerous.

② Did the pianist practice hard?

③ We ran fastly to catch the bus.

④ Jane came home late at night.

⑤ You can see the moon clearly tonight.

10 다음 (A)~(C)에 들어갈 말이 바르게 짝지어진 것은?

| · This movie is ___(A)___ interesting. |
| · We stood ___(B)___ to an exit. |
| · We ___(C)___ know each other. |

	(A)	(B)	(C)
①	highly	close	hard
②	highly	closely	hardly
③	high	closely	hard
④	highly	close	hardly
⑤	high	close	hardly

11 다음 대화의 밑줄 친 우리말과 같도록 괄호 안의 말을 배열할 때 세 번째에 오는 것은?

A: What do you eat for breakfast?
B: <u>나는 보통 아침으로 시리얼을 먹어.</u>
　　(breakfast, cereal, for, usually, eat, I)

① breakfast　　　② cereal
③ for　　　④ usually
⑤ eat

12 다음 빈칸에 too가 들어갈 수 없는 것은?

① I enjoyed reading this novel, _____.

② I cannot solve the question, _____.

③ I will join the soccer club, _____.

④ I want to eat a sandwich, _____.

⑤ I am a good swimmer, _____.

13 다음은 Amy의 주간 운동 계획표이다. <보기>와 같이 빈칸에 알맞은 말을 넣어 질문에 대한 대답을 완성하시오.

Mon	Tue	Wed	Thu	Fri	Sat	Sun
yoga	yoga	cycle	yoga	yoga	cycle	–

| <보기>　A: How often does Amy cycle? |
| 　　　　B: She _sometimes_ _cycles_. |

| A: How often does Amy swim? |
| B: She _____ _____. |

14 다음 중 어법상 바른 것은?

① Brad always is nice to everyone.

② I wear sometimes shorts to school.

③ He can often watch TV after midnight.

④ You should open never that box.

⑤ Spiders build usually webs very fast.

15 다음 중 자연스럽지 <u>않은</u> 대화는?

① A: Why are you leaving now?
   B: I need to go to school early today.
② A: I couldn't finish the math homework.
   B: I couldn't finish it, too.
③ A: Do you go to the gym every day?
   B: No. I seldom exercise these days.
④ A: Are you and Michael close friends?
   B: Yes. We usually spend time together.
⑤ A: I don't like green tea.
   B: I don't like green tea, either.

16 <보기>와 같이 괄호 안의 말을 활용하여 다음 질문에 대한 대답을 완성하시오.

<보기>	A: How often do you meet your friends?
	B: _I usually meet my friends._ (usually)

A: How often do you go out to eat?
B: _____ (sometimes)

17 다음 대화의 밑줄 친 우리말과 같도록 주어진 <조건>에 맞게 문장을 완성하시오.

A: Let's watch the soccer game on Saturday afternoon.
B: I can't because I have an art class then. <u>나는 주말에 자유 시간이 거의 없어.</u>

<조건>
1. 빈도부사를 이용하여 5단어로 쓰시오.
2. free time, have를 활용하시오.

= _____ on weekends.

18 다음 표를 <u>잘못</u> 설명한 것은?

How often do you study after school?					
	Mon	Tue	Wed	Thu	Fri
Sam	O	O	O	O	O
Luna	X	X	X	X	X
Mary	X	X	O	X	O
Jason	O	X	X	X	X
Mike	X	O	O	O	O

① Sam always studies after school.
② Luna never studies after school.
③ Mary sometimes studies after school.
④ Jason often studies after school.
⑤ Mike usually studies after school.

19 다음 중 밑줄 친 부분이 어법상 <u>어색한</u> 것은?

① He looked at the painting <u>closely</u>.
② Rick arrived <u>lately</u> for the meeting.
③ I finished my science project <u>early</u>.
④ My brother went <u>high</u> up the mountain.
⑤ It <u>hardly</u> snows in tropical countries.

20 다음 빈칸에 공통으로 들어갈 알맞은 것은?

· The volunteers picked _____ the trash on the beach.
· You should wake him _____ now.

① off   ② on   ③ down
④ in   ⑤ up

21 다음 대화의 밑줄 친 ⓐ~ⓔ 중 어법상 어색한 것을 찾아 기호를 쓰고 바르게 고쳐 쓰시오.

> *A*: I feel ⓐ<u>really</u> confident about the exam. I studied all night.
> *B*: I studied a lot, too. I ⓑ<u>hard</u> slept last night.
> *A*: Then we'll ⓒ<u>easily</u> pass the test.
> *B*: But I'm still nervous. I'm not sure I'll do ⓓ<u>good</u>.
> *A*: Don't worry. You ⓔ<u>always</u> get a great score.
> *B*: I hope you're right.

(1) _____ → _____
(2) _____ → _____

22 다음 글의 빈칸에 들어갈 말이 순서대로 짝지어진 것은?

> Sharks are great hunters. They swim _____ in the water. They also have _____ teeth and powerful jaws. So, the prey can seldom escape.
>
> *prey 먹이, 사냥감

① silent – sharply
② silently – sharpily
③ silently – sharply
④ silently – sharp
⑤ silent – sharp

[23-24] 다음 중 often이 들어갈 가장 알맞은 위치를 고르시오.

23

> Little ① babies ② sleep ③ most ④ of the ⑤ day.

24

> You ① can ② see ③ cute ④ squirrels ⑤ in Central Park.

25 다음 중 어법상 바른 것의 개수는?

> ⓐ Jisun took her jacket off on the bus.
> ⓑ Please wake up me at 8 A.M.
> ⓒ Don't throw them away.
> ⓓ You should write down your phone number.
> ⓔ Could you pick up it and give it to me?

① 1개
② 2개
③ 3개
④ 4개
⑤ 5개

26 다음 문장에서 틀린 부분을 바르게 고쳐 완전한 문장을 쓰시오.

> I turned the heater on, but Jackson turned off it.
>
> → _____
> _____

CHAPTER 13
비교구문

The cat is **as small as** the puppy. 그 고양이는 그 강아지만큼 작다.
The bird is **smaller than** the cat. 그 새는 그 고양이보다 더 작다.
The bug is **the smallest** of the four. 그 벌레는 넷 중에서 가장 작다.

위 문장에서 여러 동물들의 크기를 비교하고 있는데, 이렇게 두 가지 이상의 대상을 서로 견주어 비교하는 문장을 **비교구문**이라고 해요. 비교하는 두 대상의 정도가 비슷하거나 같음을 나타낼 때는 **원급**, 두 대상 간 정도의 차이를 나타낼 때는 **비교급**, 셋 이상의 비교 대상 중 하나의 정도가 가장 높음을 나타낼 때는 **최상급**을 써요.

기출로 적중 POINT

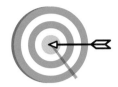

내신 100점 적중!
기출 출제율

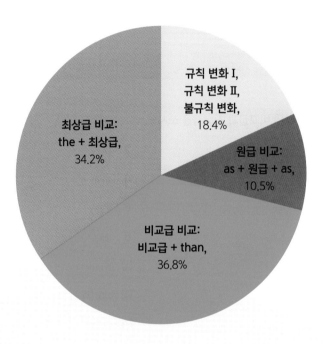

규칙 변화 I,
규칙 변화 II,
불규칙 변화,
18.4%

원급 비교:
as + 원급 + as,
10.5%

최상급 비교:
the + 최상급,
34.2%

비교급 비교:
비교급 + than,
36.8%

TOP 1 **비교급 비교: 비교급 + than (36.8%)**
비교급 비교의 형태와 쓰임 및 비교급을 강조하는 법을 묻는 문제가 자주 출제된다.

TOP 2 **최상급 비교: the + 최상급 (34.2%)**
최상급 비교의 형태와 쓰임을 묻는 문제가 자주 출제된다.

TOP 3 **규칙 변화 I, II, 불규칙 변화 (18.4%)**
형용사나 부사의 비교급과 최상급을 묻는 문제가 자주 출제된다.

규칙 변화 I

정답 p.39

원급은 형용사나 부사의 원래 형태이며, 비교급은 대부분 원급에 -(e)r을, 최상급은 대부분 원급에 -(e)st를 붙여 만든다.

비교급/최상급 만드는 법		원급	비교급	최상급
대부분의 형용사·부사	+ -er/-est	tall	tall**er**	tall**est**
-**e**로 끝나는 형용사·부사	+ -r/-st	large	larg**er**	larg**est**
「자음 + **y**」로 끝나는 형용사·부사	y를 i로 바꾸고 + -er/-est	happy	happ**ier**	happ**iest**
「단모음 + 단자음」으로 끝나는 형용사·부사	마지막 자음을 한 번 더 쓰고 + -er/-est	big	big**ger**	big**gest**

연습문제 | 다음 형용사나 부사의 비교급과 최상급을 쓰시오.

1 new – _____ – _____

2 busy – _____ – _____

3 long – _____ – _____

4 fast – _____ – _____

5 fresh – _____ – _____

6 easy – _____ – _____

7 heavy – _____ – _____

8 big – _____ – _____

9 wet – _____ – _____

10 thick – _____ – _____

11 cold – _____ – _____

12 pretty – _____ – _____

13 cheap – _____ – _____

14 cute – _____ – _____

15 light – _____ – _____

16 small – _____ – _____

17 nice – _____ – _____

18 hot – _____ – _____

19 sweet – _____ – _____

20 soft – _____ – _____

21 rich – _____ – _____

22 healthy – _____ – _____

23 thin – _____ – _____

24 warm – _____ – _____

25 slow – _____ – _____

26 weak – _____ – _____

27 huge – _____ – _____

28 noisy – _____ – _____

29 sunny – _____ – _____

30 scary – _____ – _____

31 wide – _____ – _____

32 sad – _____ – _____

정답 p.39

규칙 변화 II

기출로작중 POINT 1-2

다음 형용사나 부사의 비교급은 원급 앞에 more를, 최상급은 원급 앞에 most를 붙여 만든다.

비교급/최상급 만드는 법		원급	비교급	최상급
대부분의 2음절 이상인 형용사·부사 (-y로 끝나는 형용사 제외)	more/most + 원급	famous	more famous	most famous
「형용사 + ly」 형태의 부사		safely	more safely	most safely

연습문제 다음 형용사나 부사의 비교급과 최상급을 쓰시오.

1 popular – _____ – _____
2 important – _____ – _____
3 hard – _____ – _____
4 beautiful – _____ – _____
5 delicious – _____ – _____
6 wise – _____ – _____
7 easily – _____ – _____
8 colorful – _____ – _____
9 helpful – _____ – _____
10 slowly – _____ – _____
11 lovely – _____ – _____
12 different – _____ – _____
13 exciting – _____ – _____
14 dangerous – _____ – _____
15 difficult – _____ – _____
16 expensive – _____ – _____

불규칙 변화

일부 형용사나 부사의 비교급과 최상급은 불규칙하게 변한다.

원급		비교급	최상급	원급		비교급	최상급
good	좋은	better	best	many	(수가) 많은	more	most
well	건강한, 잘			much	(양이) 많은		
bad	나쁜	worse	worst	old	나이 든, 오래된	older	oldest
badly	나쁘게				연상의	elder	eldest
ill	아픈, 병든			far	(거리가) 먼	farther	farthest
little	(양이) 적은	less	least		(정도가) 더욱	further	furthest

연습문제 | 다음 형용사나 부사의 비교급과 최상급을 쓰시오.

1 bad　　　　　－ ＿＿＿＿＿＿＿＿　　－ ＿＿＿＿＿＿＿＿＿

2 large　　　　－ ＿＿＿＿＿＿＿＿　　－ ＿＿＿＿＿＿＿＿＿

3 high　　　　　－ ＿＿＿＿＿＿＿＿　　－ ＿＿＿＿＿＿＿＿＿

4 many　　　　－ ＿＿＿＿＿＿＿＿　　－ ＿＿＿＿＿＿＿＿＿

5 young　　　　－ ＿＿＿＿＿＿＿＿　　－ ＿＿＿＿＿＿＿＿＿

6 well　　　　　－ ＿＿＿＿＿＿＿＿　　－ ＿＿＿＿＿＿＿＿＿

7 short　　　　－ ＿＿＿＿＿＿＿＿　　－ ＿＿＿＿＿＿＿＿＿

8 ill　　　　　　－ ＿＿＿＿＿＿＿＿　　－ ＿＿＿＿＿＿＿＿＿

9 far(더욱)　　－ ＿＿＿＿＿＿＿＿　　－ ＿＿＿＿＿＿＿＿＿

10 dirty　　　　－ ＿＿＿＿＿＿＿＿　　－ ＿＿＿＿＿＿＿＿＿

11 far(먼)　　　－ ＿＿＿＿＿＿＿＿　　－ ＿＿＿＿＿＿＿＿＿

12 cool　　　　－ ＿＿＿＿＿＿＿＿　　－ ＿＿＿＿＿＿＿＿＿

13 good　　　　－ ＿＿＿＿＿＿＿＿　　－ ＿＿＿＿＿＿＿＿＿

14 much　　　　－ ＿＿＿＿＿＿＿＿　　－ ＿＿＿＿＿＿＿＿＿

15 little　　　　－ ＿＿＿＿＿＿＿＿　　－ ＿＿＿＿＿＿＿＿＿

16 great　　　　－ ＿＿＿＿＿＿＿＿　　－ ＿＿＿＿＿＿＿＿＿

17 smart　　　－ _____　－ _____

18 angry　　　－ _____　－ _____

19 old(나이 든, 오래된)　－ _____　－ _____

20 peaceful　　－ _____　－ _____

21 dark　　　　－ _____　－ _____

22 hungry　　　－ _____　－ _____

23 kind　　　　－ _____　－ _____

24 thirsty　　　－ _____　－ _____

25 special　　　－ _____　－ _____

26 old(연상의)　　－ _____　－ _____

27 quiet　　　　－ _____　－ _____

28 soon　　　　－ _____　－ _____

29 tasty　　　　－ _____　－ _____

30 carefully　　－ _____　－ _____

31 near　　　　－ _____　－ _____

32 fat　　　　　－ _____　－ _____

33 lucky　　　　－ _____　－ _____

34 loudly　　　－ _____　－ _____

35 badly　　　　－ _____　－ _____

36 bright　　　　－ _____　－ _____

37 useful　　　－ _____　－ _____

38 quick　　　　－ _____　－ _____

기출 적중문제

다음 중 원급-비교급-최상급 형태가 잘못된 것은?

① hungry – hungrier – hungriest

② happy – happier – happiest

③ many – manier – maniest

④ new – newer – newest

⑤ helpful – more helpful – most helpful

원급 비교: as + 원급 + as

정답 p.39

1. 「as + 원급 + as」는 '…만큼 ~한/하게'라는 의미로, 비교하는 두 대상의 정도가 비슷하거나 같음을 나타낸다.

   This car is **as expensive as** that car. 이 차는 저 차만큼 비싸다.

   I can run **as fast as** Jake. 나는 Jake만큼 빠르게 달릴 수 있다.

2. 「not + as[so] + 원급 + as」는 '…만큼 ~하지 않은/않게'라는 의미이다.

   My room is **not as[so] large as** Sujin's. 나의 방은 수진이의 것만큼 크지 않다.

   Ben did **not** sing **as[so] well as** his brother. Ben은 그의 형만큼 노래를 잘하지 않았다.

연습문제   우리말과 같도록 괄호 안의 말을 활용하여 빈칸에 쓰시오.

1 오늘은 어제만큼 화창하다. (sunny)

= Today is _____ _____ _____ yesterday.

2 Joey의 가방은 나의 것만큼 무겁지 않다. (heavy)

= Joey's bag is _____ _____ _____ _____ mine.

3 이 욕실은 그 부엌만큼 깨끗해 보인다. (clean)

= This bathroom looks _____ _____ _____ the kitchen.

4 나는 Alex만큼 프랑스어를 잘 말할 수 없다. (well)

= I cannot speak French _____ _____ _____ Alex.

5 서울은 모스크바만큼 춥니? (cold)

= Is Seoul _____ _____ _____ Moscow?

6 피자를 만드는 것은 파스타를 만드는 것만큼 쉽지 않다. (easy)

= Making pizza is _____ _____ _____ _____ making pasta.

기출 적중문제 ◎

<보기>와 같이 괄호 안의 말을 활용하여 다음 두 문장을 한 문장으로 바꿔 쓰시오.

> <보기> Jason can lift heavy boxes. Harry can lift heavy boxes, too.
>
> → Harry is _as strong as_ Jason. (strong)

Kate came home at 11 o'clock. Lola came home at 11 o'clock, too.

→ Lola came home _____ Kate. (late)

기출로적중 POINT 3-1 비교급 비교: 비교급 + than

정답 p.39

1. 「비교급 + than」은 '…보다 더 ~한/하게'라는 의미로, 비교하는 두 대상 간 정도의 차이를 나타낸다.

   Dad gets up **earlier than** me. 아빠는 나보다 더 일찍 일어나신다.
   My kite is flying **higher than** Cam's. 나의 연은 Cam의 것보다 더 높게 날고 있다.
   This design is **more popular than** that one. 이 디자인은 저것보다 더 인기 있다.

2. 비교급 앞에 much, even, still, far, a lot을 써서 '훨씬'이라는 의미로 비교급을 강조할 수 있다.

   Suho studies **much harder** than Soyun. 수호는 소윤이보다 훨씬 더 열심히 공부한다.
   Your advice was **far more helpful** than hers. 너의 조언은 그녀의 것보다 훨씬 더 도움이 됐다.

   (Tip) very는 비교급이 아닌 원급을 강조한다.
   I bought a very (**cheap**, ~~cheaper~~) jacket. 나는 매우 싼 재킷을 샀다.

연습문제 A 다음 그림을 보고 괄호 안의 말을 활용하여 빈칸에 쓰시오.

1

2

3

4

5

6

1 The rabbit is ＿＿＿＿＿ ＿＿＿＿＿ the snail. (fast)

2 Minsu looks ＿＿＿＿＿ ＿＿＿＿＿ Junho. (thin)

3 Amy's hair is ＿＿＿＿＿ ＿＿＿＿＿ Rachel's. (long)

4 The melon is ＿＿＿＿＿ ＿＿＿＿＿ the apple. (big)

5 The Eiffel Tower is ＿＿＿＿＿ ＿＿＿＿＿ the N Seoul Tower. (tall)

6 The necklace is ＿＿＿＿＿ ＿＿＿＿＿ ＿＿＿＿＿ the ring. (expensive)

우리말과 같도록 괄호 안의 말을 활용하여 빈칸에 쓰시오.

1 대구는 인천보다 더 덥다. (hot)

= Daegu is _____ _____ Incheon.

2 Josh는 나보다 더 놀라 보였다. (surprised)

= Josh looked _____ _____ _____ me.

3 오렌지는 레몬보다 훨씬 더 단맛이 난다. (sweet)

= Oranges taste _____ _____ _____ lemons.

4 이 매트리스는 나머지 것들보다 더 딱딱하게 느껴진다. (hard)

= This mattress feels _____ _____ the others.

5 나는 Jeff보다 역에 훨씬 더 가까이 산다. (close)

= I live _____ _____ to the station _____ Jeff.

6 Jenny는 항상 그녀의 오빠보다 더 빠르게 먹는다. (fast)

= Jenny always eats _____ _____ her brother.

7 미국에서는, 야구가 축구보다 더 인기 있다. (popular)

= In America, baseball is _____ _____ _____ soccer.

8 나의 엄마는 나의 아빠보다 훨씬 더 조심스럽게 운전하신다. (carefully)

= My mom drives _____ _____ _____ _____ my dad.

연습문제 C 괄호 안에서 알맞은 것을 고르시오.

1 Alice is (very / a lot) younger than her brother.

2 This white shirt is (large / larger) than the blue one.

3 Firefighters are (very / much) braver than other people.

4 Warm air is (lighter / more lighter) than cold air.

5 Your soup is (very / even) more delicious than mine.

6 My old computer is (noisy / noisier) than the new one.

기출 적중문제

다음 중 어법상 <u>어색한</u> 것은?

① Math is much more difficult than English.

② His camera is a lot better than yours.

③ Tigers are very bigger than cats.

④ Pears are far tastier than carrots.

⑤ This cupcake is even more colorful than that one.

> very는 비교급을 강조할 수 없어요.

기출로적중 POINT 3-2 비교급 비교: 비교급 + and + 비교급

정답 p.40

> 「비교급 + and + 비교급」은 '점점 더 ~한/하게'라는 의미이다.
>
> The tree grew **taller and taller**. 그 나무는 점점 더 높게 자랐다.
> The weather is getting **warmer and warmer**. 날씨가 점점 더 따뜻해지고 있다.
>
> (Tip) 비교급이 「more + 원급」의 형태인 경우 「more and more + 원급」으로 쓴다.
> The house is becoming **more and more expensive**. 그 집은 점점 더 비싸지고 있다.
> The story got **more and more interesting**. 그 이야기는 점점 더 흥미로워졌다.

연습문제 | 우리말과 같도록 괄호 안의 말을 활용하여 문장을 완성하시오.

1 나의 성적은 점점 더 좋아지고 있다. (good)
= My grades are getting _____.

2 Cindy의 강아지들은 점점 더 커졌다. (big)
= Cindy's puppies grew _____.

3 그 밴드는 점점 더 인기 있어졌다. (popular)
= The band became _____.

4 그는 점점 더 춥게 느꼈다. (cold)
= He felt _____.

5 그의 감기는 점점 더 나빠졌다. (bad)
= His cold got _____.

6 너의 얼굴은 점점 더 빨개지고 있다. (red)
= Your face is turning _____.

7 그 수업은 점점 더 지루해졌다. (boring)
= The class became _____.

8 그 식당은 점점 더 유명해졌다. (famous)
= The restaurant got _____.

9 하늘이 점점 더 어두워지고 있다. (dark)
= The sky is getting _____.

10 준수의 신발은 점점 더 더러워졌다. (dirty)
= Junsu's shoes became _____.

최상급 비교: the + 최상급

정답 p.40

「the + 최상급」은 '가장 ~한/하게'라는 의미로, 셋 이상의 비교 대상 중 하나의 정도가 가장 높음을 나타낸다. 최상급은 보통 in이나 of를 사용하여 비교 범위를 나타낸다.

in + 장소/집단　The blue whale is **the biggest** animal **in the world.**
　　　　　　　흰긴수염고래는 세상에서 가장 큰 동물이다.

of + 비교 대상　This box is **the heaviest** of the three.　이 상자는 셋 중에서 가장 무겁다.

연습문제　괄호 안의 말을 최상급 형태로 바꿔 문장을 완성하시오.

1 Maria is _____ of all her classmates. (smart)

2 It is _____ wallet in the shop. (expensive)

3 This movie is _____ of them. (bad)

4 Mount Everest is _____ mountain in the world. (high)

5 Tomorrow will be _____ day of the week. (sunny)

6 Venus is _____ planet in the solar system. (hot)

7 What is _____ of all subjects? (difficult)

8 My grandmother is _____ woman in my family. (wise)

9 Eric is _____ student in the math class. (good)

10 Friendship is _____ thing in my life. (important)

11 Mr. Jones is _____ teacher in my school. (strict)

12 August is _____ month of the year in South Korea. (wet)

기출 적중문제 ◎⊢⊐

우리말과 같도록 괄호 안의 말을 활용하여 문장을 완성하시오.

> 그녀는 그 도시에서 가장 유명한 요리사이다. (famous, chef)

= _____ in the city.

기출로적중 POINT 4-2 최상급 비교: one of the + 최상급 + 복수명사

정답 p.40

「one of the + 최상급 + 복수명사」는 '가장 ~한 것들 중 하나'라는 의미이다.

London Bridge is **one of the oldest bridges**. 런던교는 가장 오래된 다리들 중 하나이다.

Bill Gates is **one of the richest men** in the world.
빌 게이츠는 세상에서 가장 부유한 남자들 중 한 명이다.

One of the kindest kids in my class is Polly. 나의 반에서 가장 친절한 아이들 중 한 명은 Polly이다.

연습문제 우리말과 같도록 괄호 안의 말을 활용하여 문장을 완성하시오.

1 Gabriel은 그의 팀에서 가장 키가 큰 선수들 중 한 명이다. (tall, player)

= Gabriel is _____ in his team.

2 추석은 한국에서 가장 중요한 공휴일들 중 하나이다. (important, holiday)

= Chuseok is _____ in Korea.

3 그것은 이 도서관에서 가장 두꺼운 책들 중 하나이다. (thick, book)

= It is _____ in this library.

4 마늘은 가장 건강에 좋은 채소들 중 하나이다. (healthy, vegetable)

= Garlic is _____.

5 미국에서 가장 오래된 나무들 중 하나는 캘리포니아에 있다. (old, tree)

= _____ in America is in California.

6 저것이 그 호텔에서 가장 좋은 방들 중 하나니? (nice, room)

= Is that _____ in the hotel?

7 알버트 아인슈타인은 세상에서 가장 유명한 과학자들 중 한 명이었다. (famous, scientist)

= Albert Einstein was _____ in the world.

8 악어는 밀림에서 가장 위험한 동물들 중 하나이다. (dangerous, animal)

= A crocodile is _____ in the jungle.

9 그는 나의 나라에서 가장 대단한 배우들 중 한 명이다. (great, actor)

= He is _____ in my country.

10 바르셀로나는 가장 흥미진진한 도시들 중 하나이다. (exciting, city)

= Barcelona is _____.

11 동수는 유럽에서 가장 놀라운 롤러코스터들 중 하나를 탔다. (amazing, roller coaster)

= Dongsu rode _____ in Europe.

서술형 대비 문제

Ⓐ <보기>에서 알맞은 말을 골라 비교급 형태로 바꿔 문장을 완성하시오.

<보기>	well	small	hard

1 *A*: How do you feel now?

    B: I feel much _____ this morning.

2 *A*: This dress is too big for me.

    B: Sorry. We don't have anything _____ that.

3 *A*: These cookies are even _____ the last ones.

    B: Oh, sorry. I baked them too long.

<보기>	quick	loud	comfortable

4 *A*: I can't hear my alarm in the morning.

    B: Use mine. It's a lot _____ yours.

5 *A*: I'm late for the concert! I should take a taxi.

    B: The subway is _____ a taxi during rush hour.

6 *A*: I like the brown sofa. How about you?

    B: I prefer the white one. It looks _____ the brown one.

Ⓑ 밑줄 친 부분이 어법상 맞으면 O를 쓰고, 틀리면 바르게 고쳐 쓰시오.

1 My bed is as <u>softest</u> as my sister's.   → _____

2 This new phone is <u>thinner</u> than my old one.   → _____

3 I chose this laptop because it was the <u>powerfulest</u>.   → _____

4 The movie was far <u>exciting</u> than the book.   → _____

5 Who is the <u>most strong</u> person in the class?   → _____

6 Yura seems much <u>happyer</u> than yesterday.   → _____

7 Chocolate is <u>the most delicious</u> flavor of all.   → _____

8 The Internet is becoming <u>usefuler and usefuler</u>.   → _____

9 Sharks are not as <u>huger than</u> whales.   → _____

10 Canada is one of the most peaceful <u>countries</u> in the world. → _____

11 I can speak English <u>so fluently as</u> you. → _____

12 This summer is <u>very</u> hotter than last summer. → _____

13 That is <u>the tallest</u> building in our city. → _____

14 Charlie's cat is not <u>so old as</u> mine. → _____

15 She is one of the most popular <u>singer</u> in Korea. → _____

C 다음은 세 대의 자동차를 비교하는 표이다. 괄호 안의 말을 활용하여 문장을 완성하시오.

외관	이름	가격	무게	출시 연도
	Elysium	$50,000	2,000kg	1999
	Falcon 815	$80,000	2,000kg	2010
	Shooting Star	$30,000	1,500kg	2017

1 가격을 비교하세요.
① The Elysium is _____ the Shooting Star. (expensive)
② The Falcon 815 is _____ of the three. (expensive)
③ The Shooting Star is _____ of the three. (cheap)

2 무게를 비교하세요.
① The Elysium is _____ the Falcon 815. (heavy)
② The Shooting Star is _____ the Falcon 815. (light)

3 출시연도를 비교하세요.
① The Elysium is _____ of the three. (old)
② The Falcon 815 is _____ the Elysium. (new)
③ The Shooting Star is _____ of the three. (new)

중간·기말고사 실전 문제

[1-2] 다음 중 원급-비교급-최상급 형태가 잘못된 것을 고르시오.

1

① nice – nicer – nicest
② fat – fatter – fattest
③ bright – brighter – brightest
④ lovely – lovelier – loveliest
⑤ special – specialer – specialest

2

① pretty – prettier – prettiest
② many – more – much
③ little – less – least
④ sad – sadder – saddest
⑤ bad – worse – worst

[3-4] 다음 빈칸에 들어갈 알맞은 것을 고르시오.

3

> Hansu is _____ than his brother.

① kind
② the most kind
③ the kindest
④ more kind
⑤ kinder

4

> The Nile is _____ river in Africa.

① more longer
② the longest
③ the most long
④ longer
⑤ more long

5 다음 빈칸에 공통으로 들어갈 알맞은 것은?

> · He speaks English _____ than me.
> · The second movie was _____ than the first one.

① well
② best
③ better
④ more good
⑤ good

6 다음 중 밑줄 친 부분이 어법상 바른 것은?

① Tomorrow will be <u>cold</u> than today.
② Apples are <u>very</u> more delicious than carrots.
③ I don't talk as loudly <u>so</u> him.
④ Her teddy bear looks <u>much</u> cuter than mine.
⑤ This book is <u>the most helpful</u> than the website.

7 다음 밑줄 친 부분을 바르게 고치지 <u>못한</u> 것은?

① Pepperoni pizza is as tasty <u>so</u> cheese pizza. (→ as)
② My final grade is <u>badder</u> than yours. (→ more bad)
③ Buying a car is <u>more cheap</u> than buying a house. (→ cheaper)
④ You were as <u>braver</u> as Samuel. (→ brave)
⑤ Jacob got <u>more tired and tired</u> during gym class. (→ more and more tired)

8 다음 문장에서 어법상 어색한 부분을 찾아 쓰고 바르게 고쳐 쓰시오.

> This is larger mall in the city.

_____ → _____

9 다음 중 어법상 어색한 것은?

① The lake is not as deep as the ocean.
② He is moving as slowly as a turtle.
③ Her house is as nicer as a palace.
④ My essay is not longer than yours.
⑤ This blouse is more colorful than that one.

10 다음 빈칸에 들어갈 말이 순서대로 짝지어진 것은?

> · This sauce is as _____ as cream.
> · Which product is the _____ in this store?

① mild – useful
② mild – more useful
③ mild – most useful
④ milder – more useful
⑤ milder – most useful

11 다음 표를 보고 괄호 안의 형용사를 활용하여 문장을 완성하시오.

	Sunho	Yujin	Minji
나이	12	11	8

(1) Sunho is _____ than Yujin and Minji. (old)
(2) Minji is _____ of the three. (young)

12 다음 중 어법상 어색한 것은?

① I can run faster than Carol.
② Yesterday was the busiest day of the week.
③ Jane visited the most good restaurant in this town.
④ I can play the guitar as well as my sister.
⑤ Jejudo is one of the most beautiful islands in Korea.

13 다음 중 어법상 바른 것의 개수는?

> ⓐ Paul is the tallest of his brothers.
> ⓑ Your sweater is soft than mine.
> ⓒ A mouse is not as smaller as an ant.
> ⓓ The siren became louder and louder.
> ⓔ A gorilla is one of the toughest animal in the forest.

① 1개   ② 2개   ③ 3개
④ 4개   ⑤ 5개

14 다음 그림을 잘못 표현한 것은?

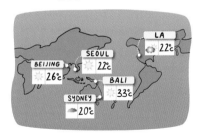

① Seoul is as warm as LA.
② Sydney is colder than Beijing.
③ LA is warmer than Sydney.
④ Seoul is the coldest of all.
⑤ Bali is the hottest of all.

[15-17] 우리말과 같도록 괄호 안의 말을 활용하여 문장을 완성하시오.

15

> 나는 나의 엄마만큼 일찍 일어나기를 원한다. (early)

= I want to get up ＿＿＿＿＿＿ my mom.

16

> 그 환자는 점점 더 건강해지고 있다. (healthy)

= The patient is getting ＿＿＿＿＿＿.

17

> Tim은 그의 반에서 가장 곱슬곱슬한 머리를 가지고 있다. (curly)

= Tim has ＿＿＿＿＿ hair in his class.

18 다음 빈칸에 들어갈 말로 어색한 것은?

> This butterfly is ＿＿＿ more beautiful than other ones.

① a lot   ② far   ③ even
④ much   ⑤ very

19 우리말과 같도록 괄호 안의 말을 활용하여 영작하시오.

> 바이올린은 비올라보다 더 작다. (the violin, the viola)

= ＿＿＿＿＿＿＿＿＿＿＿＿

[20-21] 다음 우리말을 영작할 때 빈칸에 들어갈 알맞은 것을 고르시오.

20

> 세상에서 가장 힘이 센 곤충은 무엇이니?
> = What is ＿＿＿＿＿＿＿＿＿?

① strong insect in the world
② stronger insect in the world
③ more strong insect in the world
④ the strongest insect in the world
⑤ the most strong insect in the world

21

> 강남은 한국에서 가장 붐비는 장소들 중 하나이다.
> = Gangnam is ＿＿＿＿＿＿＿＿＿.

① one of the busiest place in Korea
② the most busy places in Korea
③ one of the busiest places in Korea
④ the busier places in Korea
⑤ one of the most busy places in Korea

22 다음 빈칸에 들어갈 알맞은 것은?

> This painting is more ＿＿＿ than that one.

① big   ② wide   ③ heavy
④ good   ⑤ expensive

23 우리말과 같도록 괄호 안의 말을 알맞게 배열하시오.

> Mario는 Tom만큼 키가 크지 않다. (is, tall, Mario, not, as, Tom, so)

= ＿＿＿＿＿＿＿＿＿＿＿＿

[24-25] 괄호 안의 말을 활용하여 다음 두 문장을 한 문장으로 바꿔 쓰시오.

24

> · The beef is 60 dollars.
> · The pork is 35 dollars.

→ The pork is _____ the beef.
(cheap)

25

> · Mount Everest is 8,848m.
> · Hallasan is 1,950m.

→ Mount Everest is much _____
Hallasan. (high)

26 다음 중 어법상 어색한 것은?

① Tulips are far prettier than sunflowers.
② Jim goes to bed as late as his parents.
③ Winter is the coldest season of the four.
④ Which is more popular dress in this shop?
⑤ This movie was more interesting than that one.

27 다음 빈칸에 들어갈 말이 나머지 넷과 다른 것은?

① The Sun is larger _____ the Earth.
② My shoes are as clean _____ yours.
③ My brother swims faster _____ me.
④ This soup smells nicer _____ that one.
⑤ Studying is more boring _____ playing.

28 다음은 스키장의 두 코스를 비교하는 표이다. 다음 표를 잘못 설명한 것은?

	A course	B course
길이	400m	1km
인기도	★★★★☆	★★★☆☆
난이도	★★☆☆☆	★★★★☆

① B course is not as short as A course.
② A course is more popular than B course.
③ A course is not as difficult as B course.
④ B course is longer than A course.
⑤ B course is easier than A course.

29 다음 표를 바르게 설명한 것을 모두 고르시오.

Bagel	Doughnut	Pretzel
$2	$2	$5

① A doughnut is cheaper than a pretzel.
② A bagel is not as cheap as a doughnut.
③ A bagel is more expensive than a pretzel.
④ A doughnut is as cheap as a pretzel.
⑤ A pretzel is the most expensive of the three.

30 다음 밑줄 친 부분과 바꿔 쓸 수 없는 것은?

> Health is <u>even</u> more important than money.

① still   ② much   ③ very
④ far   ⑤ a lot

CHAPTER 14
전치사

A ball is **in** the box. 공이 상자 안에 있다.

명사 the box 앞에 **in**이 와서 '상자 안에'라는 의미를 나타냈어요. 이렇게 명사나 대명사 앞에 와서 시간, 장소, 위치, 방향 등을 나타내는 것을 **전치사**라고 해요.

기출로 적중 POINT

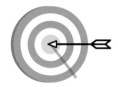

내신 100점 적중!
기출 출제율

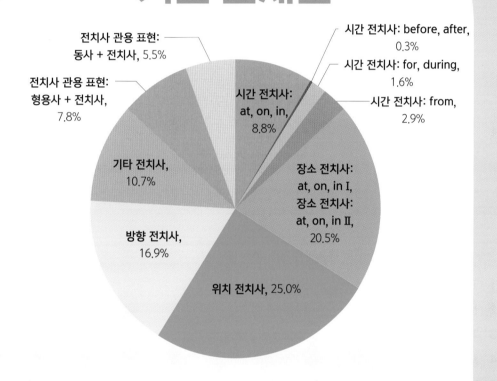

전치사 관용 표현:
동사 + 전치사, 5.5%

전치사 관용 표현:
형용사 + 전치사,
7.8%

시간 전치사: before, after,
0.3%

시간 전치사: for, during,
1.6%

시간 전치사: from,
2.9%

시간 전치사:
at, on, in,
8.8%

기타 전치사,
10.7%

방향 전치사,
16.9%

장소 전치사:
at, on, in I,
장소 전치사:
at, on, in II,
20.5%

위치 전치사, 25.0%

TOP 1 **위치 전치사 (25%)**
위치를 나타내는 전치사의 의미와 쓰임을 묻는 문제가 자주 출제된다.

TOP 2 **장소 전치사: at, on, in I, II (20.5%)**
장소를 나타내는 전치사 at, on, in의 쓰임을 묻는 문제가 자주 출제된다.

TOP 3 **방향 전치사 (16.9%)**
방향을 나타내는 전치사의 의미와 쓰임을 묻는 문제가 자주 출제된다.

시간 전치사: at, on, in

at, on, in은 '~에'라는 의미로 시간을 나타낸다.

at	시각	**at** 10 o'clock 10시에　　**at** 7:30 7시 30분에
	시점	**at** noon 정오에　　**at** night 밤에　　**at** the time 그때에
on	요일	**on** Monday 월요일에　　**on** Friday 금요일에 (Tip) 「on + 요일s」: (요일)마다　　**on** Sundays 일요일마다
	날짜, 기념일	**on** May 1 5월 1일에　　**on** August 14, 1996 1996년 8월 14일에 **on** Valentine's Day 밸런타인데이에　　**on** my birthday 나의 생일에
in	월, 계절	**in** January 1월에　　**in** winter 겨울에
	연도, 세기	**in** 2002 2002년에　　**in** the 20th century 20세기에
	아침·오후·저녁	**in** the morning/afternoon/evening 아침/오후/저녁에 (Tip) 특정한 날의 아침·오후·저녁을 나타낼 때는 on을 쓴다. 　　**on** Monday afternoon 월요일 오후에 　　**on** Christmas morning 크리스마스 아침에

연습문제　괄호 안에서 at, on, in 중 알맞은 것을 고르시오.

1 The Korean War ended (at / on / in) 1953.

2 Matt left for London (at / on / in) April 6, 2004.

3 The class starts (at / on / in) 9 o'clock every weekday.

4 Many different flowers bloom (at / on / in) spring.

5 Would you like to have lunch (at / on / in) Saturday?

6 I hate waking up (at / on / in) Monday morning.

7 The restaurant is not open (at / on / in) Tuesdays.

8 What are you going to do (at / on / in) your birthday?

 **기출 적중문제**

다음 문장에서 어법상 <u>어색한</u> 부분을 찾아 쓰고 바르게 고쳐 쓰시오.

> Mila will visit Paris on September.

_____ → _____

시간 전치사: before, after

정답 p.42

before와 after는 시간을 나타낸다.

before	~ 전에	Ms. Scott goes to work before 8 o'clock. Scott씨는 8시 전에 출근한다. Do your homework before dinner. 저녁 식사 전에 너의 숙제를 해라.
after	~ 후에	After school, she met her friend. 방과 후에, 그녀는 그녀의 친구를 만났다. They looked tired after the game. 그들은 그 경기 후에 피곤해 보였다. (Tip) '(기간) 후에'라는 의미를 나타내기 위해 「in + 기간을 나타내는 표현」을 쓸 수 있다. The cake will be ready in two hours. 그 케이크는 두 시간 후에 준비가 될 것이다.

연습문제 우리말과 같도록 before나 after와 괄호 안의 말을 활용하여 문장을 완성하시오.

1 내가 주말 전에 너의 책을 돌려줄게. (the weekend)

= I will return your book _____ .

2 점심 식사 후에 우리가 아이스크림 가게에 가도 되니? (lunch)

= Can we go to the ice cream shop _____ ?

3 크리스마스 전에, Kate는 약간의 선물을 사야 한다. (Christmas)

= _____ , Kate has to buy some presents.

4 Mindy는 11시 전에 잠이 든다. (11 o'clock)

= Mindy goes to sleep _____ .

5 9시 후에 빨래를 하지 마라. (nine)

= Don't do laundry _____ .

6 나의 형과 나는 저녁 식사 전에 비디오 게임을 했다. (dinner)

= My brother and I played video games _____ .

7 그 연극 후에, 우리는 같이 걸어서 집에 갔다. (the play)

= _____ , we walked home together.

8 아침 식사 후에 여기에서 그들을 만나자. (breakfast)

= Let's meet them here _____ .

9 나의 13번째 생일 전에, 나는 특별한 무언가를 하고 싶다. (my 13th birthday)

= _____ , I want to do something special.

10 그들은 그들의 결혼 후에 캘리포니아로 이사했다. (their marriage)

= They moved to California _____ .

시간 전치사: for, during

정답 p.42

for와 during은 둘 다 '~ 동안'이라는 의미이지만, for 뒤에는 숫자를 포함한 기간 표현이 오고 during 뒤에는 특정 기간을 나타내는 명사가 온다.

for	+ 숫자를 포함한 기간 표현	I waited for **40 minutes**. 나는 40분 동안 기다렸다. Amy played tennis for **an hour**. Amy는 한 시간 동안 테니스를 쳤다.
during	+ 특정 기간을 나타내는 명사	It is humid during **the summer**. 여름 동안에는 습하다. I traveled to the US during **the vacation**. 나는 방학 동안 미국으로 여행했다.

연습문제 다음 빈칸에 for나 during 중 알맞은 것을 쓰시오.

1 She slept _____ 12 hours last weekend.

2 Press the button _____ five seconds.

3 You performed well _____ the football game.

4 Nick lived in the Philippines _____ three years.

5 The actor hurt his knee _____ the play.

6 I have nothing to do _____ the holidays.

7 My mother bought a beautiful rug _____ her trip.

8 I didn't talk to my best friend _____ a few months.

9 My dog was scared _____ the thunderstorm.

10 We often visit our grandmother's house _____ the summer.

11 My family has lived in this town _____ hundreds of years.

기출 적중문제 ◎

다음 빈칸에 공통으로 들어갈 알맞은 것은?

> Bake the cake _____ 30 minutes, and let it cool _____ an hour.

① during   ② for   ③ before

④ on   ⑤ at

기출로적중 POINT 1-4 시간 전치사: from

정답 p.42

> **from은 '~부터'라는 의미로, 시간을 나타내는 표현 앞에서 일이 시작되는 시점을 나타낸다.**
>
> The shop is open from **7 A.M.** 그 가게는 오전 7시부터 연다.
> She worked here from **2002.** 그녀는 여기에서 2002년부터 일했다.
>
> (Tip) 「from ~ to …」는 '~부터 …까지'라는 의미로, 기간을 나타낸다.
> The shop is open from **7 A.M.** to **9 P.M.** 그 가게는 오전 7시부터 오후 9시까지 연다.
> She worked here from **2002** to **2009.** 그녀는 여기에서 2002년부터 2009년까지 일했다.

연습문제 우리말과 같도록 알맞은 전치사와 괄호 안의 말을 활용하여 문장을 완성하시오.

1 그는 매일 아침 8시부터 수업이 있다. (8 o'clock)

= He has a class _____ every morning.

2 새로운 음악 수업들은 다음 주부터 시작한다. (next week)

= New music lessons start _____.

3 나는 2005년부터 2012년까지 발리에서 살았다. (2005, 2012)

= I lived in Bali _____.

4 나는 폭풍 때문에 화요일부터 목요일까지 조깅하러 가지 않았다. (Tuesday, Thursday)

= I didn't go jogging _____ because of the storm.

5 올해부터, 나의 삶에 많은 변화들이 있을 것이다. (this year)

= _____, there will be many changes in my life.

6 그 빵집은 국경일로 오늘부터 다음 주 월요일까지 문을 닫는다. (today, next Monday)

= The bakery is closed _____ for the national holiday.

7 나는 프랑스어를 배우기 위해 9월부터 12월까지 파리에 있을 것이다. (September, December)

= I will be in Paris _____ to learn French.

기출 적중문제

우리말과 같도록 빈칸에 알맞은 말을 쓰시오.

나는 월요일부터 금요일까지 학교에 다닌다.

= I attend school _____ _____ _____ _____.

at, on, in은 장소를 나타낸다.

at ~에, ~에서	비교적 좁은 장소나 하나의 지점	**at** the station 역에	**at** the corner 모퉁이에
on ~에, ~ 위에	표면에 접촉한 상태	**on** the desk 책상 위에 **on** the floor 바닥에	**on** the wall 벽에 **on** the sofa 소파 위에
in ~에, ~ 안에	비교적 넓은 장소나 공간의 내부	**in** Seoul 서울에 **in** China 중국에 **in** the box 상자 안에 **in** the building 건물 안에	

연습문제 다음 그림을 보고 빈칸에 at, on, in 중 알맞은 것을 쓰시오.

[1-5]

[6-10]

1 There is a man _____ the room.

2 The man is standing _____ the window.

3 There are three coats _____ the closet.

4 Some teddy bears are _____ the bed.

5 A telephone is _____ the table.

6 People are waiting _____ the bus stop.

7 Lots of posters are _____ the wall.

8 A pizza box is _____ the trash can.

9 A girl is sitting _____ the bench.

10 There are books _____ the girl's bag.

기출 적중문제

다음 그림을 보고 괄호 안의 말을 활용하여 문장을 완성하시오.

A: Where is my phone?
B: It is _____. (the pillow)

at, on, in은 다양한 상황을 나타내기도 한다.

at	일상적으로 다니는 장소	at home 집에서 at school 학교에서 at work 직장에서 at the airport 공항에서 at the library 도서관에서
	행사, 모임	at a concert 콘서트에서 at a meeting 회의에서 at a party 파티에서
on	길, 층	on the street 길 위에 on the second floor 2층에
	교통수단	on a bus 버스에 on a subway 지하철에 on a train 기차에 on a plane 비행기에 (Tip) 예외: in a car 차에 in a taxi 택시에
	통신수단	on the Internet 인터넷에서 on the phone 전화로
in	자연환경	in the sky 하늘에 in the sea 바다에 in the world 세상에
	인쇄물	in a book 책에 in a dictionary 사전에 in a newspaper 신문에 in a picture 그림/사진에
	(특정 장소에서) ~하는 중인	in bed 취침 중인 in the hospital 입원 중인
	기타	in a blue shirt 파란 셔츠를 입은 in half 반으로 in danger 위험에 빠진 in a hurry 서두르는 in a line 한 줄로

연습문제 다음 빈칸에 at, on, in 중 알맞은 것을 쓰시오.

1 There are no clouds _____ the sky.

2 Monica is _____ bed now.

3 I had a great time _____ the concert.

4 There were many seats _____ the bus.

5 Please fold the paper _____ half.

6 Get _____ the car over there.

7 The woman _____ the green dress is Roxy.

8 I first met George _____ his party.

9 Our apartment is _____ the third floor.

10 Many animals in the ocean are _____ danger.

11 The guests are standing _____ a line.

12 Some people are running _____ the road.

13 The boy _____ the picture is my cousin, Adam.

14 Could you pick me up _____ the airport?

15 I read about Helen Keller _____ a book.

16 Sophie will stay _____ home all day tomorrow.

17 I like to spend the weekends _____ the café.

18 New York is one of the busiest cities _____ the world.

19 Would you like to go swimming _____ the sea?

20 I had to stand _____ the train for 30 minutes.

21 The store moved to the building _____ Main Street.

22 There was an article about me _____ the newspaper.

23 My father was _____ work when I got home yesterday.

24 There are always a lot of people _____ the subway.

25 My younger sister made many friends _____ school.

26 I often speak to my grandparents _____ the phone.

27 My aunt is _____ the hospital because she broke her leg.

28 You can look up the meanings of words _____ a dictionary.

29 Do not put your personal information _____ the Internet.

30 I was _____ a hurry this morning, so I couldn't eat breakfast.

기출 적중문제 ◎

다음 빈칸에 공통으로 들어갈 알맞은 것은?

> · Is there a bank _____ Maple Street?
> · I'm _____ the subway right now.

① at   ② on   ③ in
④ to   ⑤ from

기출로적중 POINT 3 위치 전치사

정답 p.42

다음 전치사는 위치를 나타낸다.

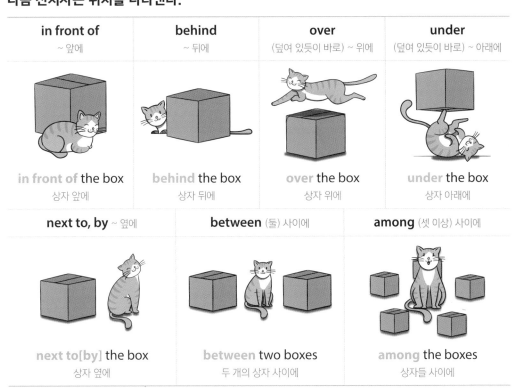

in front of ~ 앞에	**behind** ~ 뒤에	**over** (덮여 있듯이 바로) ~ 위에	**under** (덮여 있듯이 바로) ~ 아래에
in front of the box 상자 앞에	behind the box 상자 뒤에	over the box 상자 위에	under the box 상자 아래에

next to, by ~ 옆에	**between** (둘) 사이에	**among** (셋 이상) 사이에
next to[by] the box 상자 옆에	between two boxes 두 개의 상자 사이에	among the boxes 상자들 사이에

연습문제 A 우리말과 같도록 빈칸에 알맞은 전치사를 쓰시오.

1 그는 그의 차를 서점 앞에 주차했다.

= He parked his car _____ the bookstore.

2 계산대 뒤에 있는 만화책을 봐도 되나요?

= Could I see the comic book _____ the counter?

3 나는 두 명의 키가 큰 아이들 사이에 서 있었다.

= I was standing _____ two tall kids.

4 그 도시의 길 아래에는 많은 지하철 노선들이 있다.

= There are many subway lines _____ the city's streets.

5 그 약국은 은행 옆에 있다.

= The pharmacy is _____ the bank.

6 그 강 위에 20개 이상의 다리가 있다.

= There are more than 20 bridges _____ the river.

7 너는 이 다섯 개의 영화 중에 골라야 한다.

= You should choose _____ these five movies.

연습문제 **B** 다음 그림을 보고 <보기>의 전치사와 괄호 안의 말을 활용하여 문장을 완성하시오.

| <보기> under   by   between   over   behind   in front of |

1  **2**  **3**

4  **5**  **6**

1 There is a small tree _____. (the armchair)

2 The shy cat often hides _____. (the bed)

3 Everyone stood _____ for the group picture. (the statue)

4 Samuel is doing yoga _____ during class. (Nancy)

5 My dog jumped _____ and ran away. (the fence)

6 The fire station is _____. (the hospital and the library)

기출 적중문제 🎯

다음 그림을 <u>잘못</u> 표현한 것은?

① The desk is next to the bed.

② The monitor is behind the hat.

③ The guitar is on the bed.

④ The vase is between the desk and the bookshelf.

⑤ The cell phone is in front of the desk.

기출로적중 POINT 4 방향 전치사

다음 전치사는 방향을 나타낸다.

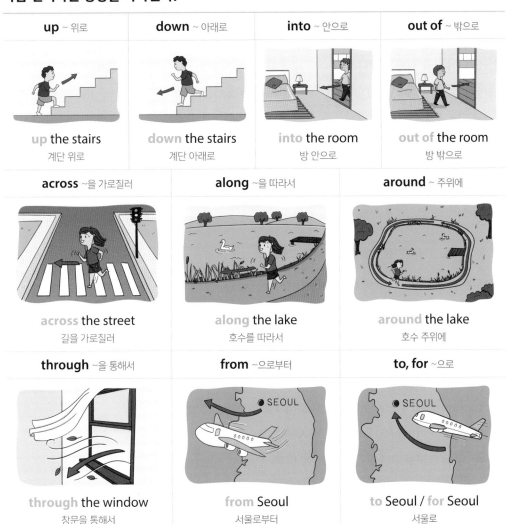

up ~ 위로	**down** ~ 아래로	**into** ~ 안으로	**out of** ~ 밖으로
up the stairs 계단 위로	down the stairs 계단 아래로	into the room 방 안으로	out of the room 방 밖으로

across ~을 가로질러	**along** ~을 따라서	**around** ~ 주위에
across the street 길을 가로질러	along the lake 호수를 따라서	around the lake 호수 주위에

through ~을 통해서	**from** ~으로부터	**to, for** ~으로
through the window 창문을 통해서	from Seoul 서울로부터	to Seoul / for Seoul 서울로

(Tip) to와 for는 둘 다 '~으로'라는 의미이지만, to는 주로 동사 go, come과 함께 쓰여 도착 지점을 나타내고, for 는 주로 동사 leave, start와 함께 쓰여 가고자 하는 방향을 나타낸다.

David **went to** Seoul. David는 서울로 갔다.
David **left for** Seoul. David는 서울로 떠났다.

우리말과 같도록 빈칸에 알맞은 전치사를 <보기>에서 골라 쓰시오.

<보기> along   around   out of   across   down   from   through   up

1 바위가 언덕 아래로 굴러가고 있다.   = A rock is rolling _____ the hill.

2 Diego는 멕시코에서 왔다.   = Diego came _____ Mexico.

3 나일강은 이집트를 통해서 흐른다.   = The Nile flows _____ Egypt.

4 사람들이 강가를 따라서 달리고 있다.   = People are running _____ the riverside.

5 갑자기, 쥐가 상자 밖으로 뛰쳐나왔다.   = Suddenly, a mouse jumped _____ the box.

6 우리들은 지금 계단 위로 올라가고 있다.   = We are going _____ the stairs now.

7 돌고래들이 그 섬 주위를 수영하고 있다.   = Dolphins are swimming _____ the island.

8 그는 물을 찾기 위해 사막을 가로질러 걸었다.   = He walked _____ the desert to find water.

괄호 안에서 가장 알맞은 전치사를 고르시오.

1 The child's ball flew (out of / over) the fence.

2 Kelly poured milk (for / into) the glass.

3 My parents go (to / for) Rome every summer.

4 My brother made a path (through / up) the snow.

5 Smoke came (for / out of) the volcano for several days.

6 The tourists threw coins (into / between) the fountain.

7 The train leaves (to / for) Busan at 10 A.M.

8 Elena likes jogging (out of / along) the river.

9 The post office is (across / into) the street from city hall.

10 The racers drove their cars (for / around) the track.

11 The hikers are climbing (up / from) the mountain.

12 There are many small restaurants (through / along) the beach.

기출 적중문제

다음 우리말을 영작할 때 빈칸에 들어갈 알맞은 전치사는?

Daniel은 그 수영장 안으로 뛰어들고 있다.
= Daniel is diving _____ the swimming pool.

① over   ② across   ③ into
④ out of   ⑤ through

기출로적중 POINT 5 기타 전치사

정답 p.43

다음 전치사는 다양한 의미를 나타낸다.

	~과 함께	Minjun plays soccer with Jiho every weekend. 민준이는 지호와 함께 주말마다 축구를 한다.
with	~을 가진	The woman with pink hair works in this shop. 분홍 머리를 가진 그 여자는 이 가게에서 일한다.
	~을 이용해서 (도구)	Cut the cake with that knife. 저 칼을 이용해서 케이크를 잘라라.
without	~ 없이	I followed him without a word. 나는 말 없이 그를 따라갔다.
by	~까지	Cory will arrive by 10 o'clock. Cory는 10시까지 도착할 것이다.
	~을 타고 (교통수단)	Yejoon is coming by train. 예준이는 기차를 타고 오고 있다. (Tip) 예외: on foot 걸어서
about	~에 대해	What is he talking about? 그는 무엇에 대해 이야기하고 있니?
like	~처럼	You swim like a fish. 너는 물고기처럼 수영한다.
	~ 같은	I like sour fruits like lemon. 나는 레몬 같은 신 과일을 좋아한다.
for	~을 위해	What can I do for you? 내가 너를 위해 무엇을 할 수 있니?
	~에 찬성하여	Half of the students were for the new rule. 학생들의 절반은 새 규칙에 찬성했다.
against	~에 반대하여/맞서	I played badminton against my older sister. 나는 나의 누나에 맞서 배드민턴을 쳤다.

연습문제 A 우리말과 같도록 빈칸에 알맞은 전치사를 <보기>에서 골라 쓰시오.

<보기> by for like about against without with on

1 그는 매일 지하철을 타고 학교에 간다.
= He goes to school _____ subway every day.

2 Joshua는 연필을 이용해서 이 그림을 그렸다.
= Joshua drew this picture _____ a pencil.

3 나는 나의 친구들을 위해 좋은 무언가를 할 것이다.
= I will do something nice _____ my friends.

4 Rangers는 Panthers에 맞선 하키 경기를 이겼다.

= The Rangers won the hockey game _____ the Panthers.

5 Jessie는 전화상에서 그녀의 엄마처럼 들린다.

= Jessie sounds _____ her mother on the phone.

6 그는 걸어서 쇼핑몰에 갔다.

= He went to the shopping mall _____ foot.

7 나의 삼촌은 초록색 눈을 가진 그 남자이다.

= My uncle is the man _____ green eyes.

8 Sam은 그의 스마트폰 없이 어디에도 가지 않는다.

= Sam doesn't go anywhere _____ his smartphone.

9 그녀는 그 여행을 취소하는 것에 찬성한다.

= She is _____ canceling the trip.

10 Mary는 유명한 탐험가에 대한 책을 읽었다.

= Mary read a book _____ a famous explorer.

11 Harrison은 지난달에 그의 형과 함께 나의 집에 왔다.

= Harrison came to my house _____ his brother last month.

12 모든 사람은 다음주 월요일까지 그들의 에세이를 제출해야 한다.

= Everyone must turn in their essays _____ next Monday.

연습문제 **B** 괄호 안에서 알맞은 전치사를 고르시오.

Last week, I went to Toronto ⓐ(by / with) my sister. She had to go there ⓑ(for / like) a violin competition. During the competition, she competed ⓒ(for / against) many young musicians. She looked very nervous, but she played ⓓ(without / like) a professional. I don't know much ⓔ(about / with) violin music, but I really enjoyed her performance. She won second prize, and I was really happy for her.

기출 적중문제 🎯

다음 빈칸에 들어갈 말이 순서대로 짝지어진 것은?

· The man _____ the beard is Bill's father.

· We must arrive at the station _____ noon.

① with - for   ② with - by   ③ for - by

④ by - for   ⑤ by - with

기출로적중 POINT 6-1 전치사 관용 표현: 형용사 + 전치사

정답 p.43

다음은 형용사와 함께 쓰이는 전치사 관용 표현이다.

be good at ~을 잘하다
be afraid of ~을 무서워하다
be full of ~으로 가득 차 있다
be famous for ~으로 유명하다
be sorry for[about] ~에 대해 미안해하다
be busy with ~으로 바쁘다
be careful with ~을 조심하다

be angry at ~에 화를 내다
be proud of ~을 자랑스러워하다
be good/bad for ~에 좋다/나쁘다
be ready for ~에 준비가 되다
be late for ~에 늦다
be familiar with ~에 익숙하다
be different from ~과 다르다

The bottle is full of juice. 그 병은 주스로 가득 차 있다.
I'm ready for bed now. 나는 이제 잘 준비가 됐다.
She is busy with work. 그녀는 일로 바쁘다.

연습문제 A 다음 빈칸에 알맞은 전치사를 쓰시오.

1 My dog is afraid _____ strangers.

2 Be careful _____ the vase.

3 My sister is good _____ swimming.

4 Chloe is angry _____ her best friend.

5 I'm sorry _____ the trouble.

6 Marie is late _____ her yoga class.

7 The teacher was proud _____ his students.

8 Exercising regularly is good _____ your health.

9 Please be ready _____ your presentation.

10 The refrigerator is full _____ fruits and vegetables.

11 Chef Renaldo is famous _____ his cream pasta.

12 The students are busy _____ their homework.

13 I am not familiar _____ this model of camera.

14 The dress was different _____ the one in the picture.

15 Watching too much TV is bad _____ your eyesight.

1 Honey is good (from / for) a sore throat.

2 The pool is full (of / for) clean water.

3 Finally, I am ready (for / of) the speech.

4 You must be proud (in / of) yourself.

5 Italy is famous (for / to) its delicious food.

6 The playground is full (from / of) children.

7 I am sorry (for / to) being late.

8 Plastic is bad (for / at) the environment.

9 Be careful (with / in) that sharp knife.

10 Pedro is afraid (from / of) spiders and snakes.

11 Glen is familiar (to / with) Korean cultures.

12 I like studying math, but I'm not good (at / for) it.

13 Sujin is busy (for / with) preparing for the event.

14 All students should be familiar (for / with) the school rules.

15 Everyone is angry (in / at) Julie for her mean behavior.

16 Everyone in my family is afraid (with / of) heights.

17 My answer was different (from / at) those of my friends.

18 The visitors should be careful (for / with) all the sculptures.

19 Several students were late (of / for) class because of the snow.

20 We made dumplings, and they were full (of / from) kimchi and pork.

기출 적중문제

다음 빈칸에 공통으로 들어갈 알맞은 것은?

· Please be careful _____ those boxes.

· I'm not familiar _____ Greek food.

· Jasmine was busy _____ the housework.

① of   ② with   ③ from

④ for   ⑤ at

POINT 6-2 전치사 관용 표현: 동사 + 전치사

정답 p.43

다음은 동사와 함께 쓰이는 전치사 관용 표현이다.

look at ~을 보다
laugh at ~을 보고/듣고 웃다, 비웃다
spend 시간/돈 on 시간/돈을 쓰다

look for ~을 찾다
listen to ~을 듣다
thank … for ~에 대해 …에게 감사해하다

wait for ~을 기다리다
ask for ~을 요청하다

Who did he **wait for**? 그는 누구를 기다렸니?
Tom **spent** two hours **on** his homework. Tom은 그의 숙제에 두 시간을 썼다.

연습문제 │ 우리말과 같도록 빈칸에 알맞은 말을 쓰시오.

1 그는 매일 음악을 듣는다.

= He _____ _____ music every day.

2 저는 당신의 초대에 대해 당신에게 감사합니다.

= I _____ you _____ your invitation.

3 태양을 직접적으로 보지 마라.

= Don't _____ _____ the sun directly.

4 Andy의 누나는 그를 비웃었다.

= Andy's sister _____ _____ him.

5 너는 어떻게 도움을 요청하는지 배워야 한다.

= You should learn how to _____ _____ help.

6 나는 너를 로비에서 기다릴 것이다.

= I will _____ _____ you in the lobby.

7 Smith씨는 수백만 달러를 요트에 썼다.

= Mr. Smith _____ millions of dollars _____ a yacht.

8 우리는 그 잃어버린 개를 찾아야 한다.

= We should _____ _____ the lost dog.

기출 적중문제

다음 빈칸에 공통으로 들어갈 알맞은 전치사를 쓰시오.

· I will ask _____ a refund.
· He is looking _____ his car key.

서술형 대비 문제

A 밑줄 친 부분이 어법상 맞으면 O를 쓰고, 틀리면 in, on, at 중 하나로 고쳐 쓰시오.

1 The fireworks start <u>in</u> night. → _____

2 Everyone <u>on</u> the plane wore a seat belt. → _____

3 Don't forget the field trip <u>on</u> Friday. → _____

4 You can see many stars <u>at</u> the sky. → _____

5 Columbus discovered America <u>on</u> 1492. → _____

6 What do people do <u>in</u> Halloween? → _____

7 The teacher's room is <u>at</u> the third floor. → _____

8 Let's have coffee <u>in</u> the afternoon. → _____

B 다음 그림을 보고 빈칸에 알맞은 전치사를 <보기>에서 골라 쓰시오.

<보기> about up by with without

A monkey stood ⓐ_____ a tall tree. The monkey was hungry. There were coconuts in the tree, but the monkey was worried ⓑ_____ climbing the tall tree. However, the monkey decided to be brave. It slowly went ⓒ_____ the tree. Suddenly, a snake ⓓ_____ sharp teeth appeared. It looked very scary. The monkey climbed down the tree ⓔ_____ a coconut. It felt angry and kicked the tree. Surprisingly, a coconut fell down!

C 다음 그림을 보고 빈칸에 알맞은 전치사를 <보기>에서 골라 쓰시오.

<보기>   next to   out of   in front of   into   on   through   over

1 There is a clock _____ the wall.

2 The cat is jumping _____ the table.

3 A girl is walking _____ the house.

4 There is a table _____ the bookshelf.

5 There are small vases _____ the sofa.

6 A bird is flying _____ the house _____ the window.

D 우리말과 같도록 빈칸에 알맞은 전치사를 <보기>에서 골라 쓰시오.

<보기>   under   at   of   by   into

1 Macy는 항상 택시를 타고 집에 간다.
   = Macy always goes home _____ taxi.

2 나는 조심하지 않아서, 구멍 안으로 빠졌다.
   = I wasn't careful, so I fell _____ a hole.

3 그 서랍은 플라스틱 숟가락들로 가득 차 있다.
   = The drawer is full _____ plastic spoons.

4 Jessica는 나무 아래에 있는 그 남자를 보고 있다.
   = Jessica is looking _____ the man _____ the tree.

<보기>   about   for   of   like   during

5 Carter는 바퀴벌레처럼 많은 다리를 가진 벌레들을 무서워한다.
   = Carter is afraid _____ bugs with many legs _____ cockroaches.

6 그 주민 센터에는 아이들을 위한 수영 강습이 있다.
   = The community center has swimming lessons _____ children.

7 Violet은 여름 방학 동안 화성에 대한 책을 읽었다.
   = Violet read a book _____ Mars _____ the summer vacation.

중간 · 기말고사 실전 문제

1 다음 빈칸에 들어갈 알맞은 것은?

> The school starts _____ March 2.

① in ② on ③ at
④ for ⑤ to

2 다음 중 밑줄 친 부분이 어법상 어색한 것은?

① It often rains in Vietnam <u>in</u> the summer.
② Many people drink coffee <u>at</u> the morning.
③ The cafeteria always serves pizza <u>on</u> Fridays.
④ The pharmacy opens <u>at</u> 8 A.M.
⑤ I got a lot of presents <u>on</u> my birthday.

3 다음 빈칸에 공통으로 들어갈 알맞은 것은?

> · Jonathan studied Spanish in Colombia _____ six months.
> · Let me carry the bag _____ you.

① in ② from ③ at
④ for ⑤ during

4 다음 우리말을 알맞게 영작한 것은?

> 그 허리케인은 3일 동안 계속되었다.

① The hurricane continued on three days.
② The hurricane continued in three days.
③ The hurricane continued before three days.
④ The hurricane continued during three days.
⑤ The hurricane continued for three days.

[5-7] 우리말과 같도록 빈칸에 알맞은 전치사를 쓰시오.

5

> 물고기들이 바위 뒤에 숨어 있다.

= The fish are hiding _____ the rocks.

6

> 열쇠들이 나의 주머니 밖으로 떨어졌다.

= The keys fell _____ my pocket.

7

> 그 벽난로 앞에 몇 개의 의자들이 있다.

= There are several chairs _____ the fireplace.

8 다음 글의 빈칸에 알맞은 전치사를 쓰시오.

> Dear Emma,
>
> My birthday is _____ October 1. Can you come to my birthday party? The party will be _____ Jimmy's Pizza Palace at 7 P.M. It is _____ Main Street. I hope to see you there!
>
> Best Regards,
> Katie

9 다음 그림을 보고 빈칸에 알맞은 전치사를 <보기>에서 골라 쓰시오.

<보기>   on   in   next to   under

(1) There is a fountain _____ the tree.

(2) A bird is sitting _____ the boy's head.

(3) The boy is reading a book _____ the tree.

10 다음 빈칸에 공통으로 들어갈 알맞은 것은?

· We just came _____ the library.
· He goes to work _____ Monday to Thursday.

① during   ② out of   ③ on
④ to   ⑤ from

11 다음 중 밑줄 친 부분이 어법상 어색한 것은?

① My parents are going to Toronto <u>at</u> June.
② Yuna was born <u>on</u> June 23, 1993.
③ The concert is <u>from</u> two to four.
④ The tournament will begin <u>in</u> a week.
⑤ We went camping <u>during</u> the summer vacation.

12 다음 중 밑줄 친 like의 쓰임이 나머지 넷과 다른 것은?

① I want to buy a wallet <u>like</u> yours.
② You look just <u>like</u> your father.
③ Rachel's hair is not <u>like</u> her sister's.
④ I <u>like</u> watching sports games.
⑤ These flowers do not smell <u>like</u> roses.

13 다음 우리말을 영작할 때 빈칸에 들어갈 알맞은 전치사는?

우리는 그 울타리를 따라서 꽃들을 심었다.
= We planted flowers _____ the fence.

① through   ② across   ③ under
④ from   ⑤ along

14 다음 빈칸에 들어갈 말이 순서대로 짝지어진 것은?

· Don't smoke _____ the building.
· Hyejin put her bag _____ the floor.

① in – on   ② to – on   ③ on – in
④ on – at   ⑤ in – at

15 다음 빈칸에 공통으로 들어갈 알맞은 것은?

· Anton likes to go hiking _____ his dog on weekends.
· Cut the cucumbers _____ this knife.

① by   ② about   ③ for
④ with   ⑤ against

16 다음 빈칸에 들어갈 말이 나머지 넷과 다른 것은?

① My family moved to Spain _____ 1999.
② Yeri is talking to her friend _____ the phone.
③ Many people are standing _____ a line.
④ Chris is the boy _____ a black shirt.
⑤ I always take a nap _____ the afternoon.

17 다음 밑줄 친 ⓐ~ⓔ 중 어법상 어색한 것을 찾아 기호를 쓰고 바르게 고쳐 쓰시오.

· Jim is looking ⓐfor his blue socks.
· What are you talking ⓑat?
· Please wait ⓒof me at the front gate.
· We cannot live ⓓwithout air and water.
· We laughed ⓔin the comedian's joke.

(1) _____ → _____
(2) _____ → _____
(3) _____ → _____

[18-19] 다음 빈칸에 들어갈 알맞은 것은?

18

James loves to listen _____ music.

① of   ② like   ③ to
④ from   ⑤ with

19

England is famous _____ its rainy weather.

① on   ② for   ③ by
④ of   ⑤ at

20 다음 빈칸에 들어갈 말이 순서대로 짝지어진 것은?

· Samantha is popular _____ her classmates.
· I was sitting _____ two children on the plane.

① among – between
② among – among
③ among – at
④ between – between
⑤ between – at

21 다음 (A)~(C)에 들어갈 말이 바르게 짝지어진 것은?

· I usually buy chocolate ____(A)____ Valentine's Day.
· The girl ____(B)____ the picture looked happy.
· The class begins ____(C)____ nine.

	(A)	(B)	(C)
①	on	on	in
②	at	at	on
③	in	at	at
④	on	in	at
⑤	at	in	on

22 다음 중 밑줄 친 부분이 어법상 어색한 것은?

① Where were you <u>in</u> Sunday evening?
② I want to go on a trip <u>with</u> my friends.
③ I often feel sleepy <u>at</u> 3 o'clock.
④ That balloon looks <u>like</u> a bear.
⑤ Can you finish your homework <u>by</u> noon?

23 다음 그림을 보고 빈칸에 들어갈 말이 순서대로 짝지어진 것을 고르시오.

A: Excuse me. Where is the library?
B: Go straight and turn left. It is _____ the post office and the bank. It is _____ city hall.

① between – by
② next to – behind
③ between – in front of
④ next to – by
⑤ among – in front of

24 다음 빈칸에 들어갈 말이 순서대로 짝지어진 것은?

· The woman put her hands _____ her pockets.
· I went for a walk _____ the riverside.

① across – of   ② across – along
③ into – of   ④ into – along
⑤ up – of

25 다음 빈칸에 들어갈 알맞은 것은?

Jaemin takes a tennis lesson _____ Saturdays.

① in   ② on   ③ at
④ to   ⑤ for

26 다음 중 어법상 어색한 것은?

① Paul stayed in Germany for five years.
② Someone was snoring during the concert.
③ Turn off your phone during class.
④ I couldn't sleep well for a month.
⑤ Let's take a break during 20 minutes.

[27-28] 다음 빈칸에 들어갈 말이 순서대로 짝지어진 것을 고르시오.

27

· My house is _____ the park.
· She was late _____ the important interview.

① next to – for   ② next to – on
③ through – on   ④ through – up
⑤ next to – down

28

· Turn left _____ the next corner.
· Go _____ the stairs.

① at – into   ② in – down
③ on – down   ④ at – down
⑤ in – into

29 다음 빈칸에 들어갈 알맞은 것은?

My cousin is good _____ playing the flute.

① to　　　② with　　　③ for
④ from　　⑤ at

30 다음 중 밑줄 친 부분이 어법상 어색한 것은?

① I can't see <u>without</u> my glasses.
② I went to school <u>by</u> taxi today.
③ I often study <u>at</u> the library.
④ I cut the apple pie <u>on</u> half.
⑤ I sing and dance <u>on</u> New Year's Eve.

31 다음 (A)~(C)에 들어갈 말이 바르게 짝지어진 것은?

· I am not ready ___(A)___ the exam.
· Are you familiar ___(B)___ this area?
· The documentary ___(C)___ sharks was interesting.

	(A)	(B)	(C)
①	for	with	by
②	to	with	by
③	for	of	about
④	for	with	about
⑤	to	of	by

32 다음 빈칸에 들어갈 말이 순서대로 짝지어진 것은?

· He is going _____ the store to get some milk.
· I met my old friend _____ the subway.

① to - with　② for - on　③ to - on
④ for - by　　⑤ to - with

33 다음 빈칸에 들어갈 알맞은 것은?

Various animals live _____ the sea.

① in　　　② to　　　③ at
④ into　　⑤ on

34 다음 (A)~(C)에 들어갈 말이 바르게 짝지어진 것은?

· Thomas is busy ___(A)___ his school project.
· Let's look ___(B)___ the stars tonight.
· Thank you ___(C)___ your service.

	(A)	(B)	(C)
①	with	to	for
②	with	at	for
③	for	to	at
④	for	at	for
⑤	with	at	at

35 다음 그림을 잘못 표현한 것은?

① There is a boy on the slide.
② A bird is flying over the trees.
③ There is a table next to the large tree.
④ There is a basket under the table.
⑤ Some dogs are lying in front of the ladder.

36 다음 (A)~(C)에 들어갈 말이 바르게 짝지어진 것을 고르시오.

· Sunmin left ___(A)___ Busan two hours ago.
· My uncle is ___(B)___ the hospital.
· The man ___(C)___ a beard often comes to this café.

	(A)	(B)	(C)
①	for	in	with
②	to	on	about
③	for	in	about
④	for	on	about
⑤	to	on	with

37 우리말과 같도록 빈칸에 알맞은 전치사를 쓰시오.

나의 아버지는 퇴근 후에 항상 체육관에서 운동하신다.

= My father always works out at the gym
_____ work.

38 다음 빈칸에 of가 들어갈 수 있는 것을 모두 고르시오.

① The box was full _____ toys.
② We asked _____ more bread.
③ Beth is afraid _____ spiders.
④ My plan is different _____ yours.
⑤ He spent lots of money _____ the new sofa.

39 다음 @~@에 들어갈 전치사가 같은 것끼리 묶인 것은?

· There were many great movies @_____ the 20th century.
· Joe is waiting for me ⓑ_____ home.
· I left my hat ⓒ_____ a bus this morning.
· Many international companies have offices ⓓ_____ New York.

① @, ⓑ   ② @, ⓒ   ③ @, ⓓ
④ ⓑ, ⓒ   ⑤ ⓑ, ⓓ

CHAPTER 15
접속사

Jason **and** Sally can speak English.   Jason과 Sally는 영어를 말할 수 있다.
단어   접속사   단어

위 문장에서 두 단어 Jason과 Sally가 **and**라는 말로 연결되어 있어요. 이렇게 단어와 단어, 구와 구, 절과 절을 연결하는 것을 **접속사**라고 해요.

기출로 적중 POINT

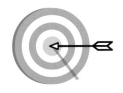

내신 100점 적중!
기출 출제율

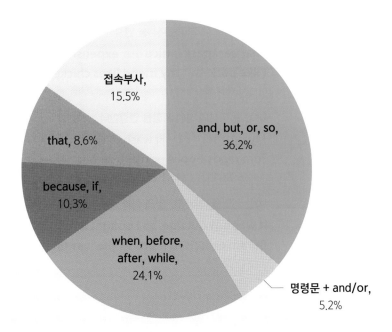

접속부사, 15.5%

that, 8.6%

because, if, 10.3%

when, before, after, while, 24.1%

and, but, or, so, 36.2%

명령문 + and/or, 5.2%

TOP 1 **and, but, or, so (36.2%)**
접속사 and, but, or, so의 의미와 쓰임을 묻는 문제가 자주 출제된다.

TOP 2 **when, before, after, while (24.1%)**
시간을 나타내는 접속사 when, before, after, while의 의미와 쓰임을 묻는
문제가 자주 출제된다.

TOP 3 **접속부사 (15.5%)**
접속부사를 지문의 문맥에 맞게 쓰는 문제가 자주 출제된다.

and, but, or, so

정답 p.45

and, but, or, so는 문법적으로 대등한 단어와 단어, 구와 구, 절과 절을 연결하는 등위접속 사이다.

and	~과, 그리고	and는 서로 대등한 내용을 연결한다. **Linda and Mark** are watching a movie. Linda와 Mark는 영화를 보고 있다. I bought **five pencils, two pens, and a notebook**. 나는 다섯 개의 연필, 두 개의 펜, 그리고 한 권의 공책을 샀다. (Tip) and는 「both A and B」의 형태로 'A와 B 둘 다'라는 의미를 나타낼 수 있다. The man can speak **both Korean and English**. 그 남자는 한국어와 영어 둘 다 말할 수 있다.
but	하지만, 그러나	but은 서로 대조되는 내용을 연결한다. That backpack is **nice but expensive**. 저 배낭은 좋지만 비싸다. I like pork, **but my friend likes chicken**. 나는 돼지고기를 좋아하지만, 나의 친구는 닭고기를 좋아한다.
or	또는, ~이거나	or는 둘 이상의 선택 사항을 연결한다. **My brother or I** will wash the car. 나의 남동생 또는 내가 세차할 것이다. Tom **reads books or plays games** on weekends. Tom은 주말마다 책을 읽거나 게임을 한다.
so	그래서, 따라서	so는 원인을 나타내는 앞의 절과 결과를 나타내는 뒤의 절을 연결한다. It was hot outside, **so I bought a fan**. 밖이 더워서, 나는 부채를 샀다. Boram exercised hard, **so she was tired**. 보람이는 열심히 운동해서 피곤했다.

(Tip) 등위접속사는 문법적으로 대등한 것들을 연결한다.

My shoes are cheap **but** (comfortable, ~~comfortably~~). 나의 신발은 저렴하지만 편하다.

연습문제 A 괄호 안에서 가장 알맞은 접속사를 고르시오.

1 Hannah (and / but) I are good friends.

2 You can order soup (or / so) a salad.

3 This dress is pretty (or / but) too small for me.

4 I had a cold, (but / so) I went to the hospital.

5 This sofa is soft, (but / so) that one is hard.

6 Is he American, French, (so / or) British?

7 Julie feels so lonely (but / and) sad.

8 Ducks can swim, (or / but) rabbits can't swim.

9 I enjoy both cycling (and / but) hiking.

10 Amy is not home yet, (so / or) you should call again later.

연습문제 B <보기>에서 가장 알맞은 접속사를 골라 다음 두 문장을 한 문장으로 연결하시오.

<보기> and but or so

1 Is today Thursday? + Is it Friday?

→ Is today Thursday _____ Friday?

2 Ostriches have wings. + They can't fly.

→ Ostriches have wings, _____ they can't fly.

3 The cake is beautiful. + It is delicious.

→ The cake is beautiful _____ delicious.

4 I was very tired. + I was hungry.

→ I was very tired _____ hungry.

5 Susan usually walks to school. + She rode a bike today.

→ Susan usually walks to school, _____ she rode a bike today.

6 Mike was very busy. + He couldn't have lunch.

→ Mike was very busy, _____ he couldn't have lunch.

7 Do you go to school by bus? + Do you go to school by subway?

→ Do you go to school by bus _____ by subway?

8 I don't like the actor in that movie. + I won't watch it.

→ I don't like the actor in that movie, _____ I won't watch it.

기출 적중문제

다음 대화의 빈칸에 들어갈 말이 순서대로 짝지어진 것은?

> *A*: How about shopping at the department store?
> *B*: I'd like to, _____ it closes in two hours.
> *A*: Then, we'd better hurry. Let's take a taxi
> _____ a bus.
> *B*: Good idea.

① or – but   ② or – or   ③ and – but
④ but – or   ⑤ but – so

명령문 + and/or

정답 p.45

1. 「명령문 + and ~」는 '…해라, 그러면 ~'이라는 의미이다.

   Wear this coat, and you'll get warm. 이 코트를 입어라, 그러면 너는 따뜻해질 것이다.

   Get some sleep, and you'll feel better. 잠을 좀 자라, 그러면 너는 기분이 나아질 것이다.

2. 「명령문 + or ~」는 '…해라, 그렇지 않으면 ~'이라는 의미이다.

   Hurry up, or you'll be late. 서둘러라, 그렇지 않으면 너는 늦을 것이다.

   Wake up early, or you can't eat breakfast. 일찍 일어나라, 그렇지 않으면 너는 아침을 먹을 수 없다.

연습문제 A 괄호 안에서 and와 or 중 알맞은 것을 고르시오.

1 Be quiet, (and / or) the baby will wake up.

2 Turn left at the corner, (and / or) you'll see the bank.

3 Put on your raincoat, (and / or) you won't get wet.

4 Bring this coupon, (and / or) you can't get a discount.

연습문제 B <보기>와 같이 다음 두 문장을 한 문장으로 연결하시오.

> **<보기>** Eat this bread. + You'll be hungry later.
> → Eat this bread, *or you'll be hungry later* .

1 Ask him. + He can help you.

   → Ask him, _____.

2 Be kind to others. + People will like you.

   → Be kind to others, _____.

3 Finish your homework. + Your teacher will be upset.

   → Finish your homework, _____.

기출 적중문제 ◎⊷

우리말과 같도록 괄호 안의 말을 활용하여 영작하시오.

> 지금 일어나라, 그러면 너는 제시간에 도착할 것이다. (get up now, arrive on time)

= _____

POINT 3-1

when, before, after, while

정답 p.45

1. when, because, if 등은 주절과 부사절을 연결하며, 부사절은 시간, 이유, 조건 등을 나타낸다.

I don't listen to music **when** I study. 나는 공부할 때 음악을 듣지 않는다.

= **When** I study, I don't listen to music.

└→ 부사절이 문장 맨 앞에 올 때는 부사절 뒤에 콤마(,)를 쓴다.

2. when, before, after, while은 시간을 나타내는 부사절을 이끈다.

when	~할 때	I was so scared **when** the power went out. 전기가 나갔을 때 나는 너무 무서웠다. (Tip) when은 '언제'라는 의미의 의문사로도 쓰인다. **When** can you call me? 너는 언제 나에게 전화할 수 있니?
before	~하기 전에	**Before** you leave the room, you should close the window. 너는 방을 나가기 전에 창문을 닫아야 한다.
after	~한 후에	I started my speech **after** everyone arrived. 모든 사람이 도착한 후에 나는 나의 연설을 시작했다.
while	~하는 동안	Maria met her friend **while** she was jogging. Maria는 조깅하고 있는 동안 그녀의 친구를 만났다.

(Tip) 시간을 나타내는 부사절에서는 미래시제 대신 현재시제를 쓴다.

After Ken (~~will have~~, **has**) dinner, he will take a shower. Ken은 저녁을 먹은 후에 샤워를 할 것이다.

연습문제 A 괄호 안에서 가장 알맞은 것을 고르시오.

1 Tracy visited me (while / before) I was sleeping.

2 (When / After) Liam took an exam, I ate lunch with him.

3 (Before / When) she is sleepy, she never drives.

4 Let's go shopping (while / after) school is over.

5 What will you do after you (finish / will finish) your project?

6 (While / After) the band was playing, we danced.

7 Take off your shoes (while / before) you enter the room.

8 I will write the letter when I (am / will be) alone.

9 (When / After) you have a question, please raise your hand.

10 Inha will call me before she (goes / will go) to the airport.

다음은 유라의 아침 일과이다. 빈칸에 before, after, while 중 알맞은 것을 쓰시오.

1 Yura eats breakfast _____ she goes jogging.

2 Yura listens to music _____ she eats breakfast.

3 Yura eats breakfast _____ she brushes her teeth.

4 Yura looks at herself in the mirror _____ she brushes her teeth.

5 Yura leaves home _____ she brushes her teeth.

연습문제 **C** 밑줄 친 when의 의미와 같은 것을 <보기>에서 골라 그 기호를 쓰시오.

<보기>   ⓐ I stay in my house <u>when</u> it rains.
ⓑ <u>When</u> do you usually have breakfast?

1 <u>When</u> I was young, I lived in France.   [　　　　]

2 <u>When</u> are you coming back?   [　　　　]

3 Take a warm bath <u>when</u> you feel cold.   [　　　　]

4 Did you cry <u>when</u> you watched this movie?   [　　　　]

5 <u>When</u> is Cassy going to leave town?   [　　　　]

기출 적중문제 ◎

(A), (B)에서 적절한 의미의 문장을 하나씩 골라 접속사 when을 이용하여 한 문장으로 연결하시오. (단, 부사절을 문장 맨 앞에 쓰시오.)

(A)	(B)
· I ride my bike.	· I play games.
· I have free time.	· I wear a helmet.

(1) _____

(2) _____

기출로적중 POINT 3-2 because, if

정답 p.46

1. because는 '~하기 때문에'라는 의미로, 이유를 나타내는 부사절을 이끈다.

I can't walk well because my leg is broken. 나의 다리가 부러졌기 때문에 나는 잘 걸을 수 없다.

(= My leg is broken, so I can't walk well.) 나의 다리가 부러져서, 나는 잘 걸을 수 없다.

Because Ben was sick, he went home early. Ben은 아팠기 때문에 일찍 집에 갔다.

(= Ben was sick, so he went home early.) Ben은 아파서 일찍 집에 갔다.

(Tip) '~ 때문에'라는 의미의 because of 뒤에는 명사(구)가 온다.

Sojin was nervous because of her test. 소진이는 그녀의 시험 때문에 초조했다.

2. if는 '만약 ~한다면'이라는 의미로, 조건을 나타내는 부사절을 이끈다.

You can watch TV if you finish your homework.

만약 네가 너의 숙제를 끝낸다면 너는 TV를 볼 수 있다.

If I go to the supermarket, I will buy milk. 만약 내가 슈퍼마켓에 간다면, 나는 우유를 살 것이다.

(Tip) 조건을 나타내는 부사절에서는 미래시제 대신 현재시제를 쓴다.

If it (will rain, rains) tomorrow, I won't go out. 만약 내일 비가 온다면, 나는 외출하지 않을 것이다.

연습문제 A <보기>와 같이 다음 문장을 because를 이용하여 바꿔 쓰시오.

<보기> I like swimming, so I joined the swim team.
→ I joined the swim team because I like swimming.
→ Because I like swimming, I joined the swim team.

1 I didn't eat breakfast, so I am very hungry.
→ _____
→ _____

2 I lied, so my parents were angry.
→ _____
→ _____

3 The sun is shining, so put on your hat.
→ _____
→ _____

4 The baby is sleeping, so we have to be quiet.
→ _____
→ _____

5 It is very cold today, so let's stay inside.

→ _____

→ _____

6 I was standing behind a tall man, so I couldn't see the stage.

→ _____

→ _____

연습문제 B 우리말과 같도록 괄호 안의 말을 활용하여 문장을 완성하시오.

1 만약 네가 도움이 필요하다면 나에게 전화해라. (need help)

= Call me _____.

2 우리는 마지막 버스를 놓쳤기 때문에 집까지 걸어와야 했다. (miss the last bus)

= _____, we had to walk home.

3 Robin은 그 재미있는 영화 때문에 많이 웃었다. (the funny movie)

= Robin laughed a lot _____.

4 그것의 커피가 맛있기 때문에 저 카페는 인기 있다. (be delicious)

= That café is popular _____.

5 만약 네가 두통이 있다면 이 약을 먹어라. (have a headache)

= Take this medicine _____.

6 만약 내가 초대장을 받는다면, 나는 그 파티에 갈 것이다. (get an invitation)

= _____, I will go to the party.

7 그 숙제가 너무 어려웠기 때문에 Janet은 포기했다. (be too difficult)

= Janet gave up _____.

8 그의 직업 때문에 Smith씨는 파리로 이사했다. (his job)

= Mr. Smith moved to Paris _____.

기출 적중문제

다음 중 어법상 어색한 것은?

① Carry was scared because she saw a snake.

② Because Tim is smart and kind, I like him.

③ We canceled the picnic because of the rain.

④ I wore a jacket because of I caught a cold.

⑤ Because my brother lost his toy, he cried.

because 뒤에는 절이 오고, because of 뒤에는 명사(구)가 와요.

기출로적중 POINT 4

that

that은 문장 안에서 주어·보어·목적어로 쓰이는 명사절을 이끄는 접속사이며, '~이라는 것'이라는 의미이다.

주어	That Jane knew my secret was surprising. Jane이 나의 비밀을 알고 있었다는 것은 놀라웠다. = It was surprising that Jane knew my secret. ↳ that절이 문장 안에서 주어로 쓰였을 때는 주로 주어 자리에 가주어 it을 쓰고 진주어 that절을 뒤로 보낸다.
보어	The news is that there will be a big storm soon. 그 뉴스는 곧 큰 폭풍이 있을 거라는 것이다. The problem was that the building was too old. 문제는 그 건물이 너무 오래되었다는 것이었다.
목적어	that절이 문장 안에서 목적어로 쓰였을 때는 that을 생략할 수 있다. I think (that) the musician is a genius. 나는 그 음악가가 천재라고 생각한다. Jim heard (that) Anne became a teacher. Jim은 Anne이 선생님이 되었다고 들었다.

Tip that은 지시대명사나 지시형용사로도 쓰인다.

지시대명사   That is my sister. 저 사람은 나의 누나이다.

지시형용사   I met that boy at a concert. 나는 콘서트에서 저 소년을 만났다.

연습문제 A   밑줄 친 that이 이끄는 절의 역할을 <보기>에서 골라 그 기호를 쓰시오.

<보기>   ⓐ 주어   ⓑ 보어   ⓒ 목적어

1   That water is heavier than oil is false.   [   ]

2   The fact is that South Korea's winters are too cold.   [   ]

3   Jasmine said that the map wasn't useful.   [   ]

4   It was nice that you cooked dinner for me.   [   ]

5   I thought that the restaurant was great.   [   ]

6   Do you know that dolphins are mammals?   [   ]

7   It was sad that I lost my favorite hat.   [   ]

8   Sumin hopes that she will get a good grade.   [   ]

9   The good news is that Joyce will join our book club.   [   ]

10   The problem is that I made the same mistake again.   [   ]

다음 문장에서 접속사 that이 들어갈 위치를 고르시오.

1 I ① think ② Ms. Scott is very friendly.

2 The problem ① is ② we don't have much time.

3 Did you ① hear ② Jisung became a soccer player?

4 Minji ① hopes ② it won't rain tomorrow.

5 It is ① true ② Kelly drew this amazing picture.

6 Do you ① know ② I can't eat any nuts?

7 It is ① a pity ② Benny broke his leg.

8 Alice ① believes ② she will become a famous singer.

9 The fact ① is ② a mushroom is not a vegetable.

10 It was ① awful ② Max had a car accident.

밑줄 친 that의 쓰임과 같은 것을 <보기>에서 골라 그 기호를 쓰시오.

<보기>	ⓐ I know that Lucas dances well.
	ⓑ That is my pencil on the desk.
	ⓒ Look at that clown over there.

1 I think that I drank too much coffee.　　　[　　　　]

2 What is that in your purse?　　　[　　　　]

3 I hope that I can see you soon.　　　[　　　　]

4 Don't buy that black shirt.　　　[　　　　]

5 I heard that someone broke the window.　　　[　　　　]

6 I have read that book many times.　　　[　　　　]

7 Kyle believes that is wrong.　　　[　　　　]

8 Alex doesn't know that man over there.　　　[　　　　]

기출 적중문제

우리말과 같도록 괄호 안의 말을 알맞게 배열하시오.

> 우리는 그것이 호랑이라고 생각했다. (a tiger, was, that, we, it, thought)

= _____

기출로 적중 POINT 5 접속부사

정답 p.46

접속부사는 앞 문장과 뒤 문장을 이어주는 접속사 역할을 하는 부사이다.

however	그러나, 하지만	Bill was sick. However, he had to go to school. Bill은 아팠다. 그러나, 그는 학교에 가야 했다.
on the other hand	반면에, 다른 한편으로는	I like dogs. On the other hand, my sister prefers cats. 나는 개를 좋아한다. 반면에, 나의 여동생은 고양이를 선호한다.
for example	예를 들어	I love dessert. For example, I like brownies and cheesecake. 나는 디저트를 좋아한다. 예를 들어, 나는 브라우니와 치즈케이크를 좋아한다.
therefore	그러므로	This milk is not fresh. Therefore, don't drink it. 이 우유는 신선하지 않다. 그러므로, 그것을 마시지 마라.

연습문제 괄호 안에서 가장 알맞은 접속부사를 고르시오.

1 I am quite short. (Therefore / On the other hand), my brother is very tall.

2 The festival will include many events. (However / For example), there will be a free art class.

3 I really like music. (However / Therefore), I am not good at singing or playing instruments.

4 I am really hungry. (For example / Therefore), I will make two sandwiches.

5 The water park has some fun areas. (For example / However), it has a big wave pool.

6 Asians usually use chopsticks. (On the other hand / For example), Europeans use forks.

7 Martin can read many languages. (For example / However), he can't speak all of them.

8 The rain was too heavy. (On the other hand / Therefore), I was late for school.

기출 적중문제

다음 글의 빈칸에 들어갈 가장 알맞은 것은?

My family does many things together on weekends. _____, we eat brunch and go to Hangang Park to ride our bikes. We sometimes watch a movie too.

① But ② Therefore ③ However
④ After ⑤ For example

A 우리말과 같도록 알맞은 접속사와 괄호 안의 말을 활용하여 문장을 완성하시오.

1 저 동물은 느리지만 강하다. (slow, strong)

= That animal is _____.

2 나는 다른 사람들을 도울 때 행복하게 느낀다. (help others)

= I feel happy _____.

3 나는 이번 겨울에 베트남이나 태국을 방문할 것이다. (Vietnam, Thailand)

= I will visit _____ this winter.

4 나의 엄마는 정원을 가지고 계셔서 채소들을 기르실 수 있다. (grow vegetables)

= My mom has a garden, _____.

5 나는 편지를 쓸 것이고, Bob이 그것을 보낼 것이다. (send it)

= I will write a letter, _____.

6 바람이 강했기 때문에, 나의 우산이 부러졌다. (be strong)

= _____, my umbrella broke.

7 이 지도를 가지고 가라, 그렇지 않으면 너는 길을 잃을 것이다. (get lost)

= Take this map, _____.

8 너는 그 콘서트가 무료인 것을 알고 있니? (be free)

= Do you know _____?

9 만약 Kerry가 사과한다면, Nathan은 그녀를 용서할 것이다. (apologize)

= _____, Nathan will forgive her.

10 어두워지기 전에 우리는 산 아래로 내려가야 한다. (get dark)

= We should go down the mountain _____.

B 다음 문장의 밑줄 친 부분을 바르게 고쳐 쓰시오.

1 She likes running but hate walking. → _____

2 Mr. Park is friendly and kindly. → _____

3 I'm good at singing and to dance. → _____

4 If you will add some salt, it will taste better. → _____

5 Jennifer cleaned her room and do her homework. → _____

6 Colin will meet his cousin when he will go to Seoul. → _____

C 다음 빈칸에 알맞은 접속부사를 <보기>에서 골라 쓰시오.

<보기> However   For example   Therefore

1 The movie was very sad. _____, everyone cried.

2 Many animals live in Australia. _____, kangaroos and koalas live there.

3 I like the color of this sweater. _____, I don't like its pattern.

4 Sandra has many hobbies. _____, she plays chess and paints pictures.

5 I ate a big lunch today. _____, I still feel hungry.

6 My old computer broke. _____, I need to buy a new one.

7 There are many tourist sites in Seoul. _____, N Seoul Tower is amazing.

D 다음 그림을 보고 빈칸에 알맞은 말을 <보기>에서 골라 쓰시오.

<보기> when   that   so   however   and   because

Jake prepared dinner for his family. He made sandwiches, pasta, ⓐ_____ a salad. There are five people in his family, ⓑ_____ Jake put five plates on the table. ⓒ_____ they came into the dining room, they were surprised to see the dishes. Everyone enjoyed the food, so Jake offered them more. ⓓ_____, they couldn't eat more ⓔ_____ they were too full. Jake's family thought ⓕ_____ he was a great cook.

중간·기말고사 실전 문제

[1-3] 다음 빈칸에 들어갈 가장 알맞은 것을 고르시오.

1

> I don't like milk, _____ my brother loves it.

① but   ② and   ③ so
④ that   ⑤ before

2

> _____ I looked at Melissa, she was smiling at me.

① And   ② That   ③ If
④ When   ⑤ But

3

> _____ Tony stayed up late last night, he is very tired now.

① Before   ② Because   ③ And
④ So   ⑤ While

4 다음 중 밑줄 친 부분이 어법상 어색한 것은?

① This flower is purple and pink.
② My music teacher is strict but nice.
③ Which do you want, coffee or tea?
④ He likes cooking, and she likes it too.
⑤ I want to visit both London or Paris.

5 우리말과 같도록 알맞은 접속사를 이용하여 다음 두 문장을 한 문장으로 연결하시오.

> · Wear a coat.
> · You'll get cold.

> 외투를 입어라, 그렇지 않으면 너는 감기에 걸릴 것이다.

= _____

6 다음 중 밑줄 친 that의 쓰임이 나머지 넷과 다른 것은?

① Mandy thinks that she can swim fast.
② It is too bad that you broke your finger.
③ I don't know that girl in our classroom.
④ It is amazing that the tree is taller than the tower.
⑤ The sad fact is that I lost my diary.

7 다음 대화의 빈칸에 들어갈 말이 순서대로 짝지어진 것은?

> A: I want to decorate this wall.
> B: Good idea. How about buying a painting _____ a photograph?
> A: We don't have much money to spend, _____ let's just get a poster.

① and – or   ② but – or   ③ but – so
④ or – and   ⑤ or – so

8 다음 빈칸에 and가 들어갈 수 없는 것은?

① Hurry up, _____ you'll miss the plane.

② I watched the play, _____ I enjoyed it.

③ Take vitamins, _____ you'll become healthy.

④ Join the club, _____ you'll make new friends.

⑤ The bike was from Dad, _____ the shoes were from Mom.

9 다음 그림을 보고 주어진 <조건>에 맞게 문장을 완성하시오.

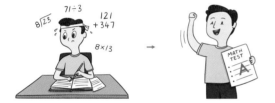

<조건>
1. will, get an A를 활용하시오.
2. 알맞은 접속사를 이용하시오.

→ Study hard, _____
  on the test.

10 다음 중 밑줄 친 부분이 문맥상 <u>어색한</u> 것은?

① I want to be strong, <u>so</u> I exercise every day.

② Tell me the problem, <u>and</u> we can solve it together.

③ Make a list, <u>or</u> you'll forget to buy some items.

④ I asked for salt, <u>so</u> he gave me pepper.

⑤ Hyeju sent me a message, <u>and</u> I replied to it.

11 우리말과 같도록 괄호 안의 말을 알맞게 배열하시오.

Cindy는 졸릴 때 커피 두 잔을 마신다. (when, two cups of coffee, she, sleepy, drinks, is)

= Cindy _____
_____ .

12 우리말과 같도록 주어진 <조건>에 맞게 다음 두 문장을 한 문장으로 연결하시오.

· I was young.
· I didn't know how to swim.

나는 어렸을 때 어떻게 수영하는지 몰랐다.

<조건>
1. 접속사를 문장 맨 앞에 쓰시오.
2. 문장 부호에 주의하시오.

= _____

13 다음 빈칸에 공통으로 들어갈 알맞은 접속사를 쓰시오.

· The news is _____ Paul won first prize.
· I hope _____ I don't get sick on the boat.

14

그 일은 힘들었지만, 우리는 우리 자신이 자랑스러웠다.

① The work was hard, and we were proud of ourselves.

② The work was hard, or we were proud of ourselves.

③ The work was hard, but we were proud of ourselves.

④ The work was hard, that we were proud of ourselves.

⑤ The work was hard, so we were proud of ourselves.

15

네가 먹고 있는 동안 소리를 내지 마라.

① Don't make noise before you are eating.

② Don't make noise while you are eating.

③ Don't make noise after you are eating.

④ Don't make noise, and you are eating.

⑤ Don't make noise, or you are eating.

16

네가 나가기 전에, 현관을 잠가라.

① When you leave, lock the front door.

② Before you leave, lock the front door.

③ Because you leave, lock the front door.

④ After you leave, lock the front door.

⑤ If you leave, lock the front door.

17 다음 두 문장의 의미가 같도록 빈칸에 알맞은 접속사를 쓰시오.

Mr. Davis set the table before the guests arrived.

= The guests arrived _____ Mr. Davis set the table.

18 다음 중 밑줄 친 when의 쓰임이 나머지 넷과 다른 것은?

① We stopped talking when the movie began.

② Did Judy meet Tyler when she was in India?

③ When I looked at my watch, it was 1 A.M.

④ Let's go snowboarding when it snows.

⑤ When did you hear the news?

19 다음 문장에서 틀린 부분을 바르게 고쳐 완전한 문장을 쓰시오.

I will return this book after I will finish reading it.

→ _____
_____

20 다음 중 밑줄 친 부분이 문맥상 어색한 것끼리 묶인 것은?

ⓐ Luke was full after he ate the whole pizza.
ⓑ This website is useful and interesting.
ⓒ She couldn't sleep while the TV was on.
ⓓ You can order chicken salad but corn soup.
ⓔ I lived in Busan if I moved to Seoul.

① ⓐ, ⓑ   ② ⓐ, ⓒ   ③ ⓑ, ⓒ
④ ⓒ, ⓓ   ⑤ ⓓ, ⓔ

21 다음 문장을 우리말로 해석한 것 중 어색한 것은?

① Jiho believed in ghosts when he was a child.
→ 지호는 아이였을 때 유령을 믿었다.
② She will study Arabic while she is in Egypt.
→ 그녀는 이집트에 있기 때문에 아랍어를 공부할 것이다.
③ After the war ended, the hero got a medal.
→ 전쟁이 끝난 후에, 그 영웅은 훈장을 받았다.
④ I called Vicky, but she wasn't at home.
→ 나는 Vicky에게 전화했지만, 그녀는 집에 없었다.
⑤ My cousin is shy, so he talks quietly.
→ 나의 사촌은 수줍음을 많이 타서 조용히 말한다.

22 다음 두 문장의 의미가 같도록 빈칸에 알맞은 접속사를 쓰시오.

I have a fever, so I can't go out.
= I can't go out _____ I have a fever.

23 우리말과 같도록 괄호 안의 말을 활용하여 문장을 완성하시오.

만약 네가 사실을 말한다면 나는 너를 용서할 것이다. (tell the truth)

= I will forgive you _____.

24 다음 빈칸에 공통으로 들어갈 알맞은 것은?

· Your hair will look nice _____ you brush it.
· The plane can't leave _____ there is a heavy storm.
· Our teacher will be angry _____ you're late for class.

① but   ② while   ③ before
④ therefore   ⑤ if

25 다음 중 밑줄 친 부분이 어법상 어색한 것은?

① We're excited because it is Friday.
② Dave went to the library because he wanted to read some books.
③ Pam got lost because she didn't have a map.
④ I will be busy tomorrow because my brother's wedding.
⑤ She likes bananas because they are sweet.

26 다음 밑줄 친 부분을 바르게 고친 것은?

The market wasn't open, but I couldn't buy any groceries.

① after　　② so　　③ when
④ because　⑤ if

27 다음 중 어법상 바른 것은?

① I had to run home because of it was raining.
② Please move the boxes quickly but very careful.
③ We will eat cheesecake after we have lunch.
④ Yunho had a snowball fight and make a snowman today.
⑤ I will give you a present if you will pass the test.

28 다음 빈칸에 공통으로 들어갈 알맞은 접속사를 <보기>에서 골라 쓰시오.

| <보기> but　when　while　that |

· I will tell you _____ I'm ready.
· Brian studies hard _____ he is in science class.
· I was hungry _____ I got home.

29 다음 중 밑줄 친 that을 생략할 수 없는 것은?

① My dad thinks that he is always right.
② I want to get that for my birthday.
③ Nina heard that Mark left the country.
④ Do you know that Sujin has a twin sister?
⑤ I believe that elephants are very smart animals.

30 우리말과 같도록 괄호 안의 말을 활용하여 영작하시오.

나는 그녀가 곧 돌아올 것이라고 생각한다. (think, return, soon)

= _____

31 우리말과 같도록 괄호 안의 말을 배열할 때 세 번째에 오는 것을 쓰시오.

나는 그들이 열심히 일한다는 것을 안다. (they, that, work, I, know, hard)

→ _____

32 다음 문장에서 어법상 어색한 부분을 찾아 쓰고 바르게 고쳐 쓰시오.

We need to buy some eggs, milk, but apples at the supermarket.

_____ → _____

33 다음 중 접속사 that이 들어갈 가장 알맞은 위치는?

① I ② hope ③ people ④ don't notice ⑤ my mistake.

[34-35] 다음 글의 빈칸에 들어갈 가장 알맞은 것을 고르시오.

34

The math test was really hard. _____, I think I did pretty well.

① When ② However
③ Or ④ Therefore
⑤ For example

35

Heather does a lot of volunteer work. _____, she spends time with poor people and cooks meals for them.

① For example ② On the other hand
③ But ④ Because
⑤ However

[36-37] 다음 글을 읽고 주어진 질문에 답하시오.

Bokyung won many contests last year. (A) 예를 들어, 그녀는 춤 대회의 우승자였다. (the winner) Also, she got first place in a singing contest. She wants to be both a singer _____ a dancer. She practices singing and dancing every day, _____ she doesn't take any lessons.

36 위 글의 밑줄 친 우리말 (A)와 같도록 괄호 안의 말을 활용하여 문장을 완성하시오.

= _____

of a dance contest.

37 위 글의 빈칸에 들어갈 말이 순서대로 짝지어진 것은?

① or – that ② or – and ③ so – but
④ and – that ⑤ and – but

38 다음 글의 빈칸에 들어갈 말이 순서대로 짝지어진 것은?

On New Year's Eve, Melanie went to Bosingak Pavilion in Jongno to see the bell at midnight. _____, there were too many people on the streets. She couldn't get close to the bell. _____, she only heard the sound of the bell.

*Bosingak Pavilion 보신각

① However – On the other hand
② However – Therefore
③ However – For example
④ Therefore – However
⑤ Therefore – On the other hand

1학년 교과서 대표 문법 한 눈에 보기

3 천재 (이재영)

	LESSON	CH	POINT	PAGE
1	be동사의 긍정문	1	1-1, 1-2	18, 20
	be동사의 부정문/의문문		1-3, 1-4	21, 23
2	일반동사의 긍정문	2	1-1	36
	일반동사의 부정문/의문문		1-2, 1-3	38, 40
3	현재진행시제	3	4-1, 4-2	65, 67
	조동사 will	4	4-1	89
4	There + be동사	9	5	188
	조동사 can	4	2-1	85
5	be동사의 과거형	1	2-1	25
	일반동사의 과거형	2	2-1, 2-2	42, 44
	동명사	8	1, 2-1, 2-2	164, 165, 166
6	to부정사의 명사적 용법	7	2-2	151
	조동사 should	4	6	95
7	to부정사의 부사적 용법	7	4	154
	접속사 when	15	3-1	315
8	4형식(수여동사)	5	2-1	109
	비교급 비교	13	3-1	273

4 천재 (정사열)

	LESSON	CH	POINT	PAGE
1	일반동사의 긍정문/부정문/의문문	2	1-1, 1-2, 1-3	36, 38, 40
	조동사 will	4	4-1	89
2	현재진행시제	3	4-1, 4-2	65, 67
	to부정사의 명사적 용법	7	2-2	151
3	일반동사의 과거형	2	2-1, 2-2	42, 44
	부가의문문	6	6	136
4	4형식(수여동사)	5	2-1	109
	to부정사의 부사적 용법	7	4	154
5	재귀대명사	10	2	206
	원급 비교	13	2	272
6	조동사 must	4	5-1	91
	동명사	8	1, 2-1, 2-2, 4	164, 165, 166, 169
7	과거진행시제	3	4-3	69
	최상급 비교	13	4-1	276
8	감탄문	6	3	125
	접속사 when	15	3-1	315

11 지학사 (민찬규)

LESSON	CH	POINT	PAGE
현재시제		1	60
1 과거시제	3	2	61
미래시제		3	63
현재진행시제	3	4-1, 4-2	65, 67
2 to부정사의 명사적 용법	7	2-2	151
to부정사의 형용사적 용법	7	3	153
3 동명사를 목적어로 쓰는 동사	8	2-1	165
접속사 when	15	3-1	315
4 조동사 should	4	6	95
to부정사의 부사적 용법	7	4	154
5 부가의문문	6	6	136
비교급 강조		3-1	273
6 최상급 비교	13	4-1	276
접속사 that	15	4	319
7 4형식(수여동사)	5	2-1	109

12 금성 (최인철)

LESSON	CH	POINT	PAGE
일반동사의 긍정문/부정문		1-1, 1-2	36, 38
1 일반동사의 의문문	2	1-3	40
현재진행시제	3	4-1, 4-2	65, 67
2 조동사 can/will/should	4	2-1, 4-1, 6	85, 89, 95
일반동사의 과거형	2	2-1, 2-2, 2-3	42, 44, 48
3 감탄문	6	3	125
2형식(감각동사)	5	1-2	107
4 접속사 when	15	3-1	315
to부정사의 명사적 용법	7	2-2	151
5 빈도부사	12	3	255
접속사 that	15	4	319
6 to부정사의 부사적 용법	7	4	154
4형식(수여동사)		2-1	109
7 5형식	5	3	113
동명사	8	1, 2-1, 2-2, 4	164, 165, 166, 169
8 비교급/최상급 비교	13	3-1, 4-1	273, 276

MEMO

최신 개정 교과서 완벽 반영

기출로적중

해커스
중학영문법
1학년

초판 8쇄 발행 2024년 12월 9일

초판 1쇄 발행 2020년 11월 4일

지은이	해커스 어학연구소
펴낸곳	㈜해커스 어학연구소
펴낸이	해커스 어학연구소 출판팀

주소	서울특별시 서초구 강남대로61길 23 ㈜해커스 어학연구소
고객센터	02-537-5000
교재 관련 문의	publishing@hackers.com
	해커스북 사이트(HackersBook.com) 고객센터 Q&A 게시판
동영상강의	star.Hackers.com

ISBN	978-89-6542-406-2 (53740)
Serial Number	01-08-01

중고등영어 1위,
해커스북 HackersBook.com

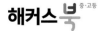

- 핵심만 담았다! **문법 암기리스트+단어 암기장 및 단어 암기장 MP3**
- 교과서 문법 포인트 학습이 쉬워지는 **1학년 교과서 대표 문법 한 눈에 보기**
- 서술형 시험을 완벽하게 대비할 수 있는 **영작/해석 워크시트**

한경비즈니스 선정 2020 한국품질만족도 교육(온·오프라인 중·고등영어) 부문 1위 해커스

해커스 중고등 교재 MAP	**나에게 맞는 교재 선택!**				

	초 5	초 6	예비중	중 1	중 2
문법			Hackers Grammar Smart Starter	Hackers Grammar Smart Level 1	Hackers Grammar Smart Level 2
				기출로 적중 해커스 중학영문법 1학년	기출로 적중 해커스 중학영문법 2학년
				해커스 중학영문법 중간·기말 대비 문제집 Level 1	해커스 중학영문법 중간·기말 대비 문제집 Level 2
서술형				해커스 쓰기 자신감 Level 1	해커스 쓰기 자신감 Level 2
구문					
독해	Hackers Reading Smart Starter Level 1	Hackers Reading Smart Starter Level 2	Hackers Reading Smart Level 1	Hackers Reading Smart Level 2	Hackers Reading Smart Level 3
				Hackers Reading Ground Level 1	Hackers Reading Ground Level 2
				Hackers Reading Path Level 1	Hackers Reading Path Level 2
					해커스 첫수능 영어 기초독해
듣기				해커스 중학영어듣기 모의고사 24회 Level 1	해커스 중학영어듣기 모의고사 24회 Level 2
어휘				해커스 3연타 중학영단어	
				해커스 보카 중학 기초	해커스 보카 중학 필수
				해커스 보카 중학 숙어	

	READING	LISTENING	VOCA
토플	 HACKERS APEX READING for the TOEFL iBT — Basic/Intermediate/Advanced/Expert	HACKERS APEX LISTENING for the TOEFL iBT — Basic/Intermediate/Advanced/Expert	HACKERS APEX VOCA for the TOEFL iBT HACKERS VOCABULARY

최신 개정 교과서 완벽 반영

기출로 적중
해커스
중학영문법

1학년

이 책을 검토해주신 선생님들

강상훈 경기 평촌비상에듀학원 / **김가영** 서울 송정중학교 / **김원덕** 경기 올림피아드학원 / **박유정** 서울 반포중학교 / **박윤정** 경기 이지베스트학원

박은혜 서울 송파중학교 / **박정은** 서울 대청중학교 / **양세희** 서울 양세희수능영어학원 / **이계윤** 서울 씨앤씨학원 / **이유빈** 서울 잉글리쉬&매쓰매니저학원

이혜원 서울 대청중학교 / **정혜은** 서울 용곡중학교 / **최다빈** 서울 최강영어 / **최승복** 경기 오른어학원 / **최지영** 경기 다른영어학원

목차

CHAPTER 5 문장의 형식

기출로 적중 POINT

CHAPTER 6 다양한 문장의 종류

기출로 적중 POINT

CHAPTER 7 to부정사

기출로 적중 POINT

CHAPTER 8 동명사

기출로 적중 POINT

목차

CHAPTER 1
be동사

기출로 적중 POINT

연습문제 A 다음 문장의 밑줄 친 부분을 we, you, he, she, it, they 중 알맞은 인칭대명사로 바꿔 쓰시오.

1 The teddy bear is brown. → _____

2 Charles and I are best friends. → _____

3 The puppies are so cute. → _____

4 You and Katie are the same age. → _____

5 Mr. Smith is my homeroom teacher. → _____

6 Olivia has to clean the room. → _____

연습문제 B 다음 빈칸에 알맞은 be동사의 현재형을 쓰시오.

1 He _____ in the car.

2 Brenda _____ tall.

3 We _____ students.

4 I _____ from Canada.

5 The paintings _____ beautiful.

6 It _____ a good book.

7 Cheetahs _____ really fast.

8 That building _____ very tall.

9 They _____ at the museum.

10 Jake and I _____ at the library.

연습문제 C 다음 문장의 밑줄 친 부분을 줄여 완전한 문장을 쓰시오.

1 You are late. → _____

2 He is at the bank. → _____

3 I am so cold. → _____

4 It is windy now. → _____

5 They are my classmates. → _____

6 We are on the bus. → _____

7 She is a famous singer. → _____

POINT 1-2 be동사 현재형의 의미

연습문제 밑줄 친 be동사의 의미와 같은 것을 <보기>에서 골라 그 기호를 쓰시오.

<보기>
@ It is a taxi.
ⓑ Jisu is pretty and kind.
ⓒ They are in the movie theater.

1 I am a writer. [　] **2** Jack is so angry. [　]

3 The train is at the station. [　] **4** The pie is delicious. [　]

5 They are my cousins. [　] **6** This movie is funny. [　]

7 My bag is under the chair. [　] **8** He is a doctor. [　]

9 My brother is at the hospital. [　] **10** Spiders are scary. [　]

POINT 1-3 be동사의 현재형: 부정문

연습문제 우리말과 같도록 괄호 안의 말을 활용하여 영작하시오.

1 나는 피곤하지 않다. (tired)
= _____

2 Liam은 무례하지 않다. (rude)
= _____

3 그들은 학교에 있지 않다. (at school)
= _____

4 그것은 그 책상 위에 있지 않다. (on the desk)
= _____

5 우리는 고등학생이 아니다. (high school students)
= _____

6 Marie와 나는 자매가 아니다. (sisters)
= _____

be동사의 현재형: 의문문

정답 p.49

연습문제 | 괄호 안에서 알맞은 것을 고르시오.

1 (Is / Are) you busy today?

2 Is the cat on the sofa? – Yes, (it / they) is.

3 (Is / Are) David your friend?

4 Is that book interesting? – No, it (is / isn't).

5 (Am / Is) I very strong?

6 Is our father at work? – No, (he / we) isn't.

7 (Is / Are) your house on this street?

8 Is your sister a basketball player? – Yes, she (is / isn't).

9 (Is / Are) the crackers salty?

10 Are you in your bedroom? – No, (I'm / you're) not.

be동사의 과거형

정답 p.49

연습문제 | 다음 빈칸에 was나 were 중 알맞은 것을 쓰시오.

1 Janet _____ a figure skater.

2 The weather _____ great.

3 Mike and Sue _____ elementary school students.

4 Lucas _____ in the swimming pool.

5 The passengers _____ on the train.

6 We _____ members of the same team.

7 He _____ happy yesterday.

8 They _____ in Africa in 2000.

9 The bank _____ closed yesterday.

10 My brother and I _____ angry at each other.

be동사의 과거형: 부정문

POINT 2-2

정답 p.49

연습문제 | 다음 문장을 부정문으로 바꿔 쓰시오.

1 It was sunny yesterday.

→ _____

2 The movie was boring.

→ _____

3 Lisa and I were tired.

→ _____

4 Peter was a math teacher.

→ _____

5 They were at home an hour ago.

→ _____

6 We were late for class.

→ _____

be동사의 과거형: 의문문

POINT 2-3

정답 p.49

연습문제 | 괄호 안의 말을 활용하여 대화를 완성하시오.

1 A: _____ pretty? (the flower)

B: Yes, it was.

2 A: _____ a lawyer? (Wendy)

B: Yes, she was.

3 A: _____ delicious? (her cupcakes)

B: Yes, they were.

4 A: _____ sharp? (the knives)

B: Yes, they were.

5 A: _____ easy? (the test)

B: No, it wasn't.

6 A: _____ at the grocery store? (your mom)

B: No, she wasn't.

1 주어와 be동사의 현재형이 <u>잘못</u> 짝지어진 것은?

① I – am
② Sally and Bob – are
③ A key – is
④ Mr. Smith – is
⑤ Tina's parents – is

[2-3] 다음 빈칸에 들어갈 말로 <u>어색한</u> 것을 고르시오.

2

> _____ are at the train station.

① Carl and I
② His grandparents
③ She
④ You
⑤ Kate and her brother

3

> _____ was upset at James last night.

① Brad and Sam
② I
③ Nelly
④ Ms. Kant
⑤ He

4 다음 빈칸에 들어갈 말이 순서대로 짝지어진 것은?

> · Bob and I _____ brothers.
> · The cat _____ on the tree.

① am – is
② am – are
③ is – are
④ are – is
⑤ are – are

5 다음 문장의 I를 Mr. Smith로 바꿔 완전한 문장을 쓰시오.

> I am a math teacher.
> → _____

6 다음 중 밑줄 친 부분이 어법상 <u>어색한</u> 것은?

① The bananas <u>are</u> delicious.
② John and his sister <u>was</u> excited.
③ We <u>are</u> in the shopping center.
④ The new apartment <u>is</u> very expensive.
⑤ You and Matt <u>are</u> my classmates.

7 다음 중 밑줄 친 be동사의 의미가 나머지 넷과 <u>다른</u> 것은?

① The cups <u>are</u> in the kitchen.
② Peter <u>is</u> kind and gentle.
③ My brothers <u>are</u> so lazy.
④ The history book <u>is</u> very boring.
⑤ I <u>am</u> so nervous now.

8 다음 중 밑줄 친 부분이 어법상 바른 것은?

① Her new jacket <u>aren't</u> warm.

② This computer game <u>not is</u> interesting.

③ The diamond on the ring <u>is</u> very small.

④ She <u>are</u> an excellent student.

⑤ I <u>amn't</u> a good singer.

9 다음 중 밑줄 친 부분을 줄여 쓸 수 <u>없는</u> 것은?

① These <u>are not</u> my mother's socks.

② His brothers <u>were not</u> angry.

③ My phone <u>was not</u> on the table.

④ I <u>am not</u> hungry anymore.

⑤ The rabbit is <u>not</u> dangerous.

10 우리말과 같도록 괄호 안의 말을 활용하여 문장을 완성하시오.

> Sonya는 어제 바쁘지 않았다. (be)

= _____ _____ _____
  yesterday.

11 다음 질문에 대한 대답으로 알맞은 것은?

> A: Are Mason and Carrie your neighbors?
> B: _____

① Yes, they aren't.　② No, they aren't.

③ Yes, you are.　④ No, you are.

⑤ Yes, he isn't.

12 다음 대화의 빈칸에 들어갈 알맞은 것은?

> A: Is Ms. Lang a violinist?
> B: _____ She is a pianist.

① Yes, she is.　② Yes, he is.

③ Yes, she isn't　④ No, she is.

⑤ No, she isn't.

13 다음 중 자연스럽지 <u>않은</u> 대화를 <u>모두</u> 고르시오.

① A: Was it cold in Russia?

　B: Yes, it was.

② A: Were the children scared?

　B: No, they weren't.

③ A: Is your mother still angry?

　B: No, she is.

④ A: Is Olivia in the living room now?

　B: Yes, I am.

⑤ A: Is that your textbook?

　B: Yes, it is.

14 다음 문장을 주어진 지시대로 바꿔 쓰시오.

> Thomas is at the supermarket.

(1) 부정문으로

    → _____

(2) 의문문으로

    → _____

15 다음 중 밑줄 친 부분이 어법상 <u>어색한</u> 것은?

> A: <u>Were</u> <u>you</u> at home yesterday?
>   ①   ②
> B: <u>No</u>, <u>I</u> <u>weren't</u>. I went to a theme park.
>   ③   ④   ⑤

16 다음 중 어법상 바른 것끼리 묶인 것은?

> ⓐ Yumi and Jake is not Amy's parents.
> ⓑ Is interesting the movie?
> ⓒ Was the swimming pool clean?
> ⓓ Selena not was happy this morning.
> ⓔ Donald and his sister were on the train.

① ⓐ, ⓑ   ② ⓐ, ⓓ   ③ ⓑ, ⓒ
④ ⓒ, ⓔ   ⑤ ⓓ, ⓔ

17 다음 빈칸에 들어갈 말이 나머지 넷과 <u>다른</u> 것은?

① Stuart _____ a doctor.
② Her hair _____ brown.
③ The cheetahs _____ very fast.
④ Nancy _____ on a boat.
⑤ He _____ too sleepy.

18 다음 중 not이 들어갈 위치는?

> ① Carl ② is ③ an ④ actor ⑤.

19 다음 우리말을 알맞게 영작한 것은?

> 너의 그림들은 아름답니?

① Your paintings is beautiful?
② You're paintings are beautiful?
③ Is your paintings beautiful?
④ Are your paintings beautiful?
⑤ Am your paintings beautiful?

20 다음 빈칸에 공통으로 들어갈 알맞은 말을 쓰시오.

· Greg and Jason ________ great athletes.
· My parents ________ kind.

21 다음 빈칸에 알맞은 말을 넣어 대화를 완성하시오.

A: ________ the rain boots yours?
B: No, ________ ________.

22 다음 밑줄 친 부분을 인칭대명사로 바르게 바꾼 것은?

① The puppies are so cute. (→ They)
② Steve is a soccer coach. (→ It)
③ Brad and you are best friends. (→ We)
④ Matt and I play chess on the weekends. (→ Its)
⑤ Wendy and Nolan live in the same city. (→ You)

23 다음은 Daniel의 가족을 소개하는 표이다. 표를 보고 문장을 완성하시오.

가족	직업	성격 / 외모
Father	a farmer	tall
Mother	a doctor	smart
Karen	a student	shy

I am Daniel and this is my family. My father ________. He is tall. This is my mother. She is a doctor, and she ________. This is my sister, Karen. Karen ________ at Seal middle school. She ________.

[24-25] 다음 글을 읽고 주어진 질문에 답하시오.

Ethan and Erica ________ my good friends. We ________ from different countries. (A) 나는 한국인이지만, 그들은 캐나다인이다. (Korean, Canadian) Ethan and Erica ________ kind and fun.

24 위 글의 빈칸에 공통으로 들어갈 알맞은 말을 쓰시오.

→ ________

25 위 글의 밑줄 친 우리말 (A)와 같도록 괄호 안의 말을 활용하여 문장을 완성하시오.

= ________, but ________ ________.

CHAPTER 2
일반동사

연습문제 A 다음 동사의 3인칭 단수형을 쓰시오.

1 live - _____

2 open - _____

3 eat - _____

4 grow - _____

5 do - _____

6 enjoy - _____

7 know - _____

8 have - _____

9 try - _____

10 play - _____

11 brush - _____

12 ring - _____

13 fly - _____

14 buy - _____

15 cook - _____

16 teach - _____

17 wash - _____

18 worry - _____

19 sleep - _____

20 get - _____

21 move - _____

22 walk - _____

23 watch - _____

24 sit - _____

25 arrive - _____

26 practice - _____

연습문제 B 괄호 안에서 알맞은 것을 고르시오.

1 Jared (know / knows) my address.

2 Minji (have / has) lunch at 12 P.M.

3 The students (listen / listens) to the teacher.

4 Beth (see / sees) her mother across the road.

5 She (carry / carries) books in her bag.

6 They (run / runs) along the river.

7 Gillian (watch / watches) TV in the morning.

8 Mr. Jones (pay / pays) for his coffee.

9 Cameron (put / puts) the paper in the box.

10 Birds (fly / flies) south for the winter.

연습문제 │ 우리말과 같도록 괄호 안의 동사를 활용하여 문장을 완성하시오.

1 그는 매우 빠르게 걷지 않는다. (walk)

= He _____ very fast.

2 나의 여동생과 나는 소고기를 먹지 않는다. (eat)

= My sister and I _____ beef.

3 그녀는 신문을 읽지 않는다. (read)

= She _____ a newspaper.

4 나는 일찍 일어나지 않는다. (wake)

= I _____ up early.

5 Nina는 그녀의 커피에 설탕을 넣는다. (put)

= Nina _____ sugar in her coffee.

6 Cameron은 자전거를 타지 않는다. (ride)

= Cameron _____ a bicycle.

7 우리는 비싼 냉장고를 가지고 있지 않다. (have)

= We _____ an expensive refrigerator.

8 지호와 혜수는 팝송을 듣지 않는다. (listen)

= Jiho and Hyesu _____ to pop music.

9 그 도서관은 토요일에 열지 않는다. (open)

= The library _____ on Saturdays.

10 여기는 나쁜 냄새가 나지 않는다. (smell)

= It _____ bad here.

11 Martin은 태권도를 배운다. (learn)

= Martin _____ taekwondo.

12 그들은 차 안에서 안전벨트를 매지 않는다. (wear)

=They _____ seat belts in a car.

13 나는 이를 하루에 세 번 닦는다. (brush)

= I _____ my teeth three times a day.

14 나의 친구는 공포 영화를 보지 않는다. (watch)

= My friend _____ horror movies.

연습문제 A 밑줄 친 부분이 어법상 맞으면 O를 쓰고, 틀리면 바르게 고쳐 완전한 문장을 쓰시오.

1 <u>Does</u> you run every day?

→ _____

2 Does Cindy <u>has</u> a red wallet?

→ _____

3 Do they <u>does</u> homework after class?

→ _____

4 <u>Does</u> he read comic books?

→ _____

5 <u>Do</u> she talk about me a lot?

→ _____

6 <u>Do</u> she do the laundry on sunny days?

→ _____

7 <u>Do</u> Maria and Dan use chopsticks well?

→ _____

8 <u>Does</u> I look good in this dress?

→ _____

연습문제 B 괄호 안에서 알맞은 것을 고르시오.

1 *A*: Do you have an umbrella?
　B: Yes, I (do / don't).

2 *A*: Does your brother like cats?
　B: No, he (does / doesn't).

3 *A*: Do they know about the concert?
　A: Yes, they (do / don't).

4 *A*: Does Tim use a laptop?
　B: No, he (does / doesn't).

5 *A*: Do you remember Tony?
　B: No, I (do / don't).

6 *A*: Do you and your friend eat Indian food?
　B: Yes, we (do / don't).

일반동사의 과거형: 규칙 변화

연습문제 A 다음 동사의 과거형을 쓰시오.

1 move - _____
2 talk - _____
3 miss - _____
4 live - _____
5 play - _____
6 study - _____
7 hurry - _____
8 share - _____
9 call - _____
10 invite - _____
11 jump - _____
12 carry - _____
13 say - _____
14 enter - _____
15 stop - _____
16 drop - _____
17 ask - _____
18 rain - _____
19 change - _____
20 hug - _____
21 stay - _____
22 jog - _____
23 visit - _____
24 laugh - _____
25 grab - _____
26 try - _____

연습문제 B 밑줄 친 부분이 어법상 맞으면 O를 쓰고, 틀리면 바르게 고쳐 쓰시오.

1 We enjoyed the festival last night. → _____

2 He arriveed at the airport at 2 P.M. → _____

3 I movd to Seoul last year. → _____

4 My friend helpped with my homework. → _____

5 Josh worryed about his grades. → _____

6 The repairman fixed the computer. → _____

7 Jimin misseed the band practice today. → _____

8 Sandra combed her hair in the morning. → _____

9 The students finishd their presentation. → _____

10 The soup tasteed like chicken. → _____

연습문제 A 다음 동사의 과거형과 과거분사형을 쓰시오.

1 feed - _____ - _____   **2** have - _____ - _____

3 catch - _____ - _____   **4** hurt - _____ - _____

5 sit - _____ - _____   **6** come - _____ - _____

7 run - _____ - _____   **8** fight - _____ - _____

9 drink - _____ - _____   **10** get - _____ - _____

11 sing - _____ - _____   **12** see - _____ - _____

13 wear - _____ - _____   **14** wake - _____ - _____

15 go - _____ - _____   **16** grow - _____ - _____

17 read - _____ - _____   **18** send - _____ - _____

19 do - _____ - _____   **20** build - _____ - _____

21 know - _____ - _____   **22** overcome - _____ - _____

23 put - _____ - _____   **24** spread - _____ - _____

25 swim - _____ - _____   **26** rise - _____ - _____

연습문제 B 괄호 안의 동사를 과거형으로 바꿔 빈칸에 쓰시오.

1 The bus driver _____ carefully. (drive)

2 They _____ delicious lemonade. (sell)

3 He _____ across the river. (swim)

4 I _____ a bad toothache yesterday. (have)

5 My friends _____ my birthday. (forget)

6 James _____ the city last month. (leave)

7 My brother _____ down the stairs. (fall)

8 Hansu _____ a new cell phone today. (buy)

연습문제 A 다음 문장을 괄호 안의 지시대로 바꿔 쓰시오.

1 Miranda finished her homework. (부정문으로)

→ _____

2 She mixed the ingredients. (의문문으로)

→ _____

3 I saw elephants at the zoo. (부정문으로)

→ _____

4 Poppy made pancakes this morning. (의문문으로)

→ _____

5 Tom wore a swimming cap. (부정문으로)

→ _____

6 Paul walked his dog last night. (의문문으로)

→ _____

연습문제 B 다음은 May와 Kevin이 오늘 한 것과 하지 않은 것을 나타낸 표이다. 빈칸에 알맞은 말을 넣어 질문에 대한 대답을 완성하시오.

	May	Kevin
walk to school	O	O
wear a coat	X	O
eat dinner	X	X
cook spaghetti	X	O

1 *A*: Did May and Kevin walk to school?

B: _____ , _____ _____ .

2 *A*: Did May wear a coat?

B: _____ , _____ _____ .

3 *A*: Did May and Kevin eat dinner?

B: _____ , _____ _____ .

4 *A*: Did Kevin cook spaghetti?

B: _____ , _____ _____ .

중간 · 기말고사 실전 문제

1 다음 빈칸에 들어갈 말로 <u>어색한</u> 것을 <u>모두</u> 고르시오.

> _____ does homework after school.

① My friend   ② Matthew   ③ They
④ She   ⑤ Kyle and Stacy

2 다음 빈칸에 들어갈 말이 순서대로 짝지어진 것은?

> · Mr. Smith _____ at this building.
> · Children _____ in the playground.

① works – plays   ② works – plaies
③ work – plaies   ④ works – play
⑤ workes – play

3 다음 중 어느 빈칸에도 들어갈 수 <u>없는</u> 것은?

> · _____ takes the bus every day.
> · _____ doesn't swim very well.

① Emma   ② My older brother
③ Their father   ④ Uncle Ethan
⑤ The students

4 다음 중 어법상 바른 것은?

① Amy doesn't likes Italian food.
② We don't talk loudly in class.
③ Greg don't go to the school on Sundays.
④ Dennis and Kate doesn't know Ms. Baker.
⑤ They don't be care about the bad
   weather.

[5-6] 우리말과 같도록 괄호 안의 동사를 활용하여 문장을 완성하시오.

5

> 몇몇의 사람들은 고기를 먹지 않는다. (eat)

= Some people _____ meat.

6

> Anne은 평일에 운동을 하지 않는다. (exercise)

= Anne _____ on
   weekdays.

7 다음 대화의 빈칸에 공통으로 들어갈 알맞은 것은?

> *A*: Does your grandfather _____ in
>   an apartment?
> *B*: No, he doesn't. But my parents
>   _____ in an apartment.

① live   ② lives   ③ livees
④ lived   ⑤ living

8 다음 중 동사의 3인칭 단수형이 <u>잘못된</u> 것은?

① worry - worries   ② catch - catches
③ learn - learns   ④ pay - payes
⑤ fly - flies

9 다음 문장을 의문문으로 바르게 바꾼 것은?

> The amusement park also has a great water park.

① Do the amusement park also has a great water park?
② Do the amusement park also have a great water park?
③ Does the amusement park also has a great water park?
④ Does the amusement park also have a great water park?
⑤ Did the amusement park also have a great water park?

10 다음 중 자연스러운 대화는?

① A: Does your brother help your parents a lot?
   B: Yes, he doesn't.
② A: Do your teachers give you lots of homework?
   B: No, they're not.
③ A: Do they sit together in class?
   B: No, they doesn't.
④ A: Do you watch the hockey game on Fridays?
   B: Yes, I am.
⑤ A: Does Bob take the subway to school?
   B: Yes, he does.

[11-12] 다음 문장을 주어진 조건에 맞게 바꿔 쓰시오.

> Minji studies history every day.

11 부정문으로 바꿔 쓰시오.

→ _____

12 의문문으로 바꿔 쓰고, 그에 대한 긍정의 대답을 쓰시오.

> A: _____
> B: _____

13 다음 글의 밑줄 친 ⓐ~ⓔ 중 어법상 어색한 것을 찾아 기호를 쓰고 바르게 고쳐 쓰시오.

> Last summer, I ⓐtravelied to Greece with my family. It ⓑwas a great vacation. We ⓒvisit Athens and ⓓlooked at old buildings. They ⓔwere amazing.

(1) _____ → _____
(2) _____ → _____

14 다음 빈칸에 들어갈 말이 순서대로 짝지어진 것은?

> · Jason and I _____ Mexican food yesterday.
> · The taxi driver _____ at Milford Street last night.

① made – stoped
② made – stopped
③ maked – stopped
④ make – stopped
⑤ maked – stoped

15 다음 중 밑줄 친 부분이 어법상 어색한 것은?

① We didn't order the pizza from Gino's.

② He buyed three pairs of pants at the store.

③ The baby bear hid behind the tree.

④ My team practiced soccer in the afternoon.

⑤ Did Billy give his friend some mint chocolate?

16 다음 질문에 대한 대답으로 알맞은 것은?

> A: Did you and Kara watch a movie last night?
> B: _____

① No, we aren't.　　② Yes, we didn't.
③ No, we did.　　　④ Yes, we are.
⑤ No, we didn't.

17 다음 중 밑줄 친 부분이 어법상 어색한 것은?

> A: Does that bus stops at the museum?
> 　　　①　　　　　　②
> B: No, it doesn't.
> 　　③ ④　⑤

[18-19] 다음 대답에 대한 질문으로 알맞은 것을 고르시오.

18

> A: _____
> B: Yes, he does. He goes to the mountain every Saturday.

① Is he go to the mountain every Saturday?

② Is he going to the mountain every Saturday?

③ Does he goes to the mountain every Saturday?

④ Does he go to the mountain every Saturday?

⑤ Did he go to the mountain every Saturday?

19

> A: _____
> B: No, he didn't. They are still on the table.

① Is he return the library books today?

② Was he return the library books today?

③ Did he return the library books today?

④ Did he returned the library books today?

⑤ Does he return the library books today?

20 다음 문장에서 어법상 어색한 부분을 찾아 쓰고 바르게 고쳐 쓰시오.

> Mike and Ben don't drinks coffee in the morning.

_____ → _____

21 다음 중 어법상 어색한 것은?

① The mushroom growed under the tree.
② Tim doesn't play volleyball.
③ I fed the baby bird in the nest.
④ Lisa dropped a coin on the ground.
⑤ This grapefruit tastes funny.

22 다음 문장을 괄호 안의 지시대로 바르게 바꾸지 못한 것은?

① Kangaroos live in Australia. (의문문으로)
  → Do kangaroos live in Australia?
② Simon walks to the gym. (부정문으로)
  → Simon don't walks to the gym.
③ You and Colin go to the gym together. (의문문으로)
  → Do you and Colin go to the gym together?
④ He bought a Christmas present for his sister. (의문문으로)
  → Did he buy a Christmas present for his sister?
⑤ Jacob flew to Iceland last winter. (부정문으로)
  → Jacob didn't fly to Iceland last winter.

23 다음 중 어법상 바른 것끼리 묶인 것은?

> ⓐ The cat didn't eat the fish.
> ⓑ Does your parents go to the church?
> ⓒ Sarah not did wear my coat yesterday.
> ⓓ Eric and Holly studies a lot.
> ⓔ Did James hike the mountain this morning?

① ⓐ, ⓒ   ② ⓐ, ⓔ   ③ ⓑ, ⓒ
④ ⓑ, ⓓ   ⑤ ⓓ, ⓔ

24 다음 글의 밑줄 친 부분을 어법에 맞게 고쳐 쓰시오.

> Mindy ⓐhave a cute puppy. Its name ⓑam Mo-Mo. It ⓒsleep on her bed every night.

ⓐ _____
ⓑ _____
ⓒ _____

25 다음은 나와 Kate가 방과 후에 하는 활동을 나타낸 표이다. 빈칸에 알맞은 말을 쓰시오.

	read books	watch TV
I	O	X
Kate	X	O

> After school, I _____ books, but I _____ TV. After school, Kate _____ books, but she _____ TV.

CHAPTER 3
시제

연습문제 A 괄호 안의 동사를 활용하여 현재시제 문장을 완성하시오.

1 Brenda _____ two younger brothers. (have)

2 Dave always _____ lunch at the cafeteria. (eat)

3 Wild panda bears _____ only in China. (live)

4 We _____ for a walk every morning. (go)

5 Mandy and Emma _____ together every day. (study)

6 Jupiter _____ the largest planet in the solar system. (be)

7 The shopping mall _____ at 10:30 A.M. (open)

8 Yuna _____ two bicycles and a skateboard. (own)

9 Minsu and I _____ strawberry milkshakes. (like)

10 Three-fourths of the earth _____ of water. (consist)

연습문제 B 우리말과 같도록 괄호 안의 말을 활용하여 빈칸에 쓰시오.

1 모든 사람은 고유의 DNA를 가진다. (have)
= Every person _____ unique DNA.

2 커피는 추운 지역에서 자라지 않는다. (grow)
= Coffee _____ _____ in cold regions.

3 Charlotte은 음악을 자주 듣니? (listen)
= _____ Charlotte often _____ to music?

4 나의 부모님은 평일에 TV를 보지 않으신다. (watch)
= My parents _____ _____ TV on weekdays.

5 아기들은 낮에 잠을 많이 자니? (sleep)
= _____ babies _____ a lot during the day?

6 Johnny는 7시 전에 일어나지 않는다. (wake)
= Johnny _____ _____ up before 7 o'clock.

7 플라스틱이 썩는 것은 450년이 걸린다. (take)
= It _____ 450 years for plastic to decay.

8 2호선 첫 지하철은 5시 30분에 신도림을 떠난다. (leave)
= The first subway on Line 2 _____ Sindorim station at 5:30 A.M.

연습문제 A <보기>와 같이 다음 문장을 과거시제로 바꿔 쓰시오.

> <보기> I eat breakfast every morning.
>   → *I ate breakfast* this morning.

1 Terry calls me every day.

→ _____ two days ago.

2 Minha studies Chinese every night.

→ _____ last night.

3 Jake plays with a robot often.

→ _____ ten years ago.

4 Does she drink tea every day?

→ _____ yesterday?

5 I go to my grandfather's house every month.

→ _____ three weeks ago.

6 Many people visit the theater on weekends.

→ _____ last weekend.

연습문제 B 밑줄 친 부분이 어법상 맞으면 O를 쓰고, 틀리면 바르게 고쳐 완전한 문장을 쓰시오.

1 Jamie bakes muffins yesterday.

→ _____

2 Chris was in the hospital now.

→ _____

3 Do you clean the bathroom an hour ago?

→ _____

4 Kate didn't come to office last Monday.

→ _____

5 She screams when she saw a snake.

→ _____

6 The Second World War ends on September 2, 1945.

→ _____

연습문제 A <보기>와 같이 다음 문장을 괄호 안의 말을 활용하여 미래시제로 바꿔 쓰시오.

> <보기> Kyle is a high school student now. (will)
> → *Kyle will be a high school student* next year.

1 They are on vacation now. (will)
→ _____ next week.

2 Lou and Sandra play golf every Saturday. (be going to)
→ _____ next Saturday.

3 Are you busy right now? (be going to)
→ _____ this weekend?

4 Matt doesn't eat spicy food. (will)
→ _____ for dinner later.

5 The class starts in the morning. (be going to)
→ _____ soon.

6 Anne takes a yoga lesson every day. (will)
→ _____ tomorrow.

7 Does he cook dinner every night? (will)
→ _____ tonight?

8 We don't go shopping on weekdays. (be going to)
→ _____ next Monday.

연습문제 B 괄호 안에서 알맞은 것을 고르시오.

1 Paul (sees / saw / will see) a play tomorrow.

2 I (finish / finished / will finish) my essay last night.

3 Jimmy (is / was / will be) a famous writer someday.

4 It (becomes / became / will become) very cold soon.

5 Dinosaurs (lives / lived / will live) a long time ago.

6 He (travels / traveled / will travel) the world next year.

7 Lisa (comes / came / will come) to my birthday party next week.

POINT 4-1

연습문제 A 다음 동사의 V-ing형을 쓰시오.

1 have - _____　　**2** buy - _____

3 blow - _____　　**4** sleep - _____

5 lie - _____　　**6** win - _____

7 see - _____　　**8** plan - _____

9 sit - _____　　**10** bake - _____

11 close - _____　　**12** wait - _____

13 run - _____　　**14** cry - _____

15 be - _____　　**16** smile - _____

17 visit - _____　　**18** ask - _____

19 tie - _____　　**20** collect - _____

21 enjoy - _____　　**22** enter - _____

연습문제 B 우리말과 같도록 괄호 안의 동사를 활용하여 문장을 완성하시오.

1 나의 어머니는 부엌에서 토스트를 만들고 계신다. (make)

= My mother _____ toast in the kitchen.

2 나는 David과 함께 도서관에서 공부하고 있다. (study)

= I _____ in the library with David.

3 Liam은 그의 가족의 그림을 그리고 있다. (draw)

= Liam _____ a picture of his family.

4 우리는 올해 그리스로 여행갈 예정이다. (travel)

= We _____ to Greece this year.

5 Dan과 Lisa는 함께 피자를 먹고 있다. (have)

= Dan and Lisa _____ pizza together.

6 아이들은 크리스마스 선물을 포장하고 있다. (wrap)

= The kids _____ the Christmas presents.

7 나는 중국에서 나의 사촌들과 좋은 시간을 보내고 있다. (have)

= I _____ a good time with my cousins in China.

연습문제 A 우리말과 같도록 괄호 안의 말을 알맞게 배열하시오.

1 그들은 그들의 숙제를 하고 있니? (their homework, doing, are, they)

= _____

2 Lewis씨는 지금 점심을 먹고 있니? (having, now, Mr. Lewis, is, lunch)

= _____

3 그 학생들은 그 수학 문제들을 풀고 있지 않다. (the students, not, the math problems, are, solving)

= _____

4 너는 지금 나의 아파트로 오고 있니? (you, coming, now, to my apartment, are)

= _____

5 그 아이는 그녀의 이를 닦고 있지 않다. (brushing, is, the kid, her teeth, not)

= _____

6 너의 오빠는 TV를 보고 있니? (TV, your older brother, is, watching)

= _____

7 나는 따뜻한 코트를 입고 있지 않다. (am, wearing, I, a warm coat, not)

= _____

연습문제 B 괄호 안의 상황에 맞게 다음 빈칸에 알맞은 말을 넣어 질문에 대한 대답을 완성하시오.

1 A: Is Sally reading a book?

B: _____, _____ _____. (Sally는 책을 읽고 있지 않음)

2 A: Are the students going into the library?

B: _____, _____ _____. (학생들은 도서관 안으로 들어가고 있음)

3 A: Is the bird building a nest?

B: _____, _____ _____. (새는 둥지를 짓고 있음)

4 A: Is Jack making a sandwich?

B: _____, _____ _____. (Jack은 샌드위치를 만들고 있지 않음)

5 A: Are people looking at the painting?

B: _____, _____ _____. (사람들은 그림을 보고 있음)

6 A: Are you studying for the history exam?

B: _____, _____ _____. (나는 역사 시험을 위해 공부하고 있지 않음)

연습문제 우리말과 같도록 괄호 안의 동사를 활용하여 빈칸에 쓰시오.

1 Sam은 두 시간 전에 아침을 만들고 있었다. (make)

= Sam _____ _____ breakfast two hours ago.

2 나의 텔레비전은 어제 작동하고 있지 않았다. (work)

= My television _____ _____ yesterday.

3 우리는 그때 학교에 걸어가고 있었다. (walk)

= We _____ _____ to school then.

4 Ramona는 한 시간 전에 통화하고 있지 않았다. (talk)

= Ramona _____ _____ on the phone an hour ago.

5 아침에 눈이 오고 있었니? – 응, 눈이 오고 있었어. (snow)

= _____ it _____ in the morning? – Yes, _____ _____ .

6 Neal은 오늘 청바지를 입고 있었니? – 아니, 그는 청바지를 입고 있지 않았어. (wear)

= _____ Neal _____ jeans today? – No, _____ _____ .

POINT 5 현재완료시제 정답 p.53

연습문제 밑줄 친 부분이 어법상 맞으면 O를 쓰고, 틀리면 바르게 고쳐 완전한 문장을 쓰시오.

1 Mia has watch her favorite movie five times.

→ _____

2 The music festival has just ends.

→ _____

3 Adam has already buy tickets for the show.

→ _____

4 Lucy has studied Spanish since 2004.

→ _____

5 We have lived in Seattle for 15 years now.

→ _____

6 Bob and I have took swimming lessons for two years.

→ _____

[1-2] 다음 빈칸에 들어갈 알맞은 것을 고르시오.

1

> Jillian _____ socks next Saturday.

① buys
② will buy
③ bought
④ was buying
⑤ has bought

2

> Last weekend, I _____ fishing with my father.

① go
② goes
③ went
④ am going
⑤ will go

3 <보기>와 같이 동사의 형태를 바꾼 것 중 잘못된 것은?

> <보기> walk → walking

① climb → climbing
② see → seeing
③ lie → lying
④ run → runing
⑤ visit → visiting

4 다음 빈칸에 공통으로 들어갈 알맞은 것은?

> · A koala typically _____ for 22 hours each day.
> · The five-year-old girl _____ with her parents every night.

① sleep
② sleeps
③ slept
④ is sleeping
⑤ have slept

[5-6] 다음 빈칸에 들어갈 알맞은 것을 <u>모두</u> 고르시오.

5

> Kelly is cooking dinner _____.

① at the moment
② yesterday
③ last night
④ now
⑤ two hours ago

6

> Will she come to the party _____?

① yesterday
② last weekend
③ tomorrow
④ five minutes ago
⑤ next Tuesday

7 다음 대화의 빈칸에 들어갈 말이 순서대로 짝지어진 것은?

> A: How did you take this photo of a dolphin _____?
> B: It suddenly _____ when my family was on a boat.

① last Tuesday – appeared
② next week – appeared
③ tomorrow – appears
④ every Saturday – appears
⑤ yesterday – will appear

8 다음 문장을 be going to를 활용하여 바꿔 쓰시오.

William will visit the museum next Friday.

→ _____

_____

11 다음 중 어법상 바른 것은?

① The Sun set in the west.

② I ate a pizza at home tomorrow night.

③ She works at the café a week ago.

④ Most animals have five senses.

⑤ Bill went to the aquarium next Tuesday.

9 다음 중 어법상 바른 것의 개수는?

ⓐ Is it going rain this Friday?

ⓑ They are going to visit us next month.

ⓒ Jackson will is in China next week.

ⓓ Carl will send the letter in two days.

ⓔ We not are going to take a trip to Mokpo this holiday.

① 1개　　　② 2개　　　③ 3개

④ 4개　　　⑤ 5개

12 다음 문장을 괄호 안의 지시대로 바꿔 쓰시오.

We are going to go to the bank tomorrow. (의문문으로)

→ _____

10 다음 (A)~(C)에 들어갈 말이 바르게 짝지어진 것은?

· He ___(A)___ at the club meeting two days ago.

· Europeans ___(B)___ in North America in 1492.

· I ___(C)___ help you to plant tulips in the garden tomorrow.

	(A)	(B)	(C)
①	wasn't	arrived	will
②	wasn't	arrived	did
③	wasn't	arrive	will
④	isn't	arrive	will
⑤	isn't	arrived	did

13 다음 밑줄 친 ⓐ~ⓔ를 바르게 고치지 <u>못한</u> 것은?

· They ⓐwill watch a Japanese film a week ago.

· She ⓑis a doctor next year.

· I ⓒwas very hungry and tired now.

· Julia ⓓtravel to Bangkok last month.

· Jennifer and Patrick ⓔwere going to Paris next Monday.

① ⓐ will watch → watched

② ⓑ is → was

③ ⓒ was → am

④ ⓓ travel → traveled

⑤ ⓔ were → are

14 다음 우리말을 영작할 때 빈칸에 들어갈 알맞은 것은?

그 아이들은 스케치북에 그림을 그리고 있다.
= The children _____ pictures in the sketchbook.

① draw
② are draw
③ drawing
④ are drawing
⑤ drew

15 다음 빈칸에 들어갈 말이 순서대로 짝지어진 것은?

· The customers are _____ outside.
· _____ Jiwon cooking dinner?

① wait - Is
② wait - Does
③ waiting - Did
④ waiting – Is
⑤ waiting - Does

16 다음 질문에 대한 대답으로 알맞은 것은?

A: Is Jack wearing his sunglasses now?
B: _____

① Yes, he does.
② Yes, he is.
③ Yes, he are.
④ No, he wasn't.
⑤ No, he doesn't.

17 우리말과 같도록 괄호 안의 말을 알맞게 배열하시오.

너의 여동생은 그녀의 이를 닦는 중이니?
(brushing, teeth, sister, her, your, is, younger)

= _____

18 다음 중 밑줄 친 부분이 어법상 어색한 것은?

① Jinho is drinking his coffee.
② Are the cats eating cooked tuna?
③ Barry isn't living in Brazil now.
④ I'm writeing my name on the paper.
⑤ She isn't driving to work.

[19-20] 다음 문장을 진행시제로 바꿔 쓰시오.

19

A leaf floats on the river.
→ _____

20

My father took a shower an hour ago.
→ _____

21 다음 두 문장을 한 문장으로 바꿀 때 빈칸에 들어갈 알맞은 것은?

> Sheldon moved to Los Angeles in 2013.
> He still lives there.
> → Sheldon _____ in Los Angeles
>   since 2013.

① is living
② lived
③ lives
④ has lived
⑤ have lived

22 다음 중 어법상 어색한 것은?

① The earth has five oceans.
② Candice walks to school every day.
③ Emma studies hard last night.
④ Marco Polo visited China in 1275.
⑤ Minju met her friends after school
   yesterday.

23 괄호 안의 동사를 활용하여 질문에 대한 대답을 완성하시오.

> A: What are they doing now?
> B: They _____ _____ a
>   sandcastle now. (build)

24 다음 문장을 괄호 안의 지시대로 바르게 바꾸지 못한 것은?

> Yura recycles cans and bottles.

① (과거시제로) Yura recycled cans and
   bottles.
② (미래시제로) Yura will recycle cans and
   bottles.
③ (현재진행시제로) Yura is recycling cans and
   bottles.
④ (과거진행시제로) Yura was recycle cans and
   bottles.
⑤ (현재완료시제로) Yura has recycled cans
   and bottles.

25 다음은 Lily의 일정표이다. 표를 보고 빈칸에 알맞은 말을 넣어 질문에 대한 대답을 완성하시오.

Yesterday	Today	Tomorrow
get a haircut	ride a bike	eat brunch

(1)
> A: What did Lily do yesterday?
> B: Lily _____ _____
>   _____ yesterday.

(2)
> A: Will Lily ride a bike tomorrow?
> B: _____, she _____.
>   She _____ _____
>   _____ tomorrow.

CHAPTER 4
조동사

기출로 적중 POINT

연습문제 **A** 괄호 안에서 알맞은 것을 고르시오.

1 Jinho (cans / can) skateboard very well.

2 We must (finish / finished) the homework today.

3 Pam (shoulds / should) pass all her exams.

4 Peter will (be able to / can) surf in the ocean.

5 Jenny can (speaks / speak) three languages.

6 My dad must (be / is) at work now.

7 The class (wills / will) start in five minutes.

8 The students may (stay / staying) home today.

9 You should (moves / move) those boxes.

10 I will (can / be able to) walk to my new school.

연습문제 **B** 밑줄 친 부분이 어법상 맞으면 O를 쓰고, 틀리면 바르게 고쳐 완전한 문장을 쓰시오.

1 It <u>may is</u> cold tonight.

→ _____

2 This printer <u>cans print</u> on both sides of the paper.

→ _____

3 We <u>should met</u> Tom at the station.

→ _____

4 You <u>must be</u> on time for class.

→ _____

5 She <u>wills listen</u> to your advice.

→ _____

6 Ken <u>can giving</u> us some tickets for the game.

→ _____

연습문제 A | 우리말과 같도록 괄호 안의 말을 알맞게 배열하시오.

1 너는 한국어를 유창하게 말할 수 있니? (speak, you, can)
= _____ Korean fluently?

2 우리는 우리의 방을 엉망으로 만들면 안 된다. (should, mess, we, not)
= _____ up our room.

3 Sam은 우리를 공항으로 태워다 줄거니? (Sam, drive, will)
= _____ us to the airport?

4 그 아기는 빠르게 걸을 수 없다. (the toddler, walk, cannot)
= _____ fast.

5 나는 지금 당장 쓰레기를 버려야 하니? (throw, should, I)
= _____ away the garbage right now?

6 윤주는 미국으로 이사를 가지 않을지도 모른다. (not, Yunju, move, may)
= _____ to the United States.

7 Wendy는 너의 생일 파티에 올 수 있니? (can, come, Wendy)
= _____ to your birthday party?

8 Katherine은 내년에 졸업하지 않을 것이다. (graduate, not, Katherine, will)
= _____ next year.

연습문제 B | 다음 빈칸에 알맞은 말을 넣어 질문에 대한 대답을 완성하시오.

1 A: Can he play the drums?
B: Yes, _____ _____.

2 A: Will she buy some snacks?
B: No, _____ _____.

3 A: Must we set the table?
B: Yes, _____ _____.

4 A: Should I wear this coat?
B: No, _____ _____.

5 A: Can you write your name in Chinese characters?
B: No, _____ _____.

연습문제 A 우리말과 같도록 can과 괄호 안의 말을 활용하여 문장을 완성하시오.

1 나는 이 퍼즐을 풀 수 있다. (solve)

= ＿＿＿＿＿＿＿＿＿＿＿＿＿＿ this puzzle.

2 Fred는 이 박스들을 들 수 있니? (lift)

= ＿＿＿＿＿＿＿＿＿＿＿＿＿＿ these boxes?

3 그는 지금 그의 왼쪽 팔을 쓸 수 없다. (use)

= ＿＿＿＿＿＿＿＿＿＿＿＿＿＿ his left arm now.

4 Jones씨는 그녀의 안경 없이 신문을 읽을 수 없다. (read)

= ＿＿＿＿＿＿＿＿＿＿＿＿＿＿ the newspaper without her glasses.

5 너는 물구나무를 설 수 있니? (stand)

= ＿＿＿＿＿＿＿＿＿＿＿＿＿＿ on your hands?

6 우리는 그 비싼 노트북을 살 수 있다. (buy)

= ＿＿＿＿＿＿＿＿＿＿＿＿＿＿ the expensive laptop.

연습문제 B <보기>와 같이 다음 두 문장의 의미가 같도록 문장을 완성하시오.

<보기> Juho can play chess.

= _Juho is able to play chess._

Are you able to speak Italian?

= _Can you speak Italian?_

1 Can Mr. Davis make seafood pasta?

= ＿＿＿＿＿＿＿＿＿＿＿＿＿＿＿＿＿＿＿＿＿＿＿

2 Snails aren't able to move that fast.

= ＿＿＿＿＿＿＿＿＿＿＿＿＿＿＿＿＿＿＿＿＿＿＿

3 Can your older brother drive?

= ＿＿＿＿＿＿＿＿＿＿＿＿＿＿＿＿＿＿＿＿＿＿＿

4 Jenna was not able to find the post office easily.

= ＿＿＿＿＿＿＿＿＿＿＿＿＿＿＿＿＿＿＿＿＿＿＿

5 Dolphins can't breathe underwater.

= ＿＿＿＿＿＿＿＿＿＿＿＿＿＿＿＿＿＿＿＿＿＿＿

POINT 2-2 can, could II

정답 p.55

연습문제 │ 밑줄 친 부분의 의미를 괄호 안에서 고르시오.

1 <u>Can</u> you please give me a ride? (능력·가능 / 허가 / 요청)

2 <u>Can</u> I go home now? (능력·가능 / 허가 / 요청)

3 Sehee <u>can</u> dance very well. (능력·가능 / 허가 / 요청)

4 You <u>can</u> borrow my umbrella. (능력·가능 / 허가 / 요청)

5 <u>Can</u> you come here please? (능력·가능 / 허가 / 요청)

6 You <u>can</u> eat your lunch here. (능력·가능 / 허가 / 요청)

7 Josh <u>can</u> play the violin. (능력·가능 / 허가 / 요청)

8 <u>Can</u> you open this jar for me? (능력·가능 / 허가 / 요청)

9 <u>Can</u> I try these shoes on? (능력·가능 / 허가 / 요청)

10 Smartphones <u>can</u> run many applications. (능력·가능 / 허가 / 요청)

POINT 3 may

정답 p.55

연습문제 │ 밑줄 친 부분이 허가, 약한 금지, 약한 추측 중 어떤 것을 나타내는지 쓰시오.

1 You <u>may</u> take a short break now. [   ]

2 He <u>may not</u> like spicy food. [   ]

3 The movie <u>may</u> be a little scary. [   ]

4 You <u>may</u> start the exam now. [   ]

5 You <u>may not</u> listen to music during class. [   ]

6 That woman <u>may</u> be an actress. [   ]

7 You <u>may not</u> bring your coffee in here. [   ]

8 Jonathan <u>may not</u> know my name. [   ]

9 <u>May</u> I use these tissues? [   ]

10 You <u>may not</u> take a photo in the museum. [   ]

연습문제 A   <보기>와 같이 다음 문장을 be going to를 활용하여 바꿔 쓰시오. (단, 줄임말을 쓰지 마시오.)

<보기>   They will travel in Europe next month.

     → *They are going to travel in Europe next month.*

1   I will make some potato soup.

   → _____

2   Jenny and I will study history together.

   → _____

3   Will Jimmy join the soccer team?

   → _____

4   She will not stay at my home next Sunday.

   → _____

5   Minho will perform on stage soon.

   → _____

6   We will not come to your Christmas party.

   → _____

7   Will it be sunny tomorrow?

   → _____

연습문제 B   우리말과 같도록 괄호 안의 말을 알맞게 배열하시오.

1   Martin은 내년에 한국을 방문할 것이다. (will, next year, Martin, visit, Korea)

   = _____

2   햄버거와 감자튀김을 주문해주겠니? (order, will, you, the hamburger and fries)

   = _____

3   Laura는 역에서 나를 만날 것이다. (Laura, is, at the station, me, to, meet, going)

   = _____

4   나랑 함께 치과에 가주시겠어요? (to the dentist, with me, you, would, go)

   = _____

5   나의 아빠는 창문으로 나의 책상을 옮길 것이다. (move, is, my desk, going, my dad, to the window, to)

   = _____

will, would Ⅱ

정답 p.55

연습문제 | 괄호 안의 주어와 would like (to)를 활용하여 문장을 완성하시오.

1 _____ a slice of pizza. (I)

2 _____ exercise more often. (I)

3 _____ a meatball sandwich. (I)

4 _____ a smaller shirt, please. (I)

5 _____ stay at the hotel? (you)

6 _____ wake up late on weekends. (I)

7 _____ donate my old toys. (I)

8 _____ more information about the show? (you)

9 _____ more sugar in my tea. (I)

10 _____ watch a documentary with me? (you)

must Ⅰ

정답 p.55

연습문제 | 우리말과 같도록 must 또는 can과 괄호 안의 동사를 활용하여 문장을 완성하시오.

1 우리는 공공장소에서 예의 바르게 행동해야 한다. (behave)

= _____ politely in a public place.

2 그녀는 두통이 있음에 틀림없다. (have)

= _____ a headache.

3 그들은 그 짧은 여행 이후에 피곤할 리가 없다. (be)

= _____ tired after the short trip.

4 너는 너의 친구들의 숙제를 베끼면 안 된다. (copy)

= _____ your friends' homework.

5 그것은 나의 잘못일 리가 없다. (be)

= _____ my fault.

6 Jason은 훌륭한 요리사임에 틀림없다. (be)

= _____ an excellent cook.

연습문제 A <보기>와 같이 다음 문장을 have to를 활용하여 바꿔 쓰시오.

> <보기> We must be quiet in the library.
>   → *We have to be quiet in the library.*

1 I must save some money.

→ _____

2 We must listen carefully to our teacher.

→ _____

3 She must go to the hospital now.

→ _____

4 The law must be fair to everyone.

→ _____

5 You must write down your name clearly.

→ _____

연습문제 B 우리말과 같도록 <보기>의 말과 괄호 안의 동사를 활용하여 문장을 완성하시오.

> <보기> must   can't   have to

1 너희들은 현장학습 날에 교복을 입을 필요가 없다. (wear)

= You _____ a uniform on the day of the field trip.

2 Patrick은 지난 밤에 바닥에서 자야 했다. (sleep)

= Patrick _____ on the floor last night.

3 저 소녀는 초등학생일 리가 없다. (be)

= That girl _____ an elementary school student.

4 너는 너의 비밀번호를 잊으면 안 된다. (forget)

= You _____ your password.

5 Jenny는 그녀의 친구들에게 모든 것을 말할 필요가 없다. (tell)

= Jenny _____ everything to her friends.

6 밖이 매우 더운 것임에 틀림없다. (be)

= It _____ very hot outside.

연습문제 우리말과 같도록 괄호 안에서 알맞은 것을 고르시오.

1 너는 이 지갑을 경찰에게 가져다 주는 것이 낫겠다.
= You (should / had better) take this wallet to the police.

2 우리는 오늘 더 따뜻하게 입어야 한다.
= We (should / had better) dress warmer today.

3 Lucy는 너무 많은 커피를 마시지 않는 것이 낫다.
= Lucy (should not / had better not) drink so much coffee.

4 그는 그의 선생님께 도움을 요청해야 한다.
= He (should / had better) ask his teacher for help.

5 너는 너의 친구에게 사과하는 것이 낫겠다.
= You (should / had better) apologize to your friend.

6 너는 너의 시간을 낭비하면 안 된다.
= You (should not / had better not) waste your time.

7 너는 그 피자 전체를 먹지 않는 것이 낫겠다.
= You (should not / had better not) eat the whole pizza.

8 너는 신호등이 바뀔 때까지 기다려야 한다.
= You (should / had better) wait for the traffic light to change.

9 나는 저 무거운 상자를 들면 안 된다.
= I (should not / had better not) lift that heavy box.

10 방문객들은 해변에 그들의 쓰레기를 버리고 가면 안 된다.
= Visitors (should not / had better not) leave their trash on the beach.

11 너는 너의 머리를 빗는 것이 낫겠다.
= You (should / had better) brush your hair.

12 우리는 서로에게 더 친절해야 한다.
= We (should / had better) be nicer to each other.

13 부모는 그들의 아이들을 잘 대우해야 한다.
= Parents (should / had better) treat their children well.

14 너는 진실을 말하는 것이 낫다.
= You (should / had better) tell the truth.

[1-2] 다음 빈칸에 들어갈 알맞은 것을 고르시오.

1

Raymond _____ golf well.

① can play   ② cans play
③ can plays   ④ cans plays
⑤ can played

2

Jake may _____ from China.

① be   ② is
③ was   ④ are
⑤ were

3 다음 우리말을 영작할 때 빈칸에 들어갈 알맞은 것은?

나의 손은 꽉 찼기 때문에 나는 너의 가방을 들어줄 수 없다. = I _____ hold your bag because my hands are full.

① didn't   ② must not
③ may not   ④ shouldn't
⑤ cannot

[4-5] 다음 밑줄 친 부분과 바꿔 쓸 수 있는 것을 고르시오.

4

My parents <u>will</u> go to Mexico next week.

① are able to   ② should
③ can   ④ are going to
⑤ must not

5

We <u>have to</u> protect our planet.

① shouldn't   ② don't have to
③ must   ④ may
⑤ can

6 우리말과 같도록 괄호 안의 말을 알맞게 배열하시오.

우리는 공기 없이 존재할 수 없다. (cannot, without air, exist, we)

= _____

7 다음 질문에 대한 대답으로 알맞은 것은?

A: Should I stretch before I exercise? B: _____

① Yes, I should.   ② Yes, you should.
③ No, I shouldn't.   ④ No, you should.
⑤ Yes, you shouldn't.

기출로 적중 해커스 중학영문법 1학년 워크북

8 다음 질문에 대한 대답으로 알맞지 <u>않은</u> 것을 <u>모두</u> 고르시오.

> A: May I borrow your eraser?
> B: _____ Here you go.

① Of course.　　② Sure.

③ Yes, you may.　　④ Sorry, you may not.

⑤ No, you may not.

9 다음 중 어법상 바른 것은?

① The story isn't may true.

② Owen are able to run quickly.

③ We must wait at the bus stop.

④ Lou shoulds clean his room.

⑤ Do can I try the hat on?

10 다음 빈칸에 들어갈 가장 알맞은 것은?

> She _____ fall asleep. It is too noisy outside.

① may　　② can't　　③ shouldn't

④ must　　⑤ will

11 다음 중 not이 들어갈 위치는?

> ① Matt ② had ③ better ④ be ⑤ late for school again.

12 다음 대화의 밑줄 친 부분과 의미가 같은 것은?

> A: <u>Can</u> I use your phone, please?
> B: Sure. It's on the table.

① Will　　② Must　　③ Should

④ May　　⑤ Do

13 다음 문장을 주어진 지시대로 바꿔 쓰시오.

> We should spend our money on a new car.

(1) 부정문으로

→ _____

_____

(2) 의문문으로

→ _____

14 다음 빈칸에 공통으로 들어갈 알맞은 것은?

> · We have a baseball game tomorrow. We _____ practice hard to win the game.
> · Jenna lost her favorite teddy bear yesterday. She _____ be upset.

① would like to　　② have to

③ cannot　　④ may

⑤ must

15 다음 우리말을 알맞게 영작한 것은?

① 그는 거기에 그의 쓰레기를 놓아 두면 된다.

= He shouldn't leave his trash there.

② 나는 다음 주말에 바쁠 지도 모른다.

= I may be busy next weekend.

③ Tanya는 훌륭한 운동 선수임이 틀림없다.

= Tanya must not be a great athlete.

④ 너는 주차 요금을 지불할 리가 없다.

= You don't have to pay a parking fee.

⑤ 너는 1분 동안 물 속에서 너의 숨을 참을 수 있니?

= Will you hold your breath underwater for a minute?

[16-17] 다음 두 문장의 의미가 같도록 빈칸에 알맞은 말을 쓰시오.

16

Sabrina can finish her science homework thanks to her sister's help.
= Sabrina _____ _____
_____ _____ her science
homework thanks to her sister's help.

17

Brad couldn't get a concert ticket last night.
= Brad _____ _____
_____ _____ a concert
ticket last night.

18 다음 대화의 빈칸에 공통으로 들어갈 알맞은 것은?

A: Danny, what are you doing?

B: I've just baked some chocolate cookies.

A: They smell good. _____ I have one?

B: Yes, of course. _____ you help me clean the kitchen later?

A: OK.

① Will　　② May　　③ Must
④ Can　　⑤ Should

19 다음 밑줄 친 can의 의미가 같은 것끼리 묶인 것은?

ⓐ Can you pass the salt?

ⓑ Eagles can fly long distances.

ⓒ Can I taste the soup?

ⓓ Emily can fix our computer.

ⓔ Can Paul speak Japanese?

① ⓐ, ⓑ　　　　　② ⓐ, ⓔ
③ ⓑ, ⓒ, ⓔ　　　④ ⓑ, ⓓ, ⓔ
⑤ ⓐ, ⓒ, ⓓ, ⓔ

20 다음 중 밑줄 친 부분이 어법상 어색한 것의 개수는?

ⓐ Neal should be not home soon.

ⓑ David may be in his room.

ⓒ Will you helping Greg with his homework?

ⓓ Adam would like to a glass of milk.

ⓔ They will have to be patient yesterday.

ⓕ Will Sally have dinner with us?

① 2개　　② 3개　　③ 4개
④ 5개　　⑤ 6개

21 다음 문장을 부정의 의미를 나타내는 문장으로 바꿔 쓰시오.

> Brandon and Bill must be twins.

→ _____

22 우리말과 같도록 have to를 활용하여 문장을 완성하시오.

(1)
> Janet은 어젯밤에 공항에 택시를 타고 가야 했다.

= Janet _____ take a taxi to the airport last night.

(2)
> Mindy는 그 오페라 입장권을 취소해야 할 것이다.

= Mindy _____ cancel the opera ticket.

23 다음은 Bill, Anne, Jack이 할 수 있는 것과 할 수 없는 것을 나타낸 표이다. 표를 보고 can을 활용하여 문장을 완성하시오.

	Bill	Anne	Jack
Dance well	O	X	O
Speak French	X	O	X

> Bill and Jack _____ well, but Anne _____ well. Anne _____ French, but Bill and Jack _____ French.

24 다음 (A)~(C)에 들어갈 말이 바르게 짝지어진 것은?

> *Liam* : Whose jacket is this?
> *Olivia*: I'm not sure, but it ___(A)___ be Greg's. I think I saw him wearing it.
> *Liam* : No, it ___(B)___ be his. I talked to him about his nice blue jacket today, but this one is black.
> *Olivia*: Really? Then you ___(C)___ ask Mike. It might be his jacket.

	(A)	(B)	(C)
①	might	can't	shouldn't
②	should	must not	should
③	may	can't	should
④	should	must not	don't have to
⑤	may	must	don't have to

25 다음은 실험실에서 지켜야 할 규칙이다. 밑줄 친 우리말 (A), (B)와 같도록 must와 괄호 안의 말을 활용하여 문장을 완성하시오.

> In the laboratory, you have to follow some rules for your safety.
> 1. (A) <u>여러분은 장갑을 껴야만 합니다.</u> (wear)
> 2. You must not bring any drinks or snacks.
> 3. (B) <u>여러분은 실험실에서 뛰면 안됩니다.</u> (run)

(A) _____ gloves.

(B) _____ in the laboratory.

CHAPTER 5
문장의 형식

연습문제 다음 밑줄 친 부분의 문장 성분을 <보기>에서 골라 쓰시오.

<보기> 주어 동사 주격 보어 수식어

1 The children laughed.
　　[　　] [　　]

2 Chloe is my friend.
　　[　　] [　　] [　　]

3 The cat jumped high.
　　[　　] [　　] [　　]

4 My uncle became a famous comedian.
　　[　　] [　　] [　　]

5 The baby slept well.
　　[　　] [　　] [　　]

6 Liam's face turned red.
　　[　　] [　　] [　　]

7 My favorite season is winter.
　　[　　] [　　] [　　]

8 Mr. Brown speaks fast.
　　[　　] [　　] [　　]

연습문제 밑줄 친 부분이 어법상 맞으면 O를 쓰고, 틀리면 바르게 고쳐 쓰시오.

1 This cake tastes cheese. → _____

2 The flowers smell nicely. → _____

3 Nancy's story sounds strange. → _____

4 Thomas looks like weak. → _____

5 The snow feels coldly. → _____

6 Your lotion smells like melons. → _____

7 The chicken soup tasted like spicy. → _____

8 The watch looked expensively. → _____

9 I feel happy about my life. → _____

10 Ken's voice sounds his dad's voice. → _____

기출로적중 POINT 2-1

연습문제 | 우리말과 같도록 괄호 안의 말을 알맞게 배열하시오.

1 Lisa는 나에게 웃긴 이야기를 말해줬다. (told, a funny story, Lisa, me)
= _____

2 나의 아버지는 우리의 집을 지으셨다. (my father, our house, built)
= _____

3 나는 재미있는 책을 읽었다. (an interesting book, read, I)
= _____

4 그는 나에게 엽서를 보냈다. (me, a postcard, he, sent)
= _____

5 Kate는 그녀의 지갑을 찾았다. (found, her wallet, Kate)
= _____

6 Dan은 민수에게 약간의 돈을 빌려줬다. (lent, Minsu, Dan, some money)
= _____

7 James는 운동화 한 켤레를 샀다. (bought, James, a pair of sneakers)
= _____

8 김 선생님은 우리에게 과학을 가르쳐주신다. (us, Ms. Kim, science, teaches)
= _____

9 그들은 한국 음식을 좋아한다. (Korean food, they, love)
= _____

10 그녀는 좋은 저녁식사를 준비했다. (a nice dinner, prepared, she)
= _____

11 나는 큰 소리를 들었다. (heard, I, a loud noise)
= _____

12 Martin은 사과 파이를 구웠다. (baked, an apple pie, Martin)
= _____

13 나는 George에게 약간의 주스를 가져다줬다. (George, brought, some juice, I)
= _____

14 그 기자는 그에게 질문을 했다. (asked, a question, the reporter, him)
= _____

연습문제 A 괄호 안에서 to, for, of 중 알맞은 것을 고르시오.

1 Raymond wrote a poem (to / for / of) Beth.

2 Neal sent an e-mail (to / for / of) his cousin.

3 My uncle built a sandcastle (to / for / of) me.

4 Sandra asked a question (to / for / of) the teacher.

5 Owen bought a concert ticket (to / for / of) Hailey.

6 Jisu made a beautiful scarf (to / for / of) her friend.

7 We showed our homework (to / for / of) our teacher.

8 I read fairy tales (to / for / of) my little sister.

연습문제 B 다음 4형식 문장은 3형식으로, 3형식 문장은 4형식으로 바꿔 쓰시오.

1 Please pass me the salt.

→ _____

2 William sent a photo to Jade by smartphone.

→ _____

3 She bought me a bunch of flowers.

→ _____

4 Dave showed us some pictures of his dogs.

→ _____

5 The bird brought a pebble to me.

→ _____

6 Can I get a cup of coffee for you?

→ _____

7 John cooked me a nice dinner.

→ _____

8 My friend lent his jacket to me.

→ _____

연습문제 A 다음 문장의 목적어에는 동그라미를 치고, 목적격 보어에는 밑줄을 치시오.

1 The hot weather makes me sweaty.

2 Don't keep our front door open.

3 He found the soup too spicy.

4 Her latest novel made Anna a famous writer.

5 The noisy neighbors kept the baby awake.

6 We found the movie boring.

7 The large hamburger made me full.

8 My father keeps his car very clean.

9 I often call my younger sister Pancake.

10 Dennis named the cat Tigger.

연습문제 B 다음 중 문장의 형식이 나머지 둘과 다른 것을 고르시오.

1 ① Katie is my best friend.
   ② The man danced very well.
   ③ The pizza smells delicious.

2 ① The song sounds terrible.
   ② Benny failed the math exam.
   ③ Minju likes the pink dress.

3 ① She gave me helpful advice.
   ② Junk food makes us unhealthy.
   ③ Dad cooked us a great meal.

4 ① Cam told me his dreams.
   ② The woman showed me the way.
   ③ Peter passed the book to me.

5 ① The mountains look beautiful.
   ② The child talked quietly.
   ③ The team members worked hard.

6 ① My friends call me Liz.
   ② She asked me a question.
   ③ I found the lecture interesting.

중간·기말고사 실전 문제

1 다음 중 문장의 형식이 <u>잘못된</u> 것은?

① 1형식: Mike smiled at the children.

② 2형식: Holly exercises regularly.

③ 3형식: The customer bought a camera.

④ 4형식: My grandma told me a story.

⑤ 5형식: Music helps me relax.

2 다음 중 2형식 문장끼리 묶인 것은?

> ⓐ Jane runs quickly.
> ⓑ The cat is brown.
> ⓒ George arrived at school.
> ⓓ My dad works in a hospital.
> ⓔ We should keep silent in the library.

① ⓐ, ⓑ   ② ⓐ, ⓓ   ③ ⓑ, ⓒ

④ ⓑ, ⓔ   ⑤ ⓓ, ⓔ

[3-4] 다음 빈칸에 들어갈 알맞은 것을 <u>모두</u> 고르시오.

3

> My hands feel like _____.

① ice   ② soft

③ rough   ④ terrible

⑤ leather

4

> This sweater looks _____.

① comfortable   ② lovely

③ candy   ④ greatly

⑤ my cat

5 다음 우리말을 영작한 것 중 <u>어색한</u> 것은?

① 그 남자는 화가 나 보였다.

= The man sounded like angry.

② 그 피자는 맛있어 보인다.

= The pizza looks tasty.

③ 너의 향수는 상쾌한 냄새가 난다.

= Your perfume smells fresh.

④ 저 소음은 자동차 엔진처럼 들린다.

= That noise sounds like a car engine.

⑤ 그 수프는 좋은 맛이 난다.

= The soup tastes good.

6 다음 중 어법상 <u>어색한</u> 것은?

① Janet looks like her mother.

② My mattress feels hard.

③ The cake tastes like delicious.

④ That movie sounds scary.

⑤ The soccer fans sounded excited.

7 다음 빈칸에 들어갈 말이 순서대로 짝지어진 것은?

> · Mr. Harper _____ us to the museum.
> · Leah's mother _____ her a birthday present.

① was - wrote   ② took - gave

③ looked - showed   ④ brought - became

⑤ sent - taught

[8-9] 우리말과 같도록 괄호 안의 말을 활용하여 문장을 완성하시오.

8

한반도는 호랑이처럼 보인다. (a tiger)

= The Korean peninsula _____.

9

얼음에 뒤덮인 길은 미끄러워 보였다. (slippery)

= The icy roads _____.

10 다음 빈칸에 들어갈 말이 나머지 넷과 다른 것은?

① Brad lent his textbook _____ Chris.
② My little sister told a lie _____ me.
③ Matt showed his new shoes _____ Lucy.
④ The history teacher read a story _____ the class.
⑤ Sally bought some chocolates _____ James.

11 다음 중 밑줄 친 부분이 어법상 어색한 것은?

Brett bought a special costume for Halloween. When he wore it, he looked like ①a dragon. It looked ②real. The fabric even ③felt like the skin of a dragon. He made monster noises while he wore it. They ④sounded like scary. He felt ⑤happy with his costume choice.

12 다음 중 주어진 문장과 문장의 형식이 <u>다른</u> 것은?

Neal eats cereal for breakfast.

① He hangs his coat in the closet.
② Martha takes a nap on the sofa.
③ That company develops computer games.
④ Brad made me a sandwich for lunch.
⑤ Carl put his books in the large bag.

[13-14] 다음 빈칸에 공통으로 들어갈 알맞은 말을 쓰시오.

13

· This building looks _____ a castle.
· The music sounds _____ jazz.

14

· Mike sent a Christmas present _____ his cousin.
· Cameron passed the book _____ Sam.

15 다음 빈칸에 들어갈 말로 <u>어색한</u> 것은?

· Cody _____ his friend a jacket.
· Nina _____ her sister new shoes.

① lent   ② got   ③ sent
④ became   ⑤ passed

16 우리말과 같도록 괄호 안의 말을 알맞게 배열하시오.

그 사고는 나의 아빠를 화나게 만들었다. (my dad, made, angry, the accident)

= _____

17 다음 빈칸에 들어갈 말로 <u>어색한</u> 것을 <u>모두</u> 고르시오.

My grandmother _____ a blanket to me.

① sent   ② made   ③ got
④ gave   ⑤ brought

18 다음 (A)~(C)에 들어갈 말이 바르게 짝지어진 것은?

· Mason cooked chicken soup ___(A)___ Carol.
· The doctor showed the X-ray ___(B)___ the patient.
· Matt asked a question ___(C)___ the tour guide.

	(A)	(B)	(C)
①	for	for	of
②	for	to	of
③	to	of	for
④	for	to	to
⑤	to	of	to

[19-20] 두 문장의 의미가 같도록 알맞은 전치사를 이용하여 문장을 완성하시오.

19

My grandfather taught us the history of the United States.
= My grandfather _____

_____ .

20

Emma made her friends some bracelets.
= Emma _____

_____ .

21 다음 중 문장의 형식이 나머지 넷과 <u>다른</u> 것은?

① His story made him a hero.

② The wind makes the temperature drop.

③ The novel makes her sleepy.

④ Mr. Cooper made us some muffins.

⑤ The snow made everything white.

22 다음 중 4형식 문장은 3형식으로, 3형식 문장은 4형식으로 바르게 바꾼 것은?

① Evan should write Fred a birthday card.

 → Evan should write a birthday card to Fred.

② Could you lend your textbook to me?

 → Could you lend me to your textbook?

③ Eve gave her friend a necklace.

 → Eve gave a necklace of her friend.

④ He bought his sister an apple.

 → He bought an apple to his sister.

⑤ Daniel built a snowman for his cousin.

 → Daniel built a snowman his cousin.

23 다음 (A)~(C)에 들어갈 말이 바르게 짝지어진 것은?

> Owen went for a hike on Saturday. The mountains looked   (A)   . He also saw a big waterfall. It   (B)   thunder. After a long walk, he became   (C)   . So, he bought some snacks at a store.

	(A)	(B)	(C)
①	beautiful	sounded like	hungry
②	beautiful	sounded	hungry
③	beautiful	sounded like	hungrily
④	beautifully	sounded	hungrily
⑤	beautifully	sounded like	hungry

24 우리말과 같도록 주어진 <조건>에 맞게 영작하시오.

> Dave는 그의 반 친구에게 그의 교과서를 빌려주었다.

> **<조건>**
> 1. lend, classmate, textbook을 활용하시오.
> 2. 6단어로 쓰시오.
> 3. 시제에 주의하시오.

= _____

25 다음 밑줄 친 ⓐ~ⓔ 중 어법상 어색한 것을 찾아 기호를 쓰고 바르게 고쳐 쓰시오.

> · Regular exercise keeps him ⓐ<u>healthily</u>.
> · The kitchen smells like ⓑ<u>apple pie</u>.
> · The strange noise made us ⓒ<u>nervous</u>.
> · Aiden found seats in the theater ⓓ<u>for</u> us.
> · Do you still ⓔ<u>feel like</u> sick?

(1) _____ → _____

(2) _____ → _____

CHAPTER 6
다양한 문장의 종류

기출로 적중 POINT

연습문제 A | 괄호 안에서 알맞은 것을 고르시오.

1 Don't (drives / drive) so fast.

2 (Be / Is) careful with the knives.

3 (Doesn't / Don't) be so angry.

4 (Speak/ Spoke) more slowly, please.

5 Don't (watch / watching) too much TV.

6 (Be / Am) friendly to the new student.

7 Never (enters / enter) the area.

8 Don't (make / made) too much noise in class.

연습문제 B | <보기>와 같이 다음 문장을 명령문으로 바꿔 쓰시오.

> <보기> You should take a taxi. → *Take a taxi.*
>
> You shouldn't take a taxi. → *Don't take a taxi.*

1 You should try that restaurant.

→ _____

2 You should exercise more often.

→ _____

3 You shouldn't play video games much.

→ _____

4 You shouldn't be rude to your teachers.

→ _____

5 You should wear a jacket.

→ _____

6 You shouldn't park here.

→ _____

7 You should sit down.

→ _____

8 You should get some rest.

→ _____

9 You shouldn't push the button.

→ _____

10 You should close the window.

→ _____

11 You should finish your homework.

→ _____

12 You shouldn't jump on the bed.

→ _____

연습문제 우리말과 같도록 괄호 안의 동사를 활용하여 문장을 완성하시오.

1 약간의 레모네이드를 마시자. = _____ some lemonade. (drink)

2 백화점에 가자. = _____ to the department store. (go)

3 저 영화를 보지 말자. = _____ that movie.(watch)

4 제가 제 자신을 소개할게요. = _____ myself. (introduce)

5 너무 늦게까지 깨어있지 말자. = _____ up too late. (stay)

6 약간의 머핀을 만들자. = _____ some muffins. (make)

7 너무 속상해하지 말자. = _____ so upset. (be)

8 제가 그 일정을 확인할게요. = _____ the schedule. (check)

9 내일 Anne의 집을 방문하자. = _____ Anne's house tomorrow. (visit)

10 오늘 테니스를 치지 말자. = _____ tennis today. (play)

연습문제 다음 문장을 감탄문으로 바꿔 쓰시오.

1 This tteokbokki tastes very spicy. → _____

2 It is a very expensive car. → _____

3 She cooks really well. → _____

4 You are really brave. → _____

5 This is very salty soup. → _____

6 This is a really interesting book. → _____

7 That movie was very scary. → _____

8 It was a very busy morning. → _____

9 The rabbit has very long ears. → _____

10 The clouds move really fast. → _____

Yes/No 의문문

정답 p.59

연습문제 <보기>와 같이 질문에 대한 대답이 괄호 안의 내용과 일치하도록 빈칸에 쓰시오.

<보기> A: Didn't you eat lunch today?   B: _Yes_ , _I_ _did_ . (I ate lunch today.)

1 A: Is the chicken cooked?   B: _____ , _____ _____ . (The chicken isn't cooked.)

2 A: Doesn't he live here?   B: _____ , _____ _____ . (He doesn't live here.)

3 A: Weren't they at home?   B: _____ , _____ _____ . (They were at home.)

4 A: Didn't Brad pay for dinner?   B: _____ , _____ _____ . (He didn't pay for dinner.)

5 A: Can you speak Spanish?   B: _____ , _____ _____ . (I can speak Spanish.)

6 A: Don't you like tomatoes?   B: _____ , _____ _____ . (I don't like tomatoes.)

7 A: Should we buy some tickets?   B: _____ , _____ _____ . (We should buy some tickets.)

8 A: Will it snow on Saturday?   B: _____ , _____ _____ . (It won't snow on Saturday.)

의문사 의문문

정답 p.59

연습문제 우리말과 같도록 괄호 안의 말을 알맞게 배열하시오.

1 너는 왜 놀랐니? (you, why, surprised, are)

= _____

2 그 케이크는 어떻게 맛이 나니? (does, the cake, how, taste)

= _____

3 너의 가족은 어디에서 머무를 거니? (where, your family, stay, will)

= _____

4 Tom은 언제 그의 지갑을 잃어버렸니? (did, lose, when, his wallet, Tom)

= _____

5 누가 불을 껐니? (turned off, who, the lights)

= _____

6 나는 지금 무엇을 할 수 있니? (can, do, now, what, I)

= _____

의문사: who

POINT 5-2

정답 p.59

연습문제 괄호 안에서 Who, Whose, Whom 중 알맞은 것을 <u>모두</u> 고르시오.

1 (Who / Whose / Whom) is that woman?

2 (Who / Whose / Whom) is the phone on the sofa?

3 (Who / Whose / Whom) should I ask?

4 (Who / Whose / Whom) birthday is it?

5 (Who / Whose / Whom) gave you this present?

6 (Who / Whose / Whom) did Patrick give the present to?

7 (Who / Whose / Whom) shoes are these?

8 (Who / Whose / Whom) is Tom talking to?

9 (Who / Whose / Whom) is your homeroom teacher?

의문사: what, which

POINT 5-3

정답 p.59

연습문제 다음 빈칸에 What이나 Which 중 알맞은 것을 넣어 대화를 완성하시오.

1 A: _____ does your sister do?   B: She is a lawyer.

2 A: _____ is bigger, a whale or a dolphin?   B: A whale.

3 A: _____ is your puppy doing?   B: He is eating.

4 A: _____ color is your bag?   B: It is red.

5 A: _____ skirt is prettier, this one or that one?   B: This one is prettier.

6 A: _____ are you making for dinner?   B: I'm making pasta.

7 A: _____ did you buy at the store?   B: I bought a scarf.

8 A: _____ team are you on, team blue or team white?   B: Team white.

9 A: _____ is longer, the Amazon River or the Nile River?   B: The Nile River.

10 A: _____ are you looking at?   B: A butterfly.

연습문제 **A** 다음 빈칸에 알맞은 의문사를 <보기>에서 골라 쓰시오.

<보기> where   when   why   how

1 A: _____ are you going to England?   B: Next month.

2 A: _____ does Raymond look?   B: He looks healthy.

3 A: _____ does the movie end?   B: It ends at 9 o'clock.

4 A: _____ is your house?   B: It is on Oak Street.

5 A: _____ do whales have a blowhole?   B: Because they breathe with it.

6 A: _____ can I get to city hall?   B: By subway.

7 A: _____ is the museum?   B: It's across the street.

8 A: _____ didn't you finish your homework?   B: Because I fell asleep.

9 A: _____ is your textbook?   B: It's in my backpack.

10 A: _____ will Michael meet us?   B: In about an hour.

연습문제 **B** <보기>와 같이 알맞은 의문사를 활용하여 대화를 완성하시오.

<보기> A: _Where does Suho live?_
        B: Suho lives in the apartment on Main Street.

1 A: _____
B: My best friend is Dustin.

2 A: _____
B: Bob was late because he missed the bus.

3 A: _____
B: The show will start at 7 P.M.

4 A: _____
B: You can buy some snacks at the grocery store across the street.

5 A: _____
B: Mr. Smith's job is a police officer.

6 A: _____
B: You can make a peach pie with this recipe.

POINT 5-5 의문사: How + 형용사/부사

정답 p.60

연습문제 <보기>의 말을 활용하여 대화를 완성하시오.

<보기>	How tall	How big	How long	How far
	How old	How often	How many	How much

1 A: _____ is the train ticket? B: $23.

2 A: _____ is the statue? B: It's over 15 meters tall.

3 A: _____ do you visit your cousin? B: Twice a month.

4 A: _____ is Brenda? B: She is nine years old.

5 A: _____ will the flight be? B: Under six hours.

6 A: _____ people came to the party? B: About 25 people came.

7 A: _____ is your apartment? B: Almost 100 square meters.

8 A: _____ is it to the subway station? B: It's about three blocks from here.

POINT 6 부가의문문

정답 p.60

연습문제 다음 빈칸에 알맞은 부가의문문을 쓰시오.

1 Sandy is your sister, _____?

2 The bus stops here, _____?

3 Your father drove you to school, _____?

4 Help me lift this box, _____?

5 I'm taller than you, _____?

6 It isn't going to rain tomorrow, _____?

7 Jake can fix your computer, _____?

8 Let's buy Sam a birthday present, _____?

9 I don't need to apologize to Linda, _____?

10 You and Dongsu aren't in the same class, _____?

중간·기말고사 실전 문제

1 다음 중 어법상 바른 것은?

① Please be call me back.
② Close the window.
③ Don't too noisy.
④ Not jump on the sofa.
⑤ Turns off the lamp, please.

2 다음 우리말을 알맞게 영작한 것은?

너무 성급하지 말자.

① Let's be too hasty.
② Let's not too hasty.
③ Let's not be too hasty.
④ Not let's be too hasty.
⑤ Let's are not too hasty.

3 다음 빈칸에 들어갈 말이 나머지 넷과 다른 것은?

① _____ smart your sister is!
② _____ tall the basketball player is!
③ _____ bad traffic it was!
④ _____ interesting this book was!
⑤ _____ comfortable this chair is!

[4-5] 우리말과 같도록 괄호 안의 말을 알맞게 배열하시오.

4

복도에서 뛰지 말아라. (run, the, hallway, in, don't)

= _____

5

대기오염에 대해서 이야기해보자. (air pollution, talk, about, let's)

= _____

6 다음 질문에 대한 대답으로 알맞은 것은?

A: Didn't you stop by the jewelry shop yesterday?   B: _____ I stayed at home all day.

① No, I wasn't.　　② No, I did.
③ No, I didn't.　　④ Yes, I did.
⑤ Yes, I didn't.

7 다음 대화의 빈칸에 공통으로 들어갈 알맞은 것은?

A: _____ are you doing this weekend?   B: I'm going to San Francisco.   A: _____ will you do there?   B: I'll visit my grandparents.

① How　　② Where　　③ When
④ Why　　⑤ What

8 다음 빈칸에 들어갈 말로 <u>어색한</u> 것은?

> Don't _____.

① touch this painting
② angry to your sister
③ eat candy before bed
④ talk loudly during class
⑤ forget our appointment

9 다음 문장을 감탄문으로 바꿔 쓰시오.

(1)
> This is a very impressive review.
> → _____ _____
> _____ _____ this is!

(2)
> The bus came really late.
> → _____ _____ the bus
> came!

10 다음 대화의 빈칸에 들어갈 가장 알맞은 것은?

> A: Beth, _____ so much noise. I'm
> trying to sleep.
> B: OK. I'll be quiet.

① make   ② makes
③ don't make   ④ not makes
⑤ doesn't make

11 다음 문장을 감탄문으로 바르게 바꾼 것은?

① It is very useful advice.
   → What useful advice is it!
② That Christmas tree is very pretty.
   → How pretty is that Christmas tree!
③ The car drives really fast.
   → What fast the car drives!
④ It is a very delicious cake.
   → What a delicious cake it is!
⑤ Emily has really long hair.
   → What Emily has long hair!

12 다음 빈칸에 들어갈 알맞은 질문은?

> A: This pie is amazing.
> B: _____
> A: Strawberries and pineapples. I can't
> believe that I can taste two flavors in
> one pie.

① What it does taste like?
② What does it taste like?
③ What taste like it does?
④ Does what it taste like?
⑤ Does it what taste like?

13 다음 빈칸에 들어갈 의문사가 나머지 넷과 <u>다른</u>
것은?

① _____ did Sarah buy at the store?
② _____ does your parrot eat?
③ _____ are you doing now?
④ _____ year were you born in?
⑤ _____ is our new neighbor?

14 다음 질문에 대한 대답으로 가장 알맞은 것은?

> *A*: Why isn't the television working?
> *B*: _____

① Around 4 P.M.
② Call the service center.
③ Because I unplugged it.
④ I like the cartoon channel.
⑤ My brother watches sports all the time.

15 다음 빈칸에 들어갈 알맞은 부가의문문은?

> I'm taller than Jinsu, _____?

① am not I   ② don't I   ③ isn't he
④ aren't I   ⑤ aren't we

16 다음 중 자연스러운 대화는?

① *A*: What did you do yesterday?
  B: It's on the second floor.
② *A*: Which house is yours?
  B: Yes, it is. It is really big.
③ *A*: Whose pen is on the desk?
  B: It's Will's pen.
④ *A*: Why is Jane crying?
  B: It's at 3 P.M.
⑤ *A*: Whom is Brad studying with?
  B: No, he isn't.

[17-18] 우리말과 같도록 괄호 안의 말을 알맞게 배열하시오.

17

> *A*: 너의 아버지는 얼마나 키가 크시니? (father, your, tall, how, is)
> *B*: He is 185cm tall.

= _____

18

> *A*: 너는 무슨 아이스크림을 좋아하니? (like, do, ice cream, you, what)
> *B*: I like mint chocolate ice cream.

= _____

19 다음 대화의 빈칸에 들어갈 말이 순서대로 짝지어진 것은?

> *A*: _____ cousins do you have?
> *B*: I have one cousin. I don't see him very often.
> *A*: Really? _____ does he live?
> *B*: In New York. He goes to university there.

① Who – Why
② Who – Where
③ How many – Where
④ What – When
⑤ How many – When

20 다음 중 어법상 바른 것끼리 묶인 것은?

ⓐ The announcement isn't fair, is it?
ⓑ Stella plays the piano, doesn't Stella?
ⓒ Close the window, will you?
ⓓ She can't ride a bike, can't she?
ⓔ It was raining this morning, wasn't it?
ⓕ Let's play a game, will you?

① ⓐ, ⓑ, ⓒ   ② ⓐ, ⓒ, ⓔ   ③ ⓐ, ⓔ, ⓕ
④ ⓑ, ⓓ, ⓕ   ⑤ ⓒ, ⓓ, ⓔ

21 우리말과 같도록 빈칸에 알맞은 말을 쓰시오.

(1)
Matt와 Danny는 같은 학교를 다니지, 그렇지 않니?

= Matt and Danny go to the same school,_____ _____?

(2)
정원에 약간의 토마토를 심자, 어떠니?

= Let's plant some tomatoes in the garden,_____ _____?

22 다음 문장을 괄호 안의 지시대로 바르게 바꾼 것을 모두 고르시오.

① It was a very long movie. (감탄문으로)
  → How a long movie it was!
② He is a very amazing artist. (감탄문으로)
  → What an amazing artist he is!
③ The sunset is really beautiful. (감탄문으로)
  → What beautiful the sunset is!
④ You take the bus. (부정 명령문으로)
  → Not take the bus.
⑤ You turn off the TV. (긍정 명령문으로)
  → Turn off the TV.

23 다음 중 자연스럽지 않은 대화는?

① A: Does David sing very well?
  B: No, he doesn't. But he plays the guitar.
② A: Why do you study in the library?
  B: Because it is very quiet.
③ A: What is Molly's job?
  B: No, it isn't. She's a lawyer.
④ A: When did you buy that jacket?
  B: Yesterday morning.
⑤ A: Didn't your father grow up in Jeonju?
  B: Yes, he did. He was born there.

24 다음 문장에서 틀린 부분을 바르게 고쳐 완전한 문장을 쓰시오.

(1)
Doesn't Melanie works at a bank?
→ _____

(2)
Not sit on the bench at the corner.
→ _____

25 다음 글의 밑줄 친 ⓐ~ⓔ 중 어법상 어색한 것을 찾아 기호를 쓰고 바르게 쓰시오.

You like to play table tennis, ⓐdo you? ⓑIs what the hardest part of playing for you? If it's using the paddles, ⓒtry Bio-ball. It is table tennis without paddles. ⓓLet's give it a shot. ⓔHitting the ball with your hands. Bio-ball is very fun and easy.

*paddle 라켓

(1) _____ → _____
(2) _____ → _____
(3) _____ → _____

CHAPTER 7
to부정사

POINT 1 to부정사의 형태와 용법

연습문제 괄호 안에서 알맞은 것을 고르시오.

1 (Eat / To eat) junk food is unhealthy.

2 I go to the library to (studied / study).

3 Ryan hates to (wake / woke) up early.

4 He needs some cold water to (drinks / drink).

5 My goal is to (visit / visiting) London.

6 Ben decided (not to open / to open not) a restaurant.

POINT 2-1 명사적 용법

연습문제 A 괄호 안의 동사를 to부정사로 바꿔 문장을 완성하고 to부정사의 쓰임을 보기에서 골라 그 기호를 쓰시오.

<보기>   ⓐ 주어   ⓑ 보어   ⓒ 목적어

1 My parents' plan is _____ a new car. (buy)   [   ]

2 Fiona tried _____ the tree. (climb)   [   ]

3 _____ in the ocean is exciting. (swim)   [   ]

4 Harry wants _____ a vacation. (take)   [   ]

5 It is fun _____ with my brother. (play)   [   ]

연습문제 B 다음 문장을 가주어 it을 사용한 문장으로 바꿔 쓰시오.

1 To bake cookies is easy.

= _____

2 To bully other friends is mean.

= _____

3 To get enough sleep is important.

= _____

4 To buy the concert tickets was impossible.

= _____

5 To play with scissors is dangerous.

= _____

연습문제 우리말과 같도록 괄호 안의 말을 활용하여 문장을 완성하시오.

1 James는 이 영화를 다시 보기를 원한다. (want, watch)

= James _____ this movie again.

2 그는 시간 내에 시험을 끝낼 것을 기대하지 않았다. (finish, expect)

= He didn't _____ the test in time.

3 수진이는 자유의 여신상을 보기를 바란다. (hope, see)

= Sujin _____ the Statue of Liberty.

4 나는 오늘 밤에 테니스를 치기를 원한다. (play, would like)

= I _____ tennis tonight.

5 Jenny와 나는 월요일에 떠나지 않기로 결심했다. (decide, leave)

= Jenny and I _____ on Monday.

6 Ken은 그의 친구들에게 편지 쓰는 것을 좋아한다. (like, write)

= Ken _____ letters to his friends.

7 Melanie는 내일 그녀의 이모를 방문하기로 계획했다. (visit, plan)

= Melanie _____ her aunt tomorrow.

8 그 말은 매우 빠르게 달리기 시작했다. (start, run)

= The horse _____ very fast.

9 Carlos는 아침에 지하철 타는 것을 싫어한다. (hate, take)

= Carlos _____ the subway in the morning.

10 Matthew는 새로운 노트북을 살 필요가 없다. (buy, need)

= Matthew doesn't _____ a new laptop.

11 우리가 집을 떠날 때 비가 오기 시작했다. (rain, begin)

= It _____ when we left the house.

12 나의 형은 강을 따라 걷는 것을 좋아한다. (walk, like)

= My brother _____ along the river.

명사적 용법: 의문사 + to부정사

연습문제 <보기>와 같이 우리말과 같도록 괄호 안의 말을 활용하여 문장을 완성하시오.

<보기> 나는 무엇을 주문할지 결정할 수 없다. (order)   = I can't decide _what to order_ .

1 나는 이 세탁기를 어떻게 사용하는지 확실하지 않다. (use)

= I'm not sure _____ this washing machine.

2 나의 재킷을 어디에 둘지 보여주겠니? (put)

= Will you show me _____ my jacket?

3 Nancy는 무엇을 살지 결정할 수 없다. (buy)

= Nancy can't choose _____ .

4 미소는 최근에 어떻게 수영하는지 배웠다. (swim)

= Miso learned _____ recently.

5 Dave는 내일 언제 우리를 만날지 아니? (meet)

= Does Dave know _____ us tomorrow?

6 너는 오늘 밤에 무엇을 볼지 골랐니? (watch)

= Did you choose _____ tonight?

형용사적 용법

연습문제 우리말과 같도록 괄호 안의 말을 활용하여 문장을 완성하시오.

1 저에게 읽을 책을 빌려주세요. (a book, read)

= Please lend me _____ .

2 너는 마실 무언가를 원하니? (something, drink)

= Would you like _____ ?

3 Paul은 입을 코트를 찾고 있다. (a coat, wear)

= Paul is looking for _____ .

4 운동하는 것은 건강해지는 가장 좋은 방법이다. (the best way, become)

= Exercising is _____ healthy.

5 우리는 해결할 심각한 문제가 있다. (a serious problem, solve)

= We have _____ .

연습문제 A 밑줄 친 to부정사의 쓰임을 <보기>에서 골라 그 기호를 쓰시오.

<보기> ⓐ 목적 ⓑ 형용사 수식 ⓒ 감정의 원인 ⓓ 결과

1 Liam will visit the store to buy a shirt.   [   ]

2 I was angry to hear the lie from her.   [   ]

3 The lake was a little cold to swim in.   [   ]

4 This mountain is very easy to climb.   [   ]

5 Sandra went to the beach to relax.   [   ]

6 My sister grew up to be a scientist.   [   ]

7 My mother was happy to meet her friend.   [   ]

8 Ms. Jones lived to be 100 years old.   [   ]

연습문제 B 밑줄 친 to부정사의 용법과 같은 것을 <보기>에서 골라 그 기호를 쓰시오.

<보기> ⓐ My parents decided to adopt a puppy.
　　　　ⓑ We have much homework to do.
　　　　ⓒ Thomas climbed the tree to pick an apple.

1 Jason's job is to sell computers.   [   ]

2 I went to the kitchen to drink some water.   [   ]

3 Nate needs someone to help him.   [   ]

4 It is fun to travel with friends.   [   ]

5 The book was difficult to understand.   [   ]

6 I was upset to see some rude people.   [   ]

7 You need to go to sleep before midnight.   [   ]

8 There are many places to visit in Europe.   [   ]

1 다음 빈칸에 들어갈 알맞은 것은?

May became one year old and she started _____ .

① speak   ② speaks
③ to speak   ④ to speaks
⑤ to spoke

2 다음 중 밑줄 친 to의 쓰임이 나머지 넷과 다른 것은?

① Brad wants to meet Bora at a café.
② I walk to school every morning.
③ Would you like to watch a movie?
④ To speak Chinese well is not easy.
⑤ Steven likes to eat eggs for breakfast.

[3-4] 다음 두 문장의 의미가 같도록 빈칸에 알맞은 말을 쓰시오.

3

To become a CEO is my goal.
= _____ is my goal _____
_____ a CEO.

4

Noah comes to my house to study on the weekends.
= Noah comes to my house
_____ _____ _____
_____ on the weekends.

5 다음 중 어법상 바른 것은?

① It is difficult to plays chess.
② To travel other countries is exciting.
③ Read a comic book is fun.
④ It is necessary wearing a seatbelt.
⑤ To collect stamps are my hobby.

6 우리말과 같도록 괄호 안의 말을 알맞게 배열하시오.

숲 속에서 혼자 걷는 것은 무섭다. (in the forest, to, scary, it, walk alone, is)

= _____

7 다음 대화의 빈칸에 들어갈 말이 순서대로 짝지어진 것은?

A: I want _____ a restaurant someday.
B: Have you decided what type of food _____ ?
A: Yes. I will prepare traditional Korean dishes.

① open - selling   ② opening - to sell
③ opening - sell   ④ to open - to sell
⑤ to open - selling

8 다음 문장에서 어법상 어색한 부분을 찾아 쓰고 바르게 고쳐 쓰시오.

> I would like ordering a Caesar salad and the salmon steak.

_____ → _____

9 괄호 안의 말을 활용하여 다음 대화의 빈칸에 알맞은 말을 쓰시오.

> A: What are you going to do this weekend?
> B: I plan _____ the furniture with my father. (paint)

[10-11] 우리말과 같도록 괄호 안의 말을 활용하여 문장을 완성하시오.

10

> Jason은 소프트웨어를 어떻게 설치할지 설명했다. (install)

= Jason explained _____ _____ _____ the software.

11

> Erica는 비행기에서 읽을 약간의 책들을 샀다. (read, books)

= Erica bought some _____ _____ _____ on the plane.

12 다음 중 밑줄 친 to부정사의 용법이 나머지 넷과 다른 것은?

① The store has many jackets to buy.
② Kyle brought enough money to pay for dinner.
③ Thomas plans to attend the graduation ceremony.
④ My dog needs something to eat.
⑤ You should choose a language to learn.

13 우리말과 같도록 괄호 안의 말을 활용하여 문장을 완성하시오.

> 우리는 Sam의 생일을 축하하기 위해 노래를 불렀다. (sing, a song, celebrate)

= We _____ .

14 주어진 <조건>에 맞게 다음 두 문장을 한 문장으로 연결하시오.

> • Joseph was excited.
> • He won the tennis game.

> <조건>
> 1. to부정사를 이용하시오.
> 2. 8단어로 쓰시오.

→ _____

15 괄호 안의 말을 활용하여 다음 대화의 빈칸에 알맞은 말을 쓰시오.

> A: You seem upset. What's wrong?
> B: I hoped _____ the shooting star last night, but I couldn't. The sky wasn't clear. (see)

16 우리말과 같도록 괄호 안의 말을 배열할 때 다섯 번째에 오는 것은?

> 그 퍼즐은 맞추기에 어렵다. (match, is, difficult, the, puzzle, to)

① is　　　　② match　　　　③ puzzle
④ difficult　　⑤ to

17 주어진 문장의 밑줄 친 to부정사와 용법이 같은 것은?

> It is fun to hang out with friends.

① My father has a lot of work to do.
② I visited the bakery to buy some bread.
③ The Korean alphabet is easy to learn.
④ Is there anything to drink in the refrigerator?
⑤ Jane's goal is to learn how to swim.

[18-19] 다음 글을 읽고 주어진 질문에 답하시오.

> ___(A)___ a dog
>
> 1. Pour warm water carefully on the dog to make it wet.
> 2. (B) 개를 씻기 위해 샴푸를 사용해라.
> 3. Rinse the shampoo off the dog with water.
> 4. Finally, dry the dog with a towel.

18 위 글의 빈칸 (A)에 들어갈 가장 알맞은 것은?

① How to wash　　② Where to wash
③ When to wash　　④ What to wash
⑤ Who to wash

19 위 글의 밑줄 친 우리말 (B)와 같도록 주어진 <조건>에 맞게 영작하시오.

> <조건>
> 1. 명령문으로 쓰시오.
> 2. use, shampoo, wash를 활용하시오.

= _____

20 다음 문장을 우리말로 가장 알맞게 해석한 것은?

> Caroline grew up to be a doctor.

① Caroline은 의사가 될 것이다.
② Caroline은 의사가 되기를 원했다.
③ Caroline은 의사와 자랐다.
④ Caroline은 의사가 되기 위해 자랐다.
⑤ Caroline은 자라서 의사가 되었다.

21 주어진 문장의 밑줄 친 to부정사와 쓰임이 같은 것은?

> To have a best friend is important in life.

① My wish is to make new friends at school.
② It is her job to water the garden.
③ The worker started to move the boxes.
④ Sandra likes to read books before dinner.
⑤ His plan was to throw a surprise party.

22 다음 중 어법상 바른 것의 개수는?

> ⓐ I washed the dishes to help my mother.
> ⓑ Sarah wants to having a hamburger and soda.
> ⓒ Jenny started to sings on the stage.
> ⓓ Feeding wild animals are not allowed.
> ⓔ Neil has a problem to discuss with his father.

① 1개   ② 2개   ③ 3개
④ 4개   ⑤ 5개

[23-24] 다음 글을 읽고 주어진 질문에 답하시오.

> Our family is visiting Egypt next month. My wish is ⓐto see the pyramids and sphinx. I plan to save some money to buy souvenirs. (A) 나는 그곳에 가게 되어 정말 신이 난다. (go, I, to, excited, am, so)
>
> *souvenir 기념품

23 위 글의 밑줄 친 ⓐ와 용법이 같은 것을 고르시오.

① This bicycle is safe to ride at night.
② It is easy to make a chocolate cake.
③ I have some money to spend.
④ Mark called Jenny to ask a question.
⑤ Beth was happy to open the gift.

24 위 글의 밑줄 친 우리말 (A)와 같도록 괄호 안의 말을 알맞게 배열하시오.

= _____ there.

25 다음 밑줄 친 to부정사의 용법이 같은 것끼리 묶인 것은?

> ⓐ Jake stayed up late to do his homework.
> ⓑ George's dream is to live in Italy.
> ⓒ My mother hates to walk in the rain.
> ⓓ Owen opened the window to see the stars.
> ⓔ The deer ran quickly to escape the lion.

① ⓐ, ⓑ, ⓒ   ② ⓐ, ⓓ, ⓔ   ③ ⓑ, ⓒ, ⓓ
④ ⓑ, ⓒ, ⓔ   ⑤ ⓒ, ⓓ, ⓔ

CHAPTER 8
동명사

연습문제 A 우리말과 같도록 괄호 안의 동사를 활용하여 빈칸에 알맞은 말을 쓰시오.

1 판타지 소설을 읽는 것은 재미있다. (read)

= _____ fantasy novels is fun.

2 Robert의 직업은 중학교에서 수학을 가르치는 것이다. (teach)

= Robert's job is _____ math in middle school.

3 나는 크리스마스 선물에 대해 생각하는 것을 계속했다. (think)

= I kept _____ about the Christmas presents.

4 Cindy는 밤에 혼자 자는 것을 무서워한다. (sleep)

= Cindy is afraid of _____ alone at night.

5 게임에서 이기는 것은 우리 팀을 신나게 만들었다. (win)

= _____ the game made our team excited.

6 그들은 저녁 식사 전에 편지 쓰는 것을 끝냈다. (write)

= They finished _____ the letter before dinner.

연습문제 B 밑줄 친 동명사의 쓰임과 같은 것을 <보기>에서 골라 그 기호를 쓰시오.

<보기> ⓐ 주어 ⓑ 보어 ⓒ 동사의 목적어 ⓓ 전치사의 목적어

1 You should avoid underline{drinking} too much coffee.　　[　　]

2 My favorite activity is underline{hiking} in the mountain.　　[　　]

3 underline{Collecting} old coins is Fred's hobby.　　[　　]

4 Emily is interested in underline{studying} other cultures.　　[　　]

5 Jenna's dream is underline{opening} her own bakery.　　[　　]

6 You should quit underline{complaining} about small things.　　[　　]

7 Jackson is good at underline{catching} mosquitoes.　　[　　]

8 underline{Living} without air and water is impossible.　　[　　]

9 underline{Eating} breakfast is important.　　[　　]

10 My hobby is underline{growing} flowers.　　[　　]

11 My friends and I talked about underline{going} to the festival.　　[　　]

12 He enjoyed underline{learning} a new language.　　[　　]

연습문제 A   우리말과 같도록 괄호 안의 말을 활용하여 문장을 완성하시오.

1 미나는 새로운 친구들을 만나는 것을 즐긴다. (meet, enjoy)

= Mina _____ new friends.

2 다리를 떠는 것을 멈춰주겠니? (stop, shake)

= Will you _____ your legs?

3 그 여행 가이드는 바다 앞에 있는 호텔에 머무르는 것을 추천했다. (stay, recommend)

= The tour guide _____ in a hotel in front of the beach.

4 그는 그 대회를 위해 매일 수영하는 것을 연습했다. (practice, swim)

= He _____ every day for the competition.

5 나는 이 퍼즐을 푸는 것을 포기했다. (solve, give up)

= I _____ this puzzle.

6 Tom은 밤에 간식을 먹는 것을 피한다. (have, avoid)

= Tom _____ snacks at night.

7 Eric은 오후 1시 전에 차를 청소하는 것을 끝냈다. (clean, finish)

= Eric _____ the car before 1 P.M.

8 Jessica는 그 귀여운 강아지에 대해 생각하는 것을 계속했다. (think, keep)

= Jessica _____ about the cute dog.

9 나는 약간의 시간을 혼자 보내는 것을 꺼리지 않는다. (spend, mind)

= I don't _____ some time alone.

연습문제 B   괄호 안에서 알맞은 것을 고르시오.

1 You shouldn't give up (following / to follow) your dreams.

2 Bob wants (getting / to get) a better grade.

3 Do you enjoy (watching / to watch) comedies?

4 I kept (waiting / to wait) for my friend at the station.

5 My sister hopes (seeing / to see) her favorite actor.

6 Carl decided (visiting / to visit) the art gallery.

7 Jenny avoids (taking / to take) taxi in the morning.

연습문제 우리말과 같도록 괄호 안의 말을 활용하여 문장을 완성하시오.

1 너는 자전거를 타는 것을 좋아하니? (like, ride)

= Do you _____ a bike?

2 우리는 여름에 소풍을 가는 것을 즐긴다. (enjoy, go)

= We _____ on a picnic in the summer.

3 나와 나의 친구들은 바다에서 수영하는 것을 좋아한다. (love, swim)

= Me and my friends _____ in the sea.

4 보미는 식료품을 온라인으로 사기 시작했다. (start, buy)

= Bomi _____ groceries online.

5 Ronald는 6주 동안 유럽에서 여행하기를 원한다. (want, travel)

= Ronald _____ in Europe for six weeks.

6 우리는 저 카페에서 영어를 말하는 것을 연습할 것이다. (speak, practice)

= We will _____ English at that café.

7 나는 보통 오후 7시에 공부하는 것을 끝낸다. (finish, study)

= I usually _____ at 7 P.M.

8 Tony는 그 창피한 순간을 잊기를 바랐다. (forget, wish)

= Tony _____ the embarrassing moment.

9 Davis씨는 매운 음식을 먹는 것을 피한다. (eat, avoid)

= Mr. Davis _____ spicy food.

10 수업이 시작했을 때 학생들은 말하는 것을 멈췄다. (talk, stop)

= The students _____ when the class started.

11 그는 사진 찍는 것을 싫어한다. (take, hate)

= He _____ pictures.

12 시간과 돈을 낭비하는 것을 그만해라. (waste, stop)

= _____ time and money.

13 나는 많은 물을 마시는 것을 추천한다. (recommend, drink)

= I _____ a lot of water.

14 그녀는 경찰에게 사실을 말하기로 결심했다. (tell, decide)

= She _____ the truth to the police officer.

동명사 vs. 진행형

정답 p.63

연습문제 밑줄 친 부분의 쓰임과 같은 것을 <보기>에서 골라 그 기호를 쓰시오.

<보기> ⓐ We finished cleaning the kitchen.
        ⓑ Carol is listening to the radio.

1 Tommy gave up studying Chinese. [   ]

2 The train is leaving from Seoul station. [   ]

3 Walking is good for your health. [   ]

4 His dream is becoming an English teacher. [   ]

5 Martha was sleeping on the sofa. [   ]

6 The cat is chasing a mouse in the garden. [   ]

7 The doctor recommended taking vitamin C. [   ]

동명사 관용 표현

정답 p.63

연습문제 우리말과 같도록 괄호 안의 말을 활용하여 문장을 완성하시오.

1 우리는 이번 주말에 쇼핑을 하러 갈 것이다. (shop)
= We will _____ this weekend.

2 Sally는 피아노 치는 것을 잘한다. (play)
= Sally _____ the piano.

3 Howard는 실수하는 것을 무서워한다. (make)
= Howard _____ mistakes.

4 불을 끄는 게 어때? (turn)
= _____ off the light?

5 Beth는 이 운동화들을 사는 데 많은 돈을 썼다. (lots of money, buy)
= Beth _____ these sneakers.

6 Paul은 한 시간 전에 파스타를 요리하느라 바빴다. (cook)
= Paul _____ pasta an hour ago.

중간·기말고사 실전 문제

1 다음 빈칸에 들어갈 알맞은 것은?

> I enjoy _____ a cup of tea in the morning.

① drink   ② to drink   ③ drank
④ drinks   ⑤ drinking

[2-3] 다음 빈칸에 들어갈 말로 어색한 것을 고르시오.

2

> Alex _____ visiting art museums.

① loves   ② likes   ③ avoids
④ wants   ⑤ recommends

3

> Wendy _____ writing poems.

① gave up   ② continued   ③ began
④ planned   ⑤ stopped

4 다음 글에서 어법상 어색한 부분을 찾아 쓰고 바르게 고쳐 쓰시오.

> I gave up to study for math test. Now I am afraid of get a bad grade.

(1) _____ → _____

(2) _____ → _____

5 주어진 문장의 밑줄 친 부분과 쓰임이 <u>다른</u> 것은?

> <u>Playing</u> chess is difficult.

① <u>Golfing</u> is Dale's hobby.
② My dream is <u>winning</u> the lottery.
③ The shark is <u>chasing</u> a fish in the sea.
④ Neal likes <u>talking</u> with his brother.
⑤ Marley kept <u>running</u> with her dog.

[6-7] 다음 빈칸에 들어갈 말이 순서대로 짝지어진 것을 고르시오.

6

> · Do you mind _____ off the TV?
> · My plan is _____ a used computer.

① turning - buy   ② to turn - buying
③ turn - buy   ④ turning - buying
⑤ turn - to buying

7

> · I love _____ coffee in the morning.
> · Mike gave up _____ a car for the trip.

① drinking - to renting   ② to drink - rent
③ to drink - to rent   ④ drinking - renting
⑤ drink - to rent

8 다음 중 밑줄 친 부분이 어법상 바른 것은?

① Tina plans spending the day at home.

② Do you recommend to take the language course?

③ Bob wanted working at a bookshop.

④ Will you stop playing the computer game?

⑤ We should avoid to sit in the sun.

9 다음 글의 밑줄 친 ⓐ~ⓔ 중 어법상 어색한 것을 찾아 기호를 쓰고 바르게 고쳐 쓰시오.

Carol began ⓐto work on her English homework on Friday. Writing two essays ⓑwere her homework. She finished ⓒto write them at 11 P.M. on Sunday. She stopped ⓓplaying computer games to write them. But she didn't mind ⓔto spend much time on the homework.

(1) _____ → _____

(2) _____ → _____

(3) _____ → _____

10 다음 빈칸에 들어갈 알맞은 것은?

The children are busy _____ in the garden.

① play   ② plays   ③ played

④ to play   ⑤ playing

[11-12] 다음 (A)~(C)에 들어갈 말이 바르게 짝지어진 것을 고르시오.

11

· Pam likes ___(A)___ her bicycle.

· Fiona practices ___(B)___ every day.

· Sam hopes ___(C)___ a new job.

	(A)	(B)	(C)
①	riding	singing	to find
②	riding	to sing	finding
③	riding	singing	finding
④	to ride	to sing	finding
⑤	to ride	singing	finding

12

· Brad enjoys ___(A)___ at a café.

· The monkey began ___(B)___ the tree.

· I wrote a book about ___(C)___ on a farm.

	(A)	(B)	(C)
①	studying	to climb	to work
②	to study	to climb	to work
③	studying	climbing	working
④	studying	climbing	to work
⑤	to study	climbing	working

13 다음 중 밑줄 친 부분의 쓰임이 나머지 넷과 다른 것은?

A: Do you know who is ①yelling there?
B: It sounds like Sarah.
A: I can see her. She's ②screaming.
B: What is she ③doing?
A: She looks upset. Her puppy is ④running away.
B: We should help her. How about ⑤catching it?
A: OK. Let's go!

14 다음 중 어법상 어색한 것은?

① The band on stage finished playing.
② The students kept talking in class.
③ She enjoys jogging in the park.
④ I look forward to meet your cousin.
⑤ Thank you for cooking a delicious meal.

15 다음 대화의 밑줄 친 우리말과 같도록 주어진 <조건>에 맞게 영작하시오.

A: Who won the talent show?
B: Greg. <u>그는 춤추는 것을 잘한다.</u>

<조건>
1. 5단어로 쓰시오.
2. good, dance를 활용하시오.

= _____

[16-17] 우리말과 같도록 괄호 안의 말을 알맞게 배열하시오.

16

그녀는 주말마다 낚시를 간다. (weekend, goes, fishing, every, she)

= _____

17

Moe는 파이를 굽는 데 시간을 쓰는 것을 좋아한다. (spending, pies, likes, Moe, time, baking)

= _____

18 다음 중 밑줄 친 부분의 쓰임이 나머지 넷과 다른 것은?

① <u>Building</u> a sandcastle was fun.
② Did you thank Kyle for <u>buying</u> lunch?
③ The deer is <u>eating</u> fresh grass.
④ Ginger liked <u>singing</u> in a musical.
⑤ Does Peter mind <u>traveling</u> by himself?

19 다음 대화에서 어법상 어색한 부분을 찾아 쓰고 바르게 고쳐 쓰시오.

A: How about to order pizza tonight?
B: Great. Let's have pepperoni pizza.

_____ → _____

[20-21] 다음은 Eastside Tennis Club의 광고이다. 밑줄 친 우리말 (A), (B)와 같도록 괄호 안의 말을 활용하여 문장을 완성하시오.

Join the Eastside Tennis Club!

Do you like playing tennis? (A) 우리 클럽에 가입하는 것이 어때?(how, join) Our group meets every Saturday at Baker Park. (B) 우리는 함께 테니스 치는 것을 연습해.(play, practice) It is a lot of fun. We hope to see you there!

20

(A) _____ our club?

21

(B) _____ together.

22 다음 대화의 밑줄 친 ⓐ~ⓔ를 바르게 고친 것은?

A: What about ⓐgo to the pool at 2 P.M.?
B: Sorry. I am busy ⓑbuy clothes online.
A: When will you finish ⓒto shopping?
B: I will stop ⓓto doing it in 30 minutes.
A: Let's go ⓔswim after that.
B: OK. I'll meet you at the pool at 3 P.M.

① ⓐ go → to go
② ⓑ buy → to buy
③ ⓒ to shopping → to shop
④ ⓓ to doing → do
⑤ ⓔ swim → swimming

23 다음 중 밑줄 친 부분이 어법상 어색한 것은?

① I spend a lot of time cleaning the house.
② Patrick will start to working at the mall.
③ My dad is busy washing the dishes.
④ She likes to eat rice cake on her birthday.
⑤ We were afraid of getting lost in the mountains.

24 다음 중 밑줄 친 부분의 쓰임이 같은 것끼리 묶인 것은?

ⓐ The cat stopped chasing the mice.
ⓑ Stealing money is a crime.
ⓒ She finished working on the project.
ⓓ Tim's dream was opening a café.
ⓔ Please start writing in your exam paper.

① ⓐ, ⓑ   ② ⓒ, ⓓ   ③ ⓐ, ⓑ, ⓓ
④ ⓐ, ⓒ, ⓔ   ⑤ ⓑ, ⓓ, ⓔ

25 다음 글의 밑줄 친 ⓐ~ⓔ 중 어법상 어색한 것의 개수는?

Sleeping well at night ⓐis important. To sleep well, experts recommend ⓑturning off your phone before you go to bed. You should also finish ⓒto eat one hour before bedtime. ⓓDo more exercise is helpful. Also, avoid ⓔwatching TV late at night.

① 1개   ② 2개   ③ 3개
④ 4개   ⑤ 5개

CHAPTER 9
명사와 관사

기출로 적중 POINT

셀 수 있는 명사와 셀 수 없는 명사

정답 p.64

연습문제 A 다음 명사가 셀 수 있는 명사이면 O, 셀 수 없는 명사이면 X를 쓰시오.

1 wallet → _____ **2** peace → _____

3 information → _____ **4** building → _____

5 flower → _____ **6** milk → _____

7 club → _____ **8** furniture → _____

9 Italy → _____ **10** desk → _____

11 sugar → _____ **12** rain → _____

13 team → _____ **14** Jinsu → _____

15 knife → _____ **16** clothing → _____

17 oxygen → _____ **18** family → _____

19 Ms. White → _____ **20** knowledge → _____

연습문제 B 밑줄 친 부분이 어법상 맞으면 O를 쓰고, 틀리면 바르게 고쳐 완전한 문장을 쓰시오.

1 James wants to drink <u>waters</u>.

→ _____

2 I spilled a lot of <u>rices</u> on the floor.

→ _____

3 Where are you meeting <u>Michael</u>?

→ _____

4 I have <u>a sand</u> in my shoe.

→ _____

5 Charlotte loves playing with <u>dolls</u>.

→ _____

6 <u>A trust</u> is important for a relationship.

→ _____

7 You can eat some <u>apple</u> in the fridge.

→ _____

8 This book has much <u>informations</u> about volcanoes.

→ _____

셀 수 있는 명사의 복수형: 규칙 변화

 POINT 2-1

정답 p.64

연습문제 | 괄호 안의 명사를 알맞은 형태로 바꿔 빈칸에 쓰시오.

1 This recipe requires two _____. (tomato)

2 Terry bought some new _____. (pencil)

3 All my _____ keep disappearing. (toy)

4 My hope is to travel to many _____. (country)

5 Roger likes reading mystery _____. (novel)

6 Did you take many _____ during the trip? (photo)

7 I have worked on my science project for ten _____. (day)

8 There are many houses with colorful _____ in the town. (roof)

9 The ground was covered with many _____. (leaf)

10 We ordered five _____ at the cafeteria. (sandwich)

셀 수 있는 명사의 복수형: 불규칙 변화

 POINT 2-2

정답 p.64

연습문제 | 우리말과 같도록 괄호 안의 말을 활용하여 빈칸에 쓰시오.

1 다섯 명의 남자들은 농구를 하고 있다. (man)

= Five _____ are playing basketball.

2 거위들은 큰 무리를 지어 이동한다. (goose)

= _____ travel in large groups.

3 나의 고양이는 마당에서 몇몇의 쥐들을 잡았다. (mouse)

= My cat caught some _____ in the yard.

4 사슴들은 모든 동물들 중에서 가장 아름다운 눈을 가지고 있다. (deer)

= _____ have the most beautiful eyes of all animals.

5 나는 토요일마다 몇몇의 아이들에게 영어를 가르쳐준다. (child)

= I teach some _____ English on Saturdays.

6 물고기들은 물 사이로 움직이기 위해 그들의 지느러미와 꼬리를 사용한다. (fish)

= _____ use their fins and tail to move through the water.

셀 수 없는 명사의 수량 표현

정답 p.64

연습문제 빈칸에 알맞은 말을 <보기>에서 한 번씩만 골라 괄호 안의 말을 활용하여 쓰시오.

<보기> slice cup bowl can

1 Ellie ate _____ for lunch. (four, pizza)

2 I'd like _____ , please. (two, salad)

3 Elena used _____ to paint the fence. (ten, paint)

4 Can I have _____ , please? (a, coffee)

<보기> loaf glass bottle piece

5 There are only _____ left on the shelf in the store. (two, ink)

6 Two men are carrying _____ into the house. (a, furniture)

7 An old lady always buys _____ on Sundays. (five, bread)

8 It is good to drink _____ every morning. (a, water)

명사 관련 표현

정답 p.65

연습문제 A 밑줄 친 부분이 어법상 맞으면 O를 쓰고, 틀리면 바르게 고쳐 쓰시오.

1 Are you going to get a new pair of <u>glass</u> today? → _____

2 Have you driven a <u>two-doors</u> car before? → _____

3 I used to live in that <u>five-story</u> building. → _____

4 I have two pairs of <u>glove</u>, so I can lend them to you. → _____

연습문제 B 다음 문장의 밑줄 친 부분과 동격인 부분에 밑줄을 치시오.

1 <u>Mr. Graham</u>, my homeroom teacher, is very strict.

2 <u>Jintae</u>, my downstairs neighbor, gave me some kimchi.

3 I'm listening to <u>Mozart</u>, an amazing composer.

4 <u>William and John</u>, the soccer players, are training in the field.

연습문제 A   우리말과 같도록 괄호 안의 말을 활용하여 빈칸에 쓰시오.

1 화장실에 두 개의 칫솔이 있다. (two, toothbrush)

= _____ _____ _____ _____ in the bathroom.

2 찬장에 한 개의 컵이 있니? (a, cup)

= _____ _____ _____ in the cupboard?

3 이 잔에는 약간의 얼음이 있다. (some, ice)

= _____ _____ _____ in this glass.

4 이 작은 마을에는 많은 버스들이 없다. (many, bus)

= _____ _____ _____ _____ in this small town.

5 바구니에 열 개의 달걀이 있다. (ten, egg)

= _____ _____ _____ in the basket.

6 식탁 아래에 한 마리의 쥐가 있다. (a, mouse)

= _____ _____ _____ under the table.

7 놀이터에 많은 그네들이 있니? (many, swing)

= _____ _____ _____ at the playground?

8 나의 커피에 설탕이 전혀 없었다. (any, sugar)

= _____ _____ _____ in my coffee.

9 농장에 많은 양들이 있었다. (many, sheep)

= _____ _____ _____ on the farm.

연습문제 B   is와 are 중 다음 빈칸에 들어갈 말이 나머지 둘과 <u>다른</u> 것을 고르시오.

1 ① There _____ a pen in the drawer.
② There _____ elephants in the field.
③ There _____ many dishes on the menu.

2 ① There _____ tissues in the bag.
② There _____ some shirts in the closet.
③ There _____ lots of water in the bucket.

3 ① There _____ sand in Irene's shoes.
② There _____ some rice in the bowl.
③ There _____ many apples on the tree.

4 ① There _____ many cars on the road.
② There _____ a fish in the fishbowl.
③ There _____ paper in the copy machine.

연습문제 다음 빈칸에 a나 an 중 알맞은 것을 쓰고, 필요하지 않으면 X를 쓰시오.

1 I call my mother twice _____ day.

2 We only have _____ hour to get ready.

3 Martin gave me some helpful _____ advice.

4 Abby is having _____ sandwich for dinner.

5 He likes having _____ tea before going to bed.

6 You have to water the plant once _____ week.

7 I bought _____ orange from the market.

8 This bakery has the best _____ cupcakes.

9 There is _____ cat in the garden.

10 What _____ excellent answer it was!

11 I found _____ old sock under my bed.

12 There is _____ university in my town.

연습문제 다음 빈칸에 a(n)이나 the 중 알맞은 것을 쓰시오.

1 _____ moon is full tonight.

2 There are people outside. Open _____ door.

3 _____ week has seven days.

4 I ate some soup. _____ soup was too spicy.

5 Howard visits the science museum once _____ month.

6 I asked the supermarket manager where I can find _____ butter.

7 _____ last day of the year is New Year's Eve.

8 Dan is _____ only person in this room.

9 Mary has played _____ violin for ten years now.

연습문제 | 알맞은 관사와 괄호 안의 말을 활용하여 문장을 완성하시오. (단, 관사가 필요하지 않으면 쓰지 마시오.)

1 You can get to Gwanghwamun by _____. (bus)

2 What are we going to have for _____? (dinner)

3 I try to study _____ every day. (history)

4 Jihoon knows how to play _____. (cello)

5 Brandon was _____ to arrive. (first person)

6 Do you have to go to _____ on weekends? (work)

7 Please send me the information by _____. (e-mail)

8 I go to the beach twice _____. (year)

9 My house is on _____. (seventh floor)

10 How about playing _____ with me? (basketball)

11 My family goes to _____ every Sunday. (church)

12 My dad came to _____ to pick me up. (school)

13 Could you give me _____? (second)

14 I borrowed a book from the library. _____ was interesting. (book)

1 다음 빈칸에 들어갈 알맞은 것은?

> Peter needs to get a _____ .

① sugar   ② money   ③ book
④ advice   ⑤ sand

2 다음 명사의 복수형이 <u>잘못된</u> 것은?

① hour – hours   ② diary - diaries
③ radio – radios   ④ address - addresses
⑤ roof - rooves

3 다음 중 어법상 바른 것은?

① Are there any churchs here?
② Many treees are planted along the road.
③ Are you going to buy the tomatos?
④ She really likes cookies.
⑤ Why don't we have boiled egges for breakfast?

4 다음 문장에서 어법상 <u>어색한</u> 부분을 찾아 쓰고 바르게 고쳐 쓰시오.

> Five sheeps and two gooses are sitting in the field.

(1) _____ → _____
(2) _____ → _____

5 다음 빈칸에 들어갈 말이 순서대로 짝지어진 것은?

> · I really need to find a pair of _____ .
> · We are having a _____ vacation in Hawaii.

① gloves – second week
② glove – two-week
③ gloves – two-weeks
④ glove – two-weeks
⑤ gloves – two-week

6 다음 <보기> 중 빈칸에 들어갈 수 있는 것의 개수는?

> <보기> foxes ants rain
>   information salmon dust

> Have you seen many _____ before?

① 2개   ② 3개   ③ 4개
④ 5개   ⑤ 6개

7 다음 중 밑줄 친 부분이 어법상 바른 것은?

① He must buy <u>a new furniture</u>.
② She would like to have <u>tea</u>.
③ This town has many <u>building</u>.
④ <u>Two car</u> are parked outside.
⑤ Ask your mother for <u>an information</u>.

8 다음 중 명사의 복수형이 바른 것끼리 묶인 것은?

ⓐ cats, leaves, oxes
ⓑ addresses, deers, glasses
ⓒ men, stories, fish
ⓓ teeth, photos, mice
ⓔ children, pianoes, women

① ⓐ, ⓑ   ② ⓐ, ⓒ   ③ ⓒ, ⓓ
④ ⓑ, ⓒ, ⓓ   ⑤ ⓑ, ⓓ, ⓔ

9 우리말과 같도록 괄호 안의 말을 활용하여 문장을 완성하시오.

Nina는 매일 아침 시리얼 두 그릇을 먹는다.
(cereal)

= Nina eats _____ every morning.

10 다음 문장에서 어법상 어색한 부분을 찾아 쓰고 바르게 고쳐 쓰시오.

My family lives in a third-floors apartment above the shop.

_____ → _____

11 다음 중 어법상 어색한 것은?

① There is a sign above the building.
② There is an egg in the refrigerator.
③ Were there ice on the road?
④ There were many children in the playground.
⑤ Is there an umbrella at the door?

12 다음 빈칸에 들어갈 말로 어색한 것은?

There are _____.

① many books in the library
② beef in this pie
③ flowers in the garden
④ five days left in this month
⑤ children in the playground

13 우리말과 같도록 빈칸에 알맞은 형태의 be동사를 쓰시오.

(1) 그 접시에 세 개의 컵케이크가 있다.

= There _____ three cupcakes on the plate.

(2) 그 주전자 안에 커피가 없다.

= There _____ coffee in the pot.

14 다음 중 밑줄 친 부분의 의미가 나머지 넷과 다른 것은?

① There are some white puppies inside the fence.
② Is there any ice cream in the freezer?
③ Look at those motorcycles over there.
④ Are there many parks in your hometown?
⑤ There is some medicine in the drawer.

15 be동사를 활용하여 다음 글의 빈칸에 알맞은 말을 쓰시오.

Yesterday, we went to a farm. There ⓐ_____ lots of animals on the farm. There ⓑ_____ cows and horses. There ⓒ_____ a very friendly sheep dog, too.

16 다음 중 밑줄 친 부분이 어법상 바른 것끼리 묶인 것은?

ⓐ Leaves are falling from the trees.
ⓑ He picked up two boxs at once.
ⓒ She went to get some dishes.
ⓓ My dentist advised me to brush my teeth three times a day.
ⓔ Please put your keies on the table.

① ⓐ, ⓒ, ⓓ   ② ⓐ, ⓑ, ⓔ   ③ ⓐ, ⓒ, ⓔ
④ ⓑ, ⓒ, ⓓ   ⑤ ⓑ, ⓓ, ⓔ

[17-18] <보기>와 같이 다음 두 문장의 의미가 같도록 빈칸에 알맞은 말을 쓰시오.

<보기>
My school has a big cafeteria.
= *There   is   a   big   cafeteria* in my school.

17

My apartment has two bathrooms.
= _____ _____ _____ _____ in my apartment.

18

The amusement park doesn't have a roller coaster.
= _____ _____ _____ _____ _____ in the amusement park.

19 다음 빈칸에 알맞은 말을 넣어 질문에 대한 대답을 완성하시오.

(1)
A: Are there pencils in this bag?
B: Yes, _____ _____.

(2)
A: Is there any meat in the refrigerator?
B: No, _____ _____.

20 우리말과 같도록 주어진 <조건>에 맞게 문장을 완성하시오.

> 나무에 11개의 코코넛이 있다.

> **<조건>**
> 1. there, coconut, be를 활용하시오.
> 2. 숫자는 영어로 쓰시오.

= _____ in the tree.

21 다음 빈칸에 들어갈 말이 나머지 넷과 <u>다른</u> 것은?

① I want _____ yellow bicycle.
② What _____ huge airplane!
③ I have _____ pet snake in my room.
④ Wanda found _____ electronic toothbrush.
⑤ My parents go hiking twice _____ day.

22 주어진 문장의 밑줄 친 부분과 의미가 <u>다른</u> 것은?

> We play badminton once <u>a</u> week.

① You should drink some water once <u>an</u> hour.
② Does the dog go for a walk three times <u>a</u> day?
③ My sister looks in the mirror twice <u>an</u> hour.
④ Sally took the science exam for <u>an</u> hour.
⑤ Does he call you three times <u>a</u> week?

23 다음 빈칸에 공통으로 들어갈 알맞은 말을 쓰시오.

> · Could you close _____ window next to the door?
> · The dentist's office is on _____ second floor.

24 다음 중 밑줄 친 부분이 어법상 <u>어색한</u> 것은?

① There is <u>a</u> chicken behind the fence.
② Water the cactus once <u>a</u> month.
③ You can always see the same side of <u>a</u> moon.
④ I often see my grandfather playing <u>the</u> guitar.
⑤ The workers went to <u>the</u> prison to repair the wall.

25 다음 밑줄 친 부분을 바르게 고치지 <u>못한</u> 것은?

① Roland often reads books after <u>the lunch</u>. (→ lunch)
② <u>New car model</u> from the company looks gorgeous. (→ The new car model)
③ Have you played <u>flute</u> before? (→ the flute)
④ Please throw out the garbage four times <u>the day</u>. (→ a day)
⑤ How can I get to the subway station, by <u>a bus</u> or on foot? (→ the bus)

CHAPTER 10
대명사

연습문제 A │ 밑줄 친 부분이 어법상 맞으면 O를 쓰고, 틀리면 바르게 고쳐 완전한 문장을 쓰시오.

1 I want to invite you to <u>me</u> house.

→ _____

2 <u>Your</u> should listen to Dad's advice.

→ _____

3 Peter came to Korea to see <u>our</u>.

→ _____

4 <u>Their</u> school is across the street.

→ _____

5 Have you seen <u>he</u> recently?

→ _____

6 My sister and I lost <u>we</u> passports.

→ _____

7 When you mix yellow and blue, <u>it</u> becomes green.

→ _____

연습문제 B │ 우리말과 같도록 괄호 안의 인칭대명사를 알맞은 형태로 바꿔 빈칸에 쓰시오.

1 (I)   ① 나의 장난감이 부러졌다.   = _____ toy is broken.
           ② 너는 나의 것을 고칠 수 있니?   = Can you fix _____ ?

2 (you)   ① 이것은 너의 여행 가방이니?   = Is this _____ suitcase?
           ② 너의 것은 매우 무겁다.   = _____ is really heavy.

3 (he)   ① 그 빨간색 스포츠카는 그의 것이다. = The red sports car is _____ .
           ② 그의 차는 근사해 보인다.   = _____ car looks fancy.

4 (she)   ① 이 팔찌는 그녀의 것이다.   = This bracelet is _____ .
           ② 그녀는 그녀의 팔찌를 직접 만들었다. = She made _____ bracelet by hand.

5 (we)   ① 우리는 우리의 개를 찾고 있다.   = We are looking for _____ dog.
           ② 우리의 것은 검정색과 하얀색 털을 가졌다. = _____ has black and white fur.

6 (they)   ① 나는 그들의 집에 방문할 것이다.   = I'm going to visit _____ house.
           ② 그들의 것은 Silver가에 있다.   = _____ is on Silver Street.

연습문제 A 괄호 안에서 알맞은 것을 고르시오.

1 Maria feels proud of (myself / herself).

2 The bird opened the cage (it / itself).

3 We (ourselves / themselves) made this pasta.

4 Paul used to like (me / myself) before.

5 I had to take care of (myself / yourself).

6 Could you bring (us / ourselves) some water?

7 My friends enjoyed (myself / themselves) at the festival.

8 Mr. Jones (him / himself) repaired the broken door.

9 The new student introduced (herself / ourselves) to us.

10 The teacher is going to give (them / themselves) helpful advice.

연습문제 B 밑줄 친 부분을 생략할 수 있으면 O를 쓰고, 생략할 수 없으면 X를 쓰시오.

1 Mark himself did the laundry. → _____

2 I'm going to trust myself more. → _____

3 You must finish your homework yourself. → _____

4 We shouldn't blame ourselves for the incident. → _____

5 They themselves built this beautiful house. → _____

6 Linda almost burned herself yesterday. → _____

7 I really don't like this skirt itself. → _____

8 Harry was angry at himself for breaking his phone. → _____

9 Did you travel in Africa by yourself? → _____

10 The reporter interviewed the president himself. → _____

연습문제 A 괄호 안에서 알맞은 것을 고르시오.

1 (That / Those) are letters from Nate.

2 (That / Those) sculpture is over 200 years old.

3 James painted (this / these) paintings himself.

4 (That / Those) are my family members.

5 I really don't like (this / these) color.

6 (This / These) are the popular menu choices.

7 Is (that / those) your laptop? - No, (it isn't / they aren't).

8 Are (this / these) seats empty? - Yes, (it is / they are).

9 Is (this / these) movie scary? - No, (it isn't / they aren't).

연습문제 B 밑줄 친 부분의 쓰임과 같은 것을 <보기>에서 골라 그 기호를 쓰시오.

<보기> ⓐ This is Jack's new phone.
　　　　ⓑ I want to sit on this bench.

1 Those are my musical instruments.　　　[　　]

2 That is our town's new middle school.　　[　　]

3 These shoes are too small for me.　　　[　　]

4 This is my home address.　　　　　　　[　　]

5 Melanie broke this window.　　　　　　[　　]

6 Those people are waiting for a celebrity.　[　　]

7 The kids shouldn't touch that.　　　　　[　　]

8 Brandon has to take that medicine.　　　[　　]

9 I haven't washed these yet.　　　　　　[　　]

10 My dad finds this article very interesting.　[　　]

비인칭 주어 it

POINT 4

연습문제 다음 중 밑줄 친 it의 쓰임이 나머지 둘과 다른 것을 고르시오.

1 ① It is Sunday today.
  ② I have it in my pocket.
  ③ It is August 31.

2 ① It was a funny joke.
  ② It is raining now.
  ③ I really liked it.

3 ① It was not a great plan.
  ② It takes 15 minutes on foot.
  ③ It is still bright outside.

4 ① Patrick lost it.
  ② I bought it at the town market.
  ③ It's already 10 o'clock.

5 ① Put it in a fridge right away.
  ② What day is it?
  ③ Where was it?

6 ① It is my sister's doll.
  ② It is November 25.
  ③ It will be summer soon.

7 ① It is quite cloudy today.
  ② It was lying on the sofa.
  ③ We ordered it for dinner.

8 ① It is two kilometers from here.
  ② What a clean room it is!
  ③ It's 3 A.M. in China now.

부정대명사: one

POINT 5-1

연습문제 다음 빈칸에 알맞은 말을 <보기>에서 골라 쓰시오.

<보기> one   ones   it   they   them

1 Have you seen my key? – Yes, _____ is on your desk.

2 Tom wants to buy a shirt. He would like a blue _____.

3 You got over ten messages. You'd better read _____ quickly.

4 These apples are too small, so I'll look for bigger _____.

5 I got those sneakers for Christmas. – _____ look comfortable.

6 Is this your umbrella? – No, mine is the longer _____.

7 There weren't any red roses. The flower shop only has white _____.

8 Your dress is very pretty. – Thanks. My mom bought _____ for me.

9 Can I eat these muffins? – Don't eat _____ now because they're still hot.

연습문제 A 다음 빈칸에 알맞은 말을 <보기>에서 한 번씩만 골라 쓰시오.

<보기> one   another   others   other   the other

1 Two cushions are on my bed. One is pink and _____ is white.

2 That is not my jacket. Mine is the _____ on the chair.

3 This restaurant is closed. Let's find _____ places to eat.

4 I already have a nice phone, so I don't need _____ one.

5 My friend, Katherine, always helps _____ .

연습문제 B 우리말과 같도록 괄호 안의 말을 활용하여 문장을 완성하시오.

1 나는 약간의 펜을 가지고 있다. 몇몇은 검정색이고, 다른 것들은 빨간색이다. (black, red)
= I have some pens. _____ , and _____ .

2 이 서랍에 열 개의 옷들이 있다. 몇몇은 바지들이고, 나머지 전부는 치마들이다. (pants, skirts)
= There are ten clothes in this drawer. _____ , and _____ .

3 두 종류의 주스가 있다. 하나는 사과 주스이고, 나머지 하나는 오렌지 주스이다. (apple juice, orange juice)
= There are two kinds of juice. _____ , and _____ .

4 박물관에 많은 외국인 관광객들이 있다. 몇몇은 중국인이고, 다른 사람들은 캐나다인이다. (Chinese, Canadians)
= There are many foreign tourists in the museum. _____ , and
_____ .

5 Jack은 슈퍼마켓에서 세 개의 채소를 샀다. 하나는 토마토이고, 다른 하나는 당근이고, 나머지 하나는 감자이다.
(a tomato, a carrot, a potato)
= Jack bought three vegetables at the supermarket. _____ ,
_____ , and _____ .

6 나의 형은 세 개의 공을 가지고 있다. 하나는 축구공이고, 다른 하나는 농구공이고, 나머지 하나는 야구공이다.
(a soccer ball, a basketball, a baseball)
= My brother has three balls. _____ , _____ , and
_____ .

연습문제 | 밑줄 친 부분이 어법상 맞으면 O를 쓰고, 틀리면 바르게 고쳐 완전한 문장을 쓰시오.

1 Every child <u>need</u> a mother's love.

→ _____

2 Everything <u>seems</u> fine.

→ _____

3 I wish to visit every <u>countries</u> in the world.

→ _____

4 All items <u>are</u> on sale right now.

→ _____

5 Each <u>members</u> has his or her own strength.

→ _____

6 All your advice <u>were</u> really helpful.

→ _____

7 Everybody <u>are</u> having a good time.

→ _____

8 Each <u>students</u> must turn in the essay.

→ _____

9 All my friends <u>likes</u> the same singer.

→ _____

10 Let's start when everyone <u>get</u> here.

→ _____

11 Every girl in my class <u>watch</u> the TV show.

→ _____

12 Each player <u>have</u> to wear the team uniform.

→ _____

13 All life <u>need</u> water to live.

→ _____

중간 · 기말고사 실전 문제

1 다음 중 밑줄 친 부분이 어법상 바른 것은?

① <u>They</u> are his textbooks.
② <u>It</u> nose is very big.
③ <u>They</u> father is a lawyer.
④ Mr. Weber bought <u>we</u> lunch.
⑤ <u>She's</u> house is across the street.

2 다음 중 밑줄 친 부분을 인칭대명사로 바르게 바꾸지 못한 것은?

① Sandra is reading <u>a magazine</u>. (→ it)
② We showed <u>our pictures</u> to Adam. (→ us)
③ <u>Mr. Lee</u> is the school's principal. (→ He)
④ Jenna fixed <u>a chair and a desk</u>. (→ them)
⑤ Mary called <u>my mother</u> last night. (→ her)

3 다음 글의 빈칸에 알맞은 인칭대명사를 쓰시오.

I like my cousin a lot. Her name is Beth. _____ hobby is skiing. _____ goes to the ski resort every weekend in the winter. I hope to go with _____ someday.

4 다음 두 문장의 의미가 같도록 빈칸에 알맞은 말을 쓰시오.

That is her car in the parking lot.
= That car in the parking lot is _____.

5 다음 (A)~(C)에 들어갈 말이 바르게 짝지어진 것은?

- ____(A)____ jokes are funny.
- This heater made ____(B)____ feel warm.
- That pen is ____(C)____.

	(A)	(B)	(C)
①	She	us	my
②	Her	us	mine
③	Her	us	my
④	Her	our	mine
⑤	She	our	my

6 다음 대화의 빈칸에 들어갈 말이 순서대로 짝지어진 것은?

A: Is this your phone on the table?
B: No, it's not _____. Maybe it's Dave's.
A: I don't think so. His is red.
B: Claire was here a few minutes ago. Maybe it's _____ phone.
A: I'll ask her.

① yours – she
② yours – hers
③ hers – her
④ mine – hers
⑤ mine – her

7 다음 글의 밑줄 친 우리말과 같도록 빈칸에 알맞은 말을 쓰시오.

I bought ice cream for you and Steve. <u>바닐라는 그의 것이고, 초콜릿은 너의 것이다.</u>

= The vanilla is _____, and the chocolate is _____.

8 다음 글의 ⓐ~ⓔ에 알맞은 말을 <보기>에서 한 번씩만 골라 쓰시오.

<보기> she they her his their

I have two pet rabbits at my home. One is a girl and the other is a boy. ⓐ＿＿＿＿＿ names are Snowy and Jelly. Snowy is very lively. She often escapes from ⓑ＿＿＿＿＿ cage. ⓒ＿＿＿＿＿ always makes a mess. Jelly is calm. He likes to sit and eat ⓓ＿＿＿＿＿ snacks. ⓔ＿＿＿＿＿ are both so cute. I love hugging them.

9 다음 중 밑줄 친 부분의 쓰임이 나머지 넷과 다른 것은?

① Brett and Paul are <u>his</u> brothers.
② Are those gloves <u>his</u> or yours?
③ I haven't met <u>his</u> parents.
④ Is <u>his</u> hair long or short?
⑤ I don't agree with <u>his</u> opinion.

10 다음 빈칸에 공통으로 들어갈 알맞은 것은?

· He likes to look at ＿＿＿＿＿ in a mirror.
· Jason painted his room ＿＿＿＿＿.

① he   ② him   ③ his
④ himself   ⑤ himselves

11 다음 중 밑줄 친 부분을 생략할 수 있는 것끼리 묶인 것은?

ⓐ She must be proud of <u>herself</u>.
ⓑ The movie <u>itself</u> was boring.
ⓒ We <u>ourselves</u> cleaned the room.
ⓓ Brad opened the door <u>himself</u>.
ⓔ The twins introduced <u>themselves</u> to their new friends.

① ⓐ, ⓑ   ② ⓐ, ⓔ   ③ ⓑ, ⓔ
④ ⓑ, ⓒ, ⓓ   ⑤ ⓒ, ⓓ, ⓔ

12 우리말과 같도록 주어진 <조건>에 맞게 영작하시오.

Jane은 그녀 자신을 전문가로 여긴다.

<조건> consider, an expert를 활용하시오.

= ＿＿＿＿＿＿＿＿＿＿＿＿＿＿＿＿＿＿＿

13 다음 중 밑줄 친 부분이 어법상 어색한 것은?

① Pass me <u>those</u> books, please.
② Did you watch <u>these</u> movie?
③ Is <u>that</u> blue sweater yours?
④ Who broke <u>this</u> dish?
⑤ <u>That</u> is a really pretty ribbon.

14 다음 대화의 밑줄 친 this와 쓰임이 같은 것을 모두 고르시오.

> A: Did you make this bracelet?
> B: No. I bought it at a store.

① Is this pepper spicy?
② This is my favorite song.
③ Whose hat is this?
④ This is Mark's new car.
⑤ This laptop is mine.

15 다음 빈칸에 들어갈 말이 나머지 넷과 다른 것은?

① This sweater is wet, so I will wear another _____.
② I lost my camera, so I bought a new _____.
③ Ethan has a green bike, and I have a red _____.
④ My sister hates broccoli, so she never eats _____.
⑤ Chris made chocolate cookies, so I tried _____.

16 우리말과 같도록 괄호 안의 말을 활용하여 문장을 완성하시오.

> 이번 주말에 비가 올 것이다. (will, rain)

= _____ this weekend.

17 다음 대화의 밑줄 친 ⓐ~ⓔ에 대한 설명이 잘못된 것을 모두 고르시오.

> A: Isn't ⓐit almost seven o'clock now?
> B: Yes. Why isn't the bus here?
> A: I don't know. ⓑIt is really late.
> B: Maybe ⓒit is late because of the weather. ⓓIt has rained a lot today.
> A: You're probably right. I hope ⓔit will get here soon.
> B: Me too. I don't want to wait any longer.

① ⓐ는 시간을 나타내는 비인칭 주어이다.
② ⓑ는 'bus'를 가리키는 대명사이다.
③ ⓑ와 ⓓ는 비인칭 주어이다.
④ ⓒ와 ⓓ는 '그것'이라고 해석하지 않는다.
⑤ ⓒ와 ⓔ는 '그것'이라고 해석한다.

18 다음 밑줄 친 it의 쓰임이 같은 것끼리 묶인 것은?

> ⓐ It's midnight now.
> ⓑ Could you give it to me?
> ⓒ It feels very soft and warm.
> ⓓ It is getting dark in here.
> ⓔ Did you see it at the gate?

① ⓐ, ⓑ   ② ⓒ, ⓓ   ③ ⓐ, ⓑ, ⓔ
④ ⓐ, ⓓ, ⓔ   ⑤ ⓑ, ⓒ, ⓔ

19 다음 글의 밑줄 친 우리말과 같도록 괄호 안의 말을 활용하여 문장을 완성하시오.

> I watched two movies on the weekend. 하나는 코미디였고, 하나는 미스터리였다. (a comedy, a mystery)

= _____, and _____

20 다음 글의 빈칸에 들어갈 말이 순서대로 짝지어진 것은?

There are two types of gorillas in Africa. _____ live in west Africa and _____ live in central Africa. Both types have a similar appearance.

① One - another
② One - the others
③ Some - another
④ Some- the others
⑤ Another - other

21 다음 중 어법상 바른 것의 개수는?

ⓐ All drivers have to be careful.
ⓑ Each desks has a computer.
ⓒ Everybody likes vacations.
ⓓ Every problems has an answer.
ⓔ All information are useful.

① 1개
② 2개
③ 3개
④ 4개
⑤ 5개

22 다음 (A)~(C)에 들어갈 말이 바르게 짝지어진 것은?

· Every ___(A)___ in the store is on sale.
· All students ___(B)___ go to school by 8 A.M.
· Each ___(C)___ must buy a ticket to get on the plane.

	(A)	(B)	(C)
①	book	have to	passengers
②	books	have to	passenger
③	book	have to	passenger
④	books	has to	passengers
⑤	book	has to	passengers

23 우리말과 같도록 괄호 안의 말을 활용하여 빈칸에 쓰시오.

그 팀의 모든 선수는 파란색 유니폼을 입는다. (player, wear)

= Every _____ on the team _____ a blue uniform.

24 다음 빈칸에 알맞은 말을 <보기>에서 한 번씩만 골라 그 기호를 쓰시오.

<보기> ⓐ one ⓑ ones ⓒ another ⓓ some ⓔ the other ⓕ the others

(1) There are three people in the car. _____ is my dad, _____ is my mom, and _____ is my sister.
(2) There are ten cars in the parking lot. _____ are old, and _____ are new.
(3) Shawn has two green shirts and three gray _____.

25 다음 빈칸에 공통으로 들어갈 알맞은 것은?

· We love the Spanish restaurant on 21st Street. _____ Spanish restaurants are not as good as that.
· I don't think my brother is handsome, but _____ people do.

① Others[others]
② Another[another]
③ Other[other]
④ This[this]
⑤ Them[them]

CHAPTER 11
형용사

기출로 적중 POINT

형용사의 용법

정답 p.68

POINT 1

연습문제 <보기>와 같이 다음 문장의 밑줄 친 형용사가 수식하거나 보충 설명하는 부분에 밑줄을 치시오.

> <보기> Look at that <u>pink</u> car.
> The teacher sounds <u>angry</u>.

1 The bus is <u>late</u>.

2 That was a <u>delicious</u> cake.

3 My father drives a <u>big</u> truck.

4 The weather is <u>terrible</u> today.

5 I watched a <u>funny</u> movie.

6 The exercise made me <u>sweaty</u>.

7 My puppy is very <u>playful</u>.

8 Greg tried to lift the <u>heavy</u> box.

9 The gift made my sister <u>happy</u>.

10 My aunt bought me an <u>expensive</u> camera.

형용사의 어순

정답 p.68

POINT 2

연습문제 밑줄 친 부분이 어법상 맞으면 O를 쓰고, 틀리면 바르게 고쳐 완전한 문장을 쓰시오.

1 Sarah saw a <u>small beautiful</u> bird.

→ _____

2 There is a <u>red round</u> table in my room.

→ _____

3 Look at that <u>pretty long yellow</u> dress.

→ _____

4 We slept in a <u>wooden old huge</u> house.

→ _____

5 That <u>long new leather</u> sofa is comfortable.

→ _____

-thing/-body + 형용사

정답 p.68

연습문제 A 괄호 안의 형용사를 알맞은 곳에 넣어 완전한 문장을 쓰시오.

1 We should order something for dessert. (sweet)

→ _____

2 There is somebody in my class. (friendly)

→ _____

3 Do you have anything? (warm)

→ _____

4 Don't pay attention to things. (small)

→ _____

5 Is there anything? (uncomfortable)

→ _____

6 I don't know anybody. (rude)

→ _____

7 Something would be good for lunch. (spicy)

→ _____

8 Anybody can solve this puzzle. (clever)

→ _____

연습문제 B 괄호 안에서 알맞은 것을 고르시오.

1 (Something loud / Loud something) woke me up last night.

2 Did you do (exciting anything / anything exciting) on Saturday?

3 I don't have (good anything / anything good) to read.

4 I heard (something funny / funny something) yesterday.

5 Lisa has some (things expensive / expensive things) in her room.

6 Did you meet (anybody interesting / interesting anybody) on your trip?

7 Let's get (special something / something special) for our teacher.

8 An adventurer enjoys exploring (new places / places new).

연습문제 A 괄호 안의 동사를 알맞은 형태로 바꿔 빈칸에 쓰시오.

1 (excite)   ① The hockey game was _____.

                  ② We were _____ about the game.

2 (interest)   ① There was an _____ article in the newspaper.

                  ② My dad was very _____ in the article.

3 (surprise)   ① Sandra was _____ by the results of the survey.

                  ② The results of the survey were _____.

4 (disappoint)   ① My parents were _____ because of my grades.

                  ② My grades were _____.

5 (confuse)   ① The riddle was _____.

                  ② Everyone was _____ by the riddle.

6 (annoy)   ① My little brother is so _____.

                  ② I'm usually _____ with him.

연습문제 B 괄호 안에서 알맞은 것을 고르시오.

1 The long bus ride was very (boring / bored).

2 My friend's injury made me (worrying / worried).

3 Is there anything (interesting / interested) to watch?

4 The noise of the thunder was (shocking / shocked).

5 He was (surprising / surprised) to see me on the street.

6 The hike to the top of the mountain was (tiring / tired).

7 The children like the (amazing / amazed) magic trick.

8 We were (confusing / confused) by the math problem.

9 I was (exciting / excited) to buy a new laptop.

10 The ending of the musical was (disappointing / disappointed).

11 A letter from my grandfather was very (moving / moved).

수사: 기수와 서수

정답 p.69

연습문제 A 다음 기수는 서수로, 서수는 기수로 바꿔 쓰시오. (단, 영어로 쓰시오.)

1 first → _____

2 ninety → _____

3 twelve → _____

4 four-hundredth → _____

5 eightieth → _____

6 seventy-three → _____

7 sixty-fifth → _____

8 twenty-five → _____

연습문제 B 우리말과 같도록 문장을 완성하시오. (단, 숫자는 영어로 쓰시오.)

1 그 물고기는 방금 수백 개의 알을 낳았다.

= The fish laid _____ eggs just now.

2 그 전시회는 보통 하루에 500명의 방문객을 끌어들인다.

= The exhibition usually attracts _____ visitors a day.

3 매년 수천 명의 사람들이 암으로 죽는다.

= _____ people die of cancer every year.

4 수백만의 사람들이 이 영화를 봤다.

= _____ people watched this movie.

수사: 정수, 소수, 분수

정답 p.69

연습문제 다음 숫자를 영어로 쓰시오.

1 0.46 → _____

2 11,000,000 → _____

3 2,464 → _____

4 82.06 → _____

5 43,454 → _____

6 $\frac{1}{3}$ → _____

7 $\frac{3}{4}$ → _____

8 $1\frac{1}{2}$ → _____

연습문제 다음 시각을 영어로 바르게 읽었으면 O를 쓰고, 틀리게 읽었으면 바르게 고쳐 쓰시오.

1 4시 53분 → four fifty-third → _____

2 7시 15분 → quarter to seven → _____

3 8시 22분 → eight twenty-two → _____

4 3시 30분 → half past four → _____

5 10시 05분 → ten-o-five → _____

6 2시 00분 → two o'clock → _____

7 5시 45분 → a quarter past six → _____

8 9시 37분 → ninth thirty-seven → _____

연습문제 다음 연도와 날짜를 영어로 쓰시오.

1 1920년 → _____

2 5월 10일 → _____

3 3월 2일 → _____

4 2012년 → _____

5 1456년 → _____

6 1940년대 → _____

7 1250년 8월 3일 → _____

8 2045년 5월 14일 → _____

수량형용사: many, much, a lot of

정답 p.69

연습문제 A 다음 빈칸에 many나 much 중 알맞은 것을 쓰시오.

1 There are _____ people at the beach.

2 I could see _____ national flags in the competition.

3 Brad does not have _____ time today.

4 The parking lot has _____ empty spaces.

5 How _____ money did you spend on dinner?

6 There wasn't _____ yellow dust this spring.

7 Pepper is a basic ingredient for _____ Korean dishes.

8 People don't pay _____ attention to others than we think.

연습문제 B 다음 문장의 밑줄 친 부분을 many나 much로 바꿔 완전한 문장을 쓰시오.

1 He bought <u>lots of</u> hats for his friends at the department store.

→ _____

2 Does the popcorn contain <u>lots of</u> salt?

→ _____

3 There aren't <u>a lot of</u> cars on the road.

→ _____

4 I couldn't find <u>a lot of</u> information on this website.

→ _____

5 The food waste attracts <u>a lot of</u> insects.

→ _____

6 Don't use <u>lots of</u> butter when you bake cookies.

→ _____

7 Was <u>lots of</u> gold found in the cave?

→ _____

8 <u>A lot of</u> workers in the United States wore jeans in 1800s.

→ _____

연습문제 A 괄호 안에서 알맞은 말을 골라 빈칸에 쓰시오.

1 (a few / a little)   ① There was _____ rain this morning.

② Jessie spent _____ days in Taiwan.

2 (few / little)   ① The subway had _____ passengers at night.

② Lisa has _____ free time these days.

3 (a few / a little)   ① My father gave me _____ advice.

② There is _____ oranges in the fridge.

4 (few / little)   ① I have _____ interest in that movie.

② _____ leaves remain on the tree.

5 (a few / a little)   ① Jack got _____ sleep last night.

② Dave brought _____ snacks for the picnic.

6 (few / little)   ① I read _____ books last month.

② There is _____ lemonade in the glass.

연습문제 B 우리말과 같도록 <보기>의 말과 괄호 안의 명사를 활용하여 문장을 완성하시오.

<보기>   a few   a little   few   little   many   much

1 너는 너의 차에 약간의 우유를 원하니? (milk)

= Would you like _____ in your tea?

2 많은 버스들이 이 정거장에 선다. (bus)

= _____ stop at this station.

3 가게 안에 손님들이 거의 없었다. (customer)

= There were _____ in the store.

4 우리는 보통 2월에 많은 눈을 볼 수 있니? (snow)

= Can we usually see _____ in February?

5 James는 나에게 늦은 것에 대한 약간의 이유들을 말해줬다. (reason)

= James told me _____ for being late.

6 박 선생님은 우리에게 숙제를 거의 주지 않는다. (homework)

= Ms. Park gives _____ to us.

연습문제 다음 빈칸에 some이나 any 중 알맞은 것을 쓰시오.

1 The child drank _____ juice from the bottle.

2 Does Patrick have _____ hobbies?

3 We ate _____ pizza for lunch.

4 I don't have _____ colored pencils.

5 Would you like _____ salad?

6 My friend lent me _____ books to read.

7 We hung _____ paintings on the wall.

8 There isn't _____ sugar in my coffee.

9 My dog didn't eat _____ food yesterday.

10 Let's put _____ ketchup on the hotdog.

11 There are _____ signs on the street.

12 Do you have _____ pets?

13 We can't think of _____ good ideas.

14 Could you give me _____ advice?

1 다음 빈칸에 들어갈 말로 어색한 것은?

Are there _____ fish in that lake?

① much   ② many   ③ any
④ a few   ⑤ a lot of

2 다음 빈칸에 들어갈 말이 순서대로 짝지어진 것은?

· Can we take a break for _____ minutes?
· He bought his parents _____ gifts.

① a few – many   ② a few – much
③ few – much   ④ a little – many
⑤ a little – much

3 다음 (A)~(C)에 들어갈 말이 바르게 짝지어진 것은?

· We couldn't find ___(A)___ cucumbers at the market yesterday.
· That movie is ___(B)___ .
· They saw ___(C)___ in the sky.

	(A)	(B)	(C)
①	some	boring	strange something
②	any	bored	something strange
③	any	boring	something strange
④	any	boring	strange something
⑤	some	bored	something strange

4 다음 문장에서 틀린 부분을 바르게 고쳐 완전한 문장을 쓰시오.

Cleaning my house made me tiring.
→ _____

5 다음 문장과 의미가 같은 것은?

It's nine thirty.

① It's a quarter to nine.
② It's a quarter past eight.
③ It's a half past eight.
④ It's a half to nine.
⑤ It's a half past nine.

6 다음 대화의 밑줄 친 우리말을 알맞게 영작한 것을 모두 고르시오.

A: When is Independence Day in the United States?
B: 7월 4일이야.

① It's July fourth.
② It's July four.
③ It's the fourteenth of July.
④ It's the four of July.
⑤ It's the fourth of July.

[7-8] 다음 중 영어로 <u>잘못</u> 읽은 것을 고르시오.

7

① 11시 45분 = a quarter to twelve

② 2025년 = two thousand twenty-five

③ 5시 10분 = ten to five

④ 8시 27분 = eight twenty-seven

⑤ 1911년 3월 1일 = March first, nineteen eleven

8

① 0.127 = zero point one two seven

② 15.91 = fifteen point ninety one

③ 1/6 = a sixth

④ 7/15 = seven-fifteenths

⑤ 5,200,043 = five million, two hundred thousand and forty-three

9 우리말과 같도록 문장을 완성하시오.

> 이 박물관은 수천 개의 그림을 가지고 있다.

= This museum has _____ paintings.

10 괄호 안의 말을 배열할 때 세 번째 오는 것을 쓰시오.

> There is a _____ in the room. (bed, blue, old, big)

→ _____

11 다음 중 기수와 서수의 형태가 <u>잘못</u> 짝지어진 것은?

① three – third

② twelve – twelveth

③ thirty-nine – thirty-ninth

④ fifty – fiftieth

⑤ ninety-two – ninety-second

12 다음 빈칸에 들어갈 수 있는 것을 <u>모두</u> 고르시오.

> They received _____ cards on Valentine's Day.

① a few   ② a little

③ much   ④ lots of

⑤ any

13 다음 밑줄 친 부분과 바꿔 쓸 수 있는 것은?

> That book didn't have <u>a lot of</u> useful information about Egyptian history.

① many   ② much   ③ few

④ a few   ⑤ a little

14 다음 빈칸에 공통으로 들어갈 알맞은 것은?

> · Did you drink _____ coffee last night?
> · There are _____ oranges in the kitchen.

① many   ② much   ③ lots of
④ a few   ⑤ a little

[17-18] 다음 문장에서 어법상 어색한 부분을 찾아 쓰고 바르게 고쳐 쓰시오.

17

> I met any people at the party. They have very different jobs.

_____ → _____

18

> Sora didn't meet interesting anyone at the book club.

_____ → _____

15 다음 빈칸에 들어갈 말이 순서대로 짝지어진 것은?

> · There isn't _____ milk in the refrigerator.
> · My uncle knows _____ funny jokes.

① a few – some   ② some – any
③ any – some   ④ any – any
⑤ a few – any

19 다음 대화의 빈칸에 공통으로 들어갈 가장 알맞은 것은?

> A: Did something bad happen? You seem _____ today.
> B: I am _____ because I had a fight with my friend last night.

① exciting   ② excited
③ annoying   ④ annoyed
⑤ amazing

16 다음 중 어법상 바른 것은?

① I bought much clothes at the store.
② There is few water in the glass.
③ We will read many stories today.
④ Would you like to drink any tea?
⑤ There isn't some soap in the bathroom.

20 주어진 문장의 밑줄 친 형용사와 용법이 다른 것은?

> Dickens was a <u>great</u> writer.

① Eagles build <u>large</u> nests.
② This photographer takes <u>beautiful</u> photos.
③ That strange man makes us <u>nervous</u>.
④ Tina wears bright <u>red</u> shoes.
⑤ Kind people say really <u>nice</u> things.

21 다음 중 밑줄 친 부분이 어법상 어색한 것은?

① He gave me a picture of a <u>cute small</u> kitty.
② She has a <u>lovely brown</u> hat with a ribbon.
③ I'll wear those <u>comfortable black</u> sneakers.
④ Carol recently bought a <u>leather big</u> sofa.
⑤ Let's throw away the <u>round old</u> table in the kitchen.

22 다음 중 어법상 어색한 것은?

① He is an amazing violinist.
② I am interested in Korean history.
③ This exercise is so tiring.
④ Everybody is excited about the news.
⑤ Failing the test was disappointed.

[23-24] 우리말과 같도록 괄호 안의 말을 활용하여 빈칸에 쓰시오.

23

> Andrew는 그 소식에 대해 충격을 받았다.
> (shock)

= Andrew was _____ by the news.

24

> 나의 친구의 이야기는 혼란스러웠다. (confuse)

= My friend's story was _____.

25 다음 글의 밑줄 친 ⓐ~ⓔ 중 어법상 어색한 것을 찾아 기호를 쓰고 바르게 고쳐 쓰시오.

> Every six months, Emily goes to the dentist. ⓐ<u>First</u>, the dentist takes ⓑ<u>a few</u> X-rays. Then, he checks Emily's teeth. This takes ⓒ<u>many</u> time. But Emily doesn't eat ⓓ<u>many</u> sweet things, so there is usually ⓔ<u>wrong nothing</u> with her teeth.

(1) _____ → _____
(2) _____ → _____

CHAPTER 12
부사

기출로 적중 POINT

연습문제 다음 문장의 밑줄 친 부사가 수식하는 부분에 밑줄을 치시오.

1 The stars shine <u>brightly</u>.

2 The movie was <u>really</u> scary.

3 Jenna checks her e-mail <u>regularly</u>.

4 <u>Sadly</u>, I lost my ticket.

5 Don't worry <u>too</u> much.

6 The patient recovered <u>very</u> slowly.

7 Bill was <u>extremely</u> hungry.

8 <u>Quickly</u>, he went down the stairs.

9 Please talk <u>nicely</u> to your sister.

10 I have visited the café <u>frequently</u>.

기출로적중 POINT 2-1 부사의 형태

정답 p.71

연습문제 괄호 안의 말을 알맞은 형태로 바꿔 빈칸에 쓰시오.

1 (simple) ① That plate has a _____ pattern.
② The textbook explains the points _____.

2 (gentle) ① The man is smart and _____.
② Add eggs to the bowl and mix _____.

3 (easy) ① This printer is _____ to use.
② The famous chef usually uses _____ available ingredients.

4 (foolish) ① _____, I left my key in the car.
② What a _____ decision!

5 (heavy) ① We could not lift the _____ sofa.
② Seoul is a _____ populated city.

6 (careful) ① Please listen to the announcement _____.
② People should be _____ on ice.

7 (good) ① Carrots are _____ for your eyes.
② I can cook Chinese food really _____.

형용사와 형태가 같은 부사

정답 p.71

연습문제 다음 중 밑줄 친 부분이 부사인 것을 고르시오.

1 ① Cheetahs are <u>fast</u> animals.
② Linda always talks too <u>fast</u>.

2 ① This mountain is so <u>high</u>.
② Some birds can't fly <u>high</u>.

3 ① We waited <u>long</u> for our friend.
② Katherine has beautiful <u>long</u> hair.

4 ① It is still <u>early</u> here.
② Minji arrived <u>early</u> at school.

5 ① Let's practice for the contest <u>hard</u>.
② Learning a new language is <u>hard</u>.

6 ① These are really <u>pretty</u> flowers.
② The sandwich tasted <u>pretty</u> good.

7 ① Don't be <u>late</u> for our appointment.
② He called me <u>late</u> at night.

-ly가 붙으면 의미가 달라지는 부사

정답 p.71

연습문제 다음 빈칸에 알맞은 말을 괄호 안에서 골라 쓰시오.

1 (late / lately)
① I have read some good books _____.
② She stayed up _____ last night.
③ _____, the weather has been warm.
④ The bus arrived at the station _____.

2 (close / closely)
① Don't stand so _____ to me.
② Look _____ at this picture.
③ We got _____ to the movie star.
④ We listened to the lecture _____.

3 (high / highly)
① We climbed _____ up the mountain.
② This necklace is _____ valuable.
③ Ms. Carrington is _____ successful.
④ The kite flew _____ above the park.

4 (hard / hardly)
① The team practiced _____.
② Did you study _____ for the test?
③ I _____ slept last night.
④ Harry _____ sees his cousins.

연습문제 **A** 우리말과 같도록 빈칸에 알맞은 빈도부사를 쓰시오.

1 Brandon은 거의 어떤 것에도 놀라지 않는다.

= Brandon is _____ surprised at anything.

2 Ginny는 항상 운동화를 신는다.

= Ginny _____ wears sneakers.

3 그 카페는 보통 많은 손님들로 가득하다.

= The café is _____ filled with many customers.

4 그 콘서트 홀은 500명 이상의 사람들을 결코 수용할 수 없다.

= The concert hall can _____ hold more than 500 people.

5 한수는 종종 아침으로 계란과 토스트를 먹는다.

= Hansu _____ have eggs and toast for breakfast.

6 너는 가끔 맑게 개인 밤에 유성을 볼 수 있다.

= You can _____ see shooting stars on clear nights.

연습문제 **B** 괄호 안의 빈도부사를 알맞은 곳에 넣어 완전한 문장을 쓰시오.

1 Eric takes a bath on weekends. (usually)

➡ _____

2 Does the bus stop here? (often)

➡ _____

3 My sister is interested in sports. (seldom)

➡ _____

4 Do you eat dinner with your family? (always)

➡ _____

5 She will fall asleep in class again. (never)

➡ _____

6 That restaurant is busy. (sometimes)

➡ _____

7 The convenience store is open at midnight. (always)

➡ _____

too, either

연습문제 | 다음 빈칸에 too나 either를 넣어 대화를 완성하시오.

1 A: The black shirt matches the jeans.　　B: The blue shirt matches the jeans, _____ .

2 A: I will visit India soon.　　B: I will visit India soon, _____ .

3 A: Minji can't fold the paper into a rose.　　B: I can't fold the paper into a rose, _____ .

4 A: They are from France.　　B: We are from France, _____ .

5 A: Jason doesn't agree with her opinion.　　B: I don't agree with her opinion, _____ .

6 A: My apartment is very small.　　B: My apartment is very small, _____ .

7 A: Greg can't solve this problem.　　B: I can't solve this problem, _____ .

8 A: They didn't have curry for lunch.　　B: We didn't have curry for lunch, _____ .

동사 + 부사

연습문제 | 다음 문장의 밑줄 친 부분을 괄호 안의 대명사로 바꿔 완전한 문장을 쓰시오.

1 Please throw away the garbage now. (it)

　→ _____

2 Write down your name and address here. (them)

　→ _____

3 You should put a warm jacket on. (it)

　→ _____

4 Why don't you take off your sunglasses inside the building? (them)

　→ _____

5 Would you like to try on this shirt? (it)

　→ _____

6 The students must hand their essays in today. (them)

　→ _____

7 Let's pick up the trash in the playground. (it)

　→ _____

중간·기말고사 실전 문제

1 다음 중 형용사와 부사의 형태가 잘못 짝지어진 것은?

① heavy – heavily ② terrible – terribly

③ similar – similarly ④ lucky – luckyly

⑤ good – well

2 다음 대화의 빈칸에 들어갈 알맞은 것은?

> A: Fred didn't like the Hawaiian pizza.
> B: Marty didn't like it, _____ .

① so   ② well   ③ too
④ either   ⑤ do

3 다음 중 어법상 바른 것은?

① Shelly never lies to her parents.

② We can go often to the beach in August.

③ Students should respect always their teachers.

④ Tigers climb sometimes trees.

⑤ David seldom is busy on the weekend.

4 다음 문장에서 어법상 어색한 부분을 찾아 쓰고 바르게 고쳐 쓰시오.

> Jeff ran rapid toward the finish line.

_____ → _____

5 다음 우리말을 영작한 것 중 어색한 것은?

① Amy는 도서관으로 조용히 걸어갔다.
   → Amy walked quietly into the library.

② Brad는 무거운 여행 가방을 쉽게 날랐다.
   → Brad easily carried the heavy suitcase.

③ 슬프게도, 나의 친구가 다른 도시로 이사를 갔다.
   → Sadly, my friend moved to another city.

④ Greg는 문을 소란하게 닫았다.
   → Greg shut the door loud.

⑤ 그 영화는 정말 웃겼다.
   → That movie was really funny.

[6-7] 다음 중 밑줄 친 부분의 쓰임이 나머지 넷과 다른 것을 고르시오.

6

① Lily studied <u>hard</u> for the test.

② The team practiced <u>hard</u> for the game.

③ Learning the new dance move was <u>hard</u>.

④ My head hurts when I concentrate <u>hard</u>.

⑤ Brad exercises <u>hard</u> every day.

7

① John goes very <u>fast</u> on his bike.

② The movie was <u>pretty</u> interesting.

③ I didn't stay at the party <u>long</u>.

④ We had an <u>early</u> lunch on Saturday.

⑤ The bus arrived 10 minutes <u>late</u>.

8 다음 중 밑줄 친 부분이 어법상 어색한 것은?

① Dolphins swim amazingly fast.

② The treasure is closely guarded.

③ Why did you sudden change your mind?

④ Lisa went to school early today.

⑤ That chemical is highly dangerous.

9 다음 빈칸에 too가 들어갈 수 없는 것은?

① I like playing baduk, _____.

② I did not pass the test, _____.

③ I will order a coffee, _____.

④ I hope to become a lawyer, _____.

⑤ I am a high school student, _____.

10 다음 대화의 밑줄 친 우리말과 같도록 주어진 <조건>에 맞게 문장을 완성하시오.

A: Let's go to an art gallery on Monday afternoon.

B: I can't. 나는 월요일 오후에 항상 친구들과 축구를 해.

<조건>
1. 빈도부사를 이용하여 7단어로 쓰시오.
2. with my friends, play soccer를 포함하시오.

= _____

on Monday afternoon.

11 다음은 Kelly의 아침 식단표이다. <보기>와 같이 빈칸에 알맞은 말을 넣어 질문에 대한 대답을 완성하시오.

Sun	Mon	Tues	Wed	Thu	Fri	Sat
salad	salad	toast	salad	toast	salad	toast

<보기> A: How often does Kelly eat salad?

B: She _usually eats_ salad.

A: How often does Kelly eat an omelet for breakfast?

B: She _____ _____ an omelet for breakfast.

12 다음 중 밑줄 친 부분이 어법상 어색한 것은?

People are ①really afraid of great white sharks when they are at the beach. But these sharks ②seldom attack humans. There are three reasons. First, they ③usually eat fish. Next, great white sharks rarely come close to shore. Lastly, lifeguards ④closely watch people at the beach. Thus, ⑤general, people are safe from great white sharks.

*great white shark 백상아리

Chapter 12 부사 **141**

13 다음 중 자연스럽지 <u>않은</u> 대화는?

① A: What did the announcement say?
   B: The train will arrive early.
② A: I watched the movie *Harry Potter* yesterday.
   B: I watched it, too.
③ A: Do you eat breakfast every day?
   B: Yes. I always eat breakfast.
④ A: Do Bill and James often play hockey?
   B: No. They seldom play hockey.
⑤ A: Nina really likes spicy food.
   B: I like spicy food, either.

14 다음 문장에서 <u>틀린</u> 부분을 바르게 고쳐 완전한 문장을 쓰시오.

> I tried on the red dress, and then I took off it.
>
> → _____

15 다음 (A)~(C)에 들어갈 말이 바르게 짝지어진 것은?

> · This art exhibition is ___(A)___ recommended.
> · After jogging for two hours, I could ___(B)___ walk.
> · He is standing ___(C)___ to the window.

	(A)	(B)	(C)
①	highly	hard	close
②	highly	hardly	closely
③	high	hard	closely
④	highly	hardly	close
⑤	high	hardly	close

16 <보기>와 같이 괄호 안의 말을 활용하여 다음 질문에 대한 대답을 완성하시오.

> <보기> A: How often do you cook at home?
>   B: *I sometimes cook at home.* (sometimes)

> A: How often does Greg exercise?
> B: _____ three times a week. (usually)

17 다음 표를 <u>잘못</u> 설명한 것은?

How often do you go to the gym?					
	Mon	Tue	Wed	Thu	Fri
Bill	X	X	X	X	X
Jake	O	X	X	X	X
Sandra	X	O	O	O	O
Lucy	O	O	O	O	O
Dave	X	X	O	X	O

① Bill never goes to the gym.
② Jake rarely goes to the gym.
③ Lucy always goes to the gym.
④ Sandra seldom goes to the gym.
⑤ Dave sometimes goes to the gym.

18 다음 중 밑줄 친 부분이 어법상 <u>어색한</u> 것은?

① This book is <u>pretty</u> difficult to read.
② It has snowed a lot <u>lately</u>.
③ Snakes can be <u>high</u> dangerous.
④ The class will finish <u>early</u> tonight.
⑤ Matt <u>hardly</u> looked at his phone during class.

[19-20] 다음 중 never가 들어갈 가장 알맞은 위치를 고르시오.

19

① My sister ② wakes ③ up ④ at 8 A.M. ⑤ on Sundays.

20

① I ② can ③ find ④ a seat ⑤ on the subway.

21 다음 대화의 밑줄 친 우리말과 같도록 괄호 안의 말을 배열할 때 네 번째에 오는 것은?

A: Do you always take the bus to school?

B: No, 나의 엄마는 때때로 나를 태워다 주셔. (me, drives, my, sometimes, mom)

① drives ② sometimes
③ mom ④ my
⑤ me

22 다음 글의 빈칸에 들어갈 말이 순서대로 짝지어진 것은?

The gorilla is a _____ animal. It can _____ lift items that weigh over 1,500 kilograms. As a result, a gorilla is very dangerous when it is angry.

① strong – easy ② strong – easily
③ strongly – easy ④ strongly – easyly
⑤ strongly – easily

23 다음 빈칸에 공통으로 들어갈 알맞은 것은?

· Neal turned _____ the TV and went to bed.
· I put _____ my homework until Sunday night.

① off ② on ③ down
④ in ⑤ up

24 다음 중 어법상 바른 것의 개수는?

ⓐ David put his leather gloves on.
ⓑ Please pick up them from the floor.
ⓒ Throw it away into the trash can.
ⓓ You can make your dreams come true, so don't give up them.
ⓔ Could you take off your shoes before entering the house?

① 1개 ② 2개 ③ 3개
④ 4개 ⑤ 5개

25 다음 대화의 밑줄 친 ⓐ~ⓔ 중 어법상 어색한 것을 찾아 기호를 쓰고 바르게 고쳐 쓰시오.

A: The weather has been so bad ⓐlately.
B: I know. It has rained ⓑhardly all day.
A: It ⓒrains never like this here.
B: Right. The heavy rain has made the weather ⓓextremely cold.
A: ⓔLuckily, it will stop early tomorrow morning according to the weather forecast.
B: That's good to hear.

(1) _____ → _____

(2) _____ → _____

CHAPTER 13
비교구문

연습문제 다음 형용사나 부사의 비교급과 최상급을 쓰시오.

1 low   - _____ - _____   **2** hot   - _____ - _____

3 hard   - _____ - _____   **4** young - _____ - _____

5 smart - _____ - _____   **6** lazy   - _____ - _____

7 big   - _____ - _____   **8** warm   - _____ - _____

9 nice   - _____ - _____   **10** heavy - _____ - _____

11 great - _____ - _____   **12** thin - _____ - _____

13 small - _____ - _____   **14** wide - _____ - _____

15 dark - _____ - _____   **16** lovely - _____ - _____

17 tasty - _____ - _____   **18** wet   - _____ - _____

19 few   - _____ - _____   **20** hungry - _____ - _____

21 wise - _____ - _____   **22** scary - _____ - _____

연습문제 다음 형용사나 부사의 비교급과 최상급을 쓰시오.

1 useful   - _____ - _____

2 strange   - _____ - _____

3 important   - _____ - _____

4 simply   - _____ - _____

5 careless   - _____ - _____

6 friendly   - _____ - _____

7 gladly   - _____ - _____

8 serious   - _____ - _____

9 interesting - _____ - _____

10 difficult - _____ - _____

불규칙 변화

POINT 1-3

정답 p.72

연습문제 다음 중 원급 – 비교급 – 최상급 형태가 잘못된 것을 고르시오.

1 ① fat – fatter - fattest
② many – much – most
③ smart – smarter - smartest

2 ① ill – worse - worst
② large – larger - largest
③ easily – easier - easiest

3 ① far – farer - farest
② good – better - best
③ strange – stranger - strangest

4 ① cold – colder - coldest
② bad – badder - baddest
③ noisy – noisier - noisiest

5 ① old – elder - eldest
② kind– more kind – most kind
③ pretty – prettier - prettiest

6 ① cute – cuter - cutest
② salty – saltier - saltiest
③ little – littler - littliest

7 ① well – better - best
② happy – happyer - happyest
③ tiring – more tiring – most tiring

8 ① useless – uselesser - uselessest
② long – longer - longest
③ badly – worse - worst

원급 비교: as + 원급 + as

POINT 2

정답 p.72

연습문제 우리말과 같도록 괄호 안의 말을 알맞게 배열하시오.

1 일몰은 일출만큼 아름답다. (a sunrise, as, a sunset, beautiful, is, as)
= _____

2 이번 여름은 작년만큼 덥지 않았다. (hot, this summer, as, was, as, last summer, not)
= _____

3 나의 지갑은 Patrick의 것만큼 가볍다. (is, my wallet, as, Patrick's, as, light)
= _____

4 프랑스어 시험은 수학 시험만큼 어려웠다. (difficult, as, the math exam, as, was, the French exam)
= _____

5 민하는 그녀의 선생님만큼 일찍 도착했다. (arrived, as, Minha, as, early, her teacher)
= _____

6 그 금속은 다이아몬드만큼 단단해 보인다. (as, looks, a diamond, the metal, as, hard)
= _____

연습문제 A <보기>와 같이 괄호 안의 말을 활용하여 다음 두 문장을 한 문장을 바꿔 쓰시오.

<보기> Ken is ten years old. Peter is thirteen years old.
→ Ken is _younger than_ Peter. (young)

1 My cat is 4 kg. Juho's cat is 7 kg.
→ My cat is _____ Juho's cat. (light)

2 Today is 2℃. Yesterday was 8℃.
→ Today is _____ yesterday. (cold)

3 Daniel is 180 cm. Ella is 161 cm.
→ Daniel is _____ Ella. (tall)

4 This movie is three hours long. That movie is two hours long.
→ This movie is _____ that movie. (long)

5 The bank is 10 km away from here. The library is 6 km away from here.
→ The bank is _____ the library from here. (far)

6 Sam gets to class at 9:00. His friends get to class at 8:45.
→ Sam gets to class _____ his friends. (late)

7 This building has nine floors. That building has twelve floors.
→ This building is _____ that building. (small)

8 Minsu studied five hours yesterday. Nina studied three hours yesterday.
→ Minsu studied _____ Nina. (much)

연습문제 B 괄호 안에서 알맞은 것을 고르시오.

1 Lemons taste (sour / sourer) than melons.

2 This airplane is (small / smaller) than the one on the left.

3 Harry is (much / very) funnier than Larry.

4 Elephants are (more heavier / heavier) than hippos.

5 Italian foods are (a lot / very) delicious.

6 Cary seemed (bored / more bored) than Emily.

7 Fleas can jump (far / very) higher than their heights.

8 He is (even / very) more famous in Korea than in any other country.

연습문제 | 우리말과 같도록 괄호 안의 말을 활용하여 문장을 완성하시오.

1 Jones씨는 점점 더 부유해졌다. (get, rich)

= Mr. Jones _____ .

2 Charlie의 개는 점점 더 뚱뚱해졌다. (become, fat)

= Charlie's dog _____ .

3 그 시험 안의 질문은 점점 더 어려워지고 있다. (get, difficult)

= The questions in the exam _____ .

4 나의 얼굴에 있는 여드름은 점점 더 커지고 있다. (grow, large)

= The pimple on my face _____ .

5 Sandy의 스페인어는 점점 더 좋아지고 있다. (become, good)

= Sandy's Spanish _____ .

6 이 영화는 끝으로 가면서 점점 더 슬퍼졌다. (get, sad)

= This movie _____ to the end.

7 그들의 밴드는 점점 더 유명해졌다. (become, famous)

= Their band _____ .

8 나의 요가 수업은 점점 더 흥미로워졌다. (get, interesting)

= My yoga class _____ .

9 그 나무는 점점 더 커졌다. (grow, tall)

= The tree _____ .

10 온라인 쇼핑은 점점 더 인기 있어지고 있다. (become, popular)

= Online shopping _____ .

11 밤은 겨울에 점점 더 길어진다. (become, long)

= The nights _____ in winter.

12 그 아이는 점점 더 불안하게 느꼈다. (feel, nervous)

= The child _____ .

연습문제 A 우리말과 같도록 괄호 안의 말을 활용하여 문장을 완성하시오.

1 이것은 우리 집에서 가장 무거운 의자이다. (heavy chair, our house)

= This is _____.

2 Carol은 그녀의 학교에서 가장 똑똑한 소녀이다. (clever girl, her school)

= Carol is _____.

3 Jim은 그 축구팀의 구성원 중에서 가장 좋은 선수이다. (good player, the soccer team's members)

= Jim is _____.

4 이번 달은 그 해 중에서 가장 더운 달일 것이다. (hot month, the year)

= This month will be _____.

5 저것은 그 서점에서 가장 흥미로운 책이다. (interesting book, the bookstore)

= That is _____.

6 나에게 서울에서 가장 인기 있는 레스토랑을 소개해 줘라. (popular restaurant, Seoul)

= Introduce me to _____.

7 우리는 세 개의 선택지 중에서 가장 큰 피자를 주문할 것이다. (large pizza, the three choices)

= We'll order _____.

8 볼가 강은 유럽에서 가장 긴 강이다. (long river, Europe)

= The Volga is _____.

9 오늘은 나의 삶에서 가장 운이 좋은 날이었다. (lucky day, my life)

= Today was _____.

연습문제 B 괄호 안의 말을 활용하여 문장을 완성하시오.

1 The motorcycle is as _____ as a car. (fast)

2 My brother is much _____ than me. (old)

3 Redwoods are _____ trees in the world. (tall)

4 What is _____ animal on earth? (strong)

5 Linda speaks Korean _____ than Cam. (well)

6 Jacob is _____ of the five. (generous)

7 My hair is not as _____ as my sister's. (thick)

8 Your plan sounds _____ than mine. (good)

연습문제 우리말과 같도록 괄호 안의 말을 활용하여 문장을 완성하시오.

1 롤러코스터는 가장 무서운 놀이 기구들 중 하나이다. (scary, ride)

= The roller coaster is _____.

2 물리학은 공부하기에 가장 어려운 과목들 중 하나이다. (difficult, subject)

= Physics is _____ to study.

3 바이칼 호는 세계에서 가장 깊은 호수들 중 하나이다. (deep, lake)

= Lake Baikal is _____ in the world.

4 떡볶이는 한국에서 가장 매운 요리들 중 하나이다. (spicy, dish)

= Tteokbokki is _____ in Korea.

5 Eric은 동아리에서 가장 어린 학생들 중 한 명이다. (young, student)

= Eric is _____ in the club.

6 저것은 동네에서 가장 큰 집들 중 하나이다. (big, house)

= That is _____ in the neighborhood.

7 그녀는 그 나라에서 가장 사랑스러운 배우들 중 한 명이다. (lovely, actor)

= She is _____ in the country.

8 이 거북이는 그 동물원에서 가장 나이가 많은 동물들 중 하나이다. (old, animal)

= This turtle is _____ in the zoo.

9 이 산의 꼭대기는 도시에서 가장 좋은 전망들 중 하나를 가지고 있다. (good, view)

= The top of this mountain has _____ in the city.

10 수영하는 것은 가장 피곤한 운동들 중 하나이다. (tiring, exercise)

= Swimming is _____.

11 '오즈의 마법사'는 세상에서 가장 훌륭한 영화들 중 하나이다. (great, movie)

= *The Wizard of OZ* is _____ in the world.

12 Dan은 그의 가족에서 가장 외향적인 아이들 중 한 명이다. (outgoing, child)

= Dan is _____ in his family.

1 다음 중 원급-비교급-최상급 형태가 <u>잘못된</u> 것은?

① far – farther – farthest

② many – much – most

③ tasty – tastier – tastiest

④ well – better – best

⑤ expensive – more expensive – most expensive

2 우리말과 같도록 괄호 안의 말을 배열할 때 일곱 번째에 오는 것은?

> David는 Marie만큼 크지 않다. (is, not, Marie, tall, as, David, as)

① Marie ② tall ③ is

④ as ⑤ not

3 다음 중 어법상 <u>어색한</u> 것은?

① Neil's test score is not so high as Mike's.

② The lamp is as brighter as the sun.

③ A tiger is not as big as an elephant.

④ Tim can climb as quickly as a monkey.

⑤ The tree is as tall as my house.

[4-5] 다음 빈칸에 들어갈 알맞은 것을 고르시오.

4

> Annie is _____ than her best friend.

① noisy ② the most noisy

③ the noisiest ④ more noisy

⑤ noisier

5

> The blue whale is _____ animal in the world.

① more larger ② the largest

③ the most large ④ larger

⑤ more large

6 다음 밑줄 친 부분을 바르게 고치지 <u>못한</u> 것은?

① Basketball players are <u>more tall</u> than soccer players. (→ taller)

② My pencil is as short <u>so</u> your pencil. (→ as)

③ Making a sandwich is <u>easy</u> than making a bowl of soup. (→ easier)

④ My neighbors are getting <u>more loud and loud</u>. (→ more and more loud)

⑤ The traffic today is <u>more heavier</u> than yesterday. (→ heavier)

7 다음 중 밑줄 친 부분이 어법상 <u>어색한</u> 것은?

① December is <u>more colder than</u> August.

② Casey was <u>even smarter than</u> Brad.

③ This dish tastes <u>spicier than</u> that one.

④ My shoes look <u>far older than</u> hers.

⑤ This car is <u>more expensive than</u> that car.

8 다음 빈칸에 공통으로 들어갈 알맞은 것은?

> · Dylan built sandcastles _____ than Laura.
> · My new phone is _____ than the last one.

① good　　　② well　　　③ gooder
④ better　　　⑤ best

9 다음 문장에서 어법상 <u>어색한</u> 부분을 찾아 쓰고 바르게 고쳐 쓰시오.

> Who is nicer student in your school?

_____ → _____

10 다음 중 어법상 바른 것은?

① This bag is more cheaper in the store.

② My dog is lazyier than my cat.

③ The giraffe is the tall animal in this picture.

④ She speaks Spanish as better as I do.

⑤ Seoul is one of the biggest cities in the world.

11 다음 빈칸에 들어갈 말이 순서대로 짝지어진 것은?

> · This sweater is as _____ as a rainbow.
> · Which animal is the _____ in the jungle?

① prettiest - dangerous

② pretty - more dangerous

③ prettier - more dangerous

④ pretty - most dangerous

⑤ prettier - most dangerous

12 다음 빈칸에 들어갈 말로 <u>어색한</u> 것은?

> This bed feels _____ more comfortable than that one.

① a lot　　　② far　　　③ even
④ still　　　⑤ very

13

Lisa의 머리는 Beth의 것만큼 짧아 보인다. (short)

= Lisa's hair looks _____ Beth's.

14

불이 점점 더 커지고 있다. (big)

= The fire is getting _____.

15

Jake의 가게는 시장에서 가장 신선한 과일을 판다. (fresh)

= Jake's store sells _____ fruits in the market.

16 다음 표를 잘못 설명한 것은?

salad	pizza	hot dog	sandwich	hamburger
$5	$15	$8	$9	$14

① A hamburger is as expensive as a sandwich.
② A salad is the cheapest of all.
③ A sandwich isn't more expensive than a pizza.
④ A pizza is the most expensive of all the dishes.
⑤ A hot dog is cheaper than a sandwich.

17 다음 중 어법상 어색한 것의 개수는?

ⓐ Kevin is the fastest runner in the race.
ⓑ That house seems big than mine.
ⓒ My room is not as larger as my brother's.
ⓓ The man ran faster and faster to catch the bus.
ⓔ Pepperoni pizza is one of the most delicious pizzas the restaurant.

① 1개   ② 2개   ③ 3개
④ 4개   ⑤ 5개

[18-19] 다음 우리말을 영작할 때 빈칸에 들어갈 알맞은 것을 고르시오.

18

세상에서 가장 큰 폭포는 어디에 있니?
= Where is _____?

① tall waterfall in the world
② taller waterfall in the world
③ more tall waterfall in the world
④ the tallest waterfall in the world
⑤ the most tall waterfall in the world

19

나의 사촌은 우리 가족 중에 가장 똑똑한 사람들 중 하나이다.
= My cousin is _____ in my family.

① one of the smartest people
② one of the smartest person
③ the most smart people
④ the smarter people
⑤ one of the most smart people

[20-21] 다음 빈칸에 들어갈 알맞은 것을 고르시오.

20

A watermelon is _____ than a lemon.

① sweet   ② sweeter
③ the sweetest   ④ more sweet
⑤ the most sweet

21

That car is more _____ than the motorcycle.

① small   ② new
③ fast   ④ nice
⑤ expensive

22 다음 중 어법상 어색한 것은?

① The roads are becoming more and more crowded during rush hour.
② Sam works as hard as his classmates.
③ Which is more spicy dish in this restaurant?
④ The Golden Gate Bridge is one of the longest bridges in the world.
⑤ Vegetables are far healthier than fried chicken.

23 다음 빈칸에 들어갈 말이 나머지 넷과 다른 것은?

① Sea lions are usually larger _____ seals.
② Swimming is more tiring _____ jogging.
③ My father runs faster _____ me.
④ This jacket looks warmer _____ that one.
⑤ My clothes are as dirty _____ yours.

24 괄호 안의 말을 활용하여 다음 두 문장을 한 문장으로 바꿔 쓰시오.

· A cheetah can run 120 km/h.
· A lion can run 80 km/h.

→ A cheetah is much _____ a lion. (fast)

25 다음 밑줄 친 부분과 바꿔 쓸 수 없는 것은?

A diamond is <u>even</u> more valuable than an emerald.

① much   ② far   ③ very
④ a lot   ⑤ still

CHAPTER 14
전치사

기출로 적중 POINT

시간 전치사: at, on, in

POINT 1-1

정답 p.74

연습문제 | 다음 빈칸에 at, on, in 중 알맞은 것을 쓰시오.

1 The music festival starts _____ April 3.

2 The Second World War ended _____ 1945.

3 Tim wakes up _____ 6 o'clock every day.

4 Leaves on trees turn brown _____ autumn.

5 Are you going to be busy _____ Monday?

6 I felt really sick _____ Tuesday morning.

7 I couldn't speak Korean _____ the time.

8 Will you have lunch with me _____ Sunday?

9 All of my relatives came to my house _____ Thanksgiving Day.

10 Elvis Presley was a famous singer _____ the 1950s.

시간 전치사: before, after

POINT 1-2

정답 p.74

연습문제 | 우리말과 같도록 괄호 안에서 before나 after 중 알맞은 것을 고르시오.

1 나는 저녁 식사 후에 산책하러 갈 것이다.

= I'm going to go for a walk (before / after) dinner.

2 연말 전에 서로를 보는 게 어때?

= How about seeing each other (before / after) the end of the year?

3 콘서트 후에, 나는 지하철역으로 걸어갔다.

= (Before / After) the concert, I walked to the subway station.

4 그의 부모님은 그가 10시 후에 TV를 보는 것을 허락하지 않으신다.

= His parents don't allow him to watch TV (before / after) ten o'clock.

5 Sandra는 보통 일출 전에 요가를 한다.

= Sandra usually does yoga (before / after) sunrise.

6 사람들은 한국에서 그들의 18번째 생일 전에 운전면허증을 받을 수 없다.

= People can't get a driver's license (before / after) their 18th birthday in Korea.

시간 전치사: for, during

정답 p.74

연습문제 다음 빈칸에 for나 during 중 알맞은 것을 쓰시오.

1 We listened carefully _____ the class.

2 I studied _____ two months for this big test.

3 Please wait here _____ ten minutes.

4 You shouldn't talk _____ the movie.

5 My friend has raised a cat _____ five years.

6 I usually take a short nap _____ the day.

7 We were so scared _____ the earthquake.

8 Minho lost his passport _____ the holiday.

9 Sally didn't leave the house _____ many months.

10 Brenda focused on writing her novel _____ the winter.

시간 전치사: from

정답 p.74

연습문제 우리말과 같도록 알맞은 전치사와 괄호 안의 말을 활용하여 문장을 완성하시오.

1 나는 평일에 저녁 7시부터 태권도 수업이 있다. (7 P.M.)
= I have a taekwondo class _____ on weekdays.

2 나의 여동생은 2006년에 태어났다. (2006)
= My little sister was born _____.

3 홍콩은 1841년부터 1997년까지 영국 식민지였다. (1841, 1997)
= Hong Kong was a British colony _____.

4 9시 이후에 악기를 연주하지 마세요. (nine)
= Please don't play an instrument _____.

5 이번 주부터, 나는 간식을 먹는 것을 멈출 것이다. (this week)
= _____, I'm going to stop eating snacks.

6 Brandon은 매일 30분 동안 그의 개를 산책시킨다. (30 minutes)
= Brandon walks his dog _____ every day.

연습문제 | 우리말과 같도록 괄호 안에서 알맞은 것을 고르시오.

1 책상 위에 바나나가 있다.   = There is a banana (on / in) the desk.

2 그 편의점은 모퉁이에 있다.   = The convenience shop is (at / in) the corner.

3 우리의 가족 사진은 벽에 걸려있다.   = Our family photo is hanging (on / in) the wall.

4 종이 상자 안에 고양이가 있다.   = There is a cat (at / in) the paper box.

5 사람들은 건물 안에서 흡연을 하면 안 된다.   = People can't smoke (on / in) the building.

6 나는 바닥에 약간의 오렌지 주스를 쏟았다.   = I spilled some orange juice (at / on) the floor.

연습문제 | 다음 빈칸에 at, on, in 중 알맞은 것을 쓰시오.

1 She is _____ a plane to Beijing.

2 Mr. Davis was _____ the hospital at that time.

3 Watch out for jellyfish when you swim _____ the sea.

4 Please cut that tomato _____ half.

5 The girl _____ red shoes is Alice.

6 My apartment is _____ the fifth floor.

7 We can't breathe without suit _____ space.

8 Linda often studies _____ the library.

9 You can look it up _____ the Internet.

10 There were too many people _____ the bus.

11 He read a fascinating article _____ a magazine.

12 I made new friends _____ Bob's birthday party.

13 Bhutan is one of the smallest countries _____ the world.

14 Martin usually goes to the supermarket _____ the Second Street.

POINT 3 위치 전치사

정답 p.75

연습문제 우리말과 같도록 빈칸에 알맞은 전치사를 <보기>에서 골라 쓰시오.

<보기> in front of   behind   under   next to   between   among

1 그 버스는 터미널 앞에 멈췄다.

= The bus stopped _____ _____ the terminal.

2 은행과 소방서 사이에 공원이 있다.

= There is a park _____ the bank and the fire station.

3 그 마술사는 그의 모자 아래에 비둘기를 숨겼다.

= The magician hid a dove _____ his hat.

4 내 뒤에 있는 아이는 너무 크게 이야기 하고 있다.

= The kid _____ me is talking too loudly.

5 저 아이돌 그룹은 청소년들 사이에서 매우 인기 있다.

= That idol group is very popular _____ teenagers.

6 Susan은 그 램프를 그녀의 침대 옆에 두었다.

= Susan put the lamp _____ her bed.

POINT 4 방향 전치사

정답 p.75

연습문제 우리말과 같도록 빈칸에 알맞은 전치사를 <보기>에서 골라 쓰시오.

<보기> down   out of   around   along   through   from   for   to

1 아마존 강은 브라질을 통해서 흐른다.   = The Amazon River flows _____ Brazil.

2 나는 나의 자전거를 언덕 아래로 타고 갔다.   = I rode my bike _____ the hill.

3 그 배는 해안을 따라서 항해하고 있다.   = The boat is sailing _____ the coast.

4 갑자기, 새가 둥지 밖으로 날아갔다.   = Suddenly, a bird flew _____ the nest.

5 이 스카프를 너의 목 주위에 둘러라.   = Wrap this scarf _____ your neck.

6 그 버스는 오전 8시에 수원으로 떠날 것이다.   = The bus leaves _____ Suwon at 8 A.M.

7 Lenny는 학교로부터 집으로 걸었다.   = Lenny walked _____ school _____ home.

연습문제 A 우리말과 같도록 빈칸에 알맞은 전치사를 <보기>에서 골라 쓰시오.

<보기> with without by about like for against

1 너는 보통 지하철을 타고 직장에 가니?

= Do you usually go to work _____ subway?

2 너는 Liam의 생일을 위해 무엇을 살 거니?

= What are you going to buy _____ Liam's birthday?

3 유라는 오늘 아침에 그녀의 지갑 없이 집을 떠났다.

= Yura left home _____ her wallet this morning.

4 나는 길 위에서 아주 긴 수염을 가진 남자를 봤다.

= I saw a man _____ a really long beard on the street.

5 당근과 브로콜리 같은 채소들을 더 많이 먹어라.

= Eat more vegetables _____ carrots and broccoli.

6 나의 부모님은 나에게 11시까지 집에 오라고 말하셨다.

= My parents told me to come home _____ 11 o'clock.

7 나는 방과 후에 나의 가장 친한 친구와 함께 카페에 갔다.

= I went to a café _____ my best friend after school.

8 모든 사람은 그 위험한 계획에 반대했다.

= Everyone was _____ the dangerous plan.

9 우리는 한 유명한 음악가에 대한 영화를 봤다.

= We watched a movie _____ a famous musician.

10 Brown씨는 새로운 정부 정책에 찬성한다.

= Ms. Brown is _____ the new government policy.

연습문제 B 괄호 안에서 알맞은 전치사를 고르시오.

This year, my family went to Spain ⓐ(for / about) Christmas. We flew to Madrid and stayed ⓑ(with / like) my uncle there. On Christmas Day, we ate seafood soup and lamb. We also had a traditional Spanish snack. It tasted ⓒ(like / without) almonds. I don't know much ⓓ(about / against) Spanish food, but it was delicious. After that, we went to Barcelona ⓔ(by / with) train. We celebrated New Year's Eve there. They had fireworks, dances, and many kinds of crazy activities.

전치사 관용 표현: 형용사 + 전치사

정답 p.75

연습문제 | 밑줄 친 부분이 어법상 맞으면 O를 쓰고, 틀리면 바르게 고쳐 쓰시오.

1 Clara is afraid <u>at</u> insects. → _____

2 Green tea is good <u>at</u> your skin. → _____

3 Be careful <u>for</u> those boxes. → _____

4 The library was full <u>of</u> students on Sunday. → _____

5 David was busy <u>at</u> his homework all day. → _____

6 Sitting like that is bad <u>at</u> your neck. → _____

7 Hyeri is good <u>with</u> speaking French. → _____

8 Kate is late <u>of</u> the meeting every time. → _____

9 Are you ready <u>of</u> your science exam? → _____

10 I'm sorry <u>for</u> laughing at your speech. → _____

11 The hotel room is different <u>to</u> the one on the website. → _____

12 Are you familiar <u>with</u> this computer program? → _____

13 They are proud <u>with</u> their children's success. → _____

전치사 관용 표현: 동사 + 전치사

정답 p.75

연습문제 | 괄호 안에서 알맞은 전치사를 고르시오.

1 I listen (to / at) podcasts every morning.

2 I'd like to thank you (to / for) your hard work.

3 David is looking (for / with) a new shirt at the mall.

4 Everyone laughed (at / to) Tammy's joke.

5 Did you ask (to / for) soy milk in your latte?

6 I had to wait (at / for) you for almost an hour.

7 We are looking (at / on) an amazing painting.

8 Alex spends much money (on / in) eating out.

중간·기말고사 실전 문제

1 다음 빈칸에 들어갈 알맞은 것은?

> The concert ends _____ 9 P.M.

① in   ② on   ③ at
④ for   ⑤ to

2 다음 우리말을 알맞게 영작한 것은?

> 그 영화는 두 시간 동안 계속되었다.

① The movie lasted for two hours.
② The movie lasted in two hours.
③ The movie lasted on two hours.
④ The movie lasted during two hours.
⑤ The movie lasted before two hours.

3 다음 빈칸에 들어갈 말이 순서대로 짝지어진 것은?

> · Hang your jacket _____ the closet.
> · Did Sam put the book _____ the shelf?

① in – on   ② to – on   ③ on – in
④ on – at   ⑤ in – at

[4-5] 다음 빈칸에 공통으로 들어갈 알맞은 것을 고르시오.

4

> · Jake exercised at the gym _____ three hours.
> · Could you open the door _____ me?

① in   ② from   ③ at
④ for   ⑤ during

5

> · A coconut fell _____ the tree.
> · I watched TV _____ 8 P.M. to 10 P.M.

① to   ② from   ③ on
④ during   ⑤ out of

6 다음 중 밑줄 친 부분이 어법상 어색한 것은?

① My family moved to Busan in 2012.
② Shawn meets his friends on the weekends.
③ The post office is open from Monday to Friday.
④ The museum tour will end in an hour.
⑤ There was a lot of rain during the last two months.

[7-9] 우리말과 같도록 빈칸에 알맞은 전치사를 쓰시오.

7

> 나는 나의 차를 건물 뒤에 주차했다.

= I parked my car _____ the building.

8

> 승객들이 비행기 밖으로 나왔다.

= The passengers got _____ the plane.

9

> 화분이 나의 책상 옆에 있다.

= There is a vase _____ my desk.

10 다음 빈칸에 들어갈 말이 나머지 넷과 <u>다른</u> 것은?

① There are few customers _____ the store.
② My summer vacation begins _____ June.
③ The dancers stood _____ a line on the stage.
④ Let's look it up _____ the Internet.
⑤ We get a lot of snow _____ the winter.

11 다음 빈칸에 공통으로 들어갈 알맞은 것은?

> · I played basketball _____ my friend last night.
> · Owen paid for the shirt _____ his credit card.

① with ② about ③ for
④ by ⑤ against

12 다음 중 밑줄 친 like의 쓰임이 나머지 넷과 <u>다른</u> 것은?

① Sarah has a necklace <u>like</u> mine.
② I <u>like</u> drawing pictures.
③ Pat's car is not <u>like</u> Leon's.
④ The museum looks <u>like</u> a castle.
⑤ This bread tastes <u>like</u> paper.

13 다음 우리말을 영작할 때 빈칸에 들어갈 알맞은 전치사는?

> 두 소년은 강을 따라서 걸었다.
> = The two boys walked _____ the river.

① around ② along ③ from
④ under ⑤ across

14 다음 빈칸에 of가 들어갈 수 있는 것을 <u>모두</u> 고르시오.

① His house is far _____ here.
② Was Lola ready _____ the science test?
③ I am proud _____ my painting.
④ This bookshelf is full _____ old books.
⑤ Thank you _____ the advice.

[15-17] 다음 빈칸에 들어갈 알맞은 것을 고르시오.

15

I went to school _____ the bus.

① of   ② for   ③ on
④ from   ⑤ with

16

Rachel is proud _____ her children.

① on   ② for   ③ by
④ of   ⑤ at

17

I saw many stars _____ the sky when I went camping.

① into   ② to   ③ at
④ in   ⑤ on

[18-20] 다음 빈칸에 들어갈 말이 순서대로 짝지어진 것을 고르시오.

18

· My house is _____ those two buildings.
· There is a deer _____ the trees.

① among – at
② between - among
③ among – among
④ between - at
⑤ among – between

19

· He walked _____ the room.
· Mark rode the bike _____ the road.

① across – of
② across – along
③ into – along
④ into – of
⑤ up – of

20

· Jane's bag is _____ the window.
· Josh was late _____ his math class.

① next to - up
② next to - at
③ next to - for
④ through – for
⑤ through – at

21 다음 그림을 보고 빈칸에 알맞은 전치사를 고르시오.

A: Where is the bank?
B: It is _____ the school and the police station.

① between   ② among
③ behind   ④ next to
⑤ by

22 다음 글의 빈칸에 알맞은 전치사를 쓰시오.

Dear Steve,
Thank you for fixing my computer _____ Saturday. It is working well now. I would like to buy you dinner _____ the new restaurant on Elm Street. Why don't we meet _____ 7 P.M. on Thursday?

Thanks again,
Matt

23 다음 빈칸에 공통으로 들어갈 알맞은 것은?

· Peter went _____ Vietnam last summer.
· James loves to listen _____ jazz music.

① by   ② for   ③ to
④ with   ⑤ from

24 우리말과 같도록 빈칸에 알맞은 전치사를 쓰시오.

우리 가족은 보통 저녁 식사 후에 함께 TV를 본다.

= Our family usually watches TV together _____ dinner.

25 다음 밑줄 친 @~ⓔ 중 어법상 어색한 것을 찾아 기호를 쓰고 바르게 고쳐 쓰시오.

· Did you listen @to the band's new album?
· Look ⓑabout that beautiful sunset!
· They are looking ⓒto their lost dog.
· Thank you ⓓfor the beautiful bouquet.
· My parents spent a lot of money ⓔat a new car.

(1) _____ → _____
(2) _____ → _____
(3) _____ → _____

해커스북 중·고등
www.HackersBook.com

CHAPTER 15
접속사

기출로 적중 POINT

연습문제 A   다음 빈칸에 알맞은 말을 괄호 안에서 한 번씩만 골라 쓰시오.

1 (and, or, but)   ① Whales _____ dolphins aren't fish.

② The hamburger was very expensive _____ too small.

③ I can meet you on Saturday _____ Sunday.

2 (and, but, so)   ① She lost her phone, _____ she bought a new one.

② The teacher looked scary, _____ she was friendly.

③ Brad ordered a hot dog _____ soda.

3 (but, or, so)   ① Do you want to go to the beach _____ the mountain?

② Mandy likes vegetables, _____ Dave doesn't like them.

③ The store is not open yet, _____ let's wait outside.

4 (and, or, so)   ① Which do you prefer, tea _____ coffee?

② Steven visited both Spain _____ Portugal last year.

③ The movie was very sad, _____ we cried a lot.

연습문제 B   다음 빈칸에 가장 알맞은 말을 <보기>에서 골라 쓰시오.

<보기>	and I will do the dishes	so he doesn't want to go to the pool
	or cold outside	but he can't speak French
	but you didn't answer	so he didn't eat lunch today
	and bought some novels	or the chess club

1 Is the weather warm _____?

2 Cam lived in Paris for three years, _____.

3 Emily will clean the table, _____.

4 Paul doesn't know how to swim, _____.

5 I called you last night, _____.

6 Sally went to the bookstore _____.

7 Benjamin can't decide to join the soccer team _____.

8 My brother wasn't hungry, _____.

명령문 + and/or

연습문제 <보기>와 같이 다음 두 문장을 한 문장으로 연결하시오.

> **<보기>** Drive carefully. + You'll get in an accident.
>
> → *Drive carefully, or you'll get in an accident.*

1 Go to Peter's birthday party. + He'll be disappointed.

→ _____

2 Study harder. + You'll pass the test.

→ _____

3 Buy a ticket. + You can't watch the play.

→ _____

4 Eat some breakfast. + You'll be hungry later.

→ _____

5 Take this medicine. + You'll be better soon.

→ _____

6 Be careful. + You may slip on the ice.

→ _____

7 Apologize to John. + He'll forgive you.

→ _____

8 Close the window. + You'll be cold.

→ _____

9 Give this gift to your mom. + She'll be happy.

→ _____

10 Exercise regularly. + You'll become healthier.

→ _____

11 Don't forget to bring a map. + You'll get lost.

→ _____

12 Run faster. + You'll arrive on time.

→ _____

연습문제 A 우리말과 같도록 <보기>의 접속사와 괄호 안의 말을 활용하여 문장을 완성하시오.

<보기> when before after while

1 나는 설거지를 하고 있는 동안 접시 하나를 깨뜨렸다. (do the dishes)

= I broke a plate _____ .

2 나는 커피를 만들고 난 후에 나의 동료들에게 약간을 줬다. (make the coffee)

= _____ , I gave some to my colleagues.

3 비가 올 때, 너는 우산을 써야 한다. (rain)

= _____ , you should use an umbrella.

4 당신이 그것을 읽은 후에 그 책을 반납하세요. (read it)

= Please return the book _____ .

5 내가 저녁 식사를 준비하는 동안, 나의 여동생은 나를 도왔다. (make dinner)

= _____ , my sister helped me.

6 네가 학교에 가기 전에 쓰레기를 가지고 나가라. (go to school)

= Take out the trash _____ .

7 그 선생님께서 말씀하실 때 우리는 주의를 기울였다. (talk)

= We paid attention _____ .

8 그 영화가 시작하기 전에, 약간의 팝콘을 사자. (start)

= _____ , let's buy some popcorn.

연습문제 B 밑줄 친 부분이 어법상 맞으면 O를 쓰고, 틀리면 바르게 고쳐 쓰시오.

1 Read the instructions before you <u>will use</u> this washing machine. → _____

2 Thomas promised to send us a postcard when he <u>is</u> in Russia. → _____

3 After the class <u>will end</u>, we will go to the shopping mall. → _____

4 When Maria <u>will visit</u> Korea, Mina will give her a tour. → _____

연습문제 C 다음 중 밑줄 친 When의 쓰임이 나머지 둘과 다른 것을 고르시오.

1 ① <u>When</u> it snows, I wear my boots.
   ② <u>When</u> is Jane meeting us?
   ③ <u>When</u> it is noisy, I can't sleep well.

2 ① <u>When</u> I feel sad, I listen to music.
   ② <u>When</u> does the soccer game start?
   ③ <u>When</u> can you call me back?

연습문제 A | <보기>와 같이 다음 문장을 because를 이용하여 바꿔 쓰시오.

> <보기> I hate taking the subway, so I just walked.
>
> → *I just walked because I hate taking the subway.*

1 He didn't study, so he failed the math test.

→ _____

2 It is snowing, so you should wear a warm jacket.

→ _____

3 I missed the bus, so I was late for the appointment.

→ _____

4 She stayed up late, so she was very tired.

→ _____

5 The comedian's joke was funny, so the audiences laughed.

→ _____

6 The Chinese restaurant is full, so let's go to the Mexican restaurant.

→ _____

연습문제 B | 우리말과 같도록 다음 빈칸에 because, because of, if 중 알맞은 것을 쓰시오.

1 만약 네가 시간이 있다면 나를 도와주겠니?

= Can you help me _____ you have time?

2 톰 크루즈는 영화 '탑건' 때문에 유명해졌다.

= Tom Cruise became famous _____ the movie *Top Gun*.

3 수프가 차가웠기 때문에 그 손님은 불평했다.

= The customer complained _____ the soup was cold.

4 일요일이기 때문에, 은행은 문을 닫았다.

= _____ it is Sunday, the bank is closed.

5 만약 네가 춥다면, 너는 에어컨을 꺼도 된다.

= _____ you are cold, you can turn the air conditioner off.

6 만약 네가 배가 고프다면 나는 너에게 샌드위치를 만들어주겠다.

= I'll make you a sandwich _____ you're hungry.

연습문제 A <보기>와 같이 다음 문장을 접속사 that을 이용하여 바꿔 쓰시오. (단, that을 생략할 수 있으면 쓰지 마시오.)

> **<보기>** Sarah invited me to her new house.
>
> → It is great _that Sarah invited me to her new house_ .

1 He lives near your apartment.

→ I heard _____ .

2 Brenda will like this present.

→ I hope _____ .

3 The weather is so great.

→ It is nice _____ .

4 The teacher canceled the quiz.

→ We didn't know _____ .

5 Jupiter is much larger than Earth.

→ It is true _____ .

6 The package arrived late.

→ The problem was _____ .

7 This laptop is too expensive.

→ I think _____ .

8 We missed our flight.

→ The bad news was _____ .

연습문제 B 다음 중 밑줄 친 that의 쓰임이 나머지 둘과 다른 것을 고르시오.

1 ① It was sad that we couldn't meet yesterday.

② That is my favorite Italian restaurant.

③ Mike hopes that he will join the basketball team.

2 ① Did you know that Thomas was an English teacher?

② Look at that huge crowd on the street.

③ I have already watched that movie.

3 ① That Kyle won the dance contest is really amazing.

② We heard that our classmate was sick.

③ Please don't turn off that light.

4 ① He said that he needed more time.

② Who was that at the door?

③ The truth is that I didn't like anything on the menu.

연습문제 괄호 안에서 알맞은 것을 고르시오.

1 Russia is a large country. (On the other hand / Therefore), Switzerland is very small.

2 My sister has many hobbies. (However / For example), she enjoys playing tennis.

3 Greg traveled to France last month. (However / Therefore), he did not visit Paris.

4 I had to work on Saturday. (On the other hand / Therefore), I could not meet my friends.

5 The city has many tourist attractions. (However / For example), it has several art museums.

6 Venus is very hot. (On the other hand / For example), Neptune is extremely cold.

7 Adam is good at many sports. (However / For example), he is not a good soccer player.

8 That movie was very interesting. (On the other hand / Therefore), I will watch it again.

9 Samuel was tired from working out so hard. (For example / Therefore), he went to bed early.

10 My sister bought a beautiful blue dress. (However / Therefore), she doesn't wear it often.

11 There are many smart animals in the world. (On the other hand / For example), monkeys and crows can use tools like humans.

12 Fish can breathe underwater. (On the other hand / For example), mammals aren't able to breathe underwater.

중간·기말고사 실전 문제

[1-2] 다음 빈칸에 들어갈 가장 알맞은 것을 고르시오.

1

> My mother bought some tomatoes, milk,
> _____ pork from the grocery store.

① and   ② but   ③ so
④ after   ⑤ that

2

> Theo is angry _____ someone stole
> his wallet.

① before   ② and   ③ because
④ so   ⑤ while

3 다음 중 밑줄 친 부분이 문맥상 어색한 것을 모두 고르시오.

① Helen wants to be a dancer, <u>so</u> she practices every day.
② Wear a thick coat, <u>or</u> you'll be warm.
③ Caroline gave me a chocolate, <u>and</u> I ate it.
④ We ordered coffee, <u>so</u> they brought us tea.
⑤ Get up early, <u>and</u> you'll have time for breakfast.

4 다음 대화의 빈칸에 들어갈 말이 순서대로 짝지어진 것은?

> A: Do you want to get something to eat?
> B: OK. How about a burger _____ some noodles?
> A: I'm not that hungry, _____ let's just have some fruit.

① or - so   ② or – and   ③ but – or
④ but – so   ⑤ and – or

5 다음 중 밑줄 친 부분이 어법상 <u>어색한</u> 것은?

① She likes jazz, <u>and</u> he likes hip-hop.
② I'd like to watch both *Iron Man* <u>or</u> *Spider-man*.
③ My friend Greg is not kind <u>but</u> funny.
④ Grandfather's shoes are dirty <u>and</u> old.
⑤ Which do you want, pizza <u>or</u> chicken?

6 우리말과 같도록 알맞은 접속사를 이용하여 다음 두 문장을 한 문장으로 연결하시오.

> · Go to bed early.
> · You will feel tired tomorrow.

> 일찍 자러 가라, 그렇지 않으면 너는 내일 피곤할 것이다.

= _____

[7-8] 다음 우리말을 알맞게 영작한 것을 고르시오.

7

> 음식이 비쌌지만, 그것은 맛이 있었다.

① The food was expensive, but it was delicious.
② The food was expensive, or it was delicious.
③ The food was expensive, that it was delicious.
④ The food was expensive, so it was delicious.
⑤ The food was expensive, and it was delicious.

8

> 네가 걷고 있는 동안 핸드폰을 보지 마라.

① Don't look at your cell phone before you
are walking.
② Don't look at your cell phone after you
are walking.
③ Don't look at your cell phone and you are
walking.
④ Don't look at your cell phone or you are
walking.
⑤ Don't look at your cell phone while you
are walking.

9 다음 빈칸에 공통으로 들어갈 알맞은 접속사를 <보기>에서 골라 쓰시오.

> <보기> while but when that

> · I was happy _____ the class ended.
> · William runs a lot _____ he plays
> football.
> · They will bring you your food _____
> it is ready.

[10-11] 다음 두 문장의 의미가 같도록 빈칸에 알맞은 접속사를 쓰시오.

10

> Rachel opened the doors before the
> plumber arrived.
> = The plumber arrived _____
> Rachel opened the doors.

11

> Jessica has a stomachache, so she
> can't play tennis.
> = Jessica can't play tennis _____
> she has a stomachache.

12 다음 중 밑줄 친 when의 쓰임이 나머지 넷과 다른 것은?

① They have picnics when it is sunny.
② Did Sandy get a haircut when he was in
Seoul?
③ When did you watch that movie?
④ We sat down when the teacher came in.
⑤ When I got out of the shower, it was 7 A.M.

13 우리말과 같도록 괄호 안의 말을 활용하여 영작하시오.

> 나는 그 소포가 오늘 도착할 것이라고 생각한다.
> (think, the package, arrive)

= _____

14 다음 중 문맥상 어색한 것의 개수는?

ⓐ We can get bananas but some oranges.

ⓑ This game is really fun and exciting.

ⓒ He couldn't read the newspaper while the noisy radio was on.

ⓓ Bill was tired after he finished exercising.

ⓔ I played the drums before I played the saxophone.

① 1개   ② 2개   ③ 3개
④ 4개   ⑤ 5개

15 다음 문장을 우리말로 해석한 것 중 어색한 것은?

① He needed to shower, but he didn't have a towel.
   → 그는 샤워를 해야 했지만, 수건이 없었다.

② William was so hungry, so he ate three burgers.
   → William은 배가 너무 고파서, 세 개의 햄버거를 먹었다.

③ Lily wanted to be a chef when she was a child.
   → Lily는 그녀가 아이였을 때 요리사가 되고 싶었다.

④ After the play ended, people clapped.
   → 연극이 끝난 후에, 사람들은 박수를 쳤다.

⑤ He will study architecture while he is in Berlin.
   → 그는 베를린에 있기 때문에 건축학을 공부할 것이다.

16 우리말과 같도록 괄호 안의 말을 활용하여 문장을 완성하시오.

만약 네가 정중하게 묻는다면 그녀는 친절히 대답할 것이다. (ask nicely)

= She will answer kindly _____.

17 다음 문장에서 틀린 부분을 바르게 고쳐 완전한 문장을 쓰시오.

Carrie will do her homework after she will watch this movie.

→ _____
   _____

18 우리말과 같도록 괄호 안의 말을 배열할 때 세 번째에 오는 것을 쓰시오.

나는 버스가 곧 올 것을 안다. (the, come, bus, soon, I, that, will, know)

→ _____

19 다음 중 접속사 that이 들어갈 가장 알맞은 위치는?

① Wendy ② thinks ③ Paul ④ likes ⑤ swimming.

20 주어진 문장의 밑줄 친 that과 쓰임이 다른 것은?

Do you know that the festival is free?

① Sandy believes that she will pass the test.

② It was a problem that she lost her wallet.

③ I saw that man at work yesterday.

④ I can't believe that the pyramid is 4,000 years old.

⑤ The fact is that Carl caused the car accident.

[21-22] 다음 글의 빈칸에 들어갈 가장 알맞은 것을 고르시오.

21

I fell off my bike yesterday. _____, I was not injured.

① When   ② Or

③ For example   ④ Therefore

⑤ However

22

My brother is an excellent student. _____, he got a perfect score on his science test last week.

① For example   ② Then

③ But   ④ However

⑤ On the other hand

[23-24] 다음 글을 읽고 주어진 질문에 답하시오.

David has visited many different countries. (A) 예를 들어, 그는 작년에 스페인과 포르투갈로 여행 갔다. (Spain, Portugal, travel, to) He enjoys experiencing different cultures. He plans to travel to Morocco _____ Egypt during his next vacation. He would like to visit both countries, _____ he won't have enough time.

23 위 글의 밑줄 친 우리말 (A)와 같도록 괄호 안의 말을 활용하여 문장을 완성하시오.

= _____

last year.

24 위 글의 빈칸에 들어갈 말이 순서대로 짝지어진 것은?

① or – and   ② so – and   ③ and – that

④ so – but   ⑤ or – but

25 다음 글의 빈칸에 들어갈 말이 순서대로 짝지어진 것은?

Amanda wants to buy a new laptop. She wants the one like her sister's. _____, that laptop is very expensive. _____, Amanda will have to save a lot of money.

① However – On the other hand

② However – Therefore

③ However – For example

④ Therefore – However

⑤ Therefore – On the other hand

MEMO

최신 개정 교과서 완벽 반영

기출로 적중
해커스
중학영문법

1학년

해설집

이 책을 검토해주신 선생님들

강상훈 경기 평촌비상에듀학원 / **김가영** 서울 송정중학교 / **김원덕** 경기 올림피아드학원 / **박유정** 서울 반포중학교 / **박윤정** 경기 이지베스트학원

박은혜 서울 송파중학교 / **박정은** 서울 대청중학교 / **양세희** 서울 양세희수능영어학원 / **이계윤** 서울 씨앤씨학원 / **이유빈** 서울 잉글리쉬&매쓰매니저학원

이혜원 서울 대청중학교 / **정혜은** 서울 용곡중학교 / **최다빈** 서울 최강영어 / **최승복** 경기 오른어학원 / **최지영** 경기 다른영어학원

CHAPTER 1
be동사
p.18

POINT 1-1 주어와 be동사의 현재형

 A

1 we	**2** she	**3** they
4 it	**5** you	**6** they
7 we	**8** he	**9** it
10 they	**11** he	**12** they
13 she	**14** you	**15** he
16 it	**17** we	**18** they

B

1 is	**2** are	**3** are
4 am	**5** is	**6** are
7 is	**8** are	**9** is
10 are	**11** is	**12** are

C

1 You're brave.   2 She's in her room.
3 I'm very thirsty.   4 It's my book.
5 They're busy now.   6 We're late for school.
7 He's a new student.

기출 적중문제
정답 ⑤
해설 be동사가 is이므로 주어는 3인칭 단수 Michael을 쓴다.

POINT 1-2 be동사 현재형의 의미

연습문제

1 ⓐ	**2** ⓑ	**3** ⓒ	**4** ⓑ
5 ⓐ	**6** ⓐ	**7** ⓑ	**8** ⓒ
9 ⓑ	**10** ⓐ	**11** ⓒ	**12** ⓒ
13 ⓑ	**14** ⓐ	**15** ⓒ	

POINT 1-3 be동사의 현재형: 부정문

연습문제 A

1 He's not / He isn't
2 We're not / We aren't
3 I'm not
4 They're not / They aren't
5 It's not / It isn't
6 She's not / She isn't
7 You're not / You aren't

연습문제 B

1 I am not[I'm not]
2 My mother is not[isn't]
3 Benny and I are not[aren't]
4 He is not[He's not/He isn't]
5 A bee is not[isn't]
6 You are not[You're not/You aren't]
7 We are not[We're not/We aren't]
8 These gloves are not[aren't]
9 Jane is not[isn't]
10 History is not[isn't]
11 My sister and I are not[aren't]
12 This movie is not[isn't]

연습문제 C

1 Jessie isn't	**2** The leaves aren't
3 Adam isn't	**4** The books aren't

기출 적중문제
정답 ②
해설 am not은 줄여 쓸 수 없다.

POINT 1-4 be동사의 현재형: 의문문

연습문제 A

1 Are you	**2** Is he
3 Is Sally	**4** Is that tomato
5 Am I	**6** Is it
7 Are you	**8** Are the coins
9 Is this yellow book	**10** Are the spoons
11 Are they	**12** Are Jacob and I

연습문제 B

1 it isn't	**2** you aren't
3 I am	**4** she isn't
5 they aren't	**6** it is
7 he isn't	**8** he is
9 we aren't	

기출 적중문제
정답 No, it isn't
해설 주어 your scarf로 묻고 있으므로 주어 it으로 대답하고 스카프가 파란색이 아니므로 No, it isn't.로 대답한다.

POINT 2-1 be동사의 과거형

연습문제

1 was	**2** were	**3** was
4 were	**5** were	**6** was
7 was	**8** were	**9** was

정답 ③

해설 was → were

POINT 2-2 be동사의 과거형: 부정문

1 He and I were not[weren't]
2 They were not[weren't]
3 The musical was not[wasn't]
4 It was not[wasn't]
5 You were not[weren't]
6 Emily was not[wasn't]
7 The stars were not[weren't]
8 My room was not[wasn't]
9 We were not[weren't]
10 The TV program was not[wasn't]
11 Leo was not[wasn't]
12 The sandwiches were not[weren't]
13 Those shoes were not[weren't]
14 The cats were not[weren't]
15 The magazine was not[wasn't]
16 My neighbors were not[weren't]

POINT 2-3 be동사의 과거형: 의문문

연습
문제
A

1 Was Debra
2 Were the glasses
3 Were the pictures
4 Was the cupcake
5 Was her son
6 Were bananas

연습
문제
B

1 I wasn't
2 they were
3 it wasn't
4 they weren't
5 she was
6 it was
7 you weren't

서술형 대비 문제

Ⓐ
1 is, aren't
2 are, isn't
3 is, aren't
4 isn't, are

Ⓑ
1 The calendar is
2 We are not [We're not/We aren't]
3 Sohee and I are
4 The dishes were
5 The park was
6 Is her classroom
7 Were they
8 My uncle is not[isn't]

9 Was Helen
10 They were not[weren't]
11 The store was not[wasn't]

Ⓒ
1 Her socks are not[aren't] purple.
2 Were they on the train to Busan?
3 Alex and I were not[weren't] very surprised.
4 Was your dog in my yard yesterday?
5 Is this white building his school?
6 It is not[It's not/It isn't] a new smartphone model.
7 Was Jimmy tired last weekend?
8 The weather was not[wasn't] wonderful a month ago.
9 Is Mr. Brown a movie director?
10 I am not[I'm not] in the science room now.
11 Are these flowers blue roses?
12 Beth is not[isn't] good at Korean.
13 The cats were not[weren't] on the roof this morning.

중간·기말고사 실전 문제

1 ④ 2 ④ 3 ① 4 ③ 5 Marie is a web designer. 6 ② 7 ③ 8 ②
9 are 10 I am, Peter is 11 My cat is not[isn't] hungry 12 ③ 13 (1) are (2) is, isn't (3) aren't
14 ④ 15 ③, ④ 16 (1) Danny is not[isn't] at the gym. (2) Is Danny at the gym? 17 ③ 18 ①
19 Yes, they were 20 Was their teacher angry?
21 ① 22 ③ 23 ⑤ 24 ⑤ 25 ②
26 Are Jim and Liam on the soccer team?
27 Her birthday was last Saturday. 28 ④
29 (A) No, he isn't (B) He is (C) Yes, he is

1 ④ your bags – are

2 be동사가 are이므로 주어는 1인칭 복수·2인칭·3인칭 복수를 쓴다. He는 3인칭 단수이므로 is를 쓴다.

3 be동사가 was이므로 주어는 1인칭 단수·3인칭 단수를 쓴다. Mike and Kerry는 3인칭 복수이므로 were를 쓴다.

4 ·주어 Nate and I는 1인칭 복수이므로 are를 쓴다.
·주어 His name은 3인칭 단수이므로 is를 쓴다.

5 주어 Marie는 3인칭 단수이므로 is를 쓴다.

6 ②: '~(에) 있다' ①③④⑤: '~(하)다'

7 ③ are[were] ①②④⑤ is[was]

8 ① are → is

③ amn't → am not

④ not is → is not[isn't]

⑤ is → are

9 첫 번째 빈칸: 주어 My classmates and I는 1인칭 복수이므로 are를 쓴다.
두 번째 빈칸: 주어 we는 1인칭 복수이므로 are를 쓴다.
세 번째 빈칸: 주어 Angela and Jimin은 3인칭 복수이므로 are를 쓴다.

10 주어 I는 1인칭 단수이므로 am을 쓰고, 주어 Peter는 3인칭 단수이므로 is를 쓴다.

11 주어 My cat은 3인칭 단수이므로 is를 쓰고 be동사의 부정문은 「be동사 + not」이다.

12 ③: am not은 줄여 쓸 수 없다.

13 (1) 주어 Evan and Olivia는 3인칭 복수이고 둘 다 키가 크다고 했으므로 are를 쓴다.
(2) 주어 Evan은 3인칭 단수이고 치과의사라고 했으므로 is를 쓰고, 주어 Olivia는 3인칭 단수이고 치과의사가 아니라고 했으므로 isn't를 쓴다.
(3) 주어 Evan and Olivia는 3인칭 복수이고 둘 다 서울에 있지 않다고 했으므로 aren't를 쓴다.

14 주어 the living room은 3인칭 단수이고 거실이 깨끗하지 않은 상황이므로 No, it isn't.로 대답한다.

15 ③: be동사의 의문문에 대한 대답: 「Yes, 주어 + be동사.」 또는 「No, 주어 + be동사 + not.」
④: 주어 you로 묻고 있으므로 주어 I로 대답한다.

16 (1) be동사의 부정문: 「be동사 + not」
(2) be동사의 의문문: 「be동사 + 주어 ~?」

17 ③ we → they

18 ① were → was

19 주어 Gilbert and Kate는 3인칭 복수이고 어제 학교에 지각했다고 했으므로 Yes, they were.로 대답한다.

20 be동사의 의문문: 「be동사 + 주어 ~?」

21 ⓑ Is interesting your job? → Is your job interesting?
ⓓ not was → was not[wasn't]
ⓔ be busy → busy

22 be동사의 부정문: 「be동사 + not」

23 ⑤ was → were

24 주어 your dogs는 3인칭 복수이므로 are를 쓰고 be동사의 의문문은 「be동사 + 주어 ~?」이다.

25 주어 you and Inho로 묻고 있으므로 주어 we로 대답하고 be동사의 의문문에 대답은 「Yes, 주어 + be동사.」 또는 「No, 주어 + be동사 + not.」이다.

26 주어 Jim and Liam은 3인칭 복수이므로 Are를 쓴다.

27 주어 Her birthday는 3인칭 단수이므로 was를 쓴다.

28 ① You → They
② It → He
③ They → You
⑤ It → They

29 (A) 주어 Nick은 3인칭 단수이고 독일이 아닌 호주에서 왔다고 했으므로 No, he isn't.로 대답한다.
(B) 주어 Nick은 3인칭 단수이고 호주에서 왔다고 했으므로 H is를 쓴다.
(C) 주어 Nick은 3인칭 단수이고 훌륭한 하키 선수라고 했으므로 Yes, he is.로 대답한다.

CHAPTER 2
일반동사

p.36

4 feels, doesn't feel

기출 적중문제

정답 ⑤

해설 주어 She는 3인칭 단수이므로 일반동사 현재형의 부정문은 「doesn't + 동사원형」이다.

POINT 1-1 일반동사의 현재형

연습문제 A

1 knows	**2** does	**3** passes
4 learns	**5** meets	**6** mixes
7 listens	**8** finishes	**9** reads
10 walks	**11** hurries	**12** sees
13 looks	**14** pushes	**15** smells
16 carries	**17** tries	**18** brushes
19 buys	**20** flies	**21** puts
22 stays	**23** touches	**24** likes
25 says	**26** fixes	**27** watches
28 enjoys	**29** runs	**30** gives
31 pays	**32** misses	**33** tastes
34 becomes	**35** catches	**36** thinks
37 makes	**38** feels	**39** asks
40 worries		

연습문제 B

1 lives	**2** studies	**3** arrives
4 has	**5** wash	**6** teaches
7 cries	**8** play	

기출 적중문제

정답 ③

해설 · 주어 She는 3인칭 단수이므로 brushes를 쓴다.
· 주어 Alex and Sally는 3인칭 복수이므로 bake를 쓴다.

POINT 1-2 일반동사의 현재형: 부정문

연습문제 A

1 He does not[doesn't] sing
2 She does not[doesn't] go
3 They do not[don't] exercise
4 Somin does not[doesn't] have
5 I do not[don't] know
6 Dan and his sister do not[don't] like
7 We do not[don't] need
8 Andy and Tina do not[don't] drink
9 My grandfather does not[doesn't] live
10 It does not[doesn't] rain
11 Steve and I do not[don't] jog
12 The museum does not[doesn't] open
13 Ms. Jones does not[doesn't] read

연습문제 B

1 rides, doesn't ride
2 practices, don't practice
3 teaches, doesn't teach

POINT 1-3 일반동사의 현재형: 의문문

연습문제 A

1 Does Liam have
2 Does Anne study
3 Does she practice
4 Do they play
5 Does he lock
6 Do his grandparents raise
7 Does Batman wear
8 Does the laptop work
9 Do Minji and Junho know
10 Do you go

연습문제 B

1 Do	**2** Does	**3** run
4 Do	**5** Does	**6** like
7 have	**8** break	**9** Does

연습문제 C

1 she does	**2** he does
3 they don't	**4** he doesn't
5 we do	**6** she does
7 they don't	**8** it doesn't

기출 적중문제

정답 **Do you live**

해설 주어 I로 대답하고 있으므로 주어 you로 묻고, 주어 you는 2인칭 단수이므로 일반동사 현재형의 의문문은 「Do + 주어 + 동사원형 ~?」이다.

POINT 2-1 일반동사의 과거형: 규칙 변화

연습문제 A

1 talked	**2** cleaned	**3** loved
4 cried	**5** worked	**6** lived
7 closed	**8** planned	**9** opened
10 hugged	**11** dropped	**12** liked
13 washed	**14** played	**15** studied
16 stopped	**17** raised	**18** visited
19 arrived	**20** married	**21** happened
22 wanted	**23** shopped	**24** danced
25 decided	**26** looked	**27** worried
28 believed	**29** listened	**30** enjoyed
31 tasted	**32** tried	**33** saved
34 stayed	**35** invited	**36** carried
37 died	**38** shouted	**39** jogged

40	smiled	41	copied	42	grabbed
43	chatted	44	hurried	45	hated
46	jumped	47	hoped	48	stepped
49	entered	50	explained		

연습문제 **B**

1	smiled	2	planned	3	studied
4	rained	5	worried	6	played
7	stayed	8	chatted		

기출 적중문제

정답 ④

해설 huged → hugged

POINT 2-2   일반동사의 과거형: 불규칙 변화

연습문제 **A**

1	laid, laid	2	sold, sold
3	drew, drawn	4	bought, bought
5	told, told	6	cut, cut
7	spoke, spoken	8	became, become
9	set, set	10	ate, eaten
11	ran, run	12	spent, spent
13	had, had	14	made, made
15	woke, woken	16	hit, hit
17	got, got(ten)	18	slept, slept
19	won, won	20	lost, lost
21	met, met	22	fed, fed
23	found, found	24	put, put
25	read, read	26	wrote, written
27	built, built	28	heard, heard
29	spread, spread	30	fought, fought
31	said, said	32	sang, sung
33	caught, caught	34	broke, broken
35	wore, worn	36	took, taken
37	did, done	38	hurt, hurt
39	went, gone	40	thought, thought
41	swam, swum	42	came, come
43	cost, cost	44	saw, seen
45	taught, taught	46	rose, risen
47	understood, understood		
48	knew, known		
49	overcame, overcome		
50	brought, brought		
51	chose, chosen	52	left, left
53	fell, fallen	54	forgot, forgotten
55	flew, flown	56	grew, grown
57	rode, ridden	58	drank, drunk
59	sat, sat	60	drove, driven
61	began, begun	62	gave, given
63	stood, stood	64	kept, kept
65	mistook, mistaken	66	sent, sent

연습문제 **B**

1	swam	2	hit	3	fell
4	gave	5	caught	6	became
7	laid	8	lost	9	bought
10	slept	11	made	12	left
13	tasted	14	did	15	ran
16	put	17	watched	18	arrived
19	won	20	dropped		

기출 적중문제

정답 ②

해설 ① readed → read
③ saveed → saved
④ stoped → stopped
⑤ faught → fought

POINT 2-3   일반동사의 과거형: 부정문과 의문문

연습문제 **A**

1	didn't have	2	Did, move	3	Did, enjoy
4	Did, finish	5	didn't pick		

연습문제 **B**

1	Aaron didn't go	2	Did you forget
3	I didn't meet	4	Did Carl take
5	Yunho didn't want		
6	Did Kevin's flight arrive		

연습문제 **C**

1	have	2	stay
3	leave, did	4	tell
5	fight, didn't	6	believe
7	hear, didn't	8	close
9	build, did	10	sing, didn't

기출 적중문제

정답 (1) He did not[didn't] send a card to his parents.
(2) Did he send a card to his parents?

해설 (1) 일반동사 과거형의 부정문: 「did not[didn't] + 동사원형」
(2) 일반동사 과거형의 의문문: 「Did + 주어 + 동사원형 ~?」

서술형 대비 문제

Ⓐ

1	looks	2	misses
3	doesn't sell	4	Do, get
5	Does, drive	6	Does, smell
7	Do, speak	8	don't believe
9	leaves	10	doesn't clean

Ⓑ

1	Yes, they do.	2	No, he doesn't.
3	Yes, she does.	4	No, they don't.
5	Yes, he does.	6	No, she doesn't

Ⓒ **1** lost **2** O **3** wake
4 feed **5** O **6** call
7 give **8** O **9** O
10 stopped

Ⓓ **1** They did not[didn't] buy a new sofa.
2 Does this garden smell like roses?
3 The baker does not[doesn't] bake bread every morning.
4 We do not[don't] watch horror movies.
5 Did the class begin at eight?
6 Do Robert and Molly work out on weekends?
7 Did she cut her finger last night?
8 I did not[didn't] break the window yesterday.

중간·기말고사 실전 문제

1 ④ **2** ③ **3** ③ **4** ③ **5** ①
6 arrives, has, plays, does **7** ① **8** ③
9 ④ **10** ⑤ **11** ⓐ goes ⓑ runs ⓒ sits
ⓓ drinks ⓔ has **12** ⓐ went ⓑ ran ⓒ sat
ⓓ drank ⓔ had **13** ⑤ **14** ④ **15** likes
16 do not[don't] trust **17** stops → stop
18 like, do not[don't] like, does not[doesn't] like, likes
19 I do not[don't] study history every day. **20** Hyeri
studies history every day. **21** ② **22** ①
23 ③ **24** ③ **25** No, he doesn't. **26** Does
Ms. Smith work at a huge company?
27 ⓐ have ⓑ gets ⓒ study ⓓ watches **28** ①
29 ⑤ **30** ④ **31** ② **32** ③ **33** ①
34 ⑤ **35** ③ **36** ③ **37** Sam did
not[didn't] buy new sneakers yesterday. **38** Did
Sam buy new sneakers yesterday? / No, he didn't.
39 ②

④ buy – buys

③ mix – mixes

③ barks → bark

동사가 takes이므로 주어는 3인칭 단수를 쓴다. They는 3인칭 복수이므로 take를 쓴다.

· 주어 They는 3인칭 복수이므로 watch를 쓴다.
· 주어 She는 3인칭 단수이므로 studies를 쓴다.

주어 Debra(She)는 3인칭 단수이므로 arrives, has, plays, does를 쓴다.

① jump – jumped

8 ③ hurt – hurt

9 ④ drive – drove – driven

10 ⑤ grow – grew – grown

11 주어 Haley(she)는 3인칭 단수이므로 goes, runs, sits, drinks, has를 쓴다.

12 어제 있었던 일이므로 일반동사의 과거형 went, ran, sat, drank, had를 쓴다.

13 ① likes → like
② don't → doesn't
③ don't watches → doesn't watch
④ be believe → believe

14 주어 We는 1인칭 복수이므로 일반동사 현재형의 부정문은 「do not[don't] + 동사원형」이다.

15 주어 My sister는 3인칭 단수이므로 likes를 쓴다.

16 주어 Joseph and Stella는 3인칭 복수이므로 일반동사 현재형의 부정문은 「do not[don't] + 동사원형」이다.

17 This elevator는 3인칭 복수이고 일반동사 현재형의 부정문은 「does not[doesn't] + 동사원형」이므로 stop을 쓴다.

18 첫 번째 빈칸: 주어 I는 1인칭 단수이고 과학을 좋아한다고 했으므로 like를 쓴다.
두 번째 빈칸: 주어 I는 1인칭 단수이고 영어를 좋아하지 않는다고 했으므로 do not[don't] like를 쓴다.
세 번째 빈칸: 주어 Yuna는 3인칭 단수이고 과학을 좋아하지 않는다고 했으므로 does not[doesn't] like를 쓴다.
네 번째 빈칸: 주어 she는 3인칭 단수이고 영어를 좋아한다고 했으므로 likes를 쓴다.

19 주어 I는 1인칭 단수이므로 일반동사 현재형의 부정문은 「do not[don't] + 동사원형」이다.

20 주어 Hyeri는 3인칭 단수이므로 studies를 쓴다.

21 ② Does ①③④⑤ Do

22 첫 번째 빈칸: 일반동사 현재형의 의문문은 「Do/Does + 주어 + 동사원형 ~?」이므로 동사원형 play를 쓴다.
두 번째 빈칸: 주어 I는 1인칭 단수이므로 play를 쓴다.

23 주어 she는 3인칭 단수이므로 일반동사 현재형의 의문문은 「Does + 주어 + 동사원형 ~?」이다.

24 일반동사 과거형의 의문문: 「Did + 주어 + 동사원형 ~?」

25 주어 Jake는 3인칭 단수이고 Jake의 머리는 빨간색이 아닌 검정색인 상황이므로 일반동사 현재형의 의문문에 대한 부정의 대답인 No, he doesn't를 쓴다.

26 주어 Ms. Smith는 3인칭 단수이므로 일반동사 현재형의 의문문은 「Does + 주어 + 동사원형 ~?」이다.

27 ⓐ 주어 I는 1인칭 단수이므로 have를 쓴다.
ⓑ 주어 She는 3인칭 단수이므로 gets를 쓴다.
ⓒ 일반동사 현재형의 부정문: 「do not[don't] + 동사원형」

ⓓ 주어 She는 3인칭 단수이므로 watches를 쓴다.

28 ① Do → Does

29 ⑤ shareed → shared

30 ・동사 visit의 과거형: visited
・동사 read의 과거형: read

31 ② breaked → broke

32 (A) 동사 take의 과거형: took
(B) 동사 walk의 과거형: walked
(C) 동사 come의 과거형: came

33 일반동사 현재형의 의문문에 대한 대답:「Yes, 주어 + do/does.」
또는「No, 주어 + don't/doesn't.」

34 일반동사 과거형의 의문문에 대한 대답:「Yes, 주어 + did.」또는
「No, 주어 + didn't.」

35 ③ aren't → don't

36 주어 your brother는 3인칭 단수이므로 일반동사 현재형의 의문
문은「Does + 주어 + 동사원형 ~?」이다.

37 일반동사 과거형의 부정문:「did not[didn't] + 동사원형」

38 A: 일반동사 과거형의 의문문:「Did + 주어 + 동사원형 ~?」
B: 일반동사 과거형의 의문문에 대한 부정의 대답:「No, 주어 +
didn't.」

39 ⓑ enjoyed → enjoy
ⓒ not did → did not[didn't]
ⓔ study she → she study

POINT 1 현재시제

 1 like **2** comes **3** turn
4 is **5** visit **6** spends
7 has

기출 적중문제

정답 I read a book
해설 현재의 습관이나 반복되는 일을 나타내고 있으므로 현재시제
를 쓴다.

POINT 2 과거시제

A
1 watched **2** cried
3 didn't rain **4** was
5 Did, buy **6** didn't drink
7 sent **8** were
9 created **10** weren't
11 didn't work

B
1 was **2** Is **3** studied
4 traveled **5** are **6** Did
7 didn't **8** doesn't **9** is
10 cried **11** walked **12** wrote
13 was, is **14** went **15** didn't
16 live

기출 적중문제

정답 ③
해설 watched → am watching

POINT 3 미래시제

A
1 I will[I'll] be
2 Luke will not[won't] watch
3 Will you be
4 Eric and Jane will go

B
1 Tommy is going to leave his home town
tomorrow.
2 I am not[I'm not] going to make a mistake
again.
3 Are you going to walk to school tomorrow?

4 Matt and Kelly are not[aren't] going to wait for me.

연습문제 C

1	will not	2	rain
3	aren't	4	come, will
5	are	6	Will, won't
7	won't	8	is not

기출 적중문제

정답 will go to the mall

해설 다음 주 일요일에 쇼핑몰에 간다고 했으므로 미래시제를 쓴다.

POINT 4-1 진행시제: 현재진행시제

연습문제 A

1	going	2	jumping	3	singing
4	sitting	5	dancing	6	beginning
7	making	8	speaking	9	seeing
10	writing	11	lying	12	putting
13	running	14	visiting	15	having
16	clapping	17	riding	18	getting
19	sleeping	20	moving	21	coming
22	winning	23	skiing	24	studying
25	watching	26	arriving	27	buying
28	talking	29	dying	30	enjoying
31	being	32	closing	33	playing
34	drawing	35	tying	36	cutting
37	planning	38	working	39	building
40	flying				

연습문제 B

1	is entering	2	are swimming
3	is baking	4	are reading
5	is lying	6	is having
7	are flying	8	are sitting

기출 적중문제

정답 ⑤

해설 '~하고 있다'라는 의미의 현재진행시제 is opening을 쓴다.

POINT 4-2 진행시제: 현재진행시제의 부정문과 의문문

연습문제 A

1 Is Tim taking a walk now?
2 Sally is not[isn't] dancing on the stage now.
3 Are they enjoying the holiday?
4 The gardener is not[isn't] watering the flowers.
5 Are the camels lying on the sand?
6 The guests are not[aren't] standing outside.
7 Is your dog jumping on the bed?
8 Sophie and Yunho are not[aren't] talking now.

연습문제 B

1 No, she isn't, is sitting
2 Yes, they are
3 No, they aren't, are painting
4 No, he isn't, is eating

연습문제 C

1	isn't	2	Is, is
3	running	4	Are, aren't
5	washing	6	is not
7	Are, are	8	Is, isn't

기출 적중문제

정답 ⑤

해설 ① not is → is not[isn't]
② listen → listening
③ sing → singing
④ be → are

POINT 4-3 진행시제: 과거진행시제

연습문제 A

1 My classmates were cleaning
2 Mina wasn't[was not] having
3 Were the students taking
4 Jamie was walking
5 Was Luke doing
6 We weren't[were not] playing
7 The students weren't[were not] listening
8 My sister and I were watching

연습문제 B

1	was exercising	2	wasn't barking
3	were chatting	4	Was, drinking, wasn't
5	were taking	6	Was, taking, was
7	Were, making, wasn't	8	weren't talking

기출 적중문제

정답 ④

해설 과거진행시제 Were ~ doing으로 묻고 있으므로 과거진행시제 「was/were + V-ing」로 대답한다.

POINT 5 현재완료시제

연습문제

1	has snowed	2	has visited
3	have gone	4	has, started
5	have lived	6	has taken
7	have traveled	8	has worked
9	has read	10	has, finished
11	have known	12	has, moved
13	have tried	14	has become

서술형 대비 문제

Ⓐ
1 They studied Korean yesterday.
2 I will not go to school tomorrow.
3 Sora plays soccer every Saturday.
4 My brother was wrapping the present.
5 Did your team win the game last week?
6 Is the cat sleeping now?
7 Juho is going to cut his hair soon.
8 The bookstore does not have good books.
9 Tom was not wearing a jacket.

Ⓑ
1 will not[won't] tell　2 will prepare
3 is going to be　4 will teach
5 going to buy
6 is not[isn't] going to leave
7 will be　8 are going to take

Ⓒ
1 is reading a book
2 are running
3 is lying on the ground
4 are making a snowman
5 are swimming

Ⓓ
1 ⓐ arrived ⓑ visited ⓒ saw ⓓ will meet
ⓔ will look
2 ⓐ lives ⓑ moved ⓒwill start ⓓ sent
ⓔ will write

중간·기말고사 실전 문제

1 ③　2 ④　3 ②　4 ①, ③
5 ③, ④　6 ③　7 ② 8 came,
ate, was 9 Will you go to the hospital this
weekend? 10 He will not[won't] stay at my
house next month. 11 Is it going to snow
tomorrow? 12 ② 13 Sarah is going to
practice the violin tomorrow. 14 ④ 15 (1) will
prepare for the speech contest (2) No, won't, will buy
some books 16 ④　17 ③　18 ③
19 ②　20 was, is　21 ⑤　22 ③
23 ③　24 ④　25 ④　26 ③
27 Jackson is tying a ribbon on the present.
28 My brother and I were shopping at the mall
30 minutes ago. 29 ③　30 was moving
31 (A) is sitting (B) has 32 (1) is throwing
(2) are eating (3) is taking 33 ②, ④ 34 ⑤
35 ②　36 ⑤　37 ④　38 ③　39 ②

---

1 tomorrow는 미래시제와 주로 함께 쓰이는 부사이다.

2 Last month는 과거시제와 주로 함께 쓰이는 부사구이다.

3 ·과학적 사실을 말하고 있으므로 현재시제를 쓰고 주어 The
Earth는 3인칭 단수이므로 goes를 쓴다.
·현재의 습관이나 반복되는 일을 나타내고 있으므로 현재시제를
쓰고 주어 She는 3인칭 단수이므로 goes를 쓴다.

4 과거시제 read가 쓰였으므로 과거시제와 주로 함께 쓰이는 부사
(구) yesterday와 two hours ago를 쓴다.

5 미래시제를 나타내는 will이 쓰였으므로 미래시제와 주로 함께 쓰
이는 부사(구) tomorrow와 next month를 쓴다.

6 첫 번째 빈칸: 현재시제 does가 쓰였으므로 현재시제와 주로 함
께 쓰이는 부사구 every Sunday와 on weekends를 쓴다.
두 번째 빈칸: 현재시제로 묻고 있으므로 현재시제로 대답한다.

7 과거시제로 묻고 있으므로 과거시제로 대답한다.

8 last night은 과거시제와 주로 함께 쓰이는 부사구이므로 과거시
제 came, ate, was를 쓴다.

9 will이 있는 미래시제의 의문문:「Will + 주어 + 동사원형 ~?」

10 will이 있는 미래시제의 부정문:「will not[won't] + 동사원형」

11 be going to가 있는 미래시제의 의문문:「be동사 + 주어 +
going to + 동사원형 ~?」

12 ⓐ is → be
ⓑ not are → are not[aren't]
ⓔ be → to be
ⓕ seeing → see

13 be going to가 있는 미래시제는「be going to + 동사원형」이
고 주어 Sarah는 3인칭 단수이므로 be동사는 is를 쓴다.

14 '~하지 않을 것이다'라는 의미의 미래시제의 부정문은「won't +
동사원형」이다.

15 (1) 미래시제 will로 묻고 있고, 다음 주 화요일에는 말하기 대
회를 준비한다고 했으므로 미래시제 will prepare for the
speech contest를 쓴다.
(2) 미래시제 Will로 묻고 있고, 다음 주 월요일에는 놀이 공원에
가지 않는다고 했으므로 will이 있는 미래시제의 의문문에 대
한 부정의 대답은「No, 주어 + won't.」이다. 다음 주 월요일
에는 약간의 책을 산다고 했으므로 미래시제 will buy some
books를 쓴다.

16 ④ is → was

17 (A) yesterday는 과거시제와 주로 함께 쓰이는 부사이므로 과
거시제 didn't를 쓴다.
(B) soon은 미래시제와 주로 함께 쓰이는 부사이므로 미래시제
를 나타내는 Will을 쓴다.
(C) 역사적인 사실을 말하고 있으므로 과거시제 walked를 쓴다.

18 ⓒ will be → was

19 Sara가 2000년에 Ken을 처음 만났고 아직도 그를 알고 있으

로 현재완료시제「have/has + p.p.」를 쓰고, 주어 Sara는 3인 칭 단수이므로 has를 쓴다.

20 첫 번째 빈칸: an hour ago는 과거시제와 주로 함께 쓰이는 부 사구이므로 과거시제를 쓰고 주어 The bus는 3인칭 단수이므로 was를 쓴다.
두 번째 빈칸: '지금은 가득 차 있다'라는 의미이므로 현재시제를 쓰고 주어 it은 3인칭 단수이므로 is를 쓴다.

21 ⑤ haveing → having

22 ③ claping → clapping

23 ① singging → singing
② makeing → making
④ lieing → lying
⑤ runing → running

24 '~하고 있다'라는 의미의 현재진행시제 are writing을 쓴다.

25 · 현재진행시제의 의문문은「Am/Is/Are + 주어 + V-ing ~?」이 고 주어 Martin은 3인칭 단수이므로 be동사는 Is를 쓴다.
· 과거진행시제의 부정문:「was/were + not + V-ing」

26 현재진행시제의 의문문에 대한 대답은「Yes, 주어 + am/is/are.」 또는「No, 주어 + am/is/are + not.」이고 주어 he는 3인칭 단 수이므로 be동사는 is를 쓴다.

27 현재시제 ties가 쓰였으므로 현재진행시제「am/is/are + V-ing」 를 쓰고 주어 Jackson은 3인칭 단수이므로 be동사는 is를 쓴다.

28 과거시제 shopped가 쓰였으므로 과거진행시제「was/were + V-ing」를 쓰고 주어 My brother and I는 1인칭 복수이므로 be 동사는 were를 쓴다.

29 현재진행시제 is ~ standing으로 대답하고 있으므로 현재진행 시제의 의문문「Am/Is/Are + 주어 + V-ing ~?」를 쓴다.

30 과거진행시제 was ~ doing으로 묻고 있으므로 과거진행시제 「was/were + V-ing」로 대답하고 주어 She는 3인칭 단수이므 로 be동사는 was를 쓴다.

31 (A) 그는 지금 벤치에 앉아있는 상황이므로 현재진행시제「am/ is/are + V-ing」를 쓰고 주어 He는 3인칭 단수이므로 be동 사는 is를 쓴다.
(B) 현재의 상태를 나타내고 있으므로 현재시제를 쓰고 주어 he 는 3인칭 단수이므로 has를 쓴다. 동사 have가 '가지다'라 는 의미일 때는 진행형으로 쓸 수 없다.

32 (1) 지희는 공을 던지고 있는 상황이고, 현재진행시제 is ~ doing 으로 묻고 있으므로 현재진행시제 is throwing을 쓴다.
(2) Molly와 Glen은 샌드위치를 먹고 있는 상황이고, 현재진 행시제 are ~ doing으로 묻고 있으므로 현재진행시제 are eating을 쓴다.
(3) Owen은 사진을 찍고 있는 상황이고, 현재진행시제 is ~ doing으로 묻고 있으므로 현재진행시제 is taking을 쓴다.

33 ① Was → Is
③ didn't → won't[am not going to]
⑤ Are they enjoying → Did they enjoy

34 ⑤ does → did

35 ⓑ don't → didn't
ⓒ begins → began
ⓓ visited → will visit[is going to visit]

36 ⑤ win → won

37 ① has went → has gone
② have lost → has lost
③ has played → have played
⑤ have became → have become

38 ③ read → reading (현재진행시제:「am/is/are + V-ing」

39 ②: 현재진행시제
①③④⑤: 미래시제를 나타내는 be going to

CHAPTER 4
조동사

p.82

POINT 1-1　조동사의 쓰임

1	work	**2**	can	**3**	should
4	ride	**5**	be	**6**	be able to
7	will	**8**	visit	**9**	be able to
10	wake				

기출 적중문제

정답　①

해설　조동사 뒤에는 동사원형이 온다.

POINT 1-2　조동사가 있는 부정문과 의문문

1 You should not[shouldn't] go
2 He cannot[can't] speak
3 Will Alice play
4 Should we order
5 Andrew may not like
6 Will Lucas watch
7 Must we wait
8 They may not be
9 Can Linda ride

1 he can		**2** you should
3 we won't		**4** you shouldn't
5 they must		**6** they will
7 she can't		**8** you must

1 Will she wash		**2** can hold
3 O		**4** O
5 may not be		**6** O
7 Must I clean		**8** won't happen

기출 적중문제

정답　④

해설　① not will → will not[won't]
　　　② Do you can → Can you
　　　③ dancing → dance
　　　⑤ Shoulds → Should

POINT 2-1　can, could I

1 Jim is able to throw
2 I am not[I'm not] able to understand
3 Dogs are not[aren't] able to see
4 Are you able to hear
5 We were not[weren't] able to find
6 They are[They're] able to sing
7 Is Alex able to solve
8 You and I are able to fix

기출 적중문제

정답　We can win the game.

해설　능력·가능(~할 수 있다)을 나타내는 can을 쓴다.

POINT 2-2　can, could II

1 ⓑ		**2** ⓐ		**3** ⓐ		**4** ⓑ
5 ⓒ		**6** ⓐ		**7** ⓒ		**8** ⓑ
9 ⓑ		**10** ⓐ		**11** ⓒ		**12** ⓑ
13 ⓒ		**14** ⓐ				

1 You can have my cookie.
2 Could you help us?
3 You can't talk in the theater.
4 Can I take a picture here?
5 Could I ask your name?
6 Jimin and Hyesu couldn't come to the picnic.
7 Can I open this window?
8 Can tigers swim well?
9 We can arrive on time.
10 Can you hold the elevator?
11 He couldn't finish the work yesterday.
12 You cannot enter this building with a pet.

기출 적중문제

정답　①

해설　①: 허가　②③④⑤: 능력·가능

POINT 3　may

1 ⓐ		**2** ⓑ		**3** ⓐ		**4** ⓑ
5 ⓑ		**6** ⓐ		**7** ⓐ		**8** ⓑ
9 ⓑ		**10** ⓐ		**11** ⓐ		**12** ⓑ
13 ⓐ		**14** ⓑ		**15** ⓑ		**16** ⓐ

기출 적중문제

정답　May[Can] I use your computer?

해설　허가(~해도 된다)를 나타내는 May 또는 Can을 쓴다.

POINT 4-1 will, would Ⅰ

1 She will join our band.
2 Will you call me later?
3 Jihye is going to buy a necklace.
4 Would you hold the door?
5 My brother will feed our dog.

기출 적중문제

정답 ④
해설 · 미래(~할 것이다)를 나타내는 will을 쓴다.
· 요청(~해주겠니?)을 나타내는 Will을 쓴다.

POINT 4-2 will, would Ⅱ

1 I would[I'd] like to		**2** I would[I'd] like	
3 I would[I'd] like to		**4** Would you like to	
5 I would[I'd] like		**6** Would you like	
7 I would[I'd] like to		**8** Would you like	
9 I would[I'd] like		**10** Would you like to	
11 Would you like		**12** I would[I'd] like to	
13 I would[I'd] like		**14** I would[I'd] like to	

POINT 5-1 must Ⅰ

1 ⓐ	**2** ⓑ	**3** ⓒ	**4** ⓑ
5 ⓑ	**6** ⓒ	**7** ⓑ	**8** ⓐ
9 ⓒ	**10** ⓑ	**11** ⓐ	**12** ⓐ
13 ⓒ	**14** ⓐ		

1 must get	**2** must be
3 can't be	**4** must not bring
5 must be	**6** must brush
7 can't be	

1 must	**2** must	**3** must not
4 must not	**5** must	**6** must not
7 must		

기출 적중문제

정답 must not ride a bike
해설 자전거를 타면 안 된다는 표지판이므로 강한 금지(~하면 안 된다)를 나타내는 must not을 쓴다.

POINT 5-2 must Ⅱ

1 I have to wait	**2** She has to print
3 You have to sign	**4** We have to think
5 You have to be	**6** They have to finish
7 Adam has to study	**8** I have to take
9 Ms. Han has to buy	
10 You and Jack have to be	
11 Uncle John has to repair	
12 My sister and I have to clean	

1 don't have to	**2** must not
3 had to	**4** will have to
5 doesn't have to	**6** must[has to]
7 must not	**8** don't have to
9 doesn't have to	**10** must[have to]
11 will have to	**12** had to

기출 적중문제

정답 ⑤
해설 택시를 타야 하는지 묻는 말에 '우리는 늦지 않았어.'라고 대답했으므로 맥락상 택시를 탈 필요가 없다고 대답해야 한다. 따라서 불필요(~할 필요가 없다)를 나타내는 don't have to를 쓴다.

POINT 6 should, had better

1 should wear
2 should repair
3 had better return
4 had better not stay
5 should not[shouldn't] waste
6 had better change
7 should not[shouldn't] make

기출 적중문제

정답 You should come home
해설 충고·의무(~해야 한다)를 나타내는 should를 쓴다.

서술형 대비 문제

1 play	**2** must
3 cannot[can't]	**4** is
5 don't have to	**6** to visit
7 sit	**8** be
9 must not	**10** you turn
11 had better not	**12** Would you

B ⓐ Yes ⓑ can ⓒ No ⓓ can't ⓔ can ⓕ can
ⓖ cannot[can't] ⓗ can

C
1 No, I won't. 　2 No, he can't.
3 Yes, we should. 　4 Yes, she can.
5 No, you may not. 　6 Yes, it will.

D
1 must not park your car
2 must fasten our seat belts
3 must not cross the street

중간·기말고사 실전 문제

1 ① 　2 ③ 　3 ④ 　4 is → be
5 Robert can play the cello. 　6 You must not
fight with your friends. 　7 ④ 　8 (1) I
should not[shouldn't] drink more water. (2) Should I
drink more water? 　9 borrow 　10 ③
11 ④ 　12 ② 　13 ③ 　14 is able to speak
15 would like to 　16 wasn't able to 　17 They
can't be in Seoul right now. 　18 ⑤ 　19 ①
20 ⑤ 　21 ⑤ 　22 (1) must wear a helmet (2)
must not make a noise 　23 ② 　24 ⑤
25 ③ 　26 ⑤ 　27 have to, will, can 28 can
swim, cannot[can't] play the drums 　29 ①
30 ④ 　31 ③ 　32 ②, ⑤ 33 ③ 　34 (A)
You should speak (B) You shouldn't eat food
35 ① 　36 ④ 　37 ② 　38 ④ 　39 ①
40 ⑤ 　41 ③ 　42 I would like to play outside
with you. 43 You had better get some rest.

1 조동사 뒤에는 동사원형이 오고 조동사는 주어의 인칭이나 수에 따라 형태가 변하지 않는다.

2 조동사 뒤에는 동사원형이 온다.

3 ① shoulds → should
② not can → cannot[can't]
③ are → is
⑤ Do may → May

4 조동사 뒤에는 동사원형이 온다.

5 조동사 뒤에는 동사원형이 온다.

6 조동사가 있는 부정문: 「조동사 + not + 동사원형」

7 had better의 부정형: had better not

8 (1) 조동사가 있는 부정문: 「조동사 + not + 동사원형」
(2) 조동사가 있는 의문문: 「조동사 + 주어 + 동사원형 ~?」

9 조동사가 있는 의문문은 「조동사 + 주어 + 동사원형 ~?」이고 전체 문장이 'May I borrow your raincoat?'이므로 세 번째에 오

는 것은 borrow이다.

10 조동사가 있는 의문문에 대한 대답은 「Yes, 주어 + 조동사.」 또는 「No, 주어 + 조동사 + not.」이고 주어 I로 묻고 있으므로 주어 you로 대답한다.

11 has to = must (의무)

12 will = be going to (미래)

13 ③: must not '~하면 안 된다 (강한 금지)'
don't have to '~할 필요가 없다 (불필요)'

14 can = be able to (능력·가능)

15 「want to + 동사원형」=「would like to + 동사원형」

16 couldn't = wasn't able to (능력·가능)

17 강한 추측(~임에 틀림없다)을 나타내는 must의 부정형: can't

18 능력·가능(~할 수 있다)을 나타내는 can의 부정형 can't를 쓴다

19 강한 충고(~하는 것이 낫다)를 나타내는 had better를 쓴다.

20 ① don't have to → can't
② Will → Can
③ must not → must
④ shouldn't → don't have to

21 귀에 통증이 있다는 말에 '너는 그렇게 크게 음악을 들으면 안 된다.'라고 대답해야 하므로 shouldn't(~하면 안 된다)를 쓴다.

22 (1) 헬멧을 써야 한다는 표지판이므로 의무(~해야 한다)를 나타내는 must를 쓴다.
(2) 소음을 내면 안 된다는 표지판이므로 강한 금지(~하면 안 된다)를 나타내는 must not을 쓴다.

23 '나는 저 상자를 들 수 없다. 그것은 너무 무겁다.'라는 의미이므로 can't(~할 수 없다)를 쓴다.

24 '젖은 머리로 밖에 나가지 마라. 너는 감기에 걸릴지도 모른다.'는 의미이므로 may(~일지도 모른다)를 쓴다.

25 첫 번째 빈칸: '그녀는 교무실에 있음에 틀림없다.'라는 의미이므로 must(~임에 틀림없다)를 쓴다.
두 번째 빈칸: '그러면 너는 그녀를 기다려야 한다'라는 의미이므로 should(~해야 한다)를 쓴다.

26 ·'나는 주원이가 춤 대회에서 이겼다는 것을 믿을 수 없다. 그녀는 매우 행복함에 틀림없다.'라는 의미이므로 must(~임에 틀림없다)를 쓴다.
·'너는 머리를 잘라야 한다. 너의 머리는 너무 길고 지저분하다.'라는 의미이므로 must(~해야 한다)를 쓴다.

27 첫 번째 빈칸: '나의 집은 나의 학교로부터 멀기 때문에 나는 학교로 버스를 타고 가야 한다'라는 의미이므로 have to(~해야 한다)를 쓴다.
두 번째 빈칸: '나의 가족은 내일 새로운 아파트로 이사할 것이다'라는 의미이므로 will(~할 것이다)을 쓴다.
세 번째 빈칸: '나는 학교로 걸어갈 수 있다'라는 의미이므로 can(~할 수 있다)을 쓴다.

28 소진이, 예리, 민호는 수영을 할 수 있다고 했으므로 can swim 을 쓴다. 소진이와 예리는 드럼을 연주할 수 없다고 했으므로 cannot[can't] play the drums를 쓴다.

29 잔디 위에서 걸으면 안 되는 상황이므로 금지를 나타내는 must not, may not, shouldn't, can't를 쓴다. don't have to는 불필요를 나타낸다.

30 첫 번째 빈칸: '제가 당신을 도와드려도 될까요?'라는 의미이므로 Can(~해도 된다)을 쓴다.
두 번째 빈칸: '저에게 당신의 여권을 보여주시겠어요?'라는 의미이므로 Can(~해주겠니?)을 쓴다.

31 ⓑⓒⓔ: 능력·가능   ⓐ: 요청   ⓓ: 허가

32 연필을 잠시 빌려도 되는지 묻는 말에 '너는 그것을 써도 된다.'라고 대답했으므로 허가를 나타내는 의문문에 대한 긍정의 대답을 쓴다.

33 ③ No, I can't. → Yes, I can.

34 (A) 조동사 뒤에는 동사원형이 온다.
(B) 조동사가 있는 부정문: 「조동사 + not + 동사원형」

35 주어진 문장과 ①: 허가   ②③④⑤: 약한 추측

36 의무(~해야 한다)를 나타내는 must의 과거형: had to

37 ②: 강한 추측   ①③④⑤: 의무

38 can = may (허가)

39 ⓒ can → have to (프린터가 정말 필요하다고 했고 '나는 나의 보고서를 출력해야 해.'라는 의미이므로 have to(~해야 한다)를 쓴다.

40 ① has to → have to
② has to → had to
③ will must → will have to
④ has to → have to

41 ⓑ would like to → would like
ⓒ should be not → should not be
ⓓ Will she can join → Will she be able to join
ⓕ Will you giving → Will you give

42 「주어 + would like to + 동사원형」 = 「주어'd like to + 동사원형」

43 「주어 + had better + 동사원형」 = 「주어'd better + 동사원형」

CHAPTER 5
문장의 형식
p.106

POINT 1-1   1형식과 2형식

 연습문제

1 1형식	**2** 2형식	**3** 1형식	**4** 2형식
5 2형식	**6** 1형식	**7** 2형식	**8** 1형식
9 2형식	**10** 2형식	**11** 1형식	**12** 2형식
13 2형식	**14** 1형식	**15** 1형식	**16** 1형식
17 2형식	**18** 1형식		

POINT 1-2   2형식: 감각동사

연습문제 A

1 soft		**2** healthy
3 strong		**4** delicious
5 happy		**6** salty
7 wonderful		**8** sweet
9 comfortable		**10** lovely
11 hungry		

연습문제 B

1 X	**2** like	**3** like	**4** X
5 X	**6** like	**7** like	

연습문제 C

1 The roller coaster looks scary.
2 A durian smells terrible.
3 This lollipop tastes like cherries.
4 My raincoat feels wet.
5 The book sounds interesting.
6 Your hair smells like roses.
7 His plan sounded impossible.

기출 적중문제

정답 ③
해설 sweetly → sweet

POINT 2-1   3형식과 4형식

 연습문제 A

1 lunch		**2** a butterfly
3 his teacher, a gift		**4** a big house
5 her, a pencil		**6** me, some advice
7 their old car		**8** them, math
9 me, a favor		**10** some medicine
11 the kids, pasta		**12** us, his new phone

연습문제 B

1 taught us English
2 bought a sweater
3 wrote his cousin a letter

4 made them pumpkin soup

5 sent Lucas many photos

6 read her daughter a fairy tale

7 asked me my name

8 made a paper airplane

9 told me a secret

정답 The boy gave the girl flowers.

해설 4형식: 「주어 + 동사 + 간접목적어(~에게) + 직접목적어(~을)」

POINT 2-2 4형식을 3형식으로 바꾸는 법

1 for **2** to **3** for **4** to

5 to **6** for **7** to **8** of

9 for

1 lent some comic books to me

2 cooked a delicious meal for us

3 told the whole story to Nancy

4 ask a favor of you

5 read a short novel to the children

6 bought a scarf for her aunt

7 wrote a poem to his parents

8 find a good job for you

9 brought the maps to us

10 made an apple pie for her classmates

11 sent an e-mail to my manager

12 give some advice to me

정답 ①

해설 ① for   ②③④⑤ to

POINT 3 5형식

1 목적어: him, 목적격보어: Teddy

2 목적어: her room, 목적격 보어: clean

3 목적어: dishes, 목적격보어: sweet

4 목적어: our fish, 목적격 보어: Dory

5 목적어: me, 목적격 보어: angry

6 목적어: the new chair, 목적격 보어: comfortable

7 목적어: the actor, 목적격 보어: a star

8 목적어: our minds, 목적격 보어: open

9 목적어: the bakery, 목적격 보어: popular

10 목적어: the story, 목적격 보어: interesting

정답 sadly → sad

해설 목적어 Emma를 보충 설명하는 목적격 보어 자리에는 형용사 sad를 쓴다.

서술형 대비 문제

A

1 looks sick

2 smells like peaches

3 tastes sour

4 feels like a cloud

5 looks like a lion

6 sounds noisy

B

1 I sent Suzy a card.

2 Mr. Smith teaches history to us.

3 He cooked his wife a special dinner.

4 My friend gave her notes to me.

5 The clown made the kids balloon animals.

6 Beth showed her new shoes to them.

7 Ms. Miller wrote the mayor a letter.

8 I will buy the concert tickets for you.

9 The waiter brought the customers coffee.

10 Can I ask some difficult questions of you?

C

1 Kelly called me a liar.

2 Henry lent his friend money.

3 Our uncle told us a scary story.

4 The police keep the town safe.

5 The weather made the pilot nervous.

6 She will give you a chance.

7 I found the math test easy.

8 He made his son a toy car.

중간·기말고사 실전 문제

1 ①, ③ **2** ②, ⑤ **3** ② **4** ②, ⑤ **5** ④

6 ④ **7** ④ **8** ④ **9** That sounded like thunder. **10** ③ **11** difficultly → difficult

12 looked like a palace **13** looks wonderful

14 ③ **15** Jimin passed Surin the pepper.

16 like **17** to **18** ② **19** ③ **20** ⑤

21 ⑤ **22** I bought my brother a birthday present.

23 ② **24** built a tree house for us **25** my artwork to the guests **26** The concert made me sleepy. **27** ③ **28** Our teacher called Tony a genius. **29** ④

1 「감각동사 + like + 명사」

2 감각동사 뒤에는 형용사가 오므로 형용사 delicious와 salty를 쓴다.

3 ② 2형식 → 1형식 (「주어 + 동사 + 수식어구」 형태의 1형식 문장이다.)

4 ②⑤: 「감각동사 + like + 명사」

5 ⓒⓓ: 2형식 ⓐⓑⓔ: 1형식

6 ④ feel → look ('~하게 보이다'라는 의미의 look을 쓴다.)

7 ④ felt like → felt

8 「make + 직접 목적어 + for + 간접 목적어」

9 감각동사의 주격 보어 자리에 명사 thunder가 왔으므로 감각동사 뒤에 like를 쓴다.

10 첫 번째 빈칸: 감각동사 뒤에는 형용사가 오므로 형용사 perfect를 쓴다.
두 번째 빈칸: 「감각동사 + like + 명사」이므로 felt like를 쓴다.

11 감각동사 뒤에는 형용사가 오므로 형용사 difficult를 쓴다.

12 '~하게 보이다'라는 의미의 look을 쓰고 감각동사의 주격 보어 자리에 명사 a palace가 왔으므로 감각동사 뒤에 like를 쓴다.

13 '~하게 보이다'라는 의미의 look을 쓰고 감각동사의 주격 보어 자리에 형용사 wonderful을 쓴다.

14 ③ looks → looks like

15 4형식: 「주어 + 동사 + 간접목적어(~에게) + 직접목적어(~을)」

16 · 감각동사의 주격 보어 자리에 명사 garbage가 왔으므로 감각동사 뒤에 like를 쓴다.
· 감각동사의 주격 보어 자리에 명사 grapes가 왔으므로 감각동사 뒤에 like를 쓴다.

17 · 「show + 직접 목적어 + to + 간접 목적어」
· 「lend + 직접 목적어 + to + 간접 목적어」

18 빈칸 뒤에 간접목적어(her sister)와 직접목적어(an umbrella)가 있으므로 수여동사가 아닌 help는 쓸 수 없다.

19 ① of → to
② my homework the teacher → the teacher my homework
④ for Carl → Carl
⑤ to → for

20 (A) 「teach + 직접 목적어 + to + 간접 목적어」
(B) 「ask + 직접 목적어 + of + 간접 목적어」
(C) 「give + 직접 목적어 + to + 간접 목적어」

21 ⑤ for ①②③④ to

22 4형식: 「주어 + 동사 + 간접목적어(~에게) + 직접목적어(~을)」

23 ⓐ text messages us → us text messages
ⓓ to → for

ⓔ for → of

24 「build + 직접 목적어 + for + 간접 목적어」

25 「show + 직접 목적어 + to + 간접 목적어」

26 5형식: 「주어 + 동사 + 목적어 + 목적격보어」

27 ③: 4형식 주어진 문장과 ①②④⑤: 3형식

28 5형식: 「주어 + 동사 + 목적어 + 목적격보어」

29 ④: 4형식 ①②③⑤: 5형식

POINT 1 명령문

1 Take this umbrella.
2 Try your best.
3 Don't[Do not] tell a lie.
4 Keep a diary.
5 Don't[Do not] miss class again.
6 Be a good person.
7 Don't[Do not] walk on the grass.
8 Be friendly to others.
9 Don't[Do not] be afraid of bugs.
10 Bring your swimsuit.
11 Don't[Do not] be angry with him.
12 Don't[Do not] use your phone in class.

1 Be   2 Go
3 Don't[Do not] open   4 Don't[Do not] feed
5 Don't[Do not] take   6 Put

1 be   2 yell
3 O   4 Clean
5 Don't[Do not] 6 speak
7 O

기출 적중문제

정답 ①
해설 부정 명령문: 「Don't + 동사원형」

POINT 2 청유문

1 Let's buy   2 Let's have
3 Let's not take   4 Let me do
5 Let's not stay   6 Let's meet
7 Let's not be   8 Let me finish
9 Let's talk   10 Let's not listen
11 Let's see

기출 적중문제

정답 going → go
해설 긍정 청유문: 「Let's + 동사원형」

POINT 3 감탄문

1 What   2 How   3 What
4 How   5 What   6 How
7 What   8 How   9 What
10 How   11 How   12 What

1 high (the mountain is)
2 a hot day (it was)
3 close friends (they are)
4 brave (she was)
5 a good dancer (Cindy is)
6 a huge building (that is)
7 colorful (this umbrella is)
8 a hard question (it was)
9 beautiful eyes (you have)
10 well he swims

1 What a heavy backpack it is!
2 How strong the wind was!
3 What a fast train this is!
4 How hard Andy studies!
5 How clever the monkeys are!

기출 적중문제

정답 ⑤
해설 What 감탄문: 「What + (a/an) + 형용사 + 명사 + (주어 + 동사)!」

POINT 4 Yes/No 의문문

1 Yes, he does.   2 No, he doesn't.
3 No, it isn't.   4 No, she didn't.
5 Yes, they were.   6 Yes, I can.
7 No, I don't   8 Yes, we should.
9 Yes, it is.   10 No, it won't.
11 Yes, I am.

POINT 5-1 의문사 의문문

1 How does my hair look?
2 Why were you sad?
3 When will the bus arrive?
4 Who is your favorite actor?
5 Where can I find a bathroom?
6 What is David watching?
7 When do you sleep?
8 Who opened this window?
9 Why are her shoes dirty?

10 How can I buy a ticket?

11 What makes you happy?

12 Where did you get those shoes?

1 is she		**2** O	
3 O		**4** speaks	
5 does he look		**6** Who can	

정답 ④

해설 의문사가 있는 일반동사 의문문은 「의문사 + do/does/did + 주어 + 동사원형 ~?」이고 주어 John은 3인칭 단수이므로 does를 쓴다.

POINT 5-2 의문사: who

1 Who	**2** Who	**3** Whose
4 Who(m)	**5** Who(m)	**6** Whose
7 Who(m)	**8** Who	**9** Who(m)
10 Whose	**11** Who	**12** Whose
13 Who	**14** Who	**15** Who(m)

POINT 5-3 의문사: what, which

1 What	**2** Which	**3** What
4 What	**5** Which	**6** What
7 Which	**8** What	**9** Which
10 Which		

1 ⓒ	**2** ⓑ	**3** ⓐ	**4** ⓔ
5 ⓓ	**6** ⓑ	**7** ⓔ	**8** ⓓ
9 ⓐ	**10** ⓒ		

정답 ②

해설 ②: Who　①③④⑤: What

POINT 5-4 의문사: where, when, why, how

1 When	**2** How	**3** Where
4 Why	**5** How	**6** Where
7 Why	**8** Where	**9** When
10 Where	**11** How	**12** Why
13 When	**14** How	**15** Why

1 ⓓ	**2** ⓑ	**3** ⓔ	**4** ⓒ
5 ⓐ	**6** ⓑ	**7** ⓓ	**8** ⓔ
9 ⓐ	**10** ⓒ		

정답 ③

해설 첫 번째 빈칸: '내가 오늘 아침에 버스를 놓쳤기 때문이야.'라고 대답했으므로 이유를 물을 때 사용하는 Why를 쓴다.

두 번째 빈칸: 'Elm가에.'라고 대답했으므로 장소를 물을 때 사용하는 Where를 쓴다.

POINT 5-5 의문사: How + 형용사/부사

1 much	**2** long	**3** often
4 tall	**5** old	**6** many
7 far	**8** big	

정답 How

해설 · 나이를 묻는 How old를 써야 하므로 How를 쓴다.

· 방법을 묻는 How를 쓴다.

· 개수를 묻는 How many를 써야 하므로 How를 쓴다.

POINT 6 부가의문문

1 aren't		**2** does
3 do		**4** wasn't
5 will		**6** didn't
7 can		**8** shall
9 isn't		**10** will
11 weren't		**12** won't
13 shouldn't		**14** are

1 wasn't it		**2** doesn't it
3 didn't he		**4** will you
5 do I		**6** aren't they
7 can't he		**8** shall we
9 aren't you		**10** aren't I
11 isn't she		**12** aren't they
13 were we		**14** does she
15 won't they		

정답 ⑤

해설 앞 문장의 동사가 긍정을 나타내는 조동사(can)이므로 can't를 쓰고 앞 문장의 주어 Hailey에 맞는 인칭대명사 she를 쓴다.

서술형 대비 문제

A
1 Turn down the volume.
2 What a popular book (this is)!
3 How fast Thomas runs!
4 Don't[Do not] step on my foot.
5 What a rainy day (it is)!
6 Don't[Do not] be late for the movie.
7 Hang the pictures on the wall.
8 How quiet (the classroom is)!
9 Get ready for school.
10 What big gloves (these are)!
11 Don't[Do not] take pictures in the gallery.
12 How lovely (the weather is)!

B
1 Let's go　　2 isn't she
3 Let's not be　　4 shall we
5 Talk　　6 can he
7 don't they
8 Don't[Do not] touch
9 won't he　　10 were they
11 will you

C
ⓐ What　ⓑ Why　ⓒ When　ⓓ Where

D
1 Where should, meet　2 What is
3 Who(m) did, go　　4 Why does, study
5 When did, see　　6 Who broke
7 How tall is

중간·기말고사 실전 문제

1 ②, ④　　　2 ②　3 ④　4 ④
5 Don't be nervous about the test.　6 Let's
meet at the subway station.　7 ③　8 ④
9 Don't[Do not] turn　10 ①　11 ⑤
12 ②　13 (1) What a great idea (2) How amazing
14 ⑤　15 ④　16 ⑤　17 ④　18 ①
19 ③　20 ④　21 ②　22 Which
23 How old is your cat?　24 What sports do
you like?　25 ④　26 ①　27 ①　28 ③
29 ②, ③　　30 ②, ⑤　　31 aren't
they　32 will you　　33 ④　34 ⑤
35 (1) No, he doesn't. (2) He likes bananas.
36 ③, ⑤　　37 ②, ⑤　　38 Turn
off your cell phone.　39 Where did you put the key?
40 ①　41 ②　42 (1) ⓐ → don't (2) ⓑ → what
will　(3) ⓓ → exercise

1　학생들이 빨간 불에 횡단보도를 건너면 안 되는 상황이므로 'Don't cross the street.(도로를 건너지 마라.)' 또는 'Wait for the green light(초록 불을 기다려라.)'라는 말이 적절하다.

2　① Opens → Open
③ Be not → Don't[Do not] be
④ be wait → wait
⑤ late → be late

3　④: 부정명령문은 「Don't + 동사원형」의 형태이므로 be rude가 되어야 한다.

4　긍정 청유문: 「Let's + 동사원형」

5　부정 명령문: 「Don't[Do not] + 동사원형」

6　긍정 청유문: 「Let's + 동사원형」

7　③ What　①②④⑤ How

8　다시는 그것을 하지 않을 것이라고 대답했으므로 '진흙에서 다시는 놀지 마라.'라는 말이 적절하다. '~하지 마라'라는 의미의 부정 명령문은 「Don't[Do not] + 동사원형」이다.

9　좌회전하면 안 된다는 표지판이므로 '좌회전하지 마라.'라는 말이 적절하다. '~하지 마라'라는 의미의 부정 명령문은 「Don't[Do not] + 동사원형」이다.

10　① is your story → your story is

11　① How → What
② am I → I am
③ What → How
④ What → How

12　'너의 형은 그 경주를 이기지 않았니?'라고 묻는 말에 그가 일등을 했다고 했으므로 긍정의 내용으로 대답한다. 부정의문문에 대답할 때는 대답의 내용이 긍정이면 Yes로 답한다.

13　(1) What 감탄문: 「What + (a/an) + 형용사 + 명사 + (주어 동사)!」
(2) How 감탄문: 「How + 형용사 + (주어 + 동사)!」

14　의문사가 있는 일반동사 의문문: 「의문사 + do/does/did + 주어 + 동사원형 ~?」

15　첫 번째 빈칸: '세 개를 가지고 있어.'라고 대답했으므로 개수를 물을 때 사용하는 How many를 쓴다.
두 번째 빈칸: '길 건너 시장에서.'라고 대답했으므로 장소를 물을 때 사용하는 Where를 쓴다.

16　⑤ When → Who (사람에 대해 물을 때 쓰는 Who를 쓴다.)

17　①: Whom(누구를)으로 묻고 있으므로 사람에 해당되는 것으로 대답한다.
②: Why(왜)로 묻고 있으므로 이유에 해당되는 것으로 대답한다.
③: What(무엇)으로 묻고 있으므로 '무엇'에 해당되는 것으로 답한다.
⑤: What time(몇 시)으로 묻고 있으므로 시간에 해당되는 것으로 대답한다.

18　① Who　②③④⑤ What

19 시간을 묻는 What time은 의문사 When으로 바꿔 쓸 수 있다.

20 첫 번째 빈칸: '*Scary Mysteries*를 보고 있어.'라고 대답했으므로 '무엇'이라는 의미의 What을 쓴다.
두 번째 빈칸: '외계 생명체와 유령에 관한 것이야.'라고 대답했으므로 '무엇'이라는 의미의 What을 쓴다.

21 Who(누구)로 묻고 있으므로 사람에 해당되는 것으로 대답한다.

22 정해진 범위 안에서의 선택을 묻고 있으므로 Which(어느 것)를 쓴다.

23 나이에 대해 묻고 있으므로 How old를 쓴다.

24 What(무슨)은 형용사처럼 쓰여 명사 앞에서 명사를 꾸밀 수 있다.

25 ① is he → isn't he
② doesn't Anna → doesn't she
③ did she → didn't she
⑤ did I → did you

26 첫 번째 빈칸: '주말마다.'라고 대답했으므로 빈도를 물을 때 쓰는 How often을 쓴다.
두 번째 빈칸: '단지 2킬로미터만 떨어져 있어.'라고 대답했으므로 거리를 물을 때 쓰는 How far를 쓴다.

27 앞 문장의 동사가 긍정을 나타내는 be동사(is)이므로 isn't를 쓰고 앞 문장의 주어 Mr. Baker에 맞는 인칭대명사 he를 쓴다.

28 ③ shall we → will we

29 부가의문문 doesn't she를 사용했으므로 앞 문장의 동사는 긍정을 나타내는 일반동사 3인칭 단수형을 쓴다.

30 ① goes Michael → Michael go
③ Let → Let's
④ drinks → drink

31 앞 문장의 동사가 긍정을 나타내는 be동사(are)이므로 aren't를 쓰고 앞 문장의 주어 Jane and Sue에 맞는 인칭대명사 they를 쓴다.

32 명령문의 부가의문문: 「명령문, will you?」

33 ⓐ do he wears → does he wear
ⓒ Monica is → is Monica
ⓕ you were → were you

34 ⑤: What(무엇)으로 묻고 있으므로 '무엇'에 해당되는 것으로 대답한다.

35 (1) 일반동사의 의문문으로 질문하고 있고 민호는 사과를 좋아하지 않는다고 했으므로 부정의 내용으로 대답한다. 부정의문문에 대답할 때는 대답의 내용이 부정이면 No로 답한다.
(2) Which(어느 것)로 묻고 있으므로 '어느 것'에 해당되는 것으로 대답한다.

36 ① What → How
② Not → Don't[Do not]
④ How → What

37 ① What kind of animal it is → What kind of animal is it

③ What it eats → What does it eat
④ is it → isn't it

38 긍정 명령문은 동사원형을 문장 맨 앞에 쓰는 형태이다.

39 의문사가 있는 일반동사 의문문: 「의문사 + do/does/did + 주어 + 동사원형 ~?」

40 ⓐ does it is → is it
ⓑ not do → don't[do not]
ⓒ you hid → did you hide

41 (A) '이것은 누구의 지갑이니?'라는 의미이므로 Whose(누구의)를 쓴다.
(B) '너는 누구를 찾고 있니?'라는 의미이므로 Whom(누구를)을 쓴다.
(C) '누가 그 창문을 깼니?'라는 의미이므로 Who(누구)를 쓴다.

42 (1) 앞 문장의 동사가 긍정을 나타내는 일반동사(want)이므로 don't를 쓴다.
(2) 의문사가 있는 조동사 의문문: 「의문사 + 조동사 + 주어 ~?」
(3) 긍정 명령문은 동사원형을 문장 맨 앞에 쓰는 형태이다.

CHAPTER 7
to부정사

p.148

POINT 1 to부정사의 형태와 용법

연습문제 A
1 to move 2 to hear 3 to read
4 to build 5 to visit 6 to play

연습문제 B
1 ⓐ   2 ⓑ   3 ⓐ   4 ⓑ
5 ⓐ

POINT 2-1 명사적 용법

연습문제 A
1 to study 2 to become 3 to grow
4 To play 5 to design

연습문제 B
1 It is difficult to be an honest person.
2 It is very interesting to collect stamps.
3 It is my plan to learn many languages.
4 It is impossible to keep my room clean.
5 It is not[isn't] easy to wake up early on Sundays.
6 It is helpful to read a lot of books.
7 It is not[isn't] good for your eyes to watch too much TV.

연습문제 C
1 ⓐ   2 ⓑ   3 ⓐ   4 ⓒ
5 ⓑ   6 ⓒ   7 ⓑ   8 ⓒ
9 ⓐ   10 ⓐ

기출 적중문제
정답 ③, ④
해설 주어진 문장과 ③④: 목적어
①⑤: 주어   ②: 보어

POINT 2-2 명사적 용법: to부정사를 목적어로 쓰는 동사

연습문제
1 expect to win 2 began to cry
3 likes to listen 4 decided to sell
5 wants to look 6 plans to leave
7 hopes to be

기출 적중문제
정답 ②
해설 walking → to walk

POINT 2-3 명사적 용법: 의문사 + to부정사

연습문제
1 what to eat 2 how to make
3 when to start 4 what to wear
5 where to buy 6 where to find
7 when to speak

기출 적중문제
정답 how
해설 「how + to부정사」 '어떻게 ~할지'

POINT 3 형용사적 용법

연습문제
1 some tea to drink
2 something to eat
3 a friend to trust
4 time to think
5 someone to look
6 a perfect place to meet
7 lots of scary stories to tell

기출 적중문제
정답 buy
해설 to부정사가 '수영복을 살 약간의 돈'이라는 의미로 명사(money)를 꾸미는 형용사적 용법으로 쓰이고 전체 문장이 'She has some money to buy a swimsuit.'이므로 여섯 번째에 오는 것은 buy이다.

POINT 4 부사적 용법

연습문제 A
1 to[in order to] see his parents
2 happy to receive
3 to[in order to] catch the bus
4 to[in order to] buy milk
5 difficult to solve
6 sad to hear
7 grew up to be
8 fun to visit
9 to[in order to] avoid people
10 disappointed to lose

연습문제 B
1 ⓒ   2 ⓐ   3 ⓐ   4 ⓑ
5 ⓐ   6 ⓑ   7 ⓒ   8 ⓒ
9 ⓒ   10 ⓑ   11 ⓐ   12 ⓒ
13 ⓐ   14 ⓑ   15 ⓒ

기출 적중문제
정답 ②
해설 주어진 문장과 ②: 부사적 용법
①③④: 명사적 용법   ⑤: 형용사적 용법

서술형 대비 문제

(A)
1 read	2 O	3 make
4 is	5 O	6 O
7 to build	8 is	9 to buy

(B)
1 It is lucky to find a four-leaf clover.
2 Vicky decided to make cookies.
3 My hobby is to play the harp.
4 We had a plan to go to the festival.
5 The lecture is hard to understand.
6 He will take an exam to become a lawyer.
7 She bought yellow paint to use on the wall.
8 I went outside to enjoy the sunshine.

(C)
1 love to play computer games
2 want to travel to Germany
3 need to walk my dog
4 hope to be an astronaut
5 would like to have a cup of coffee

(D)
1 to ask me a question
2 to see her favorite movie star
3 to leave his hometown
4 to do the homework together
5 to send a package to her grandparents

중간·기말고사 실전 문제

1 ④ 2 ④ 3 ③ 4 is dangerous to ride a bike at night 5 ① 6 to learn 7 It, to finish my homework 8 in order to make 9 drinking → to drink 10 how to use 11 ① 12 ④ 13 ③ 14 bought butter to make a cake 15 I was surprised to see Bill Gates. 16 ② 17 ⑤ 18 ⑤ 19 ① 20 ④ 21 ③ 22 ④ 23 ④ 24 ④ 25 Use a knife to spread 26 ④ 27 I was happy to win the competition. 28 ②

1 hope는 to부정사를 목적어로 쓰는 동사이므로 to buy를 쓴다.

2 ① Drink → To drink
② taught → teach
③ are → is
⑤ saves → to save

3 첫 번째 빈칸: plan은 to부정사를 목적어로 쓰는 동사이므로 to travel을 쓴다.
두 번째 빈칸: '너는 어디를 방문할지 이미 결정했니?'라는 의미이

므로 「where + to부정사」(어디를 ~할지)를 쓴다.

4 to부정사가 주어로 쓰일 때 주어 자리에 가주어 it을 쓰고 진주어 to부정사(구)를 뒤로 보낸다.

5 ①: 전치사 to   ②③④⑤: to부정사의 to

6 start는 to부정사를 목적어로 쓰는 동사이므로 to learn을 쓴다.

7 to부정사가 주어로 쓰일 때 주어 자리에 가주어 it을 쓰고 진주어 to부정사(구)를 뒤로 보낸다.

8 목적을 나타내는 to부정사의 to는 in order to로 바꿔 쓸 수 있다.

9 want는 to부정사를 목적어로 쓰는 동사이므로 to drink를 쓴다.

10 '어떻게 ~할지'라는 의미의 「how + to부정사」를 쓴다.

11 두 번째 문장은 첫 번째 문장의 명사 cookies에 대한 부연 설명이므로 명사를 뒤에서 꾸밀 수 있는 형용사적 용법의 to부정사를 쓴다.

12 ④: 명사적 용법   ①②③⑤: 형용사적 용법

13 ③ winning → win

14 '만들기 위해'라는 의미로 목적을 나타내는 부사적 용법의 to부정사를 쓴다.

15 두 번째 문장은 첫 번째 문장의 감정을 나타내는 형용사 surprised에 대한 원인이므로 감정의 원인을 나타내는 부사적 용법의 to부정사를 쓴다.

16 보기에 '무섭다'라는 의미로 형용사를 수식하는 부사적 용법의 to부정사를 쓰고 전체 문장이 'The movie is scary to watch.'이므로 다섯 번째에 오는 것은 to이다.

17 ⓑ borrowing → borrow
ⓒ falls → fall

18 주어진 문장과 ⑤: 명사적 용법(주어)
①: 부사적 용법(형용사 수식)   ②: 형용사적 용법
③④: 부사적 용법(목적)

19 주어진 문장과 ①: 부사적 용법(목적)
②: 전치사 to   ③: 명사적 용법(보어)
④: 명사적 용법(목적어)   ⑤: 명사적 용법(주어)

20 ④: 형용사적 용법   ①②③⑤: 부사적 용법

21 '(…해서 결국) ~하다'라는 의미로 결과를 나타내는 to부정사이므로 '그녀의 딸은 자라서 선생님이 되었다.'라고 해석한다.

22 '~하기 위해'라는 의미로 목적을 나타내는 to부정사이므로 'Bill은 쉬기 위해 클래식 음악을 듣는다.'라고 해석한다.

23 주어진 문장과 ④: 주어
①②: 목적어
③⑤: 보어

24 '땅콩버터 샌드위치를 어떻게 만드는지'라는 의미이므로 「how + to부정사」(어떻게 ~할지)를 쓴다.

25 '바르기 위해'라는 의미로 목적을 나타내는 부사적 용법의 to부정사를 쓴다.

26 밑줄 친 ⓐ와 ④: 명사적 용법(보어)

① : 부사적 용법(형용사 수식)　　② : 부사적 용법(목적)

③ : 형용사적 용법　　⑤ : 부사적 용법(감정의 원인)

27 '이겨서 기뻤다'라는 의미로 감정의 원인을 나타내는 부사적 용법의 to부정사를 쓴다.

28 ⓐⓒⓕ : 부사적 용법(목적)

ⓑ : 명사적 용법(보어)　　ⓓ : 명사적 용법(주어)

ⓔ : 형용사적 용법

CHAPTER 8
동명사

p.164

POINT 1 동명사의 형태와 쓰임

연습문제 **A**

1 collecting		**2** Planning	
3 exercising		**4** playing	
5 Sitting		**6** spending	

연습문제 **B**

1 ⓓ	**2** ⓒ	**3** ⓑ	**4** ⓑ
5 ⓒ	**6** ⓓ	**7** ⓐ	**8** ⓐ

POINT 2-1 동명사를 목적어로 쓰는 동사

연습문제

1 practices dancing	**2** enjoys traveling
3 kept barking	**4** finish writing
5 mind standing	**6** recommend ordering
7 avoid eating	

기출 적중문제

정답　④

해설　동명사 playing이 목적어이므로 to부정사를 목적어로 쓰는 동사 want는 쓸 수 없다.

POINT 2-2 동명사와 to부정사를 모두 목적어로 쓰는 동사

연습문제 **A**

1 hates driving[to drive]

2 begin saving[to save]

3 like listening[to listen]

4 continue improving[to improve]

연습문제 **B**

1 cycling, to cycle	**2** falling, to fall
3 smoking	**4** to ask
5 going	**6** watching, to watch
7 hiking	
8 exercising, to exercise	
9 playing, to play	**10** to go
11 waiting	**12** doing, to do

연습문제 **C**

1 closing the window	**2** crying[to cry] loudly
3 watching TV	**4** to buy a new laptop
5 eating your salad	**6** to clean the kitchen

정답 likes writing, likes to write

해설 like는 동명사와 to부정사를 모두 목적어로 쓰는 동사이므로 writing과 to write를 쓴다.

POINT 3 동명사 vs. 진행형

1 ⓐ **2** ⓑ **3** ⓐ **4** ⓐ
5 ⓑ **6** ⓐ **7** ⓐ **8** ⓑ
9 ⓑ

정답 ④

해설 ④: 동명사   ①②③⑤: 진행형의 V-ing

POINT 4 동명사 관용 표현

1 go skiing
2 are good at swimming
3 look forward to meeting
4 is afraid of sleeping
5 How[What] about ordering
6 is busy fixing
7 Thank you for answering
8 spend a lot of time eating

정답 use → using

해설 「be good at + V-ing」 '~하는 것을 잘하다'

서술형 대비 문제

Ⓐ
1 Running[To run]   **2** O
3 O
4 designing[to design] **5** painting
6 O   **7** is
8 opening   **9** waking[to wake]
10 canceling

Ⓑ
1 skating
2 listening[to listen] to jazz music
3 to have dinner with Ken
4 studying[to study] Chinese
5 playing the violin
6 closing the door
7 to join the band

Ⓒ
1 ⓐ plan to do ⓑ How about going
   ⓒ like watching[to watch]
2 ⓐ recommend going ⓑ want to come
   ⓒ need to buy ⓓ enjoy riding

중간·기말고사 실전 문제

1 ②   **2** ④   **3** ④   **4** ⑤   **5** (1) to
hike → hiking (2) spend → spending[to spend]
6 ⑤   **7** ③   **8** ②   **9** ④
10 ⓐ building ⓑ taking ⓒ climbing[to climb]
11 ⑤   **12** ③   **13** I am looking forward to
reading it. **14** ③   **15** ③   **16** (1) ⓑ → is (2) ⓒ
→ having (3) ⓔ → saving   **17** She spends two
hours cooking   **18** is good at making funny
videos   **19** ④   **20** ②, ⑤ **21** ②   **22** (1) to
go → going (2) Play → Playing[To play]   **23** ②
24 ⑤   **25** (A) Thank you for inviting (B) I enjoyed
eating

1 동명사 painting이 목적어이므로 to부정사를 목적어로 쓰는 동사 plan은 쓸 수 없다.

2 동명사 singing이 목적어이므로 to부정사를 목적어로 쓰는 동사 want는 쓸 수 없다.

3 ① to watch → watching
   ② to open → opening
   ③ diving → to dive
   ⑤ to make → making

4 ⑤: 진행형의 V-ing   주어진 문장과 ①②③④: 동명사

5 (1) enjoy는 동명사를 목적어로 쓰는 동사이므로 hiking을 쓴다.
   (2) love는 동명사와 to부정사를 모두 목적어로 쓰는 동사이므로 spending이나 to spend를 쓴다.

6 ⑤: 동명사   ①②③④: 진행형의 V-ing

7 ③ cries → crying

8 · mind는 동명사를 목적어로 쓰는 동사이므로 feeding을 쓴다.
   · 보어 자리이므로 명사 역할을 하는 동명사 getting을 쓴다.

9 · continue는 동명사와 to부정사를 모두 목적어로 쓰는 동사이므로 calling이나 to call을 쓴다.
   · mind는 동명사를 목적어로 쓰는 동사이므로 sitting을 쓴다.

10 ⓐ finish는 동명사를 목적어로 쓰는 동사이므로 building을 쓴다.
   ⓑ enjoy는 동명사를 목적어로 쓰는 동사이므로 taking을 쓴다.
   ⓒ love는 동명사와 to부정사를 모두 목적어로 쓰는 동사이므로 climbing이나 to climb을 쓴다.

11 ⑤ to rain → raining

12 (A) enjoy는 동명사를 목적어로 쓰는 동사이므로 swimming을 쓴다.
(B) give up은 동명사를 목적어로 쓰는 동사이므로 reading을 쓴다.
(C) want는 to부정사를 목적어로 쓰는 동사이므로 to go를 쓴다.

13 「look forward to + V-ing」 '~하는 것을 기대하다'

14 (A) 전치사(about)의 목적어 자리이므로 동명사 flying을 쓴다.
(B) keep은 동명사를 목적어로 쓰는 동사이므로 working을 쓴다.
(C) recommend는 동명사를 목적어로 쓰는 동사이므로 watching을 쓴다.

15 ③: 진행형의 V-ing   ①②④⑤: 동명사

16 (1) 주어로 쓰인 동명사는 항상 단수 취급하므로 is를 쓴다.
(2) enjoy는 동명사를 목적어로 쓰는 동사이므로 having을 쓴다.
(3) keep은 동명사를 목적어로 쓰는 동사이므로 saving을 쓴다.

17 「spend + 시간 + V-ing」 '~하는 데 시간을 쓰다'

18 「be good at + V-ing」 '~하는 것을 잘하다'

19 ① to write → writing
② find → finding[to find]
③ work → working[to work]
⑤ To doing → Doing[To do]

20 like는 동명사와 to부정사를 모두 목적어로 쓰는 동사이므로 to eat과 eating을 쓴다.

21 ⓒ to move → moving
ⓓ Take → Taking[To take]

22 (1) 「How about + V-ing?」 '~하는 게 어때?'
(2) 주어 자리이므로 명사 역할을 하는 동명사 Playing이나 to부정사 To play를 쓴다.

23 ② to learning → learning[to learn]

24 「be busy + V-ing」 '~하느라 바쁘다'

25 (A) 「thank … for + V-ing」 '~한 것에 대해 …에게 감사해하다'
(B) enjoy는 동명사를 목적어로 쓰는 동사이므로 eating을 쓴다.

CHAPTER 9
명사와 관사
p.178

POINT 1 셀 수 있는 명사와 셀 수 없는 명사

연습문제 A

1	O	**2**	X	**3**	X	**4**	O
5	O	**6**	X	**7**	X	**8**	O
9	X	**10**	O	**11**	O	**12**	X
13	O	**14**	X	**15**	O	**16**	O
17	X	**18**	O	**19**	O	**20**	X
21	X	**22**	X	**23**	X	**24**	O
25	X	**26**	X	**27**	O	**28**	X
29	X	**30**	O				

연습문제 B

1	coffee	**2**	Bananas	**3**	Minho
4	sugar	**5**	friends	**6**	flowers
7	a book	**8**	Honesty	**9**	furniture
10	a dollar	**11**	Vietnam	**12**	happiness

기출 적중문제

정답 ④
해설 an advice → advice

POINT 2-1 셀 수 있는 명사의 복수형: 규칙 변화

연습문제 A

1	dishes	**2**	keys	**3**	cities
4	cookies	**5**	tomatoes	**6**	leaves
7	butterflies	**8**	photos	**9**	roofs
10	cups	**11**	babies	**12**	knives
13	shirts	**14**	boxes	**15**	buses
16	diaries	**17**	wives	**18**	wolves
19	stories	**20**	radios	**21**	games
22	churches	**23**	stars	**24**	potatoes
25	addresses	**26**	dolls	**27**	legs
28	videos	**29**	benches	**30**	foxes
31	pianos	**32**	books	**33**	bottles
34	peaches	**35**	holidays	**36**	glasses
37	lives	**38**	ladies	**39**	cliffs
40	classes	**41**	watches	**42**	loaves
43	boats	**44**	countries	**45**	trees
46	shelves	**47**	brushes	**48**	questions
49	parties	**50**	dictionaries		

연습문제 B

1	potatoes	**2**	book	**3**	stories
4	Leaves	**5**	knives	**6**	roofs
7	countries	**8**	sofa		

정답 ⑤

해설 sandwich – sandwiches

POINT 2-2 셀 수 있는 명사의 복수형: 불규칙 변화

연습문제 A

1 men	**2** mice	**3** sheep
4 oxen	**5** fish	**6** feet
7 teeth	**8** deer	**9** women
10 children	**11** geese	**12** salmon

연습문제 B

1 women	**2** teeth	**3** fish
4 deer	**5** feet	**6** children
7 men	**8** sheep	

연습문제 C

1 man	**2** mice	**3** children
4 Leaves	**5** deer	**6** dog
7 women	**8** babies	**9** feet
10 geese		

정답 oxes → oxen

해설 ox(황소)의 복수형은 oxen이다.

POINT 3 셀 수 없는 명사의 수량 표현

연습문제 A

1 bottles of water	**2** glasses of juice
3 cups of coffee	**4** pieces of furniture
5 cans of soda	**6** bowls of rice
7 slices of ham	**8** loaves of bread

연습문제 B

1 glass	**2** slices	**3** cup
4 bottles	**5** bowls	**6** pieces
7 cans	**8** loaves	

연습문제 C

1 three cups of tea
2 eight glasses of water
3 a piece[slice] of cheese
4 five loaves of bread
5 six bottles of ink
6 four cans of coke
7 a bowl of cereal
8 three slices of ham

정답 three glasses of juice

해설 셀 수 없는 명사 juice는 단위명사 glass로 수량을 나타내며 three는 복수를 나타내므로 glass의 복수형 glasses를 쓴다.

POINT 4 명사 관련 표현

연습문제 A

1 gloves	**2** six-year-old	**3** pairs
4 ten-page	**5** two-month	**6** socks
7 glasses	**8** twelve-story	

연습문제 B

1 a pair of scissors	**2** five-year-old
3 two pairs of gloves	**4** four-leaf
5 three-story	**6** Four pairs of socks

연습문제 C

1 Merry	**2** Mr. Parker
3 a great writer	**4** a student in my class
5 the football players	

정답 ④

해설 ① four pair of shoes → four pairs of shoes
② two-years-old → two-year-old
③ three bottles of milks → three bottles of milk
⑤ a pair of pant → a pair of pants

POINT 5 There + be동사

연습문제 A

1 is	**2** are	**3** Is, isn't
4 is	**5** Is, is	**6** is
7 wasn't	**8** Are, are	**9** weren't
10 wasn't	**11** Were, weren't	
12 are		

연습문제 B

1 Yes, there is.	**2** No, there aren't.
3 No, there isn't.	**4** Yes, there are.

연습문제 C

1 There are three pillows
2 There weren't many children
3 Is there much milk
4 There were two cups
5 There isn't any flour
6 Are there many students

정답 ④

해설 ④ is[was] ①②③⑤ are[were]

POINT 6-1 부정관사 a(n)의 쓰임

연습문제 A

1 an	**2** a	**3** a	**4** an
5 a	**6** a	**7** a	**8** an
9 an	**10** an	**11** a	**12** a
13 an	**14** an	**15** a	**16** an

17 an	**18** a	**19** an	**20** an

연습 문제 **B**	**1** ⓐ	**2** ⓑ	**3** ⓒ	**4** ⓑ
	5 ⓐ	**6** ⓒ	**7** ⓑ	

연습 문제 **C**	**1** an	**2** a	**3** X	**4** a
	5 X	**6** a	**7** X	**8** an
	9 X	**10** a		

기출 적중문제

정답 ①

해설 · 빈칸 뒤 단어의 첫소리가 모음으로 발음되므로 an을 쓴다.
· 빈칸 뒤 단어의 첫소리가 자음으로 발음되므로 a를 쓴다.

POINT 6-2 정관사 the의 쓰임

연습 문제	**1** the	**2** the	**3** The	**4** the
	5 a	**6** the	**7** the	**8** The
	9 A	**10** the		

기출 적중문제

정답 a → the

해설 악기 이름(harp) 앞에는 정관사 the를 쓴다.

POINT 6-3 관사를 쓰지 않는 경우

연습 문제	**1** X	**2** X	**3** a	**4** the
	5 X	**6** X	**7** the	**8** X

기출 적중문제

정답 ②

해설 by the train → by train

서술형 대비 문제

ⓐ
1 salt	**2** knives
3 teeth	**4** oxen
5 sixteen-year-old	**6** O
7 happiness	**8** O
9 bowls of salad	**10** three-week
11 slices of pizza	**12** photos
13 a pair of gloves	**14** O
15 pairs of sneakers	

ⓑ ⓐ A loaf of ⓑ Two pairs of ⓒ Two bottles of
   ⓓ Three cans of

ⓒ **1** There are five children

2 There is a slide
3 There are three cookies
4 There are two orange fish
5 There is a funny clown
6 There are four books

ⓓ **1** ⓐ X ⓑ the ⓒ X ⓓ the ⓔ the
2 ⓐ the ⓑ X ⓒ X ⓓ a ⓔ X

중간·기말고사 실전 문제

1 ④	**2** ③	**3** ⑤	**4** ③	**5** ②
6 ③	**7** ②	**8** were, was		**9** ②

10 ④ **11** ⑤ **12** ⓐ sheep ⓑ foxes ⓒ men
13 ③, ④ **14** ② **15** There are five tomatoes
16 ② **17** five-stories → five-story **18** a →
the **19** ⑤ **20** ⓐ knives ⓑ potatoes
ⓒ cookies **21** (1) there isn't (2) there are **22** (1) are
(2) is not[isn't] **23** three glasses of water
24 ⑤ **25** ⑤ **26** Yes, there are. **27** ④
28 ③ **29** There are two computers **30** There
isn't a parking lot **31** ③ **32** ② **33** ③
34 ③ **35** ② **36** the, a **37** ⑤
38 (1) woman → women (2) child → children
39 ⑤ **40** the **41** ③ **42** ② **43** ①

1 ④: house는 보통명사, kindness는 추상명사이다.
  ①: 보통명사 ②: 추상명사 ③: 집합명사 ⑤: 물질명사

2 ③: cookie는 셀 수 있는 명사이므로 a와 함께 쓸 수 있다.

3 ⑤ leaf - leaves

4 ③ ox - oxen

5 빈칸 앞에 a가 있으므로 셀 수 있는 명사 중 첫소리가 자음인 단어
girl, book, building을 쓴다.

6 ① floweres → flowers
  ② photoes → photos
  ④ tomatos → tomatoes
  ⑤ sandwichs → sandwiches

7 ① a fresh air → fresh air
  ③ tree → trees
  ④ Five student → Five students
  ⑤ an advice → advice

8 첫 번째 빈칸: 「There + be동사」는 뒤따라오는 명사에 be동사
를 수일치시키고 복수명사 clowns가 있으므로 be동사는 were
를 쓴다.
  두 번째 빈칸: 「There + be동사」는 뒤따라오는 명사에 be동사
를 수일치시키고 단수명사 singer가 있으므로 be동사는 was

를 쓴다.

9 · 셀 수 없는 명사(Honesty)는 a(n)과 함께 쓸 수 없고 복수형으로도 쓸 수 없으므로 Honesty를 쓴다.
· 셀 수 있는 명사(boy) 뒤에 단수동사 is가 쓰였으므로 A boy를 쓴다.

10 · a can of와 함께 쓰이는 명사는 paint와 soda이다.
· a pair of와 함께 쓰이는 명사는 한 쌍이 짝을 이루는 명사인 pants, scissors, gloves이다.

11 · 한 쌍이 짝을 이루는 명사는 항상 복수형으로 쓰므로 sunglasses를 쓴다.
· 「숫자 + 단위명사」의 단위명사는 항상 단수형으로 쓰므로 three-day를 쓴다.

12 ⓐ 네 마리의 양이 언덕 위에 있는 상황이므로 sheep의 복수형 sheep을 쓴다.
ⓑ 두 마리의 여우가 잔디 위에 누워있는 상황이므로 fox의 복수형 foxes를 쓴다.
ⓒ 세 명의 남자가 소들에게 먹이를 주고 있는 상황이므로 man의 복수형 men을 쓴다.

13 ① deers → deer
② foots → feet
⑤ tootches → teeth

14 (A) Four는 복수를 나타내므로 bottle의 복수형 bottles를 쓴다.
(B) a는 셀 수 있는 명사의 단수형 앞에 쓰이므로 bowl을 쓴다.
(C) three는 복수를 나타내므로 piece의 복수형 pieces를 쓴다.

15 '~이 있다'라는 의미의 「There + be동사」를 쓰고 five는 복수를 나타내므로 tomato의 복수형 tomatoes를 쓴다.

16 ⓑ pianoes → pianos
ⓒ keyes → keys
ⓓ diaryes → diaries

17 「숫자 + 단위명사」의 단위명사는 항상 단수형으로 쓰므로 five-story를 쓴다.

18 악기 이름(guitar) 앞에는 정관사 the를 쓴다.

19 「There + are」 뒤에는 셀 수 있는 명사의 복수형을 쓰므로 셀 수 없는 명사 ink는 쓸 수 없다.

20 ⓐ two는 복수를 나타내므로 knife의 복수형 knives를 쓴다.
ⓑ three는 복수를 나타내므로 potato의 복수형 potatoes를 쓴다.
ⓒ ten은 복수를 나타내므로 cookie의 복수형 cookies를 쓴다.

21 (1) 「There + be동사」의 의문문에 대한 부정의 대답: 「No, there + be동사 + not.」
(2) 「There + be동사」의 의문문에 대한 긍정의 대답: 「Yes, there + be동사.」

22 (1) '~이 있다'라는 의미의 「There + be동사」를 쓰고 복수명사 bathrooms가 있으므로 be동사는 are를 쓴다.
(2) '~이 없다'라는 의미의 「There + be동사 + not」을 쓰고 셀

수 없는 명사 oil이 있으므로 be동사는 is not[isn't]를 쓴다.

23 셀 수 없는 명사 water는 단위명사 glass로 수량을 나타내며 three는 복수를 나타내므로 glass의 복수형 glasses를 쓴다.

24 ⑤ Are → Is

25 '~이 있다'라는 의미의 「There + be동사」를 쓰고 '세 조각의 피자'라는 의미의 three slices of pizza에 복수명사 slices가 있으므로 be동사는 are를 쓴다.

26 「There + be동사」의 의문문에 대한 대답은 「Yes, there + be동사.」 또는 「No, there + be동사 + not.」이고 나무에 다람쥐들이 있는 상황이므로 Yes, there are.를 쓴다.

27 ① piece → pieces
② rices → rice
③ glass of milks → glasses of milk
⑤ loaves → loaf

28 ③: '거기에, 그곳에' ①②④⑤: '~이 있다'

29 '나의 방 안에 두 대의 컴퓨터가 있다.'라는 의미이므로 「There + be동사」(~이 있다)를 쓰고 복수명사 computers가 있으므로 be동사는 are를 쓴다.

30 '이 건물에 주차장이 없다.'라는 의미이므로 「There + be동사 + not」(~이 없다)을 쓰고 단수명사 parking lot이 있으므로 be동사는 isn't를 쓴다.

31 ③: 새장 안에 새가 없는 상황이므로 '새장 안에 세 마리의 새가 있다.'는 적절하지 않다.

32 ② an ①③④⑤ a

33 ③ are[were] ①②④⑤ is[was]

34 · a: meeting/month/child/man
· an: egg/English teacher

35 ②: 식사 이름(breakfast) 앞에는 관사를 쓰지 않는다.

36 · 서수(first) 앞에는 정관사 the를 쓴다.
· '~마다'를 나타낼 때는 부정관사 a(n)을 쓰고 뒤따라오는 단어의 첫소리가 자음이므로 a를 쓴다.

37 ⑤ the church → church (장소(church)가 본래의 목적(예배)으로 쓰였으므로 관사를 쓰지 않는다.)

38 (1) Two는 복수를 나타내므로 woman의 복수형 women을 쓴다.
(2) three는 복수를 나타내므로 child의 복수형 children을 쓴다.

39 ⑤: '하나의' 주어진 문장과 ①②③④: '~마다'

40 · 서로 알고 있는 것을 말할 때는 정관사 the를 쓴다.
· only 앞에는 정관사 the를 쓴다.

41 ③ cheeses → cheese

42 ② is → are

43 ① a tennis → tennis

CHAPTER 10
대명사

p.204

POINT 1 인칭대명사

연습문제 A

1	It	2	them	3	Her	4	We
5	His	6	her	7	They	8	You
9	Their	10	its	11	us		

연습문제 B

1 ① My ② mine
2 ① yours ② your
3 ① His ② his
4 ① ours ② Our
5 ① their ② theirs

기출 적중문제

정답 ④
해설 Minsu는 3인칭 단수이고 빈칸 뒤에 소유의 대상이 되는 명사 favorite subject가 왔으므로 소유격 인칭대명사 His를 쓴다.

POINT 2 재귀대명사

연습문제 A

1	herself	2	yourself	3	myself
4	himself	5	herself	6	themselves
7	herself	8	ourselves	9	itself
10	themselves				

연습문제 B

1	X	2	O	3	X	4	O
5	O	6	X	7	O	8	X
9	O	10	X	11	X	12	X

연습문제 C

1	myself	2	herself	3	himself
4	us	5	herself	6	yourself
7	himself	8	ourselves	9	yourself
10	them				

기출 적중문제

정답 myself
해설 '나 자신'이라는 의미의 재귀대명사 myself를 쓴다.

POINT 3 지시대명사

연습문제 A

1	That	2	that
3	these	4	these
5	this, it isn't	6	This
7	those, they are	8	these
9	that	10	This
11	these, they aren't	12	those

연습문제 B

1	ⓐ	2	ⓑ	3	ⓐ	4	ⓑ
5	ⓐ	6	ⓐ	7	ⓑ	8	ⓐ
9	ⓑ	10	ⓑ				

연습문제 C

1	That rabbit	2	this ring
3	Those firefighters	4	these photos
5	those apples	6	this song

기출 적중문제

정답 ①, ③, ④
해설 주어진 문장과 ①③④: 지시대명사 ②⑤: 지시형용사

POINT 4 비인칭 주어 it

연습문제 A

1	ⓐ	2	ⓑ	3	ⓐ	4	ⓐ
5	ⓑ	6	ⓐ	7	ⓑ	8	ⓐ
9	ⓐ	10	ⓑ	11	ⓑ	12	ⓐ
13	ⓑ	14	ⓑ				

연습문제 B

1	ⓕ	2	ⓒ	3	ⓓ	4	ⓔ
5	ⓐ	6	ⓑ				

연습문제 C

1 It's cloudy 2 It's Friday
3 It's winter

기출 적중문제

정답 ①
해설 ①: 대명사 it ②③④⑤: 비인칭 주어 it

POINT 5-1 부정대명사: one

연습문제 A

1	one	2	It	3	one	4	They
5	it	6	one	7	them	8	It
9	one	10	ones	11	ones		

기출 적중문제

정답 it, one
해설 첫 번째 빈칸: 앞에서 언급된 특정한 대상(this white dress)을 가리키고 있고, this white dress는 단수이므로 it을 쓴다.
두 번째 빈칸: 앞에서 언급된 명사(dress)와 같은 종류의 불특정한 사물을 가리키고 있고, dress는 단수이므로 one을 쓴다.

POINT 5-2 부정대명사: another, other

연습문제 A

1	another	2	another
3	others	4	other

연습문제 B

1 One, the other
2 Some, the others
3 Some, others
4 One, another, the other

기출 적중문제

정답 One, the other

해설 「one ~, the other -」'(둘 중) 하나는 ~, 나머지 하나는 -'

POINT 5-3 부정대명사: each, every, all

연습문제

1 cloud	**2** has	**3** student
4 have	**5** ticket	**6** needs
7 eggs	**8** seems	**9** is
10 are		

기출 적중문제

정답 ⓒ → needs

해설 「Every + 단수명사 + 단수동사」이므로 단수동사 needs를 쓴다.

서술형 대비 문제

Ⓐ
1 Her	**2** They	**3** her
4 Its	**5** them	**6** We
7 him	**8** His	**9** Their

Ⓑ
1 Those	**2** that	**3** this
4 these		

Ⓒ
1 It is chilly	**2** Everything looks
3 All the flowers, smell	**4** It takes
5 It is dark	**6** Every teacher, is

Ⓓ
1 One is a teacher, the other is a writer
2 another was a bag, the other was a book
3 Some are listening, the others are playing
4 Some are doctors, others are patients
5 One was yellow, the other was black

중간·기말고사 실전 문제

1 them **2** Her **3** ③ **4** ② **5** His, He, him **6** ⑤ **7** yours **8** ④ **9** ② **10** ③ **11** It **12** ④ **13** ③ **14** ③ **15** ④ **16** ⑤ **17** ④ **18** One is math, the

---

other is history **19** ④ **20** It will be cold **21** ④ **22** ③, ⑤ **23** ① **24** ④ **25** yours his **26** Are those **27** (1) It is spring (2) It was Thursday **28** ④, ⑤ **29** ④ **30** ② **31** calls himself an artist **32** ④ **33** ⑤ **34** Some, the others **35** ② **36** ② **37** ③ **38** singer, has **39** ⓒ → has **40** (1) ⓑ (2) ⓐ, ⓒ, ⓓ (3) ⓕ, ⓔ **41** ②

1 3인칭 복수명사 buildings를 가리키고 빈칸이 동사 designed의 목적어 자리이므로 목적격 인칭대명사 them을 쓴다.

2 girl은 3인칭 단수이고 빈칸 뒤에 소유의 대상이 되는 명사 name이 왔으므로 소유격 인칭대명사 Her를 쓴다.

3 ① She's → Her
② It → Its
④ We → Our
⑤ their → them

4 ② he → him

5 첫 번째 빈칸: 빈칸 뒤에 소유의 대상이 되는 명사 hometown이 왔으므로 소유격 인칭대명사 His를 쓴다.
두 번째 빈칸: 빈칸이 주어 자리이므로 주격 인칭대명사 He를 쓴다.
세 번째 빈칸: 빈칸이 동사 know의 목적어 자리이므로 목적격 인칭대명사 him을 쓴다.

6 소유대명사는 「소유격 + 명사」를 대신한다.

7 소유대명사는 「소유격 + 명사」를 대신한다.

8 빈칸이 전치사 to의 목적어 자리이므로 목적격 인칭대명사 us를 쓴다.

9 ②: 목적격 인칭대명사   ①③④⑤: 소유격 인칭대명사

10 ③: 소유격 인칭대명사   ①②④⑤: 소유격 인칭대명사

11 · '그것은 내가 가장 좋아하는 색이다.'라는 의미이므로 대명사 It (그것)을 쓴다.
· '밝아지고 있다.'라는 의미이므로 명암을 나타내는 비인칭 주어 It을 쓴다.

12 · 동사 saw의 목적어가 주어 She와 같은 대상이므로 재귀대명사 herself를 쓴다. (재귀 용법)
· '나의 여동생은 그 노래를 직접 썼다.'라는 의미이므로 재귀대명사 herself를 쓴다. (강조 용법)

13 첫 번째 빈칸: yours로 묻고 있고 '응, 그것은 나의 것이야.'라는 의미이므로 소유대명사 mine을 쓴다.
두 번째 빈칸: 빈칸 뒤에 소유의 대상이 되는 명사 bag이 왔으므로 소유격 인칭대명사 her를 쓴다.

14 ③ it – itself

15 ④ ourselves → us

16 전치사 of의 목적어가 주어 we와 같은 대상이므로 재귀대명사

ourselves를 쓴다.

17 ⓑⓒⓔ: 강조 용법   ⓐⓓ: 재귀 용법

18 「one ~, the other -」'(둘 중) 하나는 ~, 나머지 하나는 -'

19 ① that → those
② these → this
③ these → this
⑤ Those → That

20 날씨를 나타내는 비인칭 주어 It을 쓴다.

21 '저것들은 치타들이니?'라고 묻는 말에 저것들은 표범이라고 했으므로 부정의 내용으로 대답한다. 지시대명사 those가 있는 의문문에 Yes나 No로 짧게 대답할 때는 주어로 they를 쓰므로 No, they aren't.로 대답한다.

22 주어진 문장과 ③⑤: 지시형용사   ①②④: 지시대명사

23 ①: 대명사 it   주어진 문장과 ②③④⑤: 비인칭 주어 it

24 ⓑⓒⓓ: 비인칭 주어 it   ⓐⓔ: 대명사 it

25 첫 번째 빈칸: '너의 것'이라는 의미의 소유대명사 yours를 쓴다.
두 번째 빈칸: '그의 것'이라는 의미의 소유대명사 his를 쓴다.

26 복수명사 purses는 지시대명사 those로 대신하고 be동사는 Are를 쓴다.

27 (1) 계절을 나타내는 비인칭 주어 It을 쓰고 현재시제로 묻고 있으므로 현재시제로 대답한다.
(2) 요일을 나타내는 비인칭 주어 It을 쓰고 과거시제로 묻고 있으므로 과거시제로 대답한다.

28 ④: ⓔ의 it은 fan을 가리키는 대명사로 '그것'이라고 해석한다.
⑤: ⓒ와 ⓔ는 fan을 가리키는 대명사이다.

29 ④ it   ①②③⑤ one

30 3인칭 복수명사 muffins를 가리키고 빈칸이 동사 baked의 목적어 자리이므로 목적격 인칭대명사 them을 쓴다.

31 '그 자신'이라는 의미의 재귀대명사 himself를 쓴다. 5형식 문장은 「주어 + 동사 + 목적어 + 목적격보어」 형태이다.

32 「one ~, another -, the other …」'(셋 중) 하나는 ~, 다른 하나는 -, 나머지 하나는 …'

33 「some ~, others -」'(여럿 중) 몇몇은 ~, 다른 것들은 -'

34 파티에서 여럿 중 몇몇은 노래를 하고 나머지 전부는 춤을 추고 있는 상황이므로 '(여럿 중) 몇몇'이라는 의미의 Some을 쓰고, '나머지 전부'라는 의미의 the others를 쓴다.

35 ・'너에게 또 다른 질문을 해도 되니?'라는 의미이므로 another(또 다른 하나)를 쓴다.
・'이 블라우스는 저에게 맞지 않아요. 저에게 다른 것을 보여주세요.'라는 의미이므로 another(또 다른 하나)를 쓴다.

36 주어 Everyone은 단수이므로 단수동사 is looking at을 쓴다.

37 (A) 「Every + 단수명사 + 단수동사」이므로 단수명사 student를 쓴다.

(B) 「All + 복수명사 + 복수동사」이므로 복수명사 customers를 쓴다.
(C) 「Each + 단수명사 + 단수동사」이므로 단수동사 has를 쓴다.

38 「Every + 단수명사 + 단수동사」이므로 단수명사 singer를 쓰고, 단수동사 has를 쓴다.

39 ⓒ: 「Each + 단수명사 + 단수동사」이므로 단수동사 has를 쓴다.

40 (1) 앞에서 언급된 명사(roses)와 같은 종류의 사물을 가리키는 ones를 쓴다.
(2) 「one ~, another -, the other …」'(셋 중) 하나는 ~, 다른 하나는 -, 나머지 하나는 …'
(3) 「some ~, the others -」'(여럿 중) 몇몇은 ~, 나머지 전부는 -'

41 ⓐ necklaces → necklace
ⓑ are → is
ⓔ are → is

CHAPTER 11
형용사

p.226

POINT 1 형용사의 용법

1	ⓑ	**2**	ⓐ	**3**	ⓐ	**4**	ⓑ
5	ⓐ	**6**	ⓑ	**7**	ⓑ	**8**	ⓐ
9	ⓑ	**10**	ⓐ	**11**	ⓑ	**12**	ⓑ
13	ⓐ	**14**	ⓐ	**15**	ⓐ	**16**	ⓑ

POINT 2 형용사의 어순

1 big red apple
2 square plastic chair
3 cute three-year-old cat
4 huge old brick castle
5 small wooden doll
6 wonderful round white moon

POINT 3 -thing/-body + 형용사

1	nobody famous	**2**	something spicy
3	Somebody rude	**4**	great things
5	nothing nice	**6**	anything cold
7	mysterious thing	**8**	something pink
9	difficult thing	**10**	anything strange
11	something good	**12**	anything useful
13	nothing serious	**14**	anybody happy

기출 적중문제

정답 fun nothing → nothing fun
해설 -thing으로 끝나는 대명사(nothing)를 꾸밀 때는 형용사 (fun)가 대명사 뒤에 온다.

POINT 4 감정형용사

A

1 ① surprising ② surprised
2 ① exciting ② excited
3 ① amazing ② amazed
4 ① shocked ② shocking
5 ① bored ② boring
6 ① disappointing ② disappointed

1	boring	**2**	tired	**3**	confused
4	interested	**5**	moved	**6**	interesting
7	annoyed	**8**	surprised		

기출 적중문제

정답 surprised
해설 The manager는 감정을 느끼는 대상이므로 V-ed 형태의 형용사 surprised를 쓴다.

POINT 5-1 수사: 기수와 서수

A

1	two	**2**	sixty
3	fortieth	**4**	twelfth
5	ninth	**6**	five
7	fifteenth	**8**	first
9	thirteen	**10**	sixty-six
11	forty-two	**12**	twenty-second
13	thirty-third	**14**	a[one] hundred

B

1 three countries, third country
2 seven candles, seventh birthday
3 twelve months, twelfth month
4 twenty-one presents, twenty-first visitor

C

1	a[one] hundred	**2**	thousands of
3	hundreds of	**4**	three thousand

기출 적중문제

정답 ninth
해설 '아홉 번째'라는 의미의 서수 ninth를 쓴다.

POINT 5-2 수사: 정수, 소수, 분수

1 (zero) point two one
2 three hundred (and) seventeen
3 nine thousand, six hundred (and) fifty-four
4 ninety three point three seven
5 twenty-four thousand, two hundred (and) five
6 fifty million, three hundred (and) forty thousand, eight hundred (and) twenty-nine
7 two point nine six eight
8 eight-fifteenths
9 three and one-half[a half]
10 three-quarters[three-fourths]
11 five and four-sevenths

POINT 5-3 수사: 시각

연습문제 A
1 six twenty-three
2 seven thirty-five
3 eight fifteen
4 twelve-o-three
5 ten fifty-two
6 three (o'clock)

연습문제 B
1 twenty after nine
2 half past eleven
3 (a) quarter to five
4 ten to two
5 five after three
6 (a) quarter past eight

POINT 5-4 수사: 연도와 날짜

연습문제
1 seventeen fifteen
2 August (the) ninth[the ninth of August]
3 January (the) third[the third of January]
4 two thousand (and) one
5 thirteen seventy-eight
6 two thousand (and) seventeen[twenty seventeen]
7 October (the) fifteenth[the fifteenth of October]
8 December (the) twenty-seventh [the twenty-seventh of December]
9 June (the) thirteenth[the thirteenth of June], two thousand (and) two
10 the nineteen thirties
11 July (the) thirty-first[the thirty-first of July], eighteen forty-two
12 the seventeen hundreds
13 March (the) twentieth[the twentieth of March], two thousand (and) twenty-six[twenty twenty-six]

POINT 6-1 수량형용사: many, much, a lot of

연습문제 A
1 many
2 much
3 much
4 many

연습문제 B
1 many
2 much
3 many
4 much

기출 적중문제
정답 ③, ⑤
해설 빈칸 뒤에 셀 수 있는 명사의 복수형(students)이 왔으므로 셀 수 없는 명사 앞에 쓰는 Much는 쓸 수 없다. Lot of는 A lot of나 Lots of의 형태로 써야 한다.

POINT 6-2 수량형용사: (a) few, (a) little

연습문제 A
1 a little
2 A few
3 few
4 a little
5 little
6 a few
7 a little
8 a few
9 little
10 few

연습문제 B
1 a few stars
2 little time
3 a little sugar
4 few students
5 a little butter
6 little syrup
7 few friends
8 a few hours

기출 적중문제
정답 ③
해설 첫 번째 빈칸: soda는 셀 수 없는 명사이고 '선미는 약간의 탄산음료를 마시기를 원했다'라는 의미이므로 a little(약간의)을 쓴다.
두 번째 빈칸: coins는 셀 수 있는 명사의 복수형이고 '그녀의 지갑 안에 동전이 거의 없었다'라는 의미이므로 few(거의 없는)를 쓴다.

POINT 6-3 수량형용사: some, any

연습문제
1 some
2 any
3 some
4 any
5 some
6 some
7 some
8 any

기출 적중문제
정답 ④
해설 부정문이므로 any를 쓴다.

서술형 대비 문제

A
1 O
2 O
3 anybody new
4 hundred
5 shocking
6 O
7 exciting
8 interested
9 something important
10 thousand

B
1 much salt
2 many questions
3 much rain
4 Many children
5 much coffee
6 much furniture
7 many good friends
8 much sleep
9 many books
10 many sheep
11 many nice restaurants

C
1 a little
2 few
3 little
4 Many
5 a few
6 much

Ⓓ ⓐ July (the) twenty-ninth[the twenty-ninth of July], two thousand (and) sixteen[twenty sixteen]
ⓑ July (the) thirtieth[the thirtieth of July]
ⓒ July (the) thirty-first[the thirty-first of July]
ⓓ August (the) first[the first of August]
ⓔ August (the) second[the second of August]

중간·기말고사 실전 문제

1 ① **2** four fifty-five[five to five]
3 August (the) fifteenth[the fifteenth of August]
4 Let's do something fun tonight. **5** long
6 new **7** ② **8** ① **9** ④ **10** fifth
11 (1) ⓓ → something nice (2) ⓔ → many[a lot of/lots of] **12** ②, ④ **13** ④ **14** ① **15** ⑤
16 millions of years **17** ③ **18** ④ **19** ③
20 ④ **21** a fantastic magic show **22** ②
23 ⑤ **24** ④ **25** ③ **26** ②, ④ **27** ④
28 ③ **29** ⑤ **30** ③ **31** any → some
32 cheap nothing → nothing cheap **33** ③
34 ③ **35** ③ **36** ② **37** surprised
38 moving **39** This puzzle makes me confused. **40** The chef's pasta was amazing.
41 ⑤ **42** ①, ②

빈칸 뒤에 셀 수 있는 명사의 복수형(schools)이 왔으므로 셀 수 없는 명사 앞에 쓰는 much는 쓸 수 없다.

현재 시간이 4시 55분이라고 했으므로 four fifty-five 또는 five to five를 쓴다.

현재 날짜가 8월 15일이라고 했으므로 August (the) fifteenth 또는 the fifteenth of August를 쓴다.

-thing으로 끝나는 대명사(something)를 꾸밀 때는 형용사(fun)가 대명사 뒤에 온다.

두 개 이상의 형용사를 함께 쓸 때는 판단, 길이, 색깔 순서로 쓰고 'nice long purple jacket'이므로 두 번째에 오는 것은 long이다.

두 개 이상의 형용사를 함께 쓸 때는 형태, 오래된 정도, 재료 순서로 쓰고 배열한 부분이 'round new glass cup'이므로 두 번째에 오는 것은 new이다.

'5시 45분이다.'는 '6시 15분 전이다.'로 바꿔 쓸 수 있으므로 It's a quarter to six.를 쓴다.

(A) 부정문이므로 any를 쓴다.
(B) marathon은 감정을 일으키는 주체이므로 V-ing 형태의 형용사 tiring을 쓴다.
(C) -thing으로 끝나는 대명사(something)를 꾸밀 때는 형용

사(new)가 대명사 뒤에 온다.

9 ④ many → much

10 '다섯 번째'라는 의미의 서수 fifth를 쓴다.

11 (1) -thing으로 끝나는 대명사(something)를 꾸밀 때는 형용사(nice)가 대명사 뒤에 온다.
(2) toys는 셀 수 있는 명사의 복수형이므로 many[a lot of/lots of]를 쓴다.

12 날짜는 서수로 읽는다.

13 · dolls는 셀 수 있는 명사의 복수형이므로 many를 쓴다.
· orange juice는 셀 수 없는 명사이고 '약간의 오렌지 주스를 먹어도 되니?'라는 의미이므로 a little(약간의)을 쓴다.

14 · 긍정문이므로 some을 쓴다.
· 부정문이고 빈칸 뒤에 셀 수 없는 명사(bread)가 왔으므로 any를 쓴다.

15 · This map은 감정을 일으키는 주체이므로 V-ing 형태의 형용사 confusing을 쓴다.
· We는 감정을 느끼는 대상이므로 V-ed 형태의 형용사 excited를 쓴다.

16 '수백만의'라는 의미의 millions of를 쓰고 뒤에 복수명사 years를 쓴다.

17 ③ twenty to three → twenty after[past] three 또는 three twenty

18 ④ two-third → two-thirds

19 · '수천의'라는 의미의 thousands of를 쓴다.
· '500'이라는 정해진 숫자를 나타낼 때는 hundred에 -s를 붙이지 않고 five hundred는 복수를 나타내므로 student의 복수형 students를 쓴다.

20 ④: 서술적 용법 ①②③⑤: 한정적 용법

21 서술적 용법의 형용사(fantastic)는 명사(magic show)를 꾸미는 한정적 용법의 형용사로 바꿔 쓸 수 있다.

22 ② nine - ninth

23 ⑤ some → any

24 '그의 새 소설'이라는 의미의 His new novel을 주어로 쓰고, His new novel은 감정을 일으키는 주체이므로 V-ing 형태의 형용사 disappointing을 쓴다.

25 ③ much ①②④⑤ many

26 빈칸 뒤에 셀 수 있는 명사의 복수형(trees)이 왔으므로 a few와 lots of를 쓴다.

27 much는 셀 수 없는 명사 앞에 쓰이므로 셀 수 있는 명사의 복수형 hamburgers는 쓸 수 없다.

28 '많은'이라는 의미의 a lot of는 many 또는 much로 바꿔 쓸 수 있고 energy는 셀 수 없는 명사이므로 much를 쓴다.

29 첫 번째 빈칸 뒤에 셀 수 없는 명사(music)와 두 번째 빈칸 뒤에

셀 수 있는 명사의 복수형(cups)이 왔으므로 셀 수 없는 명사와
셀 수 있는 명사의 복수형 앞에 쓰이는 lots of(많은)를 쓴다.

30 ⓒ great somebody → somebody great
ⓓ special nothing → nothing special

31 '나는 한 시간 전에 약간의 약을 먹었지만'이라는 의미이고 긍정문
이므로 some을 쓴다. any는 주로 부정문과 의문문에 쓴다.

32 -thing으로 끝나는 대명사(nothing)를 꾸밀 때는 형용사
(cheap)가 대명사 뒤에 온다.

33 ① letter → letters
② rains → rain
④ sugars → sugar
⑤ apple → apples

34 ③: 서술적 용법   주어진 문장과 ①②④⑤: 한정적 용법

35 ③ plastic large → large plastic

36 첫 번째 빈칸: You는 감정을 느끼는 대상이므로 V-ed 형태의 형
용사 tired를 쓴다.
두 번째 빈칸: I는 감정을 느끼는 대상이므로 V-ed 형태의 형용
사 tired를 쓴다.

37 Alice는 감정을 느끼는 대상이므로 V-ed 형태의 형용사
surprised를 쓴다.

38 Last night's play는 감정을 일으키는 주체이므로 V-ing 형태의
형용사 moving을 쓴다.

39 me는 감정을 느끼는 대상이므로 V-ed 형태의 형용사 confused
를 쓴다.

40 The chef's pasta는 감정을 일으키는 주체이므로 V-ing 형태의
형용사 amazing을 쓴다.

41 ⑤ tired → tiring

42 The movie는 감정을 일으키는 주체이므로 V-ed 형태의 형용사
annoyed와 disappointed는 쓸 수 없다.

CHAPTER 12
부사

p.250

POINT 1 부사의 쓰임

연습
문제
1 rained	**2** tired
3 studies	**4** I passed the test
5 much	**6** listen
7 good	**8** happy
9 it is time to say goodbye	
10 boring	**11** Walk
12 someone knocked on the door	
13 shines	**14** well
15 fast	

POINT 2-1 부사의 형태

연습
문제
A
1 loudly	**2** really	**3** happily
4 sadly	**5** badly	**6** gently
7 nervously	**8** specially	**9** perfectly
10 strangely	**11** similarly	**12** regularly
13 strongly	**14** seriously	**15** wonderfully
16 suddenly	**17** quietly	**18** well
19 carefully	**20** differently	**21** clearly
22 surprisingly	**23** comfortably	**24** heavily
25 noisily	**26** safely	**27** nicely
28 angrily	**29** wisely	**30** deeply
31 possibly	**32** honestly	

연습
문제
B
1 carefully	**2** perfectly
3 terribly	**4** beautiful
5 Unfortunately	**6** deeply
7 friendly	**8** kindly
9 different	**10** Amazingly
11 quietly	

 기출 적중문제
정답 Don't[Do not] speak loudly
해설 동사(speak)를 꾸미는 부사 loudly를 쓴다.

POINT 2-2 형용사와 형태가 같은 부사

연습
문제
1 ①	**2** ②	**3** ②	**4** ③
5 ①	**6** ③	**7** ②	

POINT 2-3 -ly가 붙으면 의미가 달라지는 부사

1 ① high ② highly ③ highly ④ high
2 ① hard ② hard ③ hardly ④ hardly
3 ① lately ② late ③ Lately ④ late
4 ① closely ② close ③ close ④ closely

POINT 3 빈도부사

1 always　**2** never　**3** usually
4 often　**5** sometimes　**6** usually
7 never　**8** seldom　**9** never

1 Birds V build nests in trees.
2 Do you V eat breakfast at home?
3 Will you V love me?
4 My sister's room is V clean.
5 I will V lie to my parents again.
6 Does Sally V go to the café?
7 Bears can V catch fish in rivers.
8 The restaurant V serves unhealthy food.
9 The subway is V empty in the afternoon.
10 Would you V work out with me?

1 always　**2** often　**3** sometimes
4 never

기출 적중문제
정답 I usually play soccer
해설 빈도부사는 일반동사 앞에 온다.

POINT 4 too, either

1 too　**2** either　**3** too
4 too　**5** either　**6** too
7 either　**8** too　**9** either
10 either

기출 적중문제
정답 ②
해설 ② either　①③④⑤ too

POINT 5 동사 + 부사

1 take off　**2** throw away　**3** write down
4 wake up　**5** turn on　**6** hand in
7 put off　**8** try on　**9** Turn off

10 put on　**11** give up　**12** pick up

1 turned on the computer
2 give it up
3 try them on
4 turn all the lights off, turn them off
5 take it off
6 pick your trash up, pick it up
7 put off her trip, put it off
8 write down your name
9 Hand it in
10 put a jacket on, put it on
11 wake the baby up, wake him up
12 throw them away

기출 적중문제
정답 The loud noise woke her up last night.
해설 「동사 + 부사」의 목적어가 대명사인 경우 「동사 + 목적어 + 부사」의 어순으로 쓴다.

서술형 대비 문제

Ⓐ **1** angrily　**2** politely
3 wisely　**4** bravely
5 dangerously　**6** well
7 carefully　**8** correctly
9 similarly　**10** Luckily

Ⓑ **1** hardly　**2** late
3 hard　**4** lately
5 highly　**6** close
7 closely　**8** high

Ⓒ **1** Monica is always friendly.
2 My dad sometimes buys my mom flowers.
3 Carl never eats healthy food.
4 You should often call your parents.
5 Do you usually exercise in the morning?
6 Will you always tell the truth?
7 The bakery is seldom crowded on Mondays.
8 He could never find a parking space.

Ⓓ **1** try them on　**2** O
3 O　**4** wakes me up
5 put it on　**6** O
7 Throw it away　**8** O
9 write it down

---

1 ④　　**2** ②　　**3** ⑤　　**4** ④　　**5** angry
→ angrily　**6** ④　　**7** ③　　**8** ⑤　　**9** ③
10 ④　　**11** ⑤　　**12** ②　　**13** never swims
14 ③　　**15** ②　　**16** I sometimes go out to eat.
17 I seldom have free time　**18** ④　　**19** ②
20 ⑤　　**21** (1) ⓑ → hardly　(2) ⓓ → well
22 ④　　**23** ②　　**24** ②　　**25** ③　　**26** I
turned the heater on, but Jackson turned it off.

---

1 ④ easy – easily

2 부정문에 대한 동의를 나타내는 부사 either(또한)를 쓴다.

3 ⑤ careful → carefully

4 ④: 명사 – 형용사
<보기>와 ①②③⑤: 형용사 – 부사

5 동사(shouted)를 꾸미는 부사 angrily를 쓴다.

6 ④ perfect → perfectly

7 ③: 형용사　①②④⑤: 부사

8 ⑤: 형용사　①②③④: 부사

9 ③ fastly → fast

10 (A) 형용사(interesting)를 꾸미는 '매우'라는 의미의 부사
highly를 쓴다.
(B) 동사(stood)를 꾸미는 '가까이'라는 의미의 부사 close를
쓴다.
(C) 동사(know)를 꾸미는 '거의 ~않다'라는 의미의 부사 hardly
를 쓴다.

11 빈도부사는 일반동사 앞에 오고 전체 문장이 'I usually eat
cereal for breakfast.'이므로 세 번째에 오는 것은 eat이다.

12 ② either　①③④⑤ too

13 Amy는 결코 수영을 하지 않는다고 했으므로 빈도부사 never
(결코 ~않다)를 쓴다. 빈도부사는 일반동사 앞에 오므로 never
swims를 쓴다.

14 ① always is → is always
② wear sometimes → sometimes wear
④ open never → never open
⑤ build usually → usually build

15 ② too → either

16 빈도부사는 일반동사 앞에 온다.

17 '거의 ~않다'라는 의미의 빈도부사 seldom을 쓰고 빈도부사는
일반동사 앞에 오므로 I seldom have free time을 쓴다.

18 ④: Jason은 방과 후에 공부를 거의 하지 않는다고 했으므로 빈
도부사 seldom(거의 ~않다)을 쓴다. often은 '종종, 자주'라는 의

미이므로 적절하지 않다.

19 ② lately → late ('늦게'라는 의미의 부사 late는 형용사와 형태
가 같다. 부사 lately는 '최근에'라는 의미이다.)

20 · pick up '~을 줍다'
· wake up '~를 깨우다'

21 (1) 동사(slept)를 꾸미고 있고 '나는 어젯밤 거의 잠을 자지 않았
다.'라는 의미이므로 부사 hardly(거의 ~않다)를 쓴다.
(2) 동사(do)를 꾸미고 있고 '나는 내가 잘 할지 확실하지 않다.'
라는 의미이므로 부사 well(잘)을 쓴다.

22 첫 번째 빈칸: 동사(swim)를 꾸미는 부사 silently를 쓴다.
두 번째 빈칸: 명사(teeth)를 꾸미는 형용사 sharp를 쓴다.

23 빈도부사는 일반동사(sleep) 앞에 온다.

24 빈도부사는 조동사(can) 뒤에 온다.

25 ⓑ wake up me → wake me up
ⓔ pick up it → pick it up

26 「동사 + 부사」의 목적어가 대명사인 경우 「동사 + 목적어 + 부
사」의 어순으로 쓴다.

CHAPTER 13
비교구문

p.268

POINT 1-1 규칙 변화 I

1 newer, newest	2 busier, busiest
3 longer, longest	4 faster, fastest
5 fresher, freshest	6 easier, easiest
7 heavier, heaviest	8 bigger, biggest
9 wetter, wettest	10 thicker, thickest
11 colder, coldest	12 prettier, prettiest
13 cheaper, cheapest	14 cuter, cutest
15 lighter, lightest	16 smaller, smallest
17 nicer, nicest	18 hotter, hottest
19 sweeter, sweetest	20 softer, softest
21 richer, richest	22 healthier, healthiest
23 thinner, thinnest	24 warmer, warmest
25 slower, slowest	26 weaker, weakest
27 huger, hugest	28 noisier, noisiest
29 sunnier, sunniest	30 scarier, scariest
31 wider, widest	32 sadder, saddest

POINT 1-2 규칙 변화 II

1 more popular, most popular
2 more important, most important
3 harder, hardest
4 more beautiful, most beautiful
5 more delicious, most delicious
6 wiser, wisest
7 more easily, most easily
8 more colorful, most colorful
9 more helpful, most helpful
10 more slowly, most slowly
11 lovelier, loveliest
12 more different, most different
13 more exciting, most exciting
14 more dangerous, most dangerous
15 more difficult, most difficult
16 more expensive, most expensive

POINT 1-3 불규칙 변화

1 worse, worst	2 larger, largest
3 higher, highest	4 more, most
5 younger, youngest	6 better, best

7 shorter, shortest	8 worse, worst
9 further, furthest	10 dirtier, dirtiest
11 farther, farthest	12 cooler, coolest
13 better, best	14 more, most
15 less, least	16 greater, greatest
17 smarter, smartest	18 angrier, angriest
19 older, oldest	
20 more peaceful, most peaceful	
21 darker, darkest	22 hungrier, hungriest
23 kinder, kindest	24 thirstier, thirstiest
25 more special, most special	
26 elder, eldest	27 quieter, quietest
28 sooner, soonest	29 tastier, tastiest
30 more carefully, most carefully	
31 nearer, nearest	32 fatter, fattest
33 luckier, luckiest	
34 more loudly, most loudly	
35 worse, worst	36 brighter, brightest
37 more useful, most useful	
38 quicker, quickest	

기출 적중문제

정답 ③
해설 many – more – most

POINT 2 원급 비교: as + 원급 + as

1 as sunny as	2 not as[so] heavy as
3 as clean as	4 as[so] well as
5 as cold as	6 not as[so] easy as

기출 적중문제

정답 as late as
해설 Kate는 오후 11시에 집에 왔고 Lola 또한 오후 11시에 집에 왔다고 했으므로 '…만큼 ~하게'라는 의미의 「as + 원급 + as」를 쓴다.

POINT 3-1 비교급 비교: 비교급 + than

A

1 faster than	2 thinner than
3 longer than	4 bigger than
5 taller than	6 more expensive than

B

1 hotter than
2 more surprised than
3 much[even/still/far] sweeter than
4 harder than
5 much[even/still/far] closer, than
6 faster than
7 more popular than

8 much[even/still/far] more carefully than

연습문제 C
1 a lot	**2** larger	**3** much
4 lighter	**5** even	**6** noisier

기출 적중문제

정답 ③

해설 very → much[even/still/far/a lot]

POINT 3-2 비교급 비교: 비교급 + and + 비교급

연습문제
1 better and better
2 bigger and bigger
3 more and more popular
4 colder and colder
5 worse and worse
6 redder and redder
7 more and more boring
8 more and more famous
9 darker and darker
10 dirtier and dirtier

POINT 4-1 최상급 비교: the + 최상급

연습문제
1 the smartest	**2** the most expensive
3 the worst	**4** the highest
5 the sunniest	**6** the hottest
7 the most difficult	**8** the wisest
9 the best	**10** the most important
11 the strictest	**12** the wettest

기출 적중문제

정답 She is the most famous chef

해설 '가장 ~한'이라는 의미의 「the + 최상급」을 쓴다.

POINT 4-2 최상급 비교: one of the + 최상급 + 복수명사

연습문제
1 one of the tallest players
2 one of the most important holidays
3 one of the thickest books
4 one of the healthiest vegetables
5 One of the oldest trees
6 one of the nicest rooms
7 one of the most famous scientists
8 one of the most dangerous animals
9 one of the greatest actors
10 one of the most exciting cities

---

11 one of the most amazing roller coasters

서술형 대비 문제

(A)
1 better than		**2** smaller than
3 harder than		**4** louder than
5 quicker than		
6 more comfortable than		

(B)
1 soft		**2** O
3 most powerful		**4** more exciting
5 strongest		**6** happier
7 O		
8 more and more useful		
9 huge as		**10** O
11 as fluently as		
12 much[even/still/far/a lot]		
13 O		**14** O
15 singers		

(C)
1 ① more expensive than
　② the most expensive ③ the cheapest
2 ① as heavy as ② lighter than
3 ① the oldest ② newer than ③ the newest

중간·기말고사 실전 문제

1 ⑤	**2** ②	**3** ⑤	**4** ②	**5** ③
6 ④	**7** ②	**8** larger → the largest		
9 ③	**10** ③	**11** (1) older (2) the youngest		
12 ③	**13** ②	**14** ④	**15** as early as	
16 healthier and healthier		**17** the curliest		
18 ⑤	**19** The violin is smaller than the viola.			
20 ④	**21** ③	**22** ⑤	**23** Mario is not so tall as Tom.	
		24 cheaper than	**25** higher than	
26 ④	**27** ②	**28** ⑤	**29** ①, ⑤	
30 ③				

1 ⑤ special – more special – most special

2 ② many – more – most

3 '…보다'라는 의미의 than이 있고 '한수는 그의 형보다 더 친절하다.'라는 의미이므로 비교급을 쓴다.

4 비교 범위를 나타내는 in Africa가 있고 '나일강은 아프리카에서 가장 긴 강이다.'라는 의미이므로 최상급을 쓴다.

5 • '…보다'라는 의미의 than이 있고 '그는 나보다 영어를 더 잘 말하다.'라는 의미이므로 비교급을 쓴다.

・'…보다'라는 의미의 than이 있고 '그 두 번째 영화는 첫 번째 것보다 더 나았다.'라는 의미이므로 비교급을 쓴다.

6 ① cold → colder
② very → much[even/still/far/a lot]
③ so → as
⑤ the most helpful → more helpful

7 ② more bad → worse

8 비교 범위를 나타내는 in the city가 있고 '이것은 그 도시에서 가장 큰 쇼핑몰이다.'라는 의미이므로 최상급을 쓴다.

9 ③ nicer → nice

10 ・'…만큼'이라는 의미의 as가 있고 '이 소스는 크림만큼 부드럽다.'라는 의미이므로 원급을 쓴다.
・비교 범위를 나타내는 in this store가 있고 '어느 제품이 이 가게에서 가장 유용하니?'라는 의미이므로 최상급을 쓴다.

11 (1) 선호는 유진이와 민지보다 더 나이가 많다고 했으므로 old의 비교급 older를 쓴다.
(2) 민지는 셋 중에서 가장 어리다고 했으므로 young의 최상급 the youngest를 쓴다.

12 ③ most good → best

13 ⓑ soft → softer
ⓒ smaller → small
ⓔ animal → animals

14 ④: 시드니가 가장 추운 상황이므로 '서울은 모두 중에서 가장 춥다.'는 적절하지 않다.

15 「as + 원급 + as」 '…만큼 ~하게'

16 「비교급 + and + 비교급」 '점점 더 ~한'

17 「the + 최상급」 '가장 ~한'

18 빈칸 뒤에 비교급 more beautiful이 있으므로 원급을 강조하는 very는 쓸 수 없다.

19 「비교급 + than」 '…보다 더 ~한'

20 '가장 ~한'이라는 의미의 「the + 최상급」을 쓴다. strong의 최상급은 the strongest이다.

21 '가장 ~한 것들 중 하나'라는 의미의 「one of the + 최상급 + 복수명사」를 쓴다. busy의 최상급은 busiest이다.

22 빈칸 앞에 2음절 이상인 형용사 앞에 붙는 more가 있으므로 expensive를 쓴다.

23 「not + so + 원급 + as」 '…만큼 ~하지 않은'

24 돼지고기는 소고기보다 더 저렴하다고 했으므로 cheap의 비교급 cheaper를 쓴다.

25 에베레스트 산이 한라산보다 더 높다고 했으므로 high의 비교급 higher를 쓴다.

26 ④ more → the most

27 ② as   ①③④⑤ than

28 ⑤: B코스는 A코스보다 더 어렵다고 했으므로 'B코스는 A코스보다 더 쉽다.'는 적절하지 않다.

29 ②: 베이글은 도넛과 가격이 같다고 했으므로 '베이글은 도넛만큼 저렴하지 않다.'는 적절하지 않다.
③: 베이글은 프레첼보다 더 저렴하다고 했으므로 '베이글은 프레첼보다 더 비싸다.'는 적절하지 않다.
④: 도넛은 프레첼보다 더 저렴하다고 했으므로 '도넛은 프레첼만큼 저렴하다.'는 적절하지 않다.

30 비교급 앞에서 비교급을 강조하는 even은 원급을 강조하는 very와 바꿔 쓸 수 없다.

CHAPTER 14
전치사

p.286

POINT 1-1 시간 전치사: at, on, in

1	in	2	on	3	at	4	in
5	on	6	on	7	on	8	on

기출 적중문제
정답 on → in
해설 월(September) 앞에는 전치사 in을 쓴다.

POINT 1-2 시간 전치사: before, after

1	before the weekend
2	after lunch
3	Before Christmas
4	before 11 o'clock
5	after nine
6	before dinner
7	After the play
8	after breakfast
9	Before my 13th birthday
10	after their marriage

POINT 1-3 시간 전치사: for, during

1	for	2	for	3	during
4	for	5	during	6	during
7	during	8	for	9	during
10	during	11	for		

기출 적중문제
정답 ②
해설 숫자를 포함한 기간 표현(30 minutes, an hour) 앞이므로 전치사 for(~ 동안)를 쓴다.

POINT 1-4 시간 전치사: from

1	from 8 o'clock
2	from next week
3	from 2005 to 2012
4	from Tuesday to Thursday
5	From this year
6	from today to next Monday
7	from September to December

기출 적중문제
정답 from Monday to Friday
해설 「from ~ to …」 '~부터 …까지'

POINT 2-1 장소 전치사: at, on, in I

1	in	2	at	3	in	4	on
5	on	6	at	7	on	8	in
9	on	10	in				

기출 적중문제
정답 on the pillow
해설 '그것은 침대 위에 있어.'라는 의미이므로 전치사 on(~ 위에)을 쓴다.

POINT 2-2 장소 전치사: at, on, in II

1	in	2	in	3	at	4	on
5	in	6	in	7	in	8	at
9	on	10	in	11	in	12	on
13	in	14	at	15	in	16	at
17	at	18	in	19	in	20	on
21	on	22	in	23	at	24	on
25	at	26	on	27	in	28	in
29	on	30	in				

기출 적중문제
정답 ②
해설 · 길(Maple Street) 앞에는 전치사 on을 쓴다.
· 교통수단(the subway) 앞에는 전치사 on을 쓴다.

POINT 3 위치 전치사

A
1	in front of	2	behind	3	between
4	under	5	next to[by]	6	over
7	among				

B
1	by the armchair
2	under the bed
3	in front of the statue
4	behind Nancy
5	over the fence
6	between the hospital and the library

정답 ⑤

해설 휴대폰은 책상 위에 있으므로 '휴대폰은 책상 앞에 있다.'는 적절하지 않다.

POINT 4 방향 전치사

1	down	2	from	3	through
4	along	5	out of	6	up
7	around	8	across		

1	over	2	into	3	to
4	through	5	out of	6	into
7	for	8	along	9	across
10	around	11	up	12	along

기출 적중문제

정답 ③

해설 '~ 안으로'라는 의미의 전치사 into를 쓴다.

POINT 5 기타 전치사

1	by	2	with	3	for
4	against	5	like	6	on
7	with	8	without	9	for
10	about	11	with	12	by

ⓐ with ⓑ for ⓒ against ⓓ like ⓔ about

기출 적중문제

정답 ②

해설 · '수염을 가진 그 남자는 Bill의 아버지이다.'라는 의미이므로 전치사 with(~을 가진)를 쓴다.
· '우리는 역에 정오까지 도착해야 한다.'라는 의미이므로 전치사 by(~까지)를 쓴다.

POINT 6-1 전치사 관용 표현: 형용사 + 전치사

1	of	2	with	3	at
4	at	5	for[about]	6	for
7	of	8	for	9	for
10	of	11	for	12	with
13	with	14	from	15	for

1	for	2	of	3	for	4	of
5	for	6	of	7	for	8	for
9	with	10	of	11	with	12	at

13	with	14	with	15	at	16	of
17	from	18	with	19	for	20	of

기출 적중문제

정답 ②

해설 · be careful with '~을 조심하다'
· be familiar with '~에 익숙하다'

POINT 6-2 전치사 관용 표현: 동사 + 전치사

1	listens to	2	thank, for
3	look at	4	laughed at
5	ask for	6	wait for
7	spent, on	8	look for

기출 적중문제

정답 for

해설 · ask for '~을 요청하다'
· look for '~을 찾다'

서술형 대비 문제

Ⓐ
1	at	2	O	3	O
4	in	5	in	6	on
7	on	8	O		

Ⓑ ⓐ by ⓑ about ⓒ up ⓓ with ⓔ without

Ⓒ
1	on	2	over
3	out of	4	in front of
5	next to	6	into, through

Ⓓ
1	by	2	into
3	of	4	at, under
5	of, like	6	for
7	about, during		

중간·기말고사 실전 문제

1	②	2	②	3	④	4	⑤	5	behind

6 out of 　　7 in front of
8 on, at, on 　　9 (1) next to (2) on (3) under

10	⑤	11	①	12	④	13	⑤	14	①
15	④	16	②						

17 (1) ⓑ → about (2) ⓒ → for
(3) ⓔ → at 18 ③ 　19 ② 　20 ① 　21 ④

22	①	23	③	24	④	25	②	26	⑤

1 날짜(March 2) 앞에는 전치사 on을 쓴다.

2 ② at → in

3 · 'Jonathan은 6개월 동안 콜롬비아에서 스페인어를 공부했다.' 라는 의미이고 숫자를 포함한 기간 표현(six months) 앞이므로 전치사 for(~ 동안)를 쓴다.
· '내가 너를 위해 그 가방을 들어줄게.'라는 의미이므로 전치사 for(~을 위해)를 쓴다.

4 숫자를 포함한 기간 표현(three days) 앞이므로 전치사 for(~ 동안)를 쓴다.

5 '~ 뒤에'라는 의미의 전치사 behind를 쓴다.

6 '~ 밖으로'라는 의미의 전치사 out of를 쓴다.

7 '~ 앞에'라는 의미의 전치사 in front of를 쓴다.

8 첫 번째 빈칸: 날짜(October 1) 앞에는 전치사 on을 쓴다.
두 번째 빈칸: 하나의 지점(Jimmy's Pizza Palace) 앞에는 전치사 at을 쓴다.
세 번째 빈칸: 길(Main Street) 앞에는 전치사 on을 쓴다.

9 (1) 나무 옆에 분수가 있는 상황이므로 전치사 next to(~ 옆에)를 쓴다.
(2) 새는 그 소년의 머리 위에 앉아있는 상황이므로 전치사 on (~ 위에)을 쓴다.
(3) 그 소년은 나무 아래에서 책을 읽고 있는 상황이므로 전치사 under(~ 아래에)를 쓴다.

10 · '우리는 방금 도서관으로부터 왔다.'라는 의미이므로 전치사 from(~으로부터)을 쓴다.
· '그는 월요일부터 목요일까지 출근한다.'라는 의미이므로 「from ~ to …」(~부터 …까지)를 쓴다.

11 ① at → in

12 ④: 동사 　①②③⑤: 전치사

13 '~을 따라서'라는 의미의 전치사 along을 쓴다.

14 · '건물 안에서 담배를 피지 마세요.'라는 의미이므로 전치사 in(~ 안에)을 쓴다.
· '혜진이는 바닥에 그녀의 가방을 두었다.'라는 의미이므로 전치사 on(~ 위에)을 쓴다.

15 · 'Anton은 주말마다 그의 개와 함께 등산하러 가는 것을 좋아한다.'라는 의미이므로 전치사 with(~과 함께)를 쓴다.
· '이 칼을 이용해서 그 오이들을 잘라라.'라는 의미이므로 전치사 with(~을 이용해서)를 쓴다.

16 ② on 　①③④⑤ in

17 (1) '너는 무엇에 대해 이야기하고 있니?'라는 의미이므로 전치사 about(~에 대해)을 쓴다.
(2) wait for '~을 기다리다'

(3) laugh at '~을 보고/듣고 웃다, 비웃다'

18 listen to '~을 듣다'

19 be famous for '~으로 유명하다'

20 · 'Samantha는 그녀의 반 친구들 사이에서 인기 있다.'라는 의미이고 her classmates는 셋 이상이므로 전치사 among ((셋 이상) 사이에)을 쓴다.
· '나는 비행기에서 두 명의 아이 사이에 앉아있었다.'라는 의미이고 two children은 둘이므로 전치사 between((둘) 사이에)을 쓴다.

21 (A) 기념일(Valentine's Day) 앞에는 전치사 on을 쓴다.
(B) 인쇄물(the picture) 앞에는 전치사 in을 쓴다.
(C) 시각(nine) 앞에는 전치사 at을 쓴다.

22 ① in → on

23 첫 번째 빈칸: 도서관은 우체국과 은행 사이에 있는 상황이고, the post office and the bank는 둘이므로 전치사 between ((둘) 사이에)을 쓴다.
두 번째 빈칸: 도서관은 시청 앞에 있는 상황이므로 전치사 in front of(~ 앞에)를 쓴다.

24 · '그 여자는 그녀의 주머니 안으로 그녀의 손을 넣었다.'라는 의미이므로 전치사 into(~ 안으로)를 쓴다.
· '나는 강변을 따라서 산책했다.'라는 의미이므로 전치사 along(~을 따라서)을 쓴다.

25 '재민이는 토요일마다 테니스 수업을 듣는다.'라는 의미이므로 「on + 요일s」((요일)마다)를 쓴다.

26 ⑤ during → for

27 · '나의 집은 그 공원 옆에 있다.'라는 의미이므로 전치사 next to(~ 옆에)를 쓴다.
· be late for '~에 늦다'

28 · 하나의 지점(the next corner) 앞에는 전치사 at을 쓴다.
· '계단 아래로 내려가라.'라는 의미이므로 전치사 down(~ 아래로)을 쓴다.

29 be good at '~을 잘하다'

30 ④ on → in

31 (A) be ready for '~에 준비가 되다'
(B) be familiar with '~에 익숙하다'
(C) '상어들에 대한 그 다큐멘터리는 흥미로웠다.'라는 의미이므로 전치사 about(~에 대해)을 쓴다.

32 · '그는 가게로 가고 있다'라는 의미이고 동사 go와 함께 쓰여 도착 지점을 나타내고 있으므로 전치사 to(~으로)를 쓴다.
· 교통수단(the subway) 앞에는 전치사 on을 쓴다.

33 자연환경(the sea) 앞에는 전치사 in을 쓴다.

34 (A) be busy with '~으로 바쁘다'
(B) look at '~을 보다'
(C) thank … for '~에 대해 …에게 감사해하다'

35 ④: 바구니는 그 테이블 위에 있는 상황이므로 '그 테이블 아래에 바구니가 있다.'는 적절하지 않다.

36 (A) '선민이는 부산으로 떠났다'라는 의미이고 동사 leave와 함께 쓰여 가고자 하는 방향을 나타내고 있으므로 전치사 for(~으로)를 쓴다.

(B) in the hospital '입원 중인'

(C) '수염을 가진 그 남자는 종종 이 카페에 온다.'라는 의미이므로 전치사 with(~을 가진)를 쓴다.

37 '~ 후에'라는 의미의 전치사 after를 쓴다.

38 ①③ of　② for　④ from　⑤ on

39 ⓐⓓ in　ⓑ at　ⓒ on

POINT 1　and, but, or, so

연습문제 A							
1	and	**2**	or	**3**	but	**4**	so
5	but	**6**	or	**7**	and	**8**	but
9	and	**10**	so				

연습문제 B							
1	or	**2**	but	**3**	and	**4**	and
5	but	**6**	so	**7**	or	**8**	so

기출 적중문제

정답 ④

해설 첫 번째 빈칸: '나도 그러기를 원하지만, 그것은 두 시간 후에 문을 닫아.'라는 의미이므로 but(하지만)을 쓴다.
두 번째 빈칸: '택시 또는 버스를 타자.'라는 의미이므로 or(또는)를 쓴다.

POINT 2　명령문 + and/or

연습문제 A							
1	or	**2**	and	**3**	and	**4**	or

연습문제 B	
1	and he can help you
2	and people will like you
3	or your teacher will be upset

기출 적중문제

정답 Get up now, and you'll[you will] arrive on time.
해설 「명령문 + and ~」 '…해라, 그러면 ~'

POINT 3-1　when, before, after, while

연습문제 A					
1	while	**2**	After	**3**	When
4	after	**5**	finish	**6**	While
7	before	**8**	am	**9**	When
10	goes				

연습문제 B					
1	after	**2**	while	**3**	before
4	while	**5**	after		

연습문제 C							
1	ⓐ	**2**	ⓑ	**3**	ⓐ	**4**	ⓐ
5	ⓑ						

연습문제 C	**1** ⓐ	**2** ⓑ	**3** ⓐ	**4** ⓒ
	5 ⓐ	**6** ⓒ	**7** ⓑ	**8** ⓒ

기출 적중문제

정답 We thought that it was a tiger.
해설 that은 동사 thought의 목적어로 쓰이는 명사절을 이끈다.

POINT 3-2   because, if

연습문제 A

1 I am very hungry because I didn't eat breakfast.
Because I didn't eat breakfast, I am very hungry.

2 My parents were angry because I lied.
Because I lied, my parents were angry.

3 Put on your hat because the sun is shining.
Because the sun is shining, put on your hat.

4 We have to be quiet because the baby is sleeping.
Because the baby is sleeping, we have to be quiet.

5 Let's stay inside because it is very cold today.
Because it is very cold today, let's stay inside.

6 I couldn't see the stage because I was standing behind a tall man.
Because I was standing behind a tall man, I couldn't see the stage.

연습문제 B

1 if you need help
2 Because we missed the last bus
3 because of the funny movie
4 because its coffee is delicious
5 if you have a headache
6 If I get an invitation
7 because the homework was too difficult
8 because of his job

기출 적중문제

정답 ④
해설 because of → because

POINT 4   that

연습문제 A	**1** ⓐ	**2** ⓑ	**3** ⓒ	**4** ⓐ
	5 ⓒ	**6** ⓒ	**7** ⓐ	**8** ⓒ
	9 ⓑ	**10** ⓑ		

연습문제 B	**1** ②	**2** ②	**3** ②	**4** ②
	5 ②	**6** ②	**7** ②	**8** ②
	9 ②	**10** ②		

POINT 5   접속부사

연습문제 A

1 On the other hand	**2** For example
3 However	**4** Therefore
5 For example	**6** On the other hand
7 However	**8** Therefore

기출 적중문제

정답 ⑤
해설 '나의 가족은 주말마다 많은 것들을 함께 한다. 예를 들어, 우리는 브런치를 먹고 우리의 자전거를 타기 위해 한강에 간다.'라는 의미이므로 For example(예를 들어)을 쓴다.

서술형 대비 문제

Ⓐ
1 slow but strong
2 when I help others
3 Vietnam or Thailand
4 so she can grow vegetables
5 and Bob will send it
6 Because the wind was strong
7 or you'll[you will] get lost
8 (that) the concert is free
9 If Kerry apologizes
10 before it gets dark

Ⓑ
1 hates	**2** kind	**3** dancing
4 add	**5** did	**6** goes

Ⓒ
1 Therefore	**2** For example
3 However	**4** For example
5 However	**6** Therefore
7 For example	

Ⓓ ⓐ and ⓑ so ⓒ When ⓓ However ⓔ because ⓕ that

중간·기말고사 실전 문제

1 ① **2** ④ **3** ② **4** ⑤ **5** Wear a coat, or you'll get a cold. **6** ③ **7** ⑤ **8** ① **9** and you will get an A **10** ④ **11** drinks two cups of coffee when she is sleepy **12** When I was young, I didn't know how to swim. **13** that **14** ③ **15** ④ **16** ② **17** after **18** ⑤ **19** I will return this book after I finish reading it. **20** ⑤ **21** ② **22** because **23** if you tell the truth **24** ⑤ **25** ④ **26** ② **27** ③ **28** when **29** ② **30** I think (that) she will return soon. **31** that **32** but → and **33** ③ **34** ② **35** ① **36** For example, she was the winner **37** ⑤ **38** ②

1 '나는 우유를 좋아하지 않지만, 나의 형은 그것을 좋아한다.'라는 의미이므로 but(하지만)을 쓴다.

2 '내가 Melissa를 봤을 때, 그녀는 나를 보고 미소 짓고 있었다.'라는 의미이므로 When(~할 때)을 쓴다.

3 'Tony는 어젯밤에 늦게까지 자지 않았기 때문에 지금 매우 피곤하다.'라는 의미이므로 Because(~하기 때문에)를 쓴다.

4 ⑤ or → and

5 「명령문 + or ~」 '… 해라, 그렇지 않으면 ~'

6 ③: 지시형용사   ①②④⑤: 명사절 접속사

7 첫 번째 빈칸: '그림 또는 사진을 사는 게 어때?'라는 의미이므로 or(또는)를 쓴다.
두 번째 빈칸: '우리는 쓸 많은 돈을 가지고 있지 않아서, 그냥 포스터를 사자.'라는 의미이므로 so(그래서)를 쓴다.

8 ① or   ②③④⑤ and

9 '열심히 공부해라, 그러면 너는 시험에서 A를 받을 것이다.'라는 의미이므로 「명령문 + and ~」(…해라, 그러면 ~)를 쓴다.

10 ④ so → but

11 '~할 때'라는 의미의 when으로 주절과 부사절을 연결하고, 주절의 주어 Cindy가 문장 맨 앞에 왔으므로 주절 뒤에 부사절을 쓴다.

12 '~할 때'라는 의미의 When으로 주절과 부사절을 연결하고, 접속사가 문장 맨 앞에 왔으므로 부사절 뒤에 콤마(,)를 쓴다.

13 ·명사절 접속사 that(보어 역할)
·명사절 접속사 that(목적어 역할)

14 '하지만'이라는 의미의 but을 쓴다.

15 '~하는 동안'이라는 의미의 while을 쓴다.

16 '~하기 전에'라는 의미의 before를 쓴다.

17 손님들이 도착하기 전에 Mr. Davis가 식탁을 차렸다는 것은 Mr.

Davis가 식탁을 차린 후에 손님이 왔다는 것이므로 '~한 후에'라는 의미의 after를 쓴다.

18 ⑤: 의문사   ①②③④: 접속사

19 시간을 나타내는 부사절에서는 미래시제 대신 현재시제를 쓴다.

20 ⓓ but → or
ⓔ if → before

21 ②: while은 '~하는 동안'이라는 의미이다.

22 내가 열이 있어서 나갈 수 없다는 것은 내가 열이 있기 때문에 나갈 수 없다는 것이므로 '~하기 때문에'라는 의미의 because를 쓴다.

23 '만약 ~한다면'이라는 의미의 if를 쓴다.

24 '만약 ~한다면'이라는 의미의 if를 쓴다.
· '만약 네가 너의 머리를 빗는다면 그것은 좋아 보일 것이다.'
· '만약 폭풍우가 있다면 그 비행기는 떠날 수 없다.'
· '만약 네가 수업에 늦는다면 우리의 선생님은 화가 날 것이다.'

25 ④ because → because of

26 '그 시장이 열지 않아서, 나는 약간의 식료품도 살 수 없었다.'라는 의미이므로 so(그래서)를 쓴다.

27 ① because of → because
② careful → carefully
④ make → made
⑤ will pass → pass

28 '~할 때'라는 의미의 when을 쓴다.
· '내가 준비가 될 때 나는 너에게 말할 것이다.'
· 'Brian은 과학 수업에 있을 때 열심히 공부한다.'
· '나는 집에 왔을 때 배가 고팠다.'

29 ②: 지시대명사   ①③④⑤: 명사절 접속사

30 that은 동사 think의 목적어 역할을 하는 명사절을 이끈다. that절이 문장에서 목적어로 쓰였을 때 that을 생략할 수 있다.

31 that은 동사 know의 목적어 역할을 하는 명사절을 이끌고, 전체 문장이 'I know that they work hard.'이므로 세 번째에 오는 것은 that이다.

32 '우리는 슈퍼마켓에서 약간의 달걀들, 우유, 그리고 사과들을 살 필요가 있다.'라는 의미이므로 and(그리고)를 쓴다.

33 that은 동사 hope의 목적어 역할을 하는 명사절을 이끈다.

34 '그 수학 시험은 아주 어려웠다. 그러나, 나는 꽤 잘 한 것 같다고 생각한다.'라는 의미이므로 However(그러나)를 쓴다.

35 'Heather는 많은 자원 봉사를 한다. 예를 들어, 그녀는 가난한 사람들과 시간을 보내고 그들을 위해 식사를 요리해준다.'라는 의미이므로 For example(예를 들어)을 쓴다.

36 '예를 들어'라는 의미의 For example을 쓴다.

37 첫 번째 빈칸: 'A와 B 둘 다'라는 의미의 both A and B이므로 and를 쓴다.

두 번째 빈칸: '그녀는 매일 노래하는 것과 춤추는 것을 연습하지만, 약간의 수업도 받지 않는다.'라는 의미이므로 but(하지만)을 쓴다.

38 첫 번째 빈칸: '12월 31일에, Melanie는 자정에 종을 보기 위해 종로에 있는 보신각에 갔다. 그러나, 거리에 너무 많은 사람들이 있었다.'라는 의미이므로 However(그러나)를 쓴다.

두 번째 빈칸: '그녀는 종에 가까이 갈 수 없었다. 그러므로, 그녀는 종소리만 들었다.'라는 의미이므로 Therefore(그러므로)를 쓴다.

CHAPTER 1
be동사
p.8

POINT 1-1 주어와 be동사의 현재형

연습문제 **A**

1 It	**2** We	**3** They
4 You	**5** He	**6** She

연습문제 **B**

1 is	**2** is	**3** are
4 am	**5** are	**6** is
7 are	**8** is	**9** are
10 are		

연습문제 **C**

1 You're late.
2 He's at the bank.
3 I'm so cold.
4 It's windy now.
5 They're my classmates.
6 We're on the bus.
7 She's a famous singer.

POINT 1-2 be동사 현재형의 의미

연습문제

1 ⓐ	**2** ⓑ	**3** ⓒ	**4** ⓑ
5 ⓐ	**6** ⓑ	**7** ⓒ	**8** ⓐ
9 ⓒ	**10** ⓑ		

POINT 1-3 be동사의 현재형: 부정문

습제

1 I am not[I'm not] tired.
2 Liam is not[isn't] rude.
3 They are not[They're not/They aren't] at school.
4 It is not[It's not/It isn't] on the desk.
5 We are not[We're not/We aren't] high school students.
6 Marie and I are not[aren't] sisters.

POINT 1-4 be동사의 현재형: 의문문

연습문제

1 Are	**2** it	**3** Is
4 isn't	**5** Am	**6** he
7 Is	**8** is	**9** Are
10 I'm		

POINT 2-1 be동사의 과거형

연습문제

1 was	**2** was	**3** were
4 was	**5** were	**6** were
7 was	**8** were	**9** was
10 were		

POINT 2-2 be동사의 과거형: 부정문

연습문제

1 It was not[wasn't] sunny yesterday.
2 The movie was not[wasn't] boring.
3 Lisa and I were not[weren't] tired.
4 Peter was not[wasn't] a math teacher.
5 They were not[weren't] at home an hour ago.
6 We were not[weren't] late for class.

POINT 2-3 be동사의 과거형: 의문문

연습문제

1 Was the flower	**2** Was Wendy
3 Were her cupcakes	**4** Were the knives
5 Was the test	**6** Was your mom

중간·기말고사 실전 문제

1 ⑤   **2** ③   **3** ①   **4** ④
5 Mr. Smith is a math teacher.   **6** ②
7 ①   **8** ③   **9** ④   **10** Sonya wasn't busy   **11** ②   **12** ⑤   **13** ③, ④
14 (1) Thomas is not[isn't] at the supermarket.
(2) Is Thomas at the supermarket?   **15** ⑤
16 ④   **17** ③   **18** ③   **19** ④   **20** are
21 Are, they aren't   **22** ①   **23** is a farmer, is

1   ⑤ is → are

2   be동사가 are이므로 주어는 1인칭 복수·2인칭·3인칭 복수를 쓴다. She는 3인칭 단수이므로 is를 쓴다.

3   be동사가 was이므로 주어는 1인칭 단수·3인칭 단수를 쓴다. Brad and Sam은 3인칭 복수이므로 were를 쓴다.

4   · 주어 Bob and I는 1인칭 복수이므로 are를 쓴다.
     · 주어 The cat은 3인칭 단수이므로 is를 쓴다.

5   주어 Mr. Smith는 3인칭 단수이므로 is를 쓴다.

6   ② was → were

7   ①: '~(에) 있다'   ②③④⑤: '~(하)다'

8   ① aren't → is not[isn't]
     ② not is → is not[isn't]
     ④ are → is
     ⑤ amn't → am not

9   ④: am not은 줄여 쓸 수 없다.

10   주어 Sonya는 3인칭 단수이므로 was를 쓰고 be동사의 부정문은 「be동사 + not」이다.

11   주어 Mason and Carrie로 묻고 있으므로 주어 they로 대답하고 be동사의 의문문에 대한 대답은 「Yes, 주어 + be동사.」 또는 「No, 주어 + be동사 + not.」이다.

12   주어 Ms. Lang으로 묻고 있으므로 주어 she로 대답하고 그녀는 피아니스트라고 했으므로 No, she isn't.로 대답한다.

13   ③: be동사의 의문문에 대한 대답: 「Yes, 주어 + be동사.」 또는 「No, 주어 + be동사 + not.」
     ④: 주어 Olivia로 묻고 있으므로 주어 she로 대답한다.

14   (1) be동사의 부정문: 「be동사 + not」
     (2) be동사의 의문문: 「be동사 + 주어 ~?」

15   ⑤ weren't → wasn't

16   ⓐ is → are
     ⓑ Is interesting the movie? → Is the movie interesting?
     ⓓ not was → was not[wasn't]

17   ③ are[were]   ①②④⑤ is[was]

18   be동사의 부정문: 「be동사 + not」

19   주어 your paintings는 3인칭 복수이므로 are를 쓰고 be동사의 의문문은 「be동사 + 주어 ~?」이다.

20   첫 번째 빈칸: 주어 Greg and Jason은 3인칭 복수이므로 are를 쓴다.
     두 번째 빈칸: 주어 my parents는 3인칭 복수이므로 are를 쓴다.

21   첫 번째 빈칸: 주어 the rain boots는 3인칭 복수이므로 Are를
쓴다.
     두 번째 빈칸: 주어 the rain boots로 묻고 있으므로 주어 they
로 대답하고 be동사의 의문문에 대한 대답은 「Yes, 주어 + be동사.」 또는 「No, 주어 + be동사 + not.」이다.

22   ② It → He
     ③ We → You
     ④ Its → We
     ⑤ You → They

23   첫 번째 빈칸: 주어 My father는 3인칭 단수이고 농부이므로 is a farmer를 쓴다.
     두 번째 빈칸: 주어 She는 3인칭 단수이고 똑똑하므로 is smart를 쓴다.
     세 번째 빈칸: 주어 Karen은 3인칭 단수이고 학생이므로 is a student를 쓴다.
     네 번째 빈칸: 주어 She는 3인칭 단수이고 수줍음을 많이 타므로 is shy를 쓴다.

24   첫 번째 빈칸: 주어 Ethan and Erica는 3인칭 복수이므로 are를 쓴다.
     두 번째 빈칸: 주어 We는 1인칭 복수이므로 are를 쓴다.
     세 번째 빈칸: 주어 Ethan and Erica는 3인칭 복수이므로 are를 쓴다.

25   주어 I는 1인칭 단수이므로 am을 쓰고, 주어 they는 3인칭 복수이므로 are를 쓴다.

CHAPTER 2
일반동사

p.18

POINT 1-1 일반동사의 현재형

연습문제 A

1 lives	2 opens	3 eats
4 grows	5 does	6 enjoys
7 knows	8 has	9 tries
10 plays	11 brushes	12 rings
13 flies	14 buys	15 cooks
16 teaches	17 washes	18 worries
19 sleeps	20 gets	21 moves
22 walks	23 watches	24 sits
25 arrives	26 practices	

연습문제 B

1 knows	2 has	3 listen
4 sees	5 carries	6 run
7 watches	8 pays	9 puts
10 fly		

POINT 1-2 일반동사의 현재형: 부정문

연습문제

1 does not[doesn't] walk
2 do not[don't] eat
3 does not[doesn't] read
4 do not[don't] wake
5 puts
6 does not[doesn't] ride
7 do not[don't] have
8 do not[don't] listen
9 does not[doesn't] open
10 does not[doesn't] smell
11 learns
12 do not[don't] wear
13 brush
14 does not[doesn't] watch

POINT 1-3 일반동사의 현재형: 의문문

연습문제 A

1 Do you run every day?
2 Does Cindy have a red wallet?
3 Do they do homework after class?
4 O
5 Does she talk about me a lot?
6 Does she do the laundry on sunny days?
7 O

8 Do I look good in this dress?

연습문제 B

1 do	2 doesn't	3 do
4 doesn't	5 don't	6 do

POINT 2-1 일반동사의 과거형: 규칙 변화

연습문제 A

1 moved	2 talked	3 missed
4 lived	5 played	6 studied
7 hurried	8 shared	9 called
10 invited	11 jumped	12 carried
13 said	14 entered	15 stopped
16 dropped	17 asked	18 rained
19 changed	20 hugged	21 stayed
22 jogged	23 visited	24 laughed
25 grabbed	26 tried	

연습문제 B

1 O	2 arrived	3 moved
4 helped	5 worried	6 O
7 missed	8 O	9 finished
10 tasted		

POINT 2-2 일반동사의 과거형: 불규칙 변화

연습문제 A

1 fed - fed	2 had - had
3 caught - caught	4 hurt - hurt
5 sat - sat	6 came - come
7 ran - run	8 fought - fought
9 drank - drunk	10 got - got(ten)
11 sang - sung	12 saw - seen
13 wore - worn	14 woke - woken
15 went - gone	16 grew - grown
17 read - read	18 sent - sent
19 did - done	20 built - built
21 knew - known	22 overcame - overcome
23 put - put	24 spread - spread
25 swam - swum	26 rose - risen

연습문제 B

1 drove	2 sold	3 swam
4 had	5 forgot	6 left
7 fell	8 bought	

POINT 2-3 일반동사의 과거형: 부정문과 의문문

연습문제 A

1 Miranda did not[didn't] finish her homework.
2 Did she mix the ingredients?
3 I did not[didn't] see elephants at the zoo.
4 Did Poppy make pancakes this morning?
5 Tom did not[didn't] wear a swimming cap.

6 Did Paul walk his dog last night?

1 Yes, they did   **2** No, she didn't
3 No, they didn't   **4** Yes, he did

중간·기말고사 실전 문제

1 ③,⑤ **2** ④   **3** ⑤   **4** ②   **5** do not[don't] eat   **6** does not[doesn't] exercise
7 ①   **8** ④   **9** ④   **10** ⑤
11 Minji does not[doesn't] study history every day.
12 Does Minji study history every day?, Yes, she does.   **13** (1) ⓐ → traveled (2) ⓒ → visited
14 ②   **15** ②   **16** ⑤   **17** ②   **18** ④
19 ③   **20** drinks → drink   **21** ①   **22** ②
23 ②   **24** ⓐ has ⓑ is ⓒ sleeps   **25** read, don't watch, doesn't read, watches

1 동사가 does이므로 주어는 3인칭 단수를 쓴다. They와 Kyle and Stacy는 3인칭 복수이므로 do를 쓴다.

2 ・주어 Mr. Smith는 3인칭 단수이므로 works를 쓴다.
　・주어 Children은 3인칭 복수이므로 play를 쓴다.

3 주어 The students는 3인칭 복수이므로 take, don't swim을 쓴다.

4 ① likes → like
　③ don't → doesn't
　④ doesn't → don't
　⑤ don't be care → don't care

5 주어 Some people은 3인칭 복수이므로 일반동사 현재형의 부정문은 「do not[don't] + 동사원형」이다.

6 주어 Anne은 3인칭 단수이므로 일반동사 현재형의 부정문은 「does not[doesn't] + 동사원형」이다.

7 첫 번째 빈칸: 일반동사 현재형의 의문문은 「Do/Does + 주어 + 동사원형 ~?」이므로 동사원형 live를 쓴다.
　두 번째 빈칸: 주어 my parents는 3인칭 복수이므로 동사원형 live를 쓴다.

8 ④ pay – pays

9 주어 The amusement park는 3인칭 단수이므로 일반동사 현재형의 의문문은 「Does + 주어 + 동사원형 ~?」이다.

10 ① doesn't → does
　② they're not → they don't
　③ doesn't → don't
　④ am → do

11 주어 Minji는 3인칭 단수이므로 일반동사 현재형의 부정문은 「does not[doesn't] + 동사원형」이다.

12 A: 주어 Minji는 3인칭 단수이므로 일반동사 현재형의 의문문은 「Does + 주어 + 동사원형 ~?」이다.
　B: 주어 Minji는 3인칭 단수이므로 일반동사 현재형의 의문문에 대한 긍정의 대답은 「Yes, 주어 + does.」이다.

13 ⓐ 동사 travel의 과거형: traveled
　ⓒ 동사 visit의 과거형: visited

14 ・동사 make의 과거형: made
　・동사 stop의 과거형: stopped

15 ② buyed → bought

16 일반동사 과거형의 의문문에 대한 대답: 「Yes, 주어 + did.」 또는 「No, 주어 + didn't.」

17 ② stops → stop

18 주어 he는 3인칭 단수이므로 일반동사 현재형의 의문문은 「Does + 주어 + 동사원형 ~?」이다.

19 일반동사 과거형의 의문문: 「Did + 주어 + 동사원형 ~?」

20 Mike and Ben은 3인칭 복수이므로 일반동사 현재형의 부정문은 「do not[don't] + 동사원형」이다.

21 ① growed → grew

22 ② don't walks → doesn't walk

23 ⓑ Does → Do
　ⓒ not did → did not[didn't]
　ⓓ studies → study

24 ⓐ 주어 Mindy는 3인칭 단수이므로 has를 쓴다.
　ⓑ 주어 Its name은 3인칭 단수이므로 is를 쓴다.
　ⓒ 주어 It은 3인칭 단수이므로 sleeps를 쓴다.

25 첫 번째 빈칸: 주어 I는 1인칭 단수이고 책을 읽는다고 했으므로 read를 쓴다.
　두 번째 빈칸: 주어 I는 1인칭 단수이고 TV를 보지 않는다고 했으므로 don't watch를 쓴다.
　세 번째 빈칸: 주어 Kate는 3인칭 단수이고 책을 읽지 않는다고 했으므로 doesn't read를 쓴다.
　네 번째 빈칸: 주어 she는 3인칭 단수이고 TV를 본다고 했으므로 watches를 쓴다.

POINT 1 현재시제

연습문제 A

1	has	**2**	eats	**3**	live
4	go	**5**	study	**6**	is
7	opens	**8**	owns	**9**	like
10	consists				

연습문제 B

1	has	**2**	doesn't grow
3	Does, listen	**4**	don't watch
5	Do, sleep	**6**	doesn't wake
7	takes	**8**	leaves

POINT 2 과거시제

연습문제 A

1 Terry called me
2 Minha studied Chinese
3 Jake played with a robot
4 Did she drink tea
5 I went to my grandfather's house
6 Many people visited the theater

연습문제 B

1 Jamie baked muffins yesterday.
2 Chris is in the hospital now.
3 Did you clean the bathroom an hour ago?
4 O
5 She screamed when she saw a snake.
6 The Second World War ended on September 2, 1945.

POINT 3 미래시제

연습문제 A

1 They will[They'll] be on vacation
2 Lou and Sandra are going to play golf
3 Are you going to be busy
4 Matt will not[won't] eat spicy food
5 The class is going to start
6 Anne will take a yoga lesson
7 Will he cook dinner
8 We are not[We're not/We aren't] going to go shopping

연습문제 B

1	will see	**2**	finished	**3**	will be
4	will become	**5**	lived	**6**	will travel
7	will come				

POINT 4-1 진행시제: 현재진행시제

연습문제 A

1	having	**2**	buying	**3**	blowing
4	sleeping	**5**	lying	**6**	winning
7	seeing	**8**	planning	**9**	sitting
10	baking	**11**	closing	**12**	waiting
13	running	**14**	crying	**15**	being
16	smiling	**17**	visiting	**18**	asking
19	tying	**20**	collecting	**21**	enjoying
22	entering				

연습문제 B

1	is making	**2**	am studying
3	is drawing	**4**	are traveling
5	are having	**6**	are wrapping
7	am having		

POINT 4-2 진행시제: 현재진행시제의 부정문과 의문문

연습문제 A

1 Are they doing their homework?
2 Is Mr. Lewis having lunch now?
3 The students are not solving the math problems.
4 Are you coming to my apartment now?
5 The kid is not brushing her teeth.
6 Is your older brother watching TV?
7 I am not wearing a warm coat.

연습문제 B

1	No, she isn't	**2**	Yes, they are
3	Yes, it is	**4**	No, he isn't
5	Yes, they are	**6**	No, I'm not

POINT 4-3 진행시제: 과거진행시제

연습문제 A

1 was making
2 wasn't working
3 were walking
4 wasn't talking
5 Was, snowing, it was
6 Was, wearing, he wasn't

POINT 5 현재완료시제

연습문제

1 Mia has watched her favorite movie five times.
2 The music festival has just ended.
3 Adam has already bought tickets for the show.
4 O
5 O

6   Bob and I have taken swimming lessons for two years.

중간·기말고사 실전 문제

1 ②   **2** ③   **3** ④   **4** ②   **5** ①, ④
6 ③, ⑤ **7** ①   **8** William is going to visit the museum next Friday. **9** ②   **10** ①   **11** ④
12 Are we going to go to the bank tomorrow?
13 ②   **14** ④   **15** ④   **16** ②   **17** Is your younger sister brushing her teeth?   **18** ④
19 A leaf is floating on the river.   **20** My father was taking a shower an hour ago.   **21** ④
22 ③   **23** are building   **24** ④   **25** (1) got a haircut (2) No, won't, will eat brunch

1   next Saturday는 미래시제와 주로 함께 쓰이는 부사구이다.

2   Last weekend는 과거시제와 주로 함께 쓰이는 부사구이다.

3   ④ runing → running

4   · 일반적 사실을 말하고 있으므로 현재시제를 쓰고 주어 A koala는 3인칭 단수이므로 sleeps를 쓴다.
·현재의 습관이나 반복되는 일을 나타내고 있으므로 현재시제를 쓰고 주어 The five-year-old girl은 3인칭 단수이므로 sleeps를 쓴다.

5   현재진행시제 is cooking이 쓰였으므로 현재진행을 나타내는 부사(구) at the moment와 now를 쓴다.

6   미래시제를 나타내는 Will이 쓰였으므로 미래시제와 주로 쓰이는 부사(구) tomorrow와 next Tuesday를 쓴다.

7   첫 번째 빈칸: 과거시제 did가 쓰였으므로 과거시제와 주로 쓰이는 부사구 last Tuesday를 쓴다.
두 번째 빈칸: 과거시제로 묻고 있으므로 과거시제로 대답한다.

8   be going to가 있는 미래시제는 「be going to + 동사원형」이고 주어 William은 3인칭 단수이므로 be동사는 is를 쓴다.

9   ⓐ going rain → going to rain
ⓒ is → be
ⓔ not are → are not[aren't]

10   (A) two days ago는 과거시제와 주로 함께 쓰이는 부사구이므로 과거시제 wasn't를 쓴다.
(B) 역사적인 사실을 말하고 있으므로 과거시제 arrived를 쓴다.
(C) tomorrow는 미래시제와 주로 함께 쓰이는 부사이므로 미래시제를 나타내는 will을 쓴다.

11   ① set → sets
② ate → will eat
③ works → worked
⑤ went → will go

12   be going to가 있는 미래시제의 의문문: 「be동사 + 주어 + going to + 동사원형 ~?」

13   ② was → will be (next year는 미래시제와 주로 함께 쓰이는 부사구이다.)

14   '~하고 있다'라는 의미의 현재진행시제 are drawing을 쓴다.

15   · 현재진행시제: 「am/is/are + V-ing」
· 현재진행시제의 의문문: 「Am/Is/Are + 주어 + V-ing ~?」

16   현재진행시제의 의문문에 대한 대답은 「Yes, 주어 + am/is/are.」 또는 「No, 주어 + am/is/are + not.」이고 주어 he는 3인칭 단수이므로 be동사는 is를 쓴다.

17   현재진행시제의 의문문은 「Am/Is/Are + 주어 + V-ing ~?」이고 주어 your younger sister는 3인칭 단수이므로 be동사는 Is를 쓴다.

18   ④ writeing → writing

19   현재시제 floats가 쓰였으므로 현재진행시제 「am/is/are + V-ing」를 쓰고 주어 A leaf는 3인칭 단수이므로 be동사는 is를 쓴다.

20   과거시제 took이 쓰였으므로 과거진행시제 「was/were + V-ing」를 쓰고 주어 My father는 3인칭 단수이므로 be동사는 was를 쓴다.

21   Sheldon이 2013년에 Los Angeles로 이사 갔고 아직도 그곳에 살고 있으므로 현재완료시제 「have/has + p.p.」를 쓰고, 주어 Sheldon은 3인칭 단수이므로 has를 쓴다.

22   ③ studies → studied

23   현재진행시제 are ·· doing으로 묻고 있으므로 현재진행시제 「am/is/are + V-ing」로 대답하고 주어 They는 3인칭 복수이므로 be동사는 are를 쓴다.

24   ④ recycle → recycling (과거진행시제: 「was/were + V-ing」

25   (1) 과거시제 did로 묻고 있고, 어제는 머리를 잘랐다고 했으므로 과거시제 got a haircut를 쓴다.
(2) 미래시제 Will로 묻고 있고, 내일은 자전거를 타지 않으므로 will이 있는 미래시제의 의문문에 대한 부정의 대답은 「No, 주어 + won't.」이다. 내일은 브런치를 먹을 것이라고 했으므로 미래시제 will eat brunch를 쓴다.

CHAPTER 4
조동사

p.42

POINT 1-1 조동사의 쓰임

1 can	2 finish	3 should
4 be able to	5 speak	6 be
7 will	8 stay	9 move
10 be able to		

1 It may be cold tonight.
2 This printer can print on both sides of the paper.
3 We should meet Tom at the station.
4 O
5 She will listen to your advice.
6 Ken can give us some tickets for the game.

POINT 1-2 조동사가 있는 부정문과 의문문

1 Can you speak
2 We should not mess
3 Will Sam drive
4 The toddler cannot walk
5 Should I throw
6 Yunju may not move
7 Can Wendy come
8 Katherine will not graduate

1 he can	2 she won't
3 we must	4 you shouldn't
5 I can't	

POINT 2-1 can, could I

1 I can solve	2 Can Fred lift
3 He cannot[can't] use	
4 Ms. Jones cannot[can't] read	
5 Can you stand	6 We can buy

1 Is Mr. Davis able to make seafood pasta?
2 Snails cannot[can't] move that fast.
3 Is your older brother able to drive?
4 Jenna could not[couldn't] find the post office easily.
5 Dolphins are not[aren't] able to breathe underwater.

POINT 2-2 can, could II

1 요청	2 허가	3 능력·가능
4 허가	5 요청	6 허가
7 능력·가능	8 요청	9 허가
10 능력·가능		

POINT 3 may

1 허가	2 약한 추측	3 약한 추측
4 허가	5 약한 금지	6 약한 추측
7 약한 금지	8 약한 추측	9 허가
10 약한 금지		

POINT 4-1 will, would I

1 I am going to make some potato soup.
2 Jenny and I are going to study history together.
3 Is Jimmy going to join the soccer team?
4 She is not going to stay at my home next Sunday.
5 Minho is going to perform on stage soon.
6 We are not going to come to your Christmas party.
7 Is it going to be sunny tomorrow?

1 Martin will visit Korea next year.
2 Will you order the hamburger and fries?
3 Laura is going to meet me at the station.
4 Would you go to the dentist with me?
5 My dad is going to move my desk to the window.

POINT 4-2 will, would II

1 I would[I'd] like	2 I would[I'd] like to
3 I would[I'd] like	4 I would[I'd] like
5 Would you like to	6 I would[I'd] like to
7 I would[I'd] like to	8 Would you like
9 I would[I'd] like	10 Would you like to

POINT 5-1 must I

1 We must behave
2 She must have

3 They cannot[can't] be
4 You must not copy
5 It cannot[can't] be
6 Jason must be

POINT 5-2 must II

1 I have to save some money.
2 We have to listen carefully to our teacher.
3 She has to go to the hospital now.
4 The law has to be fair to everyone.
5 You have to write down your name clearly.

1 don't have to wear **2** had to sleep
3 can't be **4** must not forget
5 doesn't have to tell **6** must be

POINT 6 should, had better

1 had better **2** should
3 had better not **4** should
5 had better **6** should not
7 had better not **8** should
9 should not **10** should not
11 had better **12** should
13 should **14** had better

중간·기말고사 실전 문제

1 ① **2** ① **3** ⑤ **4** ④ **5** ③
6 We cannot exist without air. **7** ② **8** ④, ⑤
9 ③ **10** ② **11** ④ **12** ④ **13** (1) We
should not[shouldn't] spend our money on a new car.
(2) Should we spend our money on a new car?
14 ⑤ **15** ② **16** is able to finish **17** wasn't
able to get **18** ④ **19** ④ **20** ③
21 Brandon and Bill cannot[can't] be twins.
22 (1) had to (2) will have to **23** can dance,
cannot[can't] dance, can speak, cannot[can't] speak
24 ③ **25** (A) You must wear (B) You must not
run

1 조동사 뒤에는 동사원형이 오고 조동사는 주어의 인칭이나 수에
따라 형태가 변하지 않는다.

2 조동사 뒤에는 동사원형이 온다.

3 능력·가능(~할 수 있다)을 나타내는 can의 부정형 cannot을 쓴

다.

4 will = be going to (미래)

5 have to = must (의무)

6 조동사가 있는 부정문: 「조동사 + not + 동사원형」

7 조동사가 있는 의문문에 대한 대답은 「Yes, 주어 + 조동사.」 또
는 「No, 주어 + 조동사 + not.」이고 주어 I로 묻고 있으므로 주어
you로 대답한다.

8 지우개를 빌려도 되는지 묻는 말에 '여기 있어.'라고 대답했으므로
허가를 나타내는 의문문에 대한 긍정의 대답을 쓴다.

9 ① isn't may → may not be
② are → is
④ shoulds → should
⑤ Do can I → Can I

10 '그녀는 잠들 수 없다. 바깥은 너무 시끄럽다.'라는 의미이므로
can't(~할 수 없다)를 쓴다.

11 had better의 부정형: had better not

12 can = may (허가)

13 (1) 조동사가 있는 부정문: 「조동사 + not + 동사원형」
(2) 조동사가 있는 의문문: 「조동사 + 주어 + 동사원형 ~?」

14 · '우리는 내일 야구 시합이 있다. 우리는 그 게임을 이기기 위해
열심히 연습해야 한다.'라는 의미이므로 must(~해야 한다)를
쓴다.
· 'Jenna는 어제 그녀가 가장 좋아하는 곰 인형을 잃어버렸다.
그녀는 속상함에 틀림없다.'라는 의미이므로 must(~임에 틀림
없다)를 쓴다.

15 ① shouldn't → can[may]
③ must not → must
④ don't have to → can't
⑤ Will → Can

16 can = be able to (능력·가능)

17 couldn't = wasn't able to (능력·가능)

18 첫 번째 빈칸: '내가 하나를 먹어도 되니?'라는 의미이므로 Can
(~해도 된다)을 쓴다.
두 번째 빈칸: '내가 나중에 부엌을 청소하는 것을 도와주겠니?'라
는 의미이므로 Can(~해주겠니?)을 쓴다.

19 ⓑⓓⓔ: '~할 수 있다' ⓐ: '~해주겠니?' ⓒ: '~해도 된다'

20 ⓐ should be not → should not be
ⓒ Will you helping → Will you help
ⓓ would like to → would like
ⓔ will have to → had to

21 강한 추측(~임에 틀림없다)을 나타내는 must의 부정형: can't

22 (1) 의무(~해야 한다)를 나타내는 must의 과거형: had to
(2) 의무(~해야 한다)를 나타내는 must의 미래형: will have to

23 첫 번째 빈칸: Bill과 Jack은 춤출 수 있다고 했으므로 ca

dance를 쓴다.

두 번째 빈칸: Anne은 춤출 수 없다고 했으므로 cannot[can't] dance를 쓴다.

세 번째 빈칸: Anne은 프랑스어를 말할 수 있다고 했으므로 can speak을 쓴다.

네 번째 빈칸: Bill과 Jack은 프랑스어를 말할 수 없다고 했으므로 cannot[can't] speak을 쓴다.

24 (A) '그것은 Greg의 것일 수도 있다.'라는 의미이므로 may를 쓴다.

(B) '그것은 그의 것일 리가 없다.'라는 의미이므로 can't를 쓴다.

(C) '그러면 너는 Mike에게 물어봐야 한다.'라는 의미이므로 should를 쓴다.

25 (A) 조동사 뒤에는 동사원형이 온다.

(B) 조동사가 있는 부정문: 「조동사 + not + 동사원형」

CHAPTER 5
문장의 형식
p.56

POINT 1-1 1형식과 2형식

 연습문제

1 주어, 동사		**2** 주어, 동사, 주격 보어
3 주어, 동사, 수식어		**4** 주어, 동사, 주격 보어
5 주어, 동사, 수식어		**6** 주어, 동사, 주격 보어
7 주어, 동사, 주격 보어		**8** 주어, 동사, 수식어

POINT 1-2 2형식: 감각동사

연습문제

1 tastes like		**2** nice
3 O		**4** looks
5 cold		**6** O
7 tasted		**8** expensive
9 O		**10** sounds like

POINT 2-1 3형식과 4형식

연습문제

1 Lisa told me a funny story.
2 My father built our house.
3 I read an interesting book.
4 He sent me a postcard.
5 Kate found her wallet.
6 Dan lent Minsu some money.
7 James bought a pair of sneakers.
8 Ms. Kim teaches us science.
9 They love Korean food.
10 She prepared a nice dinner.
11 I heard a loud noise.
12 Martin baked an apple pie.
13 I brought George some juice.
14 The reporter asked him a question.

POINT 2-2 4형식을 3형식으로 바꾸는 법

 연습문제 A

1 to	**2** to	**3** for
4 of	**5** for	**6** for
7 to	**8** to	

 연습문제 B

1 Please pass the salt to me.
2 William sent Jade a photo by smartphone.
3 She bought a bunch of flowers for me.
4 Dave showed some pictures of his dogs to us.

5 The bird brought me a pebble.
6 Can I get you a cup of coffee?
7 John cooked a nice dinner for me.
8 My friend lent me his jacket.

POINT 3 5형식

연습
문제
A

1 목적어: me, 목적격보어: sweaty
2 목적어: our front door, 목적격보어: open
3 목적어: the soup, 목적격 보어: too spicy
4 목적어: Anna, 목적격 보어: a famous writer
5 목적어: the baby, 목적격보어: awake
6 목적어: the movie, 목적격 보어: boring
7 목적어: me, 목적격 보어: full
8 목적어: his car, 목적격 보어: very clean
9 목적어: my younger sister, 목적격 보어: Pancake
10 목적어: the cat, 목적격 보어: Tigger

연습
문제
B

| **1** ② | **2** ① | **3** ② |
| **4** ③ | **5** ① | **6** ② |

중간·기말고사 실전 문제

1 ②　　**2** ④　　**3** ①,⑤　**4** ①,②　**5** ①
6 ③　　**7** ②　　**8** looks like a tiger
9 looked slippery　**10** ⑤　　**11** ④　　**12** ④
13 like　**14** to　　**15** ④　　**16** The accident
made my dad angry. **17** ②,③ **18** ②
19 taught the history of the United States to us
20 made some bracelets for her friends
21 ④　　**22** ①　　**23** ①　　**24** Dave lent his
classmate his textbook.　　**25** (1) ⓐ → healthy
(2) ⓔ → feel

1 ② 2형식 → 1형식 (「주어 + 동사 + 수식어구」 형태의 1형식 문장이다.)

2 ⓑⓔ: 2형식 ⓐⓒⓓ: 1형식

3 「감각동사 + like + 명사」

4 감각동사 뒤에는 형용사가 오므로 형용사 comfortable과 lovely를 쓴다.

5 ① sounded like → looked

6 ③ tastes like → tastes

7 ・빈칸 뒤에 목적어(us)가 있으므로 3형식 동사 took을 쓴다.
・빈칸 뒤에 간접목적어(her)와 직접목적어(a birthday present)가 있으므로 수여동사 gave를 쓴다.

8 '~하게 보이다'라는 의미의 look을 쓰고 감각동사의 주격 보어 자리에 명사 a tiger가 왔으므로 감각동사 뒤에 like를 쓴다.

9 '~하게 보이다'라는 의미의 look을 쓰고 감각동사의 주격 보어 자리에 형용사 slippery를 쓴다.

10 ⑤ for　　①②③④ to

11 ④ sounded like → sounded

12 주어진 문장과 ①②③⑤: 3형식
④: 4형식

13 ・감각동사의 주격 보어 자리에 명사 a castle이 왔으므로 감각동사 뒤에 like를 쓴다.
・감각동사의 주격 보어 자리에 명사 jazz가 왔으므로 감각동사 뒤에 like를 쓴다.

14 ・4형식 문장을 3형식 문장으로 바꿀 때 동사 send는 간접목적어 앞에 전치사 to를 쓴다.
・4형식 문장을 3형식 문장으로 바꿀 때 동사 pass는 간접목적어 앞에 전치사 to를 쓴다.

15 ・빈칸 뒤에 간접목적어(his friend)와 직접목적어(a jacket)가 있으므로 수여동사가 아닌 became은 쓸 수 없다.
・빈칸 뒤에 간접목적어(her sister)와 직접목적어(new shoes)가 있으므로 수여동사가 아닌 became은 쓸 수 없다.

16 5형식: 「주어 + 동사 + 목적어 + 목적격보어」

17 간접목적어(me) 앞에 전치사 to가 있으므로 4형식 문장을 3형식 문장으로 바꿀 때 간접목적어 앞에 전치사 for를 쓰는 동사 made와 got은 쓸 수 없다.

18 (A) 4형식 문장을 3형식 문장으로 바꿀 때 동사 cook은 간접목적어 앞에 전치사 for를 쓴다.
(B) 4형식 문장을 3형식 문장으로 바꿀 때 동사 show는 간접목적어 앞에 전치사 to를 쓴다.
(C) 4형식 문장을 3형식 문장으로 바꿀 때 동사 ask는 직접목적어 앞에 전치사 of를 쓴다.

19 4형식 문장을 3형식 문장으로 바꿀 때 동사 teach는 간접목적어 앞에 전치사 to를 쓴다.

20 4형식 문장을 3형식 문장으로 바꿀 때 동사 make는 간접목적어 앞에 전치사 for를 쓴다.

21 ④: 4형식 ①②③⑤: 5형식

22 ② to your textbook → your textbook
③ of → to
④ to → for
⑤ a snowman his cousin → his cousin a snowman

23 (A) 감각동사 뒤에는 형용사가 오므로 형용사 beautiful을 쓴다.
(B) 「감각동사 + like + 명사」이므로 sounded like를 쓴다.
(C) 주어 he를 보충 설명하는 주격 보어 자리에는 형용사 hungry를 쓴다.

24 4형식: 「주어 + 동사 + 간접목적어(~에게) + 직접목적어(~을)」

25 (A) 목적격 보어 자리에 부사는 올 수 없다.
(B) 감각동사의 주격 보어 자리에 형용사 sick이 왔으므로 감각동사 feel을 쓴다.

POINT 1 명령문

1 drive	**2** Be	**3** Don't
4 Speak	**5** watch	**6** Be
7 enter	**8** make	

1 Try that restaurant.
2 Exercise more often.
3 Don't play video games much.
4 Don't be rude to your teachers.
5 Wear a jacket.
6 Don't park here.
7 Sit down.
8 Get some rest.
9 Don't push the button.
10 Close the window.
11 Finish your homework.
12 Don't jump on the bed.

POINT 2 청유문

1 Let's drink	**2** Let's go
3 Let's not watch	**4** Let me introduce
5 Let's not stay	**6** Let's make
7 Let's not be	**8** Let me check
9 Let's visit	**10** Let's not play

POINT 3 감탄문

1 How spicy (this tteokbokki tastes)!
2 What an expensive car (it is)!
3 How well she cooks!
4 How brave (you are)!
5 What salty soup (this is)!
6 What an interesting book (this is)!
7 How scary (that movie was)!
8 What a busy morning (it was)!
9 What long ears (the rabbit has)!
10 How fast the clouds move!

POINT 4 Yes/No 의문문

1 No, it isn't	**2** No, he doesn't
3 Yes, they were	**4** No, he didn't
5 Yes, I can	**6** No, I don't
7 Yes, we should	**8** No, it won't

POINT 5-1 의문사 의문문

1 Why are you surprised?
2 How does the cake taste?
3 Where will your family stay?
4 When did Tom lose his wallet?
5 Who turned off the lights?
6 What can I do now?

POINT 5-2 의문사: who

1 Who	**2** Whose	**3** Who(m)
4 Whose	**5** Who	**6** Who(m)
7 Whose	**8** Who(m)	**9** Who

POINT 5-3 의문사: what, which

1 What	**2** Which	**3** What
4 What	**5** Which	**6** What
7 What	**8** Which	**9** Which
10 What		

POINT 5-4 의문사: where, when, why, how

1 When	**2** How	**3** When
4 Where	**5** Why	**6** How
7 Where	**8** Why	**9** Where
10 When		

1 Who is your best friend?
2 Why was Bob late?
3 When will the show start?
4 Where can I buy some snacks?
5 What is Mr. Smith's job?
6 How can I make a peach pie?

POINT 5-5　의문사: How + 형용사/부사

1 How much　**2** How tall　**3** How often
4 How old　**5** How long　**6** How many
7 How big　**8** How far

POINT 6　부가의문문

1 isn't she　**2** doesn't it　**3** didn't he
4 will you　**5** aren't I　**6** is it
7 can't he　**8** shall we　**9** do I
10 are you

중간·기말고사 실전 문제

1 ②　**2** ③　**3** ③　**4** Don't run in the hallway.　**5** Let's talk about air pollution.
6 ③　**7** ⑤　**8** ②　**9** (1) What an impressive review　(2) How late　**10** ③　**11** ④
12 ②　**13** ⑤　**14** ③　**15** ④　**16** ③
17 How tall is your father?　**18** What ice cream do you like?　**19** ③　**20** ②
21 (1) don't they　(2) shall we　**22** ②, ⑤　**23** ③
24 (1) Doesn't Melanie work at a bank?　(2) Don't sit on the bench at the corner.　**25** (1) ⓐ → don't
(2) ⓑ → What is　(3) ⓔ → Hit

1 ① be call → call
③ Don't too noisy → Don't be too noisy
④ Not jump → Don't jump
⑤ Turns → Turn

2 부정 청유문: 「Let's + not + 동사원형」

3 ③: What　①②④⑤: How

4 부정 명령문: 「Don't[Do not] + 동사원형」

5 긍정 청유문: 「Let's + 동사원형」

6 '너는 어제 그 보석 가게에 들르지 않았니?'라고 묻는 말에 하루 종일 집에 머물렀다고 했으므로 부정의 내용으로 대답한다. 부정의 문문에 대답할 때는 대답의 내용이 부정이면 No로 답한다.

7 첫 번째 빈칸: '나는 샌프란시스코에 갈 거야.'라고 대답했으므로 '무엇'이라는 의미의 What을 쓴다.
두 번째 빈칸: '나의 조부모님을 방문할 거야.'라고 대답했으므로 '무엇'이라는 의미의 What을 쓴다.

8 ②: 부정명령문은 「Don't + 동사원형」의 형태이므로 be angry 가 되어야 한다.

9 (1) What 감탄문: 「What + (a/an) + 형용사 + 명사 + (주어 + 동사)!」
(2) How 감탄문: 「How + 부사 + 주어 + 동사!」

10 조용히 할 것이라고 대답했으므로 '너무 많은 소음을 내지 말아라.'라는 말이 적절하다. '~하지 마라'라는 의미의 부정 명령문은 「Don't[Do not] + 동사원형」이다.

11 ① is it → it is
② is that Christmas tree → that Christmas tree is
③ What → How
⑤ What Emily has long hair → What long hair Emily has

12 의문사가 있는 일반동사 의문문: 「의문사 + do/does/did + 주어 + 동사원형 ~?」

13 ⑤: Who　①②③④: What

14 Why(왜)로 묻고 있으므로 이유에 해당되는 것으로 대답한다.

15 I'm으로 시작하는 문장이므로 「aren't I?」를 쓴다.

16 ① What(무엇)으로 묻고 있으므로 '무엇'에 해당되는 것으로 대답한다.
② Which(어느 것)로 묻고 있으므로 '어느 것'에 해당되는 것으로 대답한다.
④ Why(왜)로 묻고 있으므로 이유에 해당되는 것으로 대답한다.
⑤ Whom(누구를)으로 묻고 있으므로 사람에 해당되는 것으로 대답한다.

17 키에 대해 묻고 있으므로 How tall을 쓴다.

18 What(무슨)은 형용사처럼 쓰여 명사 앞에서 명사를 꾸밀 수 있다.

19 첫 번째 빈칸: '한 명의 사촌이 있어.'라고 대답했으므로 개수를 물을 때 사용하는 How many를 쓴다.
두 번째 빈칸: '뉴욕에서.'라고 대답했으므로 장소를 물을 때 사용하는 Where를 쓴다.

20 ⓑ doesn't Stella → doesn't she
ⓓ can't she → can she
ⓕ will you → shall we

21 (1) 앞 문장의 동사가 긍정을 나타내는 일반동사(go)이므로 don't를 쓰고 앞 문장의 주어 Matt and Danny에 맞는 인칭대명사 they를 쓴다.
(2) 긍정 청유문의 부가의문문: 「긍정 청유문, shall we?」

22 ① How → What
③ What → How
④ Not take → Do not[Don't] take

23 ③: What(무엇)으로 묻고 있으므로 '무엇'에 해당되는 것으로 대답한다.

24 (1) 일반동사가 있는 부정 의문문: 「Don't/Doesn't/Didn't + 주어 + 동사원형 ~?」
(2) 부정 명령문: 「Don't[Do not] + 동사원형」

25 ⓐ: 앞 문장의 동사가 긍정을 나타내는 일반동사(like)이므로

don't를 쓴다.
ⓑ: 의문사가 있는 be동사 의문문: 「의문사 + be동사 + 주어 ~?」
ⓔ: 긍정 명령문은 동사원형을 문장 맨 앞에 쓰는 형태이다.

CHAPTER 7
to부정사
p.78

POINT 1 to부정사의 형태와 역할

연습문제

1 To eat	**2** study	**3** wake
4 drink	**5** visit	**6** not to open

POINT 2-1 명사적 용법

연습문제 **A**

1 to buy, ⓑ	**2** to climb, ⓒ	**3** To swim, ⓐ
4 to take, ⓒ	**5** to play, ⓐ	

연습문제 **B**

1 It is easy to bake cookies.
2 It is mean to bully other friends.
3 It is important to get enough sleep.
4 It was impossible to buy the concert tickets.
5 It is dangerous to play with scissors.

POINT 2-2 명사적 용법: to부정사를 목적어로 쓰는 동사

연습문제

1 wants to watch	**2** expect to finish
3 hopes to see	**4** would like to play
5 decided not to leave	**6** likes to write
7 planned to visit	**8** started to run
9 hates to take	**10** need to buy
11 began to rain	**12** likes to walk

POINT 2-3 명사적 용법: 의문사 + to부정사

연습문제

1 how to use	**2** where to put
3 what to buy	**4** how to swim
5 when to meet	**6** what to watch

POINT 3 형용사적 용법

연습문제

1 a book to read
2 something to drink
3 a coat to wear
4 the best way to become
5 a serious problem to solve

POINT 4 부사적 용법

중간·기말고사 실전 문제

1 ③ 　 2 ② 　 3 It, to become 　 4 in order to study 　 5 ② 　 6 It is scary to walk alone in the forest. 　 7 ④ 　 8 ordering → to order 　 9 to paint 　 10 how to install 　 11 books to read 　 12 ③ 　 13 sang a song to celebrate Sam's birthday 　 14 Joseph was excited to win the tennis game. 　 15 to see 　 16 ⑤ 　 17 ⑤ 　 18 ① 　 19 Use shampoo to wash the dog. 　 20 ⑤ 　 21 ② 　 22 ② 　 23 ② 　 24 I am so excited to go 　 25 ②

1 start는 to부정사를 목적어로 쓰는 동사이므로 to speak를 쓴다.

2 ②: 전치사 to(~로) 　 ①③④⑤: to부정사의 to

3 to부정사가 주어로 쓰일 때 주로 주어 자리에 가주어 it을 쓰고 진주어 to부정사(구)를 뒤로 보낸다.

4 목적을 나타내는 to부정사의 to는 in order to로 바꿔 쓸 수 있다.

5 ① plays → play
　 ③ Read → To read
　 ④ wearing → to wear
　 ⑤ are → is

6 to부정사가 주어로 쓰일 때 주로 주어 자리에 가주어 it을 쓰고 진주어 to부정사(구)를 뒤로 보낸다.

7 첫 번째 빈칸: want는 to부정사를 목적어로 쓰는 동사이므로 to open을 쓴다.
　 두 번째 빈칸: '너는 무슨 종류의 음식을 팔지 결정했니?'라는 의미이므로 「what + to부정사」(무엇을 ~할지)를 쓴다.

8 would like는 to부정사를 목적어로 쓰는 동사이므로 to order를 쓴다.

9 plan은 to부정사를 목적어로 쓰는 동사이므로 to paint를 쓴다.

10 「how + to부정사」'어떻게 ~할지'

11 '~할'이라는 의미로 명사 books를 수식하는 형용사적 용법의 to부정사를 쓴다.

12 ③: 명사적 용법(목적어) 　 ①②④⑤: 형용사적 용법

13 '축하하기 위해'라는 의미로 목적을 나타내는 부사적 용법의 to부정사를 쓴다.

14 두 번째 문장은 첫 번째 문장의 감정을 나타내는 형용사 excited에 대한 원인이므로 감정의 원인을 나타내는 부사적 용법의 to부정사를 쓴다.

15 hope는 to부정사를 목적어로 쓰는 동사이므로 to see를 쓴다.

16 '맞추기에 어렵다'라는 의미로 형용사를 수식하는 부사적 용법의 to부정사를 쓰고 전체 문장이 'The puzzle is difficult to match.'이므로 다섯 번째에 오는 것은 to이다.

17 주어진 문장과 ⑤: 명사적 용법
　 ①④: 형용사적 용법 　 ②③: 부사적 용법

18 '개를 어떻게 씻기는지'라는 의미이므로 「how + to부정사」(어떻게 ~할지)를 쓴다.

19 '씻기 위해'라는 의미로 목적을 나타내는 부사적 용법의 to부정사를 쓴다.

20 '(…해서 결국) ~하다'라는 의미로 결과를 나타내는 to부정사이므로 'Caroline은 자라서 의사가 되었다.'라고 해석한다.

21 주어진 문장과 ②: 주어
　 ①⑤: 보어 　 ③④: 목적어

22 ⓑ having → have
　 ⓒ sings → sing
　 ⓓ are → is

23 밑줄 친 ⓐ와 ②: 명사적 용법
　 ①④⑤: 부사적 용법 　 ③: 형용사적 용법

24 '가게 되어 신이 난다'라는 의미로 감정의 원인을 나타내는 부사적 용법의 to부정사를 쓴다.

25 ⓐⓓⓔ: 부사적 용법 　 ⓑⓒ: 명사적 용법

CHAPTER 8
동명사
p.88

POINT 1 동명사의 형태와 쓰임

	1	Reading	2	teaching	3	thinking
	4	sleeping	5	Winning	6	writing

	1	ⓒ	2	ⓑ	3	ⓐ	4	ⓓ
	5	ⓑ	6	ⓒ	7	ⓓ	8	ⓐ
	9	ⓐ	10	ⓑ	11	ⓓ	12	ⓒ

POINT 2-1 동명사를 목적어로 쓰는 동사

연습문제 A
1 enjoys meeting
2 stop shaking
3 recommended staying
4 practiced swimming
5 gave up solving
6 avoids having
7 finished cleaning
8 kept thinking
9 mind spending

연습문제 B
1	following	2	to get	3	watching
4	waiting	5	to see	6	to visit
7	taking				

POINT 2-2 동명사와 to부정사를 목적어로 모두 쓰는 동사

1 like riding[to ride]
2 enjoy going
3 love swimming[to swim]
4 started buying[to buy]
5 wants to travel
6 practice speaking
7 finish studying
8 wished to forget
9 avoids eating
10 stopped talking
11 hates taking[to take]
12 Stop wasting
13 recommend drinking
14 decided to tell

POINT 3 동명사 VS. 진행형

	1	ⓐ	2	ⓑ	3	ⓐ
	4	ⓐ	5	ⓑ	6	ⓑ
	7	ⓐ				

POINT 4 동명사 관용 표현

1 go shopping
2 is good at playing
3 is afraid of making
4 How[What] about turning
5 spent lots of money buying
6 was busy cooking

중간·기말고사 실전 문제

1	⑤	2	④	3	④	4	(1) to study →

studying (2) get → getting　　5 ③　　6 ④
7 ④　　8 ④　　9 (1) ⓑ → was (2) ⓒ → writing
(3) ⓔ → spending　　10 ⑤　　11 ①　　12 ③
13 ⑤　　14 ④　　15 He is good at dancing.
16 She goes fishing every weekend.
17 Moe likes spending time baking pies.
18 ③　　19 to order → ordering　　20 How
about joining　　21 We practice playing tennis
22 ⑤　　23 ②　　24 ④　　25 ②

1 enjoy는 동명사를 목적어로 쓰는 동사이므로 drinking을 쓴다.

2 동명사 visiting이 목적어이므로 to부정사를 목적어로 쓰는 동사 want는 쓸 수 없다.

3 동명사 writing이 목적어이므로 to부정사를 목적어로 쓰는 동사 plan은 쓸 수 없다.

4 (1) give up은 동명사를 목적어로 쓰는 동사이므로 studying을 쓴다.
(2) 「be afraid of + V-ing」 '~하는 것을 무서워하다'

5 ③: 진행형의 V-ing　주어진 문장과 ①②④⑤: 동명사

6 · mind는 동명사를 목적어로 쓰는 동사이므로 turning을 쓴다.
· 보어 자리이므로 명사 역할을 하는 동명사 buying을 쓴다.

7 · love는 동명사와 to부정사를 모두 목적어로 쓰는 동사이므로 drinking이나 to drink를 쓴다.
· give up은 동명사를 목적어로 쓰는 동사이므로 renting을 쓴다.

8 ① spending → to spend
② to take → taking

③ working → to work

⑤ to sit → sitting

9 (1) 주어로 쓰인 동명사는 항상 단수 취급하므로 was를 쓴다.

(2) finish는 동명사를 목적어로 쓰는 동사이므로 writing을 쓴다.

(3) mind는 동명사를 목적어로 쓰는 동사이므로 spending을 쓴다.

10 「be busy + V-ing」 '~하느라 바쁘다'

11 (A) like는 동명사와 to부정사를 모두 목적어로 쓰는 동사이므로 riding이나 to ride를 쓴다.

(B) practice는 동명사를 목적어로 쓰는 동사이므로 singing을 쓴다.

(C) hope는 to부정사를 목적어로 쓰는 동사이므로 to find를 쓴다.

12 (A) enjoy는 동명사를 목적어로 쓰는 동사이므로 studying을 쓴다.

(B) begin은 동명사와 to부정사를 모두 목적어로 쓰는 동사이므로 climbing이나 to climb를 쓴다.

(C) 전치사(about)의 목적어 자리이므로 동명사 working을 쓴다.

13 ⑤: 동명사 ①②③④: 진행형의 V-ing

14 ④ meet → meeting

15 「be good at + V-ing」 '~하는 것을 잘하다'

16 「go + V-ing」 '~하러 가다'

17 「spend + 시간 + V-ing」 '~하는 데 시간을 쓰다'

18 ③: 진행형의 V-ing ①②④⑤: 동명사

19 「How about + V-ing?」 '~하는 게 어때?'

20 「How about + V-ing?」 '~하는 게 어때?

21 practice는 동명사를 목적어로 쓰는 동사이므로 playing을 쓴다.

22 ① to go → going

② to buy → buying

③ to shop → shopping

④ do → doing

23 ② to working → working[to work]

24 ⓐⓒⓔ: 목적어 ⓑ: 주어 ⓓ: 보어

25 ⓒ to eat → eating

ⓓ Do → Doing[To do]

CHAPTER 9
명사와 관사

p.98

POINT 1 셀 수 있는 명사와 셀 수 없는 명사

1 O	**2** X	**3** X	**4** O
5 O	**6** X	**7** O	**8** X
9 X	**10** O	**11** X	**12** X
13 O	**14** X	**15** O	**16** X
17 X	**18** O	**19** X	**20** X

1 James wants to drink water.

2 I spilled a lot of rice on the floor.

3 O

4 I have sand in my shoe.

5 O

6 Trust is important for a relationship.

7 You can eat some apples in the fridge.

8 This book has much information about volcanoes.

POINT 2-1 셀 수 있는 명사의 복수형: 규칙 변화

1 tomatoes	**2** pencils	**3** toys
4 countries	**5** novels	**6** photos
7 days	**8** roofs	**9** leaves
10 sandwiches		

POINT 2-2 셀 수 있는 명사의 복수형: 불규칙 변화

1 men	**2** Geese	**3** mice
4 Deer	**5** children	**6** Fish

POINT 3 셀 수 없는 명사의 수량 표현

1 four slices of pizza	**2** two bowls of salad
3 ten cans of paint	**4** a cup of coffee
5 two bottles of ink	**6** a piece of furniture
7 five loaves of bread	**8** a glass of water

13 a second 　　　　**14** The book

POINT 4　명사 관련 표현

1 glasses　　**2** two-door　　**3** O
4 gloves

1 my homeroom teacher
2 my downstairs neighbor
3 an amazing composer
4 the soccer players

POINT 5　There + be동사

1 There are two toothbrushes
2 Is there a cup
3 There is some ice
4 There aren't many buses
5 There are ten eggs
6 There is a mouse
7 Are there many swings
8 There wasn't any sugar
9 There were many sheep

1 ①　　　　**2** ③　　　　**3** ③
4 ①

POINT 6-1　부정관사 a(n)의 쓰임

1 a　　　**2** an　　　**3** X
4 a　　　**5** X　　　**6** a
7 an　　**8** X　　　**9** a
10 an　**11** an　**12** a

POINT 6-2　정관사 the의 쓰임

1 The　　**2** the　　**3** A
4 The　　**5** a　　　**6** the
7 The　　**8** the　　**9** the

POINT 6-3　관사를 쓰지 않는 경우

1 bus　　　　　　　**2** dinner
3 history　　　　　**4** the cello
5 the first person　**6** work
7 e-mail　　　　　**8** a year
9 the seventh floor　**10** basketball
11 church　　　　　**12** the school

중간·기말고사 실전 문제

1 ③　　**2** ⑤　　**3** ④　　**4** (1) sheeps →
sheep (2) gooses → geese　**5** ⑤　　**6** ②
7 ②　　**8** ③　　**9** two bowls of cereal
10 third-floors → third-floor　**11** ③　　**12** ②
13 (1) are　(2) is not[isn't]　**14** ③　　**15** ⓐ
were　ⓑ were　ⓒ was　　**16** ①　　**17** There
are two bathrooms　**18** There isn't a roller coaster
19 (1) there are　(2) there isn't　**20** There are eleven
coconuts　**21** ④　　**22** ④　　**23** the　　**24** ③
25 ⑤

1　③: book은 셀 수 있는 명사이므로 a와 함께 쓸 수 있다.

2　⑤ roof – roofs

3　① churchs → churches
　　② treees → trees
　　③ tomatos → tomatoes
　　⑤ egges → eggs

4　(1) Five는 복수를 나타내므로 sheep의 복수형 sheep을 쓴다.
　　(2) two는 복수를 나타내므로 goose의 복수형 geese를 쓴다.

5　· 한 쌍이 짝을 이루는 명사는 항상 복수형으로 쓰므로 gloves를
　　　쓴다.
　　· 「숫자 + 단위명사」의 단위명사는 항상 단수형으로 쓰므로
　　　two-week을 쓴다.

6　빈칸 앞에 many가 있으므로 셀 수 있는 명사의 복수형 foxes,
　　ants, salmon을 쓴다.

7　① a new furniture → new furniture
　　③ building → buildings
　　④ Two car → Two cars
　　⑤ an information → information

8　ⓐ oxes → oxen
　　ⓑ deers → deer
　　ⓔ pianoes → pianos

9　셀 수 없는 명사 cereal은 단위명사 bowl로 수량을 나타내며
　　two는 복수를 나타내므로 bowl의 복수형 bowls를 쓴다.

10　「숫자 + 단위명사」의 단위명사는 항상 단수형으로 쓰므로 third-
　　floor를 쓴다.

11　③ Were → Was

12　「There + are」 뒤에는 셀 수 있는 명사의 복수형을 쓰므로 셀 수
　　없는 명사 beef는 쓸 수 없다.

13　(1) '~이 있다'라는 의미의 「There + be동사」를 쓰고 복수명사
　　cupcakes가 있으므로 be동사는 are를 쓴다.

(2) '~이 없다'라는 의미의 「There + be동사 + not」을 쓰고 셀 수 없는 명사 coffee가 있으므로 be동사는 is를 쓴다.

14 ③: '거기에, 그곳에' ①②④⑤: '~이 있다'

15 ⓐ 「There + be동사」는 뒤따라오는 명사에 be동사를 수일치시키고 복수명사 animals가 있으므로 be동사는 were를 쓴다.
ⓑ 「There + be동사」는 뒤따라오는 명사에 be동사를 수일치시키고 복수명사 cows and horses가 있으므로 be동사는 were를 쓴다.
ⓒ 「There + be동사」는 뒤따라오는 명사에 be동사를 수일치시키고 단수명사 sheep dog가 있으므로 be동사는 was를 쓴다.

16 ⓑ boxs → boxes
ⓔ keies → keys

17 '나의 아파트에 두 개의 화장실이 있다.'라는 의미이므로 「There + be동사」(~이 있다)를 쓰고 복수명사 bathrooms가 있으므로 be동사는 are를 쓴다.

18 '그 놀이 공원에 롤러코스터가 없다.'라는 의미이므로 「There + be동사 + not」(~이 없다)을 쓰고 단수명사 a roller coaster가 있으므로 be동사는 is를 쓴다.

19 (1) 「There + be동사」의 의문문에 대한 긍정의 대답: 「Yes, there + be동사.」
(2) 「There + be동사」의 의문문에 대한 부정의 대답: 「No, there + be동사 + not.」

20 '~이 있다'라는 의미의 「There + be동사」를 쓰고 eleven은 복수를 나타내므로 coconut의 복수형 coconuts를 쓴다.

21 ④ an ①②③⑤ a

22 ④: '하나의' 주어진 문장과 ①②③⑤: '~마다'

23 ・서로 알고 있는 것을 말할 때는 정관사 the를 쓴다.
・서수(second) 앞에는 정관사 the를 쓴다.

24 ③: 유일한 것(moon) 앞에는 정관사 the를 쓴다.

25 ⑤ the bus → bus

CHAPTER 10
대명사
p.110

POINT 1   인칭대명사

 A
1 I want to invite you to my house.
2 You should listen to Dad's advice.
3 Peter came to Korea to see us.
4 O
5 Have you seen him recently?
6 My sister and I lost our passports.
7 O

연습문제 B
| 1 My, mine | 2 your, Yours | 3 his, His |
| 4 hers, her | 5 our, Ours | 6 their, Theirs |

POINT 2   재귀대명사

 A
1 herself	2 itself	3 ourselves
4 me	5 myself	6 us
7 themselves	8 himself	9 herself
10 them		

연습문제 B
1 O	2 X	3 O
4 X	5 O	6 X
7 O	8 X	9 X
10 O		

POINT 3   지시대명사

연습문제 A
1 Those	2 That	3 these
4 Those	5 this	6 These
7 that, it isn't	8 these, they are	
9 this, it isn't		

연습문제 B
1 ⓐ	2 ⓐ	3 ⓑ
4 ⓐ	5 ⓑ	6 ⓑ
7 ⓐ	8 ⓑ	9 ⓐ
10 ⓑ		

POINT 4   비인칭 주어 it

연습문제
| 1 ② | 2 ② | 3 ① | 4 ③ |
| 5 ② | 6 ① | 7 ① | 8 ② |

POINT 5-1 부정대명사: one

연습문제

1	it	**2**	one	**3**	them
4	ones	**5**	They	**6**	one
7	ones	**8**	it	**9**	them

POINT 5-2 부정대명사: another, other

연습문제 A

1	the other	**2**	one	**3**	other
4	another	**5**	others		

연습문제 B

1 Some are black, others are red
2 Some are pants, the others are skirts
3 One is apple juice, the other is orange juice
4 Some are Chinese, others are Canadians
5 One is a tomato, another is a carrot, the other is a potato
6 One is a soccer ball, another is a basketball, the other is a baseball

POINT 5-3 부정대명사: each, every, all

연습문제

1 Every child needs a mother's love.
2 O
3 I wish to visit every country in the world.
4 O
5 Each member has his or her own strength.
6 All your advice was really helpful.
7 Everybody is having a good time.
8 Each student must turn in the essay.
9 All my friends like the same singer.
10 Let's start when everyone gets here.
11 Every girl in my class watches the TV show.
12 Each player has to wear the team uniform.
13 All life needs water to live.

중간·기말고사 실전 문제

1 ① **2** ② **3** Her, She, her
4 hers **5** ② **6** ⑤ **7** his, yours
8 ⓐ Their ⓑ her ⓒ She ⓓ his ⓔ They
9 ② **10** ④ **11** ④ **12** Jane considers herself an expert. **13** ② **14** ①, ⑤ **15** ④
16 It will rain **17** ③, ④ **18** ⑤ **19** One was a comedy, the other was a mystery **20** ④

21 ② **22** ③ **23** player, wears **24** (1) ⓐ, ⓒ, ⓔ (2) ⓓ, ⓕ (3) ⓑ **25** ③

1 ② It → Its
   ③ They → Their
   ④ we → us
   ⑤ She's → Her

2 ② us → them

3 첫 번째 빈칸: 빈칸 뒤에 소유의 대상이 되는 명사 hobby가 왔으므로 소유격 인칭대명사 Her를 쓴다.
   두 번째 빈칸: 빈칸이 주어 자리이므로 주격 인칭대명사 She를 쓴다.
   세 번째 빈칸: 빈칸이 전치사 with의 목적어 자리이므로 목적격 인칭대명사 her를 쓴다.

4 소유대명사는 「소유격 + 명사」를 대신한다.

5 (A) 빈칸 뒤에 소유의 대상이 되는 명사 jokes가 왔으므로 소유격 인칭대명사 Her를 쓴다.
   (B) 빈칸이 동사 made의 목적어 자리이므로 목적격 인칭대명사 us를 쓴다.
   (C) '저 펜은 나의 것이다'라는 의미이므로 소유대명사 mine을 쓴다.

6 첫 번째 빈칸: your phone으로 묻고 있고 '아니, 그것은 나의 것이 아니야.'라는 의미이므로 mine을 쓴다.
   두 번째 빈칸: 빈칸 뒤에 소유의 대상이 되는 명사 phone이 왔으므로 소유격 인칭대명사 her를 쓴다.

7 첫 번째 빈칸: '그의 것'이라는 의미의 소유대명사 his를 쓴다.
   두 번째 빈칸: '너의 것'이라는 의미의 소유대명사 yours를 쓴다.

8 ⓐ 빈칸 뒤에 소유의 대상이 되는 명사 names가 왔으므로 소유격 인칭대명사 Their을 쓴다.
   ⓑ 빈칸 뒤에 소유의 대상이 되는 명사 cage가 왔으므로 소유격 인칭대명사 her를 쓴다.
   ⓒ 빈칸이 주어 자리이므로 주격 인칭대명사 She를 쓴다.
   ⓓ 빈칸 뒤에 소유의 대상이 되는 명사 snacks가 왔으므로 소유격 인칭대명사 his를 쓴다.
   ⓔ 빈칸이 주어 자리이므로 주격 인칭대명사 They를 쓴다.

9 ②: 소유대명사 ①③④⑤: 소유격 인칭대명사

10 · 전치사 at의 목적어가 주어 He와 같은 대상이므로 재귀대명사 himself를 쓴다. (재귀 용법)
   · 'Jason은 그의 방을 직접 페인트칠했다.'라는 의미이므로 재귀대명사 himself를 쓴다. (강조 용법)

11 ⓑⓒⓓ: 강조 용법 ⓐⓔ: 재귀 용법

12 '그녀 자신'이라는 의미의 재귀대명사 herself를 쓴다. 5형식 문장은 「주어 + 동사 + 목적어 + 목적격보어」 형태이다.

13 ② these › this

14 주어진 문장과 ①⑤: 지시형용사 ②③④: 지시대명사

15 ④ it ①②③⑤ one

16 날씨를 나타내는 비인칭 주어 It을 쓴다.

17 ③: ⓑ의 It은 the bus를 가리키는 대명사이다.
④: ⓒ의 it은 the bus를 가리키는 대명사로 '그것'이라고 해석한다.

18 ⓑⓒⓔ: 대명사 it   ⓐⓓ: 비인칭 주어 it

19 「one ~, the other -」: (둘 중) 하나는 ~, 나머지 하나는 -

20 「some ~, the others -」: (여럿 중) 몇몇은 ~, 나머지 전부는 -

21 ⓑ Each desks → Each desk
ⓓ Every problems → Every problem
ⓔ are → is

22 (A) 「Every + 단수명사 + 단수동사」이므로 단수명사 book을 쓴다.
(B) 「All + 복수명사 + 복수동사」이므로 복수동사 have to를 쓴다.
(C) 「Each + 단수명사 + 단수동사」이므로 단수명사 passenger를 쓴다.

23 「Every + 단수명사 + 단수동사」이므로 단수명사 player를 쓰고, 단수동사 wears를 쓴다.

24 (1) 「one ~, another -, the other …」: (셋 중) 하나는 ~, 다른 하나는 -, 나머지 하나는 …
(2) 「some ~, the others -」: (여럿 중) 몇몇은 ~, 나머지 전부는 -
(3) 앞에서 언급된 명사(shirts)와 같은 종류의 사물을 가리키는 ones를 쓴다.

25 · '우리는 21번가에 있는 스페인 음식점은 좋아하지만, 다른 스페인 음식점은 그곳만큼 훌륭하지 않다.'라는 의미이므로 Other (다른)를 쓴다.
· '나는 나의 남동생이 잘생겼다고 생각하지 않지만, 다른 사람들은 그렇게 생각한다.'라는 의미이므로 other(다른)을 쓴다.

CHAPTER 11
형용사

p.122

POINT 1 형용사의 용법

1	The bus	2	cake	3	truck
4	The weather	5	movie	6	me
7	My puppy	8	box	9	my sister
10	camera				

POINT 2 형용사의 어순

1 Sarah saw a beautiful small bird.
2 There is a round red table in my room.
3 O
4 We slept in a huge old wooden house.
5 O

POINT 3 -thing/-body + 형용사

(A)

1 We should order something sweet for dessert.
2 There is somebody friendly in my class.
3 Do you have anything warm?
4 Don't pay attention to small things.
5 Is there anything uncomfortable?
6 I don't know anybody rude.
7 Something spicy would be good for lunch.
8 Anybody clever can solve this puzzle.

(B)

1	Something loud	2	anything exciting
3	anything good	4	something funny
5	expensive things	6	anybody interesting
7	something special	8	new places

POINT 4 감정형용사

(A)

1 exciting, excited
2 interesting, interested
3 surprised, surprising
4 disappointed, disappointing
5 confusing, confused
6 annoying, annoyed

1	boring	**2**	worried	**3**	interesting
4	shocking	**5**	surprised	**6**	tiring
7	amazing	**8**	confused	**9**	excited
10	disappointing	**11**	moving		

POINT 5-1　수사: 기수와 서수

1	one	**2**	ninetieth
3	twelfth	**4**	four hundred
5	eighty	**6**	seventy-third
7	sixty-five	**8**	twenty-fifth

1	hundreds of	**2**	five hundred
3	Thousands of	**4**	Millions of

POINT 5-2　수사: 정수, 소수, 분수

1 (zero) point four six
2 eleven million
3 two thousand, four hundred (and) sixty-four
4 eighty-two point zero six
5 forty-three thousand, four hundred (and) fifty-four
6 one-third[a third]
7 three-quarters[three-fourths]
8 one and one-half[a half]

POINT 5-3　수사: 시각

1 four fifty-three
2 (a) quarter after[past] seven 또는 seven fifteen
3 O
4 half to four 또는 half after[past] three 또는 three thirty
5 O
6 O
7 (a) quarter to six 또는 five forty-five
8 nine thirty-seven

POINT 5-4　수사: 연도와 날짜

1 nineteen twenty
2 May (the) tenth[the tenth of May]
3 March (the) second[the second of March]
4 two thousand (and) twelve[twenty twelve]
5 fourteen fifty-six
6 the nineteen forties

7 August (the) third[the third of August], twelve fifty
8 May (the) fourteenth[the fourteenth of May], two thousand (and) forty-five[twenty forty-five]

POINT 6-1　수량형용사: many, much, a lot of

1	many	**2**	many	**3**	much
4	many	**5**	much	**6**	much
7	many	**8**	much		

1 He bought many hats for his friends at the department store.
2 Does the popcorn contain much salt?
3 There aren't many cars on the road.
4 I couldn't find much information on this website.
5 The food waste attracts many insects.
6 Don't use much butter when you bake cookies.
7 Was much gold found in the cave?
8 Many workers in the United States wore jeans in 1800s.

POINT 6-2　수량형용사: (a) few, (a) little

1	a little, a few	**2**	few, little
3	a little, a few	**4**	little, Few
5	a little, a few	**6**	few, little

1	a little milk	**2**	Many buses
3	few customers	**4**	much snow
5	a few reasons	**6**	little homework

POINT 6-3　수량형용사: some, any

1	some	**2**	any	**3**	some
4	any	**5**	some	**6**	some
7	some	**8**	any	**9**	any
10	some	**11**	some	**12**	any
13	any	**14**	some		

중간·기말고사 실전 문제

1 ①	**2** ①	**3** ③	**4** Cleaning my house made me tired.		**5** ⑤	**6** ①, ⑤	
7 ③	**8** ②	**9** thousands of	**10** blue				

11 ②	**12** ①, ④	**13** ②	**14** ③	**15** ③

16 ③　　**17** any → some　　**18** interesting
anyone → anyone interesting　　**19** ④　　**20** ③
21 ④　　**22** ⑤　　**23** shocked
24 confusing　　**25** (1) ⓒ → much[a lot of/lots
of]　(2) ⓔ → nothing wrong

---

1 빈칸 뒤에 셀 수 있는 명사의 복수형(fish)이 왔으므로 셀 수 없는 명사 앞에 쓰는 much는 쓸 수 없다.

2 ・minutes는 셀 수 있는 명사의 복수형이므로 a few를 쓴다.
　・gifts는 셀 수 있는 명사의 복수형이고 '그는 그의 부모님에게 많은 선물을 사드렸다.'라는 의미이므로 many(많은)를 쓴다.

3 (A) 부정문이므로 any를 쓴다.
　(B) movie는 감정을 일으키는 주체이므로 V-ing 형태의 형용사 boring을 쓴다.
　(C) -thing으로 끝나는 대명사(something)를 꾸밀 때는 형용사(strange)가 대명사 뒤에 온다.

4 me는 감정을 느끼는 대상이므로 V-ed 형태의 형용사 tired를 쓴다.

5 '9시 30분이다.'는 '9시 30분 후이다.'로 바꿔 쓸 수 있으므로 It's a half past nine.을 쓴다.

6 날짜는 서수로 읽는다.

7 ③ ten to five → five ten 또는 ten after[past] five

8 ② fifteen point ninety one → fifteen point nine one

9 '수천의'라는 의미의 thousands of를 쓴다.

10 두 개 이상의 형용사를 함께 쓸 때는 크기, 오래된 정도, 색깔 순서로 쓰고 배열한 부분이 'big old blue bed'이므로 세 번째 오는 것은 blue이다.

11 ② twelve - twelfth

12 빈칸 뒤에 셀 수 있는 명사의 복수형(cards)이 왔으므로 a few와 lots of를 쓴다. a little과 much는 셀 수 없는 명사 앞에 쓰고, any는 주로 부정문과 의문문에 쓴다.

13 '많은'이라는 의미의 a lot of는 many 또는 much로 바꿔 쓸 수 있고 information은 셀 수 없는 명사이므로 much를 쓴다.

14 첫 번째 빈칸 뒤에 셀 수 없는 명사(coffee)와 두 번째 빈칸 뒤에 셀 수 있는 명사의 복수형(oranges)이 왔으므로 셀 수 없는 명사와 셀 수 있는 명사의 복수형 앞에 쓰이는 lots of(많은)를 쓴다.

15 ・부정문이고 빈칸 뒤에 셀 수 없는 명사(milk)가 왔으므로 any를 쓴다.
　・긍정문이므로 some을 쓴다.

16 ① much → many
　② few → little
　④ any → some
　⑤ some → any

17 '나는 파티에서 약간의 사람들을 만났다.'라는 의미이고 긍정문이

므로 some을 쓴다. any는 주로 부정문과 의문문에 쓴다.

18 -one으로 끝나는 대명사(anyone)를 꾸밀 때는 형용사(interesting)가 대명사 뒤에 온다.

19 첫 번째 빈칸: You는 감정을 느끼는 대상이므로 V-ed 형태의 형용사 annoyed를 쓴다.
　두 번째 빈칸: I는 감정을 느끼는 대상이므로 V-ed 형태의 형용사 annoyed를 쓴다.

20 ③: 서술적 용법　주어진 문장과 ①②④⑤: 한정적 용법

21 ④ leather big → big leather

22 ⑤ disappointed → disappointing

23 Andrew는 감정을 느끼는 대상이므로 V-ed 형태의 형용사 shocked를 쓴다.

24 My friend's story는 감정을 일으키는 주체이므로 V-ing 형태의 형용사 confusing을 쓴다.

25 (1) time은 셀 수 없는 명사이므로 much[a lot of/lots of]를 쓴다.
　(2) -thing으로 끝나는 대명사(nothing)를 꾸밀 때는 형용사(wrong)가 대명사 뒤에 온다.

CHAPTER 12
부사
p.136

POINT 1 부사의 쓰임

 연습 문제
1 shine 2 scary
3 checks 4 I lost my ticket
5 much 6 slowly
7 hungry 8 he went down the stairs
9 talk 10 have visited

POINT 2-1 부사의 형태

 연습 문제
1 simple, simply 2 gentle, gently
3 easy, easily 4 Foolishly, foolish
5 heavy, heavily 6 carefully, careful
7 good, well

POINT 2-2 형용사와 형태가 같은 부사

 연습 문제
1 ② 2 ② 3 ① 4 ②
5 ① 6 ② 7 ②

POINT 2-3 -ly가 붙으면 의미가 달라지는 부사

 연습 문제
1 lately, late, Lately, late
2 close, closely, close, closely
3 high, highly, highly, high
4 hard, hard, hardly, hardly

POINT 3 빈도부사

 연습 문제 A
1 seldom 2 always 3 usually
4 never 5 often 6 sometimes

연습 문제 B
1 Eric usually takes a bath on weekends.
2 Does the bus often stop here?
3 My sister is seldom interested in sports.
4 Do you always eat dinner with your family?
5 She will never fall asleep in class again.
6 That restaurant is sometimes busy.
7 The convenience store is always open at midnight.

POINT 4 too, either

 연습 문제
1 too 2 too 3 either
4 too 5 either 6 too
7 either 8 either

POINT 5 동사 + 부사

 연습 문제
1 Please throw it away now.
2 Write them down here.
3 You should put it on.
4 Why don't you take them off inside the building?
5 Would you like to try it on?
6 The students must hand them in today.
7 Let's pick it up in the playground.

중간·기말고사 실전 문제

1 ④ 2 ④ 3 ① 4 rapid → rapidly
5 ④ 6 ③ 7 ④ 8 ③ 9 ②
10 I always play soccer with my friends 11 never eats 12 ⑤ 13 ⑤ 14 I tried on the red dress, and then I took it off. 15 ④ 16 He usually exercises 17 ④ 18 ③ 19 ②
20 ③ 21 ① 22 ② 23 ① 24 ③
25 (1) ⓑ → hard (2) ⓒ → never rains

1 ④ lucky → luckily

2 부정문에서 동의를 나타내기 위해 쓰이는 부사 either(또한)를 쓴다.

3 ② go often → often go
③ respect always → always respect
④ climb sometimes → sometimes climb
⑤ seldom is → is seldom

4 동사(ran)를 꾸미는 부사 rapidly를 쓴다.

5 ④ loud → loudly

6 ③: 형용사('힘든') ①②④⑤: 부사('열심히')

7 ④: 형용사('이른')
①: 부사('빠르게'), ②: 부사('꽤'), ③: 부사('오래'),
⑤: 부사('늦게')

8 ③ sudden → suddenly

9 ② either ①③④⑤ too

10 '항상'이라는 의미의 빈도부사 always를 쓰고 빈도부사는 일반동

사 앞에 위치하므로 I always play soccer with my friends 를 쓴다.

11 Kelly는 결코 아침으로 오믈렛을 먹지 않는다고 했으므로 빈도부사 never(결코 ~않다)를 쓴다. 빈도부사는 일반동사 앞에 위치하므로 never eats를 쓴다.

12 ⑤ general → generally

13 ⑤ either → too

14 「동사 + 부사」의 목적어가 대명사인 경우 「동사 + 대명사 + 부사」의 어순으로 쓰므로 took it off를 쓴다.

15 (A) 형용사(recommended)를 꾸미는 '매우'라는 의미의 부사 highly를 쓴다.
(B) 동사(walk)를 꾸미는 '거의 ~않다'라는 의미의 부사 hardly 를 쓴다.
(C) 동사(is standing)를 꾸미는 '가까이'라는 의미의 부사 close를 쓴다.

16 빈도부사는 일반동사 앞에 위치하므로 He usually exercises 를 쓴다.

17 ④: Sandra는 체육관에 자주 간다고 했으므로 빈도부사 usually(보통, 대개)를 쓴다. seldom은 '거의 ~않다'라는 의미이므로 적절하지 않다.

18 ③ high → highly

19 빈도부사는 일반동사(wakes) 앞에 위치한다.

20 빈도부사는 조동사(can) 뒤에 위치한다.

21 빈도부사는 일반동사 앞에 위치하고 'My mom sometimes drives me.'이므로 네 번째에 오는 것은 drives이다.

22 첫 번째 빈칸: 명사(animal)를 꾸미는 형용사 strong을 쓴다.
두 번째 빈칸: 동사(lift)를 꾸미는 부사 easily를 쓴다.

23 · turn off '~을 끄다'
· put off '~를 미루다'

24 ⓑ pick up them → pick them up
ⓓ give up them → give them up

25 (1) 동사(rained)를 꾸미고 있고 '종일 비가 심하게 내렸다.'라는 의미이므로 부사 hard(심하게)를 쓴다.
(2) 빈도부사는 일반동사 앞에 위치하므로 never rains를 쓴다.

CHAPTER 13
비교구문

p.146

POINT 1-1 규칙 변화 I

연습문제

1 lower - lowest		**2** hotter - hottest	
3 harder - hardest		**4** younger - youngest	
5 smarter - smartest		**6** lazier - laziest	
7 bigger - biggest		**8** warmer - warmest	
9 nicer- nicest		**10** heavier - heaviest	
11 greater - greatest		**12** thinner - thinnest	
13 smaller - smallest		**14** wider - widest	
15 darker - darkest		**16** lovelier - loveliest	
17 tastier - tastiest		**18** wetter - wettest	
19 fewer - fewest		**20** hungrier - hungriest	
21 wiser - wisest		**22** scarier - scariest	

POINT 1-2 규칙 변화 II

연습문제

1 more useful - most useful
2 stranger - strangest
3 more important - most important
4 more simply - most simply
5 more careless - most careless
6 friendlier - friendliest
7 more gladly - most gladly
8 more serious - most serious
9 more interesting - most interesting
10 more difficult - most difficult

POINT 1-3 불규칙 변화

연습문제

1 ②	**2** ③	**3** ①	**4** ②
5 ②	**6** ③	**7** ②	**8** ①

POINT 2 원급 비교: as + 원급 + as

연습문제

1 A sunset is as beautiful as a sunrise.
2 This summer was not as hot as last summer.
3 My wallet is as light as Patrick's.
4 The French exam was as difficult as the math exam.
5 Minha arrived as early as her teacher.
6 The metal looks as hard as a diamond.

POINT 3-1 비교급 비교: 비교급 + than

연습문제 A

1 lighter than 2 colder than 3 taller than
4 longer than 5 farther than 6 later than
7 smaller than 8 more than

연습문제 B

1 sourer 2 smaller 3 much
4 heavier 5 very 6 more bored
7 far 8 even

POINT 3-2 비교급 비교: 비교급 + and + 비교급

연습문제

1 got richer and richer
2 became fatter and fatter
3 are getting more and more difficult
4 is growing larger and larger
5 is becoming better and better
6 got sadder and sadder
7 became more and more famous
8 got more and more interesting
9 grew taller and taller
10 is becoming more and more popular
11 become longer and longer
12 felt more and more nervous

POINT 4-1 최상급 비교: the + 최상급

연습문제 A

1 the heaviest chair in our house
2 the cleverest girl in her school
3 the best player of the soccer team's members
4 the hottest month of the year
5 the most interesting book in the bookstore
6 the most popular restaurant in Seoul
7 the largest pizza of the three choices
8 the longest river in Europe
9 the luckiest day in my life

연습문제 B

1 fast 2 older
3 the tallest 4 the strongest
5 better 6 the most generous
7 thick 8 better

POINT 4-2 최상급 비교: one of the + 최상급 + 복수명사

연습문제

1 one of the scariest rides
2 one of the most difficult subjects
3 one of the deepest lakes
4 one of the spiciest dishes
5 one of the youngest students
6 one of the biggest houses
7 one of the loveliest actors
8 one of the oldest animals
9 one of the best views
10 one of the most tiring exercises
11 one of the greatest movies
12 one of the most outgoing children

중간·기말고사 실전 문제

1 ② 2 ① 3 ② 4 ⑤ 5 ②
6 ④ 7 ① 8 ④ 9 nicer → the nicest 10 ⑤ 11 ④ 12 ⑤ 13 as short as 14 bigger and bigger 15 the freshest
16 ① 17 ③ 18 ④ 19 ① 20 ②
21 ⑤ 22 ③ 23 ⑤ 24 faster than
25 ③

1 ② many – more – most

2 '…만큼 ~한'이라는 의미의 「as + 원급 + as」를 쓰고 'David is not as tall as Marie.'이므로 일곱 번째에 오는 것은 Marie이다.

3 ② brighter → bright

4 '…보다'라는 의미의 than이 있고 'Annie는 그녀의 가장 친한 친구보다 더 시끄럽다.'라는 의미이므로 비교급 noisier를 쓴다.

5 비교 범위를 나타내는 in the world가 있고 '흰긴수염고래는 세계에서 가장 크다.'라는 의미이므로 최상급 the largest를 쓴다.

6 ④ more and more loud → louder and louder

7 ① more colder than → colder than

8 · '…보다'라는 의미의 than이 있고 'Dylan은 Laura보다 모래성을 더 잘 만들었다.'라는 의미이므로 비교급 better를 쓴다.
   · '…보다'라는 의미의 than이 있고 '나의 새 전화기는 지난번 것보다 더 낫다.'라는 의미이므로 비교급 better를 쓴다.

9 비교 범위를 나타내는 in your school이 있고 '너의 학교에서 가장 친절한 학생은 누구니?'라는 의미이므로 최상급 the nicest를 쓴다.

10 ① more cheaper → the cheapest
    ② lazyier → lazier
    ③ tall → tallest
    ④ better → well

11 · '…만큼'이라는 의미의 as가 있고 '이 스웨터는 무지개만큼 예쁘다.'라는 의미이므로 원급 pretty를 쓴다.

・ 비교 범위를 나타내는 in the jungle이 있고 '정글에서 어느 동물이 가장 위험하니?'라는 의미이므로 최상급 most dangerous를 쓴다.

12 빈칸 뒤에 비교급 more comfortable이 있으므로 원급을 강조하는 very는 쓸 수 없다.

13 '…만큼 ~한'이라는 의미의 「as + 원급 + as」를 쓴다.

14 '점점 더 ~한'이라는 의미의 「비교급 + and + 비교급」을 쓴다.

15 '가장 ~한'이라는 의미의 「the + 최상급」을 쓴다.

16 ① 햄버거는 샌드위치보다 비싸다고 했으므로 '햄버거는 샌드위치만큼 비싸다.'는 적절하지 않다.

17 ⓑ big → bigger
ⓒ larger → large
ⓔ the restaurant → in the restaurant

18 '가장 ~한'이라는 의미의 「the + 최상급」을 쓴다.

19 '가장 ~한 것들 중 하나'라는 의미의 「one of the + 최상급 + 복수명사」를 쓴다. smart의 최상급은 smartest이다.

20 '…보다'라는 의미의 than이 있고 '수박은 레몬보다 더 달다.'라는 의미이므로 비교급 sweeter를 쓴다.

21 빈칸 앞에 2음절 이상인 형용사 앞에 붙는 more가 있으므로 expensive를 쓴다.

22 ③ more → the most

23 ⑤ as   ①②③④ than

24 치타가 사자보다 훨씬 더 빠르게 달릴 수 있다고 했으므로 fast의 비교급 faster를 쓴다.

25 비교급 앞에서 비교급을 강조하는 even은 원급을 강조하는 very와 바꿔 쓸 수 없다.

CHAPTER 14
전치사

p.158

POINT 1-1 시간 전치사: at, on, in

연습문제			
1 on	**2** in	**3** at
4 in	**5** on	**6** on
7 at	**8** on	**9** on
10 in		

POINT 1-2 시간 전치사: before, after

연습문제			
1 after	**2** before	**3** After
4 after	**5** before	**6** before

POINT 1-3 시간 전치사: for, during

연습문제			
1 during	**2** for	**3** for
4 during	**5** for	**6** during
7 during	**8** during	**9** for
10 during		

POINT 1-4 시간 전치사: from

연습문제		
1 from 7 P.M.	**2** in 2006
3 from 1841 to 1997	**4** after nine
5 From this week	**6** for 30 minutes

POINT 2-1 장소 전치사: at, on, in I

연습문제			
1 on	**2** at	**3** on
4 in	**5** in	**6** on

POINT 2-2 장소 전치사: at, on, in II

연습문제			
1 on	**2** in	**3** in
4 in	**5** in	**6** on
7 in	**8** at	**9** on
10 on	**11** in	**12** at
13 in	**14** on	

POINT 3 위치 전치사

연습문제
1	in front of	2	between	3	under
4	behind	5	among	6	next to

POINT 4 방향 전치사

연습문제
1	through	2	down	3	along
4	out of	5	around	6	for
7	from, to				

POINT 5 기타 전치사

연습문제 A
1	by	2	for	3	without
4	with	5	like	6	by
7	with	8	against	9	about
10	for				

연습문제 B
ⓐ	for	ⓑ	with	ⓒ	like
ⓓ	about	ⓔ	by		

POINT 6-1 전치사 관용 표현: 형용사 + 전치사

연습문제
1	of	2	for	3	with
4	O	5	with	6	for
7	at	8	for	9	for
10	O	11	from	12	O
13	of				

POINT 6-2 전치사 관용 표현: 동사 + 전치사

연습문제
1	to	2	for	3	for
4	at	5	for	6	for
7	at	8	on		

중간·기말고사 실전 문제

1 ③	2 ①	3 ①	4 ④	5 ②
6 ⑤	7 behind	8 out of	9 next to[by]	
10 ④	11 ①	12 ②	13 ②	14 ③, ④
15 ③	16 ④	17 ④	18 ②	19 ③
20 ③	21 ①	22 on, at, at		23 ③
24 after	25 (1) ⓑ → at (2) ⓒ → for (3) ⓔ → on			

---

1 시간(9 P.M.) 앞에는 전치사 at을 쓴다.

2 기간을 나타내는 표현(two hours) 앞이므로 전치사 for(~ 동안)를 쓴다.

3 · '너의 재킷을 옷장 안에 걸어라.'라는 의미이므로 전치사 in(~ 안에)을 쓴다.

· 'Sam이 그 책을 선반 위에 놓았니?'라는 의미이므로 전치사 on(~ 위에)을 쓴다.

4 · 'Jake는 세 시간 동안 체육관에서 운동했다.'라는 의미이고 기간을 나타내는 표현(three hours) 앞이므로 전치사 for(~ 동안)를 쓴다.

· '너는 나를 위해 문을 열어줄 수 있니?'라는 의미이므로 전치사 for(~를 위해)를 쓴다.

5 · '한 개의 코코넛이 나무로부터 떨어졌다.'라는 의미이므로 전치사 from(~으로부터)을 쓴다.

· '나는 오후 8시부터 10시까지 TV를 봤다.'라는 의미이므로 「from ~ to …」('~부터 …까지')를 쓴다.

6 ⑤ during → for

7 '~ 뒤에'라는 의미의 전치사 behind를 쓴다.

8 '~ 밖으로'라는 의미의 전치사 out of를 쓴다.

9 '~옆에'라는 의미의 전치사 next to[by]를 쓴다.

10 ④ on ①②③⑤ in

11 · '나는 어젯밤에 나의 친구와 함께 농구를 했다.'라는 의미이므로 전치사 with(~와 함께)를 쓴다.

· 'Owen은 그의 신용카드를 이용해서 그 셔츠의 값을 지불했다.'라는 의미이므로 전치사 with(~을 이용해서)를 쓴다.

12 ②: 동사 like ①③④⑤: 전치사 like

13 '~을 따라서'라는 의미의 전치사 along을 쓴다.

14 ③④ of ① from ②⑤ for

15 교통수단(the bus) 앞에는 전치사 on을 쓴다.

16 be proud of '~을 자랑스러워하다'

17 자연환경(the sky) 앞에는 전치사 in을 쓴다.

18 · '나의 집은 저 두 건물들 사이에 있다.'라는 의미이고 two buildings는 둘이므로 전치사 between(~ (둘) 사이에)을 쓴다.

· '나무들 사이에 한 마리의 사슴이 있다.'라는 의미이므로 전치사 among(~ (셋 이상) 사이에)을 쓴다.

19 · '그는 방 안으로 걸어 들어갔다.'라는 의미이므로 전치사 into(~ 안으로)를 쓴다.

· 'Mark는 길을 따라서 자전거를 탔다.'라는 의미이므로 전치사 along(~을 따라서)을 쓴다.

20 · 'Jane의 가방은 창문 옆에 있다.'라는 의미이므로 전치사 next to(~ 옆에)를 쓴다.

· be late for '~에 늦다'

21 은행은 학교와 경찰서 사이에 있는 상황이고, the school and the police station은 둘이므로 전치사 between(~ (둘) 사이에)을 쓴다.

22 첫 번째 빈칸: 요일(Saturday) 앞에는 전치사 on을 쓴다.
두 번째 빈칸: 하나의 지점(the new restaurant) 앞에는 전치사 at을 쓴다.
세 번째 빈칸: 시간(7 P.M.) 앞에는 전치사 at을 쓴다.

23 · 'Peter는 지난여름에 베트남에 갔다.'라는 의미이므로 전치사 to(~에, ~으로)를 쓴다.
· listen to '~을 듣다'

24 '~ 후에'라는 의미의 전치사 after를 쓴다.

25 (1) look at '~을 보다'
(2) look for '~을 찾다'
(3) spend … on '~에 …(돈/시간)을 쓰다'

POINT 1   and, but, or, so

1 ① and   ② but   ③ or
2 ① so   ② but   ③ and
3 ① or   ② but   ③ so
4 ① or   ② and   ③ so

1 or cold outside
2 but he can't speak French
3 and I will do the dishes
4 so he doesn't want to go to the pool
5 but you didn't answer
6 and bought some novels
7 or the chess club
8 so he didn't eat lunch today

POINT 2   명령문 + and/or

1 Go to Peter's party, or he'll be disappointed.
2 Study harder, and you'll pass the test.
3 Buy a ticket, or you can't watch the play.
4 Eat some breakfast, or you'll be hungry later.
5 Take this medicine, and you'll be better soon.
6 Be careful, or you may slip on the ice.
7 Apologize to John, and he'll forgive you.
8 Close the window, or you'll be cold.
9 Give this gift to your mom, and she'll be happy
10 Exercise regularly, and you'll become healthier.
11 Don't forget to bring a map, or you'll get lost.
12 Run faster, and you'll arrive on time.

POINT 3-1   when, before, after, while

1 while I was doing the dishes
2 After I made the coffee
3 When it rains
4 after you read it
5 While I was making dinner
6 before you go to school
7 when the teacher talked
8 Before the movie starts

연습문제 B

| 1 | use | 2 | O | 3 | ends |
| 4 | visits | | | | |

연습문제 C

| 1 | ② | 2 | ① |

POINT 3-2 because, if

연습문제 A

1 He failed the math test because he didn't study.
2 You should wear a warm jacket because it is snowing.
3 I was late for the appointment because I missed the bus.
4 She was very tired because she stayed up late.
5 The audiences laughed because the comedian's joke was funny.
6 Let's go to the Mexican restaurant because the Chinese restaurant is full.

연습문제 B

| 1 | if | 2 | because of | 3 | because |
| 4 | Because | 5 | If | 6 | if |

POINT 4 that

연습문제 A

1 he lives near your apartment
2 Brenda will like this present
3 that the weather is so great
4 the teacher canceled the quiz
5 that Jupiter is much larger than Earth
6 that the package arrived late
7 this laptop is too expensive
8 that we missed our flight

연습문제 B

| 1 | ② | 2 | ① | 3 | ③ |
| 4 | ② | | | | |

POINT 5 접속부사

연습문제

1	On the other hand	2	For example
3	However	4	Therefore
5	For example	6	On the other hand
7	However	8	Therefore
9	Therefore	10	However
11	For example	12	On the other hand

중간·기말고사 실전 문제

1 ① 2 ③ 3 ②,④ 4 ① 5 ②
6 Go to bed early, or you will feel tired tomorrow.
7 ① 8 ⑤ 9 when 10 after
11 because 12 ③ 13 I think (that) the package will arrive today. 14 ① 15 ⑤
16 if you ask nicely 17 Carrie will do her homework after she watches this movie.
18 that 19 ③ 20 ③ 21 ⑤ 22 ①
23 (A) For example, he traveled to Spain and Portugal 24 ⑤ 25 ②

1 '나의 엄마는 식료품점에서 약간의 토마토, 우유, 그리고 돼지고기를 사셨다.'라는 의미이므로 and(그리고)를 쓴다.

2 'Theo는 누군가 그의 지갑을 훔쳤기 때문에 화가 났다.'라는 의미이므로 because(~이기 때문에)를 쓴다.

3 ② or → and
   ④ so → but

4 첫 번째 빈칸: '햄버거나 국수가 어때?'라는 의미이므로 or(또는)를 쓴다.
   두 번째 빈칸: '나는 그렇게 배고프지 않아서, 그냥 약간의 과일을 먹자.'라는 의미이므로 so(그래서)를 쓴다.

5 ② or → and

6 '… 해라, 그렇지 않으면 ~'이라는 의미의 「명령문 + or ~」를 쓴다.

7 '하지만'이라는 의미의 but을 쓴다.

8 '~하는 동안'이라는 의미의 while을 쓴다.

9 · '~할 때'라는 의미의 when을 쓴다.
   · '수업이 끝났을 때 나는 행복했다.'
   · 'William은 미식축구를 할 때 많이 뛴다.'
   · '그들은 그것이 준비되었을 때 너에게 너의 음식을 가져다줄 것이다.'

10 배관공이 도착하기 전에 Rachel이 문을 열었다는 것은 Rachel이 문을 연 후에 배관공이 왔다는 것이므로 '~한 후에'라는 의미의 after를 쓴다.

11 Jessica가 복통이 있어서 테니스를 칠 수 없다는 것은 Jessica가 복통이 있기 때문에 테니스를 칠 수 없다는 것이므로 '~이기 때문에'라는 의미의 because를 쓴다.

12 ③: 의문사 ①②④⑤: 접속사

13 명사절 접속사 that은 동사 think의 목적어 역할을 하는 명사절을 이끈다. that절이 문장에서 목적어로 쓰였을 때 that을 생략할 수 있다.

14 ⓐ but → or[and]

15 ⑤ while은 '~하는 동안'이라는 의미이다.

16 '만약 ~한다면'이라는 의미의 if를 쓴다.

17 시간을 나타내는 부사절에서는 미래시제 대신 현재시제를 쓴다.

18 명사절 접속사 that은 동사 know의 목적어 역할을 하는 명사절을 이끌고, 'I know that the bus will come soon.'이므로 세 번째에 오는 것은 that이다.

19 명사절 접속사 that은 동사 thinks의 목적어 역할을 하는 명사절을 이끈다.

20 ③: 지시형용사   주어진 문장과 ①②④⑤: 명사절 접속사

21 '나는 어제 나의 자전거에서 떨어졌다. 그러나, 나는 다치지 않았다.'라는 의미이므로 However(그러나)를 쓴다.

22 '나의 남동생은 매우 훌륭한 학생이다. 예를 들어, 그는 지난주에 그의 과학 시험에서 만점을 받았다.'라는 의미이므로 For example(예를 들어)을 쓴다.

23 '예를 들어'라는 의미의 For example을 쓴다.

24 첫 번째 빈칸: '그는 그의 다음 휴가 동안 모로코 또는 이집트로 여행 가는 것을 계획한다.'라는 의미이므로 or(또는)를 쓴다.
두 번째 빈칸: '그는 두 나라 모두를 여행하기를 원하지만 그는 충분한 시간이 없을 것이다.'라는 의미이므로 but(하지만)을 쓴다.

25 첫 번째 빈칸: '그녀는 그녀의 여동생의 것 같은 노트북을 원한다. 하지만, 그 노트북은 매우 비싸다.'라는 의미이므로 However(그러나)를 쓴다.
두 번째 빈칸: '그 노트북은 매우 비싸다. 그러므로 Amanda는 많은 돈을 모아야 할 것이다.'라는 의미이므로 Therefore(그러므로)를 쓴다.

MEMO

MEMO

최신 개정 교과서 완벽 반영

기출로적중

해커스

중학영문법

1학년

해설집

최신 개정 교과서 완벽 반영

기출로적중

해커스
중학영문법

1학년

해커스 중학영문법이 특별한 이유!

1. 실제 중학교 내신 **기출문제 빅데이터 및 최신 개정 교과서** 완벽 반영
2. **단계별 문제풀이**를 통해 내신 시험에 확실하게 대비 가능
3. 문법 포인트 이해에 **필수적인 기초 문법**으로 체계적인 학습 시작
4. **워크북의 추가 문제를** 충분히 풀어보며 실력 완성
5. 내신 점수를 높여주는 **다양한 학습 자료** 제공

정가 **13,900**

53740

9 788965 424062

ISBN 978-89-6542-406-

해커스북(HackersBook.com)에서
본 교재에 대한 다양한 추가 학습 자료를 이용하세요!